Italian Horror Film Directors

ALSO BY LOUIS PAUL

*Tales from the Cult Film Trenches:
Interviews with 36 Actors from Horror, Science
Fiction and Exploitation Cinema* (McFarland, 2008)

BY TOM LISANTI AND LOUIS PAUL

*Film Fatales: Women in Espionage Films
and Television, 1962–1973* (McFarland, 2002)

Italian Horror Film Directors

LOUIS PAUL

with forewords by
JESS FRANCO and ANTONELLA FULCI

McFarland & Company, Inc., Publishers
Jefferson, North Carolina, and London

The present work is a reprint of the illustrated case bound edition of Italian Horror Film Directors *first published in 2005 by McFarland.*

Except where noted otherwise, all photographs
are from the author's collection.

LIBRARY OF CONGRESS CATALOGUING-IN-PUBLICATION DATA

Paul, Louis, 1960–
Italian horror film directors / Louis Paul ; with forewords
by Jess Franco and Antonella Fulci.
p. cm.
Includes filmograhies.
Includes bibliographical references and index.

ISBN 978-0-7864-6113-4
softcover : 50# alkaline paper ∞

1. Horror films — Italy — History and criticism.
2. Motion picture producers and directors — Italy. I. Title.
PN1995.9.H6P34   2011
791.4302'33'092245 — dc22   2004013465

British Library cataloguing data are available

© 2005 Louis Paul. All rights reserved

*No part of this book may be reproduced or transmitted in any form
or by any means, electronic or mechanical, including photocopying
or recording, or by any information storage and retrieval system,
without permission in writing from the publisher.*

Cover art by Mark Durr

Manufactured in the United States of America

*McFarland & Company, Inc., Publishers
Box 611, Jefferson, North Carolina 28640
www.mcfarlandpub.com*

TABLE OF CONTENTS

Foreword by Jess Franco   1
Foreword by Antonella Fulci   3
Preface   5
Introduction: The Evolution of the Italian Horror Film   9

The Leading Horror Film Directors

Dario Argento	37	Umberto Lenzi	143
Lamberto Bava	66	Antonio Margheriti	159
Mario Bava	84	Aristide Massaccesi	181
Ruggero Deodato	109	Bruno Mattei	210
Lucio Fulci	120	Michele Soavi	220

Other Significant Horror Film Directors

Marcello Avallone	229	Antonio Bido	246
Pupi Avati	230	Antonio Boccaci	247
Mariano Baino	233	Giuliano Carnimeo	248
Francesco Barilli	234	Mario Colucci	249
Sergio Bergonzelli	235	Luigi Cozzi	251
Giulio Berruti	238	Armando Crispino	256
Andrea Bianchi	239	Massimo Dallamano	258
Mario Bianchi (Montero)	243	Damiano Damiani	261

Fabrizio De Angelis	263	Sergio Martino	292
Alberto De Martino	264	Stelvio Massi	299
Rino Di Silvestro	268	Camillo Mastrocinque	301
Giorgio Ferroni	270	Emilio Miraglia	302
Al Festa	272	Sergio Pastore	303
Riccardo Freda	274	Renato Polselli	304
Mario Gariazzo	279	Massimo Pupillo	307
Gianfranco Giagni	281	Giulio Questi	310
Enzo Girolami	282	Piero Regnoli	312
Marino Girolami	287	Mario Siciliano	314
Aldo Lado	288	Paolo Solvay	315
Mario Landi	291		

Epilogue: The Future of Italian Horror Films 319

Appendix: Important Horror (and Other Genre) Films by Other Directors 323

Bibliography 341

Index 345

FOREWORD

Being, as I am, an absolute fan of American fantasy and horror movies from James Whale and Tod Browning to William Witney and Erle C. Kenton, it is understandable that my favorite Italian movies and directors were never the pretentious works of Luchino Visconti or Federico Fellini or their pupils such as Mario Bolognini or Ettore Scola, but creators in whose films I discovered myself from the times of my childhood, the same feeling that I loved in the old masterpieces from the studios of Universal and Republic.

So when I saw the first Riccardo Freda and Mario Bava horror films, I discovered anew an imagination and a creative world that was more open and free than the American films of that same period. I started to look for other Italian films and directors because I could not believe that Freda and Bava would be two isolated cases in a cinema landscape much too influenced by political or clumsy social messages. In doing so, I found old beautiful films of Carmine Gallone, Mario Camerini, Mario Soldati, Renato Castellani (I consider *Un Colpo de Pistola* [1941] a masterpiece) and, most of all, Alessandro Blasetti. I have seen the latter's *La Corona di Ferro* (a.k.a. *The Iron Crown*, with Gino Cervi, Massimo Girotti and Luisa Ferida—the lover of Mussolini) at least 20 times. Almost implicit in this film were the elements of the fantastic, erotic and horror-sadistic—the core elements of great Italian films.

Then, after a few years of "neo-realism" (a very brilliant period, it cannot be denied, but quite far from my personal preferences), the huge industry of the Italian cinema had its golden years and the gateway to imagination swung open again, its pathway, of course, blazed by Bava and Freda.

I started again to love the incredible work of their followers, as Vittorio Cottofavi, Antonio Margheriti, Umberto Lenzi, Lucio Fulci, Dario Argento, Sergio Corbucci, Sergio Solima, Sergio Leone, Fernando Di Leo and hundreds of others invaded the marketplace. Just as in the days of the "Old Hollywood," the Italian A

& B cinemas grew up together. Those brilliant men, supported by very clever and quick-minded producers, technicians, and actors and actresses, re-invented the Western, the peplum, the horror, the erotic, the thriller, the adventure and the spy films.

For 15 years that splendid machine churned out thousands of films. In reverse flattery, even Hollywood imitated them. Americans came to Almeria, Spain, to shoot their Westerns on the favorite sets of Leone and Corbucci. Unfortunately, this lesson was learned in a very short time of decadence: The Italians had re-invented the cinema and quickly killed it themselves through oversaturation.

Jess Franco (with Lina Romay). Photograph courtesy Kevin Collins.

Now the Italian cinema is almost dead. Only a handful of fairly big and intellectual films supported by the official statements—the ministries or official television or both—see the light yearly and, in general, are the kind of "prestige" films which are not to my personal taste.

Only a few persevere—such as Argento, Michele Soavi and Tinto Brass. I hope better times will come very soon. I believe in the creativity and strengths of the Italian people. Just look around in the modern American movies and you will find the likes of the Italian-Americans, Martin Scorsese, Abel Ferrara and Quentin Tarantino. Bored of talk shows, contests and series, the Italians—and all of us with them—will search again for a new renaissance of their creative, mad, bold cinema.

Jess Franco
(Jesus Franco Manera)
Fall 2004

FOREWORD

Italian horror? What's it all about? In this season of the year, when the distributors put out all that they consider trash stored in their warehouses, there is nothing on the horizon for us gore filmgoers to watch. Italian directors seem to have hidden their horror screenplays in the closet, except for the survivor, Dario Argento, who has released his *Il Fantasma dell'Opera* and *Nonhosonno*. To refresh the genre, we must look at it with a sense of humor, step back and never forget that nothing can be funnier and more satisfactory than watching a "bad" horror movie in the right mood with the right company. The magic begins when an absurd plot merges with bad acting and fits perfectly with the inaudible dialogue. In the best case, the director is very concerned about making a serious movie and the result is outstanding nonsense. I used to hear my father, Lucio Fulci, say that horror was not to be taken seriously, being the best escape from real-life cruelty.

Whenever I watch his film *Il Cavaliere Costante Nicosia Demoniaco, ovvero: Dracula in Brianza* (1975), I see his most personal point of view about the matter. Costante (Lando Buzzanca), after a trip in Romania and a wild party at the weird Count Gradulecu's castle, believes he's been bitten by the count. Back in Italy, he gets into every sort of hilarious situation to satisfy his blood thirst. Dad knew how healthy it was to laugh and he laughed 'til his very last moment. I remember our afternoons together, spent watching Amando De Ossorio's saga of the Blind Dead, especially *The Cursed Ship* (*El Buque Maldito* [1975]). My father was delighted by both the eccentric costumes and, in the Italian-language version, the outstanding dialogue, written by the now 81-year-old master of the bizarre Renato Polselli. *Riti, Magie Nere e Segrete Orge nel Trecento* (1972) and *La Verità Secondo Satana* (1971) were two of Polselli's early '70s flicks. I'm very proud I could meet with maestro Polselli once in a while and talk to him. His sense of humor and his peculiar point of view about everything were something that everybody should hear at least once.

With the few recent attempts to give dignity to the genre, it may seem snobbish

Antonella Fulci. Photograph courtesy the Blood Times Collection.

to give so much attention to movies like the most amusing and stylish Al Festa's *Fatal Frames* (1994), but if the alternative is to watch a sad, pretentious "wish I was a Hammer movie" film or the usual remake of a remake of a remake of a cult classic, well, I wish that people like Al Festa could shoot a hundred other movies like *Fotogrammi Mortali*.

There's not much more to say about actual Italian horror, except that nowadays, Italian directors seems to have all of their new masterworks locked up in the closet. With books like Louis Paul's *Italian Horror Film Directors*, perhaps some director will be encouraged to take his masterwork out ... just to see what happens.

Antonella Fulci
Summer 2004

PREFACE

My affection for the Italian horror film began many years ago. When I was younger, local independent television stations in New York aired all kinds of horror films, primarily on the weekends and at late hours of the night. I recall that I was always enthralled with foreign horror films above all others. I easily recollect countless late-night viewings of strange, atmospheric films.

When I was old enough to go to the movies alone, among my earliest viewing experiences were some of the great Hammer films from Britain and the early works of Dario Argento on the big screen, in theaters well before the age of the videocassette. Later still, when I was old enough, and brave enough, to traverse the sleazy, seedy, ominous strip of theaters on 42nd Street, I truly began to learn what the cinematic terms exploitation and sexploitation meant.

That now long-gone single city block (between Seventh and Eighth avenues) of a dozen theaters showed many older releases, re-releases and whatever they held deep in the bowels of their film storage rooms. It was a turning point in my movie going experiences and my life that I'll never forget. Therefore, I dedicate this book to the spirit of the Italian horror film as it was forged first through late-night television and then through my exposure to this strange new world in the cavernous cinemas of 42nd Street. I also dedicate this project to the actors and filmmakers, those living and those deceased whose work I cherish and who have made me realize what a unique form of entertainment the cinema is.

The seeds of *Italian Horror Film Directors* were first sown when some of the ideas expressed within first appeared in a much different form in a book titled *Inferno Italia*, published in Germany in the fall of 1998 by Bertler-Lieber Verlag. Since then, I have managed to go back to the original manuscript of that work, edit it, and update a lot of the information, which essentially means that I have added new text and expanded and updated the filmography to include films released since 1998. I have also updated other information where needed and now the work is what I originally intended it to be, an even more valuable resource to fans of Italian genre film.

Special thanks go to Kevin Clement, Kevin Collins, Torsten Dewi, John Donaldson, Craig Ledbetter, Tom Lisanti, Michael Monahan, Phil Palmieri, Mike Vraney, Tom Weaver, Stuart West and Chuck Wilson; to Jess Franco and Antonella Fulci for their thoughtful, entertaining forewords; to all those kind people who've crossed my path and made my life interesting and intriguing and whose names are too numerous too mention; to Heidi Stock for her valued assistance in editing many early versions of this project; Jennifer Barnaby for editing assistance and for great help providing the photos; and to Wendy Norris, who helped me over a substantial editing hump and made this work finally take the much-needed shape I always envisioned.

All films in this book are listed by their original Italian title (capitalized according to English-language practice). I have decided not to list the English titles for a number of reasons. Most importantly, there are a number of films for which there are many alternate titles (in English) for the American, British and other English-language releases. I found it a form of cheating to mention a film under an obscure English language title or translation, when many more knowledgeable people may know it as something entirely different.

I would like to take a moment to explain the organization of this book. The introduction discusses the origins of the Italian horror film, and takes the reader as far back as possible. I detail how France's own Grand Guignol theatrical forays, World War II and the changing political climates and mores of society contributed to the ever-changing Italian film industry. I also cover how neo-realist filmmakers like Roberto Rossellini also contributed to a newer, highly stylized sense of filmmaking, impressing upon fellow Italian directors of the early 1950s and 1960s a new sense of dramatic and cinematic possibilities. Also discussed is how the work of fiction writers like Cornell Woolrich and Edgar Wallace, among others, influenced the earliest of many Italian thrillers. This brings readers as far up-to-date as possible, mentioning as many important films in the genre as possible, and discussing some at length.

"The Leading Horror Film Directors" features in-depth profiles of ten important directors: Dario Argento, Lamberto Bava, Mario Bava, Ruggero Deodato, Lucio Fulci, Umberto Lenzi, Antonio Margheriti, Aristide Massaccesi, Bruno Mattei and Michele Soavi. All of their films are discussed, with particular attention paid to their genre contributions, which in the case of directors like Argento, Lamberto and Mario Bava and Lucio Fulci, is considerable. The following section, "Other Significant Horror Film Directors," takes a look at 39 other directors and their work. Many of these either seldom worked in the horror genre but churned out a small number of interesting features, while others made very few films at all but concentrating on the genre, hence their inclusion in this section of the book. Amongst the directors that appear here are names familiar to scholars of the genre: Pupi Avati,

Armando Crispino, Massimo Dallamano, Riccardo Freda and Aldo Lado. More obscure directors, including Francisco Barilli, Giulio Berruti, Antonio Bido, Rino Di Silvestro, Gianfranco Giagni, Emilio Miraglia and Giulio Questi receive equal attention.

An epilogue, "The Future of Italian Horror," affords an opportunity to take a look into the Italian film industry, and the horror genre in particular, and their possibilities for the future. There is an Appendix, "Important Horror (and Other Genre) Films by Other Directors," a filmography that lists horror films and other related genre offerings mentioned in the book's earliest chapters but not appearing elsewhere (because they were not directed by any of the 50 notable and not-so-notable directors profiled). A bibliography and an index conclude the book.

I have compiled exhaustive filmographies for each director. The filmography provides the film's alternate titles in various countries of release (including the United States and Great Britain) and important cast and crew credits. I have attempted to include, whenever possible, all the known names for many actors who for years have appeared in English-dubbed export prints of these films under pseudonyms.

I do hope the reader enjoys this book and will gain some knowledge and insight about the Italian film industry's greatest export, the Italian horror film. If this book leads one to discover or rediscover any number of films, genres, or personalities, then I have done my work well.

Louis Paul
Fall 2004

INTRODUCTION

The Evolution of the Italian Horror Film

One key to understanding Italian horror films can be expressed in two words: hallucinatory horror. There is no cinema with effect equal to that of the hallucinatory horror of Italian horror films. Nightmares come true, fears and phobias are given life, and the odd and the unjustifiable are held aloft for the world to see. There are other directors from other countries who have contributed mightily to the horror film genre, their names familiar today to many casual filmgoers due to their work as well as the countless articles and books and other media attention given them.

The Italian horror film has had its heyday. It has passed. So, the purpose of this book is to recount the origins of the genre, celebrate ten specific auteurs who have contributed enormously, mention the many who have made noteworthy films in this genre, and also discuss the seminal influential genres associated with the Italian horror film. Hopefully, you will enjoy reading about the obscure films, as well as reading about those that you may already be familiar with.

Curiously, it is in another country that one can begin to trace the origins of the Italian horror film. In 1897 France, the theatre of the Grand Guignol was born. Grand Guignol is a term that has entered our language to describe the most gruesome incidents and, indeed, the events that took place at this small theatre named the Grand Guignol in the section of the Parisian city of Montmarte were indeed gruesome. For over 65 years, various troupes of actors titillated Parisian audiences with one-act performances of murder, mayhem and revenge. Apparently, the Grand Guignol performance was based on the avant-garde ideas of naturalistic performances.

Originally done as short pantomimes, the performances blossomed to morality plays, then on to much more sensationalistic fare. As the age of the artisan began to peak, people from all over would just as soon pay a visit to the theater of the Grand Guignol as they would the opera or some other such place of live entertainment. According to one still-living former member of the Parisian Grand Guignol theater, the actor Robert Hossein, "The air was bewitching. It was as if the religious fervor brought devil-worshippers to the Grand Guignol. The stage manager always shouted for more blood! The rain sometimes leaked through the roof. The audience thought it was raining blood!"

What the theater of the Grand Guignol exploited was not so much the imagined or ancient fears and terrors of fantastic monsters, but the more shocking horrible truths of contemporary Paris: Ordinary people, the people you pass on the street, could be anyone — a lover, a killer, anything. Each and every night on stage, the Grand Guignol theater performed acts of such unbelievable cruelty as stabbings, mutilations, beheadings, eye gougings, torture and dismemberment, all in gloriously graphic detail.

Another surviving member of the Grand Guignol troupe, an unidentified actress, remembers many audience members who got more than just a visual thrill from the shows: "The cleaning ladies would find traces of sexual pleasure from the audience." Eventually, the Grand Guignol inspired a controversial imitator with a similar troupe based in Rome.

As the Parisian Grand Guignol theater reached its peak of popularity in the late 1920s and survived the war years with visiting German, then Allied forces, it could no longer stay contemporary with the real-life horrors of the world and closed its doors permanently in 1962. The Italian Grand Guignol theater survived from 1908 through 1928. It has been widely accepted that the Grand Guignol theater of Italy had influenced a great of the many writings of then-contemporary Italian authors.

The origins of the cinema in France and America influenced similar experiments worldwide. The first Italian forays into the fantastic were highly stylized, entertaining yet clunky renditions of mythic fables from their own history. The powerful mythological character Maciste (a Roman contemporary of the Greek Hercules) was portrayed in a series of silent films, often portrayed by real-life wrestler Bartolomeo Pagano. Outlandish sets, costumes and feats of heroism entertained the masses. The first real, documented horror film that we can trace is not actually a horror film, but a fantasy picture. This film, *L'Atketa Fantasma*, released in 1919, influenced by Pagano's Maciste films, also features a heroic wrestler (performed by Mario Guaita-Ausonia). This character is a man who becomes involved in a series of outlandish adventures (wearing a mask, to conceal his true identity), to save the life of his beloved.

In 1920 the film *Il Mostro di Frankenstein* was released, but this then-controversial film was seen by few in its original form due to the censorship of the time

Bartolomeo Pagano as he appeared in one of the many early silent films featuring the mythological character Maciste.

of many sensational images. This is now considered a lost film; no print seems to have survived the passage of time. Directed by Eugenio Testa, it told the tale of a Dr. Frankenstein (played by the film's producer, Luciano Albertini) tracking down his creation (Umberto Guarracino).

As time rolled on, so did the rise of fascism in the capitals of Italy. In 1935, the Italian dictator Benito Mussolini founded the *Centro Sperimentale di Cinematografia*, the film school for the study of the art and science of making motion pictures. Mussolini had been greatly influenced by the films of the German documentarian Leni Riefenstahl and was convinced that this was the next great art that should receive more political funding.* In the following years, the Italian cinema's

---

*The letters CSC often appeared in the opening and closing credits of Italian films throughout the '60s and early '70s. The letters were attached to the names of the cast members and technicians who had attended the Centro Sperimentale Di Cinematografia, the school funded by Mussolini in 1935 for the study and advancement of the art and science of making motion pictures. For years, at least two people per film (whether primary or minor actors or technicians) had to have the letters CSC attached to their names in order for the film to gain state funding and tax breaks. Oddly enough, even when names of cast members and technicians were anglicized into barely recognizable pseudonyms, the CSC letters were still attached, explaining, for example, why you would see Erica Bianchi Colombatto CSC and Erica Blank CSC appearing in the credits for the same film in both the original Italian language versions and then the dubbed English-language export prints. The oldest film school in Western Europe, the Centro Sperimentale di Cinematografia is still financed by the Italian government and focuses on research, publication and theory as applied to all the cinematic arts.

subversion of the CSC's rigid guidelines led to the birth of the so-called golden age of neo-realism films—movies designed to entertain the average Italian filmgoer with tales of the everyday life of the common people. Many famous Italian directors got their start in these neo-realism films, the most famous being Lucino Visconti and Roberto Rossellini.

The Italian cinema of the fantastic, however, was a genre that was rarely thought of, much less one that was encouraged. *Il Medium* in 1951 was the closest one came to a horror film at this time; even then, this production of Giancarlo Menotti's famous opera, directed by Menotti himself, did not stray far beyond the dramatic conventions of the story, remaining little more than a filmed opera.

In 1954, the immensely popular Italian film comedian known as Toto (whose real name was Antonio Vincenzo Stefanto Clemente, a.k.a. Antonio De Curtis) appeared in *Toto all'Inferno*. Toto was very popular with common audiences for his ability to spoof character types or lifestyles and social classes; the rich and the underachievers all received equal treatment by this Italian equivalent of Jacques Tati and Charlie Chaplin. In this film, Toto journeys to Hell when he commits suicide and encounters Satan as well as Belfagor, the Italian mythological embodiment of evil. Toto falls in love with Cleopatra and is banned from Hell by Satan to spend eternity as a civil servant.

The United States, a long-time contributor to the genre, had churned out many films with their successful and profitable film versions of classic horror literature in the '30s. But by the end of the '40s, the horror film in the States had virtually finished itself off as a genre. Film studios had endlessly cannibalized their own successful movies into inferior sequels and remakes. In the early '50s, Hollywood science fiction replaced horror as the fears of the imagination were replaced with the fears of possible realities to come.

By the mid-50s, an overdose of these apocalyptic horrors began to revert to the origins of the horror film and hybrid films became commonplace. During this period, one need not look far to find mad scientists breeding large insect creatures, or to view interplanetary missions to other worlds inhabited by strange alien monsters. Hardcore horror audiences yearned for more realistic terrors in their films.

Alfred Hitchcock has been called the master of terror. Yet, in reality, Hitchcock's best work can be found when he occasionally stepped outside of the rigid format that he had developed into a style. The tension-filled *Rear Window* (1954) and his espionage-themed *North by Northwest* (1959) are among his greatest achievements. It was only when Hitchcock employed graphic shock tactics, not unlike those of American B movie showman William Castle, for the film *Psycho* (1960) that he finally hit upon the perfect formula for the horror film audiences.

However, it was outside of the United States, the single biggest proponent of the horror genre for decades, that the true rebirth of the horror film would take place. *I Vampiri* in 1956 became the first official Italian horror film. While the few Italian films discussed above contain elements of the fantastic, it was this Riccardo

Freda-directed picture that truly ushered in the first wave of the Italian horror films. Originally a sculptor by trade, Freda utilized slow ethereal movements for his actors to portray mood. His film is a genuinely stark production that, at the time of its release, was far different from any of his contemporaries' work.

Set in modern-day Paris, *I Vampiri* is concerned with a scientist who drains the blood from young women to maintain the youth and beauty of his beloved aged Duchess. There are no shadowy fogs or vampire bats turning into cape-flowing humans as in the American Universal film productions of the 1940s.

Elements of the neo-realism films of the late 1940s and early 1950s are evident in the scenes of the film's protagonist, a journalist who is investigating the case of the strange disappearances of young women. Unfortunately, what mars the film are the static moments that betray Freda's former occupation as an artist and an infatuation with the concerns of the cinema of neo-realism.

Too much screen time is taken up with the young journalist walking aimlessly through the streets filled with common people going about their business and the mind-numbingly dull and endless police procedural scenes. What made *I Vampiri* stand out at the time and eventually become regarded as noteworthy (if slightly overrated) in the history of the Italian horror film, is, firstly, the director's insistence on utilizing a wonderfully macabre set design for the interiors and subterranean lair of the castle Du Grand, where the Countess makes her home. Secondly, the way in which the film anticipated the *giallo* thrillers of the years to come by utilizing prototypical devices like the black-gloved hands of the killer (Paul Mueller), in the service of the Countess, was significant. Freda has this same character stalk his prey (mainly women), and the female victims cower in fear from this advancing stalker. This person himself is exhibiting a "controlled behavior" via heroin injections that are administered by another mysterious person wearing black gloves, a wonderfully adult and prescient cinematic device. All this could have been influenced by the work of Mario Bava, the cameraman on this film, who took over the production (uncredited) when Freda reportedly left the picture uncompleted.

Freda's *Caltiki, il Mostro Immortale* (1959) is an entertaining film that revisits similar ground covered in the wonderfully amusing 1958 American film *The Blob* but adds a uniquely European spin to the proceedings. A group of archaeologists excavating an ancient Spanish ruin in South America face a bodiless, shapeless creature that oozes its way around and sears the flesh from the bones of its victims. The film begins with a methodically placed plot and the standard introduction to the main characters of the story but quickly thereafter races to its climax, a result of Freda leaving the film in mid-production. Mario Bava, the cameraman and special effects technician for the film, finished the movie (uncredited) as director.

In 1959, Stefano Vanzina (Steno), a director primarily known for his lowbrow comedy efforts, directed *Tempi Duri per i Vampiri*. Obviously modeled on the slapstick efforts of the comedies featuring the character Toto, this movie features Renato Rascel as the descendant of Baron Rodrigo (Christopher Lee), a vampire who does not appear much different from the Dracula character that Lee played in the Hammer Dracula film made before this production. Rodrigo infects Rascel with vampirism, turning the buffoonish actor into a mugging version of a nightcrawler, always chasing sexy damsel in distress Sylva Koscina, the object of his affections. The film is a comedy, but more so a horror comedy. There were not that many horror-related films made during this period, so it warrants mention alongside Marino Girolami's *Il Mio Amico Jekyll* (1960), a tale about a professor named Fabius (Raimondo Vianello) who invents a machine which changes him into handsome schoolteacher Ugo Tognazzi.

Cinematographer Mario Bava began his career chiefly as a cameraman and previously had dabbled in experimental forms of photography, painting, and so on. Bava's technique was to strip away much of the narrative story that propels the plot and just leave the bare essentials. What draws his audience into his films is his masterful way with images. When he began to work with color, Bava's technique of using various colored gels to cover particular spotlights to highlight key areas of scenes turned his films into living paintings of the grotesque. Bava's *La Maschera del Demonio*, produced and released in 1960, was the pivotal, groundbreaking film for the Italian horror film and the turning point for the genre as a whole. His work, a dark fable full of sexual wonder and ghostly malevolence, became a touchstone for a whole generation of cinephiles attuned to the dark pleasures of the horror cinema. Bava's film utilized the ghostly, pale strangeness of British actress Barbara Steele and made her an icon for the genre. His use of carefully decorated sets, sound and camera placement made one believe in the supernatural horrors that were damning a village out of time. Many of the film's highlights would, in the years to come, become staple images of the horror film genre: the laborious resurrection of an undead character as he slowly claws his way out of his grave, and the role of the hero, plagued by indecision — having to choose between the wholesome and virginal Katia (Steele) and the more compelling, sexual allure of the witch-vampire Asa (also Steele).

Bava's film would not have been made were it not for the international success of the British Hammer production *Dracula* (1958). More than Freda's *I Vampiri*, Hammer's *Dracula* seems to be the movie responsible for the birth of what eventually became known as the Italian cinema of Gothic horror films due to the fact that it highly romanticized Bram Stoker's novel and added a mood and atmosphere filled with dread, where danger lurked in the shadows and the night, and the daylight held only a brief respite from the dark.

In 1960, Renato Polselli directed *L'Amante del Vampiro*, a film that receives little respect or attention from many of today's horror film critics due to its low budget and sexploitative approach to the genre. It is, nevertheless, an important footnote in the history of Italian horror for being among the first films to blatantly

Ti Aspetterò all'Inferno (1960, Verdestella Film). One of the first dramatic films with thriller elements, it helped pave for the way for the Italian horror movie.

mix sex and horror. Strongly influenced by Hammer's *Dracula*, rather than Riccardo Freda's *I Vampiri*, *L'Amante del Vampiro* tells the tale of a group of ballet dancers who encounter the bizarre vampire servant (Walter Brandi) of a wicked vampire countess.

Polselli's film is cast with sexy actresses endowed with full, heaving bosoms that lurch out at the screen. Even the monstrous male vampire cannot resist grabbing a breast while making a move for their necks to drink their blood. The brief but effective above-the-waist nudity also adds to the air of exploitation. The film succeeds, becoming an often-uncredited early Continental influence on the daring, nudity-filled Hammer films of the late '60s.

Piero Regnoli, one of the writers for Freda's *I Vampiri*, directed the more exploitative *L'Ultima Preda del Vampiro* (1960) and took some of the ideas present in Renato Polselli's *L'Amante del Vampiro* and amplified them. Oddly, themes and plot devices that were used in Regnoli's film would be copied in the following years. Regnoli's film tells of a group of show business types stranded at the castle of Count Gabor Kernassy (Walter Brandi) when their vehicle breaks down. Far from civilization, they spend much of the screen time ogling each other (there are five women and two men in the troupe), giving the audience many titillating glimpses of bare flesh, paving the way for more sexually explicit fare later on in the decade.

L'Ultima Preda del Vampiro quickly comes to the main event when it turns out that the Count has an equally handsome twin (also Brandi), who by night is a monstrous vampire. While the Count falls in love with one of the showgirls, his twin spends the bulk of the screen time seducing, then vampirizing the rest of the young women. Regnoli's film satisfies on most levels, even the sexploitative one by having his actresses bare more than just their fangs. On an additional note: This is the very first film in this genre that contained a scene where a group of travelers are stranded at a malevolent and evil place.

Another influential film released in 1960, Giorgio Ferroni's *Il Mulino delle Donne di Petra* is a decidedly different sort of horror film. Shot in the muted colors favored by famed Dutch and Flemish painters, Ferroni's film, set in Holland, tells of a student who is attracted to the strange daughter of a professor (Wolfgang Preiss). The professor and his daughter live in an old windmill, containing a macabre array of female statues posed in a bizarre tableau. The student, who is an artist, visits this strange private museum and falls in love with the daughter, whom he is told never to see again. It turns out that the father is a scientist who is seeking to prevent the death of his daughter from a rare disease by injecting her with the blood of healthy young women and administering the transplanted genes of his victims, in order to preserve her youth and vitality. The victims, after death, are encased in wax. Ferroni's film moves at a slow, languid crawl, yet contains many memorable images (most importantly, the strange, alien landscape of the muddy reddish-clay ground that surrounds the tufts of water adjacent to the windmills, like odd versions of the standard European castles jutting out, high into the sky, amidst the forest and mountains).

Seddok (1960) is Anton Giulio Majano's re-working of the French director Georges Franju's *Les Yeux Sans Visage* (1959). Majano's film is an exploitative yet enjoyably trashy movie about an acclaimed scientist who treats a disfigured woman. He seeks to restore her beauty with the aid of a serum that has as its main ingredients the blood and tissue samples from young female victims. Although he is madly in love with the woman, the scientist eventually learns that the woman is only using his medical talents to restore her so that she may leave him. He begins to inject himself, overdosing on his own formula. Now addicted to the serum that caused him to turn into a monstrous being, he prowls the night in search of more female victims.

Influenced by the big-budget American productions that were shot in Italy as well as the early home-grown Italian Hercules productions of Pietro Francisci, to which he contributed his talents as a cameraman, Mario Bava's own *Ercole al Centro della Terra* (1961) was a colorful combination of the athletic muscleman peplum revival and Bava's own fascination with gothic imagery. It is also a study in how to make a modern adventure film with a story rich in mythological wonder.

This film led to a number of imitations attempting to graft macabre, often horrific plot devices onto the limited story structures of the sword-and-sandal genre. Very few were successful, but two films stand out: *Maciste Contro il Vampiro* (1961), Sergio Corbucci's violent and exciting film starring Gordon Scott and Gianna Maria Canale, and *Maciste all'Inferno* (also 1961), Riccardo Freda's own interpretation of the mythology cum gothic horror genre. It fails miserably when it laughably features a hero from a mythological time suddenly appearing in Scotland during the 1600s, saving a woman proclaimed a witch by superstitious villagers from certain death. Maciste (Kirk Morris) must travel to Hell, much like Reg Park's Hercules did in Bava's film. Here it is to find an ancient and powerful witch who has placed a curse of possession upon her descendant.

Quickly gaining ground as a formidable box office genre, the Italian horror film began to splinter off into many directions, some of them influenced by the visually arresting and atmospheric British film *City of the Dead* (1960). This John Moxey film, set in the supernaturally fog-enshrouded fictional New England town of Whitewood, tells of a cult of Satanic worshipers who maintain a stranglehold over the secluded village where a resurrected witch holds all in her power. The young and innocent students assigned to research local legends of witchcraft are victims unwittingly sent to their deaths by the same man (Christopher Lee) who both impersonates a gruff instructor of American legends and myths and presides over the human sacrifices.

Riccardo Freda's *L'Orribile Segreto del Dr. Hichcock* (1961) showed what one director, uninhibited by the invisible constraints of the horror genre, can do with the theme of necrophilia. This still-powerful and macabre tale is chiefly about a nineteenth century physician who can only function sexually when his bedroom partner is in an artificially created sense of death. Dr. Hichcock (Robert Flemyng) is stricken with grief when he overdoses his wife on his experimental serum and induces her death. Years later, the medical deviate returns from his self-imposed exile with a new wife (Barbara Steele) and can't help resuming his sideline practice of digging up freshly buried corpses of women to fondle their cold bodies.

Freda's film uses some oddly compelling images to make his film perverse. The doctor's home, a vine-covered mansion, exudes the warmth of the rain forest but is often shown only at night, lit in dark golds and hues of blue, which gives it a cold, dank appearance. One of the film's more resonating macabre images is of a lady in white who constantly screams during the night. Always dressed in a bridal gown, she makes her way to the family crypt, and Flemyng's nightly visits to cemeteries where he get his sexual kicks.

Mario Bava's thriller *La Ragazza Che Sapeva Troppo* (1962) blends the themes of menace and impropriety that were mainstays of the work of Alfred Hitchcock and the strictly Bava-ian approach, influenced by the Italian crime novels of the time. This became one of the influential films from which many Italian *giallo* thrillers of the '70s can be traced.

Roma Contra Roma (1963), directed by Giuseppe Vari, is a visually arresting and colorful but minor contribution to both the horror film genre and the heroic adventure sagas from which its origins sprung. Featuring American actor John Drew Barrymore as the power-crazed sorcerer Aderbal who seeks to revive legions of Rome's dead soldiers in a bid to rule the world, the film uneasily alternates between action and atmospheric horror, before succumbing to the inevitable finale where the heroic figure of the epic (Ettore Manni) will right the wrongs committed by Barrymore's wicked sorcerer, and bring the film to its fitting conclusion.

The obscure *Delitto allo Specchio* (1963) by director Jean Josipovici adds elements from Agatha Christie's classic story *Ten Little Indians* to the gothic horror genre with its tale of a seance held in a gloomy mansion filled with the usual disreputable types. One by one, each and every guest is menaced.

Riccardo Freda's *Lo Spettro* (1963) revisits some of the themes that fascinated him when he made *L'Orribile Segreto del Dr. Hichcock*. While a totally different film, *Lo Spettro* re-introduces the Dr. Hichcock character (Peter Baldwin replacing Robert Flemyng) as a driven man who suspects the infidelity of his wife (Barbara Steele). As he awaits evidence of her possible treachery, or a worse fate at the hands of her lover, Hichcock is injected with a formula that induces a death-like state. Presumed dead, he is buried. Of course, Hichcock returns to terrorize the two lovers, and, in an ending that is definitely inspired by the Grand Guignol theater, surprises his wife who is attempting to commit suicide by drinking poison. He injects her with the same formula that he himself had taken, only it is more powerful and kills her. In triumph, he drinks the nearby glass of liquid, not realizing that it is the same poison.

Mario Bava's *I Tre Volti della Paura* (1963) is a superior omnibus film featuring three stories, influenced by the work of three distinct writers of fiction (Anton Chekhov, Guy De Maupassant and Alexei Tolstoy). Wildly uneven but effective, its crowning moment of success is the gloriously atmospheric tale "The Wurdalak." A peasant family, faced with the possible threat of a cruel villain, gathers together within the confines of their small home to keep away the invader: a demon (Boris Karloff) who is vampirizing members of his own clan.

Antonio Margheriti's *La Vergine di Norimberga* (1963) is another tale of gothic horrors, but this time they take place in the contemporary Germany of 1963, at the castle of a newly married couple. A masked man in an executioner's hood stalks the nearby environs for nubile maidens to torture in the dungeons of the castle.

Il Castello dei Morti Vivi (1964) is the work of three directors: unknown Warren Keifer, Italian Luciano Ricci and British Michael Reeves. The film, about a demented count (Christopher Lee) who finds pleasure in tormenting his guests and embalming the women as statues, is an uneven and uninvolving affair despite occasional moments of pure delirium.

Camillo Mastrocinque's *La Cripta e l'Incubo* (1964) was, at the time of its release, the third version of Irish author Sheridan LeFanu's *Carmilla* on record. The film, a co-production with Spain's Hispamer Films, is peopled by a cast of uninteresting actors except for Christopher Lee as the family patriarch, concerned about an ancestral curse, a form of vampirism, that plagues the descendants, in this case, the Count's daughter.

Margheriti's *La Danza Macabre* (1964) is as near as an Italian filmmaker had gotten to reproducing the atmosphere, mood and theatrics of Mario Bava's *La Maschera del Demonio*. Utilizing the hypnotic presence of Barbara Steele as a ghostly femme fatale, Margheriti's film echoed many of the basic primal nightmares of childhood memories, including spending the night alone in a large house. Margheriti amplified this theme into a delirious paean to Steele's presence. This same director's *I Lunghi Capelli della Morte* (1964) is a much more grandiose, serious film, which could have been merely a dramatic costume picture if the horror themes had been removed. Once again, Barbara Steele is featured in the cast as a resurrected presence of revenge, out to avenge the death of herself and the treatment of others under the tyrannical ruler that preys upon a populace.

Renato Polselli's *Il Mostro dell'Opera* (1964) is a film that was beset with problems. It began production in 1961 as a follow-up to Polselli's *L'Amante del Vampiro* (1960), yet it was not finished until 1964. In this film, Polselli continues his fascination with full-bodied voluptuous actresses as well as the cheap and exploitative premise that fueled his previous work. A group of actors and dancers use an old opera house as a rehearsal hall for their next production. Amidst the scenes of writhing, scantily clad women is a vampiric creature that preys first on the women, then the men.

Partly due to the apparent failure of his macabre, ghostly and daring *La Frusta e il Corpo* (1963) to find an attentive and appreciative audience, Mario Bava struck back at cinema audiences and critics alike with the excessively violent *Sei Donne per l'Assassino* (1964). This film took elements that existed in his *La Ragazza Che Sapeva Troppo* and added touches of a heretofore-unseen sadistic nature. A stylish cinematic interpretation of the Grand Guignol ethic of shock value theatrics, *Sei Donne per l'Assassino* would, in the years to come, remain a key work for many filmmakers to reference when they were making their own *giallo* thrillers.

Mario Caiano's *Amanti d'Oltretomba* (1965) is another film where the director, obviously infatuated with his leading lady, seeks to construct the film entirely around her aura. Once again, the visage of Barbara Steele appears as the twin faces of horror as she portrays two roles in this picture loosely based on tales written by Edgar Allan Poe. As the brunette Muriel, Steele is caught with her lover (Rik Battaglia) by her husband (Paul Mueller), who tortures and kills her. As Jenny, Muriel's twin blonde sister, she is driven to near-insanity by the now-crazed husband and becomes possessed by the vengeful spirit of Muriel. Caino worked much better in the fantasy milieu of the sword-and-sandal peplums and the European spy thrillers than he did with Gothic horror.

Director Massimo Pupillo's *Il Boia Scarlatto* (1965) is a laughable yet disturbing and sadistic entry in the genre. As the Italian horror films were about to make a turn towards strictly more violent fare, Pupillo's film about a deranged former muscleman actor (Mickey Hargitay) who displays repressed homosexual tendencies is a troubling title that points to the move towards the heightened appearance of misogynism in the Italian horror films of the late '60s. Another group of stranded travelers (models accompanied by their photographers) appear at the castle of an ex-actor who is totally preoccupied with his own narcissism. At night, he oils up his torso, dons a scarlet red hangman's hood and seeks to kidnap, torture and murder his guests.

Dino Tavella's *Il Mostro di Venezia* (1965) harkens back to the same kind of dull police procedural and travelogue footage that plagues much of Freda's own *I Vampiri*. Here, a killer of women stalks the canals of Venice in his scuba diving wetsuit. When he appears out of the water to torture his victims, he dons the robes of a monk and a mask of a skull. A forgettable, nearly unwatchable, bore, it is best remembered for images contained within its promotional posters which featured the skull-faced killer and scantily clad women in chains. That same year, Michael Reeves' *La Sorella di Satana* (1965), a low-budget but occasionally effective horror film, premiered. The basic premise was about a vacationing couple and the new bride (Barbara Steele) who becomes possessed by the vengeful sprit of a witch who was persecuted and murdered in the film's prologue.

Mario Bava's science fiction–horror hybrid, *Terrore nello Spazzio* (1965) is an ingenious mix of interplanetary space travel SF and the more Earthbound horrors of parasitic, vampire-like beings who use the host bodies of murdered crewmen as a means to get off the planet on which they are stranded. Visually impressive on a low budget, this is indeed one of the finest "interplanetary space travel horror films" of the '60s, although admittedly the genre is a very small one.

Un Angelo per Satana (1966) is Camillo Mastrocinque's horror tale concerning a beautiful woman (Barbara Steele) who becomes possessed by the spirit of another deceased woman whose visage had been carved as an ancient statue. Slow, ponderous and none too involving, the film is chiefly recommended for the perverse intensity of Steele's performance as the possessed Harriet, a harrowing, unglamorous portrayal.

Steele returned to the screen in what would become her last role in an Italian genre film. In *Cinque Tombe per un Medium* (1966), she portrays Cleo, the widow of Dr. Hauff, an enigmatic scientist who was striving to complete his finest achievement prior to his death — the waking of the dead. Walter Brandi appears as the stoic hero, a lawyer who investigates the death of Dr. Hauff and witnesses (during one of the movie's more effective sequences) the macabre reviving of the dead as they, spurred on by the spirit of the late Dr. Hauff, seek to murder those responsible for his murder. Filmed in an eerie combination of stark contrasting blacks and whites, the film is often enveloped in shades of gray whenever the undead threaten key cast members. Barbara Steele has little to do but to alternately appear aloof, mys-

As a narcissistic former actor, Mickey Hargitay whips himself into a frenzy in the satiric horror film *Il Boia Scarlatto* (1965, MBS Cinematografica/International Entertainment Corporation).

terious, comely and, finally, terrified. Yet, despite the lack of anything challenging for her to do according to the confines of the script, her presence alone elevates the productions above other, similar genre films of the period. Massimo Pupillo had made two other films that have earned a place in the Italian horror pantheon, *Il Boia Scarlatto* (1965) and *La Vendetta di Lady Morgan* (1966). Yet neither of these films managed to convey the oppressive atmosphere that *Cinque Tombe per un Medium* strives for and, sometimes achieves, making it his most successful film as a director.

La Llama nel Corpo (1966) is Elio Scardamaglia's handsomely crafted gothic thriller about a physician (William Berger) who presides over an asylum full of crazed individuals and a killer who roams its corridors at night, threatening women with a sharp blade. Is this all a device intended to blame the doctor for the murders? Or is there something more sinister at hand? In the truest Italian horror film tradition, the latter is the case, as there is a hooded killer, a deformed woman locked away in one of the unused rooms and a jealous, insane wife, adding to the apparently unending list of suspicious characters for audience members to choose the culprit from.

The obscure *La Lunga Notte di Veronique* (1966) is the kind of film that aims to be a replica of the Gothic films of the early sixties, but ends up being far from the original intentions of the director, Gianni Vernuccio. A woman (Alba Rigazzi) makes a suicidal pact with an amorous Count, but he does not keep his part of the bargain. Years later, her specter returns to seduce his grandson into repeating the same kind of pact with her.

Massimo Pupillo's *La Vendetta di Lady Morgan* (1966) is cut from a similar cloth, but his film also seems more interested in the ethereal aspects of the genre, as a returning female spirit who seduces then murders her lovers and victims enacts revenge from beyond the grave. Filmed in a more careful and studied manner that any of Pupillo's other films as a director, *La Vendetta di Lady Morgan* is a successful attempt at emulating the better Gothic horror films of earlier years, but by 1966, audiences were tuned into and expecting more from the colorful and violence-soaked horror films that other filmmakers were churning out.

A change signaling the end of the Italian horror film, as we had known it, appeared on the horizon with the 1966 film *Libido*. A thriller that predates the innovative work of Dario Argento, *Libido* seems to be little influenced by the seminal work of Mario Bava in the genre and, instead, seems to exist within a cinematic vacuum of its own. Helmed by the prolific screenwriting team of Ernesto Gastaldi and Luciano Martino (with the assistance of Vittorio Salerno), the film introduces Giancarlo Giannini as Christian, a man who had witnessed his insane father murder his mistress in a room full of mirrors, then throw himself over a cliff into the sea. When Christian returns to the cliffside estate years later, accompanied by his new bride (Dominique Boschero) and friends (Mara Maryl and Luciano Pigozzi), events transpire that suggest that maybe Christian's father is not dead after all and that someone may be terrorizing his new bride. Over the course of the film, viewers learn that even this is not the case as his wife and one of his friends have learned of Christian's troubled past and have jointly agreed to drive him insane in a bid to gain his inheritance for themselves. Unknown to them, Christian has already gone insane and events from his past may repeat themselves.

Although Gastaldi and Martino would contribute to dozens of Italian genre films (as screenwriters) over the next two decades, this, their first production as directors, is ultimately an uneven affair, displaying an awkward handling of actors. Their follow-up production (released in 1982 as *Notturno con Grida*) is an equally madcap, as well as incredibly low-budget production that disappoints as a thriller, going so far as to use (colorized) footage from *Libido* as well as returning cast members Maryl and Pigozzi in a ridiculous plot device that incorporates themes from that earlier film (the picturesque cliff side setting and the insane genetic murderers) into a new plot featuring a group of people (including psychics) stranded in a forest. Flashbacks from earlier events (scenes from *Libido*) are intercut with the new footage of actors wandering around aimlessly waiting for the screenwriters to come up with something to act with.

Antonio Margheriti's *Nude ... Si Muore* (1967) is an underrated thriller set in

Caltiki, il Mostro Immortale (1959, Galatea Film [Milan]/Climax Pictures [Los Angeles–U.S.]/Allied Artists Pictures Corporation [U.S.]).

a girl's school where the killer is revealed to be a cross-dresser! The original story was written by Mario Bava. The cast is relatively full of attractive unknowns (save for Michael Rennie as the policeman investigating the murders and Mark Damon as the hero) and is notable for being one of the first films to feature frequent Margheriti character actor Luciano Pigozzi (often credited as Alan Collins) in a major role.

Malenka — La Nipote del Vampiro (1968) is another uneven vampire tale, this time an Italian and Spanish co-production directed by the Spaniard Amando De Ossorio (in his genre film debut). Featuring the original European sex bomb Anita Ekberg, the movie makes for an occasionally diverting, but ultimately unsatisfying entry in the vampire film genre. Julian Ugarte (who the previous year had appeared in *La Marca del Hombre Lobo*, the first of the numerous Paul Naschy–Waldemar Daninsky werewolf films, in a similar role) portrays the vampire count who lures his comely, mature descendent (Ekberg) to his Italian castle and reveals to her that she is the reincarnation of Malenka, his beloved lover, who was supposedly burned as a witch centuries before. In a series of confusing sequences, it is suggested that all is a ruse to force Ekberg to renounce her inheritance and that all of the bloodsucking that had come before had been part of an elaborately staged scheme. Most likely the filmmakers were aware of the problems that such material might cause in censorial regions and so two versions of the film were produced simultaneously. In one version we learn that the count really is a vampire and, at the intentional comedic fade-out in another, so are his nubile, sexy assistants.

The popularity of a wealth of adult Italian comic strips (called *fumetti* in their native country) caused some filmmakers to look to these sadistic, sexy and violent illustrated stories for their inspiration. Piero Vivarelli's *Satanik* (1968) is one such film. It tells the tale of haggard, crone-like Marnie Bannister (Magda Konopka), who murders her scientist employer to steal his new invention, a potion that changes her into a seductive killer. Marnie needs to imbibe more and more of the mysterious potion and ultimately reverts back to her true form just in time for the intervention of the authorities. Featuring such time-worn cliches as rollicking musical numbers (for the cabaret sequences) and the good-evil duality of the main character (which here is turned inside-out as the character of Marnie uses her newfound sexual allure to seduce, murder and achieve fame), Vivarelli's colorful production is merely a sporadically entertaining footnote marking time until the explosion of the thriller genre in the early '70s pointed to the new directions that the Italian horror film was taking.

Based upon the sadistic and sensual Italian comic strip (*fumetto*) called *Isabella* (created by Alessandro Angiolini in 1966), *Isabel, Duchessa del Diavoli* (1969) is the only known cinematic interpretation of the character of Isabella. This film, directed by Bruno Corbucci, concerns the birth of our sword-wielding heroine (Brigitte Skay) who, as a small child, saw her royal parents murdered by a sadistic baron. Given safety and a new identity by a troupe of traveling circus performers, Isabella is unaware of her heritage until a series of violent confrontations strike chords of vengeance within her. Trained as an expert swordsman, Isabella thinks only of revenge. While the film presents many opportunities for Corbucci, a veteran of Spaghetti Westerns, to adapt his brutal cinematic style to the costume melodrama, he botches the idea almost immediately by introducing numerous slapstick moments and scenes of soft-core copulations. The film becomes a mixed affair and only marginally a horror film by association.

Il Contronatura (1969) is Antonio Margheriti's uneven but still interesting tale of revenge. A group of travelers end up in a villa inhabited by a couple who are spiritualists. During seances that practically last the entire length of the film, the criminal past of the stranded travelers is unveiled. The spiritualists are, in fact, ghostly beings who remind the travelers of their misdeeds.

La Bambola di Satana (1969) by Ferruccio Casapinta is a strange film starring Erna Scheurer as Elizabeth, a woman who returns to her family's ancestral home after the death of her father for the reading of his will. Legends of ghostly apparitions are told, and the local village and the castle seems to be the center of these hauntings. After experiencing a series of erotic nightmares, Elizabeth is kidnapped by a hooded figure and tortured in the castle dungeon. Her boyfriend suspects that there are no ghosts, but a sinister plot to gain her family inheritance by terrorizing her. Filled with scenes depicting seemingly constant storms and howling winds, the movie is certainly rooted within the classic gothic atmosphere of early Italian horrors, but the addition of considerable nudity and a black-gloved killer clearly places *La Bambola di Satana* at the cusp of the new age. It is an indication of the changing aspects of the Italian horror film to come.

L'Uccello dalle Piume di Cristallo (1969) is the directorial debut of Dario Argento and one of the great *giallo* thrillers. It also unfortunately heralds the end of the classical Italian horror film and introduces the decade where the Italian horror film would splinter off into many separate sub-divisions. The '70s would see the growth of the *giallo* film into an outright cottage industry. Yet, before nearly every Italian horror film was presented in the guise of a thriller film, there were a few more pictures left to come out of the industry from filmmakers attempting to breathe new life into an ever-changing genre. Tonino Cervi's *Il Delitto del Diavolo* (1971) is one of those films.

In a failed attempt to introduce elements of the youth counterculture genre into the Italian horror film, director Cervi instead has *Il Delitto del Diavolo* coast along on an eerie, unsteady atmosphere resembling a macabre fairy tale. A drifter (Raymond Lovelock) is induced by the Devil (masquerading as an industrialist riding in a Rolls Royce automobile, an obvious paean to the notions of youth versus the older society that was so prevalent in the early '70s) to become involved with three eccentric women who live in a secluded house in the countryside. The challenges Cervi brings to his lead character are the many temptations of the flesh and the need for the freewheeling human to suffer (alternately) both sin and guilt. After Lovelock resigns himself to sharing the remainder of his life and abandons his quest for personal freedom, he is murdered. The film's not-surprising coda re-introduces the satanic character, who congratulates the women and sends them on their way, presumably on to a similar mission. Cervi's film is a thinly masked exploitation of the ideals exhibited by the male youth population who openly embraced the counter cultural revolution, particularly the threat to personal freedom and expression, which, in most instances, meant the ideals represented by bourgeoisie society and female companionship.

Meanwhile, Mel Welles' deliciously entertaining *La Figlia di Frankenstein* (1971), a hybrid of the '70s Hammer horror films' infatuation with nudity and sadism and the golden age of Italian horror's gothic period, appeared. This lurid sexploitation film tells of the tribulations endured by Tania (Rosalba Neri), the daughter of Dr. Frankenstein (Joseph Cotten). The icy offspring of the infamous surgeon seeks to emulate then surpass her own father's experiments by creating the ultimate creature — a stupendously well-endowed human male who sports incredible strength and an unmatched virility, the latter to equal her own carnal desires gone awry.

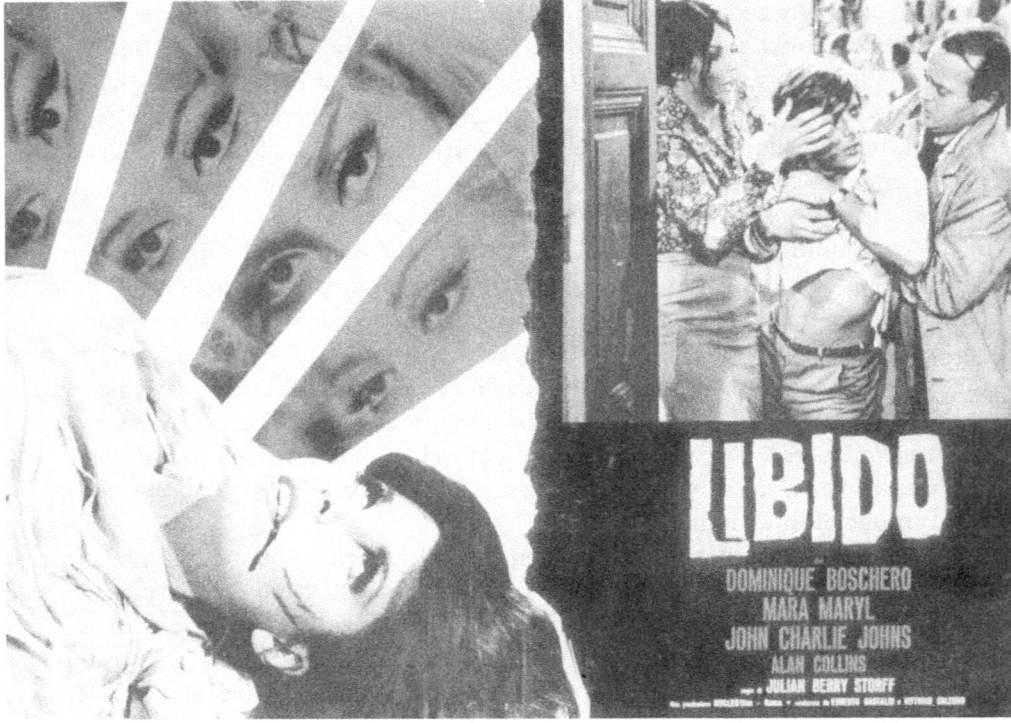

Libido (1966, Nucleo film), an early example of an Italian *giallo* thriller.

With loving attention paid to the eighteenth century–influenced set design, the film's climax (which invokes the innocent Universal horror films which preceded the Hammer Films by decades) sees torch-wielding villagers storm the castle of Frankenstein to destroy both creator and creation. But they stand at the entrance, mouths agape, as they witness the fondling, caressing hands of the monster upon the nubile body of his goddess—before they both perish in the flames.

More sexually explicit themes appeared in Emilio P. Miraglia's *La Notte Che Evelyn Uscì dalla Tomba* (1971). In this film, a sadistic count (Antonio De Teffe) is shown to be merely an innocent pawn in a scheme to drive him insane. His occasional nocturnal missions include picking up stray women, then returning with them to the castle dungeon for sex games and whippings. Then he is confronted with the ghostly reappearance of his deceased second wife (Marina Malfatti), whose corpse repeatedly rises from the grave in a plot to drive him insane and gain his inheritance. With the addition of scheming lovers, treachery and a surprising climax, the film succeeds as a thriller and is entertaining, even at a crass level with its insistence on female nudity and occasional sequences of sadism.

More experimental was director Filippo Walter Ratti's *La Notte dei Dannati* (1971). In this strange and seldom-seen film, the wife of a mystery writer and amateur detective (Pierre Brice) is invited to the estate of her family to attend the reading of a will. With a large inheritance at stake, the couple journeys to the family home only to be confronted with malevolence in the form of a reincarnated witch who has slowly turned family members to her side and made them her own private satanic coven. With his wife being visited nightly by an ethereal Satanist with lesbian tendencies, it comes time for the opium-smoking hero to finally put down his pipe and investigate the strange happenings before it is too late. Ratti's film may be too slow for some audiences, but the film moves at such an otherworldly pace that events seem to unfold like the opium smoke blowing from the hero's pipe.

Psychedelic imagery appears again in *L'Occhio nel Labirinto* (1971), Mario Caiano's bizarre, surreal horror thriller. The film begins when a woman (Rosemary Dexter) believes that she actually sees her psychiatrist-lover (Horst Frank) murdered in an underground parking garage. However, when an investigation ensues, there is no victim to be found. Suffering repeated visions of this occurrence, she enlists the aid of a strange criminal mastermind (Adolfo Celli) who lives in a castle peopled by eccentric characters. Ultimately, it is revealed that the woman is, in fact, a schizophrenic, who has murdered her lover and will repeat the act of murder unless stopped. Caino fills the film with as many of Dexter's bizarre visions (a severed head in a refrigerator, sadistic sex in a castle dungeon, an elaborate LSD trip) as to continually keep the viewing audience off guard and guessing the outcome of the tale.

In Jean Brismee and Andre Hunnebelle's Belgian-Italian co-production *La Terrificante Notte del Demonio* (1971), psychedelics play less of an integral part of the story, but are no less an implied ingredient in the production of this strange tale. Enrica Bianchi Colmobatto, a.k.a. Erica Blanc, has her most prestigious genre role as the succubus, an ungodly product of a union between the brother of an ex–SS Nazi baron and his own housekeeper. Baron Von Rumberg (Jean Servais) had been an officer during World War II and had to murder his only child, whose mother died giving birth to her. Decades later, a stranded group of travelers end up at the Von Rumberg castle and meet with a beautiful woman (Colombatto) who claims to be the baron's daughter. Seemingly innocent and virginal by day, she becomes a breast-baring, ghostly succubus by night, serving the Devil's command by killing each of the seven stranded travelers since each of the them (including a young, troubled priest) exhibits one of the seven deadly sins. Whenever they commit their particular sin, the succubus will appear. As strange as it all sounds, the often haphazard and confused direction seems to contribute to the disturbing and genuinely eerie atmosphere that soaks the film.

The Italian comic strip genre of *fumetti* was revisited once again for Corrado Farina's *Baba Yaga* (1973), a film version of the sado-fetishistic adult comics of creator Guido Crepax, featuring the heroine Valentina. In *Baba Yaga*, Valentina (Isabelle De Funes) is a photographer who enters into a series of misadventures involving crime, murder and witchcraft. Ultimately, our heroine ends up imprisoned in a sinister castle where black-clad villainous Carroll Baker (who is actually a witch) will attempt to draw her into her coven through a series of sexual and then torturous affairs. More successful than Bruno Corbucci's own earlier experiment with making of a *fumetto* a cinematic interpretation, *Baba Yaga* glides along on its own peculiar combination of sex and fashion, despite the inability of director Farina to convey a particularly needed atmosphere of menace. The Valentina character was revived in 1988 for an Italian television miniseries and then a more sexually explicit theatrical film version of three re-edited episodes from the series.

When it came to cheap exploitation, there are few Italian horror films as more offensive than *Il Castello della Paura* (1973). This Ramino Oliveros film is little more than low-budget horror at its worst. With the aid of a malevolent dwarf (Michael Dunn) and an assortment of sinister servants and hunchbacks, Count Frankenstein (Rossano Brazzi) seeks to give birth to his new creation called Goliath. However, the Count expels his diminutive assistant from the castle and this lost soul takes up with Ook, the Neanderthal Man (Salvatore Baccaro acting under the pseudonym Boris Lugosi), a prehistoric caveman–like creature. Both return to Castle Frankenstein to enact the dwarf's revenge. Filled with nudity and gore, the film meanders from one awkward camera set-up to the next; even in its cheap thrills it fails to elicit the kind of positive response that other similar, or less inspired, films have managed.

An equally strange film is Mario Mancini's *Frankenstein '80* (1973), a lurid sex film dressed as a horror movie. This misguided production follows the monster named Mosaico (Xiro Papas), the creation of Dr. Albrechtstein (Gordon Mitchell), who kills his creator and then roams the modern metropolis of contemporary Italy searching for new fresh body parts when his own start to malfunction (his body is rejecting the hastily transplanted organs attached by his creator). Although Mosaico has a mission, he is not too involved with replacing body parts to pass up molesting and raping women at night. The police investigate and eventually believe that a superhuman killer is in their midst. *Frankenstein '80* is a failed attempt at combining the most exploitive elements from sex and horror films.

Occasionally there comes an Italian horror film which, manages to fall out of the confines of a given genre. Such is the case with Gianfranco Mingozzi's *Flavia, La Monaca Musulmana* (1974). Supposedly based on actual historic events, *Flavia* tells of a fifteenth century woman (Florinda Bolkan) who was forcibly imprisoned within a convent where she endured brutal treatment and rape by the priests of the notorious Tarantula sect.

When invading Muslims overtook Italy, she joined forces with them and used them to wreak vengeance upon those who wronged her. When the Muslims left Italy, Flavia is captured and skinned alive for her punishment. Needlessly sadistic, graphic and strong sequences of mutilation highlight this film and most likely kept it from the viewing roster of most Italian horror fans. Although it fits into no known category, its bold and relentless view of religious persecution and revenge makes for a decidedly uneasy experience.

Another area seldom traversed by Italian filmmakers is the occult possession theme. Most likely due to the heavy Catholicized nature of the country, few directors have actually managed to make horror films with this subject matter and only a handful (Mario Bava and Lucio Fulci, for instance) have managed to make a film using this subject matter that is interesting.

Il Mediaglione Insanguinato (1974) is one of the more intriguing attempts at the occult possession theme popularized by the international success of the American horror film *The Exorcist* (1973). Director Massimo Dallamano's tale begins when a widowed British television director (Richard Johnson) takes his young daughter (Nicoletta Elmi) to a picturesque area to research demonic paintings. The child becomes possessed by one particularly eerie painting and, with a bizarrely inappropriate, incestuous glint in her eye, seeks to remove all those who cause concern for her and her father. At the climax, the young girl seems to overcome her possession and madly slashes away at the painting, before coming at her own father—knife in hand, leaving the question unanswered: Will she, or won't she?

The Exorcist was also spoofed in Ciccio Ingrassia's *L'Esorciccio* (1975), a misguided attempt at making a near-slapstick comedy version of that film. Ingrassia, formerly one-half of the incredibly popular Italian comedy team of Franco and Ciccio (which made dozens of films throughout the '60s and early '70s), flounders in his film without a manic figure (like former wild man Franco Franchi) to play off of.

Un Sussurro nel Buio (1976) directed by Marcello Aliprandi, models its themes of occult possession on the highly regarded *Don't Look Now* (1972), directed by Nicolas Roeg. Set in a Venetian villa (like its model), the story finds the parents of a young boy becoming alarmed when their son exhibits strange behavior. Apparently, he can see and talk with his deceased brother (who died at childbirth). The parents deny the presence of this apparition until it threatens the existence of the family. Less pretentious than its example, the film manages to tread similar ground but remains an interesting and eerie thriller.

Un Urlo dalla Tenebrae (1977) is an unusual tale of possession told from the point of view of a nun who has a young brother possessed by a demonic spirit. Offensively lurid, cheap and exploitative, the film (directed by Elo Pannaccio) becomes more soft pornography than horror film by spending considerable screen time with its key female cast members, having them disrobe at every conceivable opportunity.

The occult rears its head once again *Sensitività* (1979), Enzo Girolami's little-seen thriller. A young woman named Lillian (Leonora Fani) returns to the hometown where her mother had been murdered (sucked below the waters of a lake by phantom hands). Lillian proceeds to inhabit the family castle and deals with a witch named Kyra, nicknamed the Lady of the Lake. A curse put upon Lillian by Kyra causes her to collapse whenever she experiences sexual thoughts or an orgasm, only to revive whenever her partner dies (usually the result of the witch's incantations). Lillian also meets a strange young woman named Lillith (Caterina Boratto) and the

two begin a sexual relationship that literally sets the countryside ablaze as flames actually engulf the pair (via a ruptured gas tank) as they make love. After years directing films in the numerous sub-genres of the Italian horror film, Girolami finally achieves a poetic grandeur with this sensual, erotic horror tale. Although the film in no way approaches Girolami's best work in the Western film genre (*Kemoa* [1975], for example), it is a decidedly offbeat affair. Its flashbacks, flash-forwards and wild, frenetic crosscutting would have made the director a not-unwelcome presence in the Hong Kong Cinema style of filmmaking.

In Carlo Ausino's stylishly photographed gothic terror tale *La Villa delle Anime Maldette* (1983), set in Turin, four people inhabit a home where, years before, two men and a woman had savagely murdered each other. The new owners encounter a seemingly malevolent caretaker who is in fact some sort of sorcerer and has put a curse of the house and its inhabitants. While the film is enjoyable hokum, it is hardly considered memorable viewing.

Producer-director Augusto Caminito's *Nosferatu a Venezia* (1988), an unsanctioned semi-sequel to Werner Herzog's *Nosferatu, Phantom der Nacht* (1979), is as unusual a film as its predecessor. Featuring Klaus Kinski (who also starred in the earlier Herzog production) as the revived Count Dracula who (unlike in the earlier film) sports a mane of long, flowing blonde hair and walks the streets of Italy after awakening from a 200-year slumber in a Venetian tomb. Caminito's version of the vampire mythos has Kinski bond with outcast gypsies, win over the tireless vampire hunters (Christopher Plummer and Donald Pleasence) and gaining the girl (Barbara De Rossi), a descendant of his one true love, at the finale. Ethereal and often haunting, despite the violent vampire attacks and nudity, the film does not shame the earlier, well-regarded German production by association.

Luigi Montefiori, a.k.a. George Eastman, a frequent presence in the films of the director Aristide Massaccesi, made his directing debut (he had contributed to the scripts for many of Massaccesi's projects over the years) with *Metamorphosis* (1989), a horror movie, the likes of which were already long out of fashion with the public. The film tells of a genetic scientist (Gene Le Brock) working on aging and its effects, and pressured to produce concrete results within a short time. The scientist injects himself with his own experimental serum, which regresses him backward through the evolutionary process. Within a short time, many nubile female victims are fleeing the dinosaur-man that the scientist has become. With the addition of some (unfashionably grotesque and uncommonly politically incorrect) animal experimentation footage, *Metamorphosis* becomes little more than a bad film that, for some, cannot end soon enough.

After years of inactivity, the Mexican visionary director Alejandro Jodorowsky

Opposite: L'Uccello dalle Piume di Cristallo (1969, UMC Pictures), a thriller directed by Dario Argento, became an influential movie as filmmakers contributed to the next wave of a new breed of horror films in Italy.

Aldo Lado's *La Corta Notte delle Bambole di Vetro* (1971, Doria G. Film s.r.l.–Dunhill Cinematografica CA s.r.l.–Jadran Film-Dieter Gessler Filmproduktion) is told in flashback, narrated by the protagonist (Jean Sorel) as he lies awaiting death in a morgue.

(*El Topo* and *The Holy Mountain*) teamed up with the producer brother of Dario Argento to make *Santa Sangre* (1989), another in a series of increasingly obscure and demented films in the Jodorowsky canon. In *Santa Sangre*, young Axel Jodorowsky portrays the son of a domineering circus knife thrower (Guy Stockwell) who, upon learning of the treachery of his wife (a tattooed aerialist), brutally maims her. After killing his father, Axel will join with his armless mother (Blanca Guerra) and the two will begin a ritualistic union of domineering mother and disturbed son that will send most viewers hastily fleeing for the exit (or reaching for their remote controls). After being released from an asylum, the pair "join" for a bizarre mime act in which the man uses his own arms to function as those of his mother. This insanity leads him to more murder, building to a fittingly insane denouement. Audiences with more experimental tastes will appreciate the fierce way in which Jodorowsky thrusts the Grand Guignol influences into our faces ... with relish.

In an attempt to make more money by exporting their product to America on a pre-sold basis, some Italian filmmakers came up with a product that could be interchangeable with just about any homegrown U.S. product. Alessandro Capone's *La Streghe* (1989) is one such film. A jumbled mix of better Italian horror films (specifically those by Mario Bava and Lucio Fulci) and Sam Raimi's first *Evil Dead* installment, *La Streghe* begins interestingly enough with Deanna Lund as a witch being burned alive and then afterward causing a young woman to commit suicide. The film begins to falter at an alarmingly fast rate when, centuries later, a group of teenagers (obvious Americans stranded in Italy trying their hands at acting with little experience) descend upon a Southwestern town and meet death at the spectral hands of Lund and a ghostly suicide victim. What could have been a promising film in the Italian horror film canon quickly deteriorates into chaos with its insistence on being anything but an Italian horror film.

Over the years, the Italian horror film would gain incredible international notoriety. Cinematic offspring like zombie films, fake mondo documentaries, cannibal films and even rip-off genres that consisted of Italian versions of internationally financially successful films from other countries would virtually inhabit as many available screens worldwide that could contain them.

The course of the Italian horror film from its infancy onward will also be traced through the contributions of the directors discussed at length in this book and the subgenres of the Italian horror film that would not have existed without the earliest of the productions mentioned here.

In recent years, the Italian film industry had been plagued by a severe dearth of quality product as well as the continuation of the erosion of the profitable boom to which the Italian horror film contributed so much in its infancy. With the 2001 release of Dario Argento's *Nonhosonno* and its favorable reception in Italy and abroad, the Italian horror film may not yet be dead.

The Leading Horror Film Directors

Dario Argento

Dario Argento was born on September 7, 1940, the son of Salvatore Argento, a motion picture executive, and his wife, Elda Luxardo, a Brazilian photographer. Dario began his career as a man obsessed with the cinema. He started out as a journalist, then graduated to film criticism (for *Paesa Sera*, one of the major daily papers in Rome). While Argento was interviewing popular actor Alberto Sordi during the production of a film, Sordi was so impressed with Argento, that he cast him in the role of a young priest for the film *Scusi, Lei È Favorevole o Contrario?* (1966). Argento had once been married to a woman named Marisa with whom he fathered two daughters, Fiore and Asia. Years later, he shared a common law marriage with Italian actress Daria Nicolodi. Since *Profondo Rosso* (1975), Nicolodi appeared in many of his films and even co-wrote the screenplay for *Suspiria* (1976). While working on the film *Opera* (1987), their relationship completely collapsed. They have not worked together since. Although Argento, a slim man with a slight frame, appears tall with mysterious features and an intense stare, he is actually very friendly, given to expressive arm gestures and chain smoking (he once preferred Merit cigarettes solely).

Argento's film credits before his first directorial effort, *L'Uccello dalle Piume di Cristallo* (1969), include quite a collection of writing assignments. He had been involved with the story ideas, or had written the scripts for sexy films, romantic comedies and dramas between the years 1968 and 1970.

Among this array of titles are Franco Prosperi's *Qualcono Ha Tradito* (1967), *La Rivoluzione Sessuale*, a softcore sex film by director Riccardo Ghione, *La Stagione di Sensei*, *Commandamenti per un Gangster* (all '68) and *Metti, Una Sera a Cena* (1969) featuring Tony Musante, Florinda Bolkan and Annie Girardot. He is credited with writing or co-writing World War II action-adventure films like Armando Crispino's *Commandos* (1968) starring Lee Van Cleef, Umberto Lenzi's

La Legione dei Dannati (1968) featuring Jack Palance and *Probabilità Zero* (1968) starring Henry Silva; and the superior Westerns *Oggi a Me ... Domani a Te* (1968) and *Cimitero Senza Croci* (1968), which liberally borrows from Sergio Leone's *Per un Pugno di Dollari* (1964). One of his early credits was as a contributor to the screenplay (with the assistance of Bernardo Bertolucci) for Sergio Leone's *C'era una Volta il West* (1968), today considered one of the greatest Italian Westerns ever made. The Don Taylor film *Un Esercito di Cinque Uomini*, for which Argento wrote the story and script in 1969, is actually much better than its reputation. It stars Peter Graves, Bud Spencer and James Daly. Graves portrays the leader of a team of violent men who plan to rob a train of guarded gold from a Mexican dictator during the 1914 Mexican revolution.

Argento's first film as a director was *L'Uccello dalle Piume di Cristallo*. It is obviously influenced by the *gialli*, the lurid paperback thrillers with yellow covers popular in Italy during the early to mid–1960s. These *gialli* (*giallo* is the Italian word for the color yellow) were Italy's response to the printed Krimis, published works of criminal fiction, particularly reprints of novels by the well-known British crime authors Edgar Wallace and his son Bryan Edgar Wallace. The Wallace books enjoyed a particular vogue when they were published in Germany in the 1950s and 1960s. By the early 1960s, dozens of films were being made by German film studios and exported to other countries. These films, called Krimls, began a rebirth in the whole field of detective fiction. Edgar Wallace had been a prolific writer of fiction. His work more often than not featured the lowest criminals imaginable, femme fatales too sexy for their time, and damsels in distress who were measurably smarter than many contemporary women were depicted. His heroes (or what passed for them) were usually gamblers seeking penance, wronged men or violent felons seeking vengeance. His protagonists were almost always members of Scotland Yard's elite. If you re-read Edgar Wallace novels today, one can see almost as brutal an inclination for the same sort of nasty bits of masochism and violence that, many years later, fellow British author Ian Fleming would use for his own James Bond series of novels.

The German film versions of the Wallace stories were, and to this day are, still a unique film genre. They fall into no existing

Dario Argento (right) and the author in 1994 (photograph: Heidi Stock).

category of film. They are neither detective stories, nor horror stories, nor romantic melodramas. These are films that seem to mix all the genres together into one whole. Often these films featured some bits of graphic violence or nudity that, for some of the countries to which they were exported, were considered daring or exploitative for the time.

Although he often claims the crime writers Dashiell Hammett, Raymond Chandler and Cornell Woolrich as major influences upon his early work and writing style, it is obvious that Dario Argento had also been quite taken with these German Edgar Wallace films. He most likely enjoyed reading the *gialli*, which contained either reprints of German Krimis translated into Italian or an Italian author's own take on the format. In fact, the story idea for *L'Uccello dalle Piume di Cristallo* is said to have (incorrectly) derived from a novel by Bryan Edgar Wallace, cementing the connection of influences.

Before continuing, however, one must also be made aware of the influence that Mario Bava had on Argento as a filmmaker. In 1968, Argento was offered a position by film producer Goffredo Lombardo. His role in Lombardo's company would be to revise scripts with which the producer was dissatisfied. It was Bernardo Bertolucci's friendship that was indirectly responsible for Argento's career as a film director. Bertolucci visited Argento, carrying with him a copy of author Frederic Brown's *Screaming Mimi*. Bertolucci believed that the story, written in 1953, could be made into a great film (apparently unaware that there had already been a 1958 film version starring Anita Ekberg, directed by Gerd Oswald). For whatever reason, Bertolucci, who sought to purchase the rights to the story, never made the film. Argento, however, was impressed by many of the elements contained within the psychological thriller and thought that with changes it could prove to be an interesting film. He was impressed by the 1962 Mario Bava thriller *La Ragazza Che Sapeva Troppo* and especially its theme of the young displaced American tourist who witnesses an incredible crime (or did she?). Bava's film told of his protagonist's dilemma, not certain she can recall specific details of the crime she witnessed, or even recognize the killer (who has apparently killed several times before). The woman is hounded by the feeling of something amiss and investigates on her own. Keeping the basic story idea, but changing the sex of the main protagonist, led to the formation of some of the plot ingredients for *L'Uccello dalle Piume di Cristallo*. Directing the film was an apparent battle for Argento who, after delivering the completed script and beginning production, was on the verge of being replaced by Ferdinando Baldi. His shooting style was misunderstood and the incoming dailies not to the satisfaction of co-producer Lombardo. But Argento prevailed when he pointed out that he had provided a clause in his contract that stated that only he could direct this film from a script that he had written and he finished the project.

The synopsis of *L'Uccello dalle Piume di Cristallo* is intriguing: Sam Delmas (Tony Musante), an American writer living in Rome, finds himself suffering from writer's block, except when he contributes to the text for a volume documenting

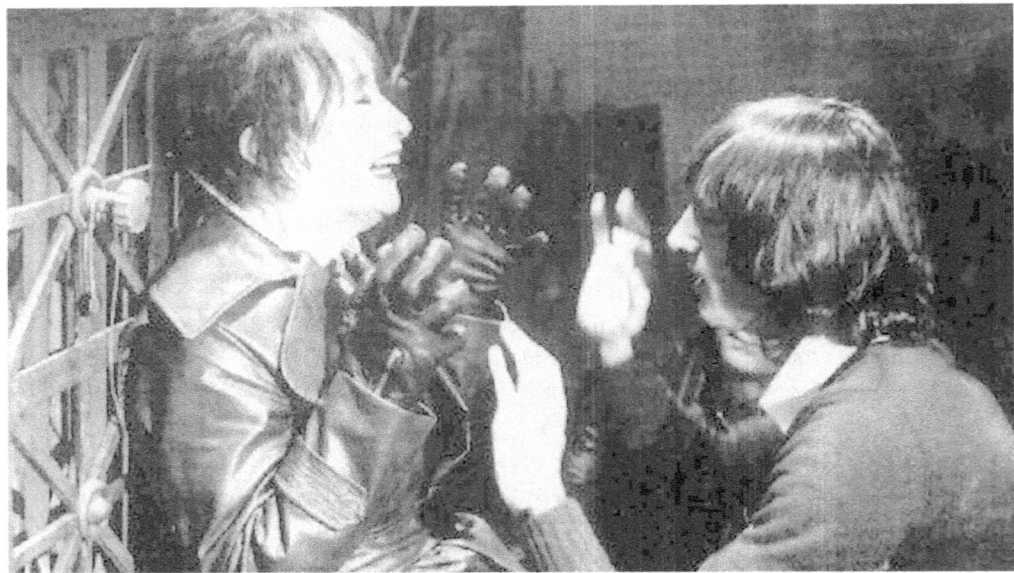

Dario Argento directs climax of *Profondo Rosso* (1975, SEDA Spettacoli Produzione for Rizzioli Films).

exotic birds. Walking through the streets one night, he witnesses an attack on a woman in an art gallery by a figure wearing a black wide-brimmed hat, black coat and black gloves. Delmas manages to save the woman's life by distracting the assailant, but instead of running to her aid, he becomes trapped in the gallery's security door system. Although the would-be killer escapes, Delmas realizes that he has glimpsed something, a vital clue perhaps, but is unable to recall what it exactly is. Delmas soon finds himself being stalked by this figure. When the bodies start piling up around him, he plans to investigate. Unwittingly, his own girlfriend (Suzy Kendall) becomes bait to trap the killer. Delmas vows to reveal the identity of the killer and search for the bizarre reason for the murders, as he becomes obsessed with solving the crimes.

The film manages to mix many of the influences previously mentioned and imbue them with a distinctly original visual outlook. Vittorio Storraro's sleek photography adds to the look of the film, which is extremely modern and realistic. Argento has the added attraction of an absolutely amazing Ennio Morricone score that is more than just a knock-off soundtrack for pay.

Morricone's soundtrack accompanies the visuals with an insistent, repetitive score that cues the viewer in on the shocking scenes to come. It shares with few other films the distinction of being one of the more successful debuts in the horror film genre. The chief elements of the Italian *giallo* film genre, which Mario Bava helped to pioneer with *La Ragazza Che Sapeva Troppo* and *Sei Donne per l'Assassino*, were refined with this film. On an added note, the director has spoken of his extreme dislike for Tony Musante, but there appears no apparent friction in the film between director and star. In fact, Musante seems to acquit himself well and becomes the first in a long line of American actors that Argento cast as his key protagonist. This is a film that fans of Italian thrillers seem to have no problem watching over and over again.

His next film, *Il Gatto a Nove Code*, teeters between thriller and horror and detective fiction more so than its predecessor does. Its plot device (the belief that an extra "Y" chromosome might cause a genetic mutation in a person's makeup, compelling him/her to commit murder during psychopathic rages) may be an idea borrowed from the similarly themed British shocker *Twisted Nerve* (1969); it seems more science fiction than actual horror.

The film succeeded in giving birth to Argento's cinematic obsession with eyes and sharp objects. Before each act of violence, the audience is exposed to an extreme close-up of eyes. Argento's cinematic world concentrates on the eyes of the killer. This way the audience will identify with this person as the malevolent presence in the film, before finding out his/her identity at the finale (through the close-up of the eyes of the murderer).

Another closer look at the story reveals many of the novel twists and turns that the filmmaker puts the audience through: Within a Rome-based medical institute that investigates chromosomal abnormalities and their possible effect on personality, a black-gloved killer (who has an XYY factor gene disorder which causes a chemical imbalance and eventual rage in its victims) murders several members of the institute staff who had discovered which person has tested positive with the XYY factor gene. Newspaperman Carlo Giordani (James Franciscus) joined by blind ex-newsman Franco Arno (Karl Malden) and his young niece try to track down the killer who has his/her eye on them.

Maybe not as fast-paced or as visually daring as its predecessor, the film, nevertheless, does feature a continued ambiance of dread and some gruesome murders (among them, a beheading by train and several stabbings) and an oddly downbeat end. The audience is left pondering the uncertain fate of the prime characters that they have been following. After the death of the killer, the camera pans to the top of an elevator shaft and we hear the cries of a small child. Has she been saved? When we last saw her, she was beaten, bound and gagged. When we last see James Franciscus' newsman, he has been seriously stabbed with a large knife and Malden's blind ex-reporter had been driven by grief to commit murder. An oddity that has continued to plague this film is the fact that it often does not end up mentioned in many authors' works on films in the horror genre. It is most disconcerting that the film is absent from Phil Hardy's valuable reference tool *The Encyclopedia of Horror Movies* (originally published by the British-based Aurum Press) and rarely discussed when Argento's work is accessed in print.

Argento spent some time after *Il Gatto a Nove Code* developing story ideas which he co-wrote with fellow genre enthusiast Luigi Cozzi. One was to have involved a seance where a medium predicts that seven members of a gathering will be killed. As seven members of the seance prepare to leave, the medium herself is murdered. The film's protagonist and the police allow another seance to be held, and the killer is revealed. When a similar approach to this idea appeared on an Italian television program and was partially used in Antonio Margheriti's film *Il Contronatura* (1969), this Argento-Cozzi project was abandoned. More unfilmed projects included ideas that involved a man who has been observed in the process of murder by someone who recognizes him. Unable to identify this person, the murderer begins to exterminate all the suspects that he can think of until he comes to a serious realization — that he should have looked closer to home. Another involved a man being followed in the night. When he confronts his stalker, the mysterious person is killed after a quarrel. The man is shocked when he realizes that someone has witnessed the crime, although he does not know who this witness is. As clues point to some close relation or friend being the possible witness to the crime, the film's protagonist methodically plans on murdering them to keep his deed a secret. With a few alterations, these projects sounds suspiciously similar to what was to become Luigi Cozzi's own giallo, *L'Assassino È Costretto ad Uccidere Ancora* (1975).

Quattro Mosche di Velluto Grigio (1971) appeared next. A nightmarish bout of casting problems stalled the film for a period when Argento could not decide on an appropriate lead actress for the film. Florinda Bolkan, Claudia Cardinale and Lisa Gastoni (among others) were considered before Mimsy Farmer received the role. As for the male lead, many interesting names were thrown around (Terence Stamp, Jean-Louis Trintignant, James Taylor, John Lennon, Ringo Starr and Michael York — who, it appeared, was selected but had to refuse because of scheduling conflicts with another project). Michael Brandon eventually was given the lead. The film is an uneven mixture of ideas: What if the hero thought he had accidentally killed someone and carried his guilt with him when, in fact, he did not kill anyone?

The last image that a dying person sees is retained on the retina of the eye, like a still photograph. In this case, it is the image of a swinging pendant. In a letter to the defunct small-press American magazine *Photon*, Luigi Cozzi recalled, "Our original draft had the retained image of a gate in the retina of the victim's eye. The hero then begins to look around at all the gates: garden gates, door gates, etc. Ultimately he realizes that it is not a gate, but a crucifix swinging fast; the crucifix, which his wife carried around her neck and was the last thing the poor victim saw. So, Dario simply changed the crucifix to a piece of jewelry containing a fly."

A highlight of this film is the appearance of the weird character called Godfrey, or God for short, a philosophizing vagrant who lives on the outskirts of town, scorning the metropolis for spawning such blackmailers and psychopaths as those that are bedeviling our hero. As played by Spaghetti Western icon Bud Spencer (Giancarlo Pedersoli), God is portrayed as such an incredible, insightful character that even his brief screen time brings the entire film to life. Wisely, the director has him return for the vengeful climax.

Introducing his audience into a world defiantly designed to keep them at a distance, Argento's film reads like an enigmatic Rubik's cube: A rock-jazz fusion band drummer (Michael Brandon) accidentally murders a stalker when the stranger follows him into a deserted theatre late one night. A masked figure appears in one of the audience boxes in the balcony and photographs the scene with Brandon standing over the body. Blackmailed and losing his circle of friends to a maniacal killer, Brandon seeks the aid of a gay private eye who has never solved a crime before. The moment he does is his last moment on Earth. Brandon's wife is starting to act very weird (as if she was not strange enough being played by the enigmatic Mimsy Farmer). At a complete loss, Brandon seeks the additional help of a psychedelicized adventurer named God (Bud Spencer).

The title of the film stems from a police test on an eyeball of a murdered victim done with a laser. Apparently, under the pretext that a victim's killer's image is retained on the retina of the eye, the laser photographs the image, which looks like four flies on gray velvet. The musical score (by Ennio Morricone) sounds somewhere between the art rock of Soft Machine and the '70s jazz-fusion experiments of Jeff Beck and keyboardist Jan Hammer. *Quattro Mosche di Velluto Grigio* remains one of Argento's most obscure but more fascinating films with plenty of gore thrown in for good measure. Unfortunately, the Paramount Pictures production did not perform well at the box office. Perhaps Michael Brandon's seemingly bland performance is something that audiences could not immediately identify with, or it could have been the obscure reason for the murders, something thrown at the audience from out of nowhere during the last five minutes. Argento has also said that he was not thrilled with Brandon's performance and originally sought out real-life musicians for the lead role. Nevertheless, Brandon's performance is quite good and he leads the audience into rooting for his survival by the film's end. This movie was to be Argento's last detective thriller until *Tenebrae* in 1982. If it were to be compared with Argento's other thrillers, surely this film will pale by comparison. Still it's an interesting thriller with a notably weird twist ending.

In 1971, Argento, in collaboration with his father Salvatore, formed the Film Company SEDA Spettacoli. Besides co-producing Argento's films under this banner, SEDA Spettacoli also produced the occasional feature by other directors. Argento and Cozzi then began work on a project that has haunted the director ever since. In 1972, they began adapting *Frankenstein* into a new version called *Frankenstein: The Modern Prometheus*. The story was written by Argento and Cozzi and offered first to Universal Pictures, then to Britain's Hammer Films. Both companies turned them down. Even with potential star Timothy Dalton attached as the lead, the duo's project collapsed. Initially, Cozzi was chosen to direct, then Argento. Possibly it was the potentially troublesome revisions that Argento and Cozzi had written: The story as planned was framed during the early days of the reign of

Adolf Hitler to draw parallels between Frankenstein's Monster and Hitler's monster, Nazism. Over the years, at various stages, Argento has attempted to revive the project, most recently in two incarnations: as a proposed (but abandoned) stage production and as a feature film that would have preceded or followed *Trauma* in 1993.

After the *Frankenstein* project was shelved, Argento, in continued collaboration with Cozzi, turned to television in 1972. Together, they worked on a miniseries of sorts. Originally their idea was for four one-hour television features to be sold to overseas markets as two complete features. But this never happened. The series was titled *La Porta sul Buio* and featured Argento, Hitchcock-style, introducing the episodes. The first film, *Il Tram*, is a thriller that Argento co-wrote and directed (using the pseudonym Sirio Bernadotte). *Il Tram* deals with a murder that takes place on a crowded surface trolley without the passengers or crew noticing. The police investigate. The second feature, *La Bambola*, is a psychological horror tale directed by Mario Foglietti and starring Erika Blanc. The third tale, *Il Vicino di Casa*, written and directed by Cozzi, revives themes from some of the original, unfilmed Argento/Cozzi material that dated back a few years. The story of a mysterious tenant at a seaside rooming house and the young couple who lives in the rooms below also incorporated ideas from previous, aborted projects (the killer who commits a crime that has been witnessed). Argento directed the fourth and final film, *Il Testimone Oculare*, allegedly after he replaced original director Roberto Pariante. Years later, Argento said that Pariante was just another pseudonym that he used, although there really is a film technician by that name who appears to have worked in some capacity on the director's earlier films.

The film tells of a woman (Marilu Tolo) who is threatened by a murderous presence. Many classic Argento touches are present, like the scene where the killer proceeds to terrorize the victim by punching a hole through the door with a thick bladed knife (shades of a similar scene from *L'Uccello dalle Piume di Cristallo*, when Suzy Kendall is terrorized in much the same manner). Unfortunately, there were no overseas sales for the quartet of films and they are only occasionally shown on Italian television today. Two episodes (the Argento-directed ones) were issued on Japanese laser disc in 1997 to capitalize on Argento's name and fame.

In 1973 Argento made his first and, to date, only non-genre feature film, the odd *Le Cinque Giornate*. An adventure film with comedic elements, it takes place during the Italian civil war of 1848. The film, which aimed for historical accuracy, performed poorly at the box office with its mix of adventure, dark black comedy and violent bloodshed. Since it was aimed primarily for the Italian market, no distributors were apparently interested in the film outside of Italy.

Profondo Rosso, released in 1975, is among the director's best work. The film opens with a sadistically sinister Christmas scene with horrific undertones: Shadows on a wall reveal a silhouette of death as two figures struggle and a bloody knife falls to the ground. The blade falls to the feet of a young child who apparently wit-

An ordinary man (David Hemmings) searching for clues to a grand mystery finds his own life in peril in Dario Argento's *Profondo Rosso* (1975, SEDA Spettacoli Produzione for Rizzioli Films).

nessed the tragic event up close. This opening scene also introduces the nursery-like children's theme, which becomes the signature audio motif heard just before murders are to occur later in the film. *Profondo Rosso* continually teases and bewilders viewers. One never gets to see the face of the true killer until the finale. The director provides hints as to this person's identity and unusual glimpses into a disturbed psyche: The killer enters a bathroom and looks into a mirror, covered with too much rust and too many scratches to provide an identification. Argento delights in mystifying the audience with another often repeated motif, a visual one that is accompanied by the children's music: a camera that pans past a floor covered with toys, some broken and other objects, then a cut to a quick shot of a knife, then a cut to an extreme close-up of someone applying black mascara to their eyes and zipping up black leather gloves. This is the point where the musical score often abruptly changes to the familiar bass heavy theme performed by Goblin. Basically, the film offers the typical Argento hero who has observed a crime but cannot let it go. In this case, it is the brutal murder of a psychic. The hero's feeling that he has overlooked something important that may prove to be a clue to the identity of the murderer haunts him.

In the film, pianist Marcus Daly (David Hemmings) sees a psychic murdered by a maniacal killer. Earlier that same day, during a conference, the same psychic had visions that someone within the room "has killed and will kill again." Daly becomes the killer's prey when he hooks up with a newswoman (Daria Nicolodi) who accidentally leaks the false story that he knows the identity of the killer. The key to this mystery is near the beginning. As the pianist watches from the street below, he sees the brutal attack take place. He rushes up the stairs to the apartment. Once through the door, he quickly walks down a long corridor adorned on both sides by grotesque paintings. It is here that Argento inserts an almost subliminal shot of the murderer standing in front of one of these paintings (visible in the letterboxed prints, barely so in the pan-and-scan versions). The newswoman, Gianna Brezzi (Nicolodi), helps Daly solve the mystery of the killer, which leads to a legendary house known as the House of the Screaming Child. This supposedly haunted house has been unoccupied for years, ever since a tragedy took place.

The bizarre, convoluted plot that leads in several different directions is all too neatly tied up at the climax. Along the way, the audience witnesses several violent murders as the killer seeks to erase anyone who might possibly identify him/her. The film is more than just a thriller. It is a horrific sensory overload of horror. There is a death by meat cleaver, a woman drowned in scalding water and several other nasty murders, making this Argento's first true excursion into ultra-violent splatter. Upon its original release, *Profondo Rosso* was often called incomprehensible in the critical reviews. Today, it more often is described as Argento's near-masterpiece, an unsung work of deep, Oedipal horror.

Profondo Rosso exists in many different versions of varying lengths. Some of the reasons for this are the unflinching scenes of graphic violence for its time. Still other cuts damaged what was thought of at the time as needless plot exposition. In fact, this particular footage itself turns out to be much more important than many of the distributor's editors probably ever realized. Essential to the plot were depictions of Daly at work with a small jazz combo and several dialogue scenes between him and the newswoman which includes banter about which is the stronger of the sexes, man or woman (a bizarre, subtle key to the riddle of the killer's identity). The three best-known versions of the film are the 100-minute print subtitled *The Hatchet Murders* that was released in America and most English-speaking countries. There is the 115-minute version titled *Suspiria 2* released on Japanese laser disc and finally there is the uncut print from Italy, which runs 122 minutes. England's Redemption Video, the popular cult-genre video label, eventually had the original, uncut Italian-language print subtitled; that is the version most Argento fans are familiar with. Similarly, Hammer and Argento film archivist (and a filmmaker as well) William Lustig, in conjunction with the Anchor Bay company, released the ultimate version of the film on DVD in 2000. About the music heard in the film: Argento initially formed Goblin as a band to provide soundtracks for his films. Since Goblin had stopped being an active group in the eighties, Claudio Simonetti (and other band members) continued working and provided the soundtrack music for many Italian genre films. Goblin reunited in 2001 to compose and perform the score for *Nonhosonno*.

Suspiria, produced in 1976, is Argento's Grand Guignol triumph. With its striking colors and its loud stereo soundtrack (music provided by Goblin), the film represents a new direction for the director. Written as a delirious combination of thriller motifs, observations on black magic and the supernatural, it is a key film in the director's oeuvre. As one character proclaims, "Bad luck isn't brought by broken mirrors but by broken minds." This is the bizarre way in which Argento devised the film, so that the situations which arise and eventually come to threaten the film's protagonist (a young ballet dancer played by Jessica Harper) are also due as much to her surroundings as her interpretations of these events. In time, they will almost cause her demise. The tale proclaims that, at a famous dance academy located in Germany, a coven of witches presides. This coven is at the service of the Three Mothers.

Anyone who discovers their deadly secret, the slow decay of death that will spread amongst the world, is targeted for death, or persecution leading to madness

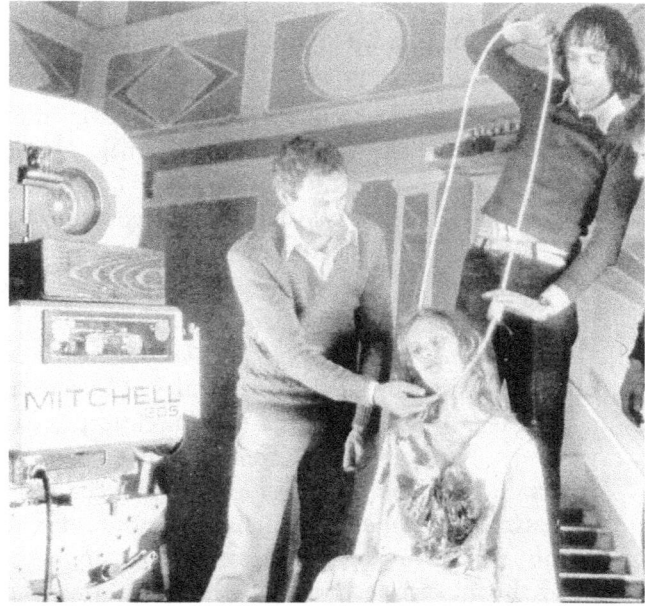

A director who likes to immerse himself into his cinematic fantasies, Argento prepares an actress for her grand death scene at the beginning of *Suspiria* (1976, SEDA Spettacoli Produzione).

or suicide. At nearly every turn, the young dancer is met with sinister, unfriendly faces. The people who claim to want to help her are manipulating her for their own purposes. From the roommate with whom she temporarily boards to the teachers at the school, everyone seems to look suspicious, casting malevolent glances at the unwelcome newcomer. *Suspiria* is also the film that introduces the concept of the Three Mothers. Argento has said that among the influences for the suggestion of the Three Mothers' story is one which is partly based on a legend of the black arts that he first noticed in a book by Thomas De Quincey, the author of *The Confessions of an Opium-Eater*.

In De Quincey's semi-autobiographical tales of drug-induced dementia and perceptions of reality, he stated that he eventually wanted to write a book about the Three Mothers. De Quincey never did write this book, but the follow-up volume to *The Confessions of an Opium-Eater,* titled *Suspiria de Profundis* (Sighs from the Depths) does contain elements that underlie the themes of the Three Mothers. Argento was interested enough to investigate the tales himself, whether they came from De Quincey's imagination or were his version of some ancient heretical mythology, and to embellish it with fictionalized additions to the story.

Most fans of the director's work have seen this film, but for the uninitiated: Suzy Banyon (Jessica Harper) is a young American ballet student who has arranged to study at the Tanzakademie, located in Germany. She arrives at night during a torrential rain just as another girl comes rushing out of the school in terror. The terrified girl, saying that the academy is evil, goes to stay with a fellow schoolmate who lives in an apartment outside the school grounds. Upon the death of these two students, Suzy returns to the school to begin her lessons. She finds out that the building once belonged to Elena Markos, an ancient witch known as the Black Queen, the Mother of Whispers, who lived hundreds of years earlier. Elena Markos still lives and she's picked Suzy Banyon as the object of her persecution.

Suspiria is Italian for the word "whispers." It was, at that time, the first film in a projected trilogy dealing with the legend of the Three Mothers: *The Mother of Whispers, The Mother of Sighs* and *The Mother of Darkness*. These were actual figures that appear in the demented tales of European author Thomas De Quincey, as well as from folklore that Argento reinterpreted and amplified into an all-new grotesque mythology. Using an old, out-of-date Technicolor film stock that bled colors off the screen in garish hues of oranges, blues and reds and one of the first successful experiments with stereo sound, affixing four-track magnetic stereo sound to the prints (or, in the case of some movie houses which were incapable of using the modern technology, blasting out the sound using a synched sound system located behind the screens), the film was a true experience to sit through in theatres.

It is, to date, Argento's first and only major horror film hit in the United States. The music score by Argento and Goblin is a true wonder in eliciting subconscious reactions to accompany the visuals. Viewed with the aid of an advanced home audio visual system, this is more readily apparent when the music reaches wild crescendos with actual whispered words filling the middle range. Listen carefully and you'll often hear the word "witch," whispered in an almost subliminal manner during the finale.

Filled with garish visions of horror like garrotings, beheadings, stabbings and slicings (including the then-controversial graphic close-up of a knife penetrating a beating heart), this film's only drawback is the muddled story filled with misinterpreted science and a wild explanation of sorcery that provokes snickers whenever explanation time comes around. Still, it looks great, making the uncut Anchor Bay DVD edition the print to own.

In 1978, Argento served as the co-producer for George A. Romero's *Dawn of the Dead*, a sequel to that director's seminal influential film about the undead, *Night of the Living Dead* (1968). Argento also provided input to the story and was often on the set of the Philadelphia-lensed production. After the film was finished, Argento made his own cut of the movie, re-edited the music score with the group Goblin and released this version in European theaters as *Zombi. Zombi*, otherwise known as *Zombi: Dawn of the Dead*, became a financial hit in Europe, spawning many imitations. The shorter Argento print contains alternate scenes, gore footage and a different order of events not in the other versions.

If *Suspiria* dealt with the subject of witchcraft and sorcery and was essentially the tale of the Mother of Whispers, Argento believed then that *Inferno* (1980) should deal with alchemy and the Mothers of Tears and Darkness. A woman named Rose (Irene Miracle) discovers a tome by Varelli, an acclaimed heretic who was an alchemist and architect. His volume on the Three Mothers, evil witches who send out sorrow, tears and darkness into the world, also tells of the three places on Earth where they can be found. The Mother of Whispers can be found in Freibourg, Germany; the Mother of Tears in Rome, Italy; and the Mother of Darkness in New York.

Inferno informs the audience as to the three keys to learning the identities of the Three Mothers. One is that the places they inhabit reek horribly of an indeterminate stench. Two is that, hidden in the cellar of each Mother's dwelling, is the picture and name of each. The third and last key is (as a key character learns) "hidden under the soles of your shoes." What this last key means is as enigmatic as it sounds. When a woman who has discovered Varelli's book encounters an old building which has in its cellar another lower chamber beneath it, entirely submerged in water, her curiosity and the loss of her keys (which she drops into the water) causes her to enter the domain of Tenebrium, the Mother of Darkness. *Inferno* continues a conceptual link begun with *Suspiria* to that of a fairy tale–like ambiance, the lost innocent among the (supernatural) world of decadence, decay and danger loses innocence and possibly life. The film is also notable for containing the last work of Mario Bava, who designed and worked on the underwater chamber sequence.

The films storyline plays out like a macabre fairy tale with all the trappings of the theater of the Grand Guignol: A neo-gothic mansion in New York City designed by Varelli, an expert in matters of the occult, figures in the disappearance of Rose, a New York student. She vanishes from her apartment complex after borrowing an antique volume (by Varelli) on witchcraft and the legend of the Three Mothers. Before vanishing, Rose describes her strange encounter with a water-filled room submerged in a letter to her brother Mark (played by American TV soap opera actor Leigh McCloskey) in Rome. This man also has an encounter with the Mother of Tears and innocently involves a classmate into the strange drama, costing her her life. The Mother of Tears and the Mother of Darkness are destroying the remaining copies of Varelli's book. It seems that Varelli had been forced to design the house to be the home for the Mother of Darkness, who may actually be the ultimate figure of death incarnate as well.

Inferno, a film like no other Argento film, is entirely composed of scenes that successfully emulate dreams and nightmares. With psychedelic colors lighting hallways, passageways and alleys, parts of *Inferno* succeed as Argento's ultimate depiction of a nightmare on film. Inhabited by a group of strange characters similar to the ones who appeared in *Suspiria*, *Inferno* definitely aims to make the connection between the two stronger. For many, the film's highlight would be the beautifully lit and designed scene that takes place in a secret underwater passage of a derelict basement room that was supervised by Mario Bava. An interesting footnote to *Inferno* is that it performed poorly in theaters in most countries. In the U.S., it had a brief, disastrous run.

Tenebrae's title suggests that it is a continuation of the Three Mothers saga when in fact it is not. As the director told the writers Luca M. Palmerini and Gaetono Mistretta in an interview for their 1994 book *Spaghetti Nightmares*, "After *Inferno*, I had the story [of the third episode] more or less ready. But by the time I'd revised it, a whole year had gone by and I realized that it lost its appeal. I decided to drop the project and instead brought forward the making of *Tenebrae* by a year ... I did take another look at the story after completing *Phenomena* and I tried to imagine the story of the Third Mother set in Rome, but once again, just as everything was ready, I gave up the idea because I simply didn't find it interesting."

Tenebrae (1982) is a return to the *giallo* format that, years earlier, the director had perfected. In the years since his first directorial effort, over 100 such films had been made, primarily in Italy. Why Argento chose to return to the format is as deep a mystery as what drives him to make these films. *Tenebrae* opens with an unseen narrator reading a book. The viewer is informed, "He realized every human obstacle, every humiliation, could be swept aside by this simple act of annihilation: Murder."

American crime novelist Peter Neal (Anthony Franciosa in a role originally written with Christopher Walken in mind) is to journey to Rome for the European launch of his latest thriller, *Tenebrae*. While there, he encounters a mad, fey film critic (John Steiner), his Italian publicity agent (John Saxon) who has the hots for Neal's wife, and a maniacal killer, hell-bent on the destruction of Neal's world and all who inhabit it. Even as the police investigate a series of gruesome murders and a disguised voice threatens Neal on the telephone, no one is anywhere near to solving the crimes committed. One victim is found with pages of Neal's book stuffed into her mouth. Neal's press agent is killed in broad daylight in full view of many lunching office workers at an outdoor plaza. An innocent woman is slaughtered when she stumbles across someone she believes to be the killer, the film critic who was sent over the edge by his hatred of women and Neal's book in particular. Of course, being a Dario Argento film, nothing is what it seems. Neal is actually the killer. It is madness (caused by recurring flashbacks to a traumatizing childhood humiliation inflicted upon him by a beautiful woman and some teenage boys) causes his secret and intense feelings of misogyny to rise to the surface and he commits acts of violence, as apparently described in his latest novel.

Argento's return to the *giallo*-thriller formula after an absence of several years is disorienting to all but his most steadfast supporters. That he swayed so effortlessly from the supernatural aspects of *Suspiria* and *Inferno* back to the *giallo* formula (with a twist) seems to have disappointed many expecting the third in the Three Mothers trilogy. The strange (imagined?) flashbacks of the author, Neal, as a young man at a beach, surrounded by other young attractive men vying for the attentions of a masochistic and beautiful woman (played by real-life transsexual Eva Robbins [formerly known as Roberto Coati] who abuses him, provides enough fodder for various Freudian interpretations of the plot. The film features some truly superb camerawork and ends with a virtual painter's splash of gore (a scene of violent dismemberment by axe that was cut from many prints throughout the world). Psychologically, *Tenebrae* is a very interesting film from Argento that tells us more about the way he really thinks, rather than the entertainment-oriented films like *Suspiria* and *Inferno* which only hint at the macabre thought processes of his mind.

Poster for the Spanish release of *Tenebrae* (1982, Sigma Cinematografica).

The next three years offered many projects either abandoned or rejected by the director. An offer to direct the cinematic version of the sprawling Stephen King volume *The Stand* attempts to make a film suggested by the works of H.P. Lovecraft and even an offer to direct an Agatha Christie story failed to see the light of a projector.

Phenomena (1985) is a strange film that points Argento in yet another bizarre new direction as an auteur (this journey is filled with a continuation of the "little girl lost" character created for *Suspiria*). Jennifer Connelly portrays a young girl named Jennifer Corvino who enrolls in a private school located deep within the border between Germany's Black Forest and Switzerland. (Sound familiar? This location resembles the one used in *Suspiria*!) The young girl shares a special psychic link with insects. Unfortunately for this young waif, her father is an American movie star and her classmates taunt her, reactivating her dormant sleepwalking habit. When she sleepwalks, she subconsciously imagines several young female classmates being brutally slain. Of course, there really is a killer roaming the area, but Jennifer cannot recognize this murderer. She even "sees" some of the murders through the eyes of the maggots that infest the killer's clothing. One recent victim was the assistant to a crippled doctor who studies insects (Donald Pleasence) and now Jennifer takes her place as his assistant. With the aid of the "Sarcophagus Fly" a purely cinematic device used to link the disparate plots, Jennifer tracks the murders to a shack. A deranged schoolteacher (Daria Nicolodi), who harbors a bizarre (and deadly) secret kidnaps her.

Aside from some outrageous gore (nasty decapitation by glass; close-up, in-your-face knifings) there is little to recommend this film that features a heroic lab chimpanzee! By the way, *Phenomena* was butchered by its U.S. distributor for its theatrical run. It lost nearly 30 minutes of screen time when it was cut from 110 minutes to 82 minutes for its 1985 theatrical release (as *Creepers*). Now that's some evidence of heavy tampering by the distributor and the MPAA, which at that time were not too crazy about horror films in general. The film also introduces Argento's new-found interest in '80s heavy metal music (heavy metal was also used primarily as the musical source material for the Argento-produced, Lamberto Bava–directed *Demoni* films). *Phenomena* was scored by ex–Goblin member Claudio Simonetti, contemporary heavy metal stalwarts Iron Maiden, the Rolling Stones' bassist Bill Wyman and others. It seemed that the director's intention was to disarm and disorient, although the film as a whole is not among his best work.

Argento's fame as a horror film director was celebrated in the 1985 documentary *Il Mondo di Dario Argento*. Directed by Michele Soavi (a former character actor who rose through the ranks of the Italian horror film industry to be an assistant director, then a director of his own productions), the documentary is noteworthy for including rare footage of Argento at work as well as notorious scenes cut from his films throughout the years. Years later, Argento returned the favor by producing and assisting with the story ideas and scripts for Soavi's films *La Chiesa* (1989) and *La Setta* (1991). During this period, Argento also hosted a late-night RAI Television series of horror films.

In 1985, before starting work on the production *Demoni*, Argento developed an idea for a fashion show presentation in Milan, Italy, for popular designer Nicola Trussardi. This production was filmed under the title *Trussardi Action*. He also directed a commercial for the Fiat Corporation in Australia. Argento then teamed up with his infrequent associate Lamberto Bava for the film *Demoni* (1985). Argento produced and co-wrote the story and screenplay for this outrageously original idea of a horror movie: People from all walks of life are given free tickets to see a premiere at a fantastic art deco theatre. The film they are to view, an untitled horror movie about a group of young adults who exhume the body of Nostradamus, the legendary alchemist, seer and magician, is about to begin on-screen. The film unreels and captivates its audience with an unusual story of how a strange mask that was imposed upon the face of Nostradamus is removed from the body and worn by one of the group. It turns one of the young men into a rampaging killer. Members of the audience slowly exhibit this same experience after a prostitute cuts her face on a replica of the mask in the theater lobby. Her wound festers into exploding boils and pours out blood and slime, before she changes into a creature. Soon, every one of the audience members that she kills or infects turns into zombie-like beast creatures, sending the remaining audience members scrambling for safety. They discover that they have been sealed in the theater. But, unknown to them, outside the whole world seems to be affected with this same strangeness. The film's over-the-top gore scene has to be a zombie-creature attack that appears a total dead end for our hero and heroine until an army helicopter crashes through the roof, providing an exit. An inferior sequel, *Demoni 2: L'Incubo Ritorna* (1986) (also co-produced and co-written by Argento), followed two years later.

Before the appearance of *Opera* (1987) in Italian theaters, Argento appeared on a weekly television news program for a four-month period (October 1987 through January 1988) to report on the horror industry. This popular spot with horror film audiences may have led to *Gli Incubi di Dario Argento* (also 1987) which was made up of short segments, directed especially for television.

By the time *Opera* was released to Italian theaters, the changing way of the world had started to affect the Italian horror film industry. Due to rising admission prices and a glut of inferior product, audience attendance began to drop off; horror films were not in vogue. It became cheaper to import the American stalk-and-slash films of the *Friday the 13th* variety than it was to produce all-new product. With the Italian economy suffering, many of their film technicians and directors in particular could find little funding for their projects, worse so for genre films. Many of these directors, Lamberto Bava for instance, turned to television for funding and have since enjoyed a lucrative career, while other genre directors began to supply the newborn cable and video markets with sexy films and dramas. *Opera* was a film that Argento insisted on making, even though it was widely misunderstood and under-appreciated at the time of its release. He is quoted as saying, "In *Opera*, love is haunted by the specter of AIDS; in fact, nobody loves in the film ... [the character of] Betty doesn't want and can't have sexual relations and relations between people are generally cold; people are distant with each other."

Opera tells the tale of Betty, a pretty young understudy, the typical show business ingenue, promoted to the lead role in a rock video-influenced version of the opera *Macbeth* by Verdi that is to be televised. An incredibly powerful maniacal killer stalks the cast and crew, then those close to Betty, taunting her along the way. *Opera* exists in many alternate and/or cut versions.

I was privileged to view an uncut director's print in Argento's presence. Although it does not explain every single bizarre motif thrown at the viewer, the uncut version helps the film to flow more smoothly. One day, this print may be available to audiences worldwide. Perhaps then the film will be more appreciated than it is today.

A hi-tech televised MTV–style opera production of *Macbeth* (which includes live ravens) is plagued by problems, most having to do with the ravens swooping down upon the show's star, Lady Macbeth, during her arias. An accident causes

Tenebrae (1982, Sigma Cinematografica). Argento (right) directs Giuliano Gemma (center) at the climax.

the temperamental star to leave the production and be replaced by her understudy. This ingenue, Betty (Christine Marsellaich), has problems of her own. It seems some maniacal killer who has overdosed on viewings of *A Clockwork Orange* is stalking her and murdering members of the cast and crew. While professing his love for her, the killer forces Betty, the heroine, to watch his sadistic murders by tying her up, applying tape to her mouth and placing tiny, sharp needles just under her eyelids to force her to watch his crimes of passion. There's a mysterious police inspector (Urbano Barberini) and many suspicious characters that lurk around (including *Chariots of Fire* star Ian Charleson and Daria Nicolodi). Eventually, we learn that the psycho killer had a very strange relationship with the ingenue's mother and seeks to repeat the same with the daughter ... at any cost.

As enigmatic and bewildering a personal film that Argento has ever made, *Opera* is also a movie that improves with viewings. Having seen the director's own personal print (with the addition of subtitles to clarify the rough edges), I maintain that it's a mess but a fascinating one. Its best moments are the already mentioned macabre needles-under-the-eyes scenes and a breathtaking special effects sequence: a bullet is fired through a door's peephole, enters the eye of an unsuspecting victim, then blasts out of the back of her head, shattering glass a room away! The whole crazy film ends with a mass of flying ravens swirling about the opera house looking for and then eventually swooping down upon the killer (more impressive camerawork courtesy of award-winning British photographer Ronnie Taylor). When the film performed less than expected in his native Italy, even Argento's co-producers R.A.I. and Orion Pictures sought to cut the film by 30 minutes to reduce the gore and the dialogue footage and to re-edit the movie into a shorter, eventually more incomprehensible version of itself. Planned U.S. and British theatrical dates were abandoned and, in most countries, *Opera* went straight to video with most but not all of the cuts eventually reinstated. The film was finally released in the United States in a completely restored version on DVD in 2002.

In 1987, Dario's father Salvatore died. Later that year, Argento co-hosted a bizarre television magazine series titled *Giallo — La Tua Impronta del Venerdi*. Besides interviews of common people, the show also featured the director explaining some of his trade secrets, like how graphic murders were depicted in his films. Highlights of the series were nine three-minute films (written and directed by Argento) which usually featured a grisly end. The films were *La Finestra sul Cortile*, *Riti Notturni*, *Il Verme*, *Amare e Morire*, *Nostalgia Punk*, *La Strega*, *Addormentarsi*, *Sammy* and *L'Incubo di Chi Voleva Interpretare l'Incubo Dario Argento*.

In 1988, Argento returned to Italian television to produce episodes of a series titled *Turno di Notte*. Consisting of 15 short films, *Turno di Notte* revolved around the thrilling misadventures that befall cab drivers during the night shift. The episodes were directed by Lamberto Bava (*Babbao Natale*, *Il Bambino Rapito*, *Buona Fine È Migliore Principio*, *E ... di Moda la Morte* and *Heavy Metal*) and Luigi Cozzi (*La Casa dello Stradivari*, *Ciak Si Muore*, *Delitto in Rock*, *L'Evasa*, *Giallo Natale*,

L'Impronta dell'Assassino, Sposarsi È un Po Morire, Il Taxi Fantasma, and *Via delle Streghe*).

Due Occhi Diabolici (1990) was the film that reunited Argento with *Dawn of the Dead* director George A. Romero. It was initially constructed to consist of four short contemporary remakes of four Edgar Allan Poe tales by four horror film directors of note. Wes Craven and John Carpenter were at one time considered but scheduling conflicts caused that idea to be abandoned. The project was reduced to the two directors who first conceived it and to two short subjects. Opening with the images of a house that Poe actually lived in and a shot of his tombstone, the film segues to the first, very disappointing short film by Romero. Essentially a remake of the Roger Corman version of Poe's *The Facts in the Case of M. Valdemar* from Corman's *Tales of Terror* (1962), the update breaks no new ground and is talky, derivative of some of Romero's earlier low-budget productions, and features amateurish performances by his actors. In the original film, Vincent Price played a wealthy man who is dying and Basil Rathbone was the mesmerist who persuades him to be hypnotized as he dies, a way of beating death until a cure is found. In the Romero remake, E.G. Marshall is the dying man and Ramy Zada is the hypnotist. But the twist is that the wife (Adrienne Barbeau) who seduces the hypnotist with her body doesn't really care about him and she just wants the old man to die. The old man never dies, he just decomposes. Of course, he seeks revenge in this state. This is a badly acted (and directed) EC Comics knock-off.

Argento's episode, *The Black Cat*, is more successful. It stars Harvey Keitel as Roderick Usher, a (Weegee-inspired) New York police photographer who works with the coroner's department. He photographs the most vile, disgusting aftermath of murders. The police are on the trail of a sick, sexual deviate who uses instruments of torture to kill. Keitel's pet cats know the truth as he slowly goes mad with the realization that his profession has put him over the edge — he realizes that he is the murderer! When the police suspect and attempt to arrest Keitel, a series of struggles result in a fascinating, bizarre death scene tableau. Fans of Tom Savini's gory special effects will salivate over the absolutely grotesque horrors on view (some of which had to be cut in many countries to achieve a reputable rating for a release). With his remake of the classic Edgar Allan Poe tale, Argento seems to show a talent that is a bit black and very twisted indeed.

In 1989, Argento opened his chain of stores called Profondo Rosso. These shops sell horror and science fiction–related merchandise. He produced and was involved with the script for *La Chiesa*, the second film by Michele Soavi. Argento also repeated the same chores on Soavi's *La Setta*, released in 1991. (More information on these Argento/Soavi collaborations can be found in the chapter on Michele Soavi.) The second of the documentaries on Argento appeared during this period. Luigi Cozzi's *Il Mondo di Dario Argento 2* pales by comparison with Soavi's 1985 documentary. The feature-length project traces the years since '85 concentrating primarily on the filming of *Opera*. The year 1992 found Argento directing an advertising spot for the Glad Pyramid air freshener for the Johnson Wax Company (for Japanese television); he also made a cameo appearance in John Landis' energetic vampire-action film *Innocent Blood*.

Trauma (1993) was the first film Argento made entirely for an American production company and on American soil (save for a few scenes done in a studio in Rome). Unfortunately, his original script was re-written by the American horror writer T.E.D. Klein to be more palatable for U.S. audiences, removing any possible thrills that the director had intended. The project utilized an accomplished but bland cast (Frederic Forrest, James Russo, Piper Laurie and Brad Dourif). *Trauma* seems to have been originally written around the showcase role of a suicidal, anorexic young woman (played by Asia Argento, the director's daughter) who teams up with an ex–drug addict TV station cameraman to investigate a series of murders. The most original item in this film is a fabulous device constructed by the killer, which decapitates people with a specially built mechanical noose.

With some not so original ideas (the Boy Who Cried Wolf: [a spectacled young pre-pubescent boy-genius investigates on his own]; is he the killer or not? [Brad Dourif doing another riff on his standard mad doctor routine]), the film cements the theory that Americans cannot make a good *giallo*. Even when one of Italy's foremost horror film directors is finally imported here, he can't transcend the problems of Americanizing his style. That Asia Argento had not yet grown to be a believable actress adds to the problem. The cast, especially the hero and the heroine, is unlikable, the plot unsavory and the denouement completely hysterical.

La Sindrome di Stendahl (1996) is Argento's attempt to utilize and take advantage of the many advances in filmmaking technology (especially in the area of special effects) that have become available in the past several years. The film also marks the return of composer Ennio Morricone. The two had not worked together since *Quattro Mosche di Velluto Grigio* in 1974. *La Sindrome di Stendahl* is a film that definitely divides the camps of Argento admirers. A policewoman (Asia Argento) is afflicted with the bizarre (apparently based on a real-life) malady called the Stendahl Syndrome, which affects the nervous system when concentrating intently on certain objects like works of art. The syndrome causes one to experience hallucinations, encounter symptoms of vertigo and other strange effects. When she is struck down after an episode at an art museum, she is kidnapped and brutally raped by a maniacal rapist-killer who has been terrorizing Rome and its vicinity. After several more attacks by the same person, including one in which she is laid side by side with another victim who is brutally slain before her eyes, the policewoman begins to undergo her own dementia, suffering complete degradation at the hands of the maniac and having repeated occurrences of the Stendahl Syndrome.

With this film, Argento reaches the pinnacle of unsavoriness by directing his own daughter, Asia, in the lead role of an Italian policewoman who has some serious problems and is brutally raped more than once. On a visit to an art museum in Rome, she encounters a period of hallucinatory dementia whilst staring at a painting. The grotesque work enthralls her and she imagines herself at one within the art as if it was a 3D object. This is explained as an occurrence of the Stendahl Syndrome. Physically she collapses to a heap. Shortly thereafter, she is brutally assaulted and raped by, apparently, the same madman who has been committing similar crimes all over Italy. As she is assaulted again by this demented being, she slowly loses touch with reality and sinks further into a near-catatonic dementia. She begins to be affected by residues of the Stendahl Syndrome without being near objects that would normally set off these reactions. As her sanity edges closer to the brink of madness, she finally strikes back at her tormentor, but the price will be her own identity as the film takes a series of sinister twists.

This film has many detractors. Its fans are few. Rape is a cinematic subject that can never be handled with delicacy. Even the most thoughtful directors have had a difficult time getting their films received as anything but another form of sexual exploitation. This film, with its many violent scenes of this act, neither titillates or informs. The fact that the rapist-killer is such a physically strong presence only amplifies the feeling of helplessness that Asia's character must endure.

Argento spent a good portion of 1996 attempting to revive the career of fellow genre film stylist Lucio Fulci. Although the two had never shared a close personal relationship, Argento intended to produce the ailing Fulci's comeback vehicle *M.D.C.— La Maschera di Wax*. When Fulci died, due to complication arising from his diabetic condition, production on this film was delayed so that the original Fulci script could be re-written and a new director sought. After briefly toying with the idea of directing the film himself, Argento decided upon Sergio Stivaletti, the special effects and make up technician who provided so many of the gruesome moments for numerous Argento productions.

In *M.D.C.— La Maschera di Wax*, a series of apparently random, disconnected sequences all come together for the rather Grand Guignol finale: a maniacal killer strikes out at a couple, slaughtering the woman and man by brutally cutting them to pieces. The life of a small child, found hiding beneath the bed, the floor covered in blood, is spared. Years later, she grows into womanhood and becomes a striking young beauty, turning the heads of many a man. When a local man (who enjoys his freewheeling life and visiting the local brothels) makes a bet to spend the night in a new, malevolent-appearing Wax Museum featuring figures of the criminally insane and true-life criminals of history, you can bet that it will be his last night alive. As for the young woman, she finds work as a costumer and seamstress at this same place. Eventually, we are introduced to the proprietor of the museum (Robert Hossein), a scarred, gentle-appearing man with a hulking brute of an assistant. The mysterious killer, whom we see only in silhouette and appearing not unlike Vincent Price's cloaked figure from Andre DeToth's *House of Wax* (1953), journeys to and from the wax museum and goes on his rounds of murder. The trail of death leads ever closer to the young woman, who suspects that her new boss may have a deeper affection for her than she welcomes. An aged police inspector (the same man who found the woman as a child, quivering beneath the blood-soaked bed) has appointed himself her pseudo-guardian and seeks to solve the unusual wave of crimes striking the city.

Argento's love for images influenced the publication of *Dario Argento Presenta 12 Racconti Sanguinari* in 1976 by his own publishing imprint, Edizioni Profondo Rosso. This was followed by a series of photo-illustrated comic books that were also anthologies containing illustrated short stories as introduced by the director. Argento is also known for authoring the following books: a novelization of *Quattro Mosche di Velluto Grigio*, titled *Quattro Mosche di Velluto Grigio: Il Terzo Film di Dario Argento* (1971); a novelization of his failed Italian civil war epic titled *Le Cinque Giornate* (1973); and *Profondo Thrilling*, a collection of his scripts (1975). *Dodici Racconti Sanguinari* (1976) was an anthology of horror literature to which Argento contributed a preface.

From the left: Claudio Simonetti (of Goblin), the author, Sergio Stivaletti (director of ***M.D.C.–La Maschera di Wax***) in 2000 (photograph: Phil Palmieri).

In addition to the countless amateur and professional genre magazine articles, a large number of books have been written about Argento, including *Dario Argento* (1980) by Demetrio Soare, a collection of interviews and observations. Other notable books are *Mostri & C.* (1982), a collection of horror and fantasy film criticisms, some by Argento, edited by Dario Argento, Luigi Cozzi and Domenico Malan. Still more tomes include *Dario Argento: Il Brivido, Il Sangue, Il Thrilling* (1986) by Fabio Giovanni, *Dario Argento* (1986) by Roberto Pugliese, *Dario Argento: Il Suo Cinema, I Suoi Personaggi e i Suoi Miti* (1991) by Luigi Cozzi, *Broken Mirrors/Broken Minds: The Dark Dreams of Dario Argento* (1991) by American author Maitland McDonagh and *Art of Darkness: The Cinema of Dario Argento* edited by Chris Gallant (2000). The latter are two of the few volumes devoted entirely to Argento and his films published entirely in English.

The films of Dario Argento are unlike any others. One can take pleasure in the director's visual style over and over. For, even though we now know the outcome of the film, who the killer or killers are, or what force is motivating them to commit violence, it is always a pleasure to follow his protagonists in detective-like fashion. In some of his more overtly supernatural-themed films, the telling of the tale is given less to a heroic figure or figures besieged by the seemingly impossible trying to unravel a mystery, and more to a dreamy, ambient state, often infused with his personal interpretations of demonology, misunderstanding of the occult or the darker side of life's inner demons. He has been dubbed the "Italian Hitchcock" because of his visual flair as a film stylist with the camera, camera movement, lighting, art direction and screenwriting. Women are often the victims in the cinematic world of Dario Argento and, at times, he has handled criticism about this. When approached by a British journalist about the apparent misogynist leanings of his films and the violence towards women in general in the genre, Argento replied, "I like women, especially the really beautiful ones. If they have a good face and figure, I would much prefer to watch them being murdered than an ugly girl or man." Strange ideas from a strange man. This does not really close the book on this subject.

Among his most recent films is a new adaptation of the Gaston Leroux classic *The Phantom of the Opera*, titled *Il Fantasma dell'Opera* (1998). Eschewing his usual screenplay collaborators in favor of Gerard Brach (who had been a long-time assistant to Roman Polanski, writing with Polanski many of that director's films since the '70s), Argento's *Phantom* leaves no excess left unexplored. Abandoned as an infant, a child is set adrift in a basket along the filthy, murky subterranean rivers and passages below the streets of Paris (the film was shot in Budapest) and raised by the rats who adopt him. Grown to manhood, the Phantom (Julian Sands) lurks in the shadows of the grand Paris Opera House, inflicting certain (and gory) deaths upon any and all who harm his beloved rats, or come too near his underground dwelling (furnished with furniture from opera productions over the years).

After spending nearly a year on the pre-production of this film, Argento chose Sands over numerous other actors (including Alan Rickman, an early original choice) to portray the anti-heroic lead of the Phantom. As in his last two productions, Argento again assigned the lead role of the heroine to his daughter, Asia. Unfortunately, the film met with disastrous results at the Italian theatrical box office and export film sales (including potential profits garnered from the lucrative cable market) had been non-existent, resulting in the movie's belated U.S. release direct to video and DVD.

Whether *Il Fantasma dell'Opera* is a good film or not, there can be little doubt in its entertainment value. Argento, the master of Italian horror films, is the director of the film and at the worst, it is a misguided attempt at remaking an often-filmed classical horror film. At its best, it could be considered another of the director's misunderstood masterpieces (which it is far from). In fact, the film is amongst the worst of the director's work. With bad performances from all (but Sands, who acquits himself well in the problematic title role) and fantastic set design, the film relies on its shallow and crude script to propel the motivations of the characters, none of it believable.

Il Fantasma dell'Opera story line reveals much in the Argento and Brach script that deviates from the many versions of the story that have become before: Left adrift as an infant and raised by sewer rats, the blond Phantom (Sands) has turned into the tall, handsome and never-masked Phantom of the Opera. Avenging the mistreatment of his adopted family of rats at the hands of insane rat catchers (who utilize a grotesque, futuristic extermination machine on wheels), the Phantom has fallen in love with the latest ingenue who has walked through the doors of the Paris Opera house, Christine (Asia Argento). Infatuated with her presence, the Phantom will do all in his power (including using his psychic abilities) to see that she becomes the new operatic singing sensation of France. But first, he must eliminate Carlotta (Nadia Rinaldi), the portly reigning diva; Raoul (Andrea Di Stefano), Christine's suitor; and anyone else who interrupts his life and personal mission to see his love as the new star on the Paris Opera stage.

Ronnie Taylor, the award-winning cinematographer who filmed Argento's *Opera*, returns to provide the same here and acquits himself well by shooting the film utilizing much of the location of the Budapest Opera House, returning to the swooping camera movements that were so much the highlight of *Opera*. Master composer Ennio Morricone also reappears to lend a hand with a thunderous romantic score, a reminder of some of his best earlier work. Still in the age of low-budget horror, this film seeks to entertain a particular brand of audience as evidenced by the following: death by sharp implements, bodies torn in half, decapitations and tongues ripped out. Unfortunately, most of the performances are bad. The idea of the two leads sharing a psychic link is one that does not work at all. In fact, the sequences where Christine "speaks" with the Phantom in her mind (but speaks aloud her thoughts to him) are risible. Further along in the film there are dubious sequences hinting at the suggested bestial nature of the Phantom as he fulfills his sensual conquest of Christine by engaging in numerous sexual acts with her and then alone with his family of rats ... one of which he shoves down his open trousers in a moment of sensual hysteria. Ultimately, *Il Fantasma dell'Opera* does not work. Whatever ideas about the project that Argento was formulating within his own mind, fail to transfer themselves to the screen and, given the director's body of work, it surely leaves the audience for this film confused and disappointed.

Rumors had circulated that Argento was working on a special project for the year 2000 and that this film might even see him reunite with Goblin, the musical group that he was instrumental in uniting. Regaining his mantle as a filmmaker of note, he released *Nonhosonno* in 2001. A delirious collection of scenes from his canon of violence, *Nonhosonno* became a critical and commercial success, reinvigorating the director's work and possibly, the Italian horror film in general.

Nonhosonno, like no Argento film before it, seems to wallow in gruesome murders and has become, in retrospect, a *giallo* for the new millennium: After a prologue where a young boy witnesses the brutal murder of his mother, the film shifts to the present day. We witness a harried whore (Barbara Lerici) rushing to leave from her latest client. As she scrambles for her belongings, she inadvertently picks up the client's notebook, actually a scrapbook of newspaper clippings and murder confessions. The killer follows her onto a commuter train in the night and murders her. Having his appetite for slaughter whetted, he then resumes a killing spree which had been interrupted for nearly 20 years. As each new grotesque murder baffles the police, they call on semi-retired Ulisse Moretti (Max Von Sydow). Moretti had once been a great cop but he now suffers from a failing memory (and constant insomnia, hence the English language translation of the title, Sleepless).

Nonhosonno is the film that Argento's followers had been waiting for the master of the macabre to make. Putting aside much of the convoluted story structures and infatuation with the supernatural that were exhibited in his earlier works, *Nonhosonno* feels like a nostalgic breath of fresh air. Argento displays a more contemporary feel for storytelling and, for the most part, a better cast of actors helps as well. Veterans Von Sydow, Rossella Falk and Gabriele Lavi acquit themselves well, despite an uneven supporting cast of new Italian faces for the young crowd. Returning to lend technical support are cinematographer Ronnie Taylor, who literally draws many of the cinematic images of grue in hues of deep crimson, and the reformed and reunited Goblin, lending pounding aural support with a score that recalls some of their great moments with the director. In summation, *Nonhossono* unspools like a "greatest hits" collection of macabre moments from the director's own oeuvre from the past.

In 2003, Argento was preparing to film *Il Cartaio* (The Card Player), a thriller about an Italian policewoman (Stefania Rocca) who is forced to play Internet poker with a serial killer named "The Card Player." If she loses the game, she is forced to witness the next victims of the killer being murdered right before her eyes. Rocca will team with a British policeman (Liam Cunningham) who is also on the trail of the killer. Argento seems poised to bring the *giallo* and his own significant style of moviemaking to the public once again.

Dario Argento Filmography

Le Cinque Giornate

A.k.a. *The Five Days* (English translation); a.k.a. *Five Days in Milan* (English title); D: Dario Argento; P: Salvatore Argento, Dario Argento; Prod. Co.: SEDA Spettacoli; SC: Dario Argento, Nanni Balestrini; C: Luigi Kuveiller; M: Giorgio Gaslini; S: Adriana Celentano, Enzo Cerusico, Marilu Tolo, Sergio Graziani.

Due Occhi Diabolici

A.k.a. *Two Evil Eyes* (English translation and title) (1990) (It., U.S.); D: George A. Romero, Dario Argento; P: Dario Argento, Achille Manzotti; Prod. Co.: ADC/Gruppo Bema; SC: George A. Romero, Dario Argento, Franco Ferrini; C: Peter Reiniers, Giuseppe Macari; SP

E: Tom Savini; S: Harvey Keitel, Adrienne Barbeau, Madeline Potter, Martin Balsam, E.G. Marshall, Ramy Zada, Bingo O'Malley, Kim Hunter, Sally Kirkland.

Il Fantasma dell'Opera

A.k.a. *The Phantom of the Opera* (English translation and title) (It., Hungary) (1998); D: Dario Argento; P: Claudio Argento, Giuseppe Colombo, Aaron Sips; Prod. Co.: A Medusa Film-Reteitalia production for Cine 2000 in association with Focus Film, Budapest and Tele +; SC: Gerard Brach, Dario Argento, based on the novel *The Phantom of the Opera* by Gaston Leroux; C: Ronnie Taylor; M: Ennio Morricone; S: Asia Argento, Julian Sands, Andrea Di Stefano, Nadia Rinaldi.

Il Gatto a Nove Code

A.k.a. *The Cat O'Nine Tails* (English translation and title); a.k.a. *Le Chat a Neuf Queue* (French title); a.k.a. *Die Neunschwanzige Katze* (German title); (1971) (It., WG, Fr.); D: Dario Argento; P: Salvatore Argento; Prod. Co.: SEDA Spettacoli/Mondial Film (Rome)/Terra Filmkunst (Munich)/Labrador Films (France); SC: Dario Argento, Luigi Collo, Dardano Sacchetti, Luigi Cozzi; C: Enrico Menczer; M: Ennio Morricone, Bruno Nicolai; S: Karl Malden, James Franciscus, Catherine Spaak, Cinzia De Carolis, Carlo Alighiero, Vittorio Congia, Pier Paolo Capponi, Corrando Olmi, Tino Carraro, Horst Frank, Emilio Marchesini, Rada Rassimov.

Inferno

(1980) (It.); D: Dario Argento; P: Claudio Argento; Prod. Co.: Produzioni Intersound (Rome); SC: Dario Argento, Daria Nicolodi (uncredited); C: Romano Albani, Lorenzo Battaglia, Mario Bava (uncredited); SP E: Germano Natali, Pino Leoni, Mario Bava (uncredited); M: Keith Emerson, and Verdi's "Va Pensiero"; S: Irene Miracle, Leigh McCloskey, Daria Nicolodi, Eleonora Giorgi, Alida Valli, Sacha Pitoeff, Feodor Chaliapin, Veronica Lazar, Gabriele Lavi, Fulvio Mingozzi.

Nonhosonno

A.k.a. *Non ho Sonno* (alternate Italian title); a.k.a. *I Can't Sleep*; a.k.a. *Sleepless* (English title) (It.) (2001); D: Dario Argento; P: Dario Argento, Claudio Argento; Prod. Co.: Opera Film for Medusa Film; SC: Dario Argento, Franco Ferrini, Carlo Lucarelli; C: Ronnie Taylor; M: Goblin; S: Max Von Sydow, Stefano Dionisi, Chiara Caselli, Rossella Falk, Paolo Maria Scalondro, Roberto Zibetti.

Opera

A.k.a. *Terror in the Opera* (U.S. video title) (1987) (It.); D: Dario Argento; P: Dario Argento, Mario and Vittorio Cecci Gori; Prod. Co.: Cecchi-Gori Group/Gruppo Tiger Cinematografica/A.D.C. Production in collaboration with R.A.I. (Radio Televisione Italiana); SC: Dario Argento, Franco Ferrini; C: Ronnie Taylor; M: Brian Eno, Roger Eno, Claudio Simonetti, Bill Wyman, Terry Taylor, The Group Steel Grave, The Northern Light, Giuseppe Verdi; SP E: Sergio Stivaletti; S: Cristina Marsillach, Urbano Barberini, Ian Charleson, Daria Nicolodi, Antonella Vitale, William McNamara, Barbara Cupisti, Antonella Vitale.

Phenomena

A.k.a. *Creepers* (English title) (1985) (It.); D: Dario Argento; P: Dario Argento; Prod. Co.: DAC Film (Rome); SC: Dario Argento, Franco Ferrini; C: Romano Albani; M: Bill Wyman,

Iron Maiden, Motorhead, Andy Sex Gang, Simon Boswell, Claudio Simonetti, Fabio Pignatelli; SP E: Sergio Stivaletti, and the Corridori Brothers; S: Jennifer Connelly, Donald Pleasence, Daria Nicolodi, Dalila Di Lazzaro, Patrick Bauchau, Fiore Argento, Federico Mastroianni, Michele Soavi.

Profondo Rosso

A.k.a. *Deep Red* (English translation and title); a.k.a. *La Tigre dei Denti a Sciabola* (Italian pre-production title; translation: *The Sabre-Toothed Tiger*); a.k.a. *The Hatchet Murders* (English title) (1975) (It.); D: Dario Argento; P: Salvatore Argento; Prod. Co.: SEDA Spettacoli Produzione for Rizzioli Films; SC: Dario Argento, Bernadino Zapponi; C: Luigi Kuveiller, Ubaldo Terzano; M: Giorgio Gaslini and Goblin, performed by Goblin; SP E: Carlo Rambaldi, Germano Natali, Guicar; S: David Hemmings, Daria Nicolodi, Gabriele Lavi, Macha Meril, Clara Calamai, Glauco Mauri, Eros Pagni, Giuliana Calandria, Nicoletta Elmi.

Quattro Mosche di Velluto Grigio

A.k.a. *Four Flies on Gray Velvet* (English translation and title); a.k.a. *Quatre Mouches De Velours Gris* (French title); a.k.a. *Four Patches of Gray* (English translation and alternate title) (1971) (It., Fr.); D: Dario Argento; P: Salvatore Argento; Prod. Co.: SEDA Spettacoli (Rome)/ Marianne Productions/Universal Productions, France (Paris); SC: Dario Argento, Luigi Cozzi, Mario Foglietti; C: Franco Di Giacomo; M: Ennio Morricone; S: Michael Brandon, Mimsy Farmer, Francine Racette, Bud Spencer a.k.a. Carlo Pedersoli, Calisto Calisti, Marisa Fabbri, Oreste Lionello, Constanza Spada.

La Sindrome di Stendahl

A.k.a. *The Stendahl Syndrome* (English translation and title) (1996) (It.); D: Dario Argento; P: Dario Argento, Giuseppe Colombo; Prod. Co.: Medusa Film/Cine 2000; SC: Dario Argento, Franco Ferrini, based on the novel *La Sindrome di Stendahl* by Grazialla Magherini; C: Giuseppe Rotunno; M: Ennio Morricone; S: Asia Argento, Thomas Kretschmann, Marco Leonardi, Luigi Diberti, Julien Lambroschini, Franco Diogene, Sonia Topazio.

Suspiria

(1976) (It.); D: Dario Argento; P: Claudio Argento; Prod. Co.: SEDA Spettacoli Produzione (Rome); SC: Dario Argento, Daria Nicolodi; C: Luciano Tovoli, Idelmo Simonelli; M: Goblin with the collaboration of Dario Argento; SP E: Germano Natali, Antonio Gabrielli; S: Jessica Harper, Stefania Casini, Udo Kier, Alida Valli, Joan Bennett, Flavio Bucci, Miguel Bose, Rudolf Schuendler, Barbara Magnolfi.

Tenebrae

A.k.a. *Tenebre*; a.k.a. *Darkness* (English translation); a.k.a. *Sotto gli Occhi dell'Assassino* (Italian pre-production title; translation: *Under the Eyes of the Killer*) a.k.a. *Unsane* (English title) (1982) (It.); D: Dario Argento; P: Claudio Argento; Prod. Co.: Sigma Cinematografica (Rome); SP: Dario Argento, George Kemp; C: Luciano Tovoli; M: Claudio Simonetti, Pignatelli, Morante; SP E: Giovanni Corridori, Luciano and Massimo Anzelloti; S: Anthony Franciosa, Daria Nicolodi, John Saxon a.k.a. Carmine Orrico, Giuliano Gemma, Cristiano Borromeo, Carola Stagnaro, Veronica Llario, John Steiner, Eva Robbins a.k.a. Eva Coatti a.k.a. Roberto Coatti, Lara Wendel, Ania Pieroni, Mirella Banti.

Testimone Oculare

A.k.a. *Eyewitness* (English translation and title) (1973) (It.); D/P: Dario Argento; Prod. Co.: RAI Radiotelevisione Italiana presents a SEDA Spettacolli S.p.A. (Rome) production; SC: Dario Argento, Luigi Cozzi; C: Elio Polacchi; M: Giorgio Gaslini; S: Marilu Tolo, Riccardo Salvino, Glauco Onorato, Altea De Nicola. Episode of the Italian television program *La Porta sul Buio* a.k.a. *The Door to Darkness*.

Il Tram

A.k.a. *The Tram* (English translation and title) (1973) (It.); D/P/SC: Dario Argento; Prod. Co.: RAI Radiotelevisione Italiana presents a SEDA Spettacoli S.p.A.; C: Elio Polacchi; M: Giorgio Gaslini; S: Enzo Cerusico, Paola Tedesco, Pier Luigi Apra, Tom Felleghi. Episode of the Italian television program *La Porta sul Buio* a.k.a. *The Door to Darkness*.

Trauma

A.k.a. *Aura's Enigma* (export English title) (1993) (It., U.S.); D/P: Dario Argento; Prod. Co.: A.D.C. S.r.l.; SC: Dario Argento, T.E.D. Klein, Franco Ferrini, Giovanni Romoli; C: Raffaele Mertes; M: Pino Donaggio; S: Asia Argento, Christopher Rydell, Frederic Forrest, Brad Dourif, Piper Laurie, Laura Johnson, James Russo, Dominique Serrano.

L'Uccello dalle Piume di Cristallo

A.k.a. *The Bird with the Crystal Plumage*; a.k.a.*The Bird with the Glass Feathers* (English translations and titles); a.k.a. *Das Geheimnis der Schwarzen Handschuhe* (German title translation: *The Secret of the Black Gloves*); a.k.a. *Sadist mit Zwarte Handschuhe* (alternate German title); a.k.a.*The Gallery Murders* (GB title); a.k.a. *The Phantom Terror* (alternate English title) (1969) (It., W.G.); D: Dario Argento; P: Salvatore Argento; Prod. Co.: C.C.C. Filmkunst (Berlin)/ SEDA Spettacoli (Rome); SC: Dario Argento, based on the novel *The Screaming Mimi* by Frederic Brown, and erroneously based on an unsourced novel by Bryan Edgar Wallace (sometimes credited in advertising); C: Vittorio Storaro; M: Ennio Morricone; S: Tony Musante, Suzy Kendall, Enrico Maria Salerno, Umberto Raho, Eva Renzi, Mario Adorf, Renato Romano, Werner Peters, Raf Valenti.

Lamberto Bava

Lamberto Bava was born in Rome, Italy, on April 3, 1944. He was born into a family where the males had worked in the world of fantasy, the movies. His grandfather, Eugenio, was a sculptor, painter and then a cameraman on film projects throughout the 1940s. Lamberto's father, Mario, was similarly involved in the visual arts and the cinema, following father Eugenio with his own career as a cinematographer. Photographing many varied projects, Mario Bava used his own experimental special effects techniques and trick photography to achieve what low-budget productions could then not really afford. Combining this useful knowledge into an art, Mario's work led him to assistant director chores on a number of films and some (uncredited) rescues of other, uncompleted or ill-financed productions. His own career as an auteur began, officially, with the 1960 film *La Maschera del Demonio*. Mario Bava seemed interested in the possibilities of the cinema of the macabre and became known primarily as a horror director. His films, among the best Italian productions of the '60s, were labeled some of the greatest horror films in the history of the cinema. Lamberto Bava's own career in movies started when he worked as an assistant director on his father's film *Terrore nello Spazio* (1965).

Lamberto continued to assist his father on the productions *La Strada per Fort Alamo* (1965), *Operazione Paura* (1966), *Le Spie Vengono dal Semifreddo* (1966), *Diabolik* (1967), the *Le Avventura di Ullise* episode of the miniseries *La Odissea* (1968), *Il Rosso Segno della Follia* (1969), *Roy Colt e Winchester Jack* (1969), *Ecologia del Delitto* (1971), *Gli Orrori del Castello di Norimberga* (1972), *Quattro Volte...Quella Notte* (1973), the unreleased (until 1998) *Cani Arrabbiati* (1974), *Lise e il Diavolo* (1975) and *Shock* (1977). On this last film, he contributed to the script as well as being credited as an assistant director. In 1978, he collaborated with his father Mario on the television film *La Venere dell'Ille*. The RAI television production, co-scripted by Lamberto, was filmed as an entry in a fantasy-related film series titled *Il Giorno del Diavolo*. *La Venere dell'Ille* was directed by both Bavas and contains themes that somewhat resemble the good/bad duality of characters that appear in Mario's *La Maschera del Demonio*. Lamberto told Italian authors Palmerini and Mistretta in the early '90s, "*La Venere dell'Ille* began as a very ambitious project approved by [the television station] RAI. They, at my father's request, put me in charge of the script along with Cesare Garboli, who wished to use some elements from my father's films that he liked, for example, the dualism's ... present in *La Maschera del Demonio*."

Lamberto worked as an assistant director on Mario Lanfranchi's *Il Baccio* (1974) and contributed to the story for the Ruggero Deodato productions *Odata di Piacere* (1975), *Ultimo Mondo Cannibale* (1976) and *Cannibal Holocaust* (1979). He is also credited as an assistant director on the last two films. An assignment from producer-director Pupi Avati led to Lamberto's first film as a director on his own, *Macabro* (1980), which he co-wrote with Pupi and Antonio Avati.

Lamberto Bava

While the atmosphere of dread that imbibes *Macabro* is as far as one could get from the stylized cinema of his father, it reveals a decidedly unusual penchant for the modern horror film of the '80s. According to Lamberto, a newspaper article inspired the film that concerns Jane (Bernice Stegers), a woman who has an affair with a man (Stanko Molnar) which reaches truly demented proportions. After his death, she keeps the severed head of her lover in the refrigerator during the day and in her bed at night, enacting some bizarre erotic tableau. *Macabro* reaches delirious levels of cinematic horror when a blind neighbor hears the sounds of intense lovemaking coming from the woman's apartment, though she is supposed to be alone. Is Jane truly a demented soul and has she completely dropped off into an abyss of insanity, or has the lover returned from the netherworld, his severed head, a detached reminder of his once-physical form? Although the film, a bizarre mix of the erotic and the fantastic, received respectful attention, years later it has come to be regarded as a work as macabre as its title suggests and an important entry in the director's filmography. Mario Bava died in 1980, shortly after completing work on Dario Argento's *Inferno*. He lived to see Lamberto's film and then said, according to Lamberto, "Now, I can die in peace." A fascinatingly original, almost baroque contemporary horror film that leaves many questions unanswered at the finale, Lamberto Bava's solo debut is a work of bizarre eroticism.

In the intervening years until Bava began his association with Dario Argento, Bava worked in the field of advertising (coincidentally, at the same firm as Ruggero Deodato) and continued to write stories, possible ideas for future film projects. One such project, *Alkmaar*, a film that was never made, was to be a thriller. Named after a port town in Holland, the movie was ready to begin filming when the cast and crew were told the production was canceled, most likely the result of a problem that may have arisen on the proposed Dutch co-production's end. When Argento approached Bava to assist him with *Tenebrae* in 1982, Bava agreed. *Tenebrae* was Argento's return to the *giallo* thriller format after years experimenting with expanding the limitations of the horror genre with films like *Suspiria* and *Inferno*.

Bava's first great film as a director, *La Casa con la Scala nel Buio,* began production and was released in 1983. Originally, this movie was developed by its producers and Dardano Sacchetti (the co-author of the screenplay) as a television film, to be shot in 16mm in four 25-minute segments and shot on an extremely low budget. Bava sought to make a much more violent film than his debut *Macabro*, so he took his small group of actors, among them Michele Soavi, and used the producer's house as the primary location. This resulted in a production (eventually blown-up to 35mm) that was not only a successful thriller in the *giallo* mold, but a production that revealed how much like his father the son had become. With just the bare essentials (Bava claims to have had use of a minimal crew and equipment), he delivered a very stylish film that, even today, remains among the best of the *gialli*. Technically, the film combines the influence of the works of his father with those of Dario Argento. It succeeds with shock theatrics when trying to manipulate its audience. However, Bava's next two productions were not as well received as this. Although they were well-made genre films, they did not capitalize on the momentum promised with *La Casa con la Scala nel Buio*.

One can see in this outline for *La Casa con la Scala nel Buio,* just how much the influences of his own father's latter-day works and those of Argento fuel the story: A composer (Andrea Occhipinti) is commissioned to write and perform the score for a horror film. In order to achieve the correct ambient mood for his music, he rents a large secluded villa. Before long, weird occurrences begin. People stop by, claiming to have befriended the vacationing owner of the villa and seek to return or borrow an object or article of clothing that they left behind; or, to just hang around. Obviously feeling bothered, the composer becomes harried when some of these female guests never seem to leave — or at least he never sees them leave. They are being murdered one by one because they share the horrific secret of the owner. Mystified by the apparent comings-but-not-goings of his visitors in the night, the composer tries to gather his thoughts and continue work on his repetitive score. He discovers an important clue when his audio recording equipment picks up a whispered exchange of words with menacing overtones. When he tries to synchronize the music (that he has recorded) to the images filmed by the female director, he discovers the beginnings of a shocking secret. The filmmaker may in fact be making a horror film based on an apparent real-life incident from her childhood, which may point to the identity of the killer who is now making threats on the life of the composer.

Bava's film is an entertaining motion picture obviously modeled on the collapsed remnants of the *giallo* genre. By 1983, after countless films, the suspense thriller had pretty much run its course. Taking inspirational cues from *Profondo Rosso* with its main protagonist, also a composer, *La Casa con la Scala nel Buio* differs considerably after that. The idea of confused sexual identity, another theme shared with an Argento film (*Tenebrae*), is explored again as an aberration of the killer's disturbed psyche based upon a childhood trauma.

Blastfighter (1983), a film rarely mentioned in genre books, is an action tale with a twist. Michael Sopkiw stars as the Rambo clone and animal-rights avenger who goes on a rampage of revenge and destruction when those close to him are threatened. Author Dardano Sacchetti originally wrote the film as a futuristic *Mad Max* remake for director Lucio Fulci, but that never happened so the script was changed. Aside from grotesque footage of animal mutilation that Bava has said was faked, the film is what it is, a nasty action movie.

Rosso nell'Oceano (1984) is a science fiction film about an artificially created, genetically mutated shark. This huge monster goes on a killing spree and it's up to two marine biologist heroes (making the *Jaws* connection even stronger) to track down the sea creature and destroy it. They discover that only fire can destroy this creature. Despite appearances by veteran actors William Berger and Gianni Garko, the film, which also stars Michael Sopkiw, cannot get around its obvious low budget and silly-looking monster shark.* Interestingly enough, elements of this film surfaced years later in Renny Harlin's *Deep Blue Sea* (1999).

Demoni, one of Lamberto Bava's great horror films, completely turns the zombie film subgenre onto its head, then sends it off reeling into the supernatural. Dario Argento produced the film and co-wrote the screenplay with Bava and with the participation of Dardano Sacchetti and Franco Ferrini. With its apparent high production values and stylish direction, the film moves along at an incredible pace. Sergio Stivaletti's special effects are gruesome and innovative, even if the story is a bit incoherent. *Demoni* was such a successful film with its fantastic plot of a movie spilling off into reality that it even garnered some accolades from the usually moribund English-language press.

---

*It is interesting to note that, on some export prints of these two films, John Old, Jr., is given as the director credit. John Old or John M. Old were pseudonyms used by Mario Bava for a few of his projects. The name appears on some English language prints of his costume adventure films with Cameron Mitchell.

Shock Transfert–Suspence–Hypnos (1977, Laser Film), the first directorial collaboration between Lamberto and Mario Bava.

A strange masked man hands out leaflets throughout a major European metropolis. The flyers offer free admittance to a sneak preview of a new film. Many people from all walks of life decide to spend a few hours at the movies. They are in for a spectacularly unsettling experience: It is an untitled horror film about young adventurers who discover the grave of Nostradamus and remove a horrific mask that had been affixed to the corpse's face. They become possessed by some kind of demonic entity, transforming them into raging monsters who prey on one another. When a prostitute who tries on a similar mask on display in the theatre lobby is scratched by it, she too turns into a zombie-demon-monster and in turn begins to infect others. As a band of survivors attempt to flee, the film reaches truly supernatural overtones as the audience finds that all the entrances have been blocked. A handful of survivors attempt to flee the theatre only find the horror is more apocalyptic than they imagined — outside the theatre, the entire city seems to be undergoing a similar fate!

This horror film mixes many genres and ends up an effective action-horror thriller. Sergio Stivaletti's makeup and special effects are quite effective and bloody. The film unspools at an unrelenting pace. It is as near to a ferocious monster movie classic as has been seen in quite some time. Its innovative story structure (a movie which spills off into reality and vice versa) was a theme not often used previously and was rarely as successful as it was here. The sequel *Demoni 2: L'Incubo Ritorno* (1986) reunited much of the production crew and some of the cast members but remains inferior to the original.

Bava's next film, *Morirai a Mezzanotte* (1986) returns to the *giallo* subgenre of the horror film that he first visited as director with 1983's *La Casa con la Scala nel Buio*. Made primarily for Italian television but apparently shown in theaters, this film, which features a cast (including Valeria D'Obici and Leonardo Treviglio) unknown to anyone not familiar with popular Italian television performers, is a fairly involving thriller. A police inspector who fought with his wife over her apparent infidelity is blamed for her murder. His co-worker, another police inspector, is assigned to find the now missing police official. The suspect seeks shelter and solace with their mutual friend, a female criminal psychologist working with the police, but all the clues lead to him. After he dies in a scuffle with the psychologist, the murders continue. But who is the killer? There are many suspects in this film, including a woman who appears androgynous and another woman who often wears men's clothing. The killings are usually seen in the dark or from odd camera angles, so the identity of the killer is kept hidden from the audience. Bava appears in a cameo role (seen as a police photographer near the beginning of the film) and signs the direction and the screenplay (authored with infrequent Argento collaborator Dardano Sacchetti) as John Old, Jr.!

Continuing a fascination with sexually confused characters which began with in *La Casa con la Scala nel Buio*, this film begins with a quite brutal, knock-down argument that almost ends in tragedy and then introduces the (mainly unseen, shadowy) killer. After this violent beginning, the tone changes dramatically when heaps of dialogue regarding the criminal investigation are thrown at the audience. The film begins to seriously lag and become a tepid thriller. Sensing this, the director reintroduces the killer as a nearly unstoppable creature of destruction. We find out at the end that the killer was an important character who became a murderer due to a traumatic experience. Bava uses touches of the macabre *giallo* thrillers of Dario Argento in key moments of terror that appear to be homages. One murder takes place in an abandoned theatre as one did in *Quattro Mosche di Velluto Grigio* and there is an encounter between the killer and a potential victim in a deserted museum, a location similar to the art gallery used in *L'Uccello dalle Piume di Cristallo*. Despite the title, *Morirai a Mezzanotte*, which translates to "Death at Midnight," the killer prefers to stalk the victims primarily in the daylight. Fairly bloodless and with little or no nudity to speak of (revealing the production's television origins), the film's exploitation quotient relies mainly on the innovative ways that Bava choreographs the assaults. Although it is unfairly maligned as an unsuccessful work, it contains many interesting ideas and is not a bad thriller.

For *Demoni 2: L'Incubo Ritorna* (1986) most of the *Demoni* production crew and even some of the cast members return (although in different roles). Again Dario Argento produced and co-wrote the screenplay (with Bava, Sacchetti and Franco Ferrini) but, this time, they bring a new slant to the story. A bizarre television program causes an outbreak of zombies in an apartment complex. As the film nearly overloads its influences (acid blood soaks through floors, as in the *Alien* series), there are also plenty of original "kitchen sink" touches like zombie dogs, zombie body builders, spectral zombies coming out of television sets (a nod to David Cronenberg's *Videodrome*) and the like. While the film does elicit a number of scares, it is not up to the terrifying first film because it ends up becoming incomprehensible. This film goes off in so many directions that it seems plotless. Characters appear, disappear, or are introduced as possible major figures in the story only to be totally forgotten as the film progresses. Rumors persist that, prior to the film's initial Italian theatrical release, the distributors cut an undetermined amount of footage and that for many export prints (and certainly the ones that appeared in English-speaking countries) additional footage was also cut. This tampering may have improved the flow of the film as far as its running time is concerned, but it leaves huge gaps in the continuity.*

Le Foto di Gioia (1987) is a superlative example of a film that uses a particular genre (the *giallo* thrillers) and expands upon it with its own sense of style. It is undoubtedly a film that betters a number of earlier, uninspired entries in the genre. Bava was preparing this film while working on *Morirai A Mezzanotte*. *Le*

Several films, including Bava's television feature La Casa dell'Orco *(1988), his 1989 remake of* La Maschera del Demonio *and a 1991 Umberto Lenzi film* (Black Demoni)*, have been distributed in various continents as* Demoni 3, *or* Demons 3.

Reproduction of a Greek video sleeve for *Le Foto di Gioia* (1987, Dania Film S.r.l./Devon Film S.r.l./Medusa Distribuzione/National Cinematografica/Filmes International in association with Reteitalia S.p.A.).

Foto di Gioia is the film that also introduced the world to Serena Grandi. As seen in this film, Grandi is a zaftig Earth mother who exudes sensuality. Besides her full figure, she has a sensuous mouth and piercing eyes. Although she had made films both before and after (mainly sexy dramas and comedies that often showcased her body, if not always her talent as a decent actress), *Le Foto di Gioia* contains one of her best performances and is among her best films. Bava claims to have had Grandi forced upon him by the producers but, whatever the truth, his cinematic eye loves her and she rides through the film's delirious thrills as its heroine.

In the film, Serena Grandi stars as Gioia (pronounced Joy), a former model for *Pussycat* magazine, now its owner. The fairly simple plot involves a grand gathering of suspects when one of Gioia's most popular models is found dead. The diverse group includes a paralyzed young man with an insatiable voyeuristic fixation on Gioia, a fey photographer (David Brandon), her old flame, B movie actor (Luigi Montefiori a.k.a. George Eastman, who appears in many films by Aristide Massaccesi), Gioia's ex–lesbian lover and the woman who got her started in the business (Capucine) and her private secretary (Daria Nicolodi). Soon other models are being killed and their corpses are artfully posed in front of huge color blow-ups of sexy photos of Gioia, to whom the pictures are sent. By the time the murderer stalks Gioia herself, most of the cast is dead. An above-average score by former Goblin member Claudio Simonetti contributes to the mood as well as the energetic direction. Bava uses colored gel lights to set the mood for the killings and weird point-of-view shots from the perspective of the killer. The killer sees his/her female victims as having one huge eye, or the heads of insects ... strange stuff!

Bava next returned to television to direct several episodes for a series of hour-long films produced by Dario Argento. Bava's contributions to the program were titled *Turno di Notte*. The hour-long Lamberto Bava–directed episodes were *E ... di Moda la Morte*, *Heavy Metal*, *Buona Fine È Migliore Principio*, *Giubetto Rosso*, *Il Bambino Rapito* and *Babbao Natale*. Bava then directed feature-length films for the Reteitalia television network program *Brivido Giallo* (1987/1988). The resulting four films were released theatrically abroad in some countries and released direct-to-video in others (English-language versions were prepared in Italy); I do not know if they ever were released to Italian theaters. The films are *Dentro al Cimitero* (a.k.a. *Una Notte nel Cimitero*), *Per Sempre*, *La Casa dell'Orco* and *Cena con il Vampiro*.

Per Sempre (variously known under its export titles *Until Death*, *Back from Hell*, *Changeling 2* and *Changeling 2: The Revenge*) stars Gioia Maria Scola and David Brandon as a couple who have murdered the woman's sadistic husband. Discovering her own pregnancy via her lover, she and her lover bury the husband's body but his spectral presence returns to haunt the couple in various ways. (Or has the woman been driven to madness?) *Per Sempre* is a film with many similarities to Mario Bava's *Shock*, to which Lamberto also contributed: A pregnant woman (Gioia Maria Scola) and her companion (David Brandon) are having a tough time trying to bury a man in the pouring rain. That he doesn't want to die makes their mission more problematic. The man they eventually kill and bury is the woman's husband. He had mistreated her, sending her into the arms of her lover (Brandon). Years later, the woman is unhappily living with the lover and is drawn to another mysterious young man. Her son exhibits strange behavior and the lover — well, let's say he's not too happy either.

In one of the best of his made-for-television horror films, Bava again deftly explores the possibilities of the duality themes of good and evil present in films such as *Shock*, his own co-production with his father. The film is loaded with routine shock sequences, most notably eerie nightmares where a rotting corpse rises from the Earth. The film's cleverest moment, which aptly displays the sheer Italian gusto of genre filmmakers, is when a key figure in the story turns his face ever so slowly to reveal that half of it is that of a dead man.

La Casa dell'Orco, also known under the titles *Demons: The Ogre* and *The Ogre*, is a wonderfully atmospheric film about a family who returns to an ancestral home in Italy. The wife (Virginia Bryant), a writer of horror fiction, is plagued by bizarre day and nightmares: weird, unusual hallucinations that stem from a childhood encounter with the unknown. Eventually, the past will come to haunt her present when the family's small child also experiences these strange sensations and the secret of the past is revealed.

At times, Bava's direction seems to resemble the heyday of the Italian Gothic cinema, in particular *Operazione Paura*. The visual talents of Riccardo Freda, Antonio Margheriti and Mario Bava are recalled with a story that slowly builds up tension towards its inevitable climax. The inventive use of lighting and camera placement reveals the thoughtful attention paid to the story, which only falters in a decidedly ridiculous and ambiguous ending.

Cena con il Vampiro, also known as *Dinner with the Vampire*, is an entertaining if not entirely successful black comedy with George Hilton as a vampire and actor who feeds on the blood of others. He will live forever as long as his image on celluloid survives. Finally, *Dentro al Cimitero* is a comic thriller about youths who encounter various terrors in a cemetery.

In 1989 and 1990, Bava filmed four features for the *Alta Tensione* television program. The titles were *L'Uuomo Che Non Volare*, *Il Maestro del Terrore*, *Il Gioko* and *Testimone Oculare* (a remake/update of Dario Argento's episode of the same name for 1972's *La Porta sul Buio* miniseries). All are handsome, well-made features with good production values, although they exhibit a much more violent, sadistic outlook than one would normally associate with Bava's work.

The year 1989 saw the appearance of Bava's *La Maschera del Demonio*, a remake of his father's horror film classic. For this film, Bava returned to the original inspiration of Nikolai Gogol's *The Vij*, then (with co-screen writers Giorgio Stegnani and Massimo De Rita) updated the story. The film is far from the classic that the 1960 feature was: A group of vacationers happens upon the ruins of a submerged underground village and a castle when one of them falls into a crevice leading to its entrance. The small town, frozen in time, contains the petrified corpse of the Princess Anibas (Debora Kinski). Anibas had been executed centuries before for committing heresy in the eyes of the church and had the Mask of Satan pounded onto her face before she was put to death. One of the vacationers pulls off the mask and then various members of the group become possessed by the spirit of Anibas, particularly Sabina, a lookalike among the group (also played by Kinski). Some of the group finds refuge in the remains of a church, where an incomprehensibly still-living priest explains to them the legend of Anibas' reign of terror. It takes the thickheaded hero some time before he comes to the realization that Sabina is Anibas spelled backwards.

Bava, whose attempt to discover the "new" Serena Grandi in his quest to cast a sexy young actress for his lead, goes amiss when it becomes quite obvious that the comely Kinski's acting abilities are not up to the challenge. Sergio Stivalleti's gruesome special effects consist of rubbery monsters when the majority of the cast has a penchant for turning into strange demonic creatures during sex. Bava's remake of his father's highly regarded film is a major miscalculation considering the reverential treatment that Mario's original 1960 film receives. It does not seem to be daring enough, covers no new ground in its approach to the subject matter and wastes the interesting cast of Kinski, Eva Grimaldi and Michele Soavi. In addition, the lighting too often betrays the sets as appearing plastic and studio-bound. The ridiculous scenario (survivors of a great catastrophe continue to live, buried beneath tons of frozen snow) brings the film closer to being a spoof of the original, rather than a continuation or an improvement over one of the classics of the horror film.

Corpo Perplessità (a.k.a. *Body Puzzle*) (1992), like *Le Foto di Gioia*, should have been a redemption of sorts for the director. But the confusing story and matter-of-fact direction restores little faith in Bava as a visual stylist. Joanna Pacula stars as the widow of a pianist. She keeps discovering body parts left in her apartment. What is so unusual for a film so obviously steeped in the *giallo* tradition is that the audience is always one step ahead of everyone. We know the identity of the killer throughout, if not exactly his motives.

The police (Tomas Arana and Gianni Garko) are at first skeptical, but begin to investigate further when they learn that the dead husband of Pacula was a promiscuous homosexual. After several more murders (including the graphic dismemberment of one victim in a public bathroom), we learn that the killer (whom we see committing these crimes) is in fact the husband who was presumed dead, his sanity sent over the edge into madness due to the death of his male lover in a car accident.

Bava's film is a likable exercise in modern horror that could have benefited by some well-chosen restraint in some of the terrifically gory sequences, turning it into a clever mystery. Bava seems up to the challenge of mystifying his audience when the most unusual clue is that all along, the audience knows the face of the killer, but is unable to identify him clearly as the woman's husband until the film's final minutes.

In 1991, Bava introduced to the world *Fantaghiro*, a television miniseries that consisted of feature-length episodes. Bava has admitted that the films were influenced by the movies *Legend, Willow* and *Ladyhawke*, popular fantasy films of the period. Essentially a fantasy set in medieval times, *Fantaghiro* is an often visually arresting work combining elements from the above influences with other original story ideas. Also, being a family-oriented production, the stylized violence is kept pretty much to a minimum. *Fantaghiro* tells the tale of a King who has sired two daughters. When his wife dies giving birth to their third child, his hopes for a boy are dashed when he discovers that it is another girl. However, she is more tomboy than female and when she grows into young adulthood and wields a sword against her enemies, this female warrior is a mean one to contend with. With the addition of fantastic images like talking trees, talking animals and magical spells, the series displays many charms one would associate with the most romantic of fairy tales. The cast is generally quite good, featuring veteran international actors Mario Adorf, Horst Bucholz and Ursula Andress. Among the dangers the princess must face are the malevolent witches who also inhabit the world. By its conclusion in 1997, the series reached eight feature-length episodes. Apparently very popular in European countries, English-dubbed export prints of the series (titled *The Cave of the Golden Rose*) had been offered for sale to English-speaking countries, However, the popularity of the series failed to gain a foothold in America, unlike the equally fantastical Australian-lensed *Hercules* or *Xena* series.

In 1994–95, Bava attempted a new, darker version of *Fantaghiro* titled *Desideria* featuring Franco Nero as the King. Among Bava's latest work: a new series titled *Sorellina e il Principe del Sogno* (1996), which explores another fantasy realm and the misadventures of the young Princess Alisea; *La Principessa e il Povero* (1997), a darker and more adult version of the themes explored in the *Fantaghiro* series, starring Anna Falchi as the comely Mirabella; and *Caraibi* (1998), yet another interpretation of the saga with Falchi and Mario Adorf. Among Lamberto Bava's most recent films is the thriller *L'Impero* (2000) starring Claudia Koll.

Lamberto Bava Filmography

Babbao Natale

(1987–88) (It.); D: Lamberto Bava; P: Dario Argento; Prod. Co.: D.A.C. Film; C: Pasquale Rachini; S: Antonella Vitale, Matteo Gazzolo, Franco Cerri, Lea Martino, Luciano Bartoli, Mauro Bosco.

Episode of the Italian television program *Turno di Notte.*

Il Bambino Rapito

(1987–88) (It.); D: Lamberto Bava; P: Dario Argento; Prod. Co.: D.A.C. Film; C: Paquale Rachini; S: Antonella Vitale, Matteo Gazzolo, Franco Cerri, Lea Martino, Ippolita Santerelli.

Episode of the Italian television program *Turno di Notte*.

Blastfighter

A.k.a. *Blastfighter l'Executeur* (French title); a.k.a. *Blastfighter— The Force of Vengeance* (English title) (1983) (It., Sp., Fr.); D: Lamberto Bava; Prod. Co.: Medusa Distribuzione S.r.l.; SC: Morand McMorand a.k.a. Morando Morandini, Luca and Max Von Ryt a.k.a. Massimo and Luca De Rita, Franco Costa a.k.a. Francesco Costa; C: Lawrence Bannon a.k.a. Gianlorenzo Battaglia; M: Andrew Barrymore a.k.a. Guido and Maurizio De Angelis; S: Michael Sopkiw, Valerie Blake a.k.a. Valentina Forte, George Eastman a.k.a. Luigi Montefiori, Michele Soavi.

Buona Fine È Migliore Principio

(1986–87) (It.); D: Lamberto Bava; P: Dario Argento; Prod. Co.: A.D.C. s.r.l.; C: Pasquale Rachini; S: Antonella Vitale, Matteo Gazzolo, Franco Cerri, Lea Martino, Stefano De Sando, Maurice Poli, Victoria Zinny.

Episode of the Italian television program *Turno di Notte*.

Caraibi

A.k.a. *Piraten der Karabik* (German title) (1998) (It., G.F.R.); D: Lamberto Bava; P: Lamberto Bava, Andrea Piazzesi; SC: Fabrizio Bettelli; C: Antonio Maccoppi; M: Paolo Buonvino; S: Anna Falchi, Mario Adorf, Jennifer Nitsch, Nicholas Rogers, Remo Girone.

La Casa con la Scala nel Buio

A.k.a. *The House with the Dark Staircase*; a.k.a. *The House with the Dark Stairway* (English translations and titles); a.k.a. *A Blade in the Dark* (English title) (1983) (It.); D: Lamberto Bava; Prod Co.: National Cinematografica/Nuova Dania Cinematografica; SC: Elisa Briganti, Dardano Sacchetti; C: Gianlorenzo Battaglia; M: Guido and Maurizio De Angelis; SP E: Giovani Corridori; S: Andrea Occhipinti, Lara Naszinski, Anny Papa, Michele Soavi, Fabiola Toledo, Valeria Cavalli, Stanko Molnar, Giovanni Frezza, Lamberto Bava.

La Casa dell'Orco

A.k.a. *Demons 3— The Ogre*; a.k.a. *The Ogre*; a.k.a. *Ghost House 2* (English titles) (1988) (It.); D/P: Lamberto Bava; SC: Lamberto Bava, Dardano Sacchetti; M: Simon Boswell; S: Virginia Bryant, Patrizio Vinci, Alice Di Giuseppe, David Flossi, Alex Serra, Paolo Malco.

Feature-length episode of the Italian television program *Brivido Giallo*.

Cena con il Vampiro

A.k.a. *Dinner with the Vampire* (English translation and title) (1988) (It.); D: Lamberto Bava; Prod. Co.: Dania Film/Surf Film/Devon Film (Rome); SC: Lamberto Bava, Dardano Sacchetti; C: Gianfranco Transunto; M: Simon Boswell, Mario Tagliaferri; S: George Hilton, Patrizia Pellegrino, Riccardo Rossi, Valerio Mililo, Yvonne Scio.

Feature-length film shot as an episode for the Italian television program *Brivido Giallo*.

Corpo Perplessità

A.k.a. *Body Puzzle* (English translation and title); a.k.a. *Misteria* (Italian theatrical re-release title); a.k.a. *La Vendetta* (Italian pre-production title) (1992) (It.); D: Lamberto Bava; Prod. Co.: P.A.C. Produzioni Atlas Consorziate S.r.l.; SC: Lamberto Bava, Teodoro Agrimi, Bruce Martin, Domenico Paolella; C: Luigi Kuveiller; M: Carlo Maria Cordio; S: Joanna Pacula, Tomas Arana, Francois Montagut, Gianni Garko, Erica Blanc a.k.a. Erica Bianchi Colombatto, Matteo Gazzolo, John Morghen a.k.a. Giovanni Lombardo Radice.

Demoni

A.k.a. *Demons* (English translation and title) (1985) (It.); D: Lamberto Bava; P: Dario Argento; Prod. Co.: DAC Film; SC: Lamberto Bava, Dario Argento, Dardano Sacchetti, Franco Ferrini; C: Gianlorenzo Battaglia; M: Claudio Simonetti, with additional musical contributions from Pat Gribben, Billy Idol, Vince Neil, Nikki Sixx, Rick Springfield and Edvard Grieg; SP E: Sergio Stivaletti; S: Urbano Barberini, Natasha Hovey, Karl Zinny, Fiore Argento, Paolo Cozzo, Fabiola Toledo, Nicoletta Elmi, Michele Soavi.

Demoni 2: L'Incubo Ritorna

A.k.a. *Demoni Due — L'Incubo Ritorna*; a.k.a. *Demons 2: The Nightmare Continues* (English translation and title); a.k.a. *Demons 2 — The Nightmare Is Back* (alternate English title); (1986) (It.); D: Lamberto Bava; P: Dario Argento, Ferdinando Caputo; Prod. Co.: DAC Film; SC: Lamberto Bava, Dario Argento, Franco Ferrini, Dardano Sacchetti; C: Gianlorenzo Battaglia; M: Simon Boswell, with additonal musical contributions from The Art of Noise, The Cult, Dead Can Dance, and Peter Murphy; S: David Knight, Coralina Cataldi Tassoni, Asia Argento, Virginia Bryant, Antonio Cantafora, Luisa Passega, Marco Vivo, Nancy Brilli.

Dentro al Cimitero

A.k.a. *Una Notte nel Cimitero* (alternate Italian title); a.k.a. *Graveyard Disturbance* (English title) (1988) (It.); D: Lamberto Bava; P: Massimo Manasse; Prod. Co.: Dania Film; SC: Lamberto Bava, Dardano Sacchetti; C: Gianlorenzo Battaglia; S: Gregory Lech Thaddeus, Lea Martino, Beatrice Ring, Gianmarco Tognazzi.
  Episode of the Italian television program *Brivido Giallo*.

Desideria

A.k.a. *Desideria e l'Anello del Drago* (alternate Italian title); a.k.a. *The Dragon Ring* (English title) (1994-995) (It.); D: Lamberto Bava; P: Lamberto Bava, Andrea Piazzesi; SC: Gianni Romoli; C: Romano Albani; M: Amadeo Minghi; SP E: Sergio Stivaletti; S: Franco Nero, Anna Falchi, Sophie Von Kessel, Joel Beeson, Ute Christensen, Stefania Sandrelli.

E ... di Moda la Morte

(1987–88) (It.); D: Lamberto Bava; P: Dario Argento; Prod. Co.: A.D.C. s.r.l.; C: Pasquale Rachini; S: Antonella Vitale, Matteo Gazzolo, Franco Cerri, Lea Martino, David Brandon A.k.a. David Caine Haughton), Vanni Corbellini.
  Episode of the Italian television program *Turno di Notte*.

Fantaghiro

A.k.a. *The Cave of the Golden Rose* (English title) (1991–97) (It.); D: Lamberto Bava; P: Roberto Bessi; SC: Lamberto Bava, Francesca Melandri, Gianni Romoli; C: Romano Albani; M: Amedeo Minghi; SP E: Aldo Mafera, Sergio Stivaletti; S: Alessandra Martines, Kim Rossi-Stuart, Mario Adorf, Jean-Pierre Cassel, Thomas Valik.

Fantaghiro II

(1992) (It.); D: Lamberto Bava; P: Lamberto Bava, Roberto Bessi; SC: Lamberto Bava, Francesca Melandri, Gianni Romoli; C: Romano Albani; M: Amedeo Minghi; SP E: Aldo Mafera, Sergio Stivaletti; S: Alessandra Martines, Kim Rossi-Stuart, Mario Adorf, Brigitte Nielsen, Stefano Davanzati.

Fantaghiro III

(1993) (It.); D: Lamberto Bava; P: Lamberto Bava, Andrea Piazzesi; SC: Lamberto Bava, Gianni Romoli; C: Romano Albani; M: Amedeo Minghi; SP E: Aldo Mafera, Sergio Stivaletti; S: Alessandra Martines, Kim Rossi-Stuart, Brigitte Nielsen, Ursula Andress, Elena D'Ippolito.

Fantaghiro IV

(1994–95) (It.); D: Lamberto Bava; P: Lamberto Bava, Andrea Piazzesi; SC: Lamberto Bava, Gianni Romoli; C: Romano Albani; M: Amedeo Minghi; SP E: Aldo Mafera, Sergio Stivaletti; S: Alessandra Martines, Horst Bucholz, Ursula Andress, Brigitte Nielsen, Marc De Jonge, Kim Rossi-Stuart.

Fantaghiro V

(1994–96) (It.); D: Lamberto Bava, Andrea Piazzesi; SC: Lamberto Bava, Gianni Romoli; C: Romano Albani; M: Amedeo Minghi; SP E: Aldo Mafera, Sergio Stivaletti; S: Alessandra Martines, Remo Girone, Brigitte Nielsen, Micheala May.

Although produced in the 1995-96 season (including some footage shot in 1994), this program was not aired on Italian television until the 1996-97 television season.

Le Foto di Gioia

A.k.a. *The Photos of Joy* (English translation and title); a.k.a. *Das Unheimliche Auge* (German title; translation: *The Uncanny Eye*); a.k.a. *Delirium* (English title) (1987) (It.); D: Lamberto Bava; P: Marco Grillo Spina, Massimo Manasse; Prod. Co.: Dania Film S.r.l./Devon Film S.r.l./Medusa Distribuzione/National Cinematografica/Filmes International in association with Reteitalia S.p.A.; SC: Luciano Martino, Gianfranco Clerici, Daniele Stroppa; C: Gianlorenzo Battaglia; M: Simon Boswell; S: Serena Grandi, Daria Nicolodi, Vanni Corbellini, Capucine, David Brandon a.k.a. David Caine Haughton, George Eastman a.k.a. Luigi Montefiori, Katrine Michelson, Karl Zinny, Sabrina Salerno.

Il Gioko

A.k.a. *School of Fear* (English title) (1989) (It.); D: Lamberto Bava; P: Lamberto Bava, Andrea Piazzesi; Prod. Co.: Reteitalia, Milan/Anfri/Silvio Berlusconi Communications; SC: Dardano Sacchetti, Giorgio Stegani; C: Gianfranco Transunto; M: Simon Boswell; S: Daria

Nicolodi, Alessandra Acciai, Jean Herbert, Stafano De Sando, Morena Turchi, Fabio Jellini, Viola Simoncioni.
   Filmed as a feature-length episode of the Italian television program *Alta Tensione*.

Giubetto Rosso

(1987–88) (It.); D: Lamberto Bava; P: Dario Argento; Prod. Co.: A.D.C. s.r.l.; C: Pasquale Rachini; S: Antonella Vitale, Matteo Gazzolo, Franco Cerri, Lea Martino, Gioia Maria Scola, Lino Salemme.
   Episode of the Italian television program *Turno di Notte*.

Heavy Metal

(1987–88) (It.); D: Lamberto Bava; P: Dario Argento; Prod. Co.: A.D.C. s.r.l.; C: Pasquale Rachini; S: Antonella Vitale, Matteo Gazzolo, Franco Cerri, Lea Martino, Vitoria Zinny, Maurice Poli.
   Episode of the Italian television program *Turno di Notte*.

L'Impero

A.k.a. *Human Currency* (English title) (2000) (It.); D: Lamberto Bava; P: Piero Amati, Marco Videtta; SC: Sergio Silva, Mimmo Rafele, Piero Murgia, Piero Bodrato; C: Romano Albani; M: Paolo Buonvino; S: Claudia Koll, Claudio Amendola, Franco Castellano, Matthieu Carriere, Maria Helena Gugenheim, Massimo De Rossi.

Macabro

A.k.a. *Macabre* (English translation and title); a.k.a. *Frozen Terror* (English title) (1980) (It.); D: Lamberto Bava; P: Gianni Minervini, Antonio Avati, Gianni Amadei; Prod. Co.: A.M.A. Film (Rome)/Medusa Distribuzione; SC: Lamberto Bava, Antonio Avati, Pupi Avati, Roberto Gandus; C: Franco Della Colli, Antonio Schiavo-Lena; M: Ubaldo Continiello; S: Bernice Stegers, Stanko Molnar, Roberto Posse, Veronica Zinny, Ferdinando Orlandi, Fernando Pannullo.

Il Maestro del Terrore

A.k.a. *The Prince of Terror* (English translation and title) (1989) (It.); D: Lamberto Bava; P: Lamberto Bava, Andrea Piazzesi; SC: Lamberto Bava, Ira Goldman, Dardano Sacchetti; C: Gianfranco Transuto; M: Simon Boswell; SP E: Sergio Stivaletti; S: Tomas Arana, Carole Andre, David Brandon, Ulisse Minervini, Joyce Pitti, Marina Viro, Virginia Bryant.
   Filmed as a feature-length episode of the Italian television program *Alta Tensione*.

La Maschera del Demonio

A.k.a. *The Mask of the Demon* (English translation and title); a.k.a. *The Mask of Satan*; a.k.a. *The Devil's Veil*; a.k.a. *The Demon's Mask*; a.k.a. *Black Sunday* (English titles) (1989) (It.); D: Lamberto Bava; P: Lamberto Bava, Andrea Piazzesi; Prod. Co.: Reteitalia (Milan)/Anfri; SC: Lamberto Bava, Massimo De Rita, Giorgio Stegani; C: Gianfranco Transunto; M: Simon Boswell; SP E: Sergio Stivaletti; S: Debora Caprioglio a.k.a. Debora Kinski, Eva Grimaldi, Giovanni Guidelli, Stanko Molnar, Michele Soavi, Laura Devoti, Alessandra Bonarota, Mary Sellers, Stefano Molinari.

Morirai a Mezzanotte

A.k.a. *To Die at Midnight*; a.k.a. *Death at Midnight* (English translations and titles); a.k.a. *You Will Die at Midnight*; a.k.a. *Carol Will Die at Midnight*; a.k.a. *Midnight Killer* (English titles) (1986) (It.); D: Lamberto Bava; P: Mark Grillo Spina, Massimo Manasse; Prod. Co.: Dania Film/Reteitalia; SC: Lamberto Bava, Dardano Sacchetti; C: Gianlorenzo Battaglia; M: Claudio Simonetti; SP E: Amedio Alessi; S: Valeria D'Obici, Leonardo Treviglio, Lea Martino, Paolo Malco, Lara Wendel.

Per Sempre

A.k.a. *Fa Sempre*; a.k.a. *Fa Sempre, Fino alla Morte* (Italian production title); a.k.a. *Until Death*; a.k.a. *Changeling 2*; a.k.a. *Changeling 2: The Return*; a.k.a. *Changeling 2: The Revenge*; a.k.a. *Back from Hell* (English titles) (1988) (It.); D: Lamberto Bava; P: Massimo Manasse, Marco Grillo Spina; Prod. Co.: Dania Film/Devon Film/Reteitalia; SC: Dardano Sacchetti; C: Gianlorenzo Battaglia; M: Simon Boswell; SP E: Fabrizio Sforza; S: Gioia Maria Scola, David Brandon a.k.a. David Caine Haughton, Giuseppe De Sando, Roberto Pedicini, Marco Vivio, Urbano Barberini.

A feature-length episode of the Italian television program *Brivido Giallo*.

La Principessa e il Povero

A.k.a. *The Princess and the Pauper* (English translation and export title); a.k.a. *Die Falsche Prinzessin* (German title) (1997) (It., G.F.R.); D: Lamberto Bava; SC: Gianni Romoli; C: Gianlorenzo Battaglia; M: Amedeo Minghi; S: Anna Falchi, Lorenzo Crespi, Nicholas Rogers, Matthieu Carriere, Thomas Kretschmann, Max Von Sydow.

Rosso nell'Oceano

A.k.a. *Red Ocean* (English translation); a.k.a. *Shark Rosso nell'Oceano* (alternate Italian title; translation: *Shark Red Ocean*); a.k.a. *Apocalypse dans l'Ocean Rouge* (French title); a.k.a. *Devouring Waves*; a.k.a. *Monster Shark* (English title) (1986) (It., Fr.); D: Lamberto Bava; Prod. Co.: Filmes Cinematografica/Nuova Dania Cinematografica/Filmes International/National Cinematografica/Films Du Griffon; SC: Vincenzo Mannino; C: Giancarlo Ferrando; M: Antony Barrymore, Guido De Angelis, Maurizio De Angelis; S: Michael Sopkiw, Valentine Monnier, Gianni Garko, William Berger, Stefano Mingardo, Garkovitch Giovanni, Emilio Conti, Iris Peynado.

Sorellina e il Principe del Sogno

A.k.a. *Prinzessin Alisea*; a.k.a. *Im Brunnen der Träume* (German titles) (1996) (It., Ger.); D: Lamberto Bava; P: Lamberto Bava, Andrea Piazzesi; SC: Gianni Romoli; C: Roberto Benevenuti; M: Amedeo Minghi; S: Christopher Lee, Jurgen Prochnow, Veronica Logan, Nicole Grimaudo, Raz Degan, Oliver Christian Rudolf, Anja Kruse, Brigitte Karner, Valeria Marini, Kamini Mathur.

Il Testimone Oculare

A.k.a. *Eyewitness* (English translation and title) (1990) (It.); D: Lamberto Bava; P: Lamberto Bava, Andrea Piazzesi; Prod. Co.: Reteitalia, Milan/Anfri/Silvio Berlusconi Communications; SC: Massimo De Rita, Giorgio Stegani; C: Gianfranco Transunto; S: Barbara Cupisti, Stefano Davanzati, Alessio Orano, Giuseppe Pianviti, Mary Sellers, Loredana

Romito, Francesco Casale; Filmed as a feature-length episode of the Italian television program *Alta Tensione*.

L'Uomo Che Non Volare

A.k.a. *The Man Who Would Not Die*; a.k.a. *The Man Who Wouldn't Die* (English translations) (1989) (It.); D: Lamberto Bava; P: Lamberto Bava, Andrea Piazzesi; Prod. Co.: Reteitalia (Milan)/Anfri; SC: Giancfranco Clerici, Giorgio Scerbanenco; C: Gianfranco Transunto; M: Simon Boswell; S: Martine Brochard, Keith Van Hooven, Gino Concari, Lino Salemme, Igor Zalewsky, Stefano Molinari, Jacques Sernas.

Filmed as a feature-length episode of the Italian television program *Alta Tensione*.

La Venere dell'Ille

A.k.a. *The Venus d'Ille* (English translation and title) (1978) (It.); D: Mario Bava, Lamberto Bava; P: Franca Franco, Carlo Tuzii; Prod. Co.: Pont-Royal-Film-TV/Raidue; SC: Lamberto Bava, Cesare Garboli, based on a story by Prosper Merimee; C: Nino Celeste; M: Ubaldo Continiello; S: Daria Nicolodi, Marc Porel, Fausti Di Bella, Mario Maranzana, Diana De Curtis, Adriana Innocenti.

Filmed as a feature-length episode of the Italian television program *Il Giorno del Diavolo*.

Mario Bava

Mario Bava was born on July 31, 1914, in San Remo, Italy. His father, Eugenio Bava, was a noted sculptor and cameraman for silent films before becoming the head of the optical effects department at the Instuto Luce. Before Mario Bava began his work as a director, he was an assistant cameraman, special effects cameraman, camera operator and also director of photography. Bava purportedly began working behind the camera when he contributed to the 1937 film *L' Avventura di Annabella*.

Working in the cavernous Cinecitta studios near Rome, Bava quickly gained a reputation as a quick problem solver on cash-strapped projects, who filmed incredibly difficult shots with speed and ingenuity. As a pioneer in trick photography with his unique use of filters and in-camera effects, he made many low-budget productions look like much more, contributing to the films of Raoul Walsh and Roberto Rossellini, among many others. Because of his talent, Bava was often asked to re-shoot scenes that a producer felt would strengthen a production. Most often, he was chosen to finish productions that were left unfinished due to the absence of the original director. *I Vampiri* was being photographed by Bava in 1956 when the director, Riccardo Freda, left the film. Freda was contracted to film the movie within a particular period of time when he went on to another project, allegedly the result of a dispute with the producers. Bava was asked to finish the project. *I Vampiri* is well remembered for its unusual atmosphere, sometimes dripping with erotic tension, mixed in with the popular detective fiction of the time; influences from pulp novels and the serious dramas that, up until then, were a staple of Italian cinema. *I Vampiri* was not a film about vampires in the traditional cinematic sense or in the mythological or literary sense either. What catapulted the film into the horror genre was the way in which it handled scenes of the beauties that were to be preyed upon; they appeared alluring and erotically wanton before being attacked by a dark figure. The U.S. distributors sought to heighten the film's erotic tension and made it a much more exploitative offering by splicing in a nude bath scene and a mild rape scene that featured brief nudity.

While its influences are rooted in the past, *I Vampiri*'s story points towards the then-current fascination for neo-realism mixed with dime store melodramatics: A scientist assists a seemingly ageless Countess in keeping her alluring and voluptuous appearance by murdering beautiful young women and transfusing their blood into the Countess. When the body count rises, a journalist and a police inspector investigate separately. Overpowered by the beauteous image of the woman, they find her villa a place where death and decay waits for all interlopers.

Mario Bava on the set of *I Tre Volti della Paura* (1963, Galatea Film [Milan]/ Emmepi Cinematografica [Rome] / Société Cinématographique Lyre [Paris]).

This overrated contribution to the early years of the Italian horror film is chiefly attributed to Riccardo Freda, although he did not entirely direct the film. The (exact) amount of Bava's assistance to this project is unquestionable, especially in the sequences that take place in the medical offices of the doctor and at the villa of the Countess. Probably due to the shift in the style of the two directors, the film is also padded with a lot of dull and repetitious travelogue footage of Italy. The lead actors, aside from Gianna Maria Canale's sinister Countess and Paul Muller's hired killer, are unmemorable.

Bava eventually got his chance to direct films when he was chosen to handle the second unit photography and direction on Pietro Francisci's seminal muscleman "sword and sandal" epics *Le Fatiche di Ercole* (1957) and *Ercole e la Regina di Lidia* (1959). When Jacques Tourneur left the film production of *La Battaglia di Maratona* (1959) without completing the battle scenes, Bava was asked to finish the film, after having already worked on the feature as its cinematographer. He also photographed Riccardo Freda's *Agi Murad, il Diavolo Bianco* in 1959. Bava re-teamed with Freda again on *Caltiki, il Mostro Immortale* (1959) as a cinematographer and finished the film at the behest of its producers, when Freda left the production. In *Caltiki*, an archeological team, accompanied by native expedition members, comes across a vengeful Aztec spirit in the form of an ever-growing blob that follows our dull heroes (two scientists and their girlfriends) back to civilization for a heavy duty rampage of violence.

Made at about the same time as *La Maschera del Demonio*, but not released to film markets outside of Italy until 1961, this film features graphic deaths for the time, and it seems to have been influenced by the Hammer films *The Quatermass Xperiment* (1955) and *X the Unknown* (1956) as well as the American *The Blob* (1958). *Caltiki*, despite its uneven pacing and thrills, still chills with its graphic killings and its unstoppable monster. If we discount Larry Hagman's spit-and-rubber band low-budget 1972 sequel, *Son of Blob* (a.k.a. *Beware, the Blob*), there was not another entertaining Blob movie until 1988's excellent *The Blob*. A note regarding the impressive special effects (contributed by Bava): The shapeless killer was actually fashioned from animal intestines purchased from a local butcher.

Purportedly, Galatea Film, the producers of *La Battaglia di Maratona*, were so impressed by Bava's skills as a rescuer of troubled productions that they offered to produce a film entirely directed by him. *La Maschera del Demonio* (1960) was the result. Claiming to have often read Nikolai Gogol's story *The Vij* to his children as a bedtime story, Bava chose this as a reference point for an idea for his first feature. Undoubtedly influenced by the successful release of Britain's *Dracula* (1958) from Hammer Films, Bava, along with screenwriter Ennio De Concini, started working on a script that would contain elements of the two.

Barbara Steele stars as the witch-vampire Princess Asa who dies horribly in the film's prologue when a steel-spiked devil's mask is nailed onto her face. Centuries later, Gorobeck (John Richardson) passes through the mist-shrouded village in the backwards country en route to a medical symposium in the company of his teacher and fellow physician Dr. Kruvajan (Andrea Checchi). They come upon the tomb of Princess Asa and Kruvajan accidentally revives her. Around the same time, Katia (also Steele) is walking her bloodhounds near the grounds of the derelict, forgotten cemetery. The sound of a ghostly wind echoes through the long-forgotten chimes of a church organ. Misty fog endlessly rolls over upon itself, spreading farther into the landscape. The few visible three-dimensional objects seen are the derelict, haunted pieces of wood, worn stone and debris that signify the remains of a cemetery. These once magisterial and ornamental tributes to life are now rotting pieces of stone and wood, signifiers of death and decay. When Dr. Gorobeck is drawn to Katia, the film begins its circular web of death. Katia also seems interested in Gorobeck, but this romance is not the story that propels the plot. Asa and her undead, centuries-old lover Javuto, after murdering and possessing the body of Dr. Kruvajan, will become more powerful after an infusion of blood. Exterminating the few of her remaining bloodline, Asa seeks to replace the virginal Katia (her last direct descendant) and, as she rejuvenates totally, she will *become* Katia!

Bava's first film as a director (and quite an accomplishment in the horror film

Barbara Steele is about to have the mask of the demon affixed to her face in Mario Bava's seminal *La Maschera del Demonio* (1960, Galatea Film [Milan]/Jolly Film [Rome]/Alta Vista Productions).

genre) launched the career of Barbara Steele as a horror film icon and helped to give birth to the cinematic Italian Gothic Horror genre. A film almost always enveloped in a mood of shadows, swirling mists and oppression, it is also fatally romantic. The simple adage that true love wins over all is attacked by a macabre visitor from the netherworld. When the hero cannot quite figure who he loves more, the sensual undead Asa or the virginal living Katia, you know you are in for something a little different. As discussed, the film which was based in part on one of Bava's favorite stories has the Russian author's fairy tale story of peasant oppression and vampiric witches adapted by Bava and company for an age where movie audiences were becoming more tolerant of what was offered to them. His daring

Christopher Lee threatens Reg Park (as Hercules) in Mario Bava's *Ercole al Centro della Terra* (1961, SPA Cinematografica).

mix of cinematography, sound and erotic underpinnings contributed to the film's success.

After the critical (and slight commercial) success of *La Maschera del Demonio*, Bava was in demand as a director while still shooting scenes, effects and other second unit work for productions such as director Anton Majano's *Seddok* (1960). He performed second unit directing chores and supervised the special effects for Henry Levin's *La Meraviglie di Aladino* (1961), a charming Arabian Nights tale which was overall just a little too juvenile for adult fans of "sword and sorcery" fantasies. As with several other Italian productions attributed to Levin as director, it is quite possible that Bava directed much more than he has been given credit for.

Following *La Maschera del Demonio*, Bava's next film as director was the sword-and-sandal film *Ercole al Centro della Terra* (1961). Bava co-wrote the screenplay (written with Duccio Tessari, Franco Prosperi and others) and photographed the film (with Ubaldo Terzano). This, his second feature, was a striking original work in the sword-and-sandal costume adventure genre. *Ercole al Centro della Terra* is a vivid action film filled with delightful colors (many bright shades of reds, greens and blues) achieved through the use of specially adapted colored gels for lighting. It is also a fantasy film filled with imagery that was far beyond its time (a nightmarish journey to Hell and a harrowing zombie attack by the undead legions led by villain Christopher Lee). Years later, Lee recalled Bava as "one of Italy's greatest cameramen."

The film, Bava's second official directing stint, remains today as part sword-and-sandal hokum and part brilliance. British body builder Reg Park stars as the heroic muscleman Hercules, returning to his kingdom after doing battle abroad only to find his sweetheart in a comatose state and his land ruled by an evil sorcerer, Lico (Christopher Lee). Hercules mistakenly believes Lico to be a fair mystic who is aiding the kingdom and the interests of the Queen; Lico instructs him to journey to Hell to retrieve a golden apple from some talking tree women to revive his now-ailing love. The end of the movie, where Lico calls forth zombies to battle the mighty Hercules, is the first zombie attack on record in a color horror film.*

The Viking adventure *Gli Invasori* followed that same year. The film's low budget is apparent despite Bava's attempt to mask this with careful set design, sexy, daring costumes for the female cast members (revealing quite a bit more skin than the norm for a genre film at this time) and some violent scenes featuring much hacking, chopping and blood.

This is Bava's first Viking film as director. Some sources claim that it was inspired by the big-budget international co-production *The Vikings* starring Kirk Douglas. In *Gli Invasori*, Cameron Mitchell stars as a heroic figure. It is most interesting for its ingenious, well-photographed battle sequences where, via in-camera effects using panes of glass and mirrors, Bava seemingly turned 30 men into over 300.

La Ragazza Che Sapeva Troppo (1962) was shot in a noir-ish, dramatic style which reflected the current interest in crime fiction on the European continent. It is often called the first important *giallo* film and is a nod to the films of Alfred Hitchcock, particularly *The Man Who Knew Too Much* (1934 and 1956), *Suspicion* (1941) and *Psycho* (1960), and is a clever audience pleaser with its mix of violence and detective fiction; it is also among the prime cinematic references (along with Bava's *Sei Donne per l'Assassino*) which became the base for Dario Argento's career as a director. A neurotic woman (Leticia Roman) who passes the time immersed in romantic novels travels to Rome to meet a dying relative. It isn't long before a series of events propel the woman to start to fantasize, hallucinate and see a murder committed ... or did she? There is something wrong with what she saw, but

---

*Bava did not direct the very interesting sequel Ercole alla Conquista di Atlantide *(1961). Riccardo Freda, the Italian Gothic cinema's other formal stylist, remade* Ercole al Centro della Terra *(sort of) with the 1962 film* Maciste all'Inferno. *This movie featured another muscular hero (played by Kirk Morris) descending into Hades to rescue the spirit of a woman who, on the surface world above, is about to be burned as a witch. Part* La Maschera del Demonio *and part delirium, this mixture of genres is pretty wild and worth viewing, if one is willing to totally suspend belief and accept the premise of a mythical warrior transported to the 1600s.*

she can't quite remember all of the details. John Saxon is an enigmatic doctor who lurks around trying to romance our now slightly schizophrenic heroine ... or is he?

A forerunner of the violent *giallo* films of the '70s, this movie takes into account that (now obvious) infamous ingredient that appears in most later *giallo* films, the question often nagging most heroes and heroines. What occurrence from a chance encounter with violence (that has sometimes resulted in a death) can they not recall, no matter how hard they try? Bava has a field day dropping subliminal clues as Roman and Saxon investigate a series of murders (dubbed the Alphabet Killings in a nod to Agatha Christie) that have plagued the city. The final outcome was far ahead of its time: the murderer is a woman who is crazy. What Roman saw one rainy night was not this woman being attacked, but rather this woman attacking someone else!

A film that improves with age, the English-language version (titled *The Evil Eye*) was not only cut, but partially re-scripted. The American distributor, American International Pictures, which had co-financed the production after the impressive box office performance of *La Maschera del Demonio*, felt that the tone of the film should be lightened, so they financed the filming of additional, comical scenes. The original Italian-language print retains a much more serious atmosphere. Most noticeable is the absence of much of Leticia Roman's narration which, in *The Evil Eye*, turned her into a Nancy Drew–type adventuress. Also absent in the English-language print is an important plot point: The heroine may have imagined the film's key murder scene due to being under the influence of a narcotic cigarette.

La Frusta e il Corpo (1963) remains today a deeply disturbing and fascinating work. It depicts some serious melding of the psychosexual maladies that plague a dysfunctional wealthy family some time before the turn of the twentieth century and the supernatural presence that might have been amplified by the strange happenings that plague the inhabitants of a royal castle.

Bava's most erotic film features Daliah Lavi as the sister-in-law of the evil masochist Kurt (Christopher Lee), who returns home to his ancestral castle after many years and then mysteriously dies after whipping and raping Lavi. She keeps on seeing his ghost, who romances her, then whips her violently ... much to her liking. This greatly disturbs other members of the family (some of whom soon meet their deaths) and Lavi's husband (Tony Kendall a.k.a. Luciano Stella). During these nightly visitations, Bava makes sure that he shows the audience little more than shadows and colored mists when Kurt appears. The rest of the family suspects that Lavi has gone insane until they find footprints in the family crypt. The denouement is both absurd and shocking.

The American distributor, Thunderbird Films, edited the film down to a bare minimum of less than 70 minutes and re-edited it in such a way that the key order of some scenes were shifted, giving more prominence to Christopher Lee.

I Tre Volti della Paura was Bava's next film that year and it signaled his growing mastery as a film director as he continued to experiment with the artificially created world of colored lighting and mists. An anthology of three stories, the final episode, "The Wurdalak," helped resurrect the then-flagging career of aged horror film icon Boris Karloff, giving him one of his scariest, worthiest latter-day roles as a malevolent family patriarch inflicted with vampirism.

The first episode, "The Telephone," is about a woman (Lydia Alfonsi) who taunts her ex-lover and neighbor (Michelle Mercier) with disguised phone calls, assuming the voice of an escaped felon, Mercier's male suitor. In the English-language prints, the film becomes a supernatural horror tale about a woman who receives calls from a dead man; when she asks her friend over to spend the night, for solace and kindness, the "dead man" appears and murders the neighbor.

Another episode is attributed to an Anton Chekhov story but is actually a combination of the literary works of Dostoevski and Guy De Maupassant. "Drop of Water" concerns a nurse (Jacqueline Pierreux) summoned to the home of the village medium who has died. The dead woman's face is a macabre and frightening visage, a grimace of terror. The nurse tidies up the dead body and arranges the corpse in a funeral gown, noticing a bright red ruby ring on the hand of the deceased. She takes the ring and puts it on her own finger, in the process spilling a glass of water. The nurse goes home to a lightning storm that knocks out the electrical power. She hears constantly dripping water from the rain outside, a wet umbrella and her kitchen and bathroom faucets. She imagines the shocking spooky grimacing woman sitting in a rocking chair and fears for her own life as she feels the icy cold hands of death approach her own throat.

The film's highlight is the longest segment, an adaptation of the Russian author Alexei Tolstoy's "The Wurdalak," with a bit of Nikolai Gogol's "The Vij" thrown in and credited to *Ivan* Tolstoi. In "The Wurdalak," Boris Karloff (who also narrates and introduces the other episodes in the English-language version) stars as the scion of a Russian peasant family living in near isolation. He journeys out in the dead of night to fell a vicious bandit who has been threatening the countryside. Days later, he returns inflicted with vampirism.

Bava again proceeds to break the walls of taboo by insisting that the family patriarch prey on the sons and daughters and smallest of grandchildren in order to spread this deadly disease of horror. Even today, "The Wurdalak" stands as a moody, spooky little piece of horror history and is still quite effective.

The original Italian-language version of this film features an alternate introduction by Karloff (he appears twice as narrator, at the film's beginning and after the last episode) and some additional running time in the individual segments. More importantly, the original score by Roberto Nicolosi is superior to the well-known brassy arrangement by Les Baxter that appears on many prints, imposed by co-producer American International Pictures.

The American co-production contract called for the rights to contributory and veto privileges for the English-language versions of the film. Besides the differences discussed above, AIP requested the addition of individual story introductions for each episode, deleting the original appearances of Karloff's on-screen narrator and re-structuring the tale "The Telephone" to heighten the films marginal thriller angle to a supernatural one by the means of dubbing and cutting.* Karloff spoke highly of Bava's directorial skills and considered his role as the family patriarch one of his greatest. It has been speculated that the pneumonia that befell Karloff shortly thereafter was a result of working in the cold climates of the Italian film studios where the film was shot, and led to the poor health that plagued him in later years.

It was Bava's celebrated, ultra-violent *Sei Donne per l'Assassino* that eventually put him on the road to cult superstardom. The 1964 movie remains perhaps the original slasher film. There had been nothing quite like it before and of course, due to its influence, there have been hundreds like it since. *Sei Donne per l'Assassino* took some of the ideas already used in *La Ragazza Che Sapeva a Troppo* and amplified them. In the film, the murders almost always took place in the dead of night, sometimes a violently stormy one. The killer is basically unseen by the audience save for some hints at a male form, or a woman masquerading as a man, attributed to the clothing, usually a black fedora-type hat with wide brim, a slick black raincoat and, almost always, black leather gloves. The killer in this film uses various ways to murder the victims, carefully keeping the audience guessing as to his (her?) identity. It could be a man (but that would be natural), but it could also be a woman (that would be unnatural thinking), and in the world of Mario Bava, that is the idea. Why couldn't a woman, whether possessed by a purposeful vengeance, vendetta or a particularly amplified, powerful presence (which, in this movie nearly all of the female cast members have), be the mysterious killer? *Sei Donne per l'Assassino* is undeniably responsible for many of the changes that took place in the horror film genre thereafter. It also signaled the coming end for the brief cycle of films in the Italian Gothic horror cinema.

For genre aficionados, this violent and colorful movie has become the ultimate Mario Bava film. To others, it is nothing more than a brutal but stylish imitation of the German Edgar Wallace thrillers that were a sensation around that same period. In either case, this film is also directly responsible for influencing the early cinematic efforts of Dario Argento and contributing to the *giallo* filmography as an invaluable reference source. Cameron Mitchell stars as the head of a fashion institute where models are being murdered via axe, spiked steel glove, hot pokers, etc., by a figure in a black hat, black leather gloves and raincoat. The reasons for the shocking murders revealed at the film's Grand Guignol finale are secondary. The assured hand and manner with which Bava's use of colors accentuate

---

*"*The Wurdalak*" episode was remade as* La Notte dei Diavoli *by Giorgio Ferroni in 1971. This modern-day version incorporates elements from the original Tolstoy tale as well as the filmed Bava-Karloff version.*

French poster image from *I Tre Volti della Paura* (1963, Galatea Film [Milan]/Emmepi Cinematografica [Rome] / Société Cinématographique Lyre [Paris]).

the mood and scenes of startling violence seem to propel the film into a world of delirium all its own.

Bava also made a Western (1964's *La Strada per Fort Alamo*) and a spy parody (1965's *Le Spie Vengeno dal Semifreddo*). *La Strada per Fort Alamo* is an above average Spaghetti Western starring Ken Clark as Arizona Bill, leader of a gang of criminals, who mends his ways after an innocent woman is killed during a robbery. *Le Spie Vengono dal Semifreddo* is a follow-up to two movies, the American *Dr. Goldfoot and the Bikini Machine* (1965) directed by Norman Taurog and the Italian film *Due Mafiosi Contra Goldginger* (1965) directed by Giorgio Simonelli. *Due Mafiosi Contra Goldginger* is a James Bond spoof featuring the immensely popular (and incredibly prolific) Italian comedy team of Franco Franchi and Ciccio Ingrassia and is a parody of several films, most obviously *Goldfinger*. It's charming and a delight to watch. However, it helps to really appreciate European spy films that copied the successful 007 formula before you approach this film. *Le Spie Vengono dal Semifreddo* re-introduces the Italian audience to Franchi and Ciccio with the addition of American pop star Fabian (replacing Frankie Avalon from the first *Dr. Goldfoot* film) as the U.S. agent on the trail of Vincent Price's humorously nefarious mad scientist. Dr. Goldfoot plans on replacing key political and military figures with his own duplicates after the originals have been kidnapped or murdered by his robot femme fatales (a startling list of many attractive Italian starlets, among them Laura Antonelli). As a sequel to two films with which he was never involved and saddled with comedic elements with which he never seemed comfortable, Bava's film remains a minor one. Look for the uncut Italian-language print as it contains footage which does not appear in the AIP version, including some more sexually suggestive scenes. Most versions feature a cameo by the director at the finale as an angel!

Bava's next film, the absolutely delirious *Terrore nello Spazio*, achieved a near-impossible mix of the science fiction and the horror film genres that had rarely been achieved before. Originally based on the story *One Night of 21 Hours* by the Italian Renato Pestriniero, itself possibly influenced by the American science fiction film *It! The Terror from Beyond Space* (1958) directed by Edward L. Cahn and written by Jerome Bixby, *Terrore nello Spazio* tells the tale of an interstellar space flight that answers a distress signal from a far-off planet only to find little but a long-dead race of beings that once inhabited the planet. But, of course, more is actually happening as otherworldly beings seeking new hosts for their abstract life forms terrorize the crews of the spaceship by first murdering them, then reviving their bodies and inhabiting them.

I Coltello del Vendicatore (1966), Bava's third film with Cameron Mitchell, depicts the titled Viking tiring of warmongering and seeking to settle down to a peaceful life with wife and children. Above-average action choreography and the battle scenes are some of the film's highlights. This is one of the first films that Bava signed as director using the pseudonym John M. Old.

French poster image from Mario Bava's *Sei Donne per l'Assassino* (1964, Emmepi Cinematografica [Rome]/Productions Georges De Beauregard [Paris]/Top Film [Munich]/Monarchia Films).

Filmed in 1966, *Operazione Paura* is one of the most thrilling ghost films in the entire Italian horror cinema. Bava used his technique of slowly building a sense of dread through the use of lighting and special effects which he put to use so well on *Terrore nello Spazio* and perfected for *Operazione Paura*. It is an immensely disturbing, scary horror film in which the director carefully builds a sense of malevolence. The film also catapulted its stars Giacomo Rossi-Stuart and Erica Blanc into a period of brief genre stardom, with numerous appearances in leading and supporting roles. Dr. Eswai (Rossi-Stuart) is sent to a rural area to a village out of time located in the mountainous terrain of Italy, isolated from any kind of modern conveniences and richly steeped in supernatural legends. He is assigned by an old acquaintance, a police inspector, to perform an autopsy on a young woman, the latest reported victim of a deadly ghost child. This ghost is a little girl (actually played by a small boy with feminine features) who appears in the dead of night, accompanied by swirling mists of colored fog, to scare people to death, or to incite their fears, leading them to commit acts of violent suicide. This, the townspeople all claim, is the curse that they all must accept because, many years earlier, as a little child lay dying from a terrible accident, no one came to her aid.

A supernaturally imbued tale, this is pure cinematic magic at its best. *Operazione Paura* contains many moments that remain indelibly marked on the psyche. Bava uses chilling subjective camera angles, a ghostly, childish giggle and shocking, near-subliminal cuts of the face of the child or its hand at a window pane to add to the mounting dread. The relationship between Dr. Eswai and Monica (Erica Blanc) has little time to get romantically charged. A good deal of the screen time normally given over to such matters is taken over by Dr. Eswai's discovery, his quest to ascertain why all the villagers are so frightened, and his subsequent investigation into the mystery surrounding Villa Grapps.*

Producer Dino De Laurentiis approached Bava to make the film version of a popular Italian comic strip character. *Diabolik* (1968) featured a budget much larger than that with which he was accustomed. John Philip Law stars as a master supercriminal called Diabolik, a Batman-type figure dressed in elaborate skin-tight costumes to hide his true identity. Diabolik lives in a huge, cavernous underground city with all of his hi-tech gadgetry and his girlfriend, a rail-thin blonde (Marisa Mell). Diabolik continually thwarts the efforts of the commissioner of police (Michel Piccoli) who is attempting to foil Diabolik's attacks on the wealthy jet set crowd. Eventually the police combine with organized crime, led by Godfather figure (and *Thunderball* villain) Adolfo Celli in order to put a stop to Diabolik's reign of

---

*In 1968, Federico Fellini and Louis Malle collaborated on the film Tre Passi nel Delirio *(Spirits of the Dead/Histoires Extraordinaires). The movie was an anthology of short films, supposedly influenced by the writings of Edgar Allan Poe. One of these short films,* Toby Dammit, *featured Terence Stamp as the titled character, a vain actor who is lured to Italy to star in a new film. Terrorized by visions of a ghost child, the actor nears a mental breakdown, then meets his fate.* Toby Dammit *wears the influence of Mario Bava proudly on its sleeve as it takes much of its influence from* Operazione Paura, *especially the ghostly visage of the little girl who terrorizes the cast in that film.*

terror before he bankrupts the country and then all of Europe. There are plenty of stunts, action, sci-fi gadgetry and colorful costumes to look at and the music score is appropriately jaunty, but it's a disappointment that we never really learn very much about the character of Diabolik. Bava probably was never interested in what drives Diabolik to commit his deeds (probably just to amass more and more wealth) but rather was attracted to the inherent possibilities of bringing a popular comic strip anti-hero to the screen in all his colorful, sexy, gaudy and psychedelic wonder.

La Odissea (1968) was released that same year via the Italian R.A.I. TV network, which funded the project. The program was a weekly fantasy series based upon the popular sword-and-sandal peplums of the early '60s and Bava assisted on particular episodes as a technical consultant and special effects cameraman. He was invited to direct an episode of his own, further chronicling the adventures of Ulysses. Apparently only a portion of that Bava-directed episode had survived in the feature film version of the series. It never played theatrically in countries where it was exported, but instead went directly to television as *La Avventure di Ulisse* (as *The Adventures of Ulysses* in some countries), re-named *The Adventures of Hercules* in most English-speaking markets (including the U.S.).

In his last western, *Roy Colt e Winchester Jack* (1969), the friendship of two men (Brett Halsey and Charles Southwood) is tested when one of them becomes the outlaw leader of a gang and the other becomes a sheriff. The two reunite to battle a common enemy, a psychopathic leader of a gang of ruthless killers.

Bava did not return to the horror film genre until *Il Rosso Segno della Follia* (1969). In the few years since *Operazione Paura*, the Italian horror film genre had changed dramatically. Audiences were used to the much more "in your face" kind of horror that Bava had helped pioneer with *Sei Donne per l'Assassino*. As one character says to another in the film, "Reality is much more horrible than fiction." The insane proprietor of a bridal fashion salon (Stephen Forsythe) kills his models and his shrew of a wife because of a deadly Oedipal complex. His many psychological conversations with himself ("No one would think to look at me that I am completely insane") reveal an extreme dementia to which the audience is privy. Bava ups the ante when he introduces possible elements of the supernatural; for example, has the wife the husband murdered returned from the grave to torment him?

In one of the most startling sequences in the film, the man stalks a couple on a train, stopping in front of their sleeping car compartment. He looks into a reflection in the mirror and sees the troubled stare of a young boy, before it reveals his own empty stare, then he proceeds to murder the couple. There are some great moments here like the voice-over narration where the killer admits to being crazy ("...I am insane"). Bava capitalizes on Forsythe's slightly feminine appearance (the actor closely resembles French screen idol Alain Delon), apparently suggesting that someone as handsome as the lead can commit an act of savage violence by amplifying his delicate physical appearance to further emphasize his appealing demeanor behind which lies confusion and dementia.

The thriller *Cinque Bambola per la Luna d'Agosto* (1970) is a return to the kind of criminal fiction and *giallo* novels that influenced some of Bava's best work. Hampered by a much lower-than-usual budget and a script that was unsure of its next turn, Bava relied too much on the zoom lens to signify tension and mood.

A group of wealthy people, their lovers, friends and servants gather at a remote house located near a beach for a weekend which ends in terror as, one by one, the guests are murdered. In yet another remake of Agatha Christie's *Ten Little Indians*, Bava shows some serious disinterest in this project from the masturbatory manner in which he furiously pumps his zoom lens in and out during the psychedelicized party scenes and the way in which he neglects the plot. Although the cast is far from worthless (*giallo* stalwarts Edwige Fenech and William Berger among them), there are only a few brief moments (the walk-in icebox where the dead are displayed in plastic, hanging like pieces of meat) where the movie perks up and makes it seem dramatically different from the Christie source material.

Another significant departure for the director was the film *Quattro Volte ... Quella Notte* (1970), where Bava jumps totally into the psychedelic swinging '70s. This odd, seldom-seen film combines comedy, drama, softcore sex and Akira Kurosawa's *Rashomon* to tell four versions of a possible seduction and rape. Daniela Giordano and Brett Halsey star.

More successful was *Ecologia del Delitto* (1971), a Grand Guignol spectacular that is markedly different from much of the director's previous work. This film is the forebear of many of the '80s slasher films. Much of the slasher genre consisted of one chief plot outline: psychopaths, whether of a natural or supernatural origin, who stalk teens, mainly nubile young women, throughout empty apartment buildings and in desolate areas. With no one around to help (those that could have had already fallen prey to the seemingly unstoppable madman), the would-be victims fend for themselves and come up with ingenious ways of self-defense.

For *Ecologia del Delitto*, Bava left behind his swirling mists and colored gels for a more natural approach. He had adopted the (for him) new technique of photographing his films in a clear, crisp manner. Possibly due to tightening budget constraints, Bava could no longer rely on his customary stylized lighting and special effects and decided on a new approach that, visually for better or worse, closely resembled the work of his successor, Dario Argento. A series of graphic murders take place but the biggest shocker in this thriller occurs right at the beginning. An elderly woman in a wheelchair is attacked by someone who throws a rope around her neck. As the chair flies out from under her she suddenly soars into the air, left hanging.

After this stupendous opening, Bava's film goes up and down like an amusement park rollercoaster; the thrills ebb, only to build again to a crescendo. A group of overage teenagers gather at the same location where the woman was murdered and, one by one, they are brutally slain. Then the film switches gears entirely when we are introduced to greedy relatives, lawyers and others, all seeking to purchase a valuable piece of land. With this film, Bava drops most of his customary specialized camera effects and cotton candy–colored lighting gels in favor of a more realistic, in-your-face appearance. The film is shot in a crystal-clear manner, utilizing the zoom lens for effect more often than not. Opportunistic American film exploitation distributors had a field day by re-editing and re-releasing the film many times. It was humorously retitled *Carnage*, *Twitch of the Death Nerve* and the more exploitative *Last House on the Left: Part 2*, implying that the Bava film was a sequel, when in fact it was not.

Gli Orrori del Castello di Norimberga (1972), Bava's next horror film, is disappointing. Like *Cinque Bambole per la Luna d'Agosto*, it relies heavily on the zoom lens to signify scenes of approaching terror, but these camera tricks soon become irritating. Little of the director's artistic style, so evident throughout much of his earlier work, is visible save for these scenes: the resurrected Baron climbing out of his grave and seeking medical attention to tend to his bloody wounds and the visits to the castle torture dungeon.

Elke Sommer stars as a museum curator who is working on the restoration of the castle Von Kleist. Centuries before, the Baron Von Kleist was a heretical sadist who dabbled in the occult and tortured countless numbers of people. It isn't long before Sommer and her young boyfriend start messing around with an ancient manuscript from the 1600s. Before you know it, the Baron has been resurrected and is up all night slaughtering the townspeople and masquerading by day as Joseph Cotten, a Von Kleist descendant.

With little to do but just stand there at times and scream her head off, the beautiful Sommer quickly becomes an irritating presence. Bava flubs the use of this actress by not utilizing her in a manner that exploits her strong sensuality. Instead, he makes her a quite hysterical heroine, waiting to be saved at every moment of endangerment. One of Bava's films to receive a decent amount of theatrical play in the U.S. upon its release in the early '70s, *Gli Orrori del Castello di Norimberga* is also, unfortunately, not among his best films, though there are a few horrific moments to recommend it to discriminating horror film audiences of today.

Lise e il Diavolo (1972), a much more personable work and an uneven contemporary horror film masterpiece, was a troubled production. With a talented cast of film veterans bringing to life his morbid fantasy characters, a Byzantine plot device and a return to the phantasmagorical style he pioneered decades back, Bava's film was thought unreleasable and was re-edited with new footage added to make it an entirely different entity. When *Lise e il Diavolo* finally appeared in 1975, it was known as *La Casa dell'Esorcismo* and became little more than another unsavory clone of *The Exorcist*.

Lise e il Diavolo is Bava's grotesque poetic homage to the surreal landscapes of master Italian painters. Elke Sommer stars as a disturbed tourist who crosses over into the netherworld where she meets a carload of weary (and horny) aristocrats en route to the gateway to Hell. After she hitches a ride with them, the car breaks down near an old villa housing the blind matriarch (Alida Valli), her bizarre son (Alessio Orano), who turns out to have strange sexual appetites, and their bald, bold family servant (Telly Savalas), who may or may not be the Devil. They all live and wait for the return (or reincarnation) of the son's former lover ... who turns out to be Sommer! As the debauched, rich wife (Sylva Koscina) of the wealthy man who gave Sommer a lift seeks every opportunity to have sex with their chauffeur, the air of depravity and strange sensuality becomes thick and acrid. Sommer begins to experience strange hallucinations featuring a man she's never met who seems to know her very intimately. Confounded by this and the strange attraction to the son of the blind woman, things come to a head. Sommer is drugged and then ravaged by Orano followed by the extermination of most of the cast members, leading to a very unusual ending.

This film, with its air of morbidity, is considered by many to be among Bava's best films. However, *Lise e il Diavolo* remains a film that had been mired in an entanglement of horrors all its own. When the film failed to garner attention from film distributors who evidently did not understand the movie and felt it unreleasable, producer Alfredo Leone induced Bava to return to the studio with Sommer and drastically re-edit the film into some kind of sellable format, so that the producer could recoup his investment and make foreign sales. American actor Robert Alda reported to the soundstage to play a priest who spends considerable screen time exorcising the bed-ridden Sommer, who is reduced to vomiting up frogs and spouting a barrage of expletives. This footage, a good 20 minutes or so, had then been inflated with some *Lise e il Diavolo* footage. When the final product was unveiled in 1975, the film became the totally incomprehensible *La Casa*

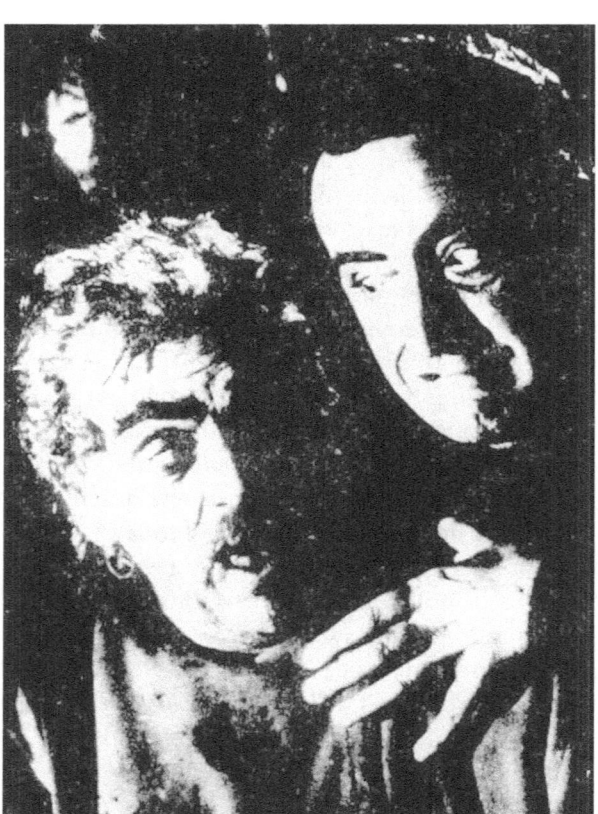

Mario Bava kids with star Boris Karloff on the set of *I Tre Volti della Paura* (1963, Galatea Film [Milan]/Emmepi Cinematografica [Rome]/Société Cinématographique Lyre [Paris]).

dell'Esorcismo. Bava's surreal, bizarre work of art had been changed into a third-rate *Exorcist* rip-off (released in the United States as *The House of Exorcism*) relegated to the bottom of grindhouse theater double bills. *La Casa dell'Esorcismo* was such a disaster that it eventually wound up released as a throwaway horror film in many countries.

Problems also plagued Bava's *Cani Arrabbiati* (1974), an experimental film that told a tale of corruption and madness, set mainly within the confines of a hijacked automobile. A personal project for the director, it was finished but never shown. Due to financial problems, it was shelved for 20 years!

A seldom-seen film (the production company that funded this film had experienced many problems), it remained in a vault buried under mounds of legal entanglements until recently when it re-surfaced. *Cani Arrabbiati* is a different kind of film for Mario Bava. It is a claustrophobic and nihilistic tale of criminals without redemption. A young boy who suffers from an illness and his chauffeur are kidnapped by some diabolical criminals on the run, who force others into their car as they elude the police. Almost the entire film takes place in the automobile as allegiances change, rape is threatened, murder takes place and things get generally more downbeat and sinister. The final moments in the film come as a bit of surprise when the audience learns that the chauffeur had intended to kidnap the child all along and that's what he had been doing when he was captured by the criminals!

Bava contributed to the special effects for the international television miniseries *Moses: The Lawgiver* (1973–75). The re-edited version of the Burt Lancaster–starring film, directed by Gianfranco De Bosin, played theatrically in some markets with *Shock* (1977).

Shock, as its title signifies, is a return to the Gothic or Grand Guignol horror of decades past. An air of perversity permeates the cinematic atmosphere that harkens back to *La Frusta e il Corpo*. A couple with a young son must pay for a devilish deed when the boy exhibits some definite un-childlike tendencies towards his mother and father. He makes attempts to caress the mother like a lover and exhibits hatred for the father. Is the boy possessed? Or is all this in the mind of the mother, who may have crossed over into dementia because she, together with her lover, may have murdered her first husband, the father of the child? A wildly uneven film punctuated by some unsettling moments, this film came too late in the genre. It was released years after the similar *Chi Sei?* (1974), and other films in the "possessed children" cycle of horror films that had been popular in the '70s such as *The Exorcist* (1973) and *The Omen* (1976).

Shock is full of themes that are often considered to be taboo, warped ideas better left in pornographic literature and the minds of deviates than filmed and splashed across the cinematic screen for all to see. It was titled *Beyond the Door II* in some markets to cash in on the surprise success of that Ovidio Assonitis film *Chi Sei?* (titled *Beyond the Door* in English-speaking markets).

Mario Bava's last film as a director was an episode of the Italian program *Il*

Giorno del Diavolo (1978). Titled *La Venere dell'Ille*, it's a melodramatic fantasy that displays some touches of the hand of one of the craft's finest technicians, telling the tale of a lovelorn man who becomes infatuated with a statue of Venus (Daria Nicolodi, fresh from her starring role in *Shock*). He brings her to life so that they may consummate their love, but tragedy results. *La Venere dell'Ille* is also the only time that Bava officially co-directed a film with his son Lamberto.

Perhaps it was fitting that Mario Bava's last contribution to film was to be a cinematographer and special effects person who assisted Dario Argento on *Inferno* (1980). His most telling legacy was the fantastically designed underwater chamber sequence. Bava died in 1980 at the age of 65. While some of his work contained moments of jarring violence, Bava will be remembered for what he did best. He formed an atmosphere of the ethereal by using carefully placed cameras and lighting and, at times, dramatic use of sound, such as silence interrupted by otherworldly tones ringing through a long-forgotten organ, or a door suddenly banging shut when there is no wind. In many of his films, Bava sought to shock the audience ... and he succeeded. Mario Bava has left a cinematic legacy of terror on film.

Mario Bava Filmography

La Battaglia di Maratona

A.k.a. *The Battle of Marathon* (English translation); a.k.a. *The Giant of Marathon* (English title) (1959) (It., Fr.); D: Jacques Tourneur, Bruno Vailati, Mario Bava (uncredited); P: Bruno Vailati; Prod. Co.: Titanus/Galatea Film (Milan)/Lux Film (Rome)/Société Cinématographique Lyre (Paris); SC: Bruno Vailati, Ennio De Concini, Augusto Frassinetti, Raffaello Pacini, Alberto Barsanti; C: Mario Bava; M: Roberto Nicolosi; S: Steve Reeves, Mylene Demongeot, Danielle Rocca, Sergio Fantoni, Ivo Garrani, Alberto Lupo, Philippe Hersent, Daniele Varga, Miranda Campa.

Caltiki, il Mostro Immortale

A.k.a. *Caltiki, the Immortal Monster* (English translation and title); a.k.a. *Caltiki*; a.k.a. *The Immortal Monster* (English title) (1959) (It., U.S.); D: Riccardo Freda, Mario Bava (uncredited); P: Samuel Schneider; Prod. Co.: Galatea Film (Milan)/Climax Pictures (Los Angeles–U.S.)/Allied Artists Pictures Corporation (U.S.); SC: Filippo Sanjust; C: Mario Bava; M: Roman Vlad, Roberto Nicolosi; SP E: Mario Bava; S: John Merivale, Gerard Herter, Didi Perego, Daniela Rocca, Gay Pearl, Daniele Vargas, Giacomo Rossi-Stuart, Arturo Dominici.

Cani Arrabbiati

A.k.a. *Wild Dogs* (English translation); a.k.a. *Semaforo Rosso* (alternate Italian title) (1974) (It.); D: Mario Bava; P: Roberto Loyola; Prod. Co.: Spera Cinematografica/Roberto Loyola Cinematografica; SC: Cesare Frugoni, Alessandro Parenzo, based on the story "A Man and a Boy" by Ellery Queen; C: Emilio Varriano, Giuseppe Alberti, Gianni Modica; M: Stelvio Cipriani; S: Riccardo Cucciolla, Maurice Poli, Lea Leander a.k.a. Lea Kruger, George Eastman a.k.a. Luigi Montefiori, Erika Dario.

Cinque Bambola per la Luna d'Agosto

A.k.a. *Five Dolls for an August Moon* (English translation and title) (1970) (It.); D: Mario Bava; P: Luigi Alessi; Prod. Co.: P.A.C. (Produzione Atlas Cinematografica); SC: Mario Di Nardo; C: Mario Bava, Antonio Rinaldi; M: Piero Umiliani; S: William Berger, Edwige Fenech, Ira Furstenberg, Howard Ross a.k.a. Renato Rossini, Helena Ronee, Maurice Poli, Ely Galleani a.k.a. Elyde Galleana.

Il Coltello del Vendicatore

A.k.a. *Knives of the Avenger* (English translation and title); a.k.a. *Raffica di Coltelli* (alternate Italian title) (1966) (It.); D: Mario Bava; P: Saro Pane, Sergio Cortona; Prod. Co.: Sider Film; SC: Mario Bava, Giorgio Simonelli, Alberto Liberati; C: Mario Bava, Antonio Rinaldi; M: Marcello Giombini; S: Cameron Mitchell, Fausto Tozzi, Giacomo Rossi-Stuart, Luciano Polletin, Amedeo Trilli, Renato Terra, Sergio Cortona, Elissa Mitchell.

Diabolik

A.k.a. *Danger: Diabolik* (1968) (It., Fr.); D: Mario Bava; P: Dino De Laurentiis; Prod. Co.: Dino De Laurentiis Cinematografica (Rome)/Marianne Productions (Pairs); SC: Mario Bava, Dino Maiuri, Adrianao Baracco, Tudor Gates, Brian Degas (U.S. version only), based on the *fumetti* (comic strips) by Angela Giussani and Luciana Giussani; C: Mario Bava, Antonio Rinaldi; M: Ennio Morricone, Bruno Nicolai; S: John Phillip Law, Marisa Mell a.k.a. Marlies Moitzi, Michel Piccoli, Adolfo Celli, Claudio Gora, Mario Donen, Renzo Palmer, Caterina Boratto, Terry-Thomas.

Ecologia del Delitto

A.k.a. *The Ecology of a Crime* (English translation); a.k.a. *Antefatto* (alternate Italian title; translation: *Before the Fact*); a.k.a. *Reazione a Catena* (alternate Italian title; translation: *Chain Reaction*); a.k.a. *Odore di Carne* (Italian pre-production title; translation: *Smell of Flesh*); a.k.a. *The Last House on the Left Part 2* (U.S. re-release title); a.k.a. *Bloodbath* (G.B. video title and Japanese video title) (1971) (It.); D: Mario Bava; P: Giuseppe Zaccariello; Prod. Co.: Nuova Linea Cinematografica; SC: Mario Bava, Giuseppe Zaccariello, Filippo Ottoni, Dardano Sacchetti, Franco Barberi, Gene Luotto; C: Mario Bava, Antonio Rinaldi; M: Stelvio Cipriani; S: Claudine Auger, Luigi Pistilli, Claudio Volonte, Anna Maria Rosati, Laura Betti, Chris Avram a.k.a. Christea Avram, Brigitte Skay, Isa Miranda, Leopoldo Trieste, Paola Rubens.

Ercole al Centro della Terra

A.k.a. *Hercules at the Center of the Earth*; a.k.a. *Hercules in the Center of the Earth* (English translations and titles); a.k.a. *Hercules in the Haunted World*; a.k.a. *Hercules vs. the Vampires*; a.k.a. *The Vampires vs. Hercules*; a.k.a. *With Hercules to the Center of the Earth* (English titles) (1961) (It.); D: Mario Bava; P: Achille Piazzi; Prod. Co.: SPA Cinematografica; SC: Mario Bava, Duccio Tessari, Alessandro Continenza, Franco Prosperi; C: Mario Bava, Ubaldo Terzano, Aristide Massaccesi (uncredited); M: Armando Trovajoli; SP E: Mario Bava; S: Reg Park, Christopher Lee, Leonora Ruffo, Giorgio Ardisson, Marisa Belli, Evelyn Stewart a.k.a. Ida Galli, Ely Draco, Grazia Collodi, Franco Giacobini, Mino Doro.

La Frusta e il Corpo

A.k.a. *The Whip and the Body*; a.k.a. *The Body and the Whip*; a.k.a. *The Way and the Body*; a.k.a. *The Whip and the Flesh*; a.k.a. *The Night Is the Phantom*; a.k.a. *Son of Satan*; a.k.a. *Incubo*; a.k.a. *What* (1963) (It., Fr.); D: Mario Bava; P: Elio Scardamaglia; Prod. Co.: Vox Film/Leone Film/Francinor (Paris)/P.I.P.–Paris International Productions; SC: Ernesto Gastaldi, Luciano Martino, Ugo Guerra; C: Mario Bava, Ubaldo Terzano; M: Carlo Rustichelli; S: Christopher Lee, Daliah Lavi, Tony Kendall a.k.a. Luciano Stella, Luciano Pigozzi, Jacques Herlin, Gustavo De Nardo, Harriet Medin White.

Gli Invasori

A.k.a. *The Invaders* (English translation and title); a.k.a. *Erik, the Conqueror* (1961) (It., Fr.); D: Mario Bava; Prod. Co.: Galatea Film (Milan)/Criterion Film (Paris)/Société Cinématographique Lyre (Paris); SC: Mario Bava, Oreste Biancoli, Piero Pierotti; C: Mario Bava, Ubaldo Terzano; M: Roberto Nicolosi; S: Cameron Mitchell, Alice Kessler, Ellen Kessler, Giorgio Ardisson, Andrea Checchi, Francoise Christophe, Folco Lulli, Franco Ressell, Joe Robinson.

Lise e il Diavolo

A.k.a. *Lisa and the Devil* (English translation and title); a.k.a. *Il Diavolo e i Morti* (alternate Italian release title; translation: *The Devil and the Dead*); a.k.a. *La Casa dell'Esorcismo* (alternate version Italian title; translation: *The House of Exorcism*; a.k.a. *The Devil in the House of Exorcism*); a.k.a. *La Maison de l'Exorcisme* (French title); a.k.a. *Die Jagd der Lebenden Leichen* (German title); a.k.a. *Der Teuflische* (alternate German title); a.k.a. *El Diablo se Lleva y los Muertos* (Spanish title) (1972) (It., Sp., W.G.); D: Mario Bava; P: Alfredo Leone; Prod. Co.: EuroAmerica/Tecisa/Roxy; SC: Mario Bava, Roberto Natale, Giorgio Manlini; C: Mario Bava, Cecilio Paniagua; M: Carlo Savina; SP E: Franco Tocci

La Casa dell'Esorcismo version: D: Mickey Lion (a.k.a. Mario Bava); SC: Alfredo Leone, Alberto Cittini; M: Rodrigo's "Concerto of Aranjuez" conducted by Paul Mauriat, "Le Sacre du Printemps" by Stravinsky; SP E: Franco Tocci; S: Elke Sommer, Telly Savalas a.k.a. Aristotle Savalas, Sylva Koscina, Alida Valli, Alessio Orano, Gabriele Tinti, Eduardo Fajardo, Carmen Silva, Franz Von Treuberg, Robert Anthony a.k.a. Espartaco Santoni.

La Casa dell'Esorcismo version: S: Robert Alda

La Maschera del Demonio

A.k.a. *The Mask of the Demon* (English translation and title); a.k.a. *Black Sunday*; a.k.a. *Revenge of the Vampire*; a.k.a. *The Demon's Mask*; a.k.a. *House of Fright* (English title) (1960) (It.); D: Mario Bava; P: Massimo De Rita, Lou Rusof (U.S. version only); Prod. Co.: Galatea Film (Milan)/Jolly Film (Rome)/Alta Vista Productions; SC: Mario Bava, Ennio De Concini, Marcello Coscia, Mario Serandrei, based on the story "The Vij" by Nikolai Gogol; C: Mario Bava, Ubaldo Terzano; M: Roberto Nicolosi, (Les Baxter, U.S. version only); SP E: Mario Bava; S: Barbara Steele, John Richardson, Ivo Garrani, Andrea Checchi, Arturo Dominici, Enrico Olivieri, Clara Bindi, Antonio Pierfederici, Tino Bianchi.

La Meraviglie di Aladino

A.k.a. *The Wonders of Aladdin* (English translation and title) (1961) (It., Fr.); D: Henry Levin, Mario Bava; Prod. Co. Lux Film (Rome)/Lux Compagnie Cinématographique de France (Paris); SC: Stefano Strucchi, Duccio Tessari, Paul Tuckaoe; C: Tonino Della Colli,

Mario Bava; M: Angelo Francesco Lavagnino; S: Donald O'Connor, Vittorio De Sica, Aldo Fabrizi, Michele Mercier, Noelle Adam.

Mario Bava is puported to be the director of credit on this film, but for export and tax reasons, American Henry Levin was solely listed as director on English-language prints.

Nebraska il Pistolero

A.k.a. *Nebraska, the Pistol* (English translation and title); a.k.a. *Gunman Called Nebraska*; a.k.a. *Ringo from Nebraska*; a.k.a. *Savage Gringo* (English title) (1966) (It., Sp.); D: Antonio Romano, Mario Bava; Prod. Co.: P.E.A.–Produzioni Europee Associate; SC: Antonio Romano; C: Guglielmo Mancori; M: Nino Oliviero; S: Ken Clark, Piero Lulli, Yvonne Bastien, Alfonso Rojas, Paco Sanz, Renato Rossini, Frank Brana, Aldo Sanbrell a.k.a. Aldo Sambrell a.k.a. Alfredo Sanchez Brell, Livio Lorenzon.

La Odissea

A.k.a. *The Odyssey* (English translation; a.k.a. *Le Avventura di Ulisse*; a.k.a. *The Adventures of Ulysses* (English translation); a.k.a. *The Adventures of Hercules* (English title) (1968) (It.); D: Franco Rossi, Mario Bava, Piero Schivazappa; P: Dino De Laurentiis; M: Carlo Rustichelli; S: Bekim Fehmiu, Irene Papas, Juliette Mayniel, Kira Bester, Renaud Verley, Marcela Velri, Constantin Nepo, Scilla Gabel.

Episode of the Italian television program *La Odissea* a.k.a.*The Odyssey*. Mario Bava's contribution was originally titled *Polifemo*.

Operazione Paura

A.k.a. *Operation Fear* (English translation and title); a.k.a. *Curse of the Living Dead*; a.k.a. *Kill, Baby, Kill* (English title) (1966) (It.); D: Mario Bava; P: Nando Pisani, Luciano Catenacci; Prod. Co.: Ful Films; SC: Mario Bava, Romano Migliorini, Roberto Natale; C: Mario Bava, Romano Rinaldi; S: Giacomo Rossi-Stuart, Erika Blanc a.k.a. Enrica Bianchi Colombatto, Fabienne Dali, Gianna Vivaldi, Piero Lulli, Giuseppe Addobbati, Franca Dominici, Micaela Esdra.

Gli Orrori del Castello di Norimberga

A.k.a. *Many Horrors in the Nuremberg Castle* (English translation); a.k.a. *Baron Vampire* (French title); a.k.a. *Damon und die Jungfrau* (German title); a.k.a. *The Chamber of Tortures*; a.k.a. *The Torture Chamber of Baron Blood*; a.k.a. *The Thirst of Baron Blood*; a.k.a. *The Chamber of Tortures*; a.k.a. *Baron Blood* (English title) (1972) (It., W.G.); D: Mario Bava; P: Alfredo Leone; Prod. Co.: Euro International Films/Dieter Geissler; SC: Mario Bava, Vincent Forte, Willibald Eser; C: Mario Bava, Antonio Rinaldi; M: Stelvio Cipriani (U.S. version: Les Baxter); SP E: Franco Tocci; S: Joseph Cotten, Elke Sommer, Antonio Cantafora, Massimo Girotti, Luciano Pigozzi, Dieter Tressler, Umberto Raho, Rada Rassimov, Nicoletta Elmi, Ely Galleani a.k.a. Elyde Galleana.

Quattro Volte ... Quella Notte

A.k.a. *Four Times That Night* (English translation); a.k.a. *Quante Volte ... Quella Notte* (alternate Italian title); a.k.a. *Una Notte Fatta di Bugie* (alternate Italian title); a.k.a. *Vier Mal Heute Nacht* (German title) (1973) (It., W.G.); D: Mario Bava; P: Alfredo Leone; Prod. Co.: Delfino Film (Rome)/Hape Film (Munich)/Arlington International Pictures; SC: Mario Bava, Gene Luotto, Mario Moroni, Charles Ross; C: Antonio Rinaldi, Salvatore Caruso;

M: Lallo Gori; S: Daniela Giordano, Pascale Petit, Brett Halsey, Dick Randall, Valeria Sabel, Rainer Basedow, Brigitte Skay, Calisto Calisti.

La Ragazza Che Sapeva Troppo

A.k.a. *The Girl Who Knew Too Much* (English translation); a.k.a. *L'Incubo* (alternate Italian title, translation: *The Nightmare*); a.k.a. *The Evil Eye* (English title) (1962) (It.); D: Mario Bava; P: Ferruccio De Martino, Salvatore Billitteri; Prod. Co.: Galatea Film S.p.a. (Milan)/Coronet Pruduzioni S.r.l. (Milan/Rome); SC: Mario Bava, Mino Guerrini, Franco Prosperi, Eliana De Sabata, Sergio Corbucci, Ennio De Concini, Neda Matteucci; C: Mario Bava, Ubaldo Terzano; M: Roberto Nicolosi (Les Baxter, U.S. version only); S: Letitia Roman, John Saxon a.k.a. Carmine Orrico, Valentina Cortese, Dante Di Paolo, Gianni Di Benedetto.

Il Rosso Segno della Follia

A.k.a. *The Red Sign of Madness* (English translation); a.k.a. *Blood Brides* (G.B. video title); a.k.a. *Una Hacha para la Luna di Miel* (Spanish title, translation: *A Hatchet for the Honeymoon*); a.k.a. *Un'Accetta per la Luna di Miel* (alternate Spanish title, translation: *An Axe for the Honeymoon*); a.k.a. *A Hatchet for the Honeymoon* (English title) (1969) (It., Sp.); D: Mario Bava; P: Manuel Cano Sanciriaco; Prod. Co.: Pan Latina Films (Madrid)/Mercury Cinematografica (Rome)/Peliculas Ibarra and Cia S.A.; SC: Mario Bava, Santiago Moncada, Mario Musy; C: Mario Bava, Antonio Rinaldi; M: Sante Romitelli; S: Stephen Forsythe, Dagmar Lassander, Laura Betti, Jesus Puente, Femi Benussi a.k.a. Eufemia Benussi, Antonia Mas, Luciano Pigozzi, Gerard Tichy, Fortunato Pasquale, Veronica Llimera.

Roy Colt e Winchester Jack

A.k.a. *Roy Colt and Winchester Jack* (English translation and title); a.k.a. *Drei Halunken und ein Halleluja* (German title) (1969) (It.); D: Mario Bava; Prod. Co.: P.A.C.–Produzioni Atlas Consorziate/Tigielle 33 (Rome); SC: Mario Di Nardo, Roberto Agrin; C: Antonio Rinaldi; M: Piero Umiliani; S: Brett Halsey, Charles Southwood, Marilu Tolo, Teodoro Corra, Guido Lollobrigida, Bruno Corazzari.

Sei Donne per l'Assassino

A.k.a. *Six Women for the Killer*; a.k.a. *Six Women for the Murderer* (English translation and titles); a.k.a. *Six Femmes pour l'Assassin* (French title); a.k.a. *Assassinats dans la Haute Couture* (French video title; translation: *Murders in the Fashion Industry*); a.k.a. *Blutige Seide* (German title; translation: *Six Women for the Murderer*); a.k.a. *Fashion House of Death*; a.k.a. *Blood and Black Lace* (English title) (1964) (It., Fr., W.G.); D: Mario Bava; P: Massimo Patrizi, Alfredo Mirabile; Prod. Co.: Emmepi Cinematografica (Rome)/Productions Georges De Beauregard (Paris)/Top Film (Munich)/Monarchia Films; SC: Mario Bava, Marcello Fondato, Giuseppe Barilla; C: Mario Bava, UbaldoTerzano; M: Carlo Rustichelli; S: Cameron Mitchell, Eva Bartok, Thomas Reiner, Dante Di Paolo, Ariana Gorini, Lea Kruger, Mary Arden, Claude Dantes, Harriet Medin White, Nadia Anty, Heidi Stroh, Franco Ressel, Massimo Righi, Luciano Pigozzi.

Shock

A.k.a. *Shock (Transfer Suspense Hypnos)* (Italian pre-production and publicity title); a.k.a *Di Via Orologio fa Sempre Freddo* (Italian pre-production title); a.k.a. *Di Via Orologio fa*

Sempre Freddo (alternate Italian pre-production title); a.k.a. *Suspense* (English pre-release export sales title); a.k.a. *Beyond the Door 2* (English title) (1977) (It.); D: Mario Bava; P: Juri Vasile, UgoValenti, Giuseppe Mangogna; Prod. Co.: Laser Film; SC: Lamberto Bava, Francesco Barbieri, Paolo Briganti, Dardano Sacchetti; C: Alberto Spagnoli, Giuseppe Maccari, Giuseppe Alberti; M: Libra (With Martino, Centofanti, Cappa); S: Daria Nicolodi, John Steiner, David Collin Jr., Ivan Rassimov, Nicola Salerno.

Le Spie Vengono dal Semifreddo

A.k.a. *The Spy Who Comes In from the Semi-Cold* (English translation); a.k.a. *Due Mafiosi dell F.B.I.* (alternate Italian title translation: *Two Mafia Guys Vs. the F.B.I.*); a.k.a. *Dr. Goldfoot and the Girl-Bombs* (English title) (1966) (It., U.S.); D: Mario Bava; P: Fulvio Lucisano (Italian version only), James H. Nicholson, Prod. Co.: Italian International Films/American International Pictures (Samuel Z. Arkoff, Louis M. Heyward, U.S. version only); SC: Castellano, Pipolo, Franco Dal Cer (Italian version only) Louis M. Heyward, Robert Kaufman, James H. Nicholson (U.S.version only); C: Antonio Rinaldi; M: Lallo Gori (Italian version), Les Baxter (U.S. version); S: Vincent Price, Fabian, Franco Franchi, Ciccio Ingrassia, Francesco Mule, Laura Antonelli, Moa Thai, George Wang.

Originally conceived as a semi-sequel to *Dr. Goldfoot and the Bikini Machine*, as well as to one of popular Italian comedy team Franco and Ciccio spy spoofs.

La Strada per Fort Alamo

A.k.a. *The Road to Fort Alamo* (English translation and title); a.k.a. *Arizona Bill* (English title) (1965) (It., Fr.); D: Mario Bava; P: Pier Luigi Torri, Achille Piazzi; Prod. Co.: Achille Piazzi Produzione/Comptoir Francais du Film Production/Protor Film/World Entertainment; SC: Franco Prosperi, Enzio Gicca Palli; C: Mario Bava, Ubaldo Terzano; M: Piero Umiliani; S: Ken Clark, Jany Clair, Michel Lemoine, Adreina Paul, Kirk Bert, Antonio Gradoli.

Terrore nello Spazzio

A.k.a. *Terror in Space* (English translation); a.k.a. *Planet of the Vampires*; a.k.a. *Terror en el Espacio* (Spanish title); a.k.a. *The Haunted Planet*; a.k.a. *Demon Planet*; a.k.a. *The Planet of the Damned*; a.k.a. *The Outlawed Planet*; a.k.a. *Space Mutants* (English titles) (1965) (It., Sp.); D: Mario Bava; P: Fulvio Lucisano, and James H. Nicholson (U.S. version only), Samuel Z. Arkoff (U.S. version only); Prod. Co.: Italian International Film/Castilla Cooperativa Cinematografica/Fulvio Lucisano/American International Pictures; SC: Mario Bava, Callisto Cosulich, Alberto Bevilacqua, Antonio Roman, Rafael J. Salvia, based on a story by Renato Pestriniero, and Ib Melchoir (U.S. version only), Louis M. Heyward (U.S. version only), based on a story by Ib Melchoir; C: Mario Bava, Antonio Rinaldi; S: Barry Sullivan, Norma Bengel, Angel Aranda, Evi Marandi, Fernando Villena, Ivan Rassimov, Rico Boido, Massimo Righi, Stelio Candelli, Mario Morales.

I Tre Volti della Paura

A.k.a. *The Three Faces of Fear*; a.k.a. *The Three Faces of Terror* (English translations); a.k.a. *Les Trois Visages de la Peur* (French title); a.k.a *Black Christmas*; a.k.a. *Black Sabbath* (English title) (1963) (It., Fr.); D: Mario Bava; P: Paolo Mercuri, Salvatore Billitteri; Prod. Co.: Galatea Film (Milan)/Emmepi Cinematografica (Rome)/Société Cinématographique Lyre (Paris); SC: Mario Bava, Marcello Fondata, Alberto Bevilacqua, Ugo Guerra, based on stories by Anton Chekov, Guy de Maupassant, and Leo Tolstoy (and F.G. Snyder); C:

Mario Bava, Ubaldo Terzano, Mario Mancini; M: Roberto Nicolosi, Les Baxter (U.S. version only); S: Boris Karloff, Michele Mercier, Lydia Alfonsi, Mark Damon, Susy Andersen a.k.a. Susan Anderson, Glauco Onorato, Rika Dialina, Jacqueline Pierreux, Milly Monti, Harriet Medin White, Gustavo De Nardo, Massimo Righi.

Anthology of three episodes: *La Goccia d'Acqua*. a.k.a. *The Drop of Water*; *Il Telefono*, a.k.a. *The Telephone*; and *Il Wurdalak*, a.k.a. *The Wurdalak*. There are substantial differences between original Italian version and English (U.S. and G.B.) prints.

I Vampiri

A.k.a. *The Vampires* (English translation and *I, Vampire* [mistaken English version]); (a.k.a. *The Lust of the Vampire*; a.k.a. *The Devil's Commandment* [English title]) (1956) (It.); D: Riccardo Freda, Mario Bava (uncredited); P: Ermanno Donati, Luigi Carpentieri; Prod. Co.: Titanus/Athena Cinematografica; SC: Riccardo Freda, Piero Regnoli, Rik Sjostrom; C: Mario Bava; M: RomanVlad; S: Giannia Maria Canale, Antoine Balpetre, Paul Mueller, Carlo D'Angelo, Wandisa Guida, Dario Michaelis, Renato Tontini, Riccardo Freda.

La Venere dell'Ille

A.k.a. *The Venus d'Ille* (English translation and title) (1978) (It.); D: Mario Bava, Lamberto Bava; P: Franca Franco, Carlo Tuzii; Prod. Co.: Pont-Royal-Film-TV/Raidue; SC: Lamberto Bava, Cesare Garboli, based on a story by Prosper Merimee; C: Nino Celeste; M: Ubaldo Continiello; S: Daria Nicolodi, Marc Porel, Fausti Di Bella, Mario Maranzana, Diana De Curtis, Adriana Innocenti.

Filmed as a feature-length episode of the Italian television program *Il Giorno del Diavolo*.

Ruggero Deodato

Ruggero Deodato was born on May 7, 1939, in Poltenza, Italy. In 1957, he entered the world of fantasy cinema through an association with famed director Roberto Rossellini. With Rossellini's help, Deodato secured a position at the famous Cinecitta Studios as his assistant director. Some years later, Deodato left to work with another director, Carlo Ludovico Bragaglia, on an assignment in Africa.

Deodato stayed with Bragaglia for several films as an assistant, then returned to Rossellini's side to gain further experience on all the technical elements of making movies. Deodato then joined other filmmakers, most notably Sergio Corbucci. With Corbucci, he worked on a number of projects, most specifically the fantasy-oriented costume adventures dubbed sword-and-sandal films, or peplums. In 1964, he became an assistant director to Antonio Margheriti for the sword-and-sandal fantasy-horror film *Ursus il Terrore dei Kirghisi*. When Margheriti left the production before shooting was finished, Deodato stepped in and finished the film. While continuing as an assistant director on other projects, he worked again with Sergio Corbucci on the Western *Django* (1967). Deodato filmed the location footage in Spain as the director Corbucci did not want to travel far from Rome. Other projects for which he was signed as an assistant director are the Corbucci Westerns *Johnny Oro* (1966) and *Un Dollaro a Testa* (1966), as well as Antonio Margheriti's science fiction films *I Criminali della Galassia* and *I Diafanoidi Vengono da Marte* (both 1965).

Deodato's first official film as director was the musical comedy *Donne ... Botte e Bersaglieri* (1967) starring Italian pop star Little Tony. That next year, Deodato followed this film with a sequel, *Vacanze sulla Costa Smeralsa*. His first fantastic effort for the cinema was the strange caper espionage adventure *Fenomenal e il Tesoro di Tutankhamen* (featuring a masked criminal named Count Norton [Mario Nicola Parenti] clad entirely in black, on the trail of an Egyptian relic) in 1967.

In 1968, he directed *Gungala, la Pantera Nuda*, a jungle adventure featuring both male and female Tarzan characters and a hunt for treasure. Deodato signed the last two films with the pseudonym Roger Rockefeller in the hopes that he could continue to work as an assistant director, if no one knew that he has already directed two popular genre films.

In 1968, he also directed a Western comedy called *I Quattro del Pater Noster*, starring the popular Italian comedian Paolo Villagio. *Zenabel* (1969) is Deodato's first film where he exhibits a unique persona as director. The sexy costume adventure featured Lucretia Love, a popular athletic star of the short-lived genre of sexy Amazon heroine films.

Deodato spent the years 1970 through 1973 directing episodes for various television programs. In 1970, he directed four episodes of the series *Triangolo Rosso*. He directed a total of 12 episodes in the next three years for the programs *All'Ultimo Minuto* and *Il Segreto di Cristina*.

In 1975, he directed *Ondata di Piacere*, a sexy drama with thriller overtones, starring his wife Silvia Dioniso, John Steiner and Al Cliver. *Uomini Si Nasce, Poliziotti Si Muore* (1976), was Deodato's contribution to the then-popular wave of police thrillers. This fast-paced, electric cops and robbers tale is notable for some extremely violent scenes and features a star-making performance by Raymond Lovelock.

Deodato was none too prolific as a feature film director during this period because he was very active as a director of television commercials and also operated within a commercial print advertising venture (along with Lamberto Bava). He claims that a *National Geographic* article on a tribe of cannibalistic aboriginal natives who lived in a cave on Mindanao, an island near the Philippines, gave him the idea to make *Ultimo Mondo Cannibale* (1976), a disgusting, abhorrent exercise in murder as entertainment. Deodato's film, much like a similar 1972 one by director Umberto Lenzi, purportedly is a documentary within an adventure film format, but that is obviously far from the truth. Besides the never-before-seen graphic torture of the cast mem-

Ruggero Deodato

bers (incredible special effects by Marcello Di Paolo) is the actual on-screen slaughter of animals indigenous to the location area. Deodato claimed in an Italian-language interview, "*Ultimo Mondo Cannibale* was shot entirely in Kuala Lampur [Malaysia] in terrible conditions using real flesh and blood cannibals." An expedition to South American jungles to locate the survivors of a brutal attack by a lost tribe of cannibalistic Indians leads to horrific adventure in the movie. Much of the cast, including Ivan Rassimov and Eurasian beauty Me Me Lai, meet a terrible fate at the hands of the cannibals—then later at the hands of critics who savaged the film in their reviews for its depiction of "staged" animal killings which were photographed and inserted into the film as the "real-life" cannibalistic rites of the South American Indian natives used for the production.

Unjustifiably praised by some audiences, this film is a vile piece of garbage and certainly there is no excuse, artistic or otherwise, for the real-life tortures that transpire on the screen. Deodato's film became very popular, but he claims, in retrospect, that he is not fond of it.

The next year he directed a melodrama. Then, in 1978, he directed *Concorde Affaire 79*, a spy-action film with an international cast including James Franciscus, Mimsy Farmer, Joseph Cotten, Edmund Purdom and Van Johnson. Unfortunately, Deodato returned to the theme of cannibals with *Cannibal Holocaust* (1979), one of the vilest pieces of celluloid on the planet. While this film exemplifies the fantastic imagination of Deodato as a filmmaker, his decision to again incorporate real-life animal death footage into his movie led to the film being confiscated in Italy. Deodato and his producers were taken to the courts and lost the case for his depiction of "art" against the judicial system's claim that needless and senseless deaths of animals occurred to make this production.

Cannibal Holocaust has an outrageous premise for a film. A sensationalist group of filmmakers journey to the South American jungles to document the brutal flesh-eating rites of cannibalistic natives, whom they incite to greater heights of violence. When they themselves go on a spree of raping, killing and torturing natives and the weaker members of their own group, the natives ultimately strike back (and film the resulting slaughter with the documentary crew's own camera equipment). Members of the film crew are beaten, the men castrated and stripped to the bone, their flesh eaten, ending in the slaughter of nearly the entire group of documentary filmmakers.

The movie purports to show the grainy, splicy "found footage" as being the real thing, as discovered in the jungles of the Amazon. The horrors of the attacks become obvious for all to see. This clever idea of using faked "found footage" by scratching the negative, adding grain to the images, photographing with amateur 16mm equipment and a slew of scenes featuring numerous zoom lens shots is admirable. However, what is reprehensible is the director's immense, questionable insistence on the (staged) gruesome slaughter of humans and (real life) animals: a woman is impaled, a wooden pole enters her through the anus and out through her mouth, while alive. A still-living fetus is ripped from the womb of another. A man is thrown into a river, live bait for actual piranha. Another man is castrated, then the flesh ripped from his still-living body. For the countless scenes of true animal cruelty, Deodato was taken to the courts by the Italian government and lost his case. His film was banned in many countries and he did not work for several years as a filmmaker.

La Casa Sperduta nel Parco (1980) was made shortly after *Cannibal Holocaust* for the same production companies. Released to Italian theaters during the *Cannibal Holocaust* scandal, the film had to be signed with the pseudonym "Roger D. Franklin" in order to insure any kind of commercial success. *La Casa Sperduta* is a lively, if unappetizing, tale of violence. The versatile David Hess is one of the main reasons to watch this film, for his incredible portrayal of a raving psychotic.

In *La Casa Sperduta nel Parco*, a gang of rough hoodlums (led by Hess) is enticed to partake in a deviate party being given by an assembly of rich and powerful people. Hoping to humiliate their lower-class guests, the wealthy partygoers are in for more than sociopolitical class struggles when the tables are turned and a mass orgy of rape, violence and murder result. When the survivors of the carnage have had enough, they decide to fight back.

This is a vicious film about corruption and society. It is also a thinly veiled remake of director Wes Craven's *Last House on the Left* and cements this connection by casting that film's psychopathic villain (Hess) in a similar role. It's as vicious and as nasty as these type of films come.

Deodato did not work again until *Predatori di Atlantide* (1983). This adventure tale with science fiction overtones involves the fabled undersea kingdom and features a cast of familiar genre names, including Christopher Connelly and George Hilton.

Inferno in Diretta (1985) was a return of sorts to the "realistic" horror films that garnered Deodato such unpopular notoriety. Bereft of extreme animal cruelty, the film, about the illicit drug trade along the South American coast and some of the cannibalistic tendencies of the natives of Columbia, was not spared the censor's blade when much of its footage of graphic human dismemberment landed on the cutting room floor.

In *Inferno in Diretta*, a television reporter and a small crew journey to the South American jungles to search for a drug smuggler who was a decorated soldier in the Vietnam War. Eventually, the horrific realization that this same person was also the man responsible for the Jonestown massacre in Guyana attributed to Jim Jones leads the group to wonder about their survival.

This potpourri of contemporary horror includes so many cinematic horror references it is astounding. The madness of war exemplified by Richard Lynch's character (no doubt influenced by Marlon Brando's performance as Col. Kurtz in Francis Ford Coppola's 1979 *Apocalypse Now*), the actual Jonestown massacre and, of course, your usual bunch of slumming South American cannibals add to the wild mess that makes up this film.

Camping del Terrore (1986) was Deodato's attempt at an Italian version of the popular American slasher films of the '80s. Partially shot on location in the United States with a cast of American genre names like Mimsy Farmer, David Hess, Charles Napier and the ubiquitous Ivan Rassimov (from *Ultimo Mondo Cannibale*), the film is well-photographed, but a derivative late entry into a cycle of films (most notably, the profitable *Friday the 13th* series and its countless imitations) that had already peaked as evidenced by its story: A couple running a camping site witness danger and terror when it is invaded by a masked psychopathic killer who prowls the grounds and the nearby woods where, years before, countless people had been slaughtered in a similar rampage.

In 1987, Deodato began a working relationship with the low-budget exploitation filmmaking production company Cannon Films. He made an adventure film starring Miles O'Keefe, *Lone Runner* (1988), and a sword-and-sandal fantasy film inspired by the success of the American *Conan* films, titled *I Barbari e Co.*

Un Delitto Poco Comune (1988) is a more assured work than Deodato had made in many years. The film is a horror tale inspired by the Hammer film, *The Man Who Could Cheat Death* (1959) and, equally, the *giallo* thrillers of Dario Argento. While the international cast (featuring Michael York, Donald Pleasence and Edwige Fenech) work well within the confines of the script, the movie begins to fall apart way before the telling climax.

In *Un Delitto Poco Commune*, a handsome pianist (Michael York) learns that he has been afflicted with a strange disease that accelerates the hormones within his body as well as the aging process. Compelled to kill the beautiful women who feel attracted to him, as well as those he feels attracted to, he taunts the investigating police inspector (Donald Pleasence) with strange phone calls after each murder. As the body count rises and the man becomes older and older, the police begin to close in on their main suspect.

An interesting update of an old theme gets the modern horror treatment, but the film's attempt to aim for a more commercial theatrical audience is betrayed by the lack of suspense during the stalking and eventual murder scenes. The cast seems disinterested and the film wastes the talents of popular *giallo* thriller presence Edwige Fenech.

Ragno Gelido, produced in the latter part of 1988 and released in 1989, was an attempt at the kind of Gothic horror that had not been made for decades. Essentially a continuation of themes that Mario Bava explored in an episode ("The Telephone") of the 1963 film *I Tre Volti della Paura*, *Ragno Gelido* falls apart on the ludicrous premise of the phone calls from Hell, despite the engaging presence of the Eurasian lead Charlotte Lewis, who gets the star treatment by spending the majority of the film acting with special effects. Undoubtedly, Deodato loves her form and spends a good deal of time photographing her, as if with a lover's caress. However, the film's central idea about a lovestruck spirit that endlessly torments a woman is taken into the realm of unbelievability. The "phone killer" starts send-

American poster art for *La Casa Sperduta nel Parco* (1980, F.D. Cinematografica).

ing out mysterious, high-pitched whines that shatter glass, kills a man by exploding his pacemaker and murders a thief by forcefully propelling coins from a pay phone. *Ragno Gelido* is a stylish but ultimately empty attempt to give an ominous presence to an inanimate object.

Deodato then returned to television to co-direct, with Tonio Valeri, the miniseries *Il Ricatto* in 1989. The year 1991 saw another return to television for the miniseries *Oceano*, featuring an international cast of genre film actors: Mario Adorf, Martin Balsam, Ernest Borgnine, Senta Berger and Lou Castel. That same year, Deodato filmed a rip-off of Hector Babenco's semi-documentary *Pixote* (1981). Deodato's version *Mamma, Ci Penso Lo* (1992), was an ill-received tale of child prostitution, drug peddling and murder in South America.

In 1993, Deodato filmed *Vortice Mortale*, an energetic thriller that successfully manages to combine heavy amounts of eroticism into a seductively complex noir mystery, complete with frequent sex scenes. It was filmed as if they were staged to be the kind of *giallo*-inspired murder scenes that were often a staple of the Italian thrillers of the '70s. Deodato's film, despite a few flaws, is one of his finest works in years and is, currently, his most recent contribution to the horror genre film.

In it, a man (Yorgo Voyagis) is found murdered, his body stuffed into a washing machine. The police investigator (Phillipe Caroit) interrogates the sisters who live in the same house. Via flashbacks, he assembles contradictory stories as to how the victim came to be involved with the women and which one may have been responsible for his murder. Caught in a slowly turning web of eroticism, the detective finds himself drawn into the strange relationship that these women have with one another. As he is more and more sexually drawn to them, he sees his own life becoming a shambles.

One of Deodato's finest genre films, *Vortice Mortale* is a movie filled with an air of morbidity and degeneracy, an ambiance that reeks of sexual tension. No small achievement given the casting of the sisters, played by a mix of heretofore unknown Italian and Hungarian actresses (Kashia Figura, Barbara Ricci and Illaria Borelli). Borelli and Figura, in particular, take a malicious joy in ruining the life of the detective. Deodato films many of the sexual encounters in a style not far removed from the heyday of the *giallo* thriller but, in this delirious exercise in psycho-sexual horror, the payoff is not murder but evil seduction.

His other recent films include *Sotto il Cielo dell'Africa* (1999) with Carol Alt and *Father Hope*, a 2002 mini-series made for Italian television.

Ruggero Deodato Filmography

I Barbari e Co.

A.k.a. *The Barbarians and Company* (English translation); a.k.a. *The Barbarians* (1987) (It., Israel, U.S.); D: Ruggero Deodato; P: Menacham Golan, Yorum Globus; Prod. Co.: Golan-

Globus Productions/Cannon Film (Los Angeles)/Cannon Italia (Rome); C: Gianlorenzo Battaglia; M: Pino Donaggio; S: David Paul, Peter Paul, Richard Lynch, Eva La Rue, Virginia Bryant.

Camping del Terrore

A.k.a. *Camping Terror* (English translation); a.k.a. *Camping della Morte* (alternate Italian title); a.k.a. *Body Count* (English title) (1986) (It.); D: Ruggero Deodato; P: Alessandro Fracassi; Prod. Co.: Racing Pictures; SC: Alex Capone a.k.a. Alessandro Capone, David Parker, Jr., a.k.a. Dardano Sacchetti, Sheila Goldberg, Luca D'Alisera; C: Emilio Loffredo; M: Claudio Simonetti; SP E: Roberto Pace; S: Mimsy Farmer, Bruce Penhall, Charles Napier, David A. Hess, Nicola Farron, Cynthia Thompson, Andrew Lederer, Ivan Rassimov, John Steiner, Luisa Maneri.

Cannibal Holocaust

A.k.a. *Jungle Holocaust*; a.k.a. *Cannibal Massacre* (English titles) (1980) (It.); D: Ruggero Deodato; P: Franco Palaggi, Franco Di Nunzio, Giovanni Masini; Prod. Co.: F.D. Cinematografica; SC: Gianfranco Clerici; C: Sergio D'Offizi, Roberto Forges Davantati; M: Riz Ortolani; SP E: Aldo Gaspari; S: Francesca Ciardi, Luca Giorgio Barbareschi, Robert Bolla a.k.a. Robert Kerman a.k.a. Richard Kerman, Salvatore Basile, Riccardo Fuentes, Gabriel Yorke, Paolo Paolini, Pio Di Savoia, Luigina Rocchi.

La Casa Sperduta nel Parco

A.k.a. *La Casa in Fondo nel Parco* (alternate Italian title); a.k.a. *The House on the Edge of the Park* (English translation and title); (1980) (It.); D: Ruggero Deodato; P: Giovanni Masini, Vito Di Bari; Prod. Co.: F.D. Cinematografica; SC: Gianfranco Clerici, Vincenzo Mannino; C: Sergio D'Offizi, Enrico Lucidi, Enrico Maggi; M: Riz Ortolani, song "Sweetly" performed by Diana Corsini, written by Riz Ortolani and Benjamin, song "Much More" performed by Charlie Cannon, Rosamaria D'Andrea and Patrizia Neri, written by Riz Ortolani and Benjamin; S: David A. Hess, Cristiana Borromeo, Annie Belle a.k.a. Annie Briand, John Morghen a.k.a. Giovanni Lombardo Radice, Lorraine De Selle, Gabrielle Di Giulio, Brigitte Petrunio.

Concorde Affaire '79

A.k.a. *The Concorde Affair 1979* (English translation and title) (1978) (It.); D: Ruggero Deodato; P: Mino Loy, Luciana Martino; Prod. Co.: National Cinematografica/Dania Film; SC: Alberto Fioretti, Ernesto Gastaldi, Renzo Genta; C: Federico Zanni; M: Stelvio Cipriani; S: James Franciscus, Mimsy Farmer, Venantino Venantini, Van Johnson, Joseph Cotten, Edmund Purdom, Mario Maranzaba.

Un Delitto Poco Comune

A.k.a. *An Uncommon Crime* (English translation); a.k.a. *Squilibrio* (Italian pre-production title; translation: *Unbalanced*); a.k.a. *The House on Percival Rubens Street*; a.k.a. *An Unusual Murder*; a.k.a. *Phantom of Death* (English titles) (1988) (It.); D: Ruggero Deodato; P: Pietro Innocenzi; Prod Co.: Globe Films S.r.l./Tandem Cinematografica S.r.l./Reteitalia/D.M.V. Distribuzione S.r.l. in association with Reteitalia S.p.A.; SC: Gianfranco Clerici, Vincenzo Mannino, Gigliola Battaglia; C: Giorgio Di Battista; M: Pino Donaggio; SP E: Fabrizio Sforza; S: Michael York, Donald Pleasence, Edwige Fenech, Mapi Galan, Caterina Boratto, Lewis Eduardo Ciannelli, Ruggero Deodato.

Donne ... Botte e Bersaglieri

A.k.a. *Man Only Cries for Love* (English title) (1967) (It.); D: Ruggero Deodato; P: Edmondo Amati; Prod. Co.: Fida Cinematografica; C: Riccardo Pallottini; M: Willy Brezza; S: Janet Agren, Little Tony, Ira Hagen, Ferruccio Amendola.

Fenomenal e il Tesoro di Tutankhamen

A.k.a. *Phenomenal and the Treasure of Tutankhamen* (English translation and title) (1967); D: Ruggero Deodato; P: Mauro Nicola Parenti; Prod. Co.: I.C.A.R.; SC: Ruggero Deodato, A.I. Capone; C: Roberto Reale; M: Bruno Nicolai; S: Mauro Nicola Parenti, Lucrezia Love, John Karlsen, Gordon Mitchell a.k.a. Charles Pendleton.

Gungala, la Pantera Nuda

A.k.a. *Gungala, the Nude Panther* (English translation and title) (1968) (It.); D: Ruggero Deodato; SC: Romano Ferrara; C: Claudio Ragona; M: Alessandro Brugnoli; S: Kitty Swan, Micaela Pignatelli, Angelo Infanti, Tiffany Anderson.

Inferno in Diretta

A.k.a. *Inferno a Diretta* (alternate Italian title); a.k.a. *Cut and Run*; a.k.a. *Hell, Live* (English titles) (1985) (It.); D: Ruggero Deodato; P: Alessandro Fracassi; Prod. Co.: Racing Pictures; SC: Cesare Frugoni, Dardano Sacchetti; C: Alberto Spagnoli; M: Claudio Simonetti; S: Lisa Blount, Leonard Mann a.k.a. Leonardo Manzella, Willie Aames, Richard Lynch, Michael Berryman, Eric La Salle, Gabriele Tinti, Valentina Forte, John Steiner, Karen Black, Barbara Magnolfi.

Lone Runner

A.k.a. *Lone Runner — Per Pugno di Diamanti* (alternate Italian title); a.k.a. *A Fistful of Diamonds*; a.k.a. *Flashfighter* (English titles) (1988) (It., U.S.); D: Ruggero Deodato; P: Maurizio Maggi, Ovidio G. Assonitis; S: Miles O'Keefe, Savina Gersak, John Steiner, Al Yamanouchi a.k.a. Haruiko Yamanouchi, Ronald Lacey.

Mamma, Ci Penso Lo

A.k.a. *Mamma, I Can Do It Alone*; a.k.a. *Mom, I Can Do It Alone* (English translations and titles) (1991) (It., Fr.); D: Ruggero Deodato; P: J. Koob, G. Bertolucci; Prod. Co.: San Francisco Film/Cinema Group Diffusion; SC: Ruggero Deodato, Andrea Manni, Oddone Cappelino; C: Roberto Forges Davanzati; S: Christopher Masterson, Dolly Carrol, Aleksei Alfonso, Hetch Mendoza, Yves Arispe, Darwin Garcia.

Oceano

(1989) (It.); D: Ruggero Deodato; P: Giovanni Berolucci; SC: Ruggero Deodato, Alberto Vazquez Figueroa; C: Luigi Verga; M: Pino Donaggio; S: Mario Adorf, Adam Arkin, Martin Balsam, Marisa Berenson, Senta Berger, William Berger, Michael Berryman, Ernest Borgnine, Lou Castel, David A. Hess, Irene Papas.

Ondata di Piacere

A.k.a. *Waves of Pleasure* (English translation); a.k.a. *Waves of Lust* (English title) (1975) (It.); D: Ruggero Deodato; P: Alberto Marras, Vincenzo Salviani; Prod. Co.: TDL Cinematografica; SC: Franco Bottari, Fabio Pittoru, Gianlorenzo Battaglia, Lamberto Bava; C: Mario Capriotti, Dante Di Palma; M: Marcello Giombini; S: Al Cliver a.k.a. Pier Luigi Conti, Silvia Dionisio, John Steiner, Elisabeth Turner.

Predatori di Atlantide

A.k.a. *The Predators of Atlantis* (English translation and title); a.k.a. *Raiders of Atlantis*; a.k.a. *The Atlantic Interceptors* (English titles) (1983) (It.); D: Ruggero Deodato; P: Maurizio and Sandro Amati for Regency Productions; Prod. Co.: Regency Productions; SC: Vincenzo Mannino, Dardano Sacchetti; C: Roberto Enrico; M: Guido and Maurizio De Angelis; S: Christopher Connelly, Gioia Maria Scola, Tony King, George Hilton, Giancarlo Prati, Michele Soavi.

I Quattro del Pater Noster

A.k.a. *In the Name of the Father* (English translation and title) (1968) (It.); D: Ruggero Deodato; Prod. Co.: Sped Film; S: Paolo Villaggio, Oreste Lionello, Lino Toffolo, Enrico Montesano.

Ragno Gelido

A.k.a. *Minaccia d'Amore* (alternate Italian title); a.k.a. *Dial Help* (English title) (1988) (It.); D: Ruggero Deodato; P: Gailiano Juso, Giovanni Bertolucci; SC: Ruggero Deodato, Joseph and Mary Caravani; C: Renato Tafuri; SP E: Germano Natali; S: Charlotte Lewis, Marcello Modugno, Mattia Sbragia, Victor Cavallo, Carola Stagnaro, Carlo Monni.

Il Ricatto

A.k.a. *Blackmail* (English title) (1989) (It.); D: Ruggero Deodato, Tonino Valeri; Prod. Co.: Reteitalia (Milan); SC: Ennio De Concini, Luigi Rossi, Massimo Ranieri; M: Riz Ortolani; S: Massimo Ranieri, Barbara Nascimbene, Luca De Filippo, Jacques Perrin, Barbara Ricci, Piero Pepe, Kim Rossi-Stuart.

Sotto il Cielo dell'Africa

A.k.a. *Thinking About Africa* (English title) (1999) (It.); D: Ruggero Deodato; P/M: Guido De Angelis, Maurizio De Angelis; SC: Piero Bodrato, Dido Castelli, Luca D'Ascanio, Guido De Angelis, Luca Manfedi, Claudio Rittore, Alberto Simone, Massimo Torre; C: Sergio D'Offizi; S: Carol Alt, Rudiger Joswig, Hans Von Borsody, Michelle Donati, John Indi, Olivia Kolbe Booysen, Richard Lynch, Daniela Poggi, Ingeborg Schoner.

Ultimo Mondo Cannibale

A.k.a. *The Last Cannibal World* (English translation); a.k.a. *Mondo Cannibale* (alternate Italian title); a.k.a. *Cannibal* (GB title); a.k.a. *The Last Survivor*; a.k.a. *Carnivorous*; a.k.a. *Jungle Holocaust*; a.k.a. *The Cannibals* (English titles) (1976) (It.); D: Ruggero Deodato; P: Giovanni Masini, Giorgio Carlo Rossi; Prod. Co.: Erre Cinematografica; SC: Tito Carpi,

Gianfranco Clerici, Renzo Genta, Giancarlo Rossi; C: Marcello Masciocchi, Giovanni Ciarla; M: Ubaldo Continello; SP E: Paolo Ricci; S: Massimo Foschi, Me Me Lai, Ivan Rassimov, Sheik Razak Shirkur, Judy Rosly, Suleiman Shamsi.

Uomini Si Nasce, Poliziotti Si Muore

A.k.a. *Live Like a Cop, Die Like a Man* (English translation and title) (It.) (1976); D: Ruggero Deodato; SC: Fernando Di Leo; S: Marc Porel, Ray Lovelock, Adolfo Celli, Silvia Dionisio, Franco Citti, Marino Masse, Sergio Ammirata, Tom Felleghy.

Vacanze sulla Costa Smerlasa

A.k.a. *Vacation on the Emerald Isle* (English translation and title) (1968) (It.); D: Ruggero Deodato; Prod. Co.: Fida Cinematografica; SC: Bruno Corbucci, Mario Amendola; C: Riccardo Pallottini; M: Willy Brezza, with songs by Little Tony; S: Little Tony, Ferruccio Amendola, Silvia Dionisio, Tony Ucci, Lucio Flauto.

Vortice Mortale

A.k.a. *Mortal Whirlpool* (English translation and title); a.k.a. *La Lavatrice* (Italian pre-production title); a.k.a. *The Washing Machine* (English title) (1993) (It., Fr., Hungary); D: Ruggero Deodato; P: Corrado and Alessandro Canzio; Prod. Co.: Esse Cinematografica (Rome)/Eurogroup Film (Paris)/Focus Film (Budapest); SC: Luigi Spagnoli; C: Sergio D'Offizi; M: Claudio Simonetti, Wolfgang Amadeus Mozart; S: Philippe Caroit, Ilaria Borrelli, Kashia Figura, Barbara Ricci, Yorgo Voyagis, Claudia Pozzi.

Zenabel

A.k.a. *Faut Pas Jouer avec les Vierges* (French title); a.k.a. *La Furie du Desir* (French hardcore re-release title) (1969) (It., Fr.); D: Ruggero Deodato; P: Nicola Parente; Prod. Co.: I.C.A.R./Pierson Productions/Gemini International Pictures; SC: Ruggero Deodato, Antonio Raccioppi; C: Roberto Reale; M: Ennio Morricone, Bruno Nicolai; S: Lucrezia Love, Mauro Nicola Parenti, Lionel Stander, John Ireland, Christine Davry

Re-released in France in 1975 under the title *La Furie du Desir*, with hardcore pornographic inserts directed by Claude Pierson a.k.a. Claude Mulot.

Lucio Fulci

Lucio Fulci was born on June 17, 1927, in Rome. The Italian director who became known for his gross-out splatter horror films began his filmmaking career as a student at Rome's Centro Sperimentale Centrale in the 1940s. In later years, Fulci admitted to brazenly attempting to gain admittance to this then-prestigious film academy by bluffing his way through academia. He reportedly told Luciano Visconti, one of the directors who taught at the school, that *Ossessione* (1942), Visconti's film adaptation of the James M. Cain novel *The Postman Always Rings Twice*, borrowed much of its imagery from the earlier works of Jean Renoir.

Fulci had originally been studying medicine at medical school and, to pay his way, had dabbled as a part-time art critic. In interviews, Fulci stated that one of the main reasons he left behind his medical studies for the world of the cinema was because he was interested in bettering his lifestyle financially. At the film school, many knowledgeable craftsmen taught him. Michelangelo Antonioni was a key instructor, as were many film theorists who taught the intricacies of filmmaking.

Fulci's first films were experimental documentaries, filmed with other technicians at the school. He graduated in 1948 and continued to make documentaries. Some of these works eventually received recognition from the Italian press. Between 1948 and 1950, he co-directed and/or co-wrote the story ideas for seven such documentaries. In 1952, Fulci began a prolific if not illustrious career as a writer. *Toto a Colori*, his first documented film script and Italy's very first color film, is a comedy adventure starring the popular Italian comic artist, Toto (a.k.a. Antonio Stefano Vincenzo Clemente). Fulci supported himself by writing a great many of these comical scripts between 1952 and 1960. He worked most often with the director Stefano Steno Vanzina who, at times, just signed the name Steno to the films that he directed. During this period, Fulci also contributed (uncredited) to the script for Steno's *Tempi Duri per i Vampiri*, a sexy 1959 horror comedy starring Christopher Lee, Sylva Koscina and the Italian comedian, Renato Rascel. During this period, Fulci worked at the Italian film criticism periodical *La Settimana Incom*.

Fulci's first feature film as a director was the 1959 *I Ladri*, a dramatic film with comedic elements about a small-time thief, starring Toto and Armando Calvo. *I Ragazzi del Juke Box* (1959), Fulci's second film, is a teenage rock 'n' roll comedy! It stars Italian pop star Adriano Celentano, Antonio De Teffe and Elke Sommer. Fulci and co-scenarist Piero Vivarelli wrote pop songs for Celentano to sing in this film and a follow-up (which Fulci did not direct).

In 1962, Fulci began his collaboration with Franco Franchi and Ciccio Ingrassia, Italy's answer to the American comedy team of Dean Martin and Jerry Lewis. Of course, the difference was that Ciccio usually got the girl and Franco, the mustached, moribund straight man of the team, didn't

Lucio Fulci

sing and *didn't* always get the girls at movie's end. Franco & Ciccio were an incredibly prolific duo who based their talents and gags on a particular dialect of the Italian language, originally based in southern Sicily. Fulci directed at least six of their movies between the years 1962 and 1967. His best films featuring Franco & Ciccio, *002 Agente Segretissimi* (1964), *002 Operazione Luna* (1965) and *Come Rubammo la Bomba Atomica* (1967), were and still remain highly enjoyable spoofs of the then-new and popular James Bond films. Espionage, gadgets, sexy women and lots of humorous sequences highlight these productions. Fulci would direct a television documentary on the life of Franco Franchi in 1978 titled *Un Uomo da Ridere* (*A Man to Laugh At*).

Fulci's 1966 Western, *Le Colt Cantarono la Morte È Fu ... Tempo di Massacro*, was the first film in his filmography to reveal an absolute interest in violent *mise-en-scène*. His star, Franco Nero, portrays a wanderer who finds a town inhabited by people being terrorized by a young tyrant and his henchman. Fulci's Western was one of the first of the new, dark breed of Italian Westerns to feature much violence and a message of despair.

In 1968, he also directed the famed American actor Edward G. Robinson in a big-budget caper film about the literary character Cardinal Brown, a minister who was also a detective. *Operazione San Pietro* was and remains a fairly obscure film in the Fulci canon. It relies more on comedy and slapstick (courtesy co-star Lando

Buzzanca) rather than the popular hi-tech gadgets that enlivened similar films from this period (Giuliano Montaldo's *Ad Ogni Costo* [1967] being a superior example of this genre).

Beatrice Cenci (1969) is a fairly misunderstood work. It is one of the films Fulci was most proud of, despite a lukewarm reception and reviews that labeled some of the film's imagery as misogynist. The violent costume drama about religious persecution during medieval times and its effect on a lithe beauty, who is wrongly labeled a practitioner of witchcraft and is subsequently tortured, is a studied but downbeat affair.

Fulci's first horror film–related credit as director was the thriller *Una sull'-Altra* (1969). A man (Jean Sorel) suspected of the murder of his wife is convicted and sentenced to death. He is awaiting execution as two people investigate the case, seeking to exonerate him. This clever film manages to build up quite an amount of suspense when it is discovered that the man's wife (whom he has been convicted of murdering) is, in fact, not dead but merely in hiding, a diabolical plan to remove the husband so that she may be with her lover.

Fulci had just viewed Romolo Guerrieri's thriller *Il Dolce Corpo di Deborah* (1968) in which Sorel (who appeared alongside Carrol Baker) made an impression on the director. Although Fulci called the Guerrieri film a *giallo*, it in fact is modeled more on the Hitchcockian idea of an innocent man framed for murder while he awaits his death at the hands of blind justice. Fulci added some violent and surprising twists to *his* film to make it, if not one of the best of the *giallo* thrillers, a fine example of a suspense film with ironic twists.

Una Lucertola con la Pelle di Donna (1971) is a film that the director was quite unhappy with, but one that is a key moment in his horror filmography. This tale of a woman (Florinda Bolkan) who experiences insane hallucinations that may reflect real-life occurrences (or is all this some sort of plot to mask the real murder of her lesbian lover?) is clever. Its momentum is only let down by the performances of the seemingly unconcerned supporting cast (including Stanley Baker). During one hallucinatory scene, the woman passes by strange corridors which appear to be tilting on their side. In this sequence, her final destination is a room that contains a truly horrific explicit image: dogs crying out like some monstrous beings with their stomachs split open, intestines spilling out to the floor. Despite this outrageous imagery (courtesy of special effects technician Carlo Rambaldi), Fulci had to endure a trial and mass media attention, when the Italian courts sought to bring the director (and the producers) to trial for alleged cruelty to animals. When Rambaldi produced the mass of rubber effects materials that the director filmed, Fulci was exonerated.

Fulci's film spends a lot of time trying to come up with new ways of surprising the audience with Bolkan's series of illusions. Although Baker's stoic cop is the movie's one rigid character anchored in reality, the actor seems ill at ease (as do some of the supporting cast members) with the outrageously plotted film. Fulci's

Italian poster art for Fulci's *Paura nella Città dei Morti Viventi* (1980, Dania Film/International Cinematografica/Medusa Distribuzioni).

most memorable dream image, a brief glimpse of the suffering dogs, is just one of an endless parade of bizarre visions: vampire bats, eyeless faces, shuffling zombies and nude corpses.

In 1972, Fulci directed *Non Si Sevizia un Paperino*, a superior whodunit enlivened by moments of incredibly sadistic violence and terror. The film, set in the rural southern part of Italy, concerns the murders of male schoolchildren and the outbreak of hysteria that results. A sexy, comedic spoof of many film genres, *All'Onorevole Piacciono le Donne ... Nonostante le Apparenze e Purchè la Nazione Non le Sappia...* (1972), followed. Perhaps as a reaction to the bad press resulting from the controversial sequences from *Una Lucertola con la Pelle di Donna*, Fulci directed two films featuring heroic dogs, *Zanna Bianca* (1973) and *Il Ritorno di Zanna Bianca* (1974). These films starred Franco Nero and a supporting cast of Alaskan wolfhounds.

Il Cavaliere Costante Nicosia Demonico, ovvero: Dracula in Brianza (1974), a comedy written by Pupi Avati, starred Lando Buzzanca as an industrialist who believes himself to be a vampire and is erotically attracted to many different women. Whether Buzzanca is, in fact, a vampire, or whether the film is actually some sort of social commentary, is left up in the air. Buzzanca, bitten by a strange person (John Steiner), is more worried about being turned into a homosexual than a vampire. When he realizes that vampirism is actually something that afflicted him, he has his factory workers donate blood to a blood bank near his factory.

Next came Fulci's second Western, *Il Quattro dell'Apocalisse* (1975), a violent, nihilistic work of art. When a vicious gang of outlaws led by a depraved gunfighter attack and terrorize a town, only four people survive. These outcasts eventually join the outlaws as they journey towards a safe haven. This Western psychopath turns into a true monster, sadistically torturing them. When he tires of his activities and moves on, they seek retribution and vengeance.

La Pretora (1976), a sexy comedy, starred the wide-eyed and voluptuous Edwige Fenech, a popular star of *giallo* thrillers and sexy comedies of the '70s. Fenech plays a demure, uptight female magistrate and her lookalike twin, who commits random acts of scandalous sexual expression with many of the men with whom she comes into contact. It's an entertaining comedy of errors, most recommended to fans of Fenech.

Sette Notte in Nero (1977) is Fulci's return to the horror genre. This ultimately unsuccessful attempt to mainstream the wild ideas he used for *Una Lucertola con la Pelle di Donna* and *Una sull'Altra* and adapt them to changing times is extremely well-photographed. Essentially, the film is a tale of a woman (Jennifer O'Neill) who possesses extrasensory perception and who "sees" a crime committed. Her husband, who is eventually imprisoned for the crime, is exonerated and released when she investigates the murder that she has witnessed with her parapsychological gift. The film takes a bizarre turn when it begins to look as though the husband may not have been innocent after all.

Much maligned by the British and U.S. fan press which usually bestows accolades on the director for his violent, shocking and gory features, *Sette Notte in Nero* remains a gem in the rough. It is a slow, sometimes elaborately paced film where the dreamlike pacing adds to the sinister implications of the story and the confusion and terror experienced by O'Neill's character.

Sella d'Argento (1978) was Fulci's third and last Western. Another violent, machismo-fueled exercise in blood and one of the last of the Italian Westerns, it appeared at the very tail end of the once-popular cycle.

Zombi 2 (1979) was a film intended as an unofficial sequel to *Zombi* when the European release version of the Argento cut of George A. Romero's *Dawn of the Dead* became a box office success in Italy. Originally, *Zombi 2* was to be written by Dardano Sacchetti, who remains uncredited for the story idea in the final prints, and Enzo Girolami was slated to direct. However, when Girolami declined to direct the film, Fulci stepped in.

Zombi's story line reinvents the zombie genre: When an aimlessly drifting sailboat appears in the waters off New York, the police investigate. They find onboard the remains of several bodies, apparently victims of a vicious attack. A decomposing but very active corpse attacks the policemen. Meanwhile, a journalist (Ian McCullough) and a woman (Tisa Farrow) searching for her sister are joined by another couple and set out for an island located in the West Indies. On this voodoo isle, a scientist (Richard Johnson) has been trying to explain the sudden multitude of revived copses of long-dead slaves and Spanish conquistadors buried on the island. These flesh-eating, rampaging creatures of destruction know no boundaries as they indiscriminately attack all in their path, turning their victims into undead, flesh-eating cannibals as well.

Zombi 2 forever changed the face of Italian horror movies. Its striking visual motifs of seemingly endless, crusty-faced legions of the undead, shambling towards helpless victims, would be used time and again, but would rarely be as immensely powerful as they are here. The Giannetto De Rossi special effects, while primitive, eschew contemporary technical achievements by utilizing gallons of blood, offal and entrails. The reason for the rise of the dead is a purely cinematic invention. Scientific experiments combined with outside voodoo forces have revived the corpses of centuries-dead black slaves and Spanish conquistadors as rabid flesh-eating ghouls. Anyone they attack and infect become like them. *Zombi 2* became such an incredible international hit that the producers reportedly offered Fulci a contract to direct more films. As he seemingly re-invented the sagging Italian horror film market, Fulci had to contend with the sudden appearance of scores of imitation films before planning his next project.

With *Paura nella Città dei Morti Viventi* (1980), Fulci finally became known as a horror film specialist. This tale is imbued with the spirit of the imagined horrors of the author H.P. Lovecraft, as well as being a salute to them. A reporter (Christopher George) rescues a young woman (Catriona MacColl) with parapsy-

U.S. theatrical trade advertisement for *Quella Villa Accanto al Cimitero* (1981, Fulvia Film S.R.L. [Rome]).

chological powers from being mistakenly buried alive, then travels with her to a New England town called Dunwich to investigate the relation between her and a priest (who apparently hung himself from a tree) who appears to her as a psychic apparition. The film soon loses all touch with reality as it heads into a nightmarish collection of unrelated gore scenes. A woman becomes possessed by the spirit of the priest and vomits up her intestines. A man driven mad by hatred and revenge drills a power tool through the brains of another. A herd of undead zombies appear to attack, then eat the flesh of the living. A seemingly calm moment between characters is interrupted by a storm of maggots. Giannetto De Rossi returned to supervise the intense special effects on this film which with the aid of a larger budget, are hard to watch. At the same time, they are so hypnotically grotesque that one finds it difficult to look away.

Fulci returned to the Gothic literature of classical American writers once again for *Il Gatto Nero* in 1981. While it shares its title and an important character with the influential story that it is supposedly based on, there is little in this film that resembles Edgar Allan Poe's macabre tale *The Black Cat*, written nearly a century before. Considering how gruesome Fulci's last film was, this one is relatively tame in the special effects department. Unfortunately, the film is a mixed-up movie full of confused ideas: A man (Patrick Magee) records messages from the dead on a tape recorder. Several murders occur in a sleepy town. A man has a battle of wills with his pet cat, which may be a demonic creature. A young couple seeking an unusual place to have sex becomes locked in a tomb. When their air runs out, they die of suffocation. The local police call in a Scotland Yard inspector (David Warbeck) to investigate their disappearance and other strange happenings (among them, a sudden fire that seems to have been purposefully ignited by the black cat). An American tourist (Mimsy Farmer), visiting the area for its quaint and eerie charm, finds a microphone atop a gravestone, and her investigation leads her to the mysterious grave taper whose attempt to hypnotize her fails when he is attacked by his own cat. With the aid of the Scotland Yard inspector, she begins to unravel the strange happenings that plague this town.

Fulci immerses himself in the macabre world of Poe and attempts a more cerebral and supernatural thriller than a violent, excessively gory monster rampage. What may keep many Italian horror fans away from this film are its deliberately paced plot and the seemingly slow, methodically paced acting of the cast.

L'Aldila (1981) is as close as Fulci has come to a masterpiece of horror. Although the special effects, again contributed by Giannetto De Rossi, are as gruesome as that of any Fulci zombie film, they are also more audacious and more carefully thought-out. With a two-tiered story which sets up a plot that centers on a remote hotel in Louisiana that leads to a doorway to Hell, Fulci's film echoes little else in the genre and is a distinctly original work. It takes great advantage of the scowling but heroic presence of leading man David Warbeck and the comely but hesitantly strange allure of the actress Catriona MacColl.

In turn-of-the-century Louisiana, a large number of torch-bearing villagers capture a man and nail him to a wall. A century later, a woman (MacColl) has inherited the hotel in hopes of renovating it into an inn. Strange happenings take place and, with the assistance of Warbeck, she investigates. They discover that the hotel is built on grounds that lead to one of the seven doorways to Hell. The man who we saw brutally murdered at the beginning was the heretical architect responsible for the design and the building of the structure. The bizarre scenes of random fantastic violence include a worker slaughtered by an unseen figure in the basement, a corpse rising from a slab to murder its wife, a pale, ghostly child and her dog and a hospital full of shuffling zombies.

Fulci's film is definitely one of the better modern Italian films of the new age of horror. His theme of the doorway to Hell echoes that of similar films, most notably the inferior *The Sentinel* (1976), but he journeys far beyond that trite film to enliven his film with large amounts of random, nightmarish images. The dark ending where a prophecy is fulfilled when the film's hero and heroine find themselves trapped in Hell, is a visually stunning and stimulating finale.

Quella Villa Accanto al Cimitero (1981) delves further into Fulci's own mythic interpretation of H.P. Lovecraft's imaginary, literary New England and the supernatural. Like *Paura nella Città dei Morti Viventi*, it maintains that certain areas of contemporary America are filled with many strange supernatural horrors.

Freudstein, an eighteenth century medical experimenter, is somehow responsible for the gruesome murders and dementia affecting the dwellers of a colonial mansion. With the addition of a ghostly child who died as a result of one of Freudstein's bizarre experiments, the film eerily segues from reality to fantasy to horror. This was the last of Fulci's classical horror films.

A couple (Catriona MacColl [again] and Giovanni De Nava) leave the claustrophobic environment of New York for the peace and tranquility of New England. They rent a home with a sinister past so that the husband, a writer, can get to work on his great novel. Before long, the couple's young child sees strange apparitions, including a ghostly young girl who eventually joins him as a playmate. The husband becomes interested in the dark past of the colonial mansion and his investigations lead him to discover the terrible secret: The house was once the home of Freudstein. Freudstein's spirit still inhabits the grounds looking for new victims.

Fulci's film is peopled with an odd cast of characters who behave in strange ways; he also indulges his habit of throwing whatever bizarre ideas that he thinks will propel his plot along onto the screen: The odd teenage housekeeper looks like she's about to stab someone at any minute. The husband always looks at his family like he's about to go off the deep end and murder them. The real estate developer returns for an unspecified reason and is slaughtered by Freudstein. Bats attack the family in the darkly lit basement. A feeling of claustrophobic terror hangs over the film. The mythic ending where the only survivor of the carnage, the young son, crosses over to the dimension of the dead to be with his new friend, the undead daughter of Dr. Freudstein, is surrounded with a poetic air that Fulci seldom attempted in the genre.

Lo Squartatore di New York (1982) is as sadistic as a horror film can come in the contemporary cinema. Maligned for its excessive, brutal and seemingly misogynist images, the film reveals little of Fulci's talent for combining shocking supernatural ideas and realistic horror that his earlier work had. In this tale, just about any female character appears to be sexually wanton, or dresses in a revealing manner, falls prey to a crazy, demented killer who enjoys cutting them up. A disappointing and gruesome work, *Lo Squartatore di New York* story reveals little imagination. The madman who is murdering these women does so because he seeks to remove the elements of sin from their lives by killing them.

Fulci's notoriously nasty and misogynist fable records every graphic slashing of eyes, breasts, abdomens and other parts of the victims in unflinching detail. The film becomes insulting and humiliating to women and men alike when the tale proposes that most women who do not subscribe to a standard code of appearance appear sexually wanton and, therefore, fair game for murdering psychotics. Even the laughable detective is apparently more disgusted with his victims than with the predator. That Fulci adds a Donald Duck–type voice to the killer to disguise his true identity affirms that the director is having fun with the film. But the graphic depictions of murder are too extreme to compliment the fun.

L'Occhio del Mal, released under the title *Manhattan Baby*, is another attempt to work with ideas outside of the normal genre conventions. In the 1982 film, an archeologist discovers an ancient amulet while on an excavation in Egypt. A curse upon the stone may be responsible for blinding him and possessing his young daughter. Although it contains some graphic murders, ultimately *L'Occhio del Mal* is a decidedly lifeless affair.

Conquest (1983) is more reminiscent of the Lucio Fulci of three years earlier. With the aid of a larger budget than his previous two films, this Italian-Mexican co-production is a startling mix of the Italian, *Conan the Barbarian*–influenced sword-and-sorcery rebirth and Fulci's own wild imagination. Set in an unspecified place, on a sun-scorched patch of land in some forgotten time, on another planet, or in a post-apocalyptic future, heroic lead Jorge Rivero and his assistant Andrea Occhipinti do battle with a tribe of cannibalistic half human-half beast creatures. These creatures, who speak, are led by Sabrina Sianni's naked (and golden-masked) evil queen. This beautiful woman with a corpse's head is not above slaughtering nubile slaves and eating their brains! The victims are ripped apart and their flesh and intestines become meals for the horde, while their brains are fed to the queen, a ritual that gives her greater powers. The two avengers do battle with the queen and her creature army. *Conquest* is a film that, despite some risible dialogue, is far better than similar Italian sword-and-sorcery contrivances of the time. The production took great advantage of the seldom-photographed scenic hills of Mexico. Rivero, as the muscular heroic figure, shines.

Fulci photographed in the Americas on location for *L'Aldila* (1981, Fulvia Film S.R.L. [Rome]).

Along with many other Italian genre directors, Fulci next contributed to the financially lucrative post-apocalypse *Mad Max* rip-off genre of Italian productions. His *I Guerrieri dell'Anno 2072* (1983) is an action-filled, if insubstantial, addition.

Murderock — Uccide a Passo di Danza (1984) is Fulci's first visit to the *giallo* thriller as director since *Una sull'Ultra* in 1969. Unfortunately, this film is weakly constructed. Heroines are again in danger: The killer who stalks and slashes with a blade is terrorizing a dance studio where they are rehearsing choreography for a televised *Flashdance* (1983)–inspired musical. The cast (including Raymond Lovelock as an investigating policeman) is game enough. However, the throbbing rock-disco score is incredibly lame and inane—surprising, since it was composed by the renowned Keith Emerson (who wrote and performed the more memorable and successful score for Dario Argento's *Inferno* in 1980).

In 1985, Fulci co-wrote (with Francesco Barilli) *La Gabbia*, an erotic drama co-starring Tony Musante and Cristina Marsillach. Cristina's sister Blanca appeared in his next film as a director. *Il Miele del Diavolo* (1986) differs in many ways from the previous few Fulci films that delved into misogynist themes. Its star, Blanca Marsillach, portrays Jessica, a freewheeling individual who enjoys kinky sexual romps with her boyfriend. A serious motorcycle accident causes her boyfriend to die on the operating table. Jessica blames the physician (Brett Halsey) for the boyfriend's death. She kidnaps the doctor, tortures him, humiliates him and on and on, until he can no longer stand her sadomasochistic abuses. *Il Miele del Diavolo* is strange work of erotic tension from the director primarily known for his zombie movies.

Fulci contributed to the American-Italian co-production *The Curse* (1986) as a designer of special optical effects and is listed in the credits (as Louis Fulci) as a co-producer for the David Keith–directed science fiction–horror film inspired by H.P. Lovecraft. Fulci followed this film with the bland possession-themed *Aenigma* (1987), the tale of a teenage schoolgirl possessed by the spirit of a once-disliked woman. The fantasy sequences are many (including the invasion of bodily orifices by snails) in this unsuccessful combination of the main plot themes from the films *Carrie* (1976), *Patrick* (1978) and *Suspiria* (1976).

Zombi 3 (1988) was a film started by Fulci and finished by Bruno Mattei. Fulci insisted he finished most of the movie; the incredibly fast-moving, rip-roaring zombie film that has become a cult favorite looks like the work of neither director.

Next followed *Quando Alice Ruppe lo Specchio* (1988), hysterical Grand Guignol spoof of films like *Bluebeard*. A middle-aged psychopathic lothario (Brett Halsey) murders same-aged women, who exhibit some sort of physical defect, for their wealth. As his crimes become more and more savage, his behavior becomes truly abhorrent, gambling the ill-gotten financial gains away and leading to a fitting end.

I Fantasmi di Sodoma (1988) was Fulci's experiment in mixing the popular erotic films of the time with the once-profitable (Italian) World War II prison camp genre. A group of overage teenagers visit an area bombed out by the war, only to find the ghostly specters of its once-lively inhabitants that seduce, then menace them.

Fulci turned to television for his next several productions. He was based at the Reteitalia network, where other contemporary genre filmmakers also found funding for their projects in an increasingly difficult theatrical marketplace. Before directing his series of television projects, Fulci is said to have produced and supervised the special effects for *I Fratti Rossi* (1988) for director Gianni Antonio Martucci (a.k.a. Joe Martucci). A moody but ultimately banal production, it tells of religious zealots who have kept their sinister sect alive throughout centuries with the use of satanic reincarnation, possession and, ultimately, the death of anyone who threatens their existence. In a 1996 interview with journalist Loris Curci, Fulci explained, "[T]he producers begged me to help promote the film. I don't even know the director."

Other films that feature his name as a presenter or supervisor (whether he actually had anything to do with the productions or not) are Giovanni Simonelli's *Hansel e Gretel* (1989), Enzo Milioni's *Fuga dalla Morte* (1989), Leandro Lucchetti's *Nel Nido del Serpente* (a.k.a. *The Snake House* and *Bloody Psycho*) (1989) and Andrea Bianchi's *Massacre* (1989), where a policeman is possessed by the satanic spirit of a vengeful monk.

The obscure 1989 thriller *Non Avere Paura della Zia Marta*, also known as *Aunt Martha Does Dreadful Things* and *The Murder Secret*, is sometimes attributed to Fulci as director, but credited to the pseudonymous Robert Martin, an alias for Mario Bianchi (Montero). This tale of greed and horror within a wealthy family of crazed psychopaths does not, however, resemble any of the other works of Fulci.

Demonia (1989), Fulci's first film for the Italian television program *Le Casa del Terrore*, is a horror tale about an archeological excavation on an island that meets with disaster. One of the team, a woman, is possessed by the spirit of a heretical nun who had been buried within the chambers of the site. There is good outdoor location photography, highlighting Fulci's apparent continuing interest in realistic horrors, but *Demonia* seems a pale imitation of similar, superior possession films.

La Dolce Casa degli Orrori (1989) is Fulci's dark fable about two children whose parents have been slaughtered by a maniacal intruder in their home. As the years pass, their ghosts, who refuse to leave the house, become a bizarre irritant to real estate personnel, prospective buyers and potential interlopers. *La Casa del Tempo* (1989) is another strange tale involving a home where all the clocks run backward. A miserably nasty elderly couple, who slaughter an innocent bird for kicks and who have killed their own heirs to retain their fortune, are about to be beset by another distant relative and her psychotic friends. This leads to a conflagration of bizarre ideas about the supernatural and the nature of life. *La Dolce Casa degli Orrori* and *La Casa del Tempo* were part of a four-part series titled *Le Casa del*

Terrore. Two films directed by Umberto Lenzi (*La Casa delle Anime Erranti* and *La Casa del Sortilegio*) completed the package.

Un Gatto nel Cervello (1990) has been called a nightmarish vanity production, but that is far from the truth. It is a remarkable autobiographical film, taking frequent imaginative journeys into the vision of a revived filmmaker. Fulci, who had often displayed a touch of the "ham" by appearing in his movies, stars as the famous Italian horror film director Lucio Fulci. Yes, Fulci plays himself, sort of. A wonderfully sweet and yet very strange performance by the director enhances the film, which was not well-received at the time for its excessive cruel imagery. Nevertheless, it remains among his very best work.

Fulci starring as himself, the famous director of horror films, has been hired to make another movie but, much to his distress, the international producers wish him to use an abundance of gore and horrific images. Fulci would rather make a simple drama, but the demands of the producers win out. Soon, the director is near a mental breakdown and begins to see images of death and murder everywhere he goes. He has a difficult time attending to his production and seeks the help of a psychiatrist who really uses the distraught director's gruesome hallucinations as fodder for his own nefarious endeavors as a mass murderer. Of course, Fulci is convinced that it is he himself who is the killer.

The film that turned out to be Fulci's swansong is a delightfully madcap but very gory spoof of himself and the genre with which he had become most associated. That the director would like the audience to take for granted this scenario, reflecting his reluctance to make horror movies, is revealed as an utter falsehood, when a number of exceedingly gory clips from recent Fulci productions fly by to pump up the running time. Fulci always had a way of astounding his audience with an excessive visual flair for the grotesque anchored in realism. This film strengthens that ideology, with a humorous twist.

Compared to the previous productions, *Voci del Profondo* (1990) is a more thoughtful, less listless film from the director. A woman is continually visited by her murdered father and assists him in locating the murderer among the heirs who are clamoring for his fortune. The film displays a definite touch of the macabre. The director seems quite interested in the several possible suspects who may have killed the man, turning the film into a supernatural version of an Agatha Christie mystery with the dead man as the investigator of the crime.

Aristide Massaccesi produced *Le Porte del Silenzio* (1991), a remake of the influential low-budget American film *Carnival of Souls* (1962). This production, filmed in America and starring John Savage, is an inventive film centered around a man investigating a murder — a murder which turns out to be his own, for he is the murdered man. However, Fulci was rumored to be ailing at the time this film was being made and, although its basic story sounds like a quite clever idea, the direction seems uninspired and lacking.

Over the next few years, Fulci became virtually inactive. Then in 1996, he was

Italian poster (locadina) for *Paura nella Città dei Morti Viventi* (1980, Dania Film/ International Cinematografica/Medusa Distribuzioni).

approached by Dario Argento about the possibility of the two collaborating on a project. Fulci had long wanted to remake the classic 1953 Vincent Price film *House of Wax*. He even developed the story and an early version of the script for the proposed production. Argento, who had never worked with Fulci before, was very involved in the pre-production on the film.

Lucio Fulci died on March 13, 1996, due to complications from diabetes. The filming of *M.D.C.— Maschera di Wax*, also known as *Gaston Leroux's Wax Mask*, was scheduled to begin within a few weeks but, due to the untimely death of its director, the project was postponed. The script was re-written and the Argento-produced film became the directorial debut of talented special effects supervisor Sergio Stivaletti.

Lucio Fulci exploited the darkest fears of man by interjecting gruesome nightmarish horrors into the real world. He pioneered the Italian zombie film and the splatter genres, virtually at the same time. The best of his films are widely recognized as unique productions that emphasize the grotesque and the gory. Although hated by mainstream film critics for his use of sometimes brutal and exploitative themes, Fulci will always be adored and revered by fans of gore-filled zombie films. After all, there's nothing quite like them.

Lucio Fulci Filmography (selected films)

002 Agente Segretissimi

A.k.a. *002 Most Secret Agents*; a.k.a. *Oh! Those Most Secret Agents* (English titles) (1964) (It.); D: Lucio Fulci; Prod. Co.: Mega Film; SC: Lucio Fulci, Amedeo Sollazzo, Vittorio Metz; C: Adalberto Albertini; M: Piero Umiliani; S: Franco Franchi, Ciccio Ingrassia, Ingrid Schoeller, Annie Gorassini.

002 Operazione Luna

A.k.a. *002 Operation: Moon* (English translation); *Dos Cosmonauts a la Fuerza* (Spanish title) (1965) (It., Sp.); D: Lucio Fulci; Prod. Co.: IMA Film (Rome)/Agata Films (Madrid); SC: Vittorio Metz, Amedeo Sollazo; C: Tino Santoni; M: Lallo Coriolano Gori; S: Francho Franchi, Ciccio Ingrassia, Monica Randall, Maria Silva, Linda Sini, Chiro Bermejo.

Aenigma

A.k.a. *Enigma* (English translation) (1987) (It., Yug.); D: Lucio Fulci; P: Ettore Spagnuolo; Prod. Co.: AM International/Sutjeska; SC: Lucio Fulci, Giorgio Mariuzzo; C: Luigi Ciccarese; SP E: Giuseppe Ferranti; S: Jared Martin, Lara Naszinski, Ulli Reinthaler, Sophie D'Aulan, Jennifer Naud, Riccardo Acerbi, Kathi Wise, Mijija Eirojvic.

L'Aldila

A.k.a. *The Beyond* (English translation and title); a.k.a. *E Tu Vivrai nel Terrore! l'Aldila!*; a.k.a. *And You Will Live in Terror! The Beyond!* (English translation); a.k.a. *Seven Doors to Death* (English title) (1981) (It.); D: Lucio Fulci; P: Fabrizio De Angelis; Prod. Co.: Fulvia Film S.R.L. (Rome); SC: Lucio Fulci, Giorgio Mariuzzo, Dardano Sacchetti; C: Sergio Salvati; SP E: Germano Natali, Giannetto De Rossi; M: Fabio Frizzi; S: Catherine MacColl a.k.a. Catriona MacColl, David Warbeck, Sarah Keller, Antoine Saint John, Veronica Lazar, Giovanni De Nava, Michele Mirabella, Al Cliver a.k.a. Pier Luigi Conti, Lucio Fulci.

All'Onorevole Piacciono le Donne ... Nonostante le Apparenze e Purchè la Nazione Non le Sappia...

A.k.a. *The Senator Likes Women ... Despite Appearances and Provided the Nation Doesn't Know* (English translation); a.k.a. *The Senator Likes Women* (U.S. theatrical title); a.k.a. *Obsede Maigre Lui* (French title); a.k.a. *The Eroticist* (English title) (1972) (It., Fr.); D: Lucio Fulci; Prod. Co.: New Film Productions/Jacques Roitfeld, Paris; SC: Lucio Fulci, Alessandro Continenza, Ottavio Jemma; M: Lucio Fred Bonqusta; S: Lando Buzzanca, Laura Antonelli, Anita Strindberg, Lionel Stander.

Beatrice Cenci

A.k.a. *The Conspiracy of Torture* and *Conspiracy* (English titles) (1969) (It.); D: Lucio Fulci; P: Giorgio Agliani, Elio Di Pietro; Prod. Co.: Filmena; SC: Lucio Fulci, Roberto Gianvita; C: Enrico Menczer; M: Angelo Francesco Lavagnino, songs and ballads by Silvano Spadaccino; S: Tomas Milian a.k.a. Tomas Rodriguez, Adrienne La Russa, Georges Wilson, Antonio Casagrabde, Raymond Pellegrin, Pedro Sanchez, Mavi, Umberto D'Orsini.

La Casa del Tempo

A.k.a. *The House of Clocks* (English translation and title) (1989) (It.); D: Lucio Fulci; SC: Gianfranco Clerici, Daniele Stroppa; C: Nino Celeste; M: Vince Tempura; S: Keith Van Hooven, Karina Huff, Paolo Paolini, Bettine Milne, Al Cliver a.k.a. Pier Luigi Conti.

Feature-length episode of the Italian television program *Le Casa Del Terrore*.

Il Cavaliere Costante Nicosia Demoniaco, ovvero: Dracula in Brianza

A.k.a. *The Gentleman Costante Nicosia Is a Demon ... Or Dracula in Brianza* (English translation); a.k.a. *Dracula in the Provinces*; a.k.a. *Young Dracula*; a.k.a. *Bite Me, Count* (English titles) (1974) (It.); D: Lucio Fulci; P: R. Marini, Alfonso Donati; Prod. Co.: Coralta Cinematografica (Rome); SC: Lucio Fulci, Pupi Avati, Bruno Corbucci, Mario Amendola, Enzo Jannacci, Giuseppe Viola; C: Sergio Salvati; M: Franco Bixio, Fabio Frizzi, Vincente Tempera; S: Lando Buzzanca, Sylva Koscina, Christa Linder, Moira Orfei, Rossano Brazzi, Valentina Cortese, Ciccio Ingrassia, John Steiner, Grazia Spadaro, Giancarlo Rossi.

Le Colt Cantarono la Morte È Fu ... Tempo di Massacro

A.k.a. *Tempo di Massacro* (alternate Italian title; translation: *Massacre Time*); a.k.a. *The Brute and the Beast*; a.k.a. *Django the Runner* (English titles) (1966) (It.); D: Lucio Fulci; P: Oreste Coltellacci; Prod. Co.: Colt Produzioni Cinematografiche/Produzioni Cinematografiche L.F./Mega Film, Rome; SC: Fernando Di Leo; C: Riccardo Pallottini; M: Lallo Gori; S: Franco Nero, George Hilton, Nino Castelnuovo, Lynn Shayne, Giuseppe Addobbati, Salvatore Borghese.

Come Rubammo la Bomba Atomica

A.k.a. *How to Steal an Atomic Bomb*; a.k.a. *How We Stole the Atomic Bomb* (English translations and titles) (1967) (It., Egypt); D: Lucio Fulci; Prod. Co.: Five Film/Fono Film (Rome)/Caprofilm (Cairo); SC: Sandro Continenza, Roberto Gianviti, Amedeo Sollazzo; C: Fausto Rossi; M: Lallo Coriolano Gori; S: Franco Franchi, Ciccio Ingrassia, Julie Anne Menard, Youssef Wahby, Franco Bonvicini.

Conquest

A.k.a. *La Conquista della Tierra Perdida* (Spanish title) (1983) (It., Sp., Mex.); D: Lucio Fulci; P: Giovanni Di Clemente; Prod. Co.: Cleminternazionale Cinematografiuca/Golden Sun/Producciones Esme; SC: Gino Capone, Jose Antonio De La Loma, Carlos Vasallo; C: Alejandro Alonso Garcia; M: Claudio Simonetti; S: Jorge Rivero, Andrea Occhipinti, Sabrina Siani a.k.a. Sabrina Seggiani, Conrado San Martin, Violeta Cela, Jose Gras Palau, Gioia Maria Scola.

Demonia

(1989) (It.); D: Lucio Fulci; Prod. Co.: Lanterna Editrice/A.M. Trading International; SC: Lucio Fulci, Piero Regnoli; C: Luigi Ciccarese; M: Giovanni Cristiani; S: Brett Halsey, Meg Register, Lino Salemme, Cristina Englehardt, Pascal Druant, Grady Thomas Clarkson, Ettore Commi, Al Cliver a.k.a. Pier Luigi Conti.

Feature-length episode of the Italian television program *Le Casa del Terrore*.

La Dolce Casa degli Orrori

A.k.a. *Sweet House of Horrors* (English translation and title) (1989) (It.); D: Lucio Fulci; SC: Lucio Fulci, Vincenzo Mannino, Gigliola Battaglini; C: Nino Celeste; M: Vince Tampera; S: Jean Christophe Bretigniere, Cinzea Monreale, Pascal Persiano, Franco Diogene.
   Feature-length episode of the Italian television program *Le Casa del Terrore*.

I Fantasmi di Sodoma

A.k.a. *The Ghost of Sodom*; a.k.a. *The Ghosts of Sodom*; a.k.a. *Sodoma's Ghosts* (English translations and titles) (1988) (It.); D: Lucio Fulci; P: Luigi Nannerni, Antonio Lucidi; Prod. Co.: Alpha Cinematografica; SC: Lucio Fulci, Carlo Alberto Alfieri; C: Silvano Tessicini; M: Carlo Maria Cordio; SP E: Angelo Mattei; S: Claus Aliot, Mary Salier, Robert Egon, Jessica Moore a.k.a. Luciana Ottaviani.

Un Gatto nel Cervello

A.k.a. *A Cat in the Brain* (English translation and title); a.k.a. *Un Gatto nel Cervello: I Volti del Terrore* (alternate Italian title; translation: *A Cat in the Brain: The Face of Terror*); a.k.a. *Nightmare Concert* (English title) (1990) (It.); D: Lucio Fulci; P: Luigi Nannerini, Antonio Lucidi; Prod. Co.: La Executive/Cine TV S.r.l; SC: Lucio Fulci, Giovanni Simonelli, Antonio Tentori; C: Alessandro Grossi; M: Fabio Frizzi; S: Lucio Fulci, David L. Thompson, Jeffrey Kennedy, Malissa Longo, Ria De Simone a.k.a. Anna Maria De Simone, Brett Halsey, Sacha Maria Darwin, Maurice Poli.
   Includes footage culled from *Le Porte dell'Inferno*, *I Fantasmi di Sodoma*, *Quando Alice Ruppe lo Specchio*, Andrea Bianchi's *Massacre*, Mario Bianchi Montero's *Non Avere Paura della Zia Marta*, Lucchetti's *Nel Nido del Serpente* and Milioni's *Fuga dalla Morte*.

Il Gatto Nero

A.k.a. *The Black Cat* (English translation and title); a.k.a. *Il Gatto di Park Lane* (alternate Italian title; translation: *The Cat of Park Lane*) (1981) (It.); D: Lucio Fulci; P: Ennio Onorati, Antonio De Padova, Giulio Sbarigia; Prod. Co.: Selenia Cinematografica (Rome); SC: Lucio Fulci, Biagio Proietti, based on "The Black Cat" by Edgar Allan Poe; C: Sergio Salvati; M: Pino Donaggio, Natale Massara; SP E: Paolo Ricci; S: Mimsy Farmer, David Warbeck, Patrick Magee, Dagmar Lassander, Daniela Dorro, Al Cliver a.k.a. Pier Luigi Conti, Bruno Corazzari, Geoffrey Copleston.

I Guerrieri dell'Anno 2072

A.k.a. *Warriors of the Year 2072* (English translation); a.k.a. *Rome 2072: I Nuovi Gladiators* (alternate Italian title); a.k.a. *Rome 2033 The Fighter Centurions*; a.k.a. *Rome 2072: The New Gladiators*; a.k.a. *The New Barbarians*; a.k.a. *The New Gladiators*; a.k.a. *Warriors of the Year 3000* (English titles) (1983) (It.); D: Lucio Fulci; Prod. Co.: Regency Productions; SC: Lucio Fulci, Dardano Sacchetti, Elisa Livia Briganti, Cesare Frugoni; C: Giuseppe Pinori; M: Riz Ortolani; S: Jared Martin, Fred Williamson, Elenora Brigliadori, Cosimo Cinieri, Mario Merola, Angela Luce, Claudio Cassinelli.

I Ladri

A.k.a. *The Thieves* (English translation) (1959) (It., Sp.); D: Lucio Fulci; Prod. Co.: Roberto Capitani and Luigi Mondello for I.C.M. [Industria Cinematografica Mondiale] (Rome)/

Fenix Film (Madrid); SC: Lucio Fulci, Marcello Coscia, Nanni Loy, Ottavo Jemma, Marino Onorati, Vittorio Vighi; C: Carlo Fiore, Manuel Berenguer; M: Carlo Innocenzi, Franco Ferrara, Fred Buscaglione; S: Antonio Vincenzo Stefano Clemente a.k.a. Antonio De Curtis a.k.a. Toto, Armando Calva, Giacomo Furia, Enzo Turco, Giovanna Ralli.

Luca il Contrabbandiere

A.k.a. *Luca, the Smuggler* (English translation); a.k.a. *Il Contrabbandiere* (alternate Italian title); a.k.a. *Vicious* (alternate Italian title); a.k.a. *The Smugglers*; a.k.a. *The Naples Connection*; a.k.a. *Contrband* (English titles) (1980) (It.); D: Lucio Fulci; P: Sandro Ifascelli, Sergio Jacobs; Prod. Co.: Primex Italiana/C.M.R. Cinematografica; SC: Lucio Fulci, Ettore Sanzo, Gianni De Chiara, Giorgio Mariuzzo; C: Sergio Salvati; M: Fabio Frizzi; S: Fabio Testi, Ivana Monti, Guido Alberti, Enrico Maisto, Giordana Falzoni, Marcel Bozzuffi, Saverio Marconi, Lucio Fulci.

Una Lucertola con la Pelle di Donna

A.k.a. *A Lizard in a Woman's Skin* (English translation and title); a.k.a. *Le Venin de la Peur* (French title; translation: *Venom of Fear*); a.k.a. *Les Salopes Vent en Enfer* (French video title; translation: *The Sluts Go to Hell*); a.k.a. *Una Lugartija con Piel de Mujer* (Spanish title); a.k.a. *Schizoid* (English title) (1971) (It., Sp., Fr.); D: Lucio Fulci; P: Edmondo Amati; Prod. Co.: Fida Cinematografica/International Apollo Film (Rome)/Les Films Corona (Paris)/Atlantida Films (Madrid); SC: Lucio Fulci, Roberto Gianviti, Jose Luis Martinez Molla, Andre Tranche; C: Luigi Kuveiller; M: Ennio Morricone, Bruno Nicolai; SP E: Carlo Rambaldi; S: Florinda Bolkan a.k.a. Florinda Bulcao, Stanley Baker, Jean Sorel, Leo Genn, Silvia Monti, Anita Strindberg, Georges Rigaud, Alberto De Mendoza, Ely Galleani a.k.a. Elyde Galleana.

Il Miele del Diavolo

A.k.a. *The Devil's Honey* (English translation and title); a.k.a. *Dangerous Obsession* (English title) (1986) (It., Sp.); D: Lucio Fulci; Prod. Co.: Selvaggia Films (Italy)/Producciones Cinematograficas Balcazar (Spain); SC: Vincenzo Salviani, Jaime Jesus Balcazar; C: Alejandro Ulloa; M: C. Natali; S: Blanca Marsillach, Brett Halsey, Corinne Clery, Paula Molina.

Murderock—Uccide a Passo di Danza

A.k.a. *Murder Rock Kill to Dance*; a.k.a. *Murderock: The Dance of Death* (English translations and titles); a.k.a. *Murder Rock* (Italian pre-production title); a.k.a. *The Demon Is Loose* (English title) (1984) (It.); D: Lucio Fulci; P: Augusto Caminito; Prod. Co.: Scena Film; SC: Lucio Fulci, Gianfranco Clerici, Vincenzo Mannino, Roberto Gianviti; C: Giuseppe Pinori; M: Keith Emerson; S: Olga Karlatos, Raymond Lovelock, Claudio Cassinelli, Cosimo Cinieri, Giuseppe Mannajuolo, Berna Maria Do Carmo, Belinda Busato, Lucio Fulci, Al Cliver a.k.a. Pier Luigi Conti.

L'Occhio del Mal

A.k.a. *The Eye of the Evil Dead* (English translation and title); a.k.a. *Possessed* (GB title); a.k.a. *Manhattan Baby* (English and alternate Italian title) (1982) (It.); D: Lucio Fulci; P: Fabrizio De Angelis; Prod.Co.: Fulvia Film; SC: Elisa Livia Briganti, Dardano Sacchetti; C: Guglielmo Mancori; M: Fabio Frizzi; S: Christopher Connelly, Martha Taylor, Brigitta Boccole, Giovanni Frezza, Cinzia De Ponti, Cosimo Cinieri, Andrea Bosic, Carlo De Mejo, Laura Levi a.k.a. Gabriella Tricca, Lucio Fulci.

Non Si Sevizia un Paperino

A.k.a. *Don't Torture Donald Duck*; a.k.a. *Don't Torture the Ugly Duckling* (English translations and titles); a.k.a. *Fanatismo* (alternate Italian title); (1972) (It.); D: Lucio Fulci; P: Renato Laboni, Felice Calaiacono, Franco Puccioni; Prod. Co.: Medusa Film Distribuzione (Rome); SC: Lucio Fulci, Gianfranco Clerici, Roberto Gianviti; C: Sergio D'Offizi; M: Riz Ortolani; S: Florinda Bolkan a.k.a. Florinda Bulcao, Barbara Bouchet a.k.a. Barbel Goutscher a.k.a. Barbel Gutchen, Tomas Milian a.k.a. Tomas Rodriguez, Irene Papas, Marc Porel, Antonello Campodifiori, Ugo D'Alessio.

Operazione San Pietro

A.k.a. *Operation St. Peter* (English translation and title); a.k.a. *Die Abenteuer des Kardinal Braun* (German title; translation: *The Adventures of Cardinal Brown*); a.k.a. *Die Seltsamen Abenteurer des Kardinal Braun* (alternate German title) (1968) (It., Fr., W.G.); D: Lucio Fulci; P: Turi Vasile; Prod. Co.: Ultra Film/Marianne Productions (Paris)/Roxy-Film (Munich); SC: Lucio Fulci, Adriano Bolzoni, Ennio De Concini, Roberto Gianviti, Paul Hengge; C: Alfio Contini, Erico Menczer; M: Armando Trovajoli, Ward Swingle; S: Edward G. Robinson, Lando Buzzanca, Heinz Ruhmann, Uta Levka, Wolfgang Kieling.

Paura nella Città dei Morti Viventi

A.k.a. *Fear in the City of the Living Dead* (English translation and title); a.k.a. *Twilight of the Dead*; a.k.a. *City of the Living Dead*; a.k.a. *The Gates of Hell* (English titles) (1980) (It.); D: Lucio Fulci; P: Giovanniu Masini; Prod. Co.: Dania Film/International Cinematografica/Medusa Distribuzioni; SC: Lucio Fulci, Dardano Sacchetti; C: Sergio Salvati; M: Fabio Frizzi; SP E: Gianetto De Rossi; S: Christopher George, Janet Agren, Catherine MacColl a.k.a. Catriona MacColl, Carlo De Mejo, Antonella Interlenghi, John Morghen a.k.a. Giovanni Lombardo Radice, Daniela Doria, Luca Paismer, Fabrizio Jovine, Lucio Fulci.

Le Porte del Silenzio

A.k.a. *The Doors to Silence* (English title) (1991) (It.); D: Lucio Fulci; P: Aristide Massaccesi; Prod. Co. Filmirage; SC: Lucio Fulci; C: Giancarlo Ferrando; M: Franco Piana; S: John Savage, Sandi Schultz, Richard Castleman, Jennifer Loeb.

La Pretora

A.k.a. *The Magistrate*; a.k.a. *The Female Magistrate* (English translation); (1976) (It.); D: Lucio Fulci; Prod. Co.: Coralta Cinematografica; SC: Franco Marotta, Laura Toscano, Franco Mercuri; C: Luciano Trasatti; M: Nico Fidenco; S: Edwige Fenech, Giancarlo Dettori, Gianni Agus, Oreste Lionello, Raf Luca, Mario Maranzana.

Quando Alice Ruppe lo Specchio

A.k.a. *When Alice Broke the Mirror* (English translation and title); a.k.a. *Touch of Death* (English title) (1988) (It.); D/S: Lucio Fulci; P: Luigi Nannerini, Antonio Lucidi; Prod. Co.:

Alpha Cinematografica; C: Silvano Tessicini; M: Carlo Maria Cordio; SP E: Angelo Mattei; S: Brett Halsey, Ria De Simone a.k.a. Anna Maria De Simone, Al Cliver a.k.a. Pier Luigi Conti, Sasha Darwin, Zora Kerova a.k.a. Zora Ulla Keslerova Tschechin, Marco Di Stefano.

Quattro dell'Apocalisse

A.k.a. *The Four of the Apocalypse* (English translation and title); a.k.a. *The Four Gunmen of the Apocalypse* (English title) (1975) (It.); D: Lucio Fulci; Prod. Co.: Coralta Cinematografica; SC: Lucio Fulci, Ennio De Concini; C: Serrgio Salvati; M: Franco Bixio, Fabio Frizzi, Vince Tempera; S: Fabio Testi, Lynne Frederick, Tomas Milian a.k.a. Tomas Rodriguez, Michael J. Pollard, Bruno Corazzari, Donald O'Brien.

Quella Villa Accanto al Cimitero

A.k.a. *The House Outside the Cemetery*; a.k.a. *The House by the Cemetery* (English translation and title); a.k.a. *La Casa Accanto al Cimitero Freudstein* (Italian pre-production title) (1981) (It.); D: Lucio Fulci; P: Fabrizio De Angelis; Prod. Co.: Fulvia Film S.R.L. (Rome); SC: Lucio Fulci, Dardano Sacchetti, Giorgio Mariuzzo; C: Sergio Salvati; M: Walter Rizzati; SP E: Gianetto De Rossi, Maurizio Trani; S: Catherine MacColl a.k.a. Catriona MacColl, Giovanni De Nava, Dagmar Lassander, Paolo Malco, Ania Pieroni, Giovanni Frezza, Silvia Collatina, Daniele Doria, Carlo De Mejo.

I Ragazzi del Juke Box

A.k.a. *The Juke Box Girls* (English translation) (1959) (It.); D: Lucio Fulci; Prod. Co.: Giovanni Addessi for Era Cinematografica; SC: Lucio Fulci, Piero Vivarelli, Vittorio Vighi; C: Carlo Montuori; M: Eros Sciorilli; S: Tony Dallara, Elke Sommer, Betty Curtis, Mario Carotenuto, Antonio Vincenzo Stefano Clemente a.k.a. Antonio De Curtis a.k.a. Toto.

Il Ritorno di Zanna Bianca

A.k.a. *The Return of White Fang* (English translation); a.k.a. *Le Retour de Croc-Blanc* (French title); a.k.a *Die Teufelsschulucht der Wilden Wolfe* (German title); a.k.a. *Challenge to White Fang* (English title) (1974) (It., Fr., W.G.); D: Lucio Fulci; P: Piero Donati; Prod. Co.: Coralta Cinematografica/Films Corona, Nanterre/C.C.C. Terra Filmkunst, Berlin; SC: Lucio Fulci, Piero Donati, Roberto Gianviti, based on characters created by Jack London; C: Silvano Ippoliti; M: Paolo Rustichelli; S: Franco Nero, Virna Lisi, John Steiner, Raimund Harmstorf, Yanti Sommer, Renato Cestie, Werner Pochath, Harry Carey, Jr., Donald O'Brien.

Sella d'Argento

A.k.a. *Silver Saddle*; a.k.a. *They Died with Their Boots On* (English titles) (1978) (It.); D: Lucio Fulci; P: Ennio De Meo, Carlo Barto; Prod. Co.: Rizzo Film; SC: Lucio Fulci, Ornella Michili; C: Sergio Salvati; M: Franco Bixio, Fabio Frizzi, Vince Tempera; S: Giuliano Gemma, Sven Valsecchi, Ettore Manni, Donald O'Brien, Aldo Sambrell, Cinzia Monreale, Licinia Lentini, Geoffrey Lewis.

Sette Notte in Nero

A.k.a. *Seven Notes in Black* (English translation); a.k.a. *Murder to the Tune of Seven Black Notes* (export title); a.k.a. *Passion e Sentimento* (Italian pre-production title; translation:

Passion and Feeling); a.k.a. *Dolce Come— Morire* (Italian pre-production title; translation: *Sweet to Die*); a.k.a. *The Psychic* (U.S. title); a.k.a. *Death Toll Times Seven* (English title) (1977) (It.); D: Lucio Fulci; P: Franco Cuccu; Prod. Co.: Cinecompany S.r.l./Rizzoli Editore; SC: Lucio Fulci, Roberto Gianviti, Dardano Sacchetti; C: Sergio Salvati; M: Franco Bixio, Fabio Frizzi, Vincente Tempera, song "With You" by Ernest, Franco Bixio, Fabio Frizzi and Vincente Tempera, performed by Linda Lee; S: Jennifer O'Neill, Gabriele Ferzetti, Marc Porel, Gianni Garko, Evelyn Stewart a.k.a. Ida Galli, Jenny Tamburi a.k.a. Luciana Della Robbia, Fabrizio Jovine, Luigi Diberti, Laura Vernier.

Lo Squartatore di New York

A.k.a. *The New York Ripper* (English translation and title); a.k.a *The Beauty Killer*; a.k.a. *Psycho Ripper*; a.k.a. *The Ripper* (English titles) (1982) (It.); D: Lucio Fulci; P: Fabrizio De Angelis; Prod. Co.: Fulvia Film S.r.l. (Rome); SC: Lucio Fulci, Gianfranco Clerici, Dardano Sacchetti, Vincenzo Mannino; C: Luigi Kuveiller; M: Francesco De Masi; S: Jack Hedley, Almanta Keller a.k.a. Antonellina Interlenghi, Paolo Malco, Howard Ross a.k.a. Renato Rossini, Alexandra Della Colli, Andrea Occhipinti, Cinzia De Ponti, Zora Kerova a.k.a. Zora Ulla Keslerova Tschechin, Rita Silva, Barbara Cupisti, Lucio Fulci.

Una sull'Altra

A.k.a. *One on Top of the Other*; a.k.a. *One After the Other* (English translations and titles); a.k.a. *Perversion Story* (French title); a.k.a. *La Macchination* (alternate French title; translation: *The Frame-Up*) (1969) (It., Fr.); D: Lucio Fulci; P: Edmondo Amati; Prod. Co.: Fida Cinematografica (Rome)/Les Productions Jacques Roitfeld (Paris)/C.C. Trebol Film (Paris); SC: Lucio Fulci, Roberto Gianviti, Jose Luis Martinez Molla; C: Alejandro Ulloa; M: Riz Ortolani; S: Marisa Mell a.k.a. Marlies Moitzi, Jean Sorel, Elsa Martinelli, John Ireland, Alberto De Mendoza, Jean Sobiesky, Giuseppe Addobbati, Faith Domergue, Riccardo Cucciolla, Lucio Fulci.

Un Uomo da Ridere

A.k.a. *A Man to Laugh* (English translation) (1978) (It.); D: Lucio Fulci
    Television documentary about Franco Franchi of the Italian comedy team, Franco and Ciccio (Ingrassia).

Voci del Profondo

A.k.a. *Il Vizio Infinito Voci dal Profondo*; a.k.a. *Urla dal Profondo* (alternate Italian titles); *Voices from Beyond* (English translation and title) (1990) (It.); D: Lucio Fulci; P: Luigi Nannerini, Antonio Lucidi; Prod. Co.: Wind Films/Scena Group/Executive Cine TV; SC: Lucio Fulci, Peiro Regnoli; C: Sandro Grossi; M: Stelvio Cipriani; E: Pino Ferranti; S: Brett Halsey, Karina Huff, Dulio Del Prete, Pascal Persiano, Lorenzo Flaherty, Damiano Azzos, Rosamaria Grauso Bettina Giovannini, Frances Nacmen, Paolo Paoloni, Sacha Maria Darwin.
    Feature-length episode of the Italian television program *Le Casa del Terrore*.

Zanna Bianca

A.k.a. *White Fang* (English translation and title); a.k.a. *White Fang and the White Hunter* (English title) (1973) (It., Sp.); D: Lucio Fulci; P: Harry Alan Towers; Prod. Co.: Oceania Produzioni Internazionali Cinematografiche/Incine Compania Industrial Cinematografica; SC: Roberto Gianviti, Piero Regnoli, Harry Alan Towers, Guy Elmes, Thom Keyes, Guillaume Roux, based on the novel by Jack London; C: Aristide Massaccesi, Pablo Ripoli, Enrico Menczer; M: Carlo Rustichelli; S: Franco Nero, Virna Lisi, Fernando Rey, John Steiner, Raimund Harmstorf, Rik Battaglia, Maurice Poli.

Zombi 2

A.k.a. *Zombie Flesh Eaters*; a.k.a. *Island of the Living Dead*; a.k.a. *Zombie*; a.k.a. *Zombies 2* (English titles) (1979) (It.); D: Lucio Fulci; P: Ugo Tucci, Fabrizio De Angelis, Antonio Mazza; Prod. Co.: Variety Film; SC: Elisa Briganti, Dardano Sacchetti (uncredited); C: Sergio Salvati, Franco Bruni, Ramon Bravo, Paolo Curfo; M: Fabio Frizzi, Giorgio Tucci; SP E: Gianetto De Rossi; S: Richard Johnson, Ian McCullough, Tisa Farrow, Al Cliver a.k.a. Pier Luigi Conti, Stefania D'Amario, Ugo Bologna, Monica Zanchi, Lucio Fulci.

Zombi 3

A.k.a. *Zombie 3* (English translation and title) (1988) (It.); D: Lucio Fulci, and Bruno Mattei; P: Franco Gaudenzi; Prod. Co.: Flora Film; SC: Claudio Fragrasso; C: Riccardo Grassetti, Luigi Ciccarese; M: Stefano Mainetti; S: Deran Serafian, Beatrice Ring, Richard Raymond, Massimo Vanni, Ulrich Reinthaller, Marina Loi, Debra Bergamini.

Umberto Lenzi

Umberto Lenzi was born on June 8, 1931, in the Massa Marittima province of Italy. Although Lenzi originally studied law as a profession, he joined the Centro Sperimentale Centrale (C.S.C.), graduating from that film school in 1956. Afterwards, Lenzi worked as a film critic and a writer and, between 1957 and 1960, wrote several detective novels and adventure stories under a pseudonym.

During this period, Lenzi began to find work on film assignments as a writer and as an assistant director. His first film credit (as a co-director), *Apocalisse sul Fiume Giallo* (1960), was an adventure set during the Chinese Civil War in 1950. His work on that film led to his first solo directorial assignment, *Le Avventure di Mary Read* (1961). A colorful costume mini-epic made at the beginning of the sword-and-sandal peplum craze of the '60s, it starred Lisa Gastoni as a pirate who becomes a member of aristocracy, only to eventually turn her back on it and return to her adventurous ways. A relatively obscure movie nowadays, this film must have performed well at the box office because it led to a number of similar assignments for Lenzi in the following years.

Lenzi directed many adventure films during the next five years. The highlights were two features about Robin Hood, *Il Trionfo di Robin Hood* (1962) and *L'Invincible Cavaliere Mascherato* (1963), and two films about a Middle Eastern hero named Sandokan starring Steve Reeves, *Sandokan la Tigre di Mompracem* (1963) and *I Pirati della Malesia* (1964). A related follow-up with Sean Flynn in the lead, *Sandokan il Maciste della Giungla* (1964), was also directed by Lenzi. He created one of the original mix-and-match genre films with *Zorro Contro Maciste* (1963).

In 1965, as the popularity of the sword-and-sandal film and the costume adventures began to wane, Lenzi turned his director's eye to the next craze of adventure movies, the European spy film. In *A008 Operazione Stermino* (1965),

Agent 008 (Ingrid Schoeller), aided by foreign Secret Service Agent 606 (Alberto Lupo), battles an evil organization of spies with ties to the Soviets and Red Chinese who have world domination on their minds. The apparent success of this well-photographed production (actual location shooting was done in Egypt) led to a duo of espionage films that Lenzi directed and filmed on location in the Middle East with Roger Browne as the star: *Superseven Chiama Cairo* (1965) and *Le Spie Amano i Fiori* (1966). In an attempt to alter the confines of the genre somewhat, Lenzi filmed *Un Milione di Dollari per Sette Assassini* (1966), also with Browne. This film featured the usually dapper actor as a master thief hired by an Egyptian nobleman to locate his drug-addicted son who had been involved in a gang of thieves, prostitutes, drug and weapons smugglers and murderers.

In 1966, Lenzi dabbled in an adventure film influenced by the Italian comic strips (*fumetti*) then appearing in the daily newspapers. *Kriminal* is a colorful movie about a masked criminal, a master of disguise who is chased by criminal gangs and the police forces of Europe.

Umberto Lenzi

Lenzi's first World War II–themed production, cashing in on the worldwide success of films like *The Dirty Dozen* (1967), was *Attentato ai Tre Grandi* (1967). Starring Ken Clark and popular German character actor Horst Frank, it is an elaborately written tale about a German mission to infiltrate the North African meeting of the Allied Command and assassinate these men. Lenzi returned to the World War II adventure theme with the Dario Argento–scripted *La Legione dei Dannati*, starring Jack Palance and Thomas Hunter in 1968.

In 1968, Lenzi made his Westerns. Like his contemporaries, he was dabbling in virtually every genre available. *Tutto per Tutto* starred Mark Damon and John Ireland and *Una Pistola per Cento Bare* featured Ireland and Peter Lee Lawrence. The latter is the better of the two films due to the horrific moment where crazed lunatics escape a nearby asylum and start to attack the locals with axes and hatchets. Maybe this film was portentous for it was after this second and last Western that Lenzi began his association with thrillers.

Orgasmo (1968), *Così Dolci ... Così Perversa* (1969), *Paranoia* (1970) and *Il Coltello di Ghiaccio* (1972) are Lenzi's quartet of thrillers starring the American actress Carroll Baker. *Orgasmo* is a tale of a wealthy widow (Baker) attracted to a younger man (Lou Castel) who becomes her lover. They enjoy an idyllic lifestyle until the arrival of the man's sister, who turns out to be crazy, and Baker must then fight for her life. *Così Dolce ... Così Perversa* features Baker in a confusing tale about the wife of a philandering adulterer. Her husband (Jean-Louis Trintignant) has an affair with a neighbor, but the woman may also be having an affair with the wife, who arranges for the husband's death to be with her lover. In *Paranoia*, Baker returns as a woman approached by the new wife of her ex-husband who wants her assistance in murdering the man. Finally in *Il Coltello di Ghiaccio*, Baker visits a wealthy family of strange characters, who eventually fall prey to a maniacal killer. This last and best of the Lenzi-Baker films is also among the best of all thrillers turned out in the glory days of the Italian *giallo*. The central story is not completely original but there's a fairly original twist at its climax, reason enough to hold it in high regard.

Reproduction of an English-language videocassette of *Paranoia* (1970, Tritone Filmindustria [Rome]/Medusa Distribuzione [Rome]/Société Nouvelle de Cinématographie/Producciones Cinematograficas D.I.A. [Madrid]).

In 1971 Lenzi made the thriller *Un Posto Ideale per Uccidere* starring Ray Lovelock, Ornella Muti and Irene Papas. An interesting psycho killer film, the movie is about two free-spirited individuals who make their way through an Italian holiday by selling naughty photos of Muti. To escape the law, they end up at the villa of Papas and think they have it made, living a sumptuous life until they discover that Papas has already murdered her husband and threatens them next.

Sette Orchidee Macchiate di Rosso (1972) was an Italian-German co-production starring Antonio Sabato, Uschi Glass and Marisa Mell. Co-financed by the

Lobby card for *Paranoia* (1970, Tritone Filmindustria [Rome]/Medusa Distribuzione [Rome]/Société Nouvelle de Cinématographie/Producciones Cinematograficas D.I.A. [Madrid]).

same company that produced the German Edgar Wallace thrillers of the '60s, it's a fine thriller that confirms how much the Wallace films had influenced the Italian *gialli*. A series of murders has plagued Europe, but they all seem unrelated until a police investigator notes a clue that may link the crimes. A medallion, a silver, half-crescent moon, has been found on the bodies, usually clutched in the hands of the victims. A newly married couple (Sabato and Glass) are terrorized when the wife is the apparent next victim of this half-moon killer. The husband takes to his car and drives all around the picturesque countryside, following any clues that could identity the killer, and saves his wife.

Until the recent revival of the new Edgar Wallace–influenced productions on German television in the mid–'90s, this film had been represented as the last official adaptation of an Edgar Wallace story from the Rialto studios, the co-producer of this movie. Purported to be based on Wallace's *The Puzzle of the Silver Half Moons*, but according to Lenzi actually taken from a little-known Cornell Woolrich story, it combines the elements of Krimis and the *giallo* into a satisfying whole. Of course, the film is also noteworthy for its updating of a noir thriller into a more contemporary setting and moving the motivation for the killings into more heretical, deviate territory by involving a seemingly kind parish priest.

Il Paese del Sesso Selvaggio (1972) is Lenzi's controversial initial foray into the lucrative cannibal film genre. A British photographer on assignment in Thailand is captured by a tribe of flesh-eating cannibals and is witness to their gruesome rituals (castration of men, slaughter of monkeys, etc.) before he is accepted as one of them and gets to marry the sexy Queen (Me Me Lai).

Lenzi supposedly, and most likely, filmed portions of this movie in Southeast Asia, before Italian filmmakers discovered that similar productions could be made in South America. With few or no questions asked, this was the place to make such a production. With the treatment of cannibalism being one of the lighter moments in this film, it is the hanging-from-the-tree sequences, not unlike those in the controversial *Man Called Horse* series, and the animal cruelty which disturb. If you've never seen this film, then truly, "You ain't seen nothing yet."

In 1973, Lenzi made his first crime film, the brutal *Milano Rovente*. In 1974, he directed *Spasmo*, which became an international horror film-thriller crossover hit. The English-language American prints are longer due to the additional footage shot by the U.S. distributor to clarify certain areas of the plot: A man (Robert Hoffman) meets a woman (Suzy Kendall) and they become romantically involved. When a mysterious killer makes an attempt on the man's life, he apparently murders the killer to defend himself, and they flee to a nearly deserted villa. Soon afterward we learn that this man has a brother (Ivan Rassimov) and that the both of them are in line for a large inheritance. It seems that the brother is driving the man insane while a murderer is killing women nearby. Can it be that *both* brothers are insane?

Lenzi's interesting approach to this horror thriller is to not show the murders on-screen. The audience has no idea who is committing these crimes and, as the film winds down to its conclusion, the possibility that there may be more than just one killer around is quite apparent. The American distributors reportedly hired American horror director George A. Romero to film an additional ten minutes of footage (including gore inserts for the murder scenes) to try to sort out any confusion that U.S. audiences might experience.

More successful was *Gatti Rossi in un Labirinto di Ventro* (1974), a film that entertains with its combination of an attractive cast and gruesome special effects. Tourists in Spain — a mentally disturbed woman (heading towards New York and a divorce), her husband, his secretary (also his lover), a deviate priest, a lesbian photographer, her fashion model lover and other quite appealing types — are menaced by a crazed killer who has a penchant for removing the eyes of his victims. Of course, in between the scenes of slaughtered victims, we are treated to several instances of sexual couplings among the cast members just to spice things up. This is another Lenzi film that performed well in its overseas theatrical release outside of Italy. It is a much-maligned work by Lenzi, but one that is enjoyable in its own sleazy '70s way: actors with big heads of hair, flare pants, lots of scenes of sexual abandon, mainly lesbian couplings featuring tons of nudity — and then there's the killings, yes the killings. What better way to gross out your audience than to remove eyes!

During the next several years, Lenzi mainly concentrated on violence-filled Mafia crime movies. Between 1974 and 1979, he directed at least a dozen of these productions. The best of these *Il Giustiziere Sfida la Città* (1975), *Il Trucido e lo Sbirro* (1976) and *Da Corleone a Brooklyn* (1978).

Mangiati Vivi (1980) saw Lenzi return to the shocking cannibal exploits of *Il Paese del Sesso Selvaggio*. Influenced by the advancements in special effects techniques as well as the controversy surrounding Ruggero Deodato's own related productions, Lenzi saw profits (or, in the case of problems with the Italian film board censors, at least overseas profits) in this new venture. Reuniting the casts from his own *Il Paese...* as well as the Deodato films, Lenzi's film is not unlike other installments in the genre. After a brutal attack from a mysterious killer in New York, a can of film is found featuring footage of atrocities committed (on humans and animals alike) in the jungle. A woman featured in the footage turns out to be the sister of Janet Agren who, with the aid of Bob Kerman (also known as Richard Bolla, a regular in '70s American porno movies), journeys to South America to learn what happened to her. Eventually, it is learned that a madman (Ivan Rassimov) who enforces his will over the natives and orders them to kill induces his followers to commit mass suicide.

It is a rough film to sit through. Just when you would think that Ruggero Deodato had the last word with the cannibal film genre, Lenzi comes back and attempts to reclaim this territory. The supporting cast, including Mel Ferrer, Paola Senatore and Me Me Lai, must have needed these paychecks badly, for their acting, such as it is, is as comical as the story. The gravest injustice is caused to the real-life animals supposedly slaughtered by the indigenous natives for the production.

Much better than this film, and, a highlight of Lenzi's horror filmography, is the wild *Incubo sulla Città Contaminata* (1980). Here, a dream-within-a-dream structure tells the tale of ferocious rampaging zombies who terrorize an entire European city, then the country with an attack of gory horror: After a nuclear power experiment goes horribly wrong, a planeload of physicians, medical and military personnel disembark at an airport in a major European city and begin a barrage of terror and death. These people had been exposed to a highly toxic substance that virtually kills the host bodies, then re-animates them into violently aggressive and very fast-moving zombies on a rampage for flesh! The circumstances begin to seem dire, the military powers can do little to curtail the onslaught of the murders of thousands, and civilians try to make their way out of the state to safety.

A very scary movie when it was released in 1981, it still retains some effective jolts. Lenzi's film moves quick — so quick, in fact, that the film's zombie-fied masses run, bearing with them axes, guns, pieces of wood, furniture and anything they can use to pry apart the human body. The film's gory special effects are quite primitive, but effective nonetheless. The story idea had been used countless times before and since, yet, there's a certain frisson to the frenzied slaughter, which reaches a highpoint when the zombies arrive at a hospital and catch the fleeing personnel. They tear at the clothing of an escaping nurse, ripping her flesh away, reaching inside her chest cavity for her warm, fresh organs. Disgusting and brutal, yet in the fantastic mind of Umberto Lenzi, this is an unsettling 90 minutes of horror to spend in a theater.

Cannibal Ferox (1981) is Lenzi's final cannibal film and one of the last in the cycle. In an attempt to explain away his reasoning for making these films, Lenzi's wacky story has a group of college graduates journey to the South American jungle to prove that the myth of cannibalism is a racist falsehood perpetrated by Caucasians. Of course, when they get to the deepest part of the jungle and encounter a crazed drug dealer who has been ruthlessly torturing the natives for his own depraved fun, these same natives retaliate in a "no holds barred" fashion. They become involved in one of the sickest slaughters ever filmed.

Rape, castration and wooden poles forced through orifices are just some of the most horrendous sites on view. Finally, the eating of the remains of the humans (not to mention what happens on-screen to animals) are among the other sick highlights of this film that frankly very few horror film cineastes would want to sit through more than once, let alone a first time. It just goes too far. After this film, Lenzi began to make sexy comedies of which *Cicciabomba* (1982) is the best.

La Casa No. 3 (a.k.a. *Ghost House*) (1987) was a return to the horror genre for Lenzi, but the familiar story, a house possessed by the vengeful ghost of a child, had by then become old and musty despite the addition of some gory effects. In 1988 Lenzi filmed *La Spiaggia del Terrore*, filmed on location in Fort Lauderdale, Florida, starring John Saxon and Michael Parks. When the leader of a violent gang of criminals is caught and executed for his crimes, murders are committed at one of the vacation resorts that American students crowd during the massive American holiday of debauchery known as Spring Break.

In 1989, Lenzi filmed two genre features for the Italian television program *Le Casa del Terrore* (a.k.a. *The House of Horrors*, or *The Houses of Doom*). Both *La Casa del Sortilegio* and *La Casa delle Anime Erranti* are disappointing thrillers. In *La Casa del Sortilegio*, a man (Andy J. Forrest) has recurring nightmares that truly horrify him. He journeys to an old house that figures into his dreams, thereby making his nightmarish dreams a reality. Although an eerie film, it is let down by its low production values. In *La Casa delle Anime Erranti*, a team of young geologists visits an abandoned hotel, only to encounter specters of horrible deeds committed in the past. These two films and Lucio Fulci's *La Casa del Tempo* and *La Dolce Casa degli Orrori* were the only four installments of the *Le Casa del Terrore* series.

However, *Le Porte dell'Inferno* (1989) is the kind of classical horror film rarely attempted by Lenzi in the past. Influences abound from the likes of Amando De

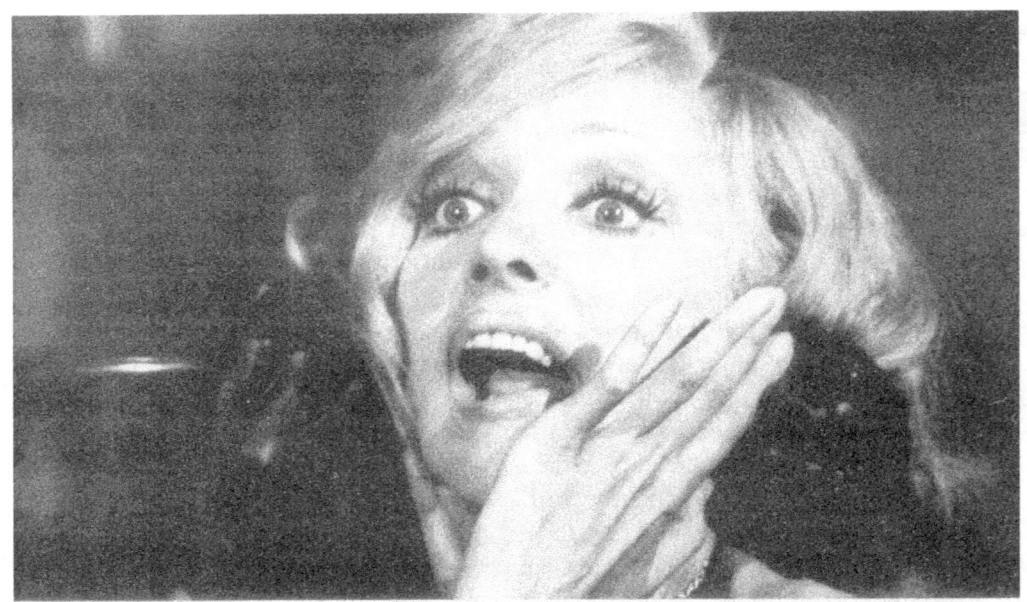

Scenes from Umberto Lenzi's *Sette Orchidee Macchiate di Rosso* (1972, Flora Film/National Cinematografica [Rome]/Rialto Film [Berlin]).

Ossorio's Templar Knights-Blind Dead series, Lamberto Bava's *Demoni* and Lucio Fulci's own *Paura nella Città dei Morti Viventi*. Here Lenzi adds his own spin. Archeologists and geologists investigating caverns located near the ruins of an ancient monastery find themselves trapped in an underground lair, menaced by a clan of undead monks. Seven centuries earlier, to the day, a group of monks, all satanic heretics, had been tortured, killed and buried in the ruins below the monastery. Now seven centuries later, they return to wreak vengeance on humankind.

Displaying a novel and chilling gothic atmosphere, Lenzi directs this horror film with a sure hand, squeezing every ounce of atmosphere from his cavernous locations. The film falters midway through when it veers into territory covered elsewhere (the superior Lamberto Bava–directed *Demoni* series), but until then, it elicits a fair share of shocks even from jaded audiences.

Paura nel Buio (1989), developed by Lenzi, produced and photographed by Aristide Massaccesi, was filmed entirely on location in Virginia. The nasty and brutal slasher movie is about a maniacal killer journeying the highways frequented by single female travelers. He is seeking victims for his obscene lust for torture and murder. Its title suggests that the film is an unofficial sequel to the superior 1986 Robert Harmon production *The Hitcher*, starring Rutger Hauer, but it is not.

In 1989, Lenzi also filmed *Cop Target*, a disappointing and violent cop buddy movie starring American B movie icons Charles Napier and Robert Ginty. In 1992 he directed David Warbeck in the first of a series of lazy adventure films called *Hornsby and Rodriguez*. To date, Lenzi's last genre credits have been *Demoni Neri* (1991), a horror film set in Brazil, and an unsuccessful 1992 attempt to film *Navigator: The Return*, an unofficial follow-up/rip-off of the clever Australian film *The Navigator* (1988). In *Demoni Neri* a group of people on holiday discover a voodoo ceremony in progress. They accidentally invoke the wrath of a priestess who conjures up black slave zombies, dead for a hundred years, to wreak vengeance upon these interlopers. Among Lenzi's most recent films is the apparently still unreleased *Sarayevo Inferno di Fuoco* (1996).

Umberto Lenzi's career has been a varied one. While he he did turn out some quite enjoyable action films in the '60s and some good thrillers in the '70s, he never consistently excelled at any one genre. In the end, he will probably be remembered most for his cannibal-themed horror films, nasty, repellent works of cinema that seemed to have found an audience of admirers looking for that extra thrill.

Umberto Lenzi Filmography

A 008 Operazione Stermino

A.k.a. *008 Operation Exterminate* (English translation), a.k.a. *A 008 Operazione Termino* (alternate Italian title) (1965) (It., Egypt); D/SP: Umberto Lenzi; Prod: Romana Film (Rome)/Coprofilm (Cairo); C: Augusto Tiezzi; M: Francesco Lavagnino; S: Ingrid Schoeller, Alberto Lupo, Ivano Staccioli, Dina De Santis, George Wang.

Apocalisse sul Fiume Giallo

A.k.a. *Apocalypse on the Yellow River*; a.k.a. *The End of the Yellow River* (English translations); a.k.a. *The Dam on the Yellow River*; a.k.a. *The Yellow River* (English titles) (1960)

(It., Fr.); D: Umberto Lenzi, Renzo Merusi; Prod. Co.: Unipictures/Major Film/Société Cinématographique Lyre (Paris); SC: Renzo Merusi, Vittoriano Petrilli, Giorgio Prosperi, Vinicio Marinucci; C: Enzo Serafin; M: Gian Stellari, Guido Robuschi; S: Anita Ekberg, Georges Marchal, Franca Bettoja, Jose Jaspe, Wang Jie, Mei Lan Chang, Milena Bettini.

Attentato ai Tre Grandi

A.k.a. *Attempt on the Three Great Powers*; a.k.a. *Attack on the Three Great Powers* (English translations); a.k.a. *Les Chiens Verts du Desert* (French title); a.k.a. *Funf Gegen Casablanca* (German title; translation: *Five Against Casablanca*); a.k.a. *Desert Commandos* (English title) (1967) (It., W.G., Fr.); D: Umberto Lenzi; P: Alberto Grimaldi; Prod. Co.: P.E.A.–Produzioni Europee Associate (Naples)/Terra Filmkunst (Berlin)/Films E.G.A. (Paris); SC: Umberto Lenzi, Johannes Billian; C: Carlo Carlini; M: Angelo Francesco Lavagnino; S: Ken Clark, Horst Frank, Jeanne Valerie, Carlo Hintermann, Gianni Rizzo.

Le Avventure di Mary Read

A.k.a. *The Adventures of Mary Read* (English translation); a.k.a. *Mary la Rousse Femme Pirate* (French title); a.k.a. *Hell Below Deck* (English title) (1961) (It., Fr.); D: Umberto Lenzi; P: Fortunato Misiano; Prod. Co.: Romana Film/Société Nouvelle de Cinématographie; SC: Luciano Martino, Ugo Guerra; C: Augusto Trezzi; M: Gino Filippini; S: Lisa Gastoni, Jerome Courtland, Walter Barnes, Germano Longo, Agostino Salvietti, Loris Gizzi, Dino De Santis.

Cannibal Ferox

A.k.a. *Make Them Die Slowly*; a.k.a. *Let Them Die Slowly* (English titles) (1981) (It.); D: Umberto Lenzi; P: Giovanni Masini; Prod. Co.: Dania Film/Medusa Distribuzione/National Cinematografica; SC: Umberto Lenzi; C: Giovanni Bergamini, Renato Doria, Maurizio Zampagni; M: Budy and Maglione, Carlo Maria Cordio; SP E: Gino De Rossi; S: Lorraine De Selle, John Morghen a.k.a. Giovanni Lombardo Radice, Zora Kerova a.k.a. Zora Ulla Keslerova Tschechin, Robert Bolla a.k.a. Robert Kerman a.k.a. Richard Kerman, Venantino Venantini.

La Casa dei Sortilegio

(1989) (It.); D: Umberto Lenzi; P: Massimo Manasse, Marco Grillo Spina; Prod. Co.: Dania Film/Natrional Cinematografica for Reteitalia, Milan; SC: Gianfranco Clerici, Daniele Stroppa; C: Giancarlo Ferrando; M: Claudio Simonetti; S: Andy J. Forrest, Sonia Petrovna, Susanna Martinkova, Marina Giulia Cavalli, Maria Stella Musy, Paul Muller a.k.a. Paul Mueller.
 Feature-length episode of the Italian television program *Le Casa del Terrore*.

La Casa della Anime Erranti

(1989) (It.); D: Umberto Lenzi; P: Massimo Manasse, Marco Grillo Spina; Prod. Co.: Dania Film/National Cinematografica for Reteitalia, Milan; SC: Umberto Lenzi; C: Giancarlo Ferrando; M: Claude King; S: Joseph Alan Johnson, Stefania Orsola Garello, Matteo Gazzolo, Laurentina Guidotti, Gianluigi Fogacci, Al Yamanouchi a.k.a. Haruiko Yamanouchi, Licia Colo, Cristiano Borromeo.
 Feature-length episode of the Italian television program *Le Casa del Terrore*.

La Casa No. 3

A.k.a. *House 3* (English translation); a.k.a. *Ghosthouse*; a.k.a. *Ghost House* (English titles) (1987) (It.); D: Umberto Lenzi; P: Aristide Massaccesi; Prod. Co.: Filmirage; SC: Cinthia McGavin (?), Shiela Goldberg; C: Franco Delli Colli; M: Piero Montanari; S: Lara Wendel, Gregg Scott, Mary Sellers, Kate Silver, Ron Houck, Martin Jay, Kristen Fougerousse.

Cicciabomba

A.k.a. *Gordinflona* (Spanish title) (1982) (It.); D: Umberto Lenzi; Prod. Co.: Emme R.T. Cineproduzione; SC: Giorgio Mariuzzo; C: Carlo Carlini; M: Claudio Rego; S: Ugo Bologna, Anita Ekberg, Paola Borboni, Adriana Russo, Dario Caporaso.

Il Coltello di Ghiaccio

A.k.a. *The Dagger of Ice*; a.k.a. *The Knife of Ice*; a.k.a. *The Knives of Ice* (English translations and titles); a.k.a. *Dietro del Silenzio* (alternate Italian title; translation: *Behind the Silence*); a.k.a. *The Ice Pick*; a.k.a. *The Ice-Pick*; a.k.a. *Silent Horror* (English titles) (1972) (It., Sp.); D: Umberto Lenzi; Prod. Co.: Tritone Cinematografica (Rome)/Mundial Film (Madrid); SC: Umberto Lenzi, Antonio Troisio; C: Jose F. Aguayo; M: Marcello Giombini; S: Carroll Baker, Alan Steel a.k.a. Sergio Ciani, Evelyn Stewart a.k.a. Ida Galli, Eduardo Fajardo, Sylvia Monelli, Jorge Rigaud.

Cop Target

(1989) (It., U.S.); D: Umberto Lenzi; P: Fabrizio De Angelis; SC: Raimondo Del Balzo; C: Giancarlo Ferrando; M: Lanfranco Parolini; S: Robert Ginty, Charles Napier, Franco Fantasia, Marsha L. McVay, Brenda Wismer.

Così Dolce ... Così Perversa

A.k.a. *So Sweet ... So Perverse* (English translation and title); a.k.a. *Si Douces, Si Perverses* (French title: *So Sweet, So Perverse*); a.k.a. *Die Süsse Sunderin* (German title; translation: *The Sweet Sinner*) (1969) (It., Fr., W.G.); D: Umberto Lenzi; P: Mino Loy, Luciano Martino; Prod. Co.: Flora Film/Tritone Filmindustria (Rome)/Zenith Cinematografica/ C.E.D.I.C. (Paris)/Rapid-Film (Munich); SC: Ernesto Gastaldi, Luciano Martino; C: Guglielmo Mancori; M: Riz Ortolani; S: Carroll Baker, Jean-Louis Trintignant, Erica Blanc a.k.a. Erica Bianchi Colombatto, Horst Frank, Helga Line a.k.a. Helga Lina Stern, Ermelinda De Felice, Gianni Di Bendetto.

Da Corleone a Brooklyn

A.k.a. *From Corleone to Brooklyn* (English translation and title) (1978) (It.); D: Umberto Lenzi; Prod. Co.: Primex Italiana; SC: Vincenzo Mannino; C: Guglielmo Mancori; M: Franco Micalizzi; S: Maurizio Merli, Mario Merola a.k.a. Mario Aufieri, Van Johnson, Laura Belli.

Demoni Neri

A.k.a. *Black Demons* (English translation and title); a.k.a. *Black Demoni* (alternate Italian title?); a.k.a. *Demoni 3* (alternate Italian title; translation: *Demons 3*) (1991) (It.); D: Umberto Lenzi; P: Giuseppe Gargiulo; Prod. Co.: Filmakers Group; SC: Umberto Lenzi, Olga Pehar;

C: Maurizio Dell'Orco; M: Franco Micalizzi; SP E: Franco Casagni; S: Keith Van Hooven, Joseph Baloghi, Sonia Curtis, Philip Murray, Juliana Texeira, Maria Alves.

Gatti Rossi in un Labirinto di Ventro

A.k.a. *Red Cats in a Labyrinth of Glass* (English translation); a.k.a. *L'Occhio Sbarrato nel Buio* (alternate Italian title; translation: *Wide-Eyed in the Dark*); a.k.a. *El Ojo en la Oscuridad* (Spanish title; translation: *The Eye in the Darkness*); a.k.a. *The Devil's Eye*; a.k.a. *Eyeball*; a.k.a. *The Secret Killer* (English titles) (1974) (It., Sp.); D: Umberto Lenzi; P: Jose Maria Cunilles; Prod. Co.: Pioneer National Cinematografica (Rome)/Estela Film (Madrid); SC: Umberto Lenzi, Felix Tusell; C: Antonio Millan; M: Bruno Nicolai; S: John Richardson, Martine Brochard, Ines Pellegrini, Andres Mejuto, Mirta Miller, Daniele Vargas, Georges Rigaud, Sylvia Solar, Raf Baldassare, Jose Maria Blanco, Marta May.

Il Giustiziere Sfida la Città

A.k.a. *One Just Man* (GB title); *Rambo's Revenge* (New Zealand and U.S. video title); a.k.a. *Syndicate Sadists* (U.S. theatrical and alternate video title) (1975) (It.); D: Umberto Lenzi; Prod. Co: Dania Film; SC: Umberto Lenzi, Daniele Alabiso; C: Vincenzo Mannino; M: Franco Micalizzi; S: Tomas Milian a.k.a. Tomas Rodriguez, Joseph Cotten, Maria Fiore, Luciano Pigozzi.

Hornsby e Rodriguez

A.k.a. *Hornsby and Rodriguez* (English translation and title); a.k.a. *Mean Tricks* (English title) (1992) (It.); D: Umberto Lenzi; Prod. Co.: Trinidad Film; SC: Vittorio M. Testa, Steven Luotto, Antonio Miglietta; C: Marco Onorato; M: Franco Micalizzi; S: David Warbeck, Charles Napier, Stefano Sabelli, Iris Peynado, David Brandon a.k.a. David Caine Haughton, Bettina Giovanni, Salvatore Lago, Stelio Candelli.

Incubo sulla Città Contaminata

A.k.a. *Nightmare of the Contaminated City* (English translation and title); a.k.a. *Horror 2* (Italian pre-production title); a.k.a. *Terror 2* (alternate Italian pre-production title); a.k.a. *Nightmare* (alternate Italian pre-production title); a.k.a. *Ataque de los Zombies Atomicos* (Spanish title); a.k.a. *La Invasión de los Zombies Atomicos* (alternate Spanish title); a.k.a. *City of the Walking Dead*; a.k.a. *Invasion by the Atomic Zombies*; a.k.a. *Invasion of the Atomic Monsters*; a.k.a. *Nightmare City* (English titles) (1980) (It., Sp.); D: Umberto Lenzi; P: Diego Alchimede, Luis Mendez, Mario Molli; Prod. Co.: Dialchi Film (Rome)/Lotus Film International (Madrid); SC: Antonio Cesare Corti, Piero Regnoli, Jose Luis Maria Delgado; C: Hans Burman, Mario Sbrenna, Giulio Battiferri; M: Stelvio Cipriani; SP E: Giuseppe Farranti, Franco Di Girolami; S: Hugo Stiglitz, Laura Trotter, Mel Ferrer, Francisco Rabal, Maria Rosaria Omaggio, Sonia Viviani, Eduardo Fajardo, Manolo Zarzo, Alejandro De Enciso.

L'Invincible Cavaliere Mascherato

(1963) (It., Fr.); D: Umberto Lenzi; P: Fortunato Misano; Prod. Co.: Romana Film (Italy)/Société Nouvelle de Cinématographie (France); SC: Gino De Sanctis, Luciano Martino, Guido Malatesta; C: Augusto Tiezzi; M: Angelo Francesco Lavagnino; S: Pierre Brice, Helene Chanel, Daniele Vargas, Massimo Serato, Aldo Bufi Landi, Carlo Latimer.

Kriminal

A.k.a. *La Mascara de Kriminal* (Spanish title) (1966) (It., Sp.); D: Umberto Lenzi; P: Claudio Teramo, Giancarlo Marchetti; Prod. Co.: Filmes Cinematografica (Rome)/Estela Films (Madrid)/Coop. Copercines (Madrid); SC: Umberto Lenzi, David Moreno Mingote; C: Angelo Lotti; M: Raymond Full, Roberto Pregadio; S: Glen Saxon a.k.a. Roel Bos, Helga Line a.k.a. Helga Lina Stern, Andrea Bosic, Armando Calvo, Mary Arden.

La Legione dei Dannati

A.k.a. *The Legion of the Damned* (English translation); a.k.a. *Die zum Teufel Gehen* (German title); a.k.a. *La Brigada de los Condenados* (Spanish title); a.k.a. *Battle of the Commandos* (English title) (1968) (It., Sp., W.G.); D: Umberto Lenzi; P: Bruno Bolognesi, Ignacio Gutierrez, Adriano Merkel; Prod. Co.: Tritone Filmindustria Roma (Rome)/Eguiluz Films (Madrid)/Hape Film (Munich); SC: Dario Argento, Rolf Grieminger, Eduardo M. [Maria] Brochero; C: Allejandro Ulloa; M: Marcello Giombini; S: Jack Palance a.k.a.Vladimir Dalamik, Thomas Hunter, Wolfgang Preiss, Helmuth Schneider, Curd Jurgens, Robert Hundar a.k.a. Claudio Undari.

Mangiati Vivi

A.k.a. *Eaten Alive* (English translation); a.k.a. *Mangiati Vivi dai Cannibali* (alternate Italian title; translation: *Eaten Alive by the Cannibals*); a.k.a. *The Emerald Forest*; a.k.a. *Doomed to Die* (English titles) (1980) (It.); D: Umberto Lenzi; P: Luciano Martino, Mino Loy, Giovanni Masini, Antonio Crescenzi; Prod. Co.: Dania Film/Nazionale Cinematografica/Medusa Distribuzione; SC: Umberto Lenzi; C: Federico Zanni, Roberto Lombardo, Guglielmo Vincioni; M: Carlo Maria Cordio, Maria Fiamma Maglione; SP E: Paolo Ricci; S: Ivan Rassimov, Janet Agren, Paola Senatore, Robert Bolla a.k.a. Robert Kerman a.k.a. Richard Kerman, Mel Ferrer, Me Me Lai, Franco Fantasia.

Milano Rovente

A.k.a. *Red-Hot Milan*; a.k.a. *Gang War in Milan* (English titles) (1973) (It.); D: Umberto Lenzi; Prod. Co.: Lombard Films (Milan); SC: Umberto Lenzi, Franco Enna; C: Lamberto Caimi; M: Carlo Rustichelli; S: Philippe Leroy, Antonio Sabato, Antonio Casagrande, Carla Romanelli, Alessandro Sperli.

Un Milione di Dollari per Sette Assassini

A.k.a. *A Million Dollars for Seven Assassins* (English translation and title); a.k.a. *Last Man to Kill* (English title) (1966) (It.); D: Umberto Lenzi; P: Fortunato Misiano; Prod. Co.: Romana Film; SC: Umberto Lenzi, Giorgio Clerici; C: Augusto Tiezzi; M: Angelo Francesco Lavagnino; S: Roger Browne, Jose Greci, Carlo Hintermann, Antonio Gradoli, Dina De Santis.

Orgasmo

A.k.a. *Orgasm*; a.k.a. *Une Folle Envie d'Amiere* (French title; translation: *The Mad Desire of Friends*); a.k.a. *Paranoia* (English title) (1968) (It., Fr.); D: Umberto Lenzi; Prod. Co.: Tritone Filmindustria (Rome)/Société Nouvelle de Cinématographie (Paris); SC: Umberto Lenzi, Ugo Moretti, Marie Claire Solleville; C: Guglielmo Mancori; M: Piero Umiliani; S: Carroll Baker, Lou Castel, Colette Descombres, Lilla Brignone, Tino Carraro, Franco Pesce, Tina Lattanzi.

Il Paese del Sesso Selvaggio

A.k.a. *Deep River Savages*; a.k.a. *The Man from Deep River*; a.k.a. *Mirage*; a.k.a. *Sacrifice!* (English titles) (1972) (It.); D: Umberto Lenzi; P: M.G. Rossi; Prod. Co.: Roas Produzione/Medusa Film Distribuzione; SC: Francesco Barilli, Massimo D'Avack; C: Riccardo Pallottini; M: Daniele Patucchi; S: Ivan Rassimov, Me Me Lai, Pratitsak Singhara, Sulallewan Suwantat, Ong Ard, Prapas Chindang, Tuan Tevan.

Paranoia

A.k.a. *Una Droga Llamada Helen* (Spanish title; translation: *A Drug Called Helen*); a.k.a. *A Quiet Place to Kill* (English title) (1970) (It., Sp.); D/P: Umberto Lenzi; Prod. Co.: Tritone Filmindustria (Rome)/Medusa Distribuzione (Rome)/Société Nouvelle de Cinématographie/Producciones Cinematograficas D.I.A. (Madrid); SC: Marcello Coscia, Rafeal Romero Merchant, Bruno Di Geronimo, Marie-Claire Solleville; C: Guglielmo Mancori; M: Gregory Garcia Segura; S: Carroll Baker, Jean Sorel, Luis Davila, Alberto Dalbes, Marina Coffa, Anna Proclemer, Hugo Blanco, Liz Halvorsen.

Paura nel Buio

A.k.a. *Fear in the Dark* (English translation); a.k.a. *Hitcher 2: Paura nel Buio* (alternate Italian title); a.k.a. *Hitcher in the Dark*; a.k.a. *Hitcher 2*; a.k.a. *The Return of the Hitcher*; a.k.a. *Camper* (English titles) (1989) (It.); D: Umberto Lenzi; P: Aristide Massaccesi; Prod. Co.: Filmirage Productions/Production Group; SC: Umberto Lenzi, Olga Pehar; M: Pietro Montanari; S: Josie Bisset, Joe Balogli, Jason Sancier, Robin Fox, Thomas Mitchell, Tom Schultheis, Todd Livingston.

Il Pirati della Malesia

A.k.a. *The Pirates of Malaysia* (English translation); a.k.a. *Les Pirates de Malaisie* (French title); a.k.a. *Los Piratos de Malasia* (Spanish title) (1964) (It., Fr., Sp.); D: Umberto Lenzi; P: Solly V. Bianco; Prod. Co.: Euro International Films/Sirius (Paris)/Ocean Film (Spain); SC: Ugo Liberatore, Nino Stresa, Gerard Cohen; C: Angelo Lotti; M: Giovanni Fusco; S: Steve Reeves, Jacqueline Sassard, Andrea Bosic, Mimmo Palmara.

Le Porte dell'Inferno

A.k.a. *The Gates of Hell*; a.k.a. *Hell's Gate* (English translations and titles) (1989) (It.); D: Umberto Lenzi; P: Umberto Lenzi, Antonio Lucidi; SC: Umberto Lenzi, Olga Pehar Lenzi; C: Sandro Mancori; M: Piero Montanari; S: Giacomo Rossi-Stuart, Barbara Cupisti, Pietro Genuardi, Mario Luzzi, Gaetano Russo.

Un Posto Ideale per Uccidere

A.k.a. *An Ideal Place for Murder*; a.k.a. *An Ideal Place to Kill* (English translation and title); a.k.a. *Un Endroit Ideal pour Tuer* (French title; translation: *An Ideal Place to Kill*); a.k.a. *Meurtre par Interim* (alternate French title; translation: *Murder in the Interim*); a.k.a. *Oasis of Fear*; a.k.a. *Deadly Trap*; a.k.a. *Dirty Pictures* (English titles) (1971) (It., Fr.); D: Umberto Lenzi; P: Carlo Ponti Cinematografica, Luciano Piperno; Prod. Co.: Champion (Rome)/Les Films Concorde (Paris); SC: Umberto Lenzi, Lucia Drudi Demby, Antonio Altoviti; C: Alfio Contini; M: Bruno Lauzi, song "How Can You Live Your Life?" performed by Raymond Lovelock; S: Irene Papas, Raymond Lovelock, Ornella Muti, Michel Bardinet, Jacques Stany, Umberto D'Orsini, Calisto Calisti, Salvatore Borgese, Giuseppe Terranova, Umberto Raho.

Sandokan il Maciste della Giungla

A.k.a. *Le Temple d'Éléphants Blancs* (French title; translation: *Temple of the White Elephants*) (1964) (It., Fr.); D: Umberto Lenzi; P: Solly V. Bianco; Prod. Co.: Filmes Cinematografica/ Capitole Films (Paris); SC: Umberto Lenzi, Fulvio Gicca-Palli, based on characters created by Emilio Salgari; C: Angelo Lotti; M: Georges Garavarentz; S: Sean Flynn, Marie Versini, Alessandra Panaro, Arturo Dominici, Giacomo Rossi-Stuart, Mimmo Palmara, Seyna Seyn, Jacques Herlin.

Sandokan la Tigre di Mompracen

A.k.a. *Sandokan le Tigre di Borneo*; a.k.a. *Sandokan*; a.k.a. *Sandokan the Great* (English titles) (1963) (It., Sp., Fr.); D: Umberto Lenzi; P: Solly V. Bianco; Prod. Co.: Filmes Cinematografica/Ocean Films (Madrid)/Comptoir Francais du Film Production (Paris); SC: Umberto Lenzi, Fulvio Gicca-Palli, based on the novel by Emilio Salgari; C: Aurelio Gutierrez Larrata, Angelo Lotti, Giovanni Scarpellini; M: Giovanni Fusco; S: Steve Reeves, Genevieve Grad, Andrea Bosic, Maurice Poli, Rik Battaglia, Joaquin Oliveras.

Sette Orchidee Macchiate di Rosso

A.k.a. *Seven Orchids Stained in Red*; a.k.a. *Seven Orchids for the Murderer* (English translations and titles); a.k.a. *Das Rätsel des Silbernen Halbmonds* (German title translation: *The Puzzle of the Silver Half Moons*) (1972) (It., W.G.); D: Umberto Lenzi; Prod. Co.: Flora Film/National Cinematografica (Rome)/Rialto Film (Berlin); SC: Umberto Lenzi, Roberto Gianviti; C: Angelo Lotti; M: Riz Ortolani; S: Antonio Sabato, Uschi Glass, Pier Paolo Capponi, Rossella Falk, Marina Malfatti, Renato Romano, Claudio Gora, Gabrielle Giorgelli, Marisa Mell a.k.a. Marlies Moitzi.

Spasmo

(1974) (It.); D: Umberto Lenzi, George A. Romero (uncredited, shot additional footage for American version); P: Ugo Tocci; Prod. Co.: UTI Produzioni Cinematiche; SC: Umberto Lenzi, Massimo Franciosa, Luisa Montagnana, Pino Boller; C: Guglielmo Mancori; M: Ennio Morricone; S: Robert Hoffman a.k.a. Hans Schmidt a.k.a. Max Lindt, Suzy Kendall, Ivan Rassimov, Adolfo Lastrett, Maria Pia Conte, Franco Silva, Monica Monet, Guido Alberti, Luigi Antonio Guerra.

La Spiaggia del Terrore

A.k.a. *The Beach of Terror* (English translation); a.k.a. *La Spiaggia del Terrore* (alternate Italian title); a.k.a *Welcome to Spring Break* (English title) (1989) (It./Panama/U.S.); D: Umberto Lenzi; P: William J. Immerman; Prod. Co.: Laguna Entertainment for Elpico S.A.; SC: Umberto Lenzi, Vittorio Rambaldi; C: Antonio Climati; M: Claudio Simonetti; S: Michael Parks, John Saxon a.k.a. Carmine Orrico, Nicolas De Toth, Sarah Buxton, Rawley Valverde, Lance Le Gault.

Le Spie Amano i Fiori

A.k.a. *The Spy Who Loved Flowers* (English translation); a.k.a *Gran Dragon Espia Invisible* (Spanish title); a.k.a. *Spies Love Flowers* (English title) (1966) (It., Sp.); D/SC: Umberto Lenzi; P: Fortunato Misano; Prod. Co.: Romana Film (Rome)/Leda Films (Madrid); C: Augusto Tiezzi; M: Angelo Francesco Lavagnino, Armando Travajoli; S: Roger Browne, Salvatore Borgese, Emma Danieli, Yoko Tani, Dario Michaelis.

Superseven Chiama Cairo

A.k.a. *Superseven Calling Cairo* (English translation and title); a.k.a. *Super 7 Appelle le Sphinx* (French title) (1965) (It., Fr.); D: Umberto Lenzi; Prod. Co.: Romana Film (Rome)/Prodex (Paris); SC: Umberto Lenzi, Piero Pierotti; C: Augusto Tiezzi; M: Angelo Francesco Lavagnino; S: Roger Browne, Massimo Serato, Fabienne Dali, Antonio Grandoli, Dina De Santis, Rosalba Neri.

Il Trionfo di Robin Hood

A.k.a. *The Triumph of Robin Hood* (English translation) (1962) (It.); D: Umberto Lenzi; P: Tiziano Longo; Prod. Co.: Buona Vista Produzione Italiana Film; SC: Giancarlo Romitelli, Moraldo Rossi, based on the stories of "Robin Hood"; C: Angelo Filippini; M: Aldo Pigga; S: Don Burnett, Gia Scala, Vincenzo Musolino, Germano Longo.

Il Trucido e lo Sbirro

A.k.a. *Free Hand for a Tough Cop* (English title) (1976) (It.); D: Umberto Lenzi; Prod. Co.: S.G.M. Film/Variety Film; SC: Umberto Lenzi, Dardano Sacchetti; C: Luigi Kuveiller, Nino Sebastiano Celeste; M: Bruno Canfora; S: Tomas Milian a.k.a. Tomas Rodriguez, Claudio Cassinelli, Nicoletta Machiavelli, Robert Hundar a.k.a. Claudio Undari, Henry Silva.

Tutto per Tutto

A.k.a. *One for All* (English translation); a.k.a. *La Hora del Coraje* (Spanish title); a.k.a. *Go for Broke*; a.k.a. *All Out*; a.k.a. *Copper Face* (English titles) (1968) (It., Sp.); D: Umberto Lenzi; Prod. Co.: P.E.A. Produzioni Europee Associate (Naples)/Estela Films (Madrid); SC: Nino Stresa, Eduardo Brochero; C: Alejandro Ulloa; M: Marcello Giombini; S: Mark Damon, John Ireland, Raf Baldassarre, Fernando Sancho, Monica Randall, Spartaco Conversi, Armando Calvo, Eduardo Fajardo.

Una Pistola per Cento Bare

A.k.a. *A Pistol for One Hundred Coffins*; a.k.a. *One Pistol for One Hundred Graves* (English translation and title); a.k.a. *La Malle de San Antonio*; a.k.a. *El Sabor del Odio* (Spanish title) (1968) (It., Sp.); D: Umberto Lenzi; Prod. Co.: Tritone/Copercines; SC: Umberto Lenzi, Vittorio Salerno, Marco Letto; C: Alejandro Ulloa; M: Angelo Francesco Lavagnino; S: Peter Lee Lawrence, John Ireland, Gloria Orsuna, Eduardo Fajardo, Victor Israel, Julio Pena, Raf Baldassare, Andrea Scotti.

Zorro Contro Maciste

A.k.a. *Samson and the Slave Queen* (English title) (1963) (It.); D: Umberto Lenzi; P: Fortunato Misiano; Prod. Co.: Romana Film; SC: Umberto Lenzi, Guido Malatesta; C: Augusto Tiezzi; M: Angelo Francesco Lavagnino; S: Pierre Brice, Alan Steel a.k.a. Sergio Ciani, Moira Orfei, Grazia Maria Spina.

Antonio Margheriti

Antonio Margheriti was born on September 19, 1930, in Rome, Italy. Initially schooled as an engineer, Margheriti joined the Centro Sperimentale Centrale (C.S.C.) film school in 1950. Upon his graduation, he found work on documentary film projects as an assistant, further exploring his interest in the cinema. Between 1957 and 1960, he worked as an assistant director, editor and screenwriter for a number of professional film projects. At some point in time, before 1960, Margheriti worked on a proposed documentary project about an actual earthquake that shattered some regions of Italy; he constructed some small-scale models to elaborate on the destruction caused. Although this film was ultimately never made, his apparent talent with model making caught the attention of that ill-fated film's producer. Coupled with his assignments as an assistant on a variety of projects, his model work helped to earn him his first feature film as a director. His debut, the science fiction film *Spazzio Uomini* (1960), was a success, partly due to it being one of the first science fiction films ever made in Italy (with special effects scenes set in space itself) and partly due to Margheriti's clever script (without the then-standard elements of racism or sexism) which cast a black male and a young white woman in prominent roles. His idea of a Utopian future must have had a lot of young men and women daydreaming about the frontiers beyond the clouds. As for the film's special effects, in retrospect they are primitive but adequately serve the purpose of the plot, given the evidently extremely low budget.

In 1961, Margheriti followed this film with *Il Pianeta degli Uomini Spenti*, another science fiction feature. This movie is not about space exploration but the combined efforts of Earth's top scientific minds to stop a colossal asteroid from slamming into the planet. The presence of aging star Claude Rains in the lead role of the main scientist adds a certain distinguished atmosphere to the proceedings

Antonio Margheriti.

and the film does maintain an eerie ambience once a spaceship lands on the asteroid in the hopes of destroying it before it reaches Earth.

In 1962, Margheriti directed his first costume adventure, *L'Arciere delle Mille e Una Notte,* starring an American teen heartthrob of the era, Tab Hunter. For the next two years, he continued to work on historical epics, making costume films on low budgets with spectacular-looking sets, courtesy of his ingenious special effects knowledge. In 1964, he directed one of the great, classic gothic horror films, *La Danza Macabre.* This film is a richly photographed (by Riccardo Pallottini) exercise about a female ghost (Barbara Steele) who is damned to spend eternity with a collection of malicious misfits in the eerie confines of a derelict mansion.

A journalist (Georges Riviere) spends a good portion of the night drinking with the famed poet and author Edgar Allan Poe in hopes of gaining an exclusive interview for his newspaper. Poe's companion, a wealthy man, puts forth a bet that if the journalist can last the night in an old mansion that is supposedly haunted, not only will he win considerable money, but Poe would surely agree to an interview the next morning. Once deposited on the grounds of the mansion, the man spends his time investigating dusty, musty, cobweb-filled rooms until strange sounds make him think that he's not alone. Before long, the stunning Elizabeth

(Steele) appears and he is immediately drawn to her. She offers little information about herself and disappears quickly. Then the man meets other inhabitants of the large estate, but he cannot interact with them and they do not seem to see *him*. Upon learning from a heretical experimenter and occultist that the rooms are all full of the undead who attempt to lure new souls to join in their revelry, the journalist thinks he's losing his mind, until Elizabeth confirms that she is in fact also dead. Still thinking that there is a way to escape the inevitableness of his situation, at dawn the journalist and Elizabeth attempt to gain their freedom and reach the gates that surround the sinister mansion.

Allegedly based upon an unpublished Poe story but in all probability influenced by his writings, Margheriti's film is one of the best of the Italian Gothic horror movies of the '60s. It revels in its haunted castle clichés, richly textured black-and-white photography and sensual crimes of passion that were responsible for the dead remaining "haunted" spirits. Steele, well-chosen to portray the mysterious, alluring and undead Elizabeth, delivers one of her finest performances, far outshining her fellow cast members.

Also in 1964, Margheriti returned to the peplum genre with *Anthar l'Invincible* and directed *Il Pelo nel Mondo*, a mondo film about the strange customs of third world nations and those of the equally strange, bourgeois and supposedly civilized European continents. That same year, as more productions moved from black-and-white to color, Margheriti made his last black-and-white Gothic horror film, *I Lunghi Capelli della Morte*. In the sixteenth century, the wife (Barbara Steele) of a wealthy count is tortured and burned at the stake as a witch, for crimes committed by the count's son (Giorgio Ardisson). Her two daughters (Steele and Halina Zalewska) witness the horrible death of their mother. Rising from the grave for vengeance, Steele frightens the count to death and, with her appearance slightly altered, garners the attention of the count's son, her next victim.

The movie, the last of the black-and-white Gothic horror films, is a fine, often dramatic supernatural exercise in romantic horror. Margheriti fills the screen in bright whites and grays, with little black to color his interesting ethereal imagery. The film's highlight of terror is when a thunderbolt splits the tomb of the dead Helen (Steele) to reveal her worm-ridden face.

Margheriti's first color horror film *La Vergine di Norimberga* (1964) is a mix of the Gothic style he used for the features *La Danza Macabre* and *I Lunghi Capelli della Morte,* and a much more aberrant tone of sadism and graphic horror. A newlywed couple (Georges Riviere and Rossana Podesta) arrives at the groom's vast estate in Germany. Podesta gets no respect from the staff or from her husband's loyal, disfigured manservant (Christopher Lee). She spends lonely hours walking the grounds during the day while her husband is away on business. Meanwhile, a hooded killer, driven insane by tortures inflicted upon him by others, captures young maidens and servants to inflict equally gruesome tortures upon them in the dungeons below.

As a ghostly presence, Barbara Steele captivates Georges Riviere before he learns her true identity in Margheriti's *La Danza Macabra* (1964, Vulsinia Film/Jolly Film [Rome]/Leo Lax Film/Ulysee Film).

The film's beautiful location photography and colorful cinematography amplify the overwhelming sense of dread on the chief location, what was essentially a sprawling castle estate. This lifeless, ominous character assists the audience in accepting the foreboding atmosphere with every sweeping camera pan (both interior and exterior). The extraordinary cruel torture scenes depict the maniac placing the victims inside a spiked Iron Maiden, or another having a small cage placed over her head with a starving rat inside. This film still achieves some effective scares and helped to point to the darker new wave of Italian horror.

Margheriti ended the year by working on two interesting sword-and-sandal projects, the horror-themed *Ursus, il Terrore dei Kirghisi* with Reg Park and the larger budgeted *I Giganti di Roma* with Richard Harrison. Margheriti never finished the *Ursus* film due to a disagreement with the film's producers and the movie was completed (uncredited) by Ruggero Deodato, his assistant at the time.

In 1965, Margheriti made a quartet of highly regarded science fiction films, *I Criminali della Galassia, I Diafanoidi Vengono da Marte, La Morte Viene dal Pianeta Aytin* and *Missione Pianeta Errante*. Initially planned as co-productions between Italian producers and American International Pictures, three of the features received funding assistance from Metro-Goldwyn-Mayer, which enabled the director to pump more money into the projects to emphasize the special effects. *I Criminali della Galassia,* which contains bizarre horror themes, stars Tony Russell as the commander of an orbiting space station under the guidance of a new quasi-political law-and-order establishment on Earth; he has his hands full trying to keep his romance with the first lieutenant (Lisa Gastoni) a secret. A scientist (Massimo Serato) with political ties on Earth has chosen to perform some strange experiments with disembodied organs (and body parts) on the station. During a drunken fight with her lover, Gastoni accepts Serato's invitation to visit his mysterious experimental planet for a holiday. Meanwhile, back on Earth, strange bald humanoid beings with several arms, wearing black vampiric cloaks, are assaulting key personnel of the Space Command as well as mere civilians who disappear mysteriously. Apparently, under the control of cruel karate-fighting women, the humanoids shrink the people to doll-size to transport them to Serato's planet for bizarre experiments.

The film foreshadows the brilliant, hyper-psychedelic, science fiction–fantasy writings of the author Michael Moorcock (especially his *The Final Programme*, a tale not dissimilar from the Frankenstein theme explored in *I Criminali della Galassia*) by several years. The sets, costumes and special effects all reveal a care and attention that rarely had been given to such product at the time.

In 1966, the director joined the profitable parade of fellow film technicians who were churning out European spy films. His contributions to this genre, *A 077 Sfida ai Killers* and *Operazione Goldman*, while entertaining, reveal their low budgets in the often poorly photographed and obviously cheaply produced models and special effects. Although enlivened with touches of science fiction themes, the films are rather flat and uninspired despite being loaded with a supporting cast of attractive genre starlets: Wandisa Guida, Diana Lorys, Janine Reynaud and Mitsouko.

An unsuccessful attempt to mold the European spy film phenomena onto the Western, *Joe l'Implacabile* (1967) was an entertaining film that failed at the box office. Margheriti's thriller *Nude ... Si Muore* (1967) is another film filled with interesting, quirky character roles for its cast members (Michael Rennie, Mark Damon, etc.). But it fails to transcend its own weakly scripted material and, despite some clever turns and twists in the plot, along with some well-staged murders, the movie crumbles under the weight of its own carelessness. The Western *Joko, Invoca Dio ... e Muori* (1968) followed. The brutal, gothic-flavored revenge film featured a man who finds the drawn and quartered remains of a friend, removes the ropes that had bound his arms and legs and seeks retribution by using the same ropes to murder those responsible, including the film's incredibly over-the-top, evil villain.

Il Contronatura (1969) is a fine horror film that has been unjustly maligned. Margheriti's penchant for combining influences and visual references from other sources into this film may be the reason *Contronatura* is a tale of the supernatural. Several travelers, all with decidedly sinister pasts, end up at an old mansion where a medium and her companion plan on holding a séance and eventually reveal the dangerous deeds committed by the attendees. The theme, that the spiritualists may, in fact, be angels of death, reminding the guests of their mortality, is one with which few genre films have experimented.

The year 1969 also saw the release of *E Dio Disse a Caino*, a fabulously dark Western, featuring a striking, nearly silent performance by Klaus Kinski. Although the film might be considered little more than a standard revenge melodrama in a western setting, it is much more than that. The film tells of the violent revenge a man has sworn to take for the years he has languished in prison. Taking place almost entirely at night, the murders of a seemingly endless array of hired hands and gunfighters are elaborately staged within high churning winds in a nearly deserted town. A clever film, it evokes elements of the horror genre at times and foreshadows the endless assaults that have become such a staple in today's action films due to the influence of the Asian director John Woo. As a point of reference, the non-stop violence often invokes contemporary comparisons with similar moments in *The Killer* (1989).

That same year, the astoundingly bad *L'Inafferabile, Invincibile Mr. Invisible* starring Dean Jones appeared. It is a failed attempt by Margheriti to combine the slapstick charms of Italian comedy with the wholesome family entertainment of a Disney film. It ends up being an empty, barren film containing a rehashed spy plot device about a nerdy professor who shows no more attention to the fabulous femme fatales than he does to his loyal dog. In the hopes that the Disney studios might be interested in a co-production, Margheriti had proposed a film about the life and adventures of Baron Munchausen. One of his dream projects throughout the early '70s, this film was designed to feature Klaus Kinski as the fabled Munchausen and Dean Jones as the last heir in the family line. The project was never made.

In 1970, Margheriti was approached by the same producer who had financed *La Danza Macabre* to direct a remake of that film. *Nella Stretta Morsa del Ragno* remains one of his best works in the genre. Strangely enough, it overshadows the earlier work *La Danza Macabre* with its more deliberate, dramatically centered performances and an even greater mood of despair whilst, at times, it is overshadowed by *La Danza Macabre*'s link to the Gothic cinema of the early '60s and the unequaled performance of Barbara Steele. The remake features the French actress Michele Mercier in the Steele role and American actor Anthony Franciosa in the Georges Riviere role of the journalist. Franciosa's role is one of his finest acting performances, ranging from quiet wonder to extreme hysteria over the course of the film. Klaus Kinski appears in a wonderfully bizarre cameo as Edgar Allan Poe.

Margheriti's remake of his own best film is one that, more often than not, has been met with unjustifiable scorn and contempt from hardcore fans of the Italian Gothic cinema. In fact, *Nella Stretta...* more than holds its own, although only Franciosa manages to register any emotional tie to the material. Mercier, a French actress who had been cast at the request of the producers, cannot hold a candle to the quiet, somnambulant terror that Barbara Steele displayed in the original film. With the modern conveniences of color, gore and a nude lesbian scene, the updated version has some qualities all its own.

During the next few years, Margheriti became attached as director to a number of projects that failed to find any release outside of his native Italy. Among these were *Finalmente ... Le Mille e Una Notte* (1972), a sex film set in historical times featuring the then-reigning queens of such films, Barbara Bouchet and Edwige Fenech, and *Novelle Galeotte d'Amore* (1972), another sex comedy set in medieval times.

In 1973, Margheriti returned to the horror genre for *La Morte negli Occhi del Gatto*. This film, about a group of nasty, hedonistic relatives out to gain a possible inheritance in a gloomy castle, has in its favor interesting sets filled with endless dark corridors and crypts with rotting corpses. The cast headed by the controversial real-life French lovers (and pop music sensations) Serge Gainsbourg and Jane Birkin seem detached and not used to working in a horror film milieu: A group of relatives have gathered at a secluded mansion for the reading of a will. Each one of them hopes to inherit a sum of money or land, left to them by the castle patriarch, an unpleasant person who had always feared that the family curse (metamorphosing into a large, feral cat creature) would overtake him. The jealous, bickering relatives are less concerned with this alleged curse and more with who among them may be the maniacal killer who is reducing their number.

Margheriti's thriller fails in its attempts to gain interest from the potential audiences for which this film was intended. The movie looks ugly and drab, courtesy of the terrible lighting and unimaginative photography by Carlo Carlini. The director's trump card, the casting of the controversial real-life lovers Birkin and Gainsbourg, does nothing for the film. They are as stiff as the rest of the cast, save for frequent Margheriti presence Luciano Pigozzi, who is always a joy to watch as he frightfully chews the scenery.

Margheriti then entered into an agreement to co-write, co-produce and direct a number of films with Giorgio Simonelli. Together they featured two actors (one of them Brad Harris) who, under the pseudonyms Fred Harris and Tom Scott, starred in a trio of comedy features. Only one of these films, the delirious action comedy *Ming, Ragazzi!* (1973), is known to have been released outside of Italy.

The controversial Andy Warhol–Paul Morrissey productions were also filmed during this period (1973). Both *Il Mostro È in Tavola ... Barone Frankenstein* (a.k.a. *Carne per Frankenstein*) and *Dracula Cerca Sangue di Vergine ... È Morì di Sete!* (a.k.a. *Sangue per Dracula*) were Italian, French and American co-productions filmed in Italy with a bizarre cast (Joe Dallesandro and Udo Kier for the former and Joe Dallesandro, Udo Kier, Vittorio De Sica and Roman Polanski for the latter), a lot of ideas and originality. For years, a controversy has raged as to who actually directed these films. These productions are equal to none of the works by Morissey, Warhol or even Margheriti if truth were told. Margheriti maintained that he supervised the filming and shot supplementary footage, and it appears that he may have directed some footage for these films. Fantastically successful releases with a bizarre combination of softcore sex, incredible gore, outrageous and campy dialogue and, in the case of the Frankenstein film, the added gimmick of 3D, these films were the favorites of college crowds for years. Margheriti's name is missing from most international prints, although on Italian versions he retains the credit "Supervised by Antonio Margheriti."

La Dove non Batte il Sole (1974) is an Italian-Chinese co-production that features Shaw Bros. veteran martial arts actor Lo Lieh as an itinerant journeyman who, along with famed gunfighter Lee Van Cleef, is searching the wild west for a number of beautiful women who have the map to a vast treasure tattooed on their backsides. The novelty of marital arts and nudity (courtesy genre veteran actresses Patty Shepard, Erika Blanc and Femi Benussi), combined with the Western, made this an entertaining, but ridiculous mix of genres. In 1975, Margheriti again featured Lee Van Cleef as one of the stars of his Western *La Parola di un Fuorilegge ... È Legge!* but, this time, the director was purely dabbling in opportunistic exploitation when his aim was to actually take advantage of the current phenomenal interest in black-oriented films. It is notable for being one of the first European productions that featured the African-American actors Jim Brown, Fred Williamson and Jim Kelly. Despite American veteran character actors in support (Dana Andrews, Barry Sullivan), the film is little more than an exploitation western, filled with the violence and gore that was so much a staple of mid–'70s films. That same year, Margheriti also directed *Controrapina*, a Mafia crime film starring Van Cleef.

A crime thriller starring Yul Brynner, *Con la Rabbia agli Occhi* followed in 1976. He made the action-adventure thriller *L'Agguato sul Fondo* (a.k.a. *Killer Fish*) (1978), about piranha terrorizing a search for treasure in the Amazon jungle with a strange cast of American television stars and B movie actors (Lee Majors, James Franciscus, Karen Black and Margaux Hemingway).

Apocalisse Domani (1980) was not only Margheriti's return to the horror film, but it also was his initial foray into the Vietnam War action-adventure genre as well. At the beginning of this film, a platoon of soldiers rescue confined American prisoners-of-war, starved for weeks and fed on nothing but rats, who have become flesh-eating cannibals. When these men savagely bite one of the team commanders operating the rescue mission (John Saxon), a gory rampage of murder and uncontrollable desires for warm flesh highlights their return to civilization. Eventually, the police shoot down these soldiers who have added to their number. Is this film an allegory for society's treatment of the returning Vietnam soldiers? Or just an incredible excuse to highlight more gruesome special effects designed by Giannetto De Rossi (Fulci's *Zombi 2*)?

Like the cannibal zombies in Umberto Lenzi's *Incubo sulla Città Contaminata*, the infected soldiers use weapons as a means to rip their victims apart, making it easier to tear the flesh and organs from their bodies. As their number grows, they attack every conceivable kind of civilian from biker gangs, to nurses and garage mechanics. No one is safe from them.

Afterwards, Margheriti took time to make *Carrera Salvaje* (1980), his disappointing science fiction action-adventure film with a seemingly uninterested cast (including Joey Travolta and John Steiner).

In 1980, Margheriti started his association with the British actor, David Warbeck. During this period, Warbeck, a veteran of early '70s sexploitation, had acted in small roles in Hammer horror films (and starred in a short-lived Robin Hood program for British television), and was enjoying full-time employment in overseas horror features, especially those filmed in Italy. He wound up working in some of the best of Lucio Fulci's films of this period, but even these horror features gave Warbeck little opportunity to shine as an actor. Margheriti's *L'Ultimo Cacciatore* (1980) gives the actor that in spades. A Vietnam war actioner (shot in the Philippines, the location used for many of Margheriti's action films), one could call *L'Ultimo Cacciatore* a horror film for the way the director approaches the horrors that one man comes up against when he faces the absolute turmoil of war. Warbeck's stoic performance is one of his best, ably supported by Margheriti regular Tony King and familiar genre faces John Steiner (as a madman military officer) and Tisa Farrow (as a photographer). *L'Ultimo Cacciatore* also inventively recycles scenes from *Apocalypse Now* (1979) and *The Deerhunter* (1978)!

Fuga dall'Arcipelago Maledetto (1981) is another Vietnam War–themed action film. Warbeck returns as a resourceful military man leading a rescue mission into the jungle. *I Cacciatori del Cobra d'Oro* (1982) is yet another war film, but, this time, a World War II action picture set in the Philippines with invading Japanese soldiers, ruthless native cannibals and a white jungle queen.

Il Mondo di Yor (1982) is a film that probably Margheriti would like to forget. Ripped apart by most reviewers at the time of its release, this low-budget film has too many influences stirred into its cold soup of a movie: the sword-and-sorcery films, the post-apocalyptic *Mad Max* rip-offs and the *Star Wars* clones, all Italian genre staples that, in the hands of less talented directors, became laughable exercises in hilarity. In Margheriti's *Yor*, which was based on a supposedly popular Italian comic strip, the society of man is apparently set in prehistoric time, but this is really a ruse. The film is actually set far into the future, after mankind has been reduced to caveman-like status, with only a ruling class of futuristic (outfitted with laser weapons!) outsiders left to keep them in check.

Margheriti returned to the adventure genre with *Tornado* (1983), another Vietnam War picture. It foreshadows Oliver Stone's *Platoon* (1986), but the movie ends in a downbeat fashion, with the hero facing sure death. *Arcobaleno Selvaggio* (1984) was Margheriti's attempt to cash in on the international success of the mercenary

Italian poster art for Margheriti's *I Lunghi Capelli della Morte* (1964, Cinegai).

thriller/action–adventure *The Wild Geese* (1978). Despite a cast of interesting actors (Lee Van Cleef, Klaus Kinski, Ernest Borgnine, Mimsy Farmer and Lewis Collins as the team commander) and well-staged action scenes, the film pales next to the action films that David Warbeck had made for Margheriti. The mercenaries fight an Asian warlord in the jungles of Burma.

I Sopravvissuti della Città Morta (1983) stars Warbeck as a clever, street-wise master thief who is tricked into joining an expedition to search for a fabled lost city and a treasure of untold riches. The film has its highlights, including some James Bond–inspired daredevil car chases and stunts, but it is more obviously influenced by the adventure film *Raiders of the Lost Ark* (1981).

La Leggenda del Rubino Malese (1984) featured Lee Van Cleef and Christopher Connelly in the kind of role that Margheriti usually intended for David Warbeck. This time, a down-on-his-luck adventurer (Connelly) unwillingly joins a group of people after a fabulous treasure in Malaysia.

Commando Leopard (1985) saw the return of the *Arcobaleno Selvaggio* cast (Collins, Kinski and John Steiner) and, this time, the remaining mercenaries are on the run from a meglomaniacal ruler who threatens a fictitious South American country.

In 1987, Margheriti made *L'Isola del Tesoro*, a huge, sprawling, special effects–dominated science fiction version of the Robert Louis Stevenson classic story *Treasure Island*. But the film, which was initially made for RAI television as a miniseries, then cut down to a three-hour feature, was too long and convoluted with too many story ideas constantly thrown at the audience. The special effects contain some of Margheriti's best work in that field, even though the miscast film veterans (Ernest Borgnine, David Warbeck, Philippe Leroy) try to hold their own against innocuous and cute child stars.

In 1988, yet another entry into the mercenaries series, *Il Triangolo della Paura*, was made by Margheriti. This time, even with Collins and Steiner, joined by Lee Van Cleef, Donald Pleasence and Brett Halsey, the film failed to find many distributors interested in a genre that, by now, had shown no beneficial monetary reason to exist. As a matter of fact, *Il Triangolo* has rarely been seen outside of Italian and German markets.

Indio (1988), an entertaining if highly ridiculous "man avenges the wrongs that have been done to nature" film, became a success on the video market. The genuinely charming, heroic presence of former heavyweight champion boxer Marvin Hagler must have made people return for more than just one rental. *Indio* was followed by two sequels, *Indio II: La Rivolta* (1990) and *Indio III* ('92), both also directed by Margheriti.

Alien degli Abissi (1989) is a return to the horror and science fiction themes that Margheriti explored in the '70s. This time, the boring script will keep even insomniacs from staying awake, and the too-few glimpses of the killer creature (created by a scientific plant's chemical spills into an Amazon jungle waterway)

DAVID WARBECK · ALMANTA SUSKA · ALAN COLLINS · JOHN STEINER
en

LOS AVENTUREROS DEL TESORO PERDIDO

Guión de: **GIANFRANCO COUYOUMDJIAN** y **T. CARPY**   Fotografía de: **S. MARSHALL**
Montaje de: **ALBERT MORTYAN**   Música de: **CHARLES SAVYN**
Una producción G.I.C.O. Cinematográfica
Dirigida por: **ANTHONY M. DAWSON**   EASTMANCOLOR

reveal it as a shoddy imitation of other similar, and equally uneven, films like *Deepstar Six* and *Leviathan* (both 1989).

To date, Margheriti's last feature film has been *Virtual Assassin* (a.k.a. *Virtual Weapon* and *Cyberflic*) (1998), a police thriller–buddy film co-starring the aforementioned Hagler and Spaghetti Western icon Terence Hill.

Besides directing, Margheriti also lent his many talents to other projects. He contributed to the special effects sequences for Primo Zeglio's *4...3...2...1...Morte!* (1967); Sergio Leone's *Giu la Testa* (1971); *L'Isola del Tesoro* (1972) and an Italian-British co-production based on the Robert Louis Stevenson *Treasure Island* (co-directed by Andrea Bianchi and John Hough). Margheriti claims that Stanley Kubrick consulted with him (about special effects techniques) before beginning production of *2001: A Space Odyssey* (1968).

Margheriti has also been fond of using an Anglo-sounding pseudonym, so Anthony Daises was born. When he realized the possible ridicule that could develop from such a fey-sounding moniker, he changed it to Anthony Dawson, then to Anthony M. Dawson to avoid confusion with the British character actor Anthony Dawson with whom he is still often confused. In recent years, besides directing *Virtual Assassin*, Margheriti had also been busy as an assistant director (on Ken Annakin's apparently unfinished 1993 film *Genghis Khan*) and contributed to the special effects for *Chicken Park* (1994), the directorial debut of Italian comedian Jerry Cala. Antonio Margheriti died on November 4, 2002.

Antonio Margheriti Filmography

A 077 Sfida ai Killers

A.k.a. *A 077 Challenge to the Killers* (English translation); a.k.a. *Sfida ai Killers* (alternate Italian title); a.k.a. *A Zero Sette Sette Sfida ai Killers* (alternate Italian title); a.k.a. *Bob Fleming ... Mission Casablanca* (French title); a.k.a. *Mission Casablanca*; a.k.a. *Challenge to the Killers*; a.k.a. *Killers Are Challenged*; a.k.a. *(The) Killers Are Challenged* (English titles) (1966) (It., Fr., Sp.); D: Antonio Margheriti; P: Mino Loy, Luciano Martino; Prod Co.: Zenith Cinematografica/Flora Film/Regina S.A.; SP: Luciano Martino, Ernesto Gastaldi, Eva Koltay; C: Riccardo Pallottini; M: Carlo Savina; S: Richard Harrison, Susy Andersen a.k.a. Susan Anderson, Wandisa Guida, Janine Reynaud, Mitsouko.

L'Agguato sul Fondo

A.k.a. *Killer Fish* (English translation); a.k.a. *The Naked Sun* (English title) (1978) (It., Brazil, U.S.); D: Antonio Margheriti; P: Alex Ponti, Olivier Perroy, Turi Vasile, Enzo Barone; Pros. Co.: Victoria Productions/Fawcett-Majors Productions/Filmar Do Brasil; SC: Giovanni Simonelli, Mark Prince, Kenneth Ross; C: Alberto Spagnoli, Giancarlo Formichi, Roberto Formichi; M: Guido and Maurizio De Angelis; S: Lee Majors, Karen Black, Mar-

Opposite: Spanish poster for *I Cacciatori del Cobra d'Oro* (1982, Gico Cinematografica).

gaux Hemingway, Marisa Berenson, James Franciscus, Dan Pastorini, Anthony Steffan a.ka. Antonio De Teffe, Gary Collins.

Alien degli Abissi

A.k.a. *Alien from the Abyss*; a.k.a. *Aliens from the Abyss*; a.k.a. *Alien from the Deep*; a.k.a. *Aliens from the Deep* (English translations and titles) (1989) (It.); D: Antonio Margheriti; P: Giancfranco Couyoumdjian; Prod. Co.: Gico Cinematografica/Dania Film/National Cinematografica/Vigo International; SC: Tito Carpi; C: Fausto Zuccoli; M: Andrea Ridolfi, Robert O'Ragland; S: Daniel Bosch, Julia McKay, Charles Napier, Luciano Pigozzi.

Anthar l'Invincible

A.k.a. *Anthar, the Invincible* (English translation and title?); a.k.a. *Il Mercante di Schive* (alternate Italian title); a.k.a. *The Slave Merchants* (English title) (1964) (It., Sp., Fr.); D: Antonio Margheriti; P: Giovanni Mazini, Renato De Pasqualis; Prod. Co.: Compagnia Cinematografica Mondiale/Fides Film, Paris/Rialto Films (Paris)/Producciones Benito Perojo (Spain); SC: Guido Malatesta; C: Alejandro Ulloa; M: Georges Garvarentz; S: Kirk Morris a.k.a. Adriano Bellini, Michele Girardon, Mario Felliciani, Renato Baldini, Tanya Lopert, Nadine Verdier, Malika Kamal.

Apocalisse Domani

A.k.a. *Apocalypse Domani*; a.k.a. *Apocalypse Tomorrow* (English translation); a.k.a. *Cannibali in Città* (Italian pre-production title; translation: *Cannibals in the City*); a.k.a. *Cannibals in the Streets*; a.k.a. *The Cannibals Are in the Streets*; a.k.a. *Canibale Apocalipsis* (Spanish title; translation: *Cannibal Apocalypse*); a.k.a. *Virus* (Spanish title); a.k.a. *Savage Apocalypse*; a.k.a. *Savage Slaughterers*; a.k.a. *Invasion of the Flesh Hunters* (English titles) (1980) (It., Sp.); D: Antonio Margheriti; P: Marizio Amati, Sandro Amati; Prod. Co.: New Fida Organization (Rome)/Jose Frade P.C. (Madrid); SC: Antonio Margheriti, Jose Luis Martinez Molla, Dardano Sacchetti; C: Fernando Arribas; M: Alessandro Blonksteiner; SP E: Giannetto De Rossi; S: John Saxon a.k.a. Carmine Orrico, Elisabeth Turner, Cindy Hamilton, Tony King, Cinzia Carolis, John Morghen a.k.a. Giovanni Lombardo Radice, Venantino Venantini.

Arciere delle Mille e Una Notte

A.k.a. *La Freccia d'Oro* (alternate Italian title); a.k.a. *The Golden Arrow* (English title) (1962) (It.); D: Antonio Margheriti; Prod. Co.: Titanus; SC: Bruno Vailati, Augusto Frassineti, Filippo Sanjust, Giorgio Prosperi, Giorgio Alorio and George Higgins III (English version only); C: Gabor Pogany; M: Mario Nascimbene, Franco Ferrara; S: Tab Hunter, Rossana Podesta, Umberto Melnati, Mario Feliciani, Dominique Boschero, Renato Baldini.

Arcobaleno Selvaggio

A.k.a. *Wild Rainbow*; a.k.a. *Savage Rainbow* (English translations); a.k.a. *Codename Wildgeese*; a.k.a. *Geheimcode Wildganse* (German title) (1984) (It., G.F.R.); D: Antonio Margheriti; P: Erwin C. Dietrich; Prod. Co.: Gico Cinematografica (Italy)/Ascot Film; SC: Michael Lester; C: Peter Baumgartner; M: Jan Nemec, Eloy; S: Lewis Collins, Ernest Borgnine, Klaus Kinski a.k.a. Klaus Gunther Nakszynksi, Manfed Lehmann, Mimsy Farmer, Thomas Dannenberg, Luciano Pigozzi.

I Cacciatori del Cobra d'Oro

A.k.a. *The Hunters of the Golden Cobra* (English translation and title); a.k.a. *Raiders of the Golden Cobra*; a.k.a. *Golden Cobra* (English title) (1982) (It.); D: Antonio Margheriti; P: Ganfranco Couyoumdjian; Prod. Co.: Gico Cinematografica; SC: Antonio Margheriti, Gianfranco Couyoumdjian; C: Sandro Mancori; M: Carlo Savina; SP E: Appolonio Abadesa; S: David Warbeck, John Steiner, Almanta Suska a.k.a. Antonella Interlenghi, Luciano Pigozzi, Reneee Abadesa, Protacio Dee.

Carrera Salvaje

A.k.a. *Car Crash* (English translation and title) (1980) (It., Sp., Mex.); D: Antonio Margheriti; P: Giovanni Di Clemente; Prod. Co.: Scorpio Cleminternazionale Cinematografica/Hesperia Film; SC: Marco Tullio Giordana; C: Hans Burman; M: Giosy Capuano, Mario Capuano; S: Joey Travolta, Vittorio Mezzogiorno, John Steiner, Francisco Rabal, Ana Maria Obregon, Riccardo Palacios.

Commando Leopard

A.k.a. *Kommando Leopard* (German title) (1985) (It., W.G.); D: Antonio Margheriti; P: Erwin C. Dietrich; Prod. Co.: Ascot Film/Prestige Film (Rome); SC: Roy Nelson; C: Peter Baumgartner; M: Goran Kuzminac, Ennio Morricone; S: Lewis Collins, Klaus Kinski a.k.a. Klaus Gunther Nakszynksi, Cristina Donadio, Manfred Lehmann, Hans Leutenegger, Francis Derosa, Thomas Dannenberg, John Steiner, Luciano Pigozzi.

Con la Rabbia agli Occhi

A.k.a. *Anger in His Eyes* (English translation); a.k.a. *Gli Indesiderabli*; a.k.a. *Death Rage*; a.k.a. *Shadow of a Killer* (English titles) (1976) (It.); D: Antonio Margheriti; P: Franco Caruso; Prod. Co.: Giovine Cinematografica; SC: Guido Castaldo, Giacomo Furia, Mark Prince, Paul Costello; C: Sergio D'Offizio; M: Guido and Maurizio De Angelis; S: Yul Brynner, Massimo Ranieri, Barbara Bouchet a.k.a. Barbel Goutscher a.k.a. Barbel Gutchen, Martin Balsam, Giancarlo Sbragia, Salvatore Borghese.

Il Contronatura

A.k.a. *The Unnaturals* (English translation and title); a.k.a. *Schreie in der Nacht* (German title; translation: *Scream in the Night*) (1969) (It., W.G.); D: Antonio Margheriti; P: Turi Vasile; Prod. Co.: CCC/EDO Cinematografica/Super International Pictures; SC: Antonio Margheriti, Hannes Dahlberg; C: Riccardo Pallottini; M: Carlo Savina; S: Joachim Fuchsberger, Marianne Koch, Dominique Boschero, Claudio Camaso, Luciano Pigozzi, Marianne Leibl, Marco Morelli, Helga Anders.

Controrapina

A.k.a. *The Rip-Off*; a.k.a. *The Squeeze* (English titles) (1977/80) (It., W.G.); D: Antonio Margheriti; P: Raymond R. Homer, Turi Vasile; Prod. Co.: Dritte Centama Gmbh; SC: Giovanni Simonelli, Mark Prince, Paul Costello; C: Sergio D'Offizi; M: Paolo Vasile; S: Lee Van Cleef, Karen Black, Edward Albert, Lionel Stander, Robert Alda, Angelo Infanti, Antonella Murgia, Peter Carsten a.k.a. Peter Ransenthaler.

I Criminali della Galassia

A.k.a. *The Criminals of the Galaxy* (English translation); a.k.a. *Wild Wild Planet* (English title) (1965) (It.); D: Antonio Margheriti; P: Antonio Margheriti, Joseph Fryd; Prod. Co.: Mercury Film International/Southern Cross Productions; SC: Renato Moreeti, Ivan Reiner; C: Riccardo Pallottini; M: Angelo Francesco Lavagnino; S: Tony Russell, Lisa Gastoni, Massimo Serato, Franco Nero, Carlo Giustini, Umberto Raho, Isarco Ravaioli, Moa Thai, Franco Ressell, Goffredo Unger.

La Danza Macabre

A.k.a. *The Macabre Dance* (English translation); a.k.a. *La Lunga Notte del Terrore* (alternate Italian title; translation: *The Long Night of Terror*); a.k.a. *La Danse Macabre* (French title); a.k.a. *Tombs of Horror*; a.k.a. *Coffin of Terror*; a.k.a. *Dimensions in Death*; a.k.a. *Castle of Blood*; a.k.a. *Castle of Terror* (English titles) (1964) (It., Fr.); D: Antonio Margheriti, Sergio Corbucci (uncredited); P: Marco Vicario, Giovanni Addessi; Prod. Co.: Vulsinia Film/Jolly Film (Rome)/Leo Lax Film/Ulysee Film; SC: Sergio Corbucci, Gianni Grimaldi; C: Riccardo Pallottini; M: Riz Ortolani; S: Barbara Steele, Georges Riviere, Margaret Robsahn, Sylvia Sorente, Henry Kruger, Silvano Tranquili, Umberto Raho.

I Diafanoidi Vengono da Marte

A.k.a. *The Deadly Diaphanoids* (English translation); a.k.a. *War of the Planets* (English title) (1965) (It.); D: Antontio Margheriti; P: Joseph Fryd, Walter Manley; Prod. Co.: Mercury Film International/Southern Cross Productions; SC: Ivan Rainer, Renato Moretti; C: Riccardo Pallottini; M: Angelo Francesco Lavagnino; S: Tony Russell, Jane Fate a.k.a. Lisa Gastoni, Franco Nero, Michel Lemoine, Umberto Raho, Carlo Giustini.

La Dove Non Batte il Sole

A.k.a. *El Karate, el Colt, y el Imposter*; a.k.a. *Blood Money*; a.k.a. *The Stranger and the Gunfighter* (English titles) (1974) (It., Sp., Hong Kong, U.S.); D: Antonio Margheriti; P: Carlo Ponti, Run Run Shaw, Gustav Berne; Prod. Co.: Compagnia Cinematografica Champion/Midega Films (Madrid)/Shaw Bros./Harbor Productions; C: Alejandro Ulloa; M: Carlo Savina; S: Lee Van Cleef, Lo Lieh, Karen Yeh, Julian Ugarte, Goiya Peralta, Al Tung, Patty Shepard, Femi Benussi a.k.a. Eufemia Benussi, Erika Blanc a.k.a. Erika Bianchi Colombatto, Jorge Rigaud, Riccardo Palacios.

Dracula Cerca Sangue di Vergine ... È Morì di Sete!

A.k.a. *Dracula Vuole Vivere: Cerca Sangue di Vergina* (alternate Italian title); a.k.a. *Du Sangue pour Dracula* (French title); a.k.a. *Blood for Dracula*; a.k.a. *Andy Warhol's Dracula*; a.k.a. *Andy Warhol's Young Dracula* (English titles) (1973) (It., Fr.); D: Paul Morrissey, Antonio Margheriti (uncredited); P: Andrew Braunsberg; Prod. Co.: CC Champion (Rome)/Jean Yanne-Jean Pierre Rassam Productions (Paris); SC: Paul Morrissey; C: Luigi Kuveiller; M: Claudio Gizzi; SP E: Carlo Rambaldi, Roberto Arcangeli; S: Udo Kier, Joe Dallesandro, Vittorio De Sica, Arno Juerging, Maxine McKendry, Milena Vukotic, Dominique Darel, Stefania Casini, Roman Polanski, Silvia Dionisio.

E Dio Disse a Caino

A.k.a. *And God Said to Cain* (English translation and title) (1969) (It.); D: Antonio Margheriti; P: Giovanni Addessi; Prod. Co.: D.C. 7 (Rome); SC: Antonio Margheriti, Giovanni Addessi; C: Luciano Trassati, Riccardo Pallottini; M: Carlo Savina; S: Klaus Kinski a.k.a. Klaus Gunther Nakszynksi, Peter Cartsen a.k.a. Peter Ransenthaler, Cella Michelangeli, Lee Burton, Antonio Cantafora, Giuliana Raffaelli, Luciano Pigozzi, Lucio De Santis.

Finalmente ... la Mille e Una Notte

A.k.a. *Bed of a Thousand Pleasures*; a.k.a. *One Thousand and One Nights*; a.k.a. *1001 Nights* (English titles) (1972) (It., Sp.); D: Antonio Margheriti; Prod. Co.: Medusa Distribuzione/Pink International Films; SC: Antonio Margheriti, Dino Verde; C: Sergio D'Offizi; M: Carlo Savina; S: Barbara Bouchet a.k.a. Barbel Goutscher a.k.a. Barbel Gutchen, Femi Benussi a.k.a. Eufemia Benussi, Barbara Marzano, Esmeralda Barros, Barbara Betti.

Fuga dall'Arcipelago Maledetto

A.k.a. *Tiger Joe* (English title) (1982) (It.); D: Antonio Margheriti; P: Gianfranco Couyoumdjian; SC: Gianfranco Couyoumdjian, Tito Carpi; C: Riccardo Pallottini; M: Carlo Savina; S: David Warbeck, Tony King, Annie Belle a.k.a. Annie Briand, Luciano Pigozzi, Giancarlo Badessi.

I Giganti di Roma

A.k.a. *The Giants of Rome* (English title) (1964) (It., Fr.); D: Antonio Margheriti; P: Mino Loy, Luciano Martino; Prod. Co.: Devon Film (Rome)/Radius Productions (Paris); SC: Ernesto Gastaldi, Luciano Martino; C: Fausto Zuccoli; M: Carlo Rustichelli; S: Richard Harrison, Wandisa Guida, Ettore Manni, Nicole Tessier, Philippe Hersent.

L'Inafferabile, Invincibile Mr. Invisible

A.k.a. *Mr. Superinvisible* (English title) (1969) (It.); D: Antonio Margheriti; P: Peter Carsten a.k.a. Peter Ransenthaler; C: Alejandro Ulloa; M: Carlo Savina; SC: Luis Marquina, Maria Laura Rocca, based on her novel; S: Dean Jones, Philippe Leroy, Gastone Moschin, Bernabe Barta Barri, Mirella Pamphili, Luciano Pigozzi, Ingeborg Schöner.

Indio

(1988) (It.); D: Antonio Margheriti; P: Filiberto Bandini; Prod. Co.: Filmauro/R.P.A. International/Reteitalia, Milan; SC: Gianfranco Bucceri, Filiberto Bandini; C: Sergio D'Offizi; M: Pino Donaggio; S: Francesco Quinn, Marvin Hagler, Brian Dennehy.

Indio II: La Rivolta

A.k.a. *Indio II: The Revolt*; a.k.a. *Indio 2* (English titles) (1990) (It.); D: Antonio Margheriti; P: Filiberto Bandini, Enrico Coletti; Prod. Co.: Filmauro/R.P.A. International; SC: Gianfranco Bucceri, Filiberto Bandini; C: Roberto Benvenuti; M: Pino Donaggio, Natale Massara; S: Marvin Hagler, Charles Napier, Frank Cuervo, Dirk Galuba, Tetchie Agbayani, Maurizio Fardo, Jacqueline Fardo.

Indio III

(1992) (It.); D: Antonio Margheriti; P: Filiberto Bandini, Enrico Coletti; Prod. Co.: Filmauro/R.P.A. International; SC: Gianfranco Bucceri, Filiberto Bandini; C: Roberto Benvenuti; M: Pino Donaggio, Natale Massara; S: Marvin Hagler, Christopher Connelly, Tetchie Agbayani.

L'Isola del Tesoro

A.k.a. *Treasure Island* (English translation); a.k.a. *Treasure Island in Space*; a.k.a. *Treasure Island in Outer Space*; a.k.a. *Space Pirates* (English titles) (1986) (It., Fr., G.F.R., Monaco); D: Antonio Margheriti; Prod. Co.: Radiotelevisione Italiana–Raidue (Rome)/T.F.1 Films Production (Paris)/Bavaria Filmkunst (Monaco); SC: Antonio Margheriti, Renato Castellani, based on ideas created by Robert Louis Stevenson in his book *Treasure Island*; C: Sandro Messina; M: Gianfranco Plenizio; S: Ernest Borgnine, Italco Nardulli, Anthony Quinn, Philippe Leroy, Klaus Lowisch, David Warbeck, Bobby Rhodes, Ira Di Benedetto.

Joe l'Implacabile

A.k.a. *Dynamite Joe* (English title) (1967) (It., Sp.); D: Antonio Margheriti; P: Seven Film/P.C. Hispamer; SC: Antonio Margheriti, Maria Del Carmin Martinez; C: Manuel Merino; M: Carlo Savina; S: Rik Van Nutter, Halina Zalewska, Mercedes Caracuel, Renato Baldini, Santiago Rivero, Barta Barry.

Joko, Invoka Dio ... e Muori

A.k.a. *Call to Your God ... and Die* (English translation); a.k.a. *Vengeance* (English title) (1968) (It., W.G.); D: Antonio Margheriti; Prod. Co.: Super International Pictures/Top Film (Munich); SC: Antonio Margheriti, Renato Savino; C: Riccardo Pallottini; M: Carlo Savina; S: Richard Harrison, Claudio Camaso, Werner Pochath, Paolo Gozlino, Sheryl Rosin, Goffredo Unger, Luciano Pigozzi, Mariangela Giordano.

La Leggenda del Rubino Malese

A.k.a. *The Legend of the Maltese Ruby* (English translation); a.k.a. *I Predatori della Jungla* (alternate Italian title); a.k.a. *Jungle Raiders*; a.k.a. *Captain Yankee* (English titles) (1984) (It.); D: Antonio Margheriti; P: Luciano Appignani; Prod. Co.: Immagine; SC: Giovanni Simonelli; C: Guglielmo Mancori; M: Cal Taormina; S: Christopher Connelly, Lee Van Cleef, Marina Costa, Luciano Pigozzi, Rene Abadeza, Julio Rodrigo.

I Lunghi Capelli della Morte

A.k.a. *The Long Hair of Death* (English translation and title); *I Lunghi Capelli di Morte* (alternate Italian title) (1964) (It.); D: Antonio Margheriti; P: Felice Testa Gay; Prod. Co.: Cinegai; SC: Bruno Valeri, Ernesto Gastaldi, Renato Caldonazzo (U.S. version only); C: Riccardo Pallottini; M: Carlo Rustichelli; S: Barbara Steele, Giorgio Ardisson, Halina Zalewska, Giuliano Raffaelli, Laura Nucci.

Ming, Ragazzi!

A.k.a. *Schiaffoni e Karati* (alternate Italian title); a.k.a. *Hercules Against Kung Fu*; a.k.a. *Mr. Hercules Vs. Karate* (1973) (It.); D: Antonio Margheriti; P: Antonio Margheriti, Carlo Ponti; Prod. Co.: Laser Film/Compagnia Cinematografica Champion; SC: Antonio Margheriti, Giorgio Simonelli, Luciano Vincenzoni, Sergio Donati; C: Luciano Trasatti; M: Carlo Savina; S: Alberto Terracina, Brad Harris, Jolina Mitchell, George Wang, Chai Lee, Seyna Seyn, Luciano Pigozzi, Giorgio Dolfin, Franco Ressel.

Missione Pianeta Errante

A.k.a. *Il Pianeta Errante* (alternate Italian title); a.k.a. *War Between the Planets*; a.k.a. *Planet on the Prowl* (English titles) (1966) (It.); D: Antonio Margheriti; P: Antonio Margheriti, Joseph Fryd, Walter Manley, Ivan Reiner; Prod. Co.: Mercury Film International; SC: Ivan Reiner, Renato Moretti; C: Riccardo Pallottini; M: Angelo Francesco Lavagnino; S: Giacomo Rossi-Stuart, Ombretta Colli, Janos Bartha, Enzo Fiermonte, Halina Zalewska, Peter Martell a.k.a. Pietro Martellanz, Marco Bogliani.

Il Mondo di Yor

A.k.a. *The World of Yor* (English translation); a.k.a. *Yor, Hunter from the Future*; a.k.a. *Yor — The Hunter from the Future* (1982) (It., Turkey); D: Antonio Margheriti; Prod. Co.: Diamant Films/Radiotelvisione Italiana/AFM, Istanbul; SC: Antonio Margheriti, Robert Bailey, based on the novel (and comic strip) "Yor" by Juan Zanotto & Ray Collins; C: Marcello Masciocchi, Guido and Maurizio De Angelis; M: Guido De Angelis, Maurizio De Angelis, John Scott; S: Reb Brown, Corinne Clery, Luciano Pigozzi, Carol Andre, Cinzia De Ponti, John Steiner, Aytekin Akkaya.

La Morte Viene dal Pianeta Aytin

A.k.a. *I Diavoli dello Spazio* (alternate Italian title; translation: *The Devils from Space*); a.k.a. *Space Devils*; a.k.a *Snow Devils* (English titles) (1965) (It.); D: Antonio Margheriti; P: Antonio Margheriti, Joseph Fryd; Prod. Co.: Mercury Film Italia; SC: Ivan Reiner, Renato Moretti; C: Riccardo Pallottini; M: Angelo Francesco Lavagnino; S: Giacomo Rossi-Stuart, Ombretta Colli, Renato Baldini, Franco Nero.

Il Mostro È in Tavola ... Barone Frankenstein

A.k.a. *Carne per Frankenstein* (alternate Italian title; translation: *Flesh for Frankenstein*); a.k.a. *The Frankenstein Experiment*; a.k.a. *Up Frankenstein*; a.k.a. *The Devil and Dr. Frankenstein*; a.k.a. *Warhol's Frankenstein*; a.k.a. *Andy Warhol's Frankenstein* (English titles) (1973) (It., Fr., W.G.); D: Paul Morrissey, Antonio Margheriti (uncredited); P: Andrew Braunsberg, Carlo Ponti Cinematografica; Prod. Co.: C.C. Champion & I (Rome)/Carlo Ponti Cinematografica (Rome)/Jean Yanne-Jean Pierre Rassam Productions (Paris); SC: Paul Morrissey; C: Luigi Kuveiller; M: Claudio Gizzi; SP E: Carlo Rambaldi, Roberto Arcangeli; S: Udo Kier, Joe Dallesandro, Monique Van Vooren, Arno Juerging, Carla Mancini, Srdjan Zelenovic, Dalila Di Lazzaro, Cristina Gaioni, Marco Liofredi, Nicoletta Elmi.

Nella Stretta Morsa del Ragno

A.k.a. *In the Web of the Spider*; a.k.a. *Web of the Spider*; a.k.a. *In the Grip of the Spider* (English translations and titles); a.k.a. *E Venne l'Alba ... Ma Tinta di Rosso* (alternate Italian title); a.k.a. *Prisonnier de l'Araignée* (French title); a.k.a. *Edgar Poe Chez les Morts Vivants* (alternate French title); a.k.a. *Les Fantômes de Hurlevent* (alternate French title); a.k.a. *Les Griffes Rouges de Hurlevent* (alternate French title); a.k.a. *Dracula im Schloss Schreckens* (German title) (1970) (It., Fr., W.G.); D: Antonio Margheriti; P: Giovanni Di Addessi; Prod. Co.: Produzione D.C.7/Paris Cannes Productions/Terra Filmkunst; SC: Bruno Corbucci, Giovanni Grimaldi; C: Sandro Mancori, Memmo Mancori; M: Riz Ortolani; S: Anthony Franciosa, Michele Mercier, Peter Carsten a.k.a. Peter Ransenthaler, Silvio Tranquili, Karin Field, Raf Baldassere, Klaus Kinski a.k.a. Klaus Gunther Nakszynksi, Irina Malewa, Paolo Goslino, Enrico Osterman.

Novelle Galeotte d'Amore

(1972) (It.); D: Antonio Margheriti; C: Guglielmo Mancori; M: Alessandro Alessandroni; S: Aldo Bufi Landi, Antonio Cantafora, Liana Del Balzo, Ada Pometti, Marlene Rahn, Eva Maria Grubmuller.

Nude ... Si Muore

A.k.a. *Naked ... One's Dead* (English translation); a.k.a. *Sette Vergini per il Diavolo* (Italian pre-production title; translation: *Seven Virgins for the Devil*); a.k.a. *The Young, the Evil, and the Savage*; a.k.a. *Schoolgirl Killer* (English titles) (1967) (It.); D: Antonio Margheriti; P: Giuseppe and Virglio De Blasi, Dante Amatulli, Laurence Woolner; Prod. Co.: Super International Pictures/B.G. A.; SC: Antonio Margheriti, Franco Bottari, Giovanni Simonelli; C: Fausto Zuccoli; M: Carlo Savina; S: Michael Rennie, Mark Damon, Eleonora Brown, Ludmilla Lvova, Vivian Stapleton, Franco DeLarosa, Luciano Pigozzi, Malisa Longo.

Operazione Goldman

A.k.a. *Operation: Goldman* (English translation and title); a.k.a. *Lightning Bolt* (English title) (1966) (It., Sp.); D: Antonio Margheriti; P: Anacleto Fontini, Joseph De Blasio; Prod. Co.: Seven Film (Rome)/B.G.A./Producciones Cinematograficas Blacazar; SC: Alfonso Balcazar, Jose Antonio De La Loma; C: Riccardo Pallottini; M: Riz Ortolani; S: Anthony Eisley, Wandisa Guida, Diana Lorys, Luisa Rivelli, Paco Sanz, Jose-Maria Caffarel, Renato Montalbano, Folco Lulli, Tito Garcia, Oreste Palella.

La Parola di un Fuorilegge ... È Legge!

A.k.a. *Take a Hard Ride* (English title) (1975) (It., U.S.); D: Antonio Margheriti; P: Harry Bernsen; Prod. Co.: Fox-Fanfare Music/Euro-General; SC: Eric Bercovici, Jerry Ludwig; C: Riccardo Pallottini; M: Jerry Goldsmith; S: Fred Williamson, Lee Van Cleef, Jim Brown, Jim Kelly, Catherine Spaak, Barry Sullivan, Harry Carey, Jr., Dana Andrews, Riccardo Palacios.

Il Pelo nel Mondo

A.k.a. *Go! Go! World*; a.k.a. *Weird Wicked World*; a.k.a. *Mondo Inferno* (English titles) (1964) (It.); D: Antonio Margheriti, Marco Vicario; P: Marco Vicario; Prod. Co.: Atlantica Cinematografica Produzione Films; SC: Marco Vicario; C: Giovanni Raffaldi, Giancarlo Lari, Marcello Gallinelli; M: Nino Oliviero, Bruno Nicolai; Narration (English language version): Stephen Garrett, John Hart

Il Pianeta degli Uomini Spenti

A.k.a. *The Planet of the Lifeless Men* (English translation); a.k.a. *Battle of the Worlds* (English title) (1961) (It.); D: Antonio Margheriti; Prod. Co.: Ultra Films; SC: Vassili Petrov; C: Marcello Masciocchi; M: Mario Migliardi; S: Claude Rains, Maja Brent, Umberto Orsini, Jacqueline Derval.

Sopravvissuti della Città Morta

A.k.a. *L' Arc del Dio Sole*; a.k.a. *The Ark of the Sun God* (English title) (1983) (It., Turkey); D: Antonio Margheriti; P: Giovanni Paolucci, Ignazio Dolce, Mutafia Gurler, Tevfik Sen,

Sedat Akdemir; Prod. Co.: Flora Film/AFM (Istanbul); SC: Giovanni Paolucci, Giovanni Simonelli; C: Sandro Mancori; M: Aldo Tamborelli; S: David Warbeck, John Steiner, Susie Sudlow, Luciano Pigozzi, Ricardo Palacios.

Spazzio Uomini

A.k.a. *Space Men* (English translation); a.k.a. *Assignment Outer Space* (English title) (1960) (It.); D: Antonio Margheriti; Prod. Co.: Ultra Film/Titanus; SC: Vassiliji Petrov; C: Marcello Masciocchi; M: Lelio Luttazzi; S: Rik Van Nutter, Gabriela Farinon, David Montresor, Archie Savage.

Tornado

A.k.a. *Tornado Strike Force* (English title) (1983) (It.); D: Antonio Margheriti; P: Gianfranco Couyoumdjian; Prod. Co.: Gico Cinematografica; SC: Tito Carpi, Gianfranco Couyoumdjian; C: Sandro Mancori; S: Timothy Brent a.k.a. Giancarlo Prete, Antonio Marsina, Luciano Pigozzi.

Il Triangolo della Paura

A.k.a. *Triangle of Fear* (English translation); a.k.a. *Der Commander* (German title) (1988) (It., G.F.R.); D: Antonio Margheriti; P: Erwin C. Dietrich; Prod. Co.: Erwin C. Dietrich/Ascot Film/Prestige Film (Rome); SC: Tito Carpi, Arne Elsholtz; C: Peter Baumgartner; M: Walter Baumgartner; S: Lewis Collins, Lee Van Cleef, John Steiner, Donald Pleasence, Bobby Rhodes, Manfred Lehman, Roman Puppo, Brett Halsey, Paul Mueller.

La Ultimo Cacciatore

A.k.a. *The Last Hunter* (English translation and title) (1980) (It.); D: Antonio Margheriti; P: Gianfranco Couyoumdjian; Prod. Co.: Gico Cinematografica/Flora Film; SC: Dardano Sacchetti; C: Riccardo Pallottini; M: Franco Mixalizzi; S: David Warbeck, Tisa Farrow, Tony King, Bobby Rhodes, Margit Evelyn Newton, John Steiner, Massimo Vanni, Luciano Pigozzi.

Ursus, il Terrore dei Kirghisi

A.k.a. *Hercules, Prisoner of Evil* (English title) (1964) (It.); D: Antonio Margheriti, Ruggero Deodato; Prod. Co.: Adelphius Cineproduzione/Societe Ambrosia; SC: Antonio Margheriti; C: Gabor Pogany; M: Franco Trinacria; S: Reg Park, Ettore Manni, Mirielle Granelli, Furio Meniconi.

La Vergine di Norimberga

A.k.a. *The Virgin of Nuremberg* (English translation and title); a.k.a *The Castle of Terror*; a.k.a. *Terror Castle*; a.k.a. *Horror Castle* (English titles) (1964) (It.); D: Antonio Margheriti; P: Marco Vicario; Prod. Co.: Atlantica Cinematografica Produzioni Films; SC: Antonio Margheriti, Ernesto Gastaldi, based on a novel by Frank Bogard; C: Riccardo Pallottini; M: Riz Ortolani; S: Rossana Podesta, Georges Riviere, Christopher Lee, Anna Delli Uberti, Luigi Severini, Luciana Milone, MirkoValentine, Lucille Saint-Simon.

Virtual Assassin

A.k.a. *Cyberflic*; a.k.a. *Virtual Weapon* (English titles) (1996/98) (It., G.F.R.); D: Antonio Margheriti; P: Edoardo Margheriti; SC: Bruno Corbucci; M: Carmelo La Bionda, Michelangelo La Bionda; S: Terence Hill a.k.a. Mario Girotti, Marvin Hagler, Gisele Blondet.

Aristide Massaccesi

Aristide Massaccesi was born on December 15, 1936, in Rome, Italy. Although Massaccesi did not adopt the anglicized pseudonym Joe D'Amato until he directed *Giubbe Rosse* (1975), it is the name with which the director is most associated, more so than his real name given to him at birth.

At the age of 14, Massaccesi, the son of a chief photographic technician in the cinema, began his career in the movies by assisting in the dubbing room for Italian film productions. He later worked with the senior Bava, Eugenio Bava, as an assistant title maker working alongside the father of Mario and grandfather of Lamberto creating credits for films.

Massaccesi graduated to working as a still photographer on the set of the 1952 motion picture *La Carroza d'Oro*. Massaccesi quickly progressed to other technical areas of film production, first as a camera operator, then cinematographer. An early, uncredited role as an assistant camera operator on Mario Bava's *Ercole al Centro della Terra* (1961) is his first genre assignment. His first assignment as a director of photography was the 1969 Silvio Amadio–directed film, *L'Isola della Svedesi*.

Massaccesi spent the next several years alternating between camera operator and director of photography positions on important films in the horror genre such as Umberto Lenzi's *Paranoia* (1970), Massimo Dallamano's *Cosa Avete Fatto a Solange?* (1971) and Alberto De Martino's *L'Assassino ... È al Telefono* (1973). However, not all of Massaccesi's work was for such well-known productions. He also worked for many low-budget directors, contributing to Guido Zurli's adventure film *Sigpress Contro Scotland Yard* (1967), Demofilo Fidani's cash-starved Western, *Inginocchiati Straniero ... i Cadaveri Non Fanno Ombra!* (1971) and Michele Lupo's *Amico, Stammi Lontano Almeno un Palmo* (1972).

In time, Massaccesi was sought out as a cinematographer by many other pro-

Aristide Massaccesi, a.k.a. Joe D'Amato.

ducers and directors because of his unique style. With the aid of special filters and his use of lighting, he created extremely stark and realistic footage. While one could not favorably compare his finest cinematographic achievements to those of fellow Italian Vittorio Storraro, Massaccesi's stark images did add a sense of heightened reality to the films on which he worked. As wonderful a cameraman as Massaccesi was, when he worked on low-budget film productions, and even when he photographed films that he directed, produced and wrote as well, his visual compositions sometimes appear hastily arranged. Still, for the most part, his work as a cameraman was far above those of his journeyman contemporaries in the field.

Aristide Massaccesi's first film as director appears to be the 1972 Western *Scansati ... Trinità Arriva en Eldorado*, utilizing the pseudonym Dick Spitfire, a delightful re-naming of producer Diego Spataro's own name. This very low-budget production was shot in only three to four days and utilized outtakes and other footage taken from other Spataro films (some made by Demofilo Fidani, including *Arrivano Django e Sartana ... È la Fine* [1970] and *Inginocchiati Straniero ... i Cadaveri Non Fanno Ombra!* [1971], both of which were photographed by Massaccesi).

Massaccesi's first film went unnoticed by critics and audiences alike, which was fine by him; he could continue as an in-demand director of photography for others. Massaccesi followed this Western with another, *Un Bounty Killer a Trinità* (1972). Although credited to an Oskar Faradine, Massaccesi actually directed and wrote the screenplay for the film, also produced by Diego Spataro and starring Jeff Cameron (Geoffredo Scarciofolo), using the Faradine pseudonym for fear that he wouldn't be hired for more director of photography assignments for other directors.

Massaccesi's next directing assignments were for the 1972 films *Sollazzevoli Storie di Mogli Gaudenti e Mariti Penitenti* (although the film is credited to Romano Gastaldi) and *Novelle Licenziose di Vergine Vogliose*. Both films were known in Italy as "Decamerotics," having been sexy, erotic takeoffs on medieval legends and Italian history. Most of the nearly 50 films that were made in the short life of this genre (1970-73) were seemingly influenced by (or ripoffs of) director Piero Paolo Pasolini's original *Decameron* (1970). *Novelle Licenziose di Vergine Vogliose* entertained a certain minor notoriety when it was repeatedly rejected by the Italian censorship board because of several scenes of strong erotic imagery. When the film was finally released in 1974, the "Decamerotics" had run their course and the film flopped. Massaccesi's next production as a director, *Eroi all'Inferno* (1973), a World War II adventure starring Klaus Kinski, showed that he could direct a film with a larger budget than those which he was previously used to.

La Morte Ha Sorriso all'Assassino (1973) is Massaccesi's first horror film as director. Klaus Kinski is featured in the cast as a medical doctor whose experiments with hypnotism and death are attempts to bring the deceased back to life. Ewa Aulin, the strange, intense star of the disastrous 1968 pop-art film *Candy*, stars as a woman restored to life. One of this odd and slow-moving film's highlights is a scene which features Aulin in bed with a male lover. When the situation becomes sexually heated, the man discovers that Aulin is now a rotting corpse. An interesting film, but not a classic in the horror film genre due to the lackluster performances and the direction that aims for ambiance and fails.

However uneven the film turned out to be it was, nevertheless, an impressive experiment: After the turn of the century, a medical doctor (Klaus Kinski) who experiments with alchemy seeks to revive the dead. One successful experiment involves the hauntingly attractive Aulin. Once she returns from death to the world of the living, she then begins to murder those men and women that seem romantically (or sexually) interested in her. Within Aulin's revived body exists the souls of many damned people. She takes different incarnations of these souls into her new life. This extremely atmospheric film has in its favor an above-average performance by Klaus Kinski and an appropriately haunted one by Ewa Aulin. The film is ultimately betrayed, in spite of an excellent script, by the confused direction that the story takes and indifference of the supporting cast members.

Massaccesi returned to the role of director of photography for Luigi Batzella's erotic vampire film *Il Plenilunio delle Vergini* (1973) and Alberto De Martino's horrendously arty *Exorcist* clone *L'Anticristo* (1974), two productions that, for purely exploitative reasons, have a following in the horror film audience.

After two years, Massaccesi returned to directing with *Giubbe Rosse* (1975). The film, starring Fabio Testi, is a variation of the popular Jack London tales *The Call of the Wild* and *White Fang* and deals with the frozen Canadian wilderness and the heroic deeds of a naturalist, adventurer and lawman. Coincidentally, Massaccesi served as an assistant director of photography for Lucio Fulci's own *Zanna Bianca* (1973), which told essentially the same story (with Franco Nero in the leading role).

In 1974, the popularity of the French sexploitation film *Emmanuelle* led to an explosion of similar, daring sexually explicit features. French director Just Jaeckin's erotic hit starred Sylvia Kristel in the role of the real-life Emmanuelle Arsan, the libertarian and free-sex jet-setter, and paved the way for dozens more films, including many French hardcore features in the international film marketplace. *Emmanuelle: The Joys of a Woman* (1975), the first official sequel to the popular film, also directed by Jaeckin and starring Kristel, featured the exotic Eurasian actress Laura Gemser as a masseuse. In 1975, low-budget Italian auteur Adalberto Bitto Albertini directed Gemser as the star of *Emmanuelle Nera*. Albertini had introduced Gemser to Massaccesi and the two became very close, but Massaccesi was already well into production on his own Emanuelle feature, *Emanuelle e Françoise*. This film, released in 1976, is a thinly veiled relation to the Just Jaeckin series with Sylvia Kristel. It starred Rosemarie Lindt as Emanuelle and Patrizia Gori as her sister, Françoise. While making this lurid tale of desire and horror, Massaccesi realized the growing attention paid to European imports with heightened violence or sex, so he prepared several alternate versions of the tale, one featuring graphic bloodletting and another with scenes of a pornographic nature.

In *Emanuelle e Françoise: Le Sorelline*, Carlo (Luigi Montefiori) has been humiliating Françoise (Patrizia Gori), both psychologically and sexually, for so long that she finally commits suicide. Emanuelle (Rosemarie Lindt), her sister, seeks revenge by drugging Carlo, then chaining him to a wall in a secret room. Emanuelle torments Carlo by starving him, beating him and then forcing him to view sexual orgies, some with his current girlfriend. Hallucinating wildly and driven to madness, Carlo breaks out of his bonds and kills Emanuelle.

Laura Gemser, frequent collaborator with Aristide Massaccesi.

It is a fascinating entry in the then-new series of alternate Emanuelle films (notice that the Massaccesi heroine's name is shorn of one M to make the distinction). The cast performs well under the strenuous circumstances and depraved situations devised by the director and co-screenwriter Bruno Mattei.

Massaccesi immediately followed this film with his own series of Emanuelle movies starring Laura Gemser. *Emanuelle Nera—Orient Reportage* (1976) was a sex film that reintroduced the Emanuelle character in the role of an international reporter and photographer; *Eva Nera* (1976) was another sex film with the protagonist this time investigating an organized crime lord (Jack Palance) and his mob in more exotic locations.

Eva Nera is another title for which Massaccesi had filmed alternate pornographic hardcore sex footage; these versions of the film, known alternately as *Emanuelle in Tahiti*, *Emanuelle on Taboo Island* and *Porno Esotic Love*, also contain other dramatic sequences that do not appear in the original film. Obviously, actor Jack Palance does not partake in any of the softcore or hardcore. *Emanuelle in America* (1976) was and is Massaccesi's crowning achievement with this series. It is a film that just defies any kind of serious critical analysis. This over-the-top film features Emanuelle (Gemser) being assigned to investigate a white slavery ring and the drug trade in South America. The astounding thing about *Emanuelle in America* is that Massaccesi's hardcore sex footage is completely nonerotic. The film's infamous and disgusting (faked) mondo scene in the uncut presentation has been the cause for concern for many a horror film buff: Brutal slavers torture and maim women for kicks, while Emanuelle spies these proceedings from a hiding place. That Massaccesi would even think to include such images

Spanish poster art for Massaccesi's *Emanuelle e gli Ultimi Cannibali* (1977, Fulvia Cinematografica/Flora Film/Gico Cinematografica).

only points to a direction of violence heretofore unseen in the Italian genre cinema.

Gemser stars as Emanuelle, the reporter and photographer intent on tracking down gunrunners, drug runners, white slavers and sleazy politicians. Her investigations lead her to the privileged world of the ultra-rich and the deviant. While at the exclusive home of an U.S. Senator who may be involved in all of this, she witnesses horrific snuff footage of women being tortured and murdered. When she is kidnapped and taken to the very island where the snuff films are being made, she attempts to put an end to the terror and expose all those responsible.

While this was one of Gemser's first film roles in a Massaccesi production, one wonders what she may have made of the outrageous plot. The film's reason for being labeled a horror feature lies in its investigative thriller subplot and the fact that Massaccesi's snuff footage appears so realistic. Using 8mm and 16mm film stock, scratching the negatives and moving the camera frantically, Massaccesi makes the disturbing scenes of women being tortured and killed seem too real.

In 1977, *Emanuelle e gli Ultimi Cannibali* followed. In this entry, Emanuelle meets up with big game hunters who are on an expedition marked for disaster. When cannibals attack the group, the survivors make an attempt to retreat from the horror and reach the safety of civilization. Graphically gory special effects by Fabrizia Spora combined with mondo footage of some sickening real-life animal abuse contribute to make this film a delight to cannibal movie lovers and a real-life horror to anyone else.

Emanuelle's visit to an asylum coincides with the escape of a crazed patient who attacks and eats another mental patient. She notices a strange tattoo on the female psycho, leading her to investigate a South American tribe of cannibals. Emanuelle joins an expedition to the jungle but eventually learns that they are actually thieves searching for a downed plane with a treasure in gems aboard. As the cannibals attack, the survivors attempt to reach safety but are only saved by Emanuelle's quick thinking. She draws a similar tattoo on her stomach and, naked, meets the cannibals head-on. They assume that she is their long-lost goddess.

Massaccesi's Emanuelle (or Black Emanuelle) series goes down stranger and darker paths with this entry. Well-photographed copulation scenes and jungle fauna add to the semi-documentary atmosphere until the cannibals arrive onscreen, throwing the whole film into gore-filled chaos. Two more sexy, occasionally violent entries in the series followed: *Emanuelle: Perchè Violenza alle Donne?* (1977) and *La Via della Prostituzione* (1977).

The obscure *Papaya dei Caraibi* (1977) is an improvement in Massaccesi's canon of erotic-adventure-horror films. The exotic Melissa Chimenti stars as the leader of a South American village of black magic worshippers and flesh-eating cannibals. Maurice Poli and Sirpa Lane, the couple who meet Chimenti, are transfixed by her hypnotic sexual aura. They are led down a path of extreme sexual desires and the supernatural. While far from being among the best of the director's work,

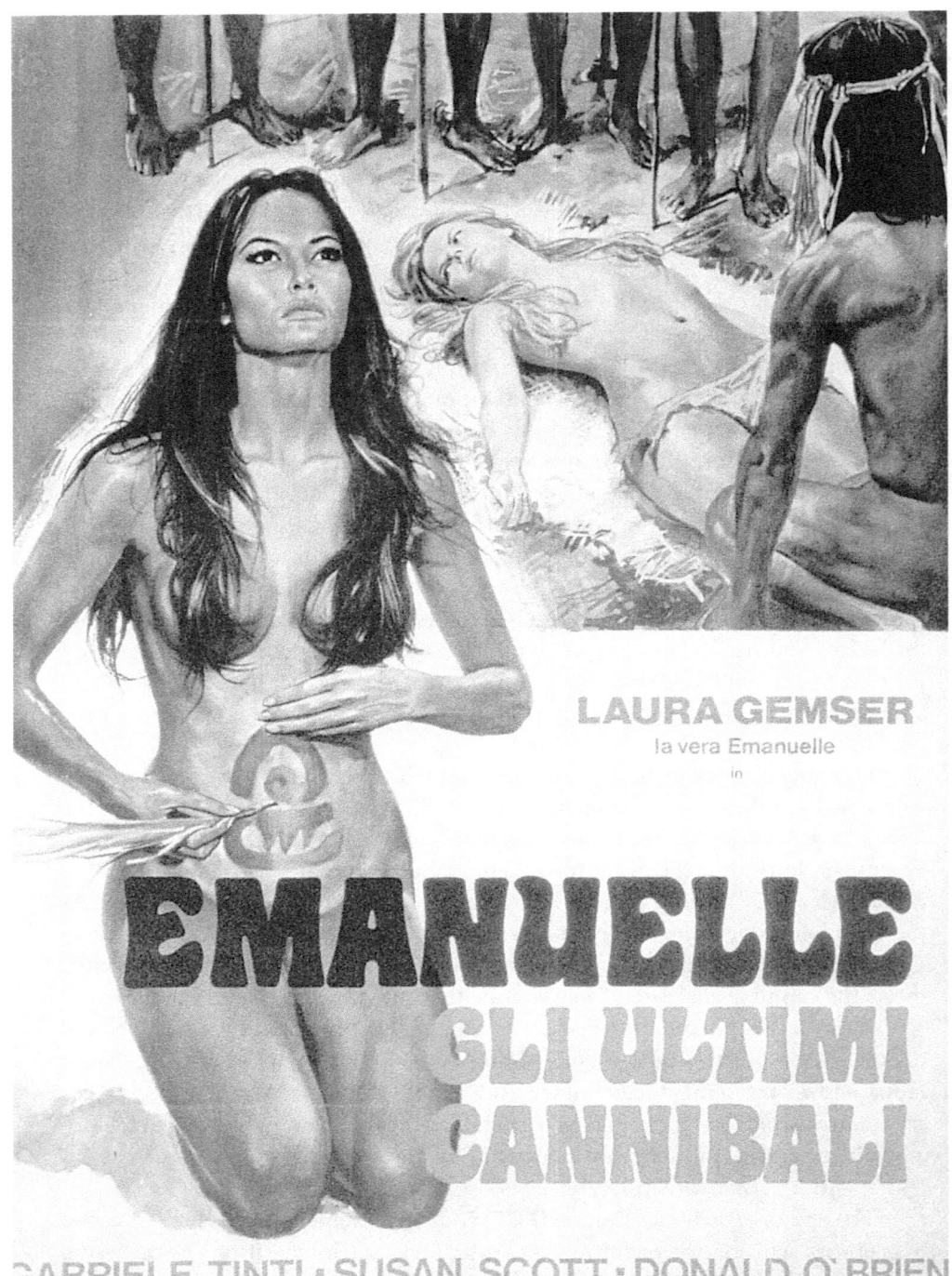

Italian poster art for Massaccesi's *Emanuelle e gli Ultimi Cannibali* (1977, Fulvia Cinematografica/Flora Film/Gico Cinematografica).

Papaya dei Caraibi at least succeeds in mixing up erotica and the supernatural to a halfway satisfying degree. The film does have an atmosphere of dread and is not designed as a disgusting taboo breaker like some other mondo or cannibal features. Unfortunately, to the detriment of the film and, ultimately, the director, is the insistence on (briefly) showing graphic animal mutilation and on-screen death to convey the flesh-eating lusts of the cannibals.

In 1978, Massaccesi directed several films. These include *Duri a Morire*, a mercenaries-at-war production, and three odd documentaries: *Emanuelle e le Porno Notti* (hosted by Laura Gemser), *Follie di Una Notte* (hosted by noted transsexual star Amanda Lear) and *Le Notti Porno nel Mondo No. 2* (co-hosted by another transsexual, Ajita Wilson and Italian porno starlet Marina Frajese).

With *Buio Omega* (1979), Massaccesi went into a total reversal, displaying a deep and profound renewed interest in the horror film genre, contributing a work of startling shock. *Buio Omega*'s tale is that of a lonely, dysfunctional man (Kieran Canter) who mourns the death of his wife (Cinzia Monreale) only to re-build her image using the pieces of the female victims that he murders. A scary housekeeper, who has pined for him for years, assists him in slaughtering a few nubile maidens in order to get an eyeball here or a fingernail there. When a young beauty (also Monreale), who resembles the dead wife, approaches the man, he begins a fairly normal relationship with her, but slowly he imagines his deceased wife (with whom he still has sexual relations) compelling him to murder her as well. Where the film obviously breaks the most taboo subject of all is in its treatment of necrophilia.

Massaccesi utilized a cast of seldom-seen actors (both before and since) to portray the bizarre deviants who people this tale of necrophilia. With the aid of a haunting score by Goblin and his own understated photography, the film plays like a perverted drama until the shock sequences begin.

That same year Massaccesi somehow became involved with two strange film projects. He edited footage of fellow exploitation filmmaker Jesus Franco's *Elles Font Tout* (1978), *Je Brûle de Partout* (1978), an unidentified Sergio Bergonzelli softcore sex film and unrelated hardcore sex footage (supplied by Massaccesi from his own productions, including outtakes) and then spliced all this together to form the film *Claire*. For the other, he edited together Franco's *Midnight Party* (1975), *Shining Sex* (1975) and an uncompleted Franco title called *Justine and Juliette*. When Massaccesi added more footage from his own hardcore films, he edited this print into a new feature titled *Justine* and released it as a film directed by Dave Tough (a frequent Massaccesi pseudonym) and supervised by Aristide Massaccesi.

Massaccesi spent the majority of the next two years working on a series of hardcore pornographic features featuring his discoveries Dirce Funari (a.k.a. Patrize or Patrizia Funari), Mark Shannon (a.k.a. Manlio Certosino), Annj Goren (a.k.a. Annamaria Naploetano), Laura Levi (a.k.a. Gabriella Tricca) and Françoise Perrot. Amidst the exploitably titled porno productions *Hard Sensations* (1979), *Blue*

Erotic Climax, Labbra Bagnate (both 1980) and others, Massaccesi directed some of his most deliriously taboo-breaking works.

Immagini di un Convento (1979) is an outrageous contribution to the then-proliferating European cycle of sexy, demented and possessed nuns in the convent films. It features Paola Senatore as the object of affection of her fellow nuns, an exorcist and a possible demonic presence. The film manages to convey a resemblance to the work of fellow director Walerian Borowczyk, most notably his *Interno d'un Convento* (1977), in its depiction of repressed society and sexuality. Massaccesi even depicted his nuns in lesbian trysts and in orgies that far exceeded what Ken Russell had done with the same subject matter in *The Devils* (1971).

The delirious, scandalous plot of *Immagini di un Convento*: When a new nun (Paola Senatore) arrives at a convent, she encounters a cloistered world of sexual repression and the loss of identity. As she discovers that this is really a cover for the depraved cruelty and sexual obsession that lies beneath its surface, she finds herself attracting, and being attracted to, her fellow nuns. Hints of demonic possession appear when it seems that a religious statue may actually be responsible for the strange happenings. An exorcist (Donald O'Brien) is called in to deal with the madness taking place, but even he is affected by the sexual allure of the nuns. Massaccesi's superior handling of the atmosphere of eroticism and occult mystery successfully broaches the barriers of taste. Paola Senatore and co-star Marina Frajese both went on to careers in pornography in the '80s.

Porno Holocaust (1979) sounds like just another outrageously titled porno, but is far from that. In this film, science fiction and horror combine with deliriously choreographed sex scenes to tell the tale of an island inhabited by a hulking giant who is a deformed humanoid beast (radiation from nuclear fallout is to blame) and a group of debauched investigators (Luigi Montefiori, Mark Shannon, Dirce Funari, Annj Goren and others). This monster attempts to kill all the men and rape the women. He drags one victim to his cave lair because she resembles his dead wife, in a hilarious attempt to elicit sympathy from the audience. Combining the hardcore porn film into the horror genre had been attempted before, most assuredly in such American productions as *The Devil in Miss Jones* (1972) and *The Devil Within Her* (1975), but, with Massaccesi's film, his intention is to have a scary monster commit the most heinous acts imaginable.

It is unclear what kind of audience Massaccesi intended to attract with this film. It neither excites sexually (a problem apparent in more than a few of his '80s porno films) nor horrifies one wholly. The central device that nuclear testing responsible for radiation fallout has created a creature of destruction has been used countless times before. What Massaccesi strove to achieve with this film is the completely ludicrous principle that even such a creature would still be amorous and that even fleeing survivors of an untold horrific carnage would take the time out for a quick sex fling. Who would take this film seriously?

Anthropophagus (1980) is no calmer. Compared to his hardcore productions, it is a decidedly tamer affair, but more crazed in other ways. Vacationers (Tisa Farrow and friends) happen upon a seemingly deserted seaport town where a cannibalistic creature (Luigi Montefiori) has caused the many deaths. The scenes of gut-munching violence are true stomach turners. Audiences exposed to the ritualistic flesh eating of George Romero's *Dawn of the Dead* are in for a real surprise with this film. *Anthropophagus* shares many visual ideas with the films of Italy's major gore director Lucio Fulci. In fact, the "in your face" gore scenes from this film rival and, at times, exceed in its own low-budget way those of Fulci's *Zombie* and *L'Aldila*. Gross scenes of entrails and flesh being torn from still-living victims makes one quite aware of the shock theatrics for which the production aims. The main gross-out scene comes late in the movie when Montefiori's rabid creature attacks a pregnant woman (Serena Grandi) and rips the living fetus from her stomach and chows down, only to be topped by the absurd climax, featuring the killer literally eating *himself* to death.

Even though *Anthropophagus* was a success as a horror film, Massaccesi continued to churn out hardcore sex films at a regular pace and still found time to return to the recently exploited themes of cannibalism and sex which leads to *Le Notti Erotiche dei Morti Viventi* (1980), a film that is pure cinema horror trash, but watchable nonetheless. In the history of the Italian horror film there is no other feature film quite like it. That's not to say that there are no similarities to a movie like *Porno Holocaust* either, but *Le Notti Erotiche dei Morti Viventi* is an altogether different form of weirdness. Basically, the film consists of flashbacks to an idyllic vacation on an island where a boatload of friends happen upon some tribal black magic rites and the supernatural events that result, including a fierce madness to screw each other to death. Frequent Massaccesi muse Laura Gemser makes an appearance and the film climaxes with a strange twist.

What can one say about this incredible title other than Massaccesi has taken the previously successful experiments with the horror and sex genre, pioneered by the Spanish director Jess Franco, to its ultimate conclusion. Besides Laura Gemser (who does not participate in any of the sexually graphic scenes), the cast includes future Massaccesi porn regulars Mark Shannon and Dirce Funari.

Orgasmo Nero (1980) also tampers with themes of the supernatural and sex. This time, a better-than-average cast including Richard Harrison and Susan Scott (Nieves Navarro) enliven this film about a dysfunctional couple and a beautiful ebony voodoo priestess (Lucia Ramirez) who enters into their lives, seducing the man, then the woman. On an idyllic Caribbean island, a strange, forlorn couple played by Harrison and Scott come across, then virtually adopt the silent beauty (Ramirez) they find on the beach. Sexually attracted to the striking beauty, the couple deals with their frustrations in many ways by having sex with others. When one of Scott's female friends can't quite keep her hands off of her strange new visitor, she finally realizes her own lust and enters into a sexual relationship she never before dreamed of. When the husband comes home and finds the wife in bed with

Spanish poster art for *Anthropophagus* (1980, P.C.M. International/Filmirage).

Ramirez, he deflowers the girl. She reveals to the audience (and to her new lovers) that she is, in fact, a voodoo priestess, and the trio takes a short trip to a neighboring island where the husband is killed during a ceremony, leaving the women alone to explore their desires.

This is one of Massaccesi's more successful mixes of eroticism and horror. His camera photographs everything in an ambient, deliberate manner. Again, Massaccesi seems to be borrowing visual cues from the work of Jess Franco. In fact, Franco used many of the ideas explored in this film for his own *Macumba Sexual* (1981), which co-starred Ajita Wilson. *Orgasmo Nero* is also notable for the appearance of actor Harrison, internationally known for his roles in action movies of the '60s, and Scott, who can be seen in a number of '70s *gialli* and mysteries. A newcomer to film, Ramirez exudes a scintillating amount of sexual energy and serves Massaccesi's script well with her slow, deliberate movements and exotic appearance.

Massaccesi spent the majority of 1981 making yet more porno films and the occasional softcore drama, but none of these films seemed to show that the director was attempting something different within either genre. The one film he directed that year that was a horror title without any heavy sexual content was *Anthropophagus II* (a.k.a. *Rosso Sangue*), an outrageously bloody, campy mix of theatrics and gore (à la Lucio Fulci) and a rip-off of the popular American *Halloween* films series.

In *Rosso Sangue*, a priest is seen chasing a man through the night. The man is impaled upon an iron fence while making his escape, but manages to stagger away as his entrails pour from his body. Eventually, he collapses and appears to die. However, the man fully recovers on the operating table and murders a nurse before making his escape. The police discover that the mysterious regenerative man is of Greek heritage and that the priest is really a scientist whose experiments with biochemistry could have resulted in the murderous being that he was chasing at the film's beginning. The killer continues his rampage of gory murder until he ends up at the home of a young girl who is disabled and bedridden.

Massaccesi manages to loosely tie this film to his successful *Anthropophagus*, but really seems intent on copying American stalker and slasher films like John Carpenter's *Halloween* and Sean S. Cunningham's *Friday the 13th*. Featuring dollops of extreme gore and violence à la Lucio Fulci, *Rosso Sangue* ends up an entertaining, if patchwork hybrid of genres resulting in a not entirely successful mix, notwithstanding its disgusting gore-filled scenes. Despite forays into the sword-and-sorcery genre (with his Ator series starring Miles O'Keefe) and his science fiction apocalypse films influenced by the international success of the Australian hit *Mad Max*, this was Massaccesi's last official horror film until *Ritorno dalla Morte* in 1992.

In 1982, to cash in on the international success of *Conan, the Barbarian*, Massaccesi contributed to the Italian sword-and-sorcery genre, producing and directing the handsome-looking *Ator l'Invincibile*, the success of which led to many more imitations. Massaccesi's revision of Tinto Brass' *Caligula* (1979), titled *Caligola — La Storia della Raccontata* (1982), is notorious for its combination of dramatic history, bloody violence and hardcore porn sequences which feature primary cast members. He followed this film with the similar-themed, but lower-budgeted *Messalina — Orgasmo Imperiale* (1982). Massaccesi next followed up with a sequel to the internationally successful Ator film, *Ator 2 l'Invincibile Orion* (1983). Then the *Mad Max* imitations became a necessary commodity for fringe Italian filmmakers. Massaccesi's contributions to this genre, *Endgame — Bronx Lotta Finale* (1983) and *Anno 2020: I Gladiatori del Futuro* (1984), are well-photographed, violent entries into this science fiction–holocaust genre with more than a little hint of homoeroticism.

To compete with the growing videocassette market interest in films of all kinds, Massaccesi began to churn out many softcore sex dramas, some with hysterical plot devices. *L'Alcova* (1985) and others were rip-offs of popular American films; another case in point being the *Flashdance* (1983) makeover *Prison Dancer* (1985).

In 1986, Massaccesi created his own production company, Filmirage. With an influx of invested money, many of his productions from this period exhibited higher-than-usual production values and a sleeker, more professional look. *La Casa No. 3* (a.k.a. *Ghost House*) (1987) was directed by Umberto Lenzi and produced by Massaccesi with some directorial assistance. Nevertheless, it is a fair, but inconsequential, attempt to cash in on the American *House* series. That same year, Massaccesi produced Michele Soavi's horror directorial debut *Deliria*, Deran Serafian's science fiction film *Interzone* and Claudio Lattanzi's *Raptors*, which Massaccesi finished directing after disagreements during production with the assigned director.

In order to compete even more with the lucrative and growing cable television market, Massaccesi turned his cinematic eye back to sexy films. *Top Model* (1987), *Pomeriggio Caldo* (a.k.a. *Afternoon*) (1988) and *Ogni Volta, un Gioco* (a.k.a.

Aristide Massaccesi (left) and the author four months before the filmmaker died in January 1999.

Any Time, Any Place) (1989) were just three of the many softcore dramas and thrillers that he made in 1987–89. These productions may have performed well financially for Massaccesi because he was able to direct a third feature in his Ator series, produce Luigi Montefiori's directorial debut *Metamorphosis* (1989) and produce and photograph Umberto Lenzi's *Paura nel Buio* (1989), a horrific thriller about a serial killer.

As Massaccesi continued to make softcore sex films tailored to the cable and video markets,* he returned to the horror genre for *Sharks: Deep Blood* (1989), a *Jaws* clone (which was terrible). He produced both *Troll 2* and *Troll 3* (a.k.a. *Creepers*) (both 1990), violent and yet childish copies of the *Gremlins* (1984) series, and ended up finishing them as director in an attempt to save the productions that even he deemed poorly filmed and unreleasable.

Troll 2, directed by Claudio Fragrasso, is an abominable sequel to the low-budget American film *Troll*. The original movie wasn't much better, but at least that film featured a scene where Sonny Bono morphed into an asparagus mutation and it wasn't filmed in Utah with an amateur cast like this movie.

Troll 3 was directed by Fabrizio Laurenti. As with *Troll 2*, producer Massaccesi stepped in and rescued the movie from the shelf (where it sat for three years) and tried to edit the film into something more presentable for the fickle international cable and video marketplace. Radiation released in Alaska causes scary root monsters that seek warm-blooded prey.

Massaccesi also produced Lucio Fulci's last horror film *Le Porte del Silenzio* (1991) starring John Savage (*The Deer Hunter* [1978]). *Le Porte del Silenzio* was filmed in America. Afterwards, he attempted to make a number of films that were never realized including *Anthropophagus 3* and *The Amazing Kung Fu Bat Teens* (a film Massaccesi had intended to pattern on the international box office success of the *Teenage Mutant Ninja Turtle* series).

Massaccesi's genuine return to horror was with 1991's disappointing *Ritorno dalla Morte* (a.k.a. *Frankenstein 2000*). However, this project suffers from an obvious lack of enthusiasm, which even affects the cast.

In an unspecified contemporary metropolis that resembles a futuristic police state, a couple strives to continue a normal life despite the outside threat of violence from gangs of hoodlums. When the woman is brutally attacked and placed on a life support system in the hospital, her only chance of revenge is to psychically link to Donald O'Brien's character via an electronic machine. Through him she will enact her vengeance.

Massaccesi's version of Frankenstein is an unsuccessful attempt at a comeback within the confines of the science fiction and horror genres. Filmed on an obvious low budget with little money left for decent actors or special effects, the movie

---

*Undici Giorni, Undici Notti (*a.k.a. 11 Days, 11 Nights*) (1987), its sequel* Undici Giorni, Undici Notti 2 *(1990) and* La Signora di Wall Street *(a.k.a. High Finance Woman) (1989).*

clumsily drags from one scene to another. The presence of aged genre villain O'Brien adds nothing to the film which, reportedly, was not released to theaters, television, cable or video for several years.

Apparently, the kind of sexy films that Massaccesi was churning out for cable and television during these past few years had also run their course. Now independent, low-budget American companies were making these same kind of films even cheaper than *he* did, and selling them to the same once-lucrative markets at packaged discount prices. With the cultish attention towards Hong Kong films reaching a fever pitch, his attention was drawn to the erotic Category III films of the Asian island. The huge success of the Chinese film *Sex and Zen* (1993) and similar movies impressed Massaccesi enough to film his own series of Oriental sex films. In fact, he even considered a Hong Kong co-production featuring Asian and European actors.

Massaccesi journeyed to Hong Kong to investigate co-production funding, but this property never got off the ground and he thought of returning home. Returning to Italy via the Philippines, he attempted several more Asian softcore productions with European performers and indigenous locals in the leading roles. These sex movies, filmed and co-financed in the Philippines, had such delirious titles as *China and Sex*, *Chinese Kama Sutra* and *Sex and Chinese Food* (all 1993). Oddly, many of these titles have yet to appear in many markets outside of Hong Kong (where some of these reputedly played theatrically), and they have yet to even appear on Italian cable television, although they did appear briefly on videocassette in that country.

In 1992, the Italian Eden Video label packaged a collection of erotic videotapes for the lucrative consumer sales markets. The collection, which was approved and edited by Massaccesi, was sold to audiences as four separate videotapes titled *Il Vizio Infinito*, *Donne di Piacere*, *Così Fan Tutti* and *Mio Dio Come Sono Caduta in Basso?*, which hilariously translates into English as *My God, Have I Fallen So Low?* These tapes were all re-edited highlights from Massaccesi's sexy films and, if not spanning his entire career, did certainly concentrate on his later '80s and '90s product.

In 1993, the American hardcore sex on video phenomena had become a financial boom for filmmakers. At this same time, there began in Italy an incredible explosion of pornography as well. Italian B movie and horror film actresses whose careers were derailed by scandal and/or drugs found new welcome arms in those of porno film producers. Seeing the unlimited possibilities to reap financial profits in the new pornographic video marketplace, Massaccesi entered into a partnership with film producer Luca Damiano a.k.a. Franco LoCascio. Their production companies Golden Hawk and Capital Film have churned out many hardcore sex films in the years since and they still do. Initially, the project began with a collection of movies that had some kind of Asian flavor. Titles like *1001 Oriental Nights* (1993), *Aladino X* (1993/1994) and *L'Alcova dei Perversi Piaceri* (1994) suggested

Massaccesi's horror thriller *Buio Omega* (1979, D.R. Produzioni per Communicazioni di Massa).

Asian connection, if not in cast, at least in their themes. Like in the early '80s, Massaccesi also assembled his own stable of performers, some who appeared in many, if not nearly all of these features. The women were, for the most part, unlike the silicone freaks seen so often in the American hardcore product. Massaccesi usually cast his female roles in his films looking for a certain combination of natural beauty and some kind of acting ability as well. Among the names one usually finds in most of these productions are Simona Valli, Giulia Chanel, Pussycat, Shalima and (the men), Rocco Siffredi and Christopher Clark. For the quickly shot, low, low-budget, independently financed productions, Massaccesi seemed content to churn out these films which, although beautifully photographed, utilized minimalist sets and dialogue to convey the "set-up" and spent the rest of the running time finding new ways to photograph gynecological close-ups. Of late, these productions had exhibited a certain kind of maturity. Massaccesi who, if truth be told, always made films in styles similar to others, but with a decidedly lurid, sexual twist, apparently decided to turn every fairy tale and mythological story and idea he could possible think of into a well-photographed piece of pornography. His productions *Tarzan X* (1994), *Al Capone* (1995) and *Ulisse* (1994) exhibit more care than usual for a film in this genre, in terms of locales, costume design and lighting. *Amleto* (1993) and *Primal Instinct* (1996) are epic-length films (with running times approximating and, in some cases, exceeding two hours!), based on Shakespeare, the '60s American television show *The Untouchables* and the Sharon Stone thriller *Basic Instinct*. Aristide Massaccesi may have improved the future of pornography.

Massaccesi's career as a horror film director of note seemed to be behind him. Rumors persisted in his last years about another return to the horror film genre. If *Ritorno dalle Morte* was any indication, maybe the genre just did not interest him any more, although his sex thriller *Sul Filo del Rasio* (1992) indicated that he was still more fascinated by sexual situations and their depictions on-screen than indulging in the conventions of the thriller genre. Fans of Massaccesi can have a field day trying to track down all of the director's films that appear in his filmography and then some, due to his use of numerous pseudonyms. Among the aliases most often used by Aristide Massaccesi are Joe D'Amato (of course), David Hills, Michael Wotruba, Peter Newton, Peter McCoy, Luca Damiano, Alexandre Borsky, Alexander Borsky, Joan Russell, Dario Donati, and Lucky Farr Delly (sometimes listed as Lucky Farradelly in credits). That name was also used by Demofilo Fidani (who also directed films in a variety of genres using the names Miles Deem, Dick Spitfire and Lucky Dickerson), by Franco LoCascio (who also sometimes uses the Luca Damiano pseudonym) and others.

Aristide Massaccesi Filmography

Al Capone

A.k.a. *The Hot Love Life of Al Capone* (English title) (1995) (It.); D/P/SC/C: Aristide Massaccesi; S: Simona Valli, Clarrisa Bruni, Tony Montana.

Aladino X

A.k.a. *Aladdin X* (English translation); a.k.a. *The Erotic Adventures of Aladdin X*; a.k.a. *The Erotic Dreams of Aladdin X* (English titles) (1993/94) (It.); D: Aristide Massaccesi, Franco Lo Cascio, credited to the pseudonym, Luca Damiano; Prod. Co.: Golden Hawk films; C: Aristide Massaccesi; S: Christopher Clark, Giulia Chanel, Pussycat, Luca Bazzocca, Joe Danila, Simona Valli, Tabitha Cash.

L'Alcova

A.k.a. *The Alcove* (English translation and title); a.k.a. *Lust* (1985) (It.); D/C: Aristide Massaccesi; Prod. Co.: M.A.D. Film; SC: Ugo Moretti; M: Manuel De Sica; S: Lilli Carati a.k.a. Lileana Caravati, Laura Gemser, Annie Belle a.k.a. Annie Briand, Al Cliver a.k.a. Pier Luigi Conti, Roberto Caruso.

L'Alcova dei Perversi Piaceri

A.k.a. *The Alcove of Perverse Pleasures* (English translation); a.k.a. *L'Alcova dei Desideri Perversi* (alternate Italian title; translation: *The Alcove of Perverse Desires*) (1994) (It.); D/P/SC: Aristide Massaccesi, Franco Lo Casio, credited to the pseudonym, Luca Damiano; Prod. Co.: Golden Hawk Films; S: Giulia Chanel, Simona Valli, Pussycat, Christopher Clark.

Amleto

A.k.a. *Hamlet* (English translation); a.k.a. *X Hamlet*; a.k.a. *Hamlet II* (English titles) (1993) (It.); D/C: Aristide Massaccesi; P: Golden Hawk Films; S: Sarah Young, Christopher Clark, Richard Lengin, Maeva, Roberto Malone, Aristide Massaccesi, Tanya La Riviere, Carole Nash, Vicky Valentina Martinez, Shalimar.

This epic-length production was released to the PAL, SECAM and VHS videocassette formats in two parts.

Anno 2020 i Gladiatori Del Futuro

A.k.a. *Anno 2028: I Gladiatori del Futuro* (alternate Italian title); a.k.a. *Year 2020 Gladiators of the Future* (English translation); a.k.a. *Futoro* (alternate Italian title); a.k.a. *2020 Texas Gladiators*; a.k.a. *Texas 2000*; a.k.a. *2020: Freedom Fighters*; a.k.a. *2020: The Rangers of Texas*; a.k.a. *2020: Texas Freedom Fighters*; a.k.a. *Sudden Death* (English titles) (1984) (It.); D: Aristide Massaccesi, George Eastman a.k.a. Luigi Montefiori [uncredited]; P/C: Aristide Massaccesi; Prod. Co.: Eureka Cinematografica; SC: George Eastman a.k.a. Luigi Montefiori; M: Carlo Maria Cordio; S: Al Cliver a.k.a. Pier Luigi Conti, Harrison Mueller, Daniel Stephen, Peter Hooten, Al Yamanouchi a.k.a. Haruiko Yamanouchi, Sabrina Siani a.k.a. Sabrina Seggiani, Isabella Rocchietta, Donald O'Brien, Michele Soavi.

Anthropophagus

A.k.a. *Anthropophagus — the Beast*; a.k.a. *Man Beast*; a.k.a. *Man-Eater*; a.k.a. *The Grim Reaper*; a.k.a. *The Savage Island* (English titles) (1980) (It.); D: Aristide Massaccesi; P: Oscar Santaniello, Aristide Massaccesi; Prod. Co.: P.C.M. International/Filmirage; SC: Aristide Massaccesi, George Eastman a.k.a. Luigi Montefiori; C: Aristide Massaccesi, Enrico Biribicchi; M: Marcello Giombini; S: Tisa Farrow, George Eastman a.k.a. Luigi Montefiori, Saverio Vallone, Vanessa Steiger a.k.a. Serena Grandi, Mark Bodin, Zora Kerova a.k.a. Zora Ulla Keslerova Tschechin.

Anthropophagus II

A.k.a. *Rosso Sangue* (alternate Italian title); a.k.a. *Red Blood*; a.k.a. *Absurd*; a.k.a. *Grim Reaper II*; a.k.a. *Monster Hunter*; a.k.a. *The Grim Reaper II*; a.k.a. *Zombie 6: Monster Hunter* (English titles) (1981) (It.); D/P/SC/C: Aristide Massaccesi; Prod. Co.: Filmirage/Metaxa Corporation; M: Carlo Maria Cordio; S: George Eastman a.k.a. Luigi Montefiori, Edmund Purdom, Annie Belle a.k.a. Annie Briand, Katya Berger, Ian Danby, Cristiano Borromeo, Ted Rusoff, Anja Kochansky, Michele Soavi, Mark Shannon a.k.a. Manlio Certosino, Dirce Funari a.k.a. Patrize Funari a.k.a. Patrizia Funari

Ator 2 l'Invincibile Orion

A.k.a. *Ator 2: The Invincible Orion*; a.k.a. *Orion — Ator 2: The Invincible* (English translations); a.k.a. *Ator II*; a.k.a. *Ator l'Invincibile II* (alternate Italian title); a.k.a. *Vendetta di Ator* (alternate Italian title; translation: *The Vengeance of Ator*); a.k.a. *Ator the Invincible* (G.B.); a.k.a *The Blade Master* (English titles) (1983) (It.); D/P/C: Aristide Massaccesi; Prod. Co.: Filmirage; M: Carlo Rustichelli; S: Miles O'Keefe, Lisa Foster, Cristiano Borromeo, Chen Wong, David Brandon a.k.a. David Cain Haughton.

Ator l'Invincibile

A.k.a. *Ator the Invincible* (English translation and title); a.k.a. *Ator, the Fighting Eagle* (1982) (It.); D: Aristide Massaccesi, Michele Soavi (uncredited); P: Aristide Massaccesi, Helen Sarlui; Prod. Co.: Filmirage S.r.l./Metaxa Corporation S.A.; SC: Aristide Massaccesi, Jose Maria Sanchez; C: Aristide Massaccesi; M: Carlo Maria Cordio; S: Miles O'Keefe, Sabrina Siani a.k.a. Sabrina Seggiani, Ritza Brown, Edmund Purdom, Laura Gemser, Chandra Vazzoler, Michele Soavi, Brooke Hart.

Blue Erotic Climax

A.k.a. *Symphonique Erotique* (French title) (1980) (It.); D/P/SC/C: Aristide Massaccesi, Claudio Bernabei (uncredited); S: Laura Levi a.k.a. Gabriella Tricca, Mark Shannon a.k.a. Manlio Certosino, Sandy Samuels a.k.a. Clare Colosimo.

Un Bounty Killer a Trinità

A.k.a. *A Bounty Killer in Trinity*; a.k.a. *A Bounty Hunter in Trinity* (English translation and titles) (1972) (It.); D/C: Aristide Massaccesi; P: Avis Films; SC: Aristide Massaccesi, Romano Scandariato; M: Vasil Kojucharov; S: Jeff Cameron, Paul McCren, Pat Miner, Attilio Dottesio, Carla Mancini, Antonio Cantafora.

Buio Omega

A.k.a. *Blue Holocaust* (English translation); a.k.a. *In Quella Casa* (Italian re-release title); a.k.a. *In Quella Casa ... Buio Omega* (Italian video title); a.k.a. *Beyond the Darkness*; a.k.a. *Buried Alive* (English titles) (1979) (It.); D: Aristide Massaccesi; P: Marco Rossetti, Oscar Santaniello; Prod. Co.: D.R. Produzioni per Communicazioni Di Massa; SC: Ottavio Fabbri, Giacomo Guerrini; C: Aristide Massaccesi, Enrico Biribicchi; M: Goblin; S: Kieran Canter, Cinzia Monreale, Franca Stoppa, Sam Modesto, Anna Cardini, Lucia D'Elia, Simonetta Allodi, Klaus Rainer.

Caligola—La Storia della Raccontata

A.k.a. *Caligula—the Untold Story* (English translation and title); a.k.a. *Caligula 2*; a.k.a. *Caligula 2: The Forbidden Story*; a.k.a. *The Emperor Caligula* (English titles) (1982) (It.); D/P/C/SC: Aristide Massaccesi; Prod. Co.: Metaxa Corporation S.A.; M: Carlo Mario Cordio; S: David Brandon a.k.a. David Cain Haughton, Laura Gemser, Cristiano Borromeo, Fabiora Toledo, Sasha D'Arc, Michele Soavi

China and Sex

A.k.a. *The Flower of Desire* (English title) (1993) (It., Philippines); D/P/C: Aristide Massaccesi; SC: Chang Chun (?); Prod. Co.: Music Box Film Presents A Golden Dragon Production; S: Lora Luna, Marc Gonsalvez, Nongkok Kok, Li Yu, Chin Yong, Lim Yao.

Chinese Kama Sutra

A.k.a. *Chinese Kamasutra*; a.k.a. *Kamasutra Cinese* (English titles) (1993) (It., Philippines); D/C: Aristide Massaccesi; P: Eduard Lao, Gloria Chen; SC: Fu Chun; Prod. Co.: Butterfly Motion Pictures; S: Giorgia Emerald, Marc Gonsalvez, Leo Gambao, Li Yu, Liezl Santos, Lim Yao.

Claire

(1979) (It., Sp., Fr.); D/P/SC/C: Jess Franco, Aristide Massaccesi; S: Didier Aubriot, Marius Clavier, Martine Flety, Susan Hemingway, Ursula Maris, Lina Romay, Beni Touxa.
Features footage from Franco's *Elles Font Tout* (Fr., 1978).

Duri a Morire

A.k.a. *Tough to Kill* (English translation and title); a.k.a. *Hard to Kill*; a.k.a. *Strike Force* (English titles) (1978) (It.); D: Aristide Massaccesi; P: Giuseppe Zaccariello; Prod. Co.: Nucleo Internazionale S.R.L. Produzioni Cinematografica; SC: Sergio Donati, Joseph McLee; C: Aristide Massaccesi; M: Stelvio Cipriani; S: Luc Meranda, Donald O'Brien, Laurence Stark, Piero Vida, Percy Hogan, Wolfgango Soldati, Isarco Ravaiolo, Alessandro Haber, Lorenza Rodriguez Lopez.

Emanuelle e Françoise—Le Sorelline

A.k.a. *Emanuelle and Françoise — The Little Sisters* (English translation); a.k.a. *Emmanuelle e Françoise*; a.k.a. *Emanuelle and Françoise* (G.B.); a.k.a. *Blood Vengeance* (alternate G.B. title); a.k.a. *Emanuelle's Revenge* (English titles) (1976) (It.); D: Aristide Massaccesi; P: Manlio Camastro, Oscar Santaniello; Prod. Co.: Matra Cinematografica; SC: Aristide Massaccesi, Bruno Mattei; C: Aristide Massaccesi; M: Gianni Marchetti; S: George Eastman a.k.a. Luigi Montefiori, Rosemarie Lindt, Patrizia Gori, Karole Annie Edel, Massimo Vanni.

Emanuelle e gli Ultimi Cannibali

A.k.a. *Emanuelle and the Last Cannibals* (English translation and title); a.k.a. *Emanuelle's Amazon Adventure*; a.k.a. *Trap Them and Kill Them* (English titles) (1977) (It.); D: Aristide Massaccesi; P: Fabrizio De Angelis, Gianfranco Couyoumdjian; Prod. Co.: Fulvia Cinematografica/Flora Film/Gico Cinematografica; SC: Aristide Massaccesi, Romano Scandariato; C: Aristide Massaccesi; M: Nico Fidenco, Giacomo Dell'Orso; SP E: Fabrizio De Angelis; S: Laura Gemser, Gabriele Tinti, Susan Scott a.k.a. Nieves Navarro, Donald O'Brien, Percy Hogan, Monica Zanchi, Annemarie Clementi, Dirce Funari a.k.a. Patrize Funari a.k.a. Patrizia Funari.

Emanuelle e le Porno Notti

A.k.a. *Emanuelle: Le Porno Notti nel Mondo*; a.k.a. *Emanuelle and the Porno Nights in the World* (English translation) (1978) (It.); D/SC/C: Aristide Massaccesi; Prod. Co.: Stefano Film/Sorgente Cinematografica; Narration: Laura Gemser; S: Laura Gemser.

Emanuelle in America

A.k.a. *Brutal Nights*; a.k.a. *Emanuelle in America* (English title) (1976) (It.); D: Aristide Massaccesi; P: Fabrizio De Angelis; Prod. Co.: New Film Productions presentana Fida Cinematografica; SC: Aristide Massaccesi, Ottavio Alessi, Piero Vivarelli, Maria Pia Fusco; C: Aristide Massaccesi, Enrico Biribicchi; M: Nico Fidenco, Giacomo Dell'Orso, songs "Celebrate Myself," "Goodbye and Farewell" performed by Armonium; SP E: Cine Audio Effects; S: Laura Gemser, Gabriele Tinti, Roger Browne, Riccardo Salvino, Maria Pia Regoli, Giulio Bianchi, Efrem Appel, Matilde Dell'Aglio, Carlo Foschi, Maria Renata Franco, Giulio Massimini, Stefania Nocilli, Paola Senatore, Marina Frajese a.k.a. Marina Hedman a.k.a. Marina Lotar

Emanuelle Nera

A.k.a. *Black Emanuelle* (English translation and title); a.k.a. *Emanuelle Negra*; a.k.a. *Emanuelle in Africa* (English title) (1975) (It.); D/SC: Adalberto Bitto Albertini; P: Mario Mariana; Prod. Co.: San Nicola Produzione Cinematografica/Flaminia Produzione Cinematografica; C: Carlo Carlini, Massimo Carlini; M: Nico Fidenco, Giacomo Dell'Orso; songs "Black Emanuelle" by The Bulldogs, "An Impossible Love" by Don Powell; S: Laura Gemser, Karin Schubert, Gabriele Tinti, Angelo Infanti, Isabelle Marchali, Don Powell, Venantino Venantini.

Emanuelle Nera—Orient Reportage

A.k.a. *Black Emanuelle in Bangkok*; a.k.a. *Black Emanuelle Goes East*; a.k.a. *Black Emanuelle 2 Goes East* (G.B.); a.k.a. *Emanuelle in Bangkok* (English titles) (1976) (It.); D: Aristide Massaccesi; P: Ulderico Arditi, Oscar Santaniello; Prod. Co.: San Nicola Produzione Cinematografica/Flaminia Produzione Cinematografica/Kristel Film; SC: Maria Pia Fusco, Piero Vivarelli, Ottavio Alessi; C: Aristide Massaccesi; M: Nico Fidenco, Giacomo Dell'Orso; songs "Black Emanuelle" performed by The Bulldogs, "Sweet Leaving Thing" performed by Silky Sound Singers; S: Laura Gemser, Gabriele Tinti, Ely Galleani a.k.a. Elyde Galleana, Ivan Rasimov, Venantino Venantini, Giacomo Rossi-Stuart, Chris Avram a.k.a. Christea Avram, Debra Berger, Koike Manoco, Gaby Bourgois.

Emanuelle: Perchè Violenza alle Donne?

A.k.a. *Emanuelle Vs. Violence Against Women* (English translation;) a.k.a. *Confessions of Emanuelle* (G.B.); a.k.a. *Degradation of Emmanuelle*; a.k.a. *Emanuelle Around the World*; a.k.a. *Black Emanuelle Around the World*; a.k.a. *She's Seventeen and Anxious* (English titles) (1977) (It.); D: Aristide Massaccesi; P: Fabrizio De Angelis; Prod. Co.: Embassy Film; SC: Maria Pia Fusco, Giancarlo Clerici; C: Aristide Massaccesi, Luigi Conversi; M: Nico Fidenco; song "A Picture of Love" performed by Fire Fly (written by Nico Fidenco, Carfin, Cascia); S: Laura Gemser, Karin Schubert, Ivan Rassimov, Don Powell, George Eastman a.k.a. Luigi Montefiori, Brigitte Petronio, Paola Maiolini, Marino Masé, Aristide Massaccesi.

Endgame—Bronx Lotta Finale

A.k.a. *Bronx Lotta Finale* (alternate Italian title); a.k.a. *Gioco Finale* (alternate Italian title); a.k.a. *Endgame* (English title) (1983) (It.); D/P/C: Aristide Massaccesi; Prod. Co.: Filmirage; SC: George Eastman a.k.a. Luigi Montefiori; M: Carlo Maria Cordio; S: Al Cliver a.k.a. Pier Luigi Conti, Laura Gemser, George Eastman a.k.a. Luigi Montefiori, Al Yamanouchi a.k.a. Haruiko Yamanouchi, Gabriele Tinti, Gordon Mitchell a.k.a. Charles Pendleton, Michele Soavi.

Eroi all'Inferno

A.k.a. *Heroes in Hell* (English translation and title) (1973) (It.); D/SC/C: Aristide Massaccesi; P: Walter Bigari; M: Vassili Kojucharov, Paolo Bruni, Gianfranco Simoncelli; S: Klaus Kinski a.k.a. Klaus Gunther Nakszynksi, Lars Bloch, Rosemarie Lindt, Ettore Manni.

Eva Nera

A.k.a. *Black Eva* (English translation); a.k.a. *Emanuelle in Tahiti* (alternate pornographic version); a.k.a. *Emanuelle on Taboo Island* (alternate pornographic version); a.k.a. *Black Cobra*; a.k.a. *Erotic Eva*; a.k.a. *Erotic Negra* (English titles) (1976) (It.); D/C: Aristide Massaccesi; P: Aristide Massaccesi, Oscar Santaniello; Prod Co.: Airone Cinematografica; SC: Aristide Massaccesi, G. Egle; M: Piero Umiliani; S: Laura Gemser, Jack Palance a.k.a. Vladimir Dalamik, Gabrielle Tinti, Michelle Starck, Ely Galleani a.k.a. Elyde Galleana, Sigrid Zanger, G. Mariotti, Dirce Funari a.k.a. Patrize Funari a.k.a. Patrizia Funari.

Follie di Una Notte

A.k.a. *Pornofolie di Notte* (alternate Italian title); a.k.a. *Ladies of the Night*; a.k.a. *Madness in the Night* (English titles) (1978) (It.); D/P/SC/C: Aristide Massaccesi; P: Mario Paladini; M: Piero Umiliani; Narration: Amanda Lear; S: Amanda Lear

Gangland Bangers

(1995) (It.); D/P/SC/C: Aristide Massaccesi; S: Julie Ashton, Sofia Ferrari, Steven St. Croix, Sean Michaels, Tony Montana, Roxanne Hall.

Giubbe Rosse

A.k.a. *Red Coat* (English translation and title); a.k.a. *Cormack of the Mounties* (English title) (1975) (It.); D/P/C: Aristide Massaccesi; Prod. Co.: Coralta Cinematografica; SC: Aristide Massaccesi, Claudio Bernabei; M: Carlo Rustichelli; S: Fabio Testi, Guido Mannari, Renato Cestie, Lynne Frederick, Lionel Stander.

Hard Sensations

A.k.a. *Hard Sensation* (English title) (1979) (It.); D/P: Aristide Massaccesi; SC: Aristide Massaccesi, George Eastman a.k.a. Luigi Montefiori; C: Enrico Biribicchi, Enzo Frattari; M: Alessandro Alessandroni; S: George Eastman a.k.a. Luigi Montefiori, Annj Goren a.k.a. Annamaria Napoletano, Dirce Funari a.k.a. Patrize Funari a.k.a. Patrizia Funari, Lucia Ramirez, Mark Shannon a.k.a. Manlio Certosino.

Immagini di un Convento

A.k.a. *Images in the Convent* (English translation and title); a.k.a. *Porno Immagini di un Convento* (alternate Italian title; translation: *Porno Images in the Convent*) (1979) (It.); D: Aristide Massaccesi; P: Oscar Santaniello; Prod. Co.: Kristal Film; SC: Tom Salina a.k.a. Bartolemeo Scavia; C: Aristide Massaccesi; M: Nico Fidenco, Giacomo Dell'Orso; S: Paola Senatore, Donald O'Brien, Angelo Arquilla, Marina Frajese a.k.a. Marina Hedman a.k.a. Marina Lotar, Paola Maiolini, Marina Ambrosini, Rosaria Riuzzi.

Inginocchiati Straniero ... i Cadaveri Non Fanno Ombra!

A.k.a. *On Your Knees Stranger ... Corpses Cast No Shadows!*; a.k.a. *Stranger That Kneels Beside the Shadow of the Cross* (English translations and titles) (1970) (It.); D: Demofilo Fidani, Aristide Massaccesi; P: Tarquina Film; SC: Demofilo Fidani; C: Aristide Massaccesi; M: Coriolana Gori; S: Hunt Powers, Chet Davis, Gordon Mitchell a.k.a. Charles Pendleton, Simone Blondell.

Justine

(1979) (It., Sp., Fr.); D: Jess Franco, Aristide Massaccesi; P: Jess Franco, Aristide Massaccesi; C: Jess Franco, Aristide Massaccesi; SC: Jess Franco, Aristide Massaccesi; Supervision: Aristide Massaccesi; M: Nico Fidenco (Italian version only); S: Alice Arno, Lina Romay, Gilda Arancio, Alain Pettit, Jess Franco, Monica Swinn.

This is a film consisting of re-edited sequences taken from the following Jess Franco films: *Midnight Party* (Fr., 1975), *Shining Sex — La Fille au Sexe Brillant* (Fr., 1975), and the uncompleted *De Sade's Juliette* (Fr., 1975).

Labbra Baggnate

A.k.a. *Wet Lips* (English translation and title) (1980) (It.); D/SC/C: Aristide Massaccesi; P: Claudio Bernabei; Prod. Co.: Cinema 80; M: Nico Fidenco; S: Françoise Perrot, Mark Shannon a.k.a. Manlio Certosino, Pauline Teutscher, Sonia Bennet.

Lussuria

(1985) (It.); D/P/C: Aristide Massaccesi; Prod. Co.: Cinema '80; SC: Aristide Massaccesi, Rene Rivet; M: Guido Anelli, Stefano Mainetti; S: Lilli Carati a.k.a. Illeana Caravati, Valerie Chezkoff, Al Cliver a.k.a. Pier Luigi Conti, Ursula Foti.

Messalina — Orgasmo Imperiale

A.k.a. *Messalina — Orgasmo Infernale* (alternate Italian title) (1982) (It.); D: Aristide Massaccesi; P: Aristide Massaccesi, Claudio Bernabei; Prod. Co.: La Cinema 80; SC: David Jones, Jim Black, Aristide Massaccesi; C: Aristide Massaccesi; M: Carlo Maria Cordio; S: Tiffany Roussos, Nadine Roussial (same actresss as Tiffany Roussos?), Rita Landers, Mark Smith, Pauline Teutscher.

La Morte Ha Sorriso all'Assassino

A.k.a. *Death Smiles on a Murderer*; a.k.a. *Death Smiles on Murder*; a.k.a. *Death Smiles at Murder* (English translations and titles); a.k.a. *La Morte Sorride all'Assassino* (alternate Italian title); a.k.a. *Sette Strani Cadaveri* (1972) (It.); D/C: Aristide Massaccesi; P: Franco Gaudenzi; Prod. Co.: Dany Film; SC: Aristide Massaccesi, Gianfranco Simoncelli, Claudio Bernabei; M: Berto Pisani; S: Ewa Aulin, Klaus Kinski a.k.a. Klaus Gunther Nakszynksi, Angela Bo, Sergio Doria, Attilo Dottesio, Marco Mariani, Luciano Rossi, Giacomo Rossi-Stuart, Franco Cerulli, Carla Mancini.

Le Notti Porno nel Mondo N. 2

A.k.a. *The Porno Nights of the World 2* (English translation); a.k.a. *Scandinavian Erotica* (G.B.); a.k.a. *Sexy Night Report N.2* (English title) (1978) (It.); D/P/SC/C: Aristide Massaccesi; M: Gianni Marchetti; S: Ajita Wilson (also Narration), Marina Frajese a.k.a. Marina Hedman a.k.a. Marina Lotar

Le Notti Erotiche dei Morti Viventi

A.k.a. *The Erotic Nights of the Living Dead* (English translation and title); a.k.a. *La Notte degli Zombies* (alternate Italian title); a.k.a. *La Regina degli Zombie* (alternate Italian title); a.k.a. *Notti Erotiche* (Italian video title); a.k.a. *Night of the Zombies*; a.k.a. *The Island of the Zombies*; a.k.a. *Sexy Nights of the Dead*; a.k.a. *Emanuelle on the Island of the Zombies*; a.k.a. *Island of the Zombies* (English titles) (1980) (It.); D/P/SC/C: Aristide Massaccesi; P: Oscar Santaniello, Massimo Albertini; M: Pluto Kennedy; S: Laura Gemser, George Eastman a.k.a. Luigi Montefiori, Mark Shannon a.k.a. Manlio Certosino, Dirce Funari a.k.a. Patrize Funari a.k.a. Patrizia Funari.

Novelle Licenzione di Vergine Vogliose

A.k.a. *Mille e Una Notte di Boccaccio a Canterbury* (alternate Italian title); a.k.a. *Diary of a Roman Virgin* (English title) (1972) (It.); D: Aristide Massaccesi; SC: Aristide Massaccesi, Diego Spataro; S: Gabriella Giorgelli, Rose Margaret Keil, Enza Sbordone, Mimmo Poli.

1001 Oriental Nights

A.k.a. *One [or A] Thousand and One Oriental Nights* (alternate title) (1993/94) (It.); D/P/SC/C: Aristide Massaccesi, Franco LoCasico; direction credited to the pseudonym "Luca Damiano"; S: Christopher Clark, Tabitha Cash, Simona Valli, Pussycat, Giulia Chanel, Luca Bazzocca, Giulio Strong.

Ogni Volta, un Gioco

A.k.a. *Any Time, Any Place*; a.k.a. *Any Time, Any Play* (English translations and titles) (1989) (It.); D/P/C: Aristide Massaccesi; P: John Gelardi; Prod. Co.: Filmirage; SC: Helen Drake, Marc Carpenter; M: Piero Montanari; S: Ruth Collins, Robert Labrosse, Wayne Camp, Sal Maggiore, Bill Messman, Cristine Frischnertz, John Wessel, Roberta Germaine.

Orgasmo Nero

A.k.a. *Black Orgasm* (English translation); a.k.a. *Caraibi: Orgasmo Nero* (alternate Italian title); a.k.a. *Voodoo Baby* (English title) (1980) (It., Santo Domingo); D/P/SC: Aristide Massaccesi; C: Alberto Spagnoli; M: Stelvio Cipriani; S: Susan Scott a.k.a. Nieves Navarro, Richard Harrison, Lucia Ramirez, Annj Goren a.k.a. Annamaria Napoletano, Mark Shannon a.k.a. Manlio Certosino.

Papaya dei Caraibi

A.k.a. *Papaya of the Caribbean* (English translation); a.k.a. *Papaya, die Liebesgöttin der Cannibalen* (German title; translation: *Papaya, Love Goddess of the Cannibals*) (1978) (It.); D: Aristide Massaccesi; P: Carlo Maietto; Prod. Co.: Mercury Cinematografica; SC: Roberto Gandus, Roberto Maietto; C: Aristide Massaccesi; M: Stelvio Cipriani; S: Melissa Chimenti, Sirpa Lane, Maurice Poli.

Pomeriggio Caldo

A.k.a. *11 Days, 11 Nights Part 3* (G.B.); a.k.a. *Eleven Days, Eleven Nights: The Final Chapter*; a.k.a. *Afternoon* (English titles) (1988) (It.); D/P/C: Aristide Massaccesi; P: Cleo Lori; SC: David Resseguier; M: Sergio Montanari; S: Valentine Demy a.k.a. Marissa Parra, Allen Cort, Carey Salley, Robert La Brosse, Laura Gemser.

Porno Esotic Love

A.k.a. *Porno Erotic Love* (English translation); a.k.a. *Porno Esotic Amore* (alternate Italian title); a.k.a. *Amor Porno Exotico* (alternate Italian title); a.k.a. *Tahitian Love*; a.k.a. *A Night in Tahiti*; a.k.a. *Exotic Love*; a.k.a. *Sexy Erotic Love*; a.k.a. *Exotic Love* (English titles) (1980) (It.); D/P: Aristide Massaccesi; SC: Giacinto Bonacquista; C: Aristide Massaccesi, Enrico Biribicchi, Enzo Frattari; M: Alessandro Alessandroni; S: Laura Gemser, Gabriele Tinti, Mark Shannon a.k.a. Manlio Certosino, Dirce Funari a.k.a. Patrize Funari a.k.a. Patrizia Funari, Annj Goren a.k.a. Annamaria Napoletano, Michelle Stark.

Porno Holocaust

A.k.a. *Delizie Erotiche in Porno Holocaust* (alternate Italian title) (1979) (It.); D/P/SC/C: Aristide Massaccesi; Prod. Co.: Kristal Film; M: Nico Fidenco; S: George Eastman a.k.a. Luigi Montefiori, Dirce Funari a.k.a. Patrize Funari a.k.a. Patrizia Funari, Annj Goren a.k.a. Annamaria Napoletano, Mark Shannon a.k.a. Manlio Certosino.

Primal Instinct

(1996) (It.); D/P/SC/C: Aristide Massaccesi; S: Sindee Coxx, Kaitlyn Ashley, Monica Orsini, Nyrobi Knight, Cleo Patra, Bobby Vitale.

Prison Dancer

A.k.a. *Can't Shake the Beat*; a.k.a. *Jailbird Rock* (English titles) (1985) (It.); D: Kevin Mancuso, Aristide Massaccesi; P: Joseph Pastore, Eduard Sarlui; C: Aristide Massaccesi; SC: Kevin Mancuso, Claudio Fragrasso; M: Rick Nowells; S: Michelle Gibson, Isabelle Ripley, Joanna Morris.

Raptors

A.k.a. *Raptors: gli Uccelli Assassini* (alternate Italian title); a.k.a. *Raptors—Dark Nights of the Scarecrow*; a.k.a. *Dark Eyes of the Zombies*; a.k.a. *The Killing Birds*; a.k.a. *Killing Birds* (English titles) (1987) (It.); D: Claudio Lattanzi, Aristide Massaccesi (uncredited); P: Aristide Massaccesi; Prod. Co.: Filmirage/Flora Film; SC: Daniele Stroppa, Claudio Lattanzi, Sheila Goldberg; C: Aristide Massaccesi; M: Carlo Maria Cordio; SP E: Harry Harris III (?), Robert Gould (?); S: Lara Wendel, Timothy Watts, Leslie Cummins, James Villemaire, Sal Maggiore, James Sutterfield, Lin Gaithright, Robert Vaughn.

Co-writer and co-director Lattanzi is also credited as Claude Milliken in some sources.

Ritorno dalla Morte

A.k.a. *Return from Death* (English translation and title); a.k.a. *Frankenstein 2000* (English title) (1992) (It.); D/SC: Aristide Massaccesi; Prod. Co.: Filmirage; C: Daniele Massaccesi, Aristide Massaccesi; M: Piero Montanari; S: Donald O'Brien, Cinzia Monreale.

Scansati ... Trinità Arriva Eldorado

A.k.a. *Trinità Arriva ad Eldorado* (alternate Italian title); a.k.a. *Get Away! Trinity Has Arrived in Eldorado* (English title) (1972) (It.); D/C: Aristide Massaccesi; P: Massimo Bernhardi, Diego Spataro; SC: Romano Scandariato; M: Giancarlo Chiaramello; S: Stan Cooper a.k.a. Stelvio Rossi, Gordon Mitchell a.k.a. Charles Pendleton, Craig Hill, Daniela Giordano.

Sex and Chinese Food

(1993) (It., Philippines); D/P/SC: Aristide Massaccesi (using the psudonym Young Sean Bean Lui); S: Licy Li, Lebyi Ngai, Dragon Luk, Dodo Ho, Kurt Nuk.

Sharks: Deep Blood

A.k.a. *Sharks the Challenge*; a.k.a. *Deep Blood* (English titles) (1989) (It.); D/P: Aristide Massaccesi; SC: George Nelson; Prod. Co.: Filmirage/Variety Film; C: Aristide Massaccesi; M: Carlo Maria Cordio; S: Frank Baroni, Allen Cort, Keith Kelsch, James Camp, Tody Bernard, John K.Brune, Margaret Hanks, Van Jensens, Don Perrin, Claude File, Charles Brill.

La Signora di Wall Street

A.k.a. *Wall Street Woman* (English translation and title); a.k.a. *Confessions of a Wall Street Woman*; a.k.a. *The Loves of a Wall Street Woman*; a.k.a. *High Finance Woman* (English titles) (1989) (It.); D/P/C: Aristide Massaccesi; SC: Danielle Stroppa; Prod. Co.: Filmirage; M: Piero Montanari; S: Tara Buckman, Charlie Edwards, Paul Van Gent, Dan Smith, Julia Howard, Louie Elias, Sashin Sardot, Laura Gemser.

Sollazzevoli Storie di Mogli Gaudenti e Mariti Penitenti

A.k.a. *More Sexy Canterbury Tales*; a.k.a. *More Filthy Canterbury Tales* (G.B.) (English titles) (1972) (It.); D: Aristide Massaccesi (using Romano Gastaldi name), Massimo Pupillo (English version uncredited); P: Sergio Rosa, Aristide Massaccesi; Prod. Co.: Transglobe Italiana; SC: Aristide Massaccesi; C: Aristide Massaccesi, Enrico Biribicchi; M: Franco Salina, Roberto Pregadio; S: Monica Audras, Marzia Damon a.k.a. Caterina Chiani, Francesca Romana, Attilio Ottesio, Ari Hanow.

Some Like It Hard

(1995) (It.); D/P/SC/C: Aristide Massaccesi; S: Sofia Ferrari, Nikki Randall, Selen a.k.a. Selena, Steven St. Croix, Tony Montana.

Sul Filo del Rasio

A.k.a. *Death on the Edge of a Razor Blade* (English translation and title); a.k.a. *Instinct* (English title) (1992) (It.); D/P: Aristide Massaccesi; SC: Daniele Stroppa; C: Daniel Massaccesi; M: Piero Montanari; Prod. Co.: Filmirage; S: Gala Orlova, Theo Losito, Walter Toschi, Susanna Burgatti, Maurice Poli, Elisabeth Rossler.

Tarzan X

A.k.a. *Tharzan X Figlio della Jungula* (alternate Italian title; translation: *Tarzan X: Son of the Jungle*); a.k.a. *Tharzan la Vera Storia de Figlio della Giungla* (alternate Italian title; translation: *Tarzan the True Story of the Son of the Jungle*); a.k.a. *Tarzan X the Shame of Jane*; a.k.a. *Tarzan X — Shame of Jane*; a.k.a. *Tarzan*; a.k.a. *Jungle Heat* (English titles) (1994) (It.); D/P/SC: Aristide Massaccesi; Prod. Co.: Butterfly Motion Picture/Capital Film; S: Rocco Siffredi, Rosa Caracciolo, Nikita Gross, Attila Schulter, Swetta Silvestru, Cintya Raffaell, Barbara Dobsom, Zoltan Kabay Tao.

Top Model

A.k.a. *Eleven Days, Eleven Nights, Part II* (English title) (1987) (It.); D/P/C: Aristide Massaccesi; P: George Bertuccelli; Prod. Co.: Filmirage; SC: Sarah Asproon, Gloria Miles, based on the novel, "Top Model" by Sarah Asproon; M: Piero Montanari; S: Jessica Moore a.k.a. Luciana Ottaviani, James Sutterfield, Axel Dugas, Laura Gemser, Jason Saucier.

This film should not be confused with the other Aristide Massaccesi film *Undici Giorni, Undici Notte 2*, which is also translated as (and titled in English as) *Eleven Days, Eleven Nights Part 2*.

Troll 2

A.k.a. *Trolls 2* (English title) (1990) (It.); D: Claudio Fragrasso, Aristide Massaccesi (uncredited); P: Aristide Massaccesi; SC: Claudio Fragrasso; Prod. Co.: Filmirage; C: Giancarlo Ferrando; M: Carlo Maria Cordio; S: Michael Stephenson, George Hardy, Margo Prey, Connie McFarland, Robert Ormsby, Deborah Reed, Jason Wright, Darren Ewing, Jason Steadman, David McConnell, Gary Carlson.

Troll 3

A.k.a. *Contamination Point 7*; a.k.a. *Crawlers*; a.k.a. *Creepers* (English titles) (1990) (It.); D: Fabrizio Laurenti, Aristide Massaccesi (uncredited); P: Aristide Massaccesi; Prod. Co.: Filmirage; SC: Danielle Stroppa, Albert Levene; C: Aristide Massaccesi; M: Carlo Maria Cordio; S: Mary Sellers, Jason Saucier, Bubba Reeves, Chelsi Stahr, Vince O'Neil, Edy Eby, Jaymzlinn Saxton, Dennis Fitzmorris, Patrick Collins, Kevin Kroft, Merrill Weech, Carol Kroft.

Ulisse

A.k.a. *Ulysses* (English title) (1994) (It.); D/P/SC/C: Aristide Massaccesi; S: Erika Bella a.k.a. Anjelica Bella, Djolth Walthon, Maria Swalloy, Regina Silpo.

Undici Giorni, Undici Notti

A.k.a. *11 Days, 11 Nights*; a.k.a. *Eleven Days, Eleven Nights* (English translations and titles) (1987) (It.); D/P/C: Aristide Massaccesi; Prod. Co.: Filmirage; SC: Sarah Asproon, Claudio Fragrasso; M: Piero Montanari; S: Jessica Moore a.k.a. Luciana Ottaviani, Joshua McDonald, Mary Sellers, Laura Gemser.

Undici Giorni, Undici Notti 2

A.k.a. *11 Days, 11 Nights 2* (English translation and title); a.k.a. *Eleven Days, Eleven Nights, the Sequel* (G.B.) (English title) (1990) (It.); D/P/C: Aristide Massaccesi; SC: Sarah Asproon;

Prod. Co.: Filmirage/Variety Film; M: Piero Montanari; S: Kristine Rose, Ruth Collins, Frederick Lewis, Maurice Dupre, Kristin Cuadraro, Alex Dexter, Fred Woodruff, James Jackson, Laura Gemser.

La Via della Prostituzione

A.k.a. *Emanuelle and the White Slave Trade*; a.k.a. *Emanuelle and the White Slave Trade Today* (English titles) (1977) (It.); D: Aristide Massaccesi; P: Fabrizio De Angelis; Prod. Co.: Fulvia Film/Flora Cinematografica/Gico Cinematografica; SC: Aristide Massaccesi, Romano Scandariato; C: Aristide Massaccesi; M: Nico Fidenco; S: Laura Gemser, Ely Galleani a.k.a. Elyde Galleana, Gabriele Tinti, Venantino Venantini.

Bruno Mattei

Born on July 30, 1931, in Rome, Italy, Bruno Mattei, like most of his fellow Italian film technicians, studied at the national film school, the Centro Sperimentale Centrale (C.S.C.). Upon his graduation in 1951, he worked primarily as a film editor and a sound technician. Eventually, Mattei tried his hand at screenwriting and contributed to a number of features. By Mattei's own admission, he had worked on more than 100 films as an editor before he directed his first film, a claim that is difficult to verify.

Mattei began his cinema career in 1956 with the dramatic costume film *Giovanni dalle Bande Nere*. His work as a sound technician or a film editor graces a number of productions between 1965 and 1969. Of the many films with which Mattei has been associated, most notable are the peplum *Tharus, Figlio di Attila* (1962) and the European spy films *Agente 3S3: Passaporto per l'Inferno* (1965), *Agente 3S3: Massacro al Sole* (1966), *Goldface, il Fantastico Superman* (1967), Jess Franco's *99 Mujeres* (1968), *Venus im Pelz* (1968), *El Conde Dracula* (1969) and the exploitation film *Africa Sexy* (1963).

Mattei's first film as director appears to be the romantic melodrama *Armida, il Dramma di Una Sposa* (1970), about which little is known. His next production as a director, the 1976 film *Cuginetta ... Amore Mio!*, is a sexy exploitation film starring Rita De Simone, a popular actress in bargain basement sexy films of the period. That same year, Mattei made *La Casa Privata per le SS*, a nasty and brutal addition to the women-in-prison genre that became quite popular in Italy in the mid– to late–'70s. Mattei followed with the even more controversial *KZ9 Lager di Stermino* (1976). His mondo documentaries, *Le Notti Porno nel Mondo* (1977) and *Emanuelle le Porno Notti del Mondo N. 2* (1978), both with Laura Gemser as on-screen narrator, were released to capitalize on the growing public interest in the local Italian sex scene as well as other assorted weird happenings in the Italian night world. *Cicciolina, Amore Mio* (1979) featured the extremely popular porno actress Ilona Staller, under her Cicciolina pseudonym. Billed as a softcore sex comedy, this obscure title could actually have been a porno film.

In 1980, Mattei directed two films in the "possessed nuns" cycle. *L'Altro Inferno* is an exploitation film (which became his first horror movie) in which a clerical investigation into strange happenings at a secluded convent uncovers an outbreak of hysteria among the inhabitants of the nunnery. As copulating nuns go at it, torturing themselves and others, it is finally revealed that this is all the result of a union between one of the nuns and the Devil, which has produced a daughter.

Bruno Mattei

Ending with a literal catastrophic storm of fire and brimstone, Mattei's possession film is one of the better, seemingly literate offerings of the genre. Obviously, it is an exploitable offering as it seemingly revels in displaying naked nuns in heat and near-naked clerics whipping themselves into an orgiastic frenzy. As blasphemous as it all sounds, if you took this kind of thing seriously, you would not be reading this book.

Its companion piece, *La Vera Storia della Monaca di Monza*, tells of a young woman forced to reside in a convent to resist the carnal temptations of the outside world but inside the cloistered walls finds depravity, sensuality and murder.

The zombie-cannibal epic *Inferno dei Morti-Viventi* (1981) is among the most gruesome of that genre, with a high body count and a seemingly endless amount of these horrific beings slaughtering cast members: Deep within the bowels of a secret military installation located in the jungles of South America, strange experiments are conducted; all hell breaks loose when an infected rat enters a worker's isolation suit and gore and grue burst forth. In true zombie and cannibal film fashion, nearly all of the research institute's workers are also infected and become rampaging, flesh-eating zombie cannibals.

Despite some poorly photographed location footage shot in the South American jungles, the film does move at an incredibly swift pace, maybe fast enough for most discerning audiences to gasp in disbelief as hordes of zombies attack the populace and indigenous animals.

Mattei followed with *Nerone e Poppea* (1981), a hilariously over-the-top sex film which features tons of graphic gore as well as the prerequisite gratuitous nudity. The similar *Caligola e Messalina* (1982) followed right on its heels and was more of the same: violence, sex and gore. Curiously enough, English dubbing has turned both of these films into wild, free-for-all sex comedies with devil-may-care scripting, making these productions akin to something as odd as *Monty Python and the Holy Grail* (1975).

In 1982, Mattei tried his hand at directing an Emmanuelle film, *Emanuelle— Violenza in un Carcere Femminile*, starring Laura Gemser and Gabriele Tinti. Despite their presence, the film meanders from one cruel visual to another, more influenced by the women-in-prison films of Jess Franco than the Gemser Emanuelle films directed by Aristide Massaccesi.

I Sette Magnifici Gladiatori (1984), an enjoyable entry in the brief peplum revival of the '80s, is one of Mattei's better efforts. The film even resurrects two '60s sword-and-sandal actors, the aging Brad Harris and Dan Vadis, to repeat their roles as heroic adventurers beside the large physical presences of Lou Ferrigno and Sybil Danning.

Rats— Notte di Terrore (1985) is a decidedly nasty post-apocalyptic science fiction–horror film. Some time after an unspecified apocalyptic war, survivors journey out into the night to find food and shelter. Roving bands of disease-ridden psychopaths prey on these poor people but, soon, both will have to contend with hordes of plague-infested, flesh-eating rats.

This is another unwelcome addition to the already crowded post-apocalypse cycle of films inspired by the 1978 international hit *Mad Max* and its sequel *The Road Warrior* (1982). Although few, if any, of the Italian productions even came close to duplicating the visceral thrills of these brilliant Australian classics of science fiction, films like *Rats— Notte di Terrore* are surely at the bottom of the barrel. Rape, dismemberment and murder are on view, as well as the on-screen killing of hundreds of real-life rats. (Is all this cruelty really necessary in the name of art?)

Hanna D (a.k.a. *La Ragazza del Vondel Park*) (1985), which Mattei co-directed, is his poor contribution to the waning Mafia crime film genre. *L'Apache Bianco* (filmed in 1984, but not released until 1986) is a violent, sadistic Western and not even recommended for the curious. *Scalps* (also filmed in 1984 and not released until 1987), Mattei's other Western, is so gruesome and gory that it may only be of interest to cinema masochists curious to see how much they can endure.

In an attempt to duplicate the success that Antonio Margheriti enjoyed with the Vietnam War– and World War II–themed films and his action-adventures starring David Warbeck, Mattei made his own series: *Doppio Bersaglio* (1987) with Miles O'Keefe, *Strike Commando* (1987) with Reb Brown and Christopher Connelly and *Strike Commando 2* (1987) with Brent Huff. In most countries, these films

Poster for *Inferno dei Morti-Viventi* (1981, Beatrice Film S.R.L. [Rome]/Films Dara [Barcelona]).

went directly to the exploitation end of the video chain.

Appuntamento a Trieste (1987) was Mattei's contribution to the miniseries genre of long, dramatic thrillers. Made for RAI television, the four-part series has an interesting cast: William Berger, Tony Musante, Edmund Purdom and Jacques Sernas. However, it remains an obscure title, little seen after its initial telecast.

Zombi 3 (1988) was a production started by director Lucio Fulci, who filmed several weeks on location. Whether Fulci was struck with an illness or had a dispute with the producers remains unclear, but Mattei replaced him. The film, a highlight of the flesh-eating zombie films of the '80s, is hated by some fans and admired by others. It delivers its share of scares and bizarre images, like an infamous flying severed head scene. In South America, a covert operation funded by international medical concerns is conducting experiments at their secret base. Zombie-like creatures that had overrun a tropical island are being experimented on, with the hopes that the medical establishment can put an end to this terrible plight. When one creature breaks loose and attacks and infects others, an infected medical assistant breaches the security of the base and runs into the jungle. Vacationing youths on holiday are soon forced to fight for their lives as a swarm of the undead and ruthless military personnel, outfitted in contamination gear, seek to exterminate all that are infected and are witness to this plague of horror.

Robowar (1988), a failed attempt to mix ideas from the more successful movies *The Terminator* and *Alien,* is set in the South American jungles. In 1989, Mattei again attempted to film a mixture of two successful films in the hopes that he could make a good exploitable hybrid. *Spectres à Venise* (1989) is set some time in the future after an apocalyptic war has devastated mankind. In the dark caverns beneath a city, a unisex team of commandos investigates an enemy stronghold to find a killer, a robotic, shape-shifting creature that decimates their number. This last attempt to milk the waning interest in the post-apocalypse genre of film sees Mattei add elements of *The Terminator* and other popular science fiction films to the mix. Lots of firepower, dark corridors and cheap but effective special effects add up to little more than another exploitative offering from Bruno Mattei.

Many of Mattei's films since *Spectres à Venise* have been sexy dramas and crime thrillers. Some of his few recent films have evidently not been received well in his native Italy and they have even stopped appearing as export releases to video or cable.

However, more notable later genre titles include *Attrazione Pericolosa* (1993), an erotic thriller starring Monique Seller and David Warbeck, *Gli Occhi Dentro* (1993) a gory, nudity-filled trashy horror starring Gabriele Gori, with the killer gouging out the eyes of his victims, and the thriller *L'Assassino ... È al Telefono* (1994), in which a killer wearing a clown mask murders female phone sex operators. These films are all exploitative features, but near-essential viewing to genre aficionados seeking to document Mattei's efforts to continue to make genre product. *Cruel Jaws* (1995), a rip-off of the classic 1975 Steven Spielberg film *Jaws* and an exact replica of Enzo Girolami's *L'Ultimo Squalo,* was one of the director's more recent efforts as a filmmaker. His most recent film, reportedly titled *Night of the Zombies,* was scheduled for production in 2001.

Bruno Mattei has obviously made a career for himself as a director of copycat movies. Whenever a film or a genre became popular, he directed his own (unsanctioned) remake or unofficial sequel. What makes these films so popular could be his apparent insistence on adding even more exploitable elements to these productions. Mattei utilizes an array of pseudonyms so, if you want to track down any of his releases but are not sure of if they are actually Mattei films, here's a list of aliases: Jordan B. Matthews, Jimmy Matheus, Axel Berger, Stefan Oblowsky and Vincent Dawn.

Bruno Mattei Filmography

L'Altro Inferno

A.k.a. *The Other Hell* (English translation and title); a.k.a. *Guardian from Hell*; a.k.a. *Innocents from Hell* (English titles) (1980) (It.); D: Bruno Mattei; P: Arcangelo Picchi, Silvio Colecchia; SC: Claudio Fragrasso; C: Giuseppe Berardini; M: Goblin; S: Carlo De Mejo, Franca Stoppa, Franco Garofalo, Francesca Carmeno, Paola Montenero, Susan Forget, Andrea Aureli.

L'Apache Bianco

A.k.a. *White Apache* (English translation and title) (1986) (It., Sp.); D: Bruno Mattei; Prod. Co.: Beatrice Film; SC: Bruno Mattei, Franco Prosperi; C: Luis Ciccarese, Julio Burgos; M: Luigi Ceccarelli; S: Sebastian Harrison, Lola Forner, Alberto Farnese, Cinzia De Ponti.

Appuntamento a Trieste

A.k.a. *Appointment in Trieste* (English translation and title); a.k.a. *Rendezvous in Trieste* (English title) (1987) (It.); D: Bruno Mattei; Prod. Co.: Tiber Cinematografica International/Radiotelevisione Italiana; SC: Lucio Manlio Battistrada, Silvio Maestranzi, Claudio Fragrasso, based on the novel *Appuntamento a Trieste* by Giorgio Scerbaneco; C: Riccardo Grassetti; M: Stefano Mainetti; S: William Berger, Tony Musante, Cristiana Borghi, Edmund Purdom, Jacques Sernas, Lidia Coslovic, Laura Trotter, Cinzia De Ponti.

Filmed as an Italian television program for the RAI network.

Armida, il Dramma di Una Sposa

(1970) (It.); D: Bruno Mattei; Prod. Co.: Filmar Compagnia Cinemtatografica; S: Franca Parisi, Maria Kiriakis, Peter Hunter, Frank Sherman.

L'Assassino ... È al Telefono

A.k.a. *The Killer Is on the Phone*; a.k.a. *The Killer Is on the Telephone* (English translations and titles); a.k.a. *Omicidio al Telefono* (alternate Italian title) (1994) (It., Sp.); D: Bruno Mattei; SC: Bruno Mattei, Nini Grassia; C: Luis Ciccarese; M: Nina Grassia, Aldo Tamborelli; S: Odette Cardinali, Patrizia Del Principe, Daniela Mango, Stefania Mega.

Attrazione Pericolosa

A.k.a. *Dangerous Attraction* (English translation and title) (1993) (It.); D: Bruno Mattei; P: Giovanni Paolucci; Prod. Co.: Europe Communications; SC: Bruno Mattei, Giovanni Paolucci; C: Luigi Ciccarese; M: Flipper Music; S: David Warbeck, Monique Seller, Gabriele Gori, Tracy Kelly, Anthony Zequilla, Anthony Berner.

Caligola e Messalina

A.k.a. *Caligula and Messalina* (English translation and title); a.k.a. *Caligula et Messaline* (French title); a.k.a. *The Fall and Rise of the Roman Empire* (G.B.) (English title) (1982) (It., Fr.); D: Bruno Mattei, Antonio Passalia; P: Pierre Hanin, Sergio Cortona, Silvia Colecchia; Prod. Co.: Beatrice Film (Rome)/ItalFrane (Paris); SC: Antonio Passalia; C: Jean Jacques

Renaun, Luigi Ciccarese; M: Giacomo Dell'Orso; S: Vladimir Brajovic, Betty Roland, Francoise Blanchard, Antonio Passalia, Raoul Cabrera, John Turner a.k.a. Valimir Brajovic, Angelo Arquilla, Piotr Stanislas, Florence Guerin.

La Casa Privata per le SS

A.k.a. *The Private House for the SS* (English translation); a.k.a. *SS Girls*; a.k.a. *SS Girls Camp* (English titles) (1976) (It.); D: Bruno Mattei; P: Oscar Santaniello; Prod. Co.: Dar Cinematografica; SC: Bruno Mattei, Giacinto Bonacquista; C: Emilio Giannini, Roberto Alzani; M: Gianni Marchetti, extracts from Johan Sebastian Bach; S: Gabriele Canara, Marina D'Aunia, Macha Magall, Tamara Triffez, Vassili Karras a.k.a.Vassili Karamesinis, Luce Gregory, Walter Bigari, Ivano Staccioli, Luciano Pigozzi.

Cicciolina, Amore Mio

A.k.a. *Cicciolina, My Love* (English translation); a.k.a. *The Goodnight Girl* (English title) (1979) (It.); D: Bruno Mattei, Amasi Damiani; Prod. Co.: Elea Cinematografica; SC: Amasi Damiani, Riccardo Schicchi; C: Antonio Piazza; M: Gianni Marchetti; S: Cicciolina a.k.a. Ilona Staller, Patrizia Basso, Giancarlo Marinangeli, Enrico Nessieres, Paolo Ludovico Barbanera.

Cruel Jaws

A.k.a. *The Beast* (alternate English title) (1995) (It., U.S.); D: Bruno Mattei, William Snyder; SC: Bruno Mattei, Robert Feen, Linda Morrison,William Snyder, Peter Benchley, based on his book *The Beast*; C: Luis Ciccarese, Ben Jackson; M: Michael Morahan; S: Richard Dew, Scott Silveria, Kirsten Urso, George Barnes, Jr.

Cuginetta ... Amore Mio!

A.k.a. *Cuginetta ... My Love!* (English translation); a.k.a. *Love Sacrifice* (English title) (1976) (It.); D: Bruno Mattei; SC: Bruno Mattei, Giacinto Bonaquisti, Luigi Montefiori; C: Oberdan Troiani; M: Alessandro Alessandroni; S: Ziggy Zanger a.k.a. Zizi Zanger, Gino Pagnani, Ria De Simone a.k.a. Anna Maria De Simone, Paola Maiolini.

Doppio Bersaglio

A.k.a. *Double Target* (English translation and title); a.k.a. *Fuga Dall'Inferno* (alternate Italian title) (1987) (It.); D: Bruno Mattei; Prod. Co.: Variety Film (Rome); SC: Bruno Mattei, Claudio Fragrasso; C: Riccardo Grassetti; M: Stefano Mainetti; S: Miles O'Keefe, Donald Pleasence, Bo Svenson, Kristine Erlandson, Luciano Pigozzi.

Emanuelle e le Porno Notti del Mondo N. 2

A.k.a. *Emanuelle and the Porno Nights in the World N. 2* (English translation) (1978) (It.); D: Bruno Mattei; Prod. Co.: Stefano Film/Sorgente Cinematografica; Narration: Laura Gemser; S: Laura Gemser, Marina Frajese a.k.a. Marina Hedman a.k.a. Marina Lotar.

Emanuelle—Violenza in un Carcere Femminile

A.k.a. *Emanuelle—Reportage da un Carcere Femminile*; a.k.a. *Emanuelle Reports from a Women's Prison*; a.k.a. *Caged Women*; a.k.a. *Hell Penitentiary*; a.k.a. *Women's Penitentiary*

(English titles) (1982) (It., Fr.); D: Bruno Mattei; Prod. Co.: Beatrice Film/Films Jacques Leitienne (Paris); SC: Palmambroglio Molteni, Oliver LeMat; C: Luigi Ciccarese; M: Luigi Ceccarelli; S: Laura Gemser, Gabriele Tinti, Lorraine De Selle, Maria Romano, Ursula Flores, Raul Cabrera.

Hanna D

A.k.a. *La Ragazza del Vondel Park* (alternate Italian title); a.k.a. *A Seize Ans dans l'Enfer d'Amsterdam* (French title); a.k.a. *The Girl from Vondel Park* (English title) (1985) (It., Fr.); D: Rino Di Silvestro a.k.a. Salvatore Di Silvestro, Bruno Mattei; Prod. Co.: Beatrice Film/Films Jacques Leitienne (Pairs); C: Franco Delli Colli; S: Ana Gisel Glass, Sebastiano Somma, Antonio Serrano, Karin Schubert, Jacques Stany, Donatella Damiani, Cristiano Borremeo.

Inferno dei Morti-Viventi

A.k.a. *Hell of the Living Dead* (English translation and title); a.k.a. *Virus—L'Inferno dei Morti Viventi* (alternate Italian title; translation: *Virus—Hell of the Living Dead*); a.k.a. *Apocalipsis Canibal* (Spanish title); a.k.a. *Night of the Zombies*; a.k.a. *Zombie Creeping Flesh* (English titles) (1981) (It., Sp.); D: Bruno Mattei; P: Sergio Cortona, Walter Bigari, Marcellino Riba-Abizani, Isabela Mula; Prod. Co.: Beatrice Film S.R.L. (Rome)/Films Dara (Barcelona); SC: Claudio Fragrasso, J.M. Cunilles; C: Juan Cabrera, Carlo Aquari, Jose Gusi; M: Goblin (music sources: other Goblin soundtracks, notably *Dawn of the Dead* and *Contamination*); S: Margit Evelyn Newton, Franco Garofalo, Selena Karay, Robert O'Neal, Gaby Renom, Luis Fonoll, Piero Fumelli, Patrizia Costa, Victor Isreal.

KZ9—Lager di Stermino

A.k.a. *KZ9—Extermination Camp* (English translation); a.k.a. *Women's Camp 119*; a.k.a. *SS Extermination Camp* (English titles) (1976) (It.); D: Bruno Mattei; P: Marcello Berni, Domenico Battista; Prod. Co.: Three Stars '76 Production; SC: Bruno Mattei, Aureliano Luppi, Giancinto Bonacquisti; C: Luigi Ciccarese, Marco Sperduti; M: Alessandro Alessandroni; S: Ivano Staccioli, Ria De Simone a.k.a. Anna Maria De Simone, Sonia Viviani, Lorraine De Selle, Nello Rivie, Gabrielle Carrara, Giovanni Attanasio, Sonia Hutzar, Gotha Kopert, Miriam Gravina, Manuela Mura, Pino Pupella.

Nerone e Poppea

A.k.a. *Nero and Poppea* (English translation); a.k.a. *Les Aventures Sexuelles de Néron et de Poppée* (French title); a.k.a. *Nero and Poppea: An Orgy of Power*; a.k.a. *Caligula Reincarnated as Nero* (English titles) (1981) (It., Fr.); D: Bruno Mattei; P: Sergio Cortona; Prod. Co.: Beatrice (Rome)/Italfrance (Paris); SC: Bruno Mattei, Antonio Passalia; C: Luigi Ciccarese; M: Giacomo Dell'Orso; S: Rudy Adams, Patricia Derek, John Turner a.k.a. Valimir Brajovic, Anthony Freeman a.k.a. Mario Novelli, Susan Forget, Caterina Catambrone.

Le Notti Porno nel Mondo

A.k.a. *The Porno Nights of the World* (English translation); a.k.a. *Emanuelle Nera e le Notti Porno nel Mondo* (alternate Italian title); a.k.a. *Mondo Erotico*; a.k.a. *Sexy Night Report* (English titles) (1977) (It.); D/SC: Bruno Mattei; P: Mario Paladini; Prod. Co.: Esagono Cinematografica; C: Enrico Birbicchi; M: Gianni Marchetti; Narration: Laura Gemser; S: Laura Gemser, Marina Frajese a.k.a. Marina Hedman a.k.a. Marina Lotar.

Gli Occhi Dentro

A.k.a. *Eyes Without a Face* (English translation and title); a.k.a. *Occhi Senza Volto* (alternate Italian title) (1993) (It.); D: Bruno Mattei; P: Giovanni Paolucci; Prod. Co.: Europe Communications (Rome); SC: Lorenzo De Luca; C: Luigi Ciccarese; S: Gabriele Gori, Sylvie Pariset, Carol Farres, Antonio Zequisa, Emi Valentino, Carlo Granchi, Achille Brugnini.

Rats — Notte di Terrore

A.k.a. *Rats — The Night of Terror* (English translation and title) a.k.a. *Les Rats — Notte di Terrore de Manhattan* (French title) (1985) (It., Fr.); D: Bruno Mattei, Claudio Fragrasso; Prod. Co.: Beatrice Film s.r.l. (Rome)/IMP. FX.CI (Nice); SC: Bruno Mattei, Claudio Fragrasso, Herve Piccini; C: Franco Della Colli; M: Luigi Ceccarelli; S: Richard Raymond, Janna Ryann, Massimo Vanni a.k.a. Alex McBride, Ann Gisel Glass, Cindy Ledbetter.

Robowar

A.k.a. *Robowar Robot da Guerra* (alternate Italian title) (1988) (It.); D: Bruno Mattei; P: Franco Gaudenzi; Prod. Co.: Flora Film; SC: Claudio Fragrasso, Rossella Drudi; C: Riccardo Grassetti; M: Daniele Alabiso; S: Reb Brown, Catherine Hickland, Massimo Vanni, Romano Puppo, John P. Dulaney, Mel Davidson.

Scalps

(1986) (It.); D: Bruno Mattei; Prod. Co.: Flora Film; SC: Bruno Mattei, Richard Harrison; C: Julio Burgos; M: Luigi Ceccarelli; S: Vassili Karras a.k.a. Vassili Karamesinis, Mary Galan, Charlie Bravo, Alberto Farese.

I Sette Magnifici Gladiatori

A.k.a. *The Seven Magnificent Gladiators* (English translation and title) (1984) (It., U.S.); D: Bruno Mattei; P: Alexander Hacohen; Prod. Co.: Cannon Releases; SC: Claudio Fragrasso, loosely based on the events in the film *The Magnificent Seven*; C: Silvano Ippoliti; M: Dov Seltzer; S: Lou Ferrigno, Sybil Danning a.k.a. Sybille Johanna Danninger, Brad Harris, Dan Vadis, Carla Ferrigno, Barbara Pesante, Yehuda Efroni, Mandy Rice-Davies, Robert Mura.

Spectres à Venise

A.k.a. *Spectres à Venise — Shocking Dark* (alternate title); a.k.a. *Shocking Dark*; a.k.a. *Terminator 2 Shocking Dark*; a.k.a. *Shocking Dark Terminator 2 Alien 3*; a.k.a. *Terminator 2 Alien 3!* (English titles) (1989) (It.); D: Bruno Mattei, Claudio Fragrasso (uncredited); P: Franco Gaudenzi, Giovanni Paolucci; SC: Claudio Fragrasso; C: Riccardo Grassetti; M: Carlo Maria Cordio, Vangelis (music source: other soundtracks); S: Chris Ahrens, Haven Tyler, Geretta Field, Tony Lombardo, Mark Steinborn, Domenica Coulson.

Strike Commando

(1987) (It.); D: Bruno Mattei; Prod. Co.: Flora Film; SC: Bruno Mattei, Claudio Fragrasso; M: Luigi Ceccarelli; S: Reb Brown, Christopher Connelly, Luciano Pigozzi, Alex Vitale, Francesca Giardi.

Strike Commando 2

A.k.a. *Trappola Diabolica* (alternate Italian title) (1987) (It.); D: Bruno Mattei; P: Franco Guadenzi; Prod. Co.: Flora Film; SC: Claudio Fragrasso, Rossella Druidi; C: Riccardo Grassetti; M: Stefano Mainetti; S: Brent Huff, Romano Puppo, Luciano Pigozzi, Ottaviano Dell'Acqua.

La Vera Storia della Monaca di Monza

A.k.a. *The True Story of the Nuns of Monza* (English translation and title) (1980) (It.); D: Bruno Mattei; P: Arcangelo Picchi; Prod. Co.: Cinemec Produzioni; SC: Arcangelo Picchi, Claudio Fragrasso; C: Giuseppe Berardini; M: Gianni Marchetti; S: Zora Kerova a.k.a. Zora Ulla Keslerova Tschechin, Franco Garofalo, Paola Corazzi, Paola Montenero, Franca Stoppa.

Violenza da un Carcere Femminile

A.k.a. *Violence in a Women's Prison* (English translation and title); a.k.a *Pentencier de Femmes* (French title); a.k.a. *Revolte au Pentencier des Filles* (alternate French title); a.k.a. *Women's Prison*; a.k.a. *Women's Prison Massacre*; a.k.a. *Caged Women*; a.k.a. *Blade Violent*; a.k.a. *Emanuelle's Escape from Hell* (English titles) (1983) (It., Fr.); D: Bruno Mattei; P: Sergio Cortona; Prod. Co.: Beatrice Film S.r.l. (Rome)/Imp. Ex. Ci. S.A. (Nice)/Les Films Jacques Leitienne (Paris); SC: Palmanbroglio Molteni, Oliver Lefait; C: Luigi Ciccarese; M: Marcello Di Paolo; E: Armando Grilli; S: Laura Gemser, Gabriele Tinti, Maria Romano, Ursula Flores, Antonella Giacomini, Françoise Perrot, Lorraine De Selle, Leila Ducci, Franca Stoppa.

Zombi 3

A.k.a. *Zombie 3* (1988) (It.); D: Lucio Fulci, and Bruno Mattei; P: Franco Gaudenzi; Prod. Co.: Flora Film; SC: Claudio Fragrasso; C: Riccardo Grassetti, Luigi Ciccarese; M: Stefano Mainetti; S: Deran Serafian, Beatrice Ring, Richard Raymond, Massimo Vanni, Ulrich Reinthaller, Marina Loi, Debra Bergamini.

Michele Soavi

Michele Soavi was born on July 3, 1957, in Milan, Italy. According to various reference sources, Soavi decided to abandon his scholastic education, quit his studies and begin taking acting lessons (he had been eager to enter the world of filmmaking for some time).

As an actor, he first appeared in the sexploitation film *Piccole Labbra* (1978). In 1979, he worked as an actor, co-producer and assistant director on a film titled *Bambule* and, as an actor, in *Il Figlio delle Stelle*. His next role and his first appearance in a genre film was in Ciro Ippolito's *Alien 2 sulla Terra* (1980).

In 1980, Soavi purportedly made repeated attempts to contact Dario Argento, both as a fan and as a potential screenwriter. The two did meet and then struck up a friendship. Soavi then met Lucio Fulci and appeared in that director's *Paura nella Città dei Morti Viventi* (1980), also helping with set decoration. In 1981, Soavi became associated with Aristide Massaccesi and appeared in the following five Massaccesi productions: *Rosso Sangue* (1981), *Caligola — La Storia della Raccontata* (1982), *Ator l'Invincibile* (1982), *Endgame Bronx Lotta Finale* (1983) and *Anno 2020: I Gladiatori del Futoro* (1984). On these last two productions, Soavi also worked as an assistant director and he co-wrote the script for the Ator film. In 1982, he was hired by Dario Argento to appear in and assist with the direction of *Tenebrae*.

In 1983, he appeared in and worked as a technical assistant on Ruggero Deodato's *I Predatori di Atlantide* and Lamberto Bava's *La Casa con la Scala nel Buio* (in which he also appeared, in a major supporting role) and *Blastfighter*. In 1985, Soavi returned to assist Argento on *Phenomena*. While working on this film, Soavi received his first directing assignment, helming two of the music videos that were used to promote it. In 1985, Soavi worked on Lamberto Bava's *Demoni* (as a technical assistant and appearing in the role of the mute, silver-masked man who gives away tickets to the horror movie premiere at the art deco palace). He directed his first film, a feature-length documentary on the man who had influenced his career greatly, Dario Argento. This documentary, *Il Mondo di Dario Argento*, was a successful experiment and not only explained on-screen many of the mysterious motivations behind some of Argento's films, but also gave audiences brief glimpses of the man at work. In 1987, Soavi was put in charge of all of the second unit direction work on Argento's *Opera*, an experience which helped him immeasurably when his first film, *Deliria* (1987), was made.

Michele Soavi

Deliria, which was financed by Aristide Massaccesi, is a superb example of what one can do by redefining and expanding the by-now routine plots of the Italian thriller genre, obviously affected by the countless American slasher films of the '80s.

A pretentious theatrical director is rehearsing a modern dance version of the exploits of Jack the Ripper, with the actor playing the killer wearing an oversize mask resembling an owl's head. A sleazy producer wants the work to premiere within a short time, so they have been rehearsing the actors and dancers around the clock. Nearby, at an asylum, the maniacal killer (and former actor) Irving Wallace escapes. Wallace hides in the trunk of a car and finds himself at the theater where the cast is rehearsing. Once locked in for the night, the remaining dancers and technical staff become prime targets for the unhinged, real-life killer who is on a rampage of violence.

This familiar tale of a psycho killer stalking the inhabitants of a theater is enlivened by Soavi's utilization of the methods of Dario Argento as a filmmaker. Soavi films every terrifying dash for freedom as if he is working on an art film rather than a horror movie. He highlights seemingly normal occurrences with a great deal of drama and apprehension. There is a key that looms in the foreground as the heroine (Barbara Cupisti) scrambles for safety. There are artistically arranged corpses and portions of bodies set on stage by the killer, a macabre tableau of violence. Finally, there are attempts at a humorous holiday feel from scads of feathers flying about the blood and grue at the same time as a mattress and pillows are chainsawed by the killer, resembling a psychotic Christmastime tableau.

Based upon story ideas suggested by Massaccesi and Luigi Montefiori (a.k.a.

George Eastman), *Deliria* was successful, winning a prize at the Avoriaz Fantasy Film Festival held in Brussels. It was there that Soavi met Terry Gilliam, the Monty Python member and director of *Brazil*. The two struck up a very close friendship. Based on his own impressions of *Deliria*, Gilliam invited Soavi to work with him on his epic film *The Adventures of Baron Munchhausen* (1988). Soavi worked on the second unit direction, filming many of the epic battle scenes for the climax. The production and the post-production work would drag on for nearly two years. During this time, Soavi contributed his talents as a director to a segment of a rock music miniseries for Italian television (*Voglia di Rock*). In 1989, Soavi appeared in Lamberto Bava's *La Maschera del Demonio*.

La Chiesa is a film that eerily combines many elements of both fantasy and horror. Produced and co-written by Dario Argento, it tells the tale of a heretical order of knights who went on a massive witch-hunt in medieval times. Upon the graves of the dead stands a huge Gothic cathedral in which several people from all walks of life will be trapped. Filmed with great attention paid to the architectural details of the structure itself, *La Chiesa* is not unlike Lamberto Bava's *Demoni*, with its *mise-en-scène* characters trying to elude what seems like a certain death, but is far superior in its appropriation of the macabre, gothic atmosphere of the Italian horror films of the '60s.

Soavi's film is the first sign of his growing proclivity for utilizing surreal set pieces and making them a living, breathing monstrosity as horrifying as any physical presence. The crowd who is trapped in the church consists of a fashion photographer and his models shooting a layout for a bridal magazine, some teenagers and the local priests. Demonic possession rears its ugly head when those who become possessed reach out and infect others (much like Lamberto Bava's *Demoni*). The film's highlight is when areas of the building start to morph into something more sinister, including glimpses of Hell with a fornicating Satanic creature.

In 1991, Soavi appeared as an actor in Luigi Cozzi's *Il Gatto Nero* and filmed *La Setta*, which was again produced and co-written by Dario Argento. An ambitious film, *La Setta* is about a mass murderer and his cult of followers who thrived in the turbulent '60s; they somehow survive into the '90s, their murderous ideals intact, targeting a schoolteacher (Kelly Curtis) to bear Satan's child. At times absurd and gruesome, at other times incredibly baroque and mystifying, *La Setta* makes a good argument for the maturing of the talents of Soavi as a filmmaker. Utilizing some of the themes often explored in the films of Terry Gilliam, most notably those of alienation and withdrawal, he combines them with his own penchant for brilliantly realizing the most macabre of normal-seeming occurrences.

La Setta, a deliriously strange bit of filmmaking, conceives a fairly standard and unimaginative plot device and enlivens it, sending it reeling with huge doses of bizarre set pieces. Among the many eerie images is villain Herbert Lom "impregnating" Curtis by inserting a sacred scarab into her nostrils, and Curtis thrown into an Art Deco well so that she may be enticed to give birth in cold water. Most

German poster art for Michele Soavi's *Aquarius* (1987, Filmirage).

unusual is the strange face-pulling sequence where a woman has her face graphically ripped off by hooks. Finally, there's the great score with a contribution by minimalist composer Philip Glass. This is a film that gets better with successive viewings. For whatever reason, Soavi did not direct another film until 1994.

Dellamorte, Dellamore (1994), a work of fantasy and horror has received many accolades, but, ultimately crumbles beneath the weight of its own self-importance. It details the phantasmagoric life of Francesco Dellamore (Rupert Everett) who is both a loner and a loser. Unable to communicate with those in the real world, he is quite content to supervise the local cemetery. At night the dead rise and Dellamore has to shoot them in the head to put them down and rebury them, but it's all in a night's work. Eventually, Dellamore sees his "fantasy dream woman" (Anna Falchi) wherever he goes. She appears as the lover of a motorcyclist who has died in a fiery crash and as a mourner who visits a grave every day. Dellamore fantasizes having sex with this woman, driving him further over the edge. His only companion in life, Gnaghi, a misshapen, lumpen and mute oaf (Francois Hadji Lazaro), who has been hiding the living, severed head of his lover in his room, doesn't understand him either, but what the hell. When one of Falchi's apparitions suggests that Dellamore's manhood is not needed, he seeks to castrate himself, but, falling completely into madness, he seeks out the company of a prostitute and may or may not be responsible for the death of this woman and her roommate. At the film's climax, Dellamore and his companion attempt to flee the city, only to end up at the edge of the abyss of the world.

The film was apparently based on the phenomenally successful Italian *fumetti* (comic strips, then illustrated novels) of Tiziano Sclavi, called *Dylan Dog*. Some people may not know that Soavi's film is, in fact, based on the same-titled novel *Dellamorte, Dellamore* (also by Sclavi), which was the forerunner for the *fumetti* of *Dylan Dog*. Though the visuals are, at times, quite striking and Everett seems to be a living, breathing incarnation of the title *Dylan Dog* character, the movie, which appropriates the colors and stylish look of comic books, fails to involve the audience in any way. Soavi's decision to film this movie in a surreal manner leaves a severe, empty gaping hole in the place where characterizations should be. Photographed in a combination of deeply saturated, bright colors, the film bares an obvious attempt to emulate the look of a Dario Argento film.

However, Soavi's more recent movies were the disappointing made-for-television films *Ultimo 2 — La Sfida* (1999), *Uno Bianco* (2001) and *Il Testimone* (2001), *San Francesco* (2003) and *L'Ultima Pallottola* (2002). Soavi's most recent film is reportedly a comedy, *Arrivederci Amore, Ciao* (2003).

Michele Soavi Filmography

Uno Bianco

(2001) (It.); D: Michele Soavi; P: Pietro Valsecchi; SC: Michele Soavi, Marco Melega, Gabrielle Romagnoli, Stefano Rulli, based on Marco Melega's book *Baglioni e Costanza*; C: Giovanni Mammolotti; M: Gianni Bella; S: Kim Rossi-Stuart, Dino Abbrescia, Bruno Armando, Pietro Bontemps, Claudio Botosso.

La Chiesa

A.k.a. *The Church* (English translation and title); a.k.a. *The Cathedral*; a.k.a. *Demon Cathedral*; a.k.a. *Return to the Land of Demons* (English titles) (1989) (It.); D: Michele Soavi; P: Dario Argento; Prod. Co.: Associazione Direttori Cineproduzione/Cecchi Gori Group/Tiger Cinematografica/Reteitalia, Milan; SC: Michele Soavi, Dario Argento, Franco Ferrini; C: Renato Tafuri; M: Keith Emerson, with the songs "Floe," "Civil Wars" by Philip Glass; "Floe" performed by Martin Goldray; "Civil Wars" performed by Goblin. "Go to Hell" written by Carola and Rinaldi, performed by Zooming on the Zoo. "The Wire Blade" written and performed by A. Manzo. "Imagination" written and performed by Simon Boswell; S: Hugh Quarshie, Asia Argento, Tomas Arana, Feodor Chailiapin, Barbara Cupisti, Antonella Vitale, John Morghen a.k.a. Giovanni Lombardo Radice, John Karlsen, John Richardson.

Deliria

A.k.a. *Aquarius*; a.k.a. *Bloody Bird*; a.k.a. *Stagefright*; a.k.a. *Stage Fright* (English titles) (1987) (It.); D: Michele Soavi; P: Aristide Massaccesi; Prod. Co.: Filmirage; SC: Michele Soavi, George Eastman a.k.a. Luigi Montefiore, Sheila Goldberg; C: Renato Tafuri; M: Simon Boswell; SP E: Gianfranco Mecacci; S: Barbara Cupisti, David Brandon a.k.a. David Caine Haughton, Roberto Gugorov, Martin Philip, Loredana Parella, Jo Ann Smith, Mary Sellers, John Morghen a.k.a. Giovanni Lombardo Radice, Sheila Goldberg, Michele Soavi.

Dellamorte, Dellamore

A.k.a. *Cemetery Man*; a.k.a. *The Cemetery Man* (English titles) (1994) (It., Fr., G.F.R.); D: Michele Soavi; P: Michele Soavi, Tilde Corsi, Gianni Romoli; Prod. Co.: Audifilm/Urania Film/K.G. Productions/BIBO Films/Silvio Berlusconi Communications/Studio Canal Plus; SC: Gianni Romoli, based on characters created by Taziano Sclavi; C: Mauro Marchetti; M: Manuel De Sica; S: Rupert Everett, Francoise Hadji-Lazaro, Anna Falchi, Stefano Masciarelli, Mickey Knox, Clive Riche, Fabiana Formica.

Il Mondo di Dario Argento

A.k.a. *The World of Dario Argento* (English translation and title); a.k.a. *Dario Argento's World of Horror* (English title) (1985) (It.); D/SC: Michele Soavi; Prod. Co.: Dacfilm (Rome); C: Giamlorenzo Battaglia, Stefano Ricciotti, Enrico Cortese; M: Goblin, Keith Emerson, Claudio Simonetti, Elsa Morante, Fabio Pignatelli, Iron Maiden, Bill Wyman, Terry Taylor.

Features interviews with Dario Argento and excerpts (and some cast and crew interviews) from all of Argento's films up to and including *Phenomena*.

La Setta

A.k.a. *The Sect* (English translation and title); a.k.a *The Devil's Daughter* (English title) (1991) (It.); D: Michele Soavi; P: Dario Argento, Mario & Vittorio Cecci Gori; Prod. Co.: ADC/Penta Film; SC: Michele Soavi, Dario Argento, Gianni Romolo; C: Raffaele Mentes; M: Pino Donaggio; SP E: Rosario Prestopino; S: Kelly Curtis, Herbert Lom, Mariangela Giordano, Michel Adatte, Carla Cassola, Angelika Maria Boeck, Tomas Arana.

Il Testimone

(2001) (It.); D: Michele Soavi; P: Pietro Valsecchi, Carmilla Narbitt; SC: Pietro Valsecchi, Leonardo Fasoli; S: Raoul Bova, Ennio Fantastichini, Aisha Cerami, Giulia Lombardi, Dino Abrescia.

L'Ultima Pallottola

(2002) (It.); D: Michele Soavi; Prod. Co: Antenna Italia Free/Mediaset s.p.a.; SC: Caprara Walter, Pietro Valsecchi; C: Mammolotti Gianni; S: Scarpati Giulio, Cecchi Carlo, Catania Antonio, Mazzotta Max, Guglielman Lavinia.

Ultimo 2 — La Sfida

(1999) (It.); D: Michele Soavi; SC: Pino Corrias, Nicola Lusuardi, Renato Pezzini, Paolo Rossi; S: Raoul Bova, Francesco Benigno, Simone Corrente, Giorgio Tirabassi, Mariano Rigillo, Ricky Memphis.

Other Significant Horror Film Directors

Marcello Avallone

Marcello Avallone (born in 1938) directed two interesting films in the horror genre, *Spettri* (1987) and *Maya* (1989). *Spettri* is the wildly uneven tale of a demon unleashed upon the excavators of an archaeological dig. Talky and with too few scares, the film betrays its obvious origins as a television feature. *Maya*, on the other hand, is an obscure gem. Shooting in the hot, humid jungles of South America, Avallone weaves a tale about an archaeologist (William Berger) who discovers the terrifying secret behind a series of gruesome murders in a poor village near a Mayan ruin. When an adventurer enters the story, his sexual relationship with a shapely beauty only points him in a direction of unrelenting horror. An evil Mayan prince has been reborn and this spirit not only inhabits the bodies of key cast members, but is also responsible for the series of murders. People are hacked apart and hearts are ripped from bodies. Avallone's film lovingly displays the kind of pulchritrudinous female flesh that often fills the screen, as if he cast his female roles from the pages of *Playboy* magazine. It is an overlooked film. Avallone continues in the genre with *The Last Cut* (1997) being his most recent effort as a director.

Marcello Avallone

Marcello Avallone Filmography (selected films)

Maya

(1989) (It.); D: Marcello Avallone; Prod. Co.: Reteitalia (Milan); SC: Marcello Avallone, Maurizio Tedesco, Andrea Purgatori, based on the short story "At School with the Warlock" by Fernao Lopez; C: Silvio Ippolito; M: Gabriele Ducros; S: William Berger, Mariella Valentini, Peter Phelps, Cyrus Elias, Mirella D'Angelo.

Spettri

A.k.a. *Specters* (English translation and title) (1987) (It.); D: Marcello Avallone; P: Maurizio Tedesco; SC: Marcello Avallone, Maurizio Tedesco, Dardano Sacchetti; C: Silvano Ippoliti; M: Lele Marchitelli, Danilo Rea; SP E: Sergio Stivaletti; S: John Pepper, Katrine Michelsen, Donald Pleasence.

Pupi Avati

Pupi Avati, who was born Giuseppe Avati in 1938, is a director of many different kinds of features, very few of them horror films. He is primarily known to horror audiences for *La Casa dalle Finestre Che Ridono* (1976), *Zeder* (1982) and *L'Arcano Incantatore* (1996).

Zeder is a trip down a dark path where, for first-time audiences, even the most knowledgeable viewers cannot ascertain what direction the filmmaker will take them.

In this film, a struggling writer (Gabriele Lavi) is given an old typewriter as a gift. He discovers a used ribbon in the machine from which he then deciphers a bizarre text relating to ancient rituals which would lead to reviving the dead. After transcribing the information, he seeks out additional enlightenment as to the meaning of the mysterious "K Zones" mentioned in the text. Decades earlier, the heretic Zeder disappeared during such an experiment. The writer discovers that Zeder had experimented with the "K Zones," the areas where the dead lay between Heaven and Hell and that an international group of well-financed individuals with ties to all forms of government are attempting to continue Zeder's experiments and revive the dead. In a story that will eventually evolve into a worldwide conspiracy involving high-ranking members of the Church, politicos and the police, the writer will discover that all is definitely not what it seems.

Avati's 1986 film *La Casa dalle Finestre Che Ridono* is a masterpiece of horror.

An artist (Lino Capolicchio) is hired to restore a fresco on the wall of an old church in a small village located within an isolated island community. Within a short time, he realizes that the painting that he is working on, a picture of St. Sebastian being tortured by two angels, is a key to the strange happenings that have affected this village. People with whom the artist comes in contact are murdered or end up missing and the local police are reluctant to investigate.

As a morbid air of degeneracy fills the frames, Avati slowly offers the hero (and the audience) clues to the mystery. The artist decides to investigate the background and life of the painter of the original mural, discovering the artist to be a deranged man who had an incestuous relationship with his two sisters and, as a result, committed suicide at a young age. In time, he finds himself heading toward a conclusion that he would have best steered away from. Avati's film chillingly evokes the atmosphere of classic black-and-white Italian horror films and yet features a heightened sense of realism as well. One of the most shocking sequences involves the artist fleeing in terror from an unseen predator. He rushes into town and yet no one answers his pleas for help. The locals are too afraid to be involved in the plight of this outsider who may have discovered the terrible secret that holds the village in terror.

Pupi Avati

A more recent Avati film in the horror genre is *L'Arcano Incantatore* (1996), which is a film set in Italy during the sixteenth century and concerns the misadventures of a defrocked cleric (Stefano Dionisi) who takes up with a banished heretic who has become an experimenter in the black arts, The Arcane Enchanter (Carlo Cecchi). A stately and yet eerie production, the film often harkens back to the heyday of the Italian gothic cinema, at the same time acknowledging the work of pioneers in the field like Mario Bava with its reliance on mood and ambiance. With these films, Pupi Avati proves that he is capable of making a movie, combining elements of the best of the early Italian Gothics. Looking forward to a mature sensibility for the genre, he acknowledges that the successes of the past cannot be repeated without paving the way for a resurrection in the genre utilizing moviemaking techniques that allow even non-horror filmgoers to appreciate the material. One of his more recent films, *I Cavalieri Che Fecero l'Impesa* (2001) concerns five brave young knights on a mission that takes them to Thebes in Greece to recover the sacred Shroud of Turin. He is currently beginning production on *Il Cuore Altrove* (2003).

Pupi Avati Filmography (selected films)

L'Arcano Incantatore

A.k.a. *The Arcane Enchanter* (English translation and title); a.k.a. *The Mysterious Enchanter*; a.k.a. *The Mysterious Encounter* (English titles) (1996) (It.); D/S: Pupi Avati; P: Antonio Avati, Aurelio De Laurentiis; C: Cesare Bastelli; M: Pino Donaggio; S: Carlo Cecchi, Stefano Dionisi, Arnaldo Ninchi, Andrea Scorzoni, Consuela Ferrera, Renzo Rinaldi.

La Casa dalle Finestre Che Ridono

A.k.a.*The House with the Windows That Laugh*; a.k.a. *The House with the Windows That Laughed* (English translations and titles); (1976) (It.); D: Pupi Avati; P: Gianni Minervini, Antonio Avati; Prod. Co.: A.M.A. Film S.r.l.; SC: Pupi Avati, Gianni Cavina, Maurizio Costanzo, Antonio Avati; C: Pasquale Rachini, Giorgio Urbinelli; M: Amedeo Tommasi; S: Lino Capolicchio, Francesca Marciano, Gianni Cavina, Giulio Pizzirani, Vanna Busoni, Andrea Matteuzzi, Pietro Brambilla, Ferdinand Orlandi, Ines Ciaschetti, Eugene Walter.

I Cavilieri Che Fecero l'Impesa

A.k.a. *The Knights Who Made the Enterprise* (English translation); a.k.a. *The Knights of the Quest* (English title) (2001) (It.); D: Pupi Avati; P: Antonio Avati, Tarak Ben Ammar, Mark Lombardo; C: Pasquale Rachini; M: Riz Ortolani; S: Raoul Bova, Edward Furlong, Marco Leonardi, Stanislas Merhar, Thomas Kreutschmann, F. Murray Abraham, Edmund Purdom.

Il Cuore Altrove

A.k.a. *A Heart Elsewhere*; a.k.a. *The Heart Is Everywhere* (English titles and translations) (2003) (It.); D/SC: Pupi Avati; P: Antonio Avati; M: Riz Ortolani; C: Pasquale Rachini; S: Neri Marcore, Giancarlo Giannini, Vanessa Incontrada, Nino D'Angelo, Vanessa Gallipoli, Sandro Milo.

Zeder

A.k.a. *Zeder-Voices from Beyond*; a.k.a. *Voices from the Beyond*; a.k.a. *Revenge of the Dead* (English titles) (1982) (It.); D: Pupi Avati; P: Gianni Minervini, Antonio Avati; Prod. Co.: AMA Film; SC: Pupi Avati, Antonio Avati, Maurizio Costanzo; M: Riz Ortolani; C: Franco Della Colli; S: Gabriele Lavi, Anne Canovas, Bob Tonelli, Paola Tanziani, Cesare Barbetti, Aldo Sassi, Veronica Moriconi.

Mariano Baino

This young filmmaker has already made one very impressive short film and one absolutely deranged feature. *Caruncula* (1992) is the first effort from the Italian-born director who works out of England. Running approximately 20 minutes, this film is so obviously influenced by the work of Dario Argento (particularly *Suspiria* and *Inferno*) that only in its bizarre plot and tyro filmmaking can one discern that this is in fact not an Argento short film.

Caruncula is about a timeless time in a universe that could just as well be inhabited by the same sort of Lynchian characters that people *Eraserhead* (1976) or, for that matter, the appalling American splatter film *Combat Shock* (1987). A young woman lives a dour lifestyle in a cramped, dark apartment with her strange relatives. Something happens to this ironic "nuclear" family when people end up dead. The film ends in the local cinema, peopled by more shocking characters.

Dark Waters (1994) is the film that should have made Baino a household name in horror film directing, if it were not so damned strange. Filmed on location in Russia, *Dark Waters* is about a woman (Louise Salter) who journeys far across the alien landscape of the Ukraine to find out why she stopped receiving letters from her sister who joined a convent on an isolated island. Once she arrives, the air reeks of malevolence and evil as this supposedly holy place, built upon the rocky cliffs that jut over the sea, is filled with strange nuns who attempt to drive insane, or murder, our heroine.

Baino's film is filled with all manner of strange characters, from silent Russian farmers who seem to be harboring a deadly secret, to the stone convent's inhabitants, who are supposed to practice Catholicism and yet yield themselves and their allegiances to a darker force. This film has its own ancestor in the popular "possessed nuns" cycle of films of the 1970s, but is stranger than any before it, particularly with the weird set design (filmed in actual caverns that form the unholy halls of the convent) and brutal murders, becoming a shock-filled ode to the work of Argento.

As a footnote, it might be interesting to point out that Baino had to practically smuggle his film out of Russia due to the high tax tariffs and demands of certain illegal cartels to keep the film footage from leaving the country. Once he returned to England, Baino spent nearly a year or more editing his footage and finally premiered the film to horror festival audiences worldwide. Only in recent years has it received a videocassette release in England and the U.S.

Mariano Baino Filmography

Caruncula

(1992) (G.B.); D: Mariano Baino; P: Bob Portal; Prod. Co.: Colstar; SC: Mariano Baino; C: Mark Milsome; S: Rosalind Furlong, Jonathan Jaynes, Peter Waddington, Joan Hicks.

Dark Waters

(1994) (G.B., It., Russia); D: Mariano Baino; P: Victor Zulev; SC: Mariano Baino, Andrew Bark; C: Alex Howe; M: Igor Clarke; S: Louise Salter, Verena Simmons, Maria Kapnist, Valerity Bassell, Sergei Bassell, Alvina Skarga.

Francesco Barilli

Born in 1943, Francesco Barilli has made few films in his career as a director, but his horror feature *Il Profumo della Signora in Nero* (1973) is certainly a striking, original work in the genre, if overall an uneven film. A woman (Mimsy Farmer) finds herself always running from shadowy figures. She imagines some sort of grand persecution plot or conspiracy at work while, all around her, those that know her well fear that she may, in fact, be becoming insane. The film follows a shaky course somewhere near to the *giallo* thriller with strange, stalking figures following Farmer's every move. Barilli's film jumps right into a completely unforeseen climax when Farmer is actually chosen by a mysterious sect of satanic cannibals to be their next prime rib meal!

Another Barilli film of note is the mean-spirited *Pensione Paura* (1978). Leonora Fani portrays Rose, a young woman who is helping family members operate a secluded, decaying hotel. However, the building is packed with sadistic, decadent types who commit murder and rape Rose. An unseen killer hacks away with an axe at her attackers; afterwards, in gratitude to her unknown savior, she hides the bodies in the basement of the hotel. Then several guests appear to force her to join them in an orgy. Again, her savior appears and shoots all of them dead, sending the film towards a surprising climax. Barilli's attempt to combine elements of the thriller genre with a study of repressed sexuality and resulting psychosis is not dissimilar from themes explored in the earlier *Il Profumo della Signora in Nero*. Barilli's most recent project is the Italian miniseries titled *Giorni da Leone* (2002).

Francesco Barilli Filmography (selected films)

Giorni da Leone

(2002) (It.); D/SC: Francesco Barilli; M: Savio Riccardi; S: Luca Barbareschi, Roberto Abbati, Simone Ascani, Edy Angelillo, Sergio Bini Bustric, Laura Cleri.

Pensione Paura

A.k.a. *Hotel Fear* (English translation); a.k.a. *La Violación de la Señorita Julia* (Spanish title) (1978) (It., Sp.); D: Francesco Barilli; Prod. Co.: Aleph Cinematografica (Rome)/Alessandra Cinematografica (Madrid); SC: Francesco Barilli, Barbara Alberti, Amedeo Pagani; C: Gualitiero Manozzi; M: Adolfo Waitzman; S: Leonora Fani a.k.a. Eleonora Cristofani, Francisco Rabal, Luc Meranda, Iole Fierro, Lidia Biondi, Jose Maria Prada.

Il Profumo delle Signora in Nero

A.k.a. *The Perfume of the Woman in Black*; a.k.a *The Perfume of the Lady in Black* (English translations and title) (1973) (It.); D: Francesco Barilli; P: Giovanni Bertolucci; Prod. Co.: Euro International Films; SC: Francesco Barilli, Massimo D'Avack; C: Mario Masini; M: Nicola Piovani; S: Mimsy Farmer, Mario Scaccia, Maurizio Bonuglia, Nike Arrighi, Daniela Barnes, Alexandra Barnes, Alexandra Paiza, Renata Zamengo.

Sergio Bergonzelli

Born in 1924, Sergio Bergonzelli has had a long cinema career. He is not the most talented of filmmakers, but occasionally he can make enjoyably hokum like *Missione Mortale Molo 83* (1966), an action-packed entry into the European spy film phenomenon of the mid-'60s.

Bergonzelli's body of work is all over the place. From his incomprehensible sex comedies in the '70s to graphic pornos featuring frequent Jess Franco star Ajita Wilson in the '80s, Bergonzelli proves that he can make just about any kind of film. One of his erotic thrillers is also one of his best contributions to the *giallo* thriller genre, *Nelle Pieghe della Carne* (1970). In this film, a cast including Eleonora Rossi-Drago and Anna Maria

Sergio Bergonzelli

Pierangeli act out the craziest family of psychopaths you are apt to find in the cinema. After disposing of her ex-husband in the ocean (an act witnessed by an escaped criminal), Rossi-Drago returns to the family household 13 years later and sees the son of the man she killed strangle his own dog to death. Falaise (Pierangeli), the daughter of the man she killed, stabs Rossi-Drago to death. When a would-be suitor arrives and attempts to seduce Falaise, he ends up literally losing his head over her ... decapitated. Finally, the criminal who witnessed the murder of the father arrives and proceeds to threaten the family before his own life is forfeited. By the time the police have arrived and attempt to bring to the killers to justice, your head will be spinning. It's just Bergonzelli having fun by dragging classy actresses through the mud and having a wild time with the format.

Delirio di Sangue (1988) is undoubtedly his best effort in the horror film genre. Starring John Philip Law as a demented pianist who pines over the death of a loved one, and former peplum muscleman Gordon Mitchell as the family servant with a taste for necrophilia, the film is as deliriously sick as can be. More than once, Law has to restrain Mitchell from abusing a female corpse and Law himself is a sick bastard. He just can't quite get it together for his new love interest and believes that a painting of his former love, painted with the blood of his current amour, could be a work of art.

Other noteworthy genre contributions by director Bergonzelli include the erotic thriller *Malizia Oggi* (1990), the Turkish crime film–cum-sexploitative shocker *La Mondana Nuda* (1980) and an erotic religious irony epic with some elements of a thriller, *La Cristina Monaca Indemoniata* (1971). Bergonzelli is also credited with the direction of the Mario Siciliano film *Erotic Family* (1980), but if anything, the film could have been a problematic one plagued by post-production problems and finished by Bergonzelli, given Siciliano's penchant for splicing in hardcore pornographic footage amongst the comedy-drama co-starring Giorgio Ardisson.

Sergio Bergonzelli Filmography (selected films)

La Cristina la Monaca Indemoniata

A.k.a. *Cristiana, the Possessed Nun* (English translation); a.k.a. *Our Lady of Lust*; a.k.a. *The Loves of a Nymphomaniac* (English titles) (1971) (It.); D/SC: Sergio Bergonzelli; Prod. Co.: MGB Films/Vera Cine'/Cine' Cast; C: Antonio Maccoppi; M: Nevil Cameron, Elvio Monti; S: Magda Konopka, Toti Achilli, Eva Czemerys a.k.a. Eva Cemerys, Vassili Karras a.k.a.Vassili Karamesinis.

Delirio di Sangue

A.k.a. *Blood Delirium* (English translation and title) (1988) (It.); D: Sergio Bergonzelli; P: Raffaella Mertes; Prod. Co.: Cine Decima; SC: Fratelli Cordi; C: Marce De Stefano; S: John Phillip Law, Gordon Mitchell a.k.a. Charles Pendleton, Brigitte Christensen.

Erotic Family

A.k.a. *Las Veredes Vacaciones de una Familia Bien* (Spanish title) (1980) (It., Sp.); D: Sergio Bergonzelli, Mario Siciliano; Prod. Co.: Metheus Film (Rome)/Llorca Films (Madrid)/ Films Dara (Barcelona) C: Juan Gelpi; M: Nico Fidenco; S: Karin Well, Raquel Evans, Giorgio Ardisson, Alfonso De Real, Berta Cabre.

Sergio Bergonzelli is credited as the sole director on the Italian video release, which also features pornographic footage, possibly directed by Siciliano (the film appears on his credits on numerous occasions) and added to the film after the initial Italian theatrical release.

Malizia Oggi

A.k.a. *Malizia Today* (English translation) (1990) (It.); D/SC: Sergio Bergonzelli; Prod. Co.: Cinedecima/Skorpion Entertainment; C: Roberto Girometti; S: Valentine Demy a.k.a. Marissa Parra, Deborah Cali, Mario Pirovano.

Missione Mortale Molo 83

A.k.a. *M.M.M. 83* (alternate Italian title); a.k.a. *Objectif Hambourg Mission 083* (French title) (1966) (It., Sp., Fr.); D: Sergio Bergonzelli; P: Sergio Bergonzelli, Adalberto Albertini; Prod. Co.: Film d'Equipe (Rome)/Olympic P.C. Madrid (Spain)/France Cinema Productions, Paris; SC: Sergio Bergonzelli, Victor A. Catena, Adalberto Albertini; C: Eloy Mella; M: Piero Piccionil; S: Fred Beir, Gerard Blain, Anna Maria Pierangeli, Sylvia Solar.

La Mondana Nuda

A.k.a. *Beklenen Sahit* (Turkish title) (1980) (It., Turkey); D: Vural Pakel, Sergio Bergonzelli, Guido Zurli; S: Richard Harrison, Malisa Longo, Karin Well, Mary Aar.

This film originally began production in Turkey in 1979 as *Beklenen Sahit*, under the direction of Vural Pakel, which could be a pseudonym for Bergonzelli, who is known to have directed a number of feature films in Turkey in the '70s and '80s. Guido Zurli is also credited with assistant direction chores in the *Dizionario del Cinema Italiano 1970–79* volume 4.

Nelle Pieghe della Carne

A.k.a. *In the Folds of the Flesh* (English translation and title); a.k.a. *Las Endemoniadas* (Spanish title; translation: *The Possessed*) (1970) (It., Sp.); D/P: Sergio Bergonzelli; Prod. Co.: M.B.G. Cinematografica (Rome)/Talia Films (Madrid); SC: Sergio Bergonzelli, Fabio De Agostini, Mariano Caiano a.k.a. Mario Caiano; C: Mario Pacheco; M: Jesus Villa Rojo; S: Eleonora Rossi-Drago, Anna Maria Pierangeli, Fernando Sancho, Alfredo Mayo, Emilio G. Caba, Maria Rosa Schlauza.

Giulio Berruti

Giulio Berruti is virtually unknown to horror film audiences but for one film, *Suor Omicidi* (1978). Anita Ekberg, the zaftig sex symbol of the '60s, plays a drug-addicted, sexually repressed nun in a convent. She often succumbs to her drug addiction with fits of dementia during which she hallucinates all manner of strange anti-clerical imagery. When a new arrival at the convent (Laura Nucci) stirs the sexual cravings in Ekberg's loins, she literally doffs her restricting religious clothing, wears a sexy black dress and goes out for a night on the town to release her pent-up desires. With the arrival of the new resident doctor (Joe Dallesandro), who immediately begins to sexually satisfy the cravings of Nucci, strange things begin to happen. Ekberg develops psychopathic rages and then blacks out. When she awakens, more than once a corpse is found nearby. Can Ekberg be the murderer, or is there more happening here than meets the eye? A definite slap in the face to viewers who are sensitive to anti-religious films of any kind, Berruti's picture features a vibrant, hateful and quite impressive performance by Ekberg, but still wallows in the obvious exploitative sub-genre of the "possessed nun" films that were popular in the '70s.

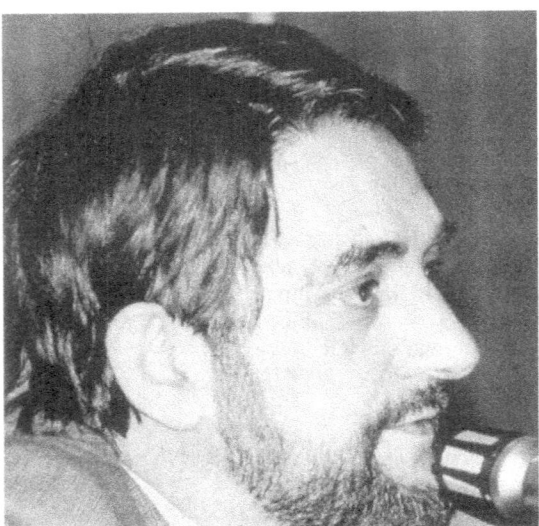
Giulio Berruti

Giulio Berruti Filmography

Suor Omicidi

A.k.a. *Sister Homicide* (English translation); a.k.a. *Killer Nun*; a.k.a. *The Deadly Habit* (English titles) (1978) (It.); D: Giulio Berruti; P: Enzo Gallo, Marcello Papaleo; Prod. Co.: Cinesud in colloboration with Gruppo Di Lavoro Calliope; SC: Giulio Berruti, Alberto Tarallo; C: Tonino Maccoppi, Pippo Carta, Gianfranca Battaglia; M: Alessandro Alessadroni; S: Anita Ekberg, Laura Nucci, Paola Morra, Alida Valli, Massimo Serato, Lou Castel, Joe Dallesandro, Alice Gherardi.

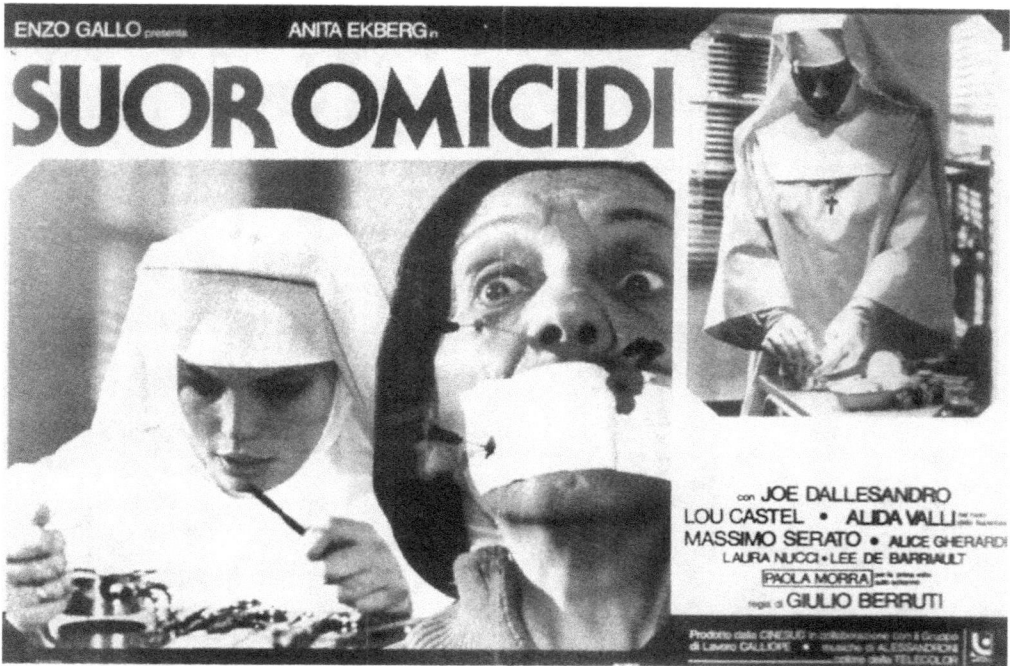

In Giulio Berruti's *Suor Omicidi* (1978, Cinesud in collaboration with Gruppo di Lavoro Calliope), a cleric (Anita Ekberg) murders her charges — or does she?

Andrea Bianchi

Born in Rome, Italy, on March 31, 1925, Andrea Bianchi is a director who genuinely seems to enjoy dabbling in the more sexploitative offerings of the related horror film genres. In 1972, he co-directed (with John Hough) a film version of the Robert Louis Stevenson tale *Treasure Island* (titled *L'Isola del Tesoro*). However, since the '80s Bianchi has been wasting his talent, primarily making pornographic films. Unable to recover from the mire of constrictions that that genre can offer, alas, none of his porno films have been memorable. His five major horror movies are *Nude per l'Assassino* (1975), *Malabimba* (1979), *Le Notti del Terrore* (1980), *Mania* (1988) and *Massacre* (1989).

Nude per l'Assassino adheres to the basic story structure of the thriller and makes little attempt to break out of the confines of the rigid *giallo* format. When a failed abortion results in the death of a young woman, a mysterious killer (wearing black leather clothing and a motorcycle helmet) goes about murdering those held responsible. Bianchi milks the exploitative elements for all their worth with

Andrea Bianchi's lurid thriller *Nude per l'Assassino* (1975, Fral Cinematografica).

this sometimes briefly, genuinely creepy, low-budget production. Of course, the film wallows in cheap sexploitation (Italian softcore starlets Femi Benussi and Edwige Fenech are featured), but this is worth viewing as it is one of the rare thrillers with a female killer!

Malabimba (1979) is a different sort of film altogether. When a seance at an old castle releases the decadent spirit of a playful sexual entity, a whole family becomes entranced in one sexual escapade after another. The sexy spirit eventually decides to possess the young, lithesome body of the proudly virginal Katell Laennac, who walks around wearing little but a sheer nightgown. All this strangeness drives the resident nun, Mariangela Giordano, completely crazy with lust ... ending in a violent sex session with young Laennac, after which she jumps to her death from the castle's high walls! Copulating couples galore is what Bianchi aims for and undemanding audiences will get that in spades, featuring plenty of close-up crotch shots which often are so glistening wet with humidity that the camera lens fogs over.*

Le Notti del Terrore (1980), Bianchi's sick, sick, sick zombie film, is unrelated

---

**For collectors and obscure trivia buffs: While researching this project, I have located three versions of this film. The most notorious one is the hardcore sex print featuring a combination of inserts and footage featuring actors from the original version of the film getting down to the nitty gritty.*

to the Fulci Zombie movies to which it attaches itself (it was even titled *Zombie 3* in some English-language sales markets). What we have here is a bunch of horny travelers all expecting a weekend of sexual thrills until the local horde of revived gut-munchers come along and start chomping on body parts galore. The film's highlight: When the zombified son of Mariangela Giordano (again!) wants to fulfill his incestuous cravings even in death, Mom lets him do so, but he bites off a bloody chunk of her breast! There are some moments that contain some genuine scares, but they are all of the Grand Guignol variety, with various members of the cast screaming at top volume as their intestines are being pulled from their bodies.

In Bianchi's 1988 production *Mania*, set in France, a sect of fanatical cultists kidnap women and chain them in a cellar where they are then whipped and tortured. This deranged group seeks to expel the sins of lust from these young and beautiful women.

The Italian video sleeve art for Andrea Bianchi's *Nude per l'Assassino* (1975, Fral Cinematografica) accentuates curvy actress Edwige Fenech.

When a high-priced prostitute is kidnapped, the local crimelord and a mysterious count join forces to locate her and put an end to this strange cult. Bianchi is in way over his head with this Eurocine co-production that, it seems, may have been designed for the cult sexploitation master Jess Franco. The film features a strange cast of slumming American actors (Chuck Connors, Bo Svenson and Robert Ginty) who perform their roles with such indifference that they have little trouble masking the fact that they can't wait to get out of this mess. Even an experienced exploitation filmmaker like Bianchi displays an inability to deliver a watchable film as the director botches both the (brief) action sequences and the (too many) scenes of torture inflicted upon women.

Bianchi filmed *Massacre* in 1989. Essentially, the production (released under the banner of Lucio Fulci) was thought of as a Fulci-directed film for a number of years before the matter was finally straightened out due to a series of investigative searches. Fulci was asked by his producers (Luigi Nannerini and Antonini Lucidi) to endorse a group of films that they were releasing which included *Massacre*, essentially an Old Dark House tale enlivened with copious amounts of blood and gore. It is one of Bianchi's worst films.

Bianchi's most recent film was *Formula 3 — I Ragazzi dell'Autodromo* (1993), a sexy melodrama starring sensual screen siren Carmen Di Pietro.

Andrea Bianchi Filmography (selected films)

Formula 3 — I Ragazzi dell'Autodrommo

A.k.a. *Hot Laps* (English title) (1993) (It.); D: Andrea Bianchi; Prod. Co.: Film 90; SC: Piero Regnoli; C: Renato Doria; S: Carmen Di Pietro, Theo Connor, Chritine Reynolds, Paul Green.

L'Isola del Tesoro

A.k.a. *Treasure Island* (English translation and title) (1972) (It., G.B., Fr., Sp., W.G.); D: Andrea Bianchi, John Hough; P: Harry Alan Towers, George Davis; Prod. Co.: Massfilms/Productions F.D.L./C.C.C. Filmkunst/Eguiluz Films (Madrid); SC: Orson Welles, Wolf Mankowitz, based on the novel *Treasure Island* by Robert Louis Stevenson; C: Cecilio Paniagua, Ginger Gemmell; M: Natale Massara; S: Orson Welles, Kim Burfield, Lionel Stander, Walter Slezak, Angel Del Pozo, Rik Battaglia, Maria Rohm, Paul Mueller, Jean Lefevbre, Aldo Sanbrell a.k.a. Aldo Sambrell a.k.a. Alfredo Sanchez Brell, Victor Israel.

Malabimba

(1979) (It.); D: Andrea Bianchi; P: Gabriele Crisanti; Prod. Co.: Filmarte; SC: Piero Regnoli; C: Franco Villa; M: Elisio Mancuso, Berto Pisano; S: Katell Laennec, Patrizia Webley a.k.a. Patrizia De Rossi, Mariangela Giordano, Enzo Fiscichella, Giuseppe Marrocu, Elisa Mainardi, Giancarlo Del Luca, Claudio Zucchet.

Mania

A.k.a. *Maniac Killer* (English title) (1988) (Fr.); D: Andrea Bianchi; P: Daniel Lesoeur, Ilona Kunesova; Prod. Co.: Eurocine (Paris); SC: A.L. Mariaux; C: Henri Frogers; M: Luis Enriquez Bacalov; S: Bo Svenson, Robert Ginty, Suzanne Andrews, Chuck Connors, Dora Doll, Henri Lambert.

Massacre

(1989) (It.); D/SC: Andrea Bianchi; Presented by: Lucio Fulci; Prod. Co.: Cold Duck; C: Silvano Tessicini; M: Luigi Ceccarelli; S: Pier Maria Cecchini, Gino Concari, Silvia Conti, Danny Degli Espositi, Patrizia Falcone, Anna Maria Placido, Paul Mueller, Maurice Poli.

Le Notti del Terrore

A.k.a. *The Nights of Terror* (English translation and title); a.k.a. *Zombie Horror*; a.k.a. *Burial Ground*; a.k.a. *Zombie 3: The Nights of Terror* (English titles) (1980) (It.); D: Andrea Bianchi; P: Gabriele Crisanti; Prod. Co.: Esteban Cinematografica; SC: Piero Regnoli; C: Gianfranco Maioletti; M: Elsio Mancuso, Berto Pisano; SP E: Giannetto De Rossi, Gino De Rossi; S: Karin Well, Mariangelo Giordano, Gian Luigi Chirizzi, Peter Bark, Simone Mattioli, Antonella Antinori, Roberto Caporali.

Nude per l'Assassino

A.k.a. *Naked for the Killer*; a.k.a. *Nude for an Assassin* (English translations and titles); a.k.a. *Strip Nude for the Killer*; a.k.a. *Strip Nude for Your Killer* (English titles) (1975) (It.); D: Andrea Bianchi; P: Silvestro De Rossi, Sergio Simonetti; Prod. Co.: Fral Cinematografica; SC: Andrea Bianchi, Massimo Felisatti; C: Franco Della Colli, Enzo Tosi; M: Berto Pisano; S: Edwige Fenech, Nino Castelnuovo, Femi Benussi a.k.a. Eufemia Benussi, Solvi Stubing, Giuliana Cecchini, Erna Schurer a.k.a. Erna Scheurer, Franco Diogene, Giuliana Cecchini.

Mario Bianchi (Montero)

After years directing a variety of features including the mondo film *Africa Sexy* (1963), Mario Bianchi (Montero's) *La Bimba di Satana* (1980) is credited to Alan W. Cools, a pseudonym. Bianchi, a director of sleazy sexploitation and pornographic films (often using a pseudonymous name), is the son of the director Roberto (Bianchi) Montero and is the filmmaker credited with the direction on this film. Essentially a remake of the Andrea Bianchi (no relation) film *Malabimba* (1979), *La Bimba di Satana* is as delirious a film as the original. The body of a countess lies in state within a remote castle, the dead woman's spirit infecting all her relatives, male and female, with a powerful sexual psychosis. Mariangela Giordano, one of the stars of *Malabimba*, is back for more sleazy fun alongside porno starlet Marina Frajase as the countess.

Another genre film by Bianchi is *Non Avere Paura della Zia Marta* (a.k.a. *The Murder Secret*), filmed and released in 1989. Released as a film "supervised" by Lucio Fulci, for obvious reasons, it was often confused as being a Lucio Fulci–directed production (most likely due to the fact that Fulci's name was associated with the film). Although the initial credit on the film reads "Lucio Fulci Presents" and, along with the director credit, an insert reads "Supervised by Lucio Fulci," the grand man of Italian horror had little to do with this film aside from lending his name to its release. Coincidentally, the director of photography on *Non*

Italian poster art for Mario Bianchi's *La Bimba di Satana* (1980, Filmarte).

Avere Paura della Zia Marta is Silvano Tessicini and the editor is Vincenzo Tomassi, two people who had worked with Fulci.

Mario Bianchi (Montero) takes great care in the Old Dark House–type plotting in the story of a group of relatives who arrive for a reading of a will, only to find horrors awaiting them as the night progresses. Although the Fulci name was prominently displayed on the marketing and sales of this film (much as it was with Andrea Bianchi's *Massacre* in 1989), in all likelihood these films could have been left unfinished by Bianchi and Fulci could have been asked by the original producers or production company to re-assemble them into a form that could be released to the general public. But, even if this was the fact, the threadbare production values and lack of marquee names, even in their native Italy, condemned these films to oblivion; they received limited video release in Italy and surrounding European countries. Mario Bianchi (Montero) spent the majority of the '90s directing pornographic films (like 1996's *Milly: Photo Live* with popular hardcore actress Milly D'Abbraccio) in Italy using the pseudonyms Nicholas Moore, Tony Yanker and Martin White.

Mario Bianchi (Montero) Filmography (selected films)

Africa Sexy

(1963) (It.); D: Mario Bianchi (Montero); Prod. Co.: Cineproduzioni Associate; C: Giuseppe La Torre, Francesco Izzarelli, Carlo Bellero, Renato Spinotti, Giorgio Mason; M: Marcello Giombini.

La Bimba di Satana

A.k.a. Satan's Baby Doll (English translation and title) (1980) (It.); D: Mario Bianchi (Montero); P: Gabriele Crisanti, Marcello Spingi; Prod. Co.: Filmarte; SC: Piero Regnoli; C: Angelo Lanutti, Franco Campanile, Maurizio Fiorentini; M: Nico Catanese; S: Maria Angela Giordano, Jacqueline Dupre, Aldo Sanbrell a.k.a. Aldo Sambrell a.k.a. Alfredo Sanchez Brell, Marina Frajese a.k.a. Marina Hedman a.k.a. Marina Lotar.

Director Mario Bianchi is the son of director Roberto Bianchi Montero. Mario Bianchi is often confused with Andrea Bianchi. For years, it was presumed the pseudonym Alan W. Cools was used by Andrea Bianchi, when in fact it belonged to Mario Bianchi.

Milly: Photo Live

(1996) (It.); D: Mario Bianchi (Montero); S: Milly D'Abbraccio.

Non Avere Paura della Zia Marta

A.k.a. *Aunt Martha Does Dreadful Things*; a.k.a. *Don't Be Afraid of Aunt Martha*; a.k.a. *The Murder Secret* (English titles) (1989) (It.); D/SC: Mario Bianchi (Montero); P: Luigi Nannerini, Antonio Lucidi; Presented and supervised by Lucio Fulci; Prod. Co.: Alpha Distribuzione Cinematografica; C: Silvano Tessicini; M: Gianni Esposito; S: Adriana Russo, Gabriele Tinti, Anna Maria Placido, Jessica Moore a.k.a. Luciana Ottaviani, Maurice Poli, Massimiliano Massimi, Sacha Maria Darwin.

Antonio Bido

Antonio Bido's *Solamente Nero* (1978) is his best film. A *giallo* thriller, it involves a series of murders on a sunny European isle, a plot involving vengeance for a misdeed of the past. That the killer is revealed to be a psychotic priest (Craig Hill) is a revelation that pales next to the real reason to see the film: Stelvio Cipriani's pulse-pounding score, an exact duplication of the soundscapes created by the group Goblin for some of Dario Argento's productions. Bido's other thriller of note, *Il Gatto dagli Occhi di Giada* (1977), is a tedious, overly talky film about a woman who witnesses a murder and the attempts of the killer to eliminate her. Among Bido's later credits is *Blue Tornado* (1991), a *Top Gun* manqué starring Dirk Benedict.

Antonio Bido Filmography (selected films)

Blue Tornado

(1991) (It., U.S.); D: Antonio Bido; P: Giovanni Di Clemente, Domenico Lo Zito; SC: Antonio Bido, Gino Capone; M: Fabio Massimo Colasanti, Marco De Angelis, Elivio Moratto; C: Maurizio Dell'Orco; S: Dirk Benedict, Ted McGinley, Patsy Kensit, David Warner, Christopher Ahrens.

Il Gatto dagli Occhi di Giada

A.k.a. *The Cat with the Jade Eyes* (English translation); a.k.a. *The Cat's Victims*; a.k.a. *Watch Me When I Kill* (English titles) (1977) (It.); D: Antonio Bido; P: Gabriella Nardi; Prod. Co.: Elis Cinematografica; SC: Antonio Bido, Vittorio Schiraldi, Roberto Natale, Aldo Serio; C: Mario Vulpiani, Maurizio Maggi; M: Trans Europa Express; S: Corrado Pani, Paola Tedesco, Franco Citti, Fernando Cerulli, Giuseppe Addobbati, Gianfranco Bullo, Yill Pratt, Bianca Toccafondi, Inna Alexeiva, Paolo Malco, Cristina Piras.

Solamente Nero

A.k.a. *Only Blackness* (English translation and title); a.k.a. Dietro Angolo Terrore (Italian pre-production title translation: *Terror Behind the Corner*); a.k.a. *The Bloodstained Shadow*

(G.B. title) (1978) (It.); D: Antonio Bido; P: Teodoro Agrimi; Prod. Co.: P.A.C. Produzione/ Atlas Consortziate S.r.l.; SC: Antonio Bido, Domenico Malan, Marisa Andalo; C: Mario Vulpiani, Maurizio Maggi; M: Stelvio Cipriani; S: Lino Capolicchio, Stefania Casini, Craig Hill, Attilo Duse, Massimo Serato, Laura Nucci, Juliette Meynie.

Antonio Bido

Antonio Boccaci

Directing under the pseudonym Anthony Krystye (or Kristye), Antonio Boccaci filmed one of the most obscure of Italian horror productions, *Metempsycho* (1963). *Metempsycho* is a film that is seldom mentioned whenever film reference books come around to discussing the Italian horror films of the '60s. Photographed in an almost experimental style, which includes a concentration on a lot of sepia-toned colors, often bathing entire scenes in bright blues and garish browns, the film is more than just the mean-spirited horror movie that it appears to be. High in the mountains of an unspecified European country is a castle that has been left to decay by its owners. Two young girls are the latest victims of the cannibalistic, deformed killer who preys on young women venturing too near the castle grounds. Peopled by a bunch of misfit characters (a mystical Eastern practitioner of white magic, the returning ingenue who is loved by two men, the suspicious lover), the film's true moments of cinematic delirium come whenever the camera chooses to show the dimly lit dungeon of terror where the cannibal killer (under the control of another individual) brings a new victim to the castle's dungeons for even more torture. Thirty-five years after this obscure film was produced, it still remains an enigmatic footnote in the history of Italian horror. Boccaci's other known credit is as a co-writer of a mean-spirited sexploitative film titled *I Giorni della Violenza* (1967) starring Rosalba Neri.

Antonio Boccaci Filmography

Metempsycho

A.k.a. *Tomb of Torture* (English title) (1963) (It.); D: Antonio Boccaci; P: Frank Campitelli, Richard Gordon; SC: Antonio Boccaci, Giorgio Simonelli; C: William Grace; M: Armando Sciascia; S: Annie Albert, Adriano Micantoni, Marco Mariani, Flora Caroselli, Bernard Blay, Enny Eco, Antonio Boccaci.

Giuliano Carnimeo

Giuliano Carnimeo is the director of over 30 films. Born in 1932, Carnimeo (who sometimes used the pseudonym Anthony Ascott) directed comedies, dramas and Westerns. Many of his Westerns are above-average (including the second film in the Sartana Western series, 1969's *Sono Sartana, il Vostro Becchino*). *Perchè Quelle Strane Gocce di Sangue sul Corpo di Jennifer?* (1972) remains his most important genre film credit and his only horror film. In an apartment complex in the middle of a cosmopolitan Italian city, beautiful model types are being murdered. When two female roommates move into an apartment where a killing recently took place, they too become potential victims. Carnimeo cast his film with a lot of familiar faces to fans of the *giallo* genre (Edwige Fenech, George Hilton and Luciano Pigozzi). This is a well-made thriller, even if the reason for the killings (a father, ruined by his gay daughter's promiscuity, seeks vengeance on all sexually alluring women) is a disturbing one.

Possibly Carnimeo's worst film as a director is *Quella Villa in Fondo al Parco* (1987), where diminutive actor Nelson De La Rosa (wearing pasted-on fur and fangs) leaps on aspiring actresses and threatens them before disappearing into cupboards. Slumming genre stars David Warbeck and Janet Agren walk through the film with extreme disinterest. The low production values and treatment of the physically challenged De La Rosa reek of exploitation at its worst.

Giuliano Carnimeo Filmography (selected films)

Perchè Quelle Strane Gocce di Sangue sul Corpo di Jennifer?

A.k.a. *Why Those Strange Drops of Blood on the Body of Jennifer?*; a.k.a. *What Are Those Strange Drops of Blood Doing on the Body of Jennifer?*; a.k.a. *What Are Those Strange Drops of Blood Doing on the Lips of Jennifer?* (English translations and titles); a.k.a. *Una Strana Orchidea con Cinque Gocce di Sangue* (Italian pre-production title; translation: *A Strange Orchid with Five Drops of Blood*); a.k.a. *Erotic Blue* (G.B. title); a.k.a. *The Case of the Bloody Iris* (English title) (1972) (It.); D: Giuliano Carnimeo; P: Luciano Martino; Prod. Co.: Galassia Film/Lea Film; SC: Ernesto Gastaldi; C: Stelvio Massi; M: Bruno Nicolai; S: Edwige Fenech, George Hilton, Paola Quattrini, Giampiero Albertini, Framco Agostini, Oreste Lionello, Ben Carra, Carla Brait, Gianni Pulone, Carla Mancini, Georges Rigaud, Annabella Incontrera, Luciano Pigozzi.

Quella Villa in Fondo al Parco

A.k.a. *Rat Man* (English title) (1987) (It.); D: Giuliano Carmineo; Prod. Co.: Fulvia Film; SC: Elisa Livia Briganti; C: Roberto Girometti; M: Stefano Mainetti; SP E: Franco Giannini; S: David Warbeck, Janet Agren, Eva Grimaldi, Nelson De La Rosa, Luisa Menon, Werner Pochath.

Sono Sartana, il Vostro Becchino

A.k.a. *Sartana, the Gravedigger*; a.k.a. *I Am Sartana, Your Angel of Death* (English titles) (1969) (It.); D: Giuliano Carnimeo; SC: Tito Carpi, Enzo Dell'Aqua; C: Giovanni Bergamini; M: Vasco and Mancuso; S: Gianni Garko, Frank Wolff, Klaus Kinski a.k.a. Klaus Gunther Nakszynksi, Gordon Mitchell a.k.a. Charles Pendleton, Ettore Manni.

Mario Colucci

Mario Colucci seems to have just one film to his credit as a director (although he is credited in some sources as contributing to the story ideas for several Italian spy thrillers of the '60s, and often worked as a composer). *Qualcosa Striscia nel Buio* (1970) is a bright shiny gem in a sea of "what the hell kind of movie is that?" films. This incredible title needs a subgenre of its own because it contains so many references to so many other films. In the dead of night, a charming psychopathic killer (Farley Granger) leads the police on a high-speed chase that ends when all involved discover that a fierce storm has destroyed the nearest bridge. Various groups of people, all on their way to their own destinations and all strangers to each other, end up at a castle ... because the bridge is destroyed. The owner of the castle is long dead and her horny stepdaughter still lives there and dallies with the handyman to pass time. Everyone stays the night seeking shelter from the storm. During a power failure, everyone lights candles and decides to hold a seance. Before the night is through, we will be treated to ghostly possessions, murder, sexual couplings, murder, a romantic interlude between the killer and one of the guests and more murder. This is an underrated film that is waiting to be rediscovered.

A montage of scenes from Mario Colluci's *Qualcosa Striscia nel Buio* (1970, Akia Productions S.P.A.).

Mario Colucci Filmography

Qualcosa Striscia nel Buio

A.k.a. *Something Creeping in the Dark*; a.k.a. *Something Is Creeping in the Dark*; a.k.a. *Something Strikes in the Dark* (English translations and titles); a.k.a. *The Phantom Assassin* (alternate English title) (1970) (It.); D/SC: Mario Colucci; P: Dino Fazio; Prod. Co.: Akia Productions S.P.A.; C: Giuseppe Aquari; M: Angelo Francesco Lavagnino; SP E: C.I.P.A.; S: Farley Granger, Lucia Bose, Giacomo Rossi-Stuart, Stan Cooper a.k.a. Stelvio Rossi, Mia Genberg, John Hamilton, Francesco Lavagnino, Dino Fazio, Loredana Nusciak.

Luigi Cozzi

Born in 1947, Luigi Cozzi already has a place reserved for himself in the Italian horror reference books as an assistant to Dario Argento during that director's formative early years. On his own, Cozzi is an uneven filmmaker. Cozzi's own favorite films are science fiction or adventure stories, so it is no surprise that among his more entertaining features are *Scontri Stellari Oltre la 3a Dimensione* (1978), *Ercole* (1983) and *Le Avventure dell'Incredibile Ercole* (1984), whilst his personal favorites include the short experimental film *Isabell, a Dream* (1968) and *Il Tunnel Sotto il Mondo* (1969), his debut feature, which remains an uneven homage to the fiction of Ray Bradbury and J.G. Ballard, among others.

Besides his 1972 television feature *Il Vicino di Casa* (where a couple rents a coastal vacation home and discovers that their upstairs neighbor is a killer), which was produced for Argento's television series *La Porta sul Buio*, Cozzi's *L'Assassino È Costretto ad Uccidere Ancora* (1975) uses a novel idea: A man seeks to have his wife murdered by a professional killer but, when the deed is done, not only is it apparent that someone else knows of the plan, but that some idiots have stolen the car containing the corpse. The rest of the film alternates between the police investigation of the wife's disappearance (and their suspicion of

Luigi Cozzi

the husband) and the killer menacing the hedonistic, fun-loving youths who unknowingly have stolen the evidence. *Contaminazione* (1980) is a science fiction–horror thriller that succeeds on the power of its sheer momentum, rather than its weak story. Much like Lucio Fulci's *Zombi*, the film begins when a ship sails into the New York harbor containing a mysterious alien creature that sears the flesh from the bone and turns people into exploding hunks of gore. A mission to a South American jungle finds that an alien intelligence has entered Earth's atmosphere and, from there, seeks to rule the world, sending out egg-like lifeforms to threaten mankind. American astronaut Ian McCullough (also in Fulci's *Zombi*) has to save the world.

In 1988, Argento produced *Turno di Notte*, a series of 15 short films for Italian television. The shorts consisted of a batch of tales that revolved around the thrilling misadventures that befall cab drivers assigned the night shift. The episodes were directed by Lamberto Bava (*Babbao Natale, Il Bambino Rapito, Buona Fine È Migliore Principo, E ... di Moda la Morte* and *Heavy Metal*) and Cozzi (*La Casa dello Stradivari, Ciak Si Muore, Delitto in Rock, L'Evasa, Giallo Natale, L'Impronta dell'Assassino, Sposarsi È un Po Morire, Il Taxi Fantasma* and *Via delle Streghe*).

Nobody likes *Paganini Horror* (1990), Cozzi included, but someone has to take the blame for this putrid mess. An all-girl rock 'n' roll band shooting an MTV–style video are suddenly inspired by an ancient lost manuscript by the virtuoso violinist Paganini. At the nearly deserted villa where the crew and band gather, someone in a strange costume carrying a violin menaces the cast.

Il Gatto Nero (1991) caused a rift in the close friendship between Cozzi and Argento because this film continued the Three Mothers story idea that Argento originated with *Suspiria* and *Inferno*. Cozzi's film is a movie within a movie about a planned film sequel to *Inferno* that will consist of a great revelation about the Three Mothers mythology. Unexplained murders plague the set and cast and then possession rears its ugly head once again when it is implied that otherworldly beings could be to blame. Containing a major role for British '70s Hammer film starlet Caroline Munro, the film languished on the shelf (as unreleasable) before making a belated appearance on British video and American cable in the late '90s.

In 1991, the second of the feature-length documentaries on Dario Argento appeared. Cozzi's *Il Mondo di Dario Argento 2* pales by comparison with Michele Soavi's 1985 (similarly titled) documentary. The project traces the years since the Soavi documentary and concentrates primarily on the filming of *Opera*.

Cozzi's most recent contribution to cinema is another documentary on Argento. Titled *Il Mondo di Dario Argento 3: Il Museo degli Orrori di Dario Argento* (1997), this shot-on-video tribute features interviews with the director, the casts and crews of the films that he has made since *Opera*, and a tourist's guide look into Profondo Rosso, the store that Argento and Cozzi own in Italy.

Luigi Cozzi Filmography

L'Assassino È Costretto ad Uccidere Ancora

A.k.a. *The Killer Is Forced to Kill Again*; a.k.a. *The Murderer Must Kill Again*; a.k.a. *The Killer Must Strike Again*; a.k.a. *The Killer Strikes Again*; a.k.a. *The Dark Is Death's Friend* (G.B.) (English translations and titles); a.k.a. *Il Ragno* (alternate Italian title; translation: *The Spider*); a.k.a. *Le Morte È Come un Ragno* (alternate Italian title) (1975) (It., Fr.); D: Luigi Cozzi; P: Giuseppe Tortorella, Umberto Lenzi; Prod. Co.: Albione Cinematografica (Milan)/GIT Internationzale Film (Milan)/Paris Cannes Production (Paris); SC: Luigi Cozzi, Daniele Del Giudice, Adriano Bolzoni; C: Riccardo Pallottini, Piergiorgio Pozzi; M: Nando De Luca; S: George Hilton, Michel Antoine, Femi Benussi a.k.a. Eufemia Benussi, Cristina Galbo, Eduardo Fajardo, Teresa Velasquez, Alessio Orano, Sydne Rome.

Le Avventure dell'Incredibile Ercole

A.k.a. *The Incredible Adventures of Hercules* (English translation); a.k.a. *The Adventures of Hercules*; a.k.a. *Hercules II* (English titles) (1984) (It.); D/SC: Luigi Cozzi; P: Menachem Golan, Goram Globus; Prod. Co.: Cannon Italia; C: Alberto Spagnoli; M: Pino Donaggio; S: Lou Ferrigno, Sonia Viviani, William Berger, Berto Marini, Federica Moro, Carla Ferrigno, Pamela Prati, Serena Grandi, Ivan Rassimov, Eva Robbins a.k.a. Eva Coatti a.k.a. Roberto Coatti.

La Casa dello Stradivari

(1987/88) (It.); D: Luigi Cozzi; P: Dario Argento; Prod. Co.: A.D.C. s.r.l.; C: Pasquale Rachini; S: Antonella Vitale, Matteo Gazzolo, Franco Cerri, Lea Martino, Jinny Stefan, Jasmine Maimone.

Episode of the Italian television program *Turno di Notte*.

Ciak Si Muore

(1987/88); D: Luigi Cozzi; P: Dario Argento; Prod. Co.: A.D.C. s.r.l.; C: Pasquale Rachini; S: Antonella Vitale, Matteo Gazzolo, Franco Ferri, Lea Martino, Corinne Clery, Loris Loddi, Michele Soavi (uncredited).

Episode of the Italian television program *Turno di Notte*.

Contaminazione

A.k.a. *Contamination* (English translation and title); a.k.a. *Contaminazione: Alien Arriva sulla Terra* (Italian pre-production title); a.k.a. *Astaron — Brut des Schreckens* (German title); a.k.a. *Alien Contamination*; a.k.a. *Alien Spawn*; a.k.a. *Alien 2*; a.k.a. *Contamination: Alien on Earth*; a.k.a. *Spawn*; a.k.a. *Toxic Spawn* (English titles) (1980) (It., W.G.); D: Luigi Cozzi; P: Claudio Mancini, Ugo Valenti; Prod. Co.: Alex Cinematografica S.r.l. (Rome)/Barthonia/Lisa Film (Munich); SC: Luigi Cozzi, Erich Tomek; C: Giuseppe Pinori, Carlo Tafani, Adolfo Bartoli; M: Goblin, Bixio Cemsa; SP E: Giovanni Corridori; S: Ian McCullough, Louise Marleau, Gisela Hahn, Marino Mase', Siegfried Rausch, Carlo De Mejo, Carlo Nonni.

Delitto in Rock

(1987/88) (It.); D: Luigi Cozzi; P: Dario Argento; Prod. Co.: A.D.C. s.r.l.; C: Pasquale Rachini; S: Antonella Vitale, Matteo Gazzolo, Franco Cerri, Lea Martino, Gianni Miani, Cinzia Farolfi.

Episode of the Italian television program *Turno di Notte*.

Ercole

A.k.a. *Hercules* (English translation and title) (1983) (It., U.S.?); D/SC: Luigi Cozzi; P: Menahem Golan, Yoram Globus; Prod. Co.: Cannon Films; C: Alberto Spagnoli; M: Pino Donaggio; S: Lou Ferrigno, Brad Harris, Sybil Danning a.k.a. Sybille Johanna Danninger, Rossana Podesta, Ingrid Anderson, Mirella D'Angelo, William Berger, Gianni Garko, Yehuda Efroni, Eva Robbins a.k.a. Eva Coatti a.k.a. Roberto Coati.

L'Evasa

(1987/88) (It.); D: Luigi Cozzi; P: Dario Argento; Prod. Co.: A.D.C. s.r.l.; C: Pasquale Rachini; S: Antonella Vitale, Matteo Gazzolo, Lea Martino, Matteo Gazzolo, Micaela Pignatelli.

Episode of the Italian television program *Turno di Notte*.

Il Gatto Nero

A.k.a. *The Black Cat* (English translation and title); a.k.a. *Edgar Allan Poe's The Black Cat*; a.k.a. *De Profundis* (alternate Italian title; translation: *Out of the Depths*) (1991) (It.); D: Luigi Cozzi; P: Lucio Lucidi; Prod. Co.: World Pictures/21st Century; SC: Luigi Cozzi; C: Pasquale Rachini; M: Vince Tempera; SP E: Antonio Corridori, Armando Valcuada; S: Florence Guerin, Urbano Barberini, Caroline Munro, Brett Halsey, Luisa Maneri, Karina Huff, Alessandra Accai, Jasmine Maimone, Antonio Marsina, Michele Soavi.

Giallo Natale

(1987/88) (It.); D: Luigi Cozzi; P: Dario Argento; Prod. Co.: A.D.C. s.r.l.; C: Pasquale Rachini; S: Antonella Vitale, Matteo Gazzolo, Lea Martino, Franco Cerri, Asia Argento, Daria Nicolodi.

Episode of the Italian television program *Turno di Notte*.

L'Impronta dell'Assassino

(1987/88); D: Luigi Cozzi; P: Dario Argento; Prod. Co.: A.D.C. s.r.l.; C: Pasquale Rachini; S: Antonella Vitale, Matteo Gazzolo, Franco Cerri, Lea Martino, Mirella D'Angelo, Brett Halsey.

Episode of the Italian television program *Turno di Notte*.

Il Mondo di Dario Argento 2

A.k.a. *The World of Dario Argento 2* (English translation and title); a.k.a. *Dario Argento: Master of Horror* (English title) (1991) (It.); D: Luigi Cozzi, Dario Argento; P: Lillo Capoano; Prod. Co.: ADC s.r.l.; SC: Luigi Cozzi, Fabio Giovanni.

Features interviews with Argento and excerpts (as well as cast and crew interviews) from

Argento's films post–*Phenomena*. Includes scenes from *Tenebrae*, *Opera*, *La Chiesa*, *Due Occhi Diabolici* and *La Setta*.

Il Mondo di Dario Argento 3: Il Museo degli Orrori di Dario Argento

A.k.a. *The World of Dario Argento 3: The Museum of Horror as Presented by Dario Argento*; a.k.a. *Dario Argento's Museum of Horror* (English translations and titles) (1997) (It.); D: Luigi Cozzi; Dario Argento; Asia Argento, Prod. Co.: Profondo Rosso presents a Profondo Rosso S.a.s. Production; SC: Luigi Cozzi, Nicola Lombardi; M: Claudio Simonetti, Bill Wyman, Ennio Morricone, Goblin.

Primarily consists of interviews conducted with Dario Argento on location in the store Profondo Rosso in Rome. Film footage consists of some Argento productions of recent years, up to and including some short films made for Italian television, produced by Argento.

Paganini Horror

(1990) (It.); D: Luigi Cozzi; P: Fabrizio De Angelis; Prod. Co.: Fulvia Film; SC: Luigi Cozzi, Daria Nicolodi; C: Franco Lecca; M: Vince Tempera; SP E: Casagni-Prestopino; S: Daria Nicolodi, Jasmine Main, Pascal Persiano, Donald Pleasence, Maria Cristina Mastrangeli, Michele Klippstein, Pietro Genuardi, Luana Ravagnini, Roberto Giannini, Giada Cozzi, Elena Pompei, Perla Agostini.

Scontri Stellari Oltre la 3a Dimensione

A.k.a. *The Adventures of Stella Star*; a.k.a. *Star Crash* (English titles) (1978) (It., U.S.); D: Luigi Cozzi; P: Nat Wachsberger, Patrick Wachsberger; Prod. Co.: Columbia Pictures Corporation/American International Pictures/Film Enterprise; SC: Luigi Cozzi, Nat Wachsberger; C: Paul Beeson, Roberto Ettore Piazzoli, Roberto Girometti; M: Aurelio Crugnola; S: Caroline Munro, Marjoe Gortner, Christopher Plummer, David Hasselhoff, Robert Tessier, Joe Spinell, Nadia Cassini, Judd Hamilton, Daniela Giordano, Hamilton Camp.

Sposarsi È un Po Morire

(1987/88) (It.); D: Luigi Cozzi; P: Dario Argento; Prod. Co.: A.D.C. s.r.l.; C: Pasquale Rachini; S: Antonella Vitale, Matteo Gazzolo, Franco Cerri, Lea Martino, Bruno Bilotta, David Dingeo.

Episode of the Italian television program *Turno di Notte*.

Il Taxi Fantasma

(1987/88) (It.); D: Luigi Cozzi; P: Dario Argento; Prod. Co.: A.D.C. s.r.l.; C: Pasquale Rachini; S: Antonella Vitale, Matteo Gazzolo, Franco Cerri, Lea Martino, Sonia Vivani.

Episode of the Italian television program *Turno di Notte*.

Via delle Streghe

(1987/88) (It.); D: Luigi Cozzi; P: Dario Argento; Prod. Co.: A.D.C. s.r.l.; S: Antonella Vitale, Matteo Gazzolo, Lea Martino, Franco Cerri, Elena Pompei, Bruno Corazzari.

Episode of the Italian television program *Turno di Notte*.

Il Vicino di Casa

A.k.a. *The Man Upstairs*; a.k.a *The Neighbor* (English translations and titles) (1973) (It.); D/SC: Luigi Cozzi; P: Dario Argento; Prod. Co.: RAI Radiotelevisione Italiana presents a SEDA Spettacoli S.p.A. (Rome) production; C: Elio Polacchi; M: Giorgio Gaslini; S: Aldo Reggiani, Laura Belli, Mimmo Palmara, Alberto Atenari.

Episode of the Italian television program *La Porta sul Buio* a.k.a. *The Door to Darkness*.

Armando Crispino

During his lengthy career, Armando Crispino (born 1925) has directed a number of films, nearly all of them entertaining movies. From the strange psychedelic western *John il Bastardo* (1967) to the World War II action epic *Commandos* (1968), Crispino has dabbled in the art of adding touches of realism to his films set in the cinema of the fantastic. However, with his horror features *L'Etrusco Uccide Ancora* (1972) and *Macchie Solari* (1974), realism is something that rarely appears.

L'Etrusco Uccide Ancora is an uneven tale about an excavation of an ancient Etruscan tomb. The entity that may have been released is murdering members of this group and terrorizing the financial benefactors of the dig. Eventually the audience learns that an insane person is really to blame for the murders. Only the possibility of possession by an ancient Etruscan demon led to the anxiety of "being possessed" for cast members that we had, up until the climax, suspected of being the killer or killers. What the heck is that all about? Crispino wants his audience to swallow this thin excuse for the murders by simply explaining that characters in the film were so scared of being possessed that they became briefly possessed? This is one important reason why this Crispino film disappoints. He has his cast admit at the finale that they were not possessed after all; it was just their fears.

Macchie Solari is a much more successful horror film in that it delves into the psychosexual problems of a woman (Mimsy Farmer) plagued by hallucinations and phobias. The dead return to life in various stages of decay and some display amorous advances towards her. A friendly priest may be a sinister person, maybe not. It turns out that all this has been caused by the repressed sexuality of the woman. Then Crispino throws the audience a curve at the film's climax.

One of his last productions as a director was the seldom-seen *Frankenstein all'Italiana* (1976), an uneven madcap farce with dollops of sophisticated humor and sexploitation.

Armando Crispino Filmography (selected films)

Commandos

A.k.a. *Sullivan's Marauders* (English title) (1968) (It., West Germany); D: Armando Crispino; P: Alfonso Sansone, Enrico Chrosciciki, Arthur Brauner, Menahem Golan; Prod. Co.: P.E.C./C.C.I. (Rome)/C.C.C. (Berlin); SC: Armando Crispino, Lucio Battistrada, Stefano Stucchi, Dario Argento; C: Benito Frattari; M: Mario Nascimbene; S: Lee Van Cleef, Jack Kelly, Giampiero Albertini, Marilu Tolo, Joachim Fuchsberger, Gotz George.

L'Etrusco Uccide Ancora

A.k.a. *Das Geheimnis der Gelben Grabes* (German title; translation: *The Mystery of the Gold Diggers*); a.k.a. *Ubica Dolazi iz Groba* (Yugoslavian title); a.k.a. *The Dead Are Alive* (English title)(1972) (It., Yugo, W.G.); D: Armando Crispino; Prod. Co.: Mondial Te. FI. (Rome)/Inex Films (Belgrade)/C.C.C. Filmkunst G.M.B.H. (Berlin); SC: Armando Crispino, Lucio Battistrada; C: Enrico Menczer; M: Riz Ortolani; S: Alex Cord, Samantha Eggar, John Marley, Nadja Tiller, Horst Frank, Enzo Tarascio, Enzo Cerusico, Carlo De Mejo, Vladan Milasinovic, Daniela Surina.

Frankenstein all'Italiana

A.k.a. *Frankenstein Italian Style* (English translation and title); a.k.a. *Prendini, Straziami, Che Brucio di Passione* (Italian re-release title) (1976) (It.); D: Armando Crispino; P: Filiberto Bandini; Prod. Co.: R.P.A. (Registi Pubblicitari Associati) Cinematografica; SC: Massimo Franciosa, Maria Luisa Montagnana; C: Giuseppe Acquari, Carlo Acquari; M: Stelvio Cipriani; SP E: Sergio Chiusi, Paolo Patrizi; S: Aldo Maccione, Gianrico Tedeschi, Ninetto Davoli, Jenny Tamburi a.k.a. Luciana Della Robbia, Anna Mazzanauro, Lorenza Guerrieri.

John il Bastardo

A.k.a. *John, the Bastard* (English translation and title) (1967) (It.); D: Armando Crispino; P: Nino Battistrada; SC: Armando Crispino, Romano Scavolini; C: Sante Achilli; M: Nico Fidenco; S: John Richardson, Claudio Camaso, Martine Beswicke, Claudio Gora, Glauco Onorato, Gordon Mitchell a.k.a. Charles Pendleton

Macchie Solari

A.k.a. *Sun Spots* (English translation); a.k.a. *Le Victime* (French title; translation: *The Victim*); a.k.a. *The Victim*; a.k.a. *Autopsy* (English titles) (1974) (It.); D: Armando Crispino; P: Leonardo Pescarolo; Prod. Co.: Clodio Cinematografica; SC: Armando Crispino, Lucio Battistrada; C: Carlo Carlini; M: Ennio Morricone; S: Mimsy Farmer, Barry Primus, Raymond Lovelock, Angela Goodwin, Massimo Serato, Carlo Cattaneo.

Armando Crispino

Massimo Dallamano

Born in 1917, Massimo Dallamano has directed a number of thrillers, including *La Morte Non Ha Sesso* (1968). He excelled as a director of films that were charitably called sexploitation. Despite this, some of Dallamano's horror features warrant mention here, particularly *Il Dio Chiamato Dorian* (1970), *Cosa Avete Fatto a Solange?* (1971), *La Polizia Chiede Aiuto* (1974) and *Il Medaglione Insanguinato* (1975), and they are as different as night and day.

La Morte Non Ha Sesso is a tale which involves elements of the police procedural drama and the thriller. John Mills stars as an Italian police inspector who suspects his wife (Luciana Paluzzi) of infidelity and then manages to coerce career criminal Robert Hoffman into agreeing to murder her. However, Hoffman falls in love with the woman, and a cat-and-mouse game between the inspector and the criminal takes up most of the running time.

Il Dio Chiamato Dorian is a tale set at the birth of the swinging '70s, when free love, free money, free everything and narcissism reign supreme. Helmut Berger plays the Dorian Gray role as an apparently never-aging bisexual stud. However, when certain individuals find out about Dorian's secret to longevity, it leads to a murder or two, then the expectant climax. In the course of the film, the audience will be treated to numerous heterosexual and (implied) homosexual sequences highlighting the sexually explicit nature of the film.

The much more serious *Cosa Avete Fatto a Solange?* had a tenuous attachment to the Edgar Wallace films of the '60s (German actors Joachim Fuchsberger and Karin Baal appear and the film was co-produced by one of the German film companies responsible for the successful Wallace film adaptations). It tells of a repressed schoolgirl who undergoes a botched abortion operation. Meanwhile, her sexually active female schoolmates are all clamoring over hot stud teacher Fabio Testi. When they start showing up as corpses, Testi isn't the only one who's a suspect. A film notorious for its graphic and shocking sex and murder scenes, it was one of the first Italian genre films to introduce the next wave of graphic horror in the industry.

La Polizia Chiede Aiuto attempts to revisit themes that Dallamano explored in *Solange*, but also spends a great deal of time on police procedurals, a not-uncommon trait for films of this period. The '70s also saw a growth in production of the Euro Crime or Police Action genre and this movie seems like an attempt to combine this with the *giallo*. *La Polizia Chiede Aiuto* examines the death of a young teenaged girl connected with a criminal ring involving girls having sex with other minors and politicals. As the police investigate, a killer dressed in dark motorcycle leathers (including a crash helmet) begins to stalk anyone involved.

Massimo Dallamano's *Cosa Avete Fatto a Solange?* (1971, Clodio Cinematografica/Italian International Film [Rome]/Rialto Film Preben Philipsen [Berlin]).

Il Mediaglione Insanguinato, one of Dallamano's later productions, was a sometimes effective (and eerie) but ultimately unsuccessful entry into the then-popular possession genre.

Massimo Dallamano Filmography (selected films)

Cosa Avete Fatto a Solange?

A.k.a. *Che Cosa Avete Fatto a Solange?* (alternate Italian title); a.k.a. *What Have You Done to Solange?*; a.k.a. *What Have They Done to Solange?* (English translations and titles); a.k.a. *Das Geheimnis der Grunen Stecknalden* (German title; translations: *The Secret of the Green Pin* and *The Mystery of the Green Pin*); a.k.a. *The School That Couldn't Scream*; a.k.a. *Terror in the Woods* (English titles) (1971) (It., W.G.); D: Massimo Dallamano; P: Leonardo Pescarolo, Fulvio Lucisano; Prod. Co.: Clodio Cinematografica/Italian International Film (Rome)/Rialto Film Preben Philipsen (Berlin); SC: Massimo Dallamano, Bruno Di Geronimo, Peter M. Thouet; C: Aristide Massaccesi; M: Ennio Morricone; S: Fabio Testi, Joachim Fuchsberger, Karin Baal, Camille Keaton, Cristina Galbo, Maria Monti, Gunther M. Stoll, Claudia Botenuth, Pilar Castel, Giovanna Di Bernardo, Rainer Penkert, Antonio Casale.

Il Dio Chiamato Dorian

A.k.a. *And God Said to Dorian* (English translation); a.k.a. *Le Dépravé* (French title); a.k.a. *Das Bildnis des Dorian Gray*; a.k.a. *Dorian Gray*; a.k.a. *The Secret of Dorian Gray*; a.k.a. *The Evils of Dorian Gray* (English titles) (1970) (It., W.G., G.B., Fr.); D: Massimo Dallamano; P: Harry Alan Towers; Prod. Co: Terra Film (Berlin)/Sargon Film (Rome)/Towers of London; SC: Massimo Dallamano, Marcello Costa, based on the novel by Oscar Wilde; C: Otello Spila; M: Peppino De Luca, Carlo Pes; S: Helmut Berger, Richard Todd, Herbert Lom, Marie Liljedahl, Margaret Lee, Maria Rohm, Beryl Cunningham, Isa Miranda, Eleonora Rossi-Drago, Renato Romano.

Il Medaglione Insanguinato

A.k.a. *The Cursed Medallion* (English translation and title); a.k.a. *Perchè?!* (alternate Italian title); a.k.a. *Emilia, la Donna delle Tenebre* (alternate Italian title); a.k.a. *The Night Child* (English title) (1975) (It.); D: Massimo Dallamano; P: William C. Reich, Fulvio Lucisano; Prod. Co.: Magdalena Produzione/Italian International; SC: Massimo Dallamano, Franco Marotta, Laura Toscano; C: Franco Della Colli; M: Stelvio Cipriani; S: Richard Johnson, Nicoletta Elmi, Joanna Cassidy, Evelyn Stewart a.k.a. Ida Galli, Lila Kedrova, Edmund Purdom.

La Morte Non Ha Sesso

A.k.a. *Death Has No Sex* (English translation); a.k.a. *Das Geheimnis der Jungen Witwe* (German title); a.k.a. *A Black Veil for Lisa*; a.k.a. *Showdown* (English titles) (1968) (It., W.G.); D: Massimo Dallamano; Prod. Co.: Filmes Cinematografica (Rome)/Pan Film (Dusseldorf)/Top Film (Munich); SC: Massimo Dallamano, Giuseppe Belli, Vittoriana Petrilli, Audrey Nohra; C: Angelo Lotti; M: Gianfranco Reverberi; S: John Mills, Luciana Paluzzi, Robert Hoffman a.k.a. Hans Schmidt a.k.a. Max Lindt, Renate Kasche, Carlo Hintermann.

La Polizia Chiede Aiuto

A.k.a. *The Police Cry for Help* (English translation); a.k.a. *The Co-Ed Murders*; a.k.a. *What Have They Done to Our Daughters* (English titles) (1974) (It.); D: Massimo Dallamano; P: Paolo Infascelli; Prod. Co.: Primex Italiana; SC: Massimo Dallamano, Ettore Sanzo; C: Franco Della Colli; M: Stelvio Cipriani; S: Farley Granger, Giovanni Ralli, Claudio Cassinelli, Mario Adorf, Franco Fabrizi, Marina Berti, Paola Turco, Corrado Gaipa, Micaela Pignatelli, Sherry Buchanan a.k.a. Cheryl Lee Buchanan

Damiano Damiani

Born in 1922, Damiano Damiani directed *La Strega in Amore*, an underrated and spellbinding tale of dementia and lust. In the 1966 melodrama, a historian (Richard Johnson) is invited to edit the memoirs of a deceased person. His predecessor (Gian Maria Volonte) resents the intrusion of this young, virile man into the household apparently only occupied by him and an aged widow. What Johnson does not know is that the old woman frequently turns into a beautiful succubus (Rosanna Schiaffino) and has enticed Volonte with her body. Now, she pits both men against each other as she disorients them by flitting back and forth between both personas. Eventually Johnson will be compelled to murder. This was the best of Damiani's horror productions.

Damiani contributed to the birth of the European crime film genre with the above-average *Confessione di un Commissario di Polizia al Procuratore della Repubblica* (1971), and his Western *Quien Sabe?* (1966) is among the best of the Spaghetti Westerns. He journeyed to America in 1982 to make *Amityville II: The Possession*, an entry in the briefly popular haunted house–possession film genre which became profitable due to the success of the first film in the series (based on actual reports of supernatural activity and a best-selling book) *The Amityville Horror*.

Damiani's most recent films include *Alex l'Ariete* (2001), an action film starring real-life policeman Alberto Tromba as a super cop fighting against crime and corruption in contemporary Italy, and *Assassino dei Giorni di Festa* (2002).

Damiano Daminani Filmography (selected films)

Alex l'Ariete

(2000) (It.); D: Damiano Damiani; SC: Dardano Sacchetti; S: Alberto Tromba, Corinne Clery, Tony Kendall a.k.a. Luciano Stella, Orso Maria Guerrini.

Damiano Damiani

Amityville II: The Possession

A.k.a. *Amityville II* (English title) (1982) (U.S., It.); D: Damiano Damiani; P: Dino De Laurentiis, Stephen R. Greenwald, Jose Lopez Rodero, Ira N. Smith; SC: Dardano Sacchetti, Hans Holzer, Tommy Lee Wallace; C: Franco Di Giacomo; M: Lalo Schifrin; S: James Olson, Burt Young, Rutanya Alda, Andrew Prine, Moses Gunn, Leonardo Cimino.

Assassino dei Giorni di Festa

(2002) (It.); D: Damiano Damiani; SC: Giovanni Ammendola, Marco Denevi, Giampaolo Serra; M: Beppe D'Onghia; S: Sara D'Amario, Domenico Fortunato, Carmen Maura, Agnese Nano, Riccardo Reim.

Confessione di un Commissario di Polizia al Procuratore della Repubblica

A.k.a. *Confessions of a Police Commissioner to the District Attorney* (English translation); a.k.a. *Confessions of a Police Captain* (English title) (1971) (It.); D: Damiano Damiani; P: Mario Montanari, Bruno Turchetto; SC: Damiano Damiani, Salvatore Laurani; C: Claudio Ragona; M: Riz Ortolani; S: Franco Nero, Martin Balsam, Marilu Tolo, Claudio Gora, Luciano Catenaccim, Giancarlo Prete, Arturo Dominici.

Quien Sabe?

A.k.a. *A Bullet for the General* (English title) (1966) (It.); D: Daminao Damiani; P: Bianco Manini, Ferruccio De Martino; Prod. Co.: M.C.M.; SC: Salvatore Laurani, Franco Solinas; C: Antonio Secchi; M: Luis Enriquez Bacalov; S: Gian Maria Volonte, Klaus Kinski a.k.a. Klaus Gunther Nakszynksi, Martine Beswicke, Lou Castel, Jaime Fernandez, Andrea Checchi, Spartaco Conversi.

La Strega in Amore

A.k.a. *The Witch in Love* (English translation and title); a.k.a. *La Strege* (alternate Italian title); a.k.a. *The Witch* (English translation); a.k.a. *Aura*; a.k.a. *The Strange Obsession* (English titles) (1966) (It.); D: Damiano Damiani; P: Alfredo Bini; Prod. Co.: Arco Film; SC: Damiano Damiani, Ugo Liberatore, based on the novel by Carlo Fuentes; C: Leonida Barboni; M: Luis Enriquez Bacalov; S: Rosanna Schiaffino, Richard Johnson, Gian Maria Volonte, Sarah Ferrati, Margherita Guzzinati.

Fabrizio De Angelis

Born in Rome, Italy, on November 15, 1940, Fabrizio De Angelis would become known as a director of action films that copied the success of other, more noteworthy productions. Although he came into his own as a director in the middle '80s, with adventurous clones of the popular Sylvester Stallone movies featuring the John Rambo character, De Angelis would have a prominent place in Italian cinematic history as the producer of a number of genre films for other directors. He produced Aristide Massaccesi's Emanuelle films (with Laura Gemser), some of Lucio Fulci's best '80s horror films (*Zombi 2*, *L'Aldila*, *Quella Villa Accanto al Cimitero*) and a number of Enzo Girolami's futuristic action films. De Angelis' production companies were named Fulvia Film, Fulvia Cinematografica and Deaf International Films. In 1988, he directed (using the pseudonym Larry Ludman) his only horror films (to date) *Killer Crocodile*, an homage to Steven Spielberg's *Jaws* and a remake (of sorts) of Sergio Martino's *Il Fiume del Grande Caimano*. He produced the sequel (*Killer Crocodile 2*, released in 1989) and co-directed it (with Italian special effects technician Giannetto Di Rossi). Among his recent titles is the obscure revenge drama *The Iron Girl* (1994).

Fabrizio De Angelis Filmography (selected films)

Killer Crocodile

(1988) (It.); D/P: Fabrizia De Angelis; SC: Fabrizio De Angelis, Dardano Sacchetti; M: Riz Ortolani; C: Sergio D'Offizi, Federico Del Zoppo; S: Anthony Crenna, Ennio Girolami, Julian Hampton, Van Johnson, Sherrie Rose.

Killer Crocodile II

(1989) (It.); D: Giannetto Di Rossi, Fabrizio De Angelis (uncredited); P: Fabrizio De Angelis; SC: Fabrizio De Angelis, Dardano Sacchetti, Giannetto Di Rossi; M: Riz Ortolani; S: Anthony Crenna, Ennio Girolami, Debra Karr, Dardano Sacchetti.

Alberto De Martino

Born in 1929, Alberto De Martino has made a number of entertaining movies, many of them in the spy action-espionage and adventure genres. *Upperseven l'Uomo da Uccidere* (1966), *Missione Speciale Lady Chaplin* (1966) and *O.K. Connery* (1967) are among the best of these titles. Essentially, his films are nearly always derivative, if enjoyable, copies of better-known international hits. Among his horror films are *Horror* (1963), *L'Assassino ... È al Telefono* (1973), *L'Anticristo* (1974), the thriller *L'Uomo dagli Occhi di Ghiaccio* (1971), *Holocaust 2000* (1977), *Extrasensorial* (1983), *7, Hyden Park — la Casa Maledetta* (1985) and *Miami Golem* (1986).

Horror is a gothic tale about a young woman (Helga Line) who journeys to her ancestral home where she is terrorized. All of this is a plan to gain her inheritance. De Martino also contributed to the *giallo* thriller genre with *L'Uomo dagli Occhi di Ghiaccio*. Combining elements of the police procedural and detective film into the thriller format, it concerns a crusading journalist (Antonio Sabato) investigating a murder (which he finds was an assassination) of a U.S. electorate member in a Southwestern U.S. city. An intriguing web of corruption envelops the investigator as he finds danger and murder at every turn. Also appearing are Barbara Bouchet, Faith Domergue and Victor Buono. De Martino returned to similar territory with *L'Assassino ... È al Telefono*, starring an emaciated Anne Heywood and an apparently disinterested cast, which also included Telly Savalas as the killer. *L'Anticristo* was De Martino's *Exorcist* clone, focusing on the enticing body of Carla Gravina as the young daughter of a wealthy prince, possessed by an ancestor, a heretical member of the family who was burned at the stake centuries earlier. *Holocaust 2000* stars Kirk Douglas as a wealthy industrialist, the father of a young boy (Simon Ward) who may turn out to be the Antichrist. This film was influenced by and essentially duplicates the main thematic storyline in the American film *The Omen* (1976). *Extrasensorial* is a violent and unengaging thriller despite the care which De Martino invested into the Italian-German co-production. Possibly the casting of enigmatic American actor Michael Moriarty (a veteran of the films of the American director Larry Cohen) is the reason for audience's inability to respond favorably to the film. Moriarty appears as twins, one an acclaimed American doctor and the other a psychopathic killer who lives in Germany. The siblings share a strong psychic link that enables the sinister brother Keith to murder and blackmail and insinuate Craig, his twin, who travels to Germany when he becomes alarmed by the psychic visions of murder in crimes that *he* (Keith) committed. One of the problems in De Martino's film is that, while the evil Keith is a madman, the other brother, Craig, is little better. Being a liar to his lover, he seems he will be bouncing off the walls any moment (a trait commonly found in some of Moriarty's

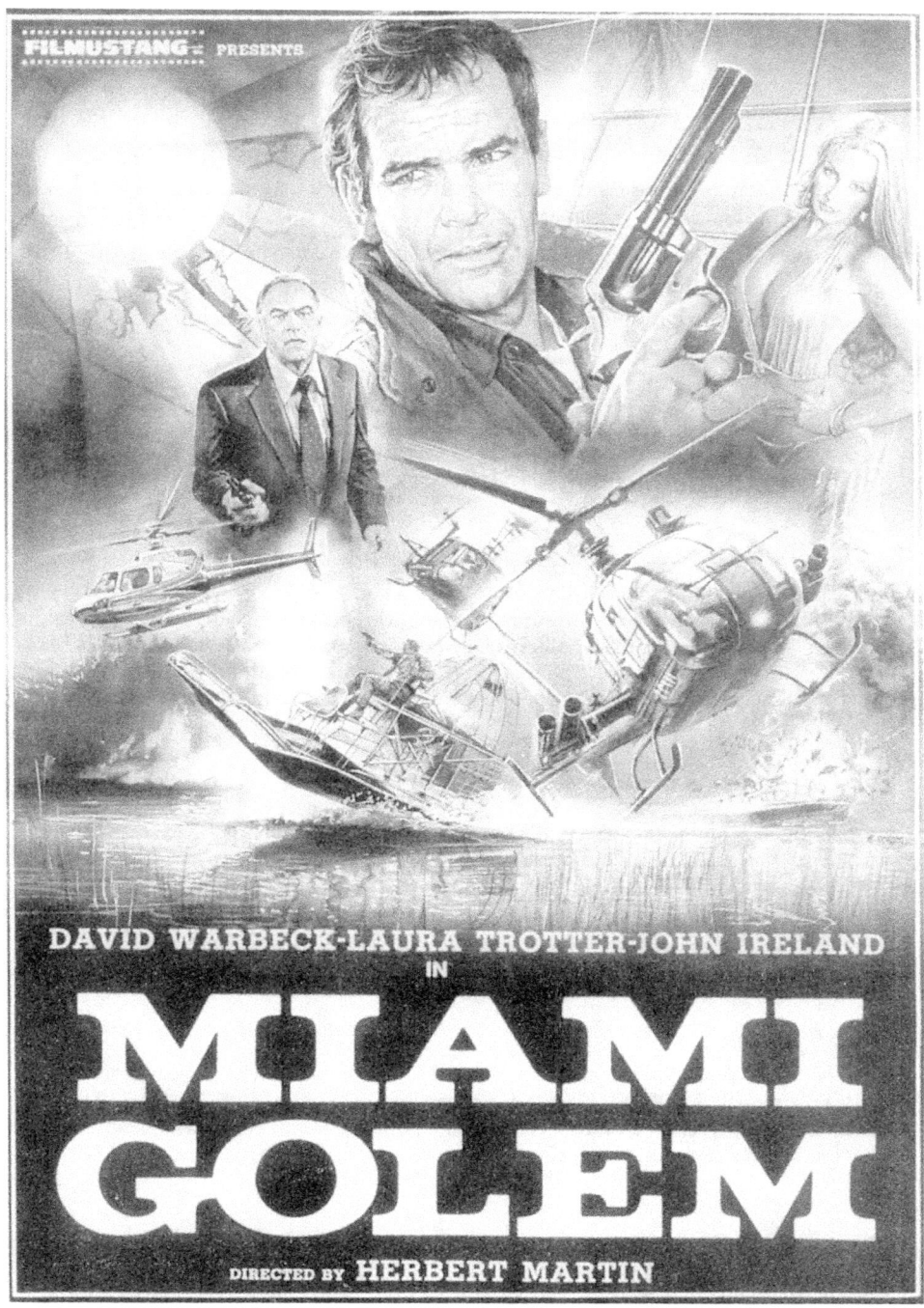

De Martino's *Miami Golem* (1986, Panther Entertainment/Filmustang Productions/ Twin Towers Enterprises).

performances in '80s films, and most likely traceable to his New York acting school roots).

Two De Martino films that are entirely original (or almost) are *7, Hyden Park — la Casa Maledetta* and *Miami Golem*. The former stars David Warbeck, a British actor known for his roles as the heroic good guy in a number of Italian genre films by directors such as Lucio Fulci and Antonio Margheriti. With *7, Hyden Park — la Casa Maldetta*, De Martino twists and bends the thriller aspects of the film and Warbeck is revealed as the psycho killer responsible for the deaths throughout. *Miami Golem* is a laughable attempt to combine horror and science fiction elements and ends up as a complete mess with Warbeck back where he belongs, as the hero attempting to keep an alien creature out of the hands of criminal organizations and the military.

Alberto De Martino Filmography (selected films)

L'Anticristo

A.k.a. *The Antichrist* (English translation and title); a.k.a. *The Tempter* (English title) (1974) (It.); D: Alberto De Martino; P: Edmondo Amati, Alfredo Nicolai; Prod. Co.: Capitolina Produzioni Cinematografiche; SC: Alberto De Martino, Gianfranco Clerici, Vincenzo Mannino; C: Aristide Massaccesi; M: Ennio Morricone, Bruno Nicolai; SP E: Biamonte Cinegroup; S: Carla Gravina, Mel Ferrer, George Coulouris, Alida Valli, Umberto Orsini, Anita Strindberg, Ernesto Colli.

L'Assassino ... È al Telefono

A.k.a. *The Killer Is on the Phone*; a.k.a. *The Killer Is on the Telephone* (English translations); a.k.a. *Scenes from a Murder*; a.k.a. *The Final Curtain* (G.B.) (English titles) (1972) (It.); D: Alberto De Martino; P: Vittorio Bartattolo, Aldo Scavarda, Guy Luongo; Prod. Co.: Difnei Cinematografica (Rome); SC: Alberto De Martino, Vincenzo Mannino, Adriano Bolzoni, Renato Izzo; C: Aristide Massaccesi; M: Stelvio Cipriani; S: Anne Heywood, Telly Savalas a.k.a. Aristotle Savalas, Rossella Falk, Giorgio Piazza.

Extrasensorial

A.k.a. *The Link*; a.k.a. *Blood Link* (English titles) (1983) (W.G., It.); D: Alberto De Martino; P: Roberto Palaggi; Prod. Co.: Zadar Filmgesellschaft m.b.H.; SC: Alberto De Martino, Theodore Apstein, Massimo De Rita; C: Romano Albani; M: Ennio Morricone; S: Michael Moriarty, Penelope Milford, Cameron Mitchell, Sarah Langenfeld, Virginia McKenna.

Holocaust 2000

A.k.a. *The Chosen* (English title) (1977) (It., G.B.); D: Alberto De Martino; P: Edmondo Amati; Prod. Co.: Embassy Productions (Rome)/Aston Film (London); SC: Alberto De Martino, Sergio Donati, Michael Robson; C: Enrico Menczer; M: Ennio Morricone; SP E: Giorgio De Rossi, Gino De Rossi; S: Kirk Douglas, Simon Ward, Agostina Belli a.k.a.

Agostina Maria Magnoni, Anthony Quayle, Virginia McKenna, Romolo Valli, Adolfo Celli, Alexander Knox, Geoffrey Keen, Ivo Garrani.

Horror

A.k.a. *The Blancheville Monster* (English title) (1963) (It., Sp.); D: Alberto De Martino; P: Alberto Aguilera; Prod. Co.: Film Columbus (Italy)/Llama Films (Madrid); SC: Sergio Corbucci, Gianni Grimaldi; C: Alejandro Ulloa; M: Francis Clark (?); S: Helga Line a.k.a. Helga Lina Stern, Gerard Tichy, Joan Hills, Leo Anchoriz, Iran Eory.

Miami Golem

A.k.a. *Miami Horror*; a.k.a. *Alien Killer*; a.k.a. *Cosmic Killer*; a.k.a. *Cosmos Killers* (English titles) (1986) (It., U.S.); D: Alberto De Martino; P: Giorgio Salvoni; Prod. Co.: Panther Entertainment/Filmustang Productions/Twin Towers Enterprises; SC: Giancfranco Clerici, Vincenzo Mannino; C: Gianlorenzo Battaglia, Paolo D'Ottavi; M: Detto Mariano; S: David Warbeck, Laura Trotter, John Ireland, Lawrence Loddi, Alessandra Camale.

Missione Speciale Lady Chaplin

A.k.a. *Special Mission: Lady Chaplin* (English translation and title); a.k.a. *Operazione Lady Chaplin* (alternate Italian title; translation: *Operation Lady Chaplin*) (1966) (It., Fr., Sp.); D: Alberto De Martino; P: Edmondo Amati; Prod. Co.: Fida Cinematografica/Productions Jacques Roitfeld, Paris/Sincronia; SC: Sandro Continenza, Marcello Coscia, Hipolito De Diego Lopez, Giovanni Simonelli; C: Alejandro Ulloa, Federico G. Larraya; M: Bruno Nicolai, song "Lady Chaplin" sung by Bobby Solo; S: Ken Clark, Daniela Bianchi, Helga Line a.k.a. Helga Lina Stern, Philippe Hersent, Jacques Bergerac.

O.K. Connery

A.k.a. *Operation Kid Brother*; a.k.a. *Secret Agent 00* (English titles) (1967) (It.); D: Alberto De Martino; P: Dario Sabatello; Prod. Co.: Dario Sabatello Productions; SC: Paolo Levi, Vincenzo Mannino, Carlo Tritto; C: Alejandro Ulloa; M: Ennio Morricone, Bruno Nicolai; S: Neil Connery, Daniela Bianchi, Adolfo Celli, Agata Flori, Bernard Lee, Lois Maxwell, Lee Burton a.k.a. Guido Lollobrigida, Anthony Dawson.

7, Hyden Park—la Casa Maledetta

A.k.a. *7 Hyde Park — The Cursed House*; a.k.a. *Seven Hyde Park — The Cursed House* (English translations); a.k.a. *Formula for a Murder* (English titles) (1985) (It.); D: Alberto De Martino; P: David Colby (?); Prod. Co.: Fulvia International Films S.r.l.; SC: Alberto De Martino, Vincenzo Mannino; C: Gianlorenzo Battaglia; M: Francesco De Masi; S: Christina Nagy, David Warbeck, Carol Blumenberg, Rossano Brazzi, Andrea Bosic, Loris Loddi.

L'Uomo dagli Occhi di Ghiaccio

A.k.a. *The Man with the Icy Eyes* (English translation and title) (1971) (It.); D: Alberto De Martino; P: Felice Testa Gay for Cinegai/Panta Cinematografica; SC: Alberto De Martino, Massimo De Rita, Arduino Mauriuri, Vincenzo Mannino, Adriano Bolzoni; C: Gabor Pogany; M: Peppino De Luca, Gino Marinacci; S: Antonio Sabato, Barbara Bouchet a.k.a. Barbel Goutscher a.k.a. Barbel Gutchen, Faith Domergue, Victor Buono, Keenan Wynn.

Upperseven l'Uomo da Uccidere

A.k.a. *Upperseven: The Man to Kill* (English translation and title); a.k.a. *Der Mann mit den 1000 Masken* (German title) (1966) (It., W.G.); D: Alberto De Martino; Prod. Co.: European Incorporation/Roxy Film (Munich); SC: Alberto De Martino, Emo Bistolfi; C: Mario Fioretti, Remo Grisanti, Romolo Paradisi; M: Carlo Rustichelli; S: Paul Hubschmid, Karin Dor, Vivi Bach, Nando Gazzolo, Rosalba Neri, Guido Lollobrigida.

Rino Di Silvestro

Born in 1932, Rino Di Silvestro (born Salvatore Di Silvestro) is another in a long line of Italian film technicians who graduated to director. But Di Silvestro seemed content to spend the bulk of his career grounded in cheap exploitation dramas: films about prostitution, sex comedies and Nazi women-in-prison atrocity movies.

La Lupa Mannera (1976) is his only horror film and even this entry overdoses on the sexploitation angle. If we accept the delirious demands bestowed upon the screenplay that Di Silvestro has fashioned for this ugly-looking sex film, women who experience powerful sex drives can possibly display tendencies towards lycanthropy. Annik Borel is the (very) shapely and strange woman who has sex with men and women alike. When her raging hormones throw her into overdrive, she becomes a naked female psychopath (but not a werewolf as the film's title, and a brief, pre-credits dream sequence suggest). After a number of murders, Borel must escape the practically torch-bearing crowds of villagers out to put her down.

Another Di Silvestro film of note is *Prostituzione* (1974) which primarily concentrates on the police investigation surrounding the murder of a young prostitute who was employed by a criminal gang into blackmailing their workers. Attempting to make a thriller with elements of neo-realism, Di Silvestro tries to show the hard life of these working class women, but copious amounts of flesh and risible dialog like "Wow, what an ass she's got!" make the film seem little more than an exploitative affair. Unfortunately, subsequent films directed by Di Silvestro failed to reach such heights of delirium and the later productions *Diario Segreto da un Carcere Femminile* (1974), *Le Deporate della Sezione Speciale SS* (1977), *Sogno Erotici di Cleopatra* (1983) and *Hanna D* (1985) wallowed in an uneven excess of nudity, sadism and melancholy.

Rino Di Silvestro Filmography (selected films)

Le Deportate della Sezione Speciale SS

A.k.a. *Deported Women of the SS Special Section* (English title) (1977) (It.); D/SC: Rino Di Silvestro a.k.a. Salvatore Di Silvestro; P: Giuseppe Zaccariello; C: Sergio D'Offizi; M: Stelvio Cipriani; S: John Steiner, Lina Polito, Stefania D'Amario, Erna Schurer a.k.a. Erna Scheurer, Sara Sperati, Solvi Stubbing, Rik Battaglia.

Diario Segreto da un Carcere Femminile

A.k.a. *Secret Diary in a Woman's Prison* (English translation); a.k.a. *Love and Death in a Woman's Prison*; a.k.a. *Love in a Women's Prison*; a.k.a. *Women in Cell Block 7*; a.k.a. *Hell Prison*; a.k.a. *Girls in Distress* (English titles) (1974) (It.); D: Rino Di Silvestro a.k.a. Salvatore Di Silvestro; P: Massimo Pupillo; Prod. Co.: Angry Films; SC: Rino Di Silvestro a.k.a. Salvatore Di Silvestro, Angelo Sangermano; C: Fausto Rossi; M: Franco Bixio; S: Anita Strindberg, Eva Czemerys a.k.a. Eva Cemerys, Jenny Tamburi a.k.a. Luciana Della Robbia, Valeria Fabrizi, Cristina Gaioni, Paola Senatore, Umberto Raho, Massimo Serato.

Hanna D

A.k.a. *La Ragazza del Vondel Park* (alternate Italian title); a.k.a. *A Seize Ans dans l'Enfer d'Amsterdam* (French title); a.k.a. *The Girl from Vondel Park* (English title) (1985) (It., Fr.); D: Rino Di Silvestro a.k.a. Salvatore Di Silvestro, Bruno Mattei; Prod. Co.: Beatrice Film/Films Jacques Leitienne (Pairs); C: Franco Delli Colli; S: Ana Gisel Glass, Sebastiano Somma, Antonio Serrano, Karin Schubert, Jacques Stany, Donatella Damiani, Cristiano Borremeo.

La Lupa Mannera

A.k.a. *The Werewolf Woman* (English translation); a.k.a. *Naked Werewolf Woman* (G.B. title); a.k.a. *Werewolf Woman* (export title); a.k.a. *Legend of the Wolfwoman*; a.k.a. *Daughter of a Werewolf*; a.k.a. *Legend of the She-Wolf*; a.k.a. *Terror of the She-Wolf* (English titles) (1976) (It.); D: Rino Di Silvestro a.k.a. Salvatore Di Silvestro; P: Diege Alchimdede, Bruno Evangelisti; SC: Rino Di Silvestro a.k.a. Salvatore Di Silvestro, Renato Rossini; C: Mario Capriotti; M: Coriolano Lallo Gori; S: Annik Borel, Frederick Stafford a.k.a. Frederick Strobel Von Stein, Dagmar Lassander, Renato Rossini, Tino Carraro, Osvaldo Ruggieri, Felicita Fanny, Andrea Scotti, Elio Zamuto.

Prostituzione

A.k.a. *Prostitution* (English translation and title); a.k.a. *Dossier di un Prostituzione* (alternate Italian title); a.k.a. *The Red Light Girls*; a.k.a. *Love Angels*; a.k.a. *Sex Slayer* (English titles) (1974) (It.); D: Rino Di Silvestro a.k.a. Salvatore Di Silvestro; P: Giuliano Anellucci; Prod. Co.: Angry Film Productions; SC: Rino Di Silvestro a.k.a. Salvatore Di Silvestro; C: Salvatore Caruso; M: Marcello Raimono, Roberto Fogu; S: Maria Fiore, Aldo Giuffre, Elio Zamuto, Krista Nell, Orchidea De Sanctis, Andrea Scotti, Lucrezia Love, Umberto Raho, Magda Konopka, Cristina Gaioni, Luciano Rossi.

Sogno Erotici di Cleopatra

A.k.a. *Erotic Dreams of Cleopatra*; a.k.a. *Cleopatra Regina d'Ettigo* (alternate Italian titles) (1983) (It., Fr.); D/P: Rino Di Silvestro a.k.a. Salvatore Di Silvestro; Prod. Co: 2T Produzione Distribuzione Film (Rome)/Nasa Film (Paris); SC: Rino Di Silvestro a.k.a. Salvatore Di Silvestro, Marcel Albertini; C: Giovanni Bergamini; M: Romulad; S: Marcella Petrelli, Jacques Stany, Rita Silva, M. Laura De Benedittis, Monica Ciprari, Andrea Coppola.

Filmed in Italy, and intended as an Italian theatrical release, this movie ended up as an export only and appeared in Great Britain as *Erotic Dreams of Cleopatra*. It has rarely been screened in its native Italy under its original production title.

Giorgio Ferroni

Left: Italian poster art for Giorgio Ferroni's *La Notte dei Diavoli* (1972, Filmes Cinematografica/Due Cinematografica/Copercines).

Giorgio Ferroni, born in 1908, made numerous action movies, peplums, dramas and comedies with a workmanlike skill; some filmed and released (to English-speaking countries) with Ferroni using his Anglicized pseudonym Calvin Jackson Padget. He died in 1981.

His two horror features, *Il Mulino delle Donne di Pietra* (1960) and *La Notte dei Diavoli* (1972), are entertaining, if occasionally static movies. *Il Mulino delle Donne di Pietra* in particular is shot in a style that emulates the muted colors of classic Dutch painters of the nineteenth century. A tale of gothic terror, *Il Mulino delle Donne di Pietra* is a study in the warped world of lust and scientific experimentation. A young artist studying at a conservatory falls in love with the mysterious daughter of an instructor. The girl lives with her father in an old windmill, far from the prying eyes of the civilized world. The young woman suffers from a condition which leaves her father, a sculptor and alchemist by trade, no choice but to kill young women and

Left: Scenes from Giorgio Ferroni's *La Notte dei Diavoli* (1972, Filmes Cinematografica/Due Cinematografica/Copercines).

transfuse their blood and genes into her body. Ferroni's film is memorable for its funereal pace and scenes of the embalmed victims arranged in an erotic tableau of death, camouflaged as statues.

La Notte dei Diavoli is a virtual remake of the "Wurdalak" episode from Mario Bava's *I Tre Volti della Paura* (1963). Ferroni's version of the tale, set in an unspecified European town in the contemporary '70s, stars Gianni Garko as a stranded traveler who ends up at a farmhouse in the middle of nowhere and falls for the young daughter of the family patriarch who is away on mysterious business. As the returning father figure slowly vampirizes the cast, Garko realizes what terrors lay in store for him and, together with his new love, makes a dash for freedom before becoming a victim of the family of bloodsuckers. With nudity and more blood than could have been shown in the earlier version of this same story, Ferroni's is an effective film, even if it in no way approaches the level of cinematic art that Bava's production did.

Giorgio Ferroni Filmography (selected films)

Il Mulino delle Donne di Pietra

A.k.a. *The Mill of the Stone Women*; a.k.a. *The Mill of the Stone Maidens* (English translations and titles); a.k.a. *Le Moulin des Femmes de Pierre* (French title); a.k.a. *Horror of the Stone Women*; a.k.a. *The Horrible Mill Women*; a.k.a. *Drops of Blood* (English titles) (1960) (It., Fr.); D: Giorgio Ferroni; P: Gianpaolo Bigazzi, Lucien Vittet; Prod. Co.: Vanguard Film/Faro Film/Explorer Film/CEC; SC: Giorgio Ferroni, Remigio Del Grosso, Ugo Liberatore, Giorgio Stegani; C: Pierludovico Pavoni; M: Carlo Innocenzi; S: Pierre Brice, Wolfgang Preiss, Scilla Gabel, Dany Carrel, Liana Orfei, Marco Guglielmi, Herbert Boehme, Olga Solbelli.

La Notte dei Diavoli

A.k.a. *The Night of the Devils* (English translation and title); a.k.a. *La Noche de los Diablos* (Spanish title) (1972) (It., Sp.); D: Giorgio Ferroni; P: Luigi Mariani, Diego Alchimide; Prod. Co.: Filmes Cinematografica/Due Cinematografica/Copercines; SC: Romano Migliorini, Giambattista Mussetto, Eduardo M. Brochero; C: Manuel Berenguer; M: Giorgio Gaslini; SP E: Carlo Rambaldi; S: Gianni Garko, Agostina Belli a.k.a. Agostina Maria Magnoni, Cinzia De Carlos, Teresa Gimpera, Umberto Raho, Luis Suarez, Sabrina Tamborra, Rosa Toros, Stefano Oppedisano, Maria Monti.

Al Festa

Beginning his professional career as a composer of music and as a sound technician (he had worked on a few productions for the director Bruno Mattei), Al Festa began his career as a director of rock music videos and promotional videos for struggling Italian musical acts with suffering record sales. Festa became a filmmaker, entering into Italy's weakened horror film market and delivering a pair of strange efforts. *Gipsy Angel* (1994), his first feature, is an overlong but admirable attempt at a romantic thriller in the *giallo* mold, but the quick cuts and music video–like editing distracts from the core plot about a disillusioned pop starlet who stumbles onto a deadly mystery. More successful, in a surreal manner, is Festa's *Fotogrammi Mortali* (a.k.a. *Fatal Frames*) (1996). An epic (nearly 140 minutes!) tribute to the Italian horror films of the '70s and '80s, *Fotogrammi Mortali* assembles a "who's who" rogues gallery of suspicious felons for the audience to marvel at, bringing together David Warbeck, Donald Pleasence, Angus Scrimm, Linnea Quigley, Rossano Brazzi, Alida Valli and others. Festa proposed to wrap around these actors' cameo moments a film that may have seemed interesting on paper, but falls flat due to the inexperienced hand of the director (working in an alien milieu) and a baffling performance by lead actress Stefania Stella. Stella, the real-life partner of Festa, is the true star of the film…appearing as herself as a would-be pop star who becomes involved in a series of murders taking place in the pop art *haute couture* world of music video filmmaking. Actually, the film proposes to tell the story of American video director Rick Gianisi, haunted by apparitions and a deadly stalker who leaves dead bodies in his/her wake. Gianisi's character confronts Stella's marble-mouthed (but strangely alluring) presence as he is assigned to make the popular Italian television actress into a real-life rock star. Confounding *Fotogrammi Mortali* at every turn is Stella's inability to act and to speak the English language (the film was shot twice, once in an Italian-language version and then in an English-language version for export reasons) and the fact that, aside from a few gruesome murders (with makeup effects courtesy Steve Johnson), the production is in bad shape. To make matters worse, both Pleasence and Brazzi died during the making of the film. An anonymous actor wearing a Donald Pleasence mask, doing a bad imitation of the actor's recognizable voice, replaced Pleasence, whose major role had to be shortened for obvious reasons. At well over two hours, the film stumbles chaotically until its mind-blowing finale, which makes as little sense as everything that had come before. *Fotogrammi Mortali* is one of the most unusual and failed Italian horror films.

Al Festa

Al Festa Filmography

Fotogrammi Mortali

A.k.a. *Fatal Frames* (English translation and title) (1996) (It.); D: Al Festa; P: Stefania Di Giandomenico; Prod. Co.: Sail Productions in association with Mediaset; SC: Al Festa, Alessandro Monese; C: Giuseppe Berardini; M: Al Festa, songs written by Al Festa; SP E: Steve Johnson; S: Stefania Stella a.k.a. Stefania Di Giandomenico, Rick Gianasi, David Warbeck, Ugo Pagliali, Alida Valli, Geoffrey Copleston, Linnea Quigley, Rossano Brazzi, Ciccio Ingrassia, Angus Scrimm, Donald Pleasence, Massimo Lavagnini.

Gipsy Angel

A.k.a. *Gypsy Angel* (alternate Italian title and English title) (1994) (It.); D/M: Al Festa; S: Carroll Baker, Danja Gazzara, Dario Casalini, Walter Faitanini

Riccardo Freda

Riccardo Freda

Born in 1909 in Alexandria, Egypt, Riccardo Freda is a problematic figure in the history of Italian horror films. While he has contributed a number of atmospheric chillers to the genre, his earliest works in the field, which are considered by many Italian horror cinemaphiles as prime examples of the finest directorial achievements in the genre, are, in fact, pedestrian and rigid exercises in filmmaking.

Freda made spy thrillers based on the James Bond canon, *Coplan FX 18 Casse Tout* (1965) being his best in that genre, and numerous adventure films like *Agi Murad, il Diavolo Bianco* (1959), a costume spectacular starring Steve Reeves. Another early film, *Maciste all'Inferno* (1961), was an interpretation of mythology cum the gothic horror genre. The film features a hero (Maciste, played by Kirk Morris, whose real name was

Adriano Belli) from an earlier time period suddenly appearing in Scotland during the 1600s. The muscle-bound Maciste saves a woman (proclaimed a witch by superstitious villagers) from certain death, and must travel to Hell to find an ancient and powerful witch who has placed a curse of possession upon her descendant.

Many of Freda's films seem static, and many of their praised moments of grandeur owe more to the technicians that supported him and, in some cases, finished the productions that he abandoned in midstream. *I Vampiri* (1956), *Caltiki, il Mostro Immortale* (1959), *L'Orribile Segreto del Dr. Hichcock* (1961) and *Lo Spettro* (1963) are films that share few themes and are as different from each other as any movies can be. For example, *I Vampiri* is a static, unconventional tale of modern-day vampirism mixed with science fiction ideas (borrowed from pulp novels). The film is plagued by seemingly endless scenes of characters walking aimlessly about for no specific purpose, except to pad out the running time. However, its redeeming features are the moody camerawork and the creative set design (both credited to Mario Bava).

Italian poster art for *L'Orribile Segreto del Dr. Hichcock* (1961, Panda Società per l'Industria Cinematografica).

Caltiki, il Mostro Immortale is an outright old-fashioned monster movie that hides the fact that it's based on a number of low-budget yet superior American (*The Blob*) and British (*Quatermass II*, *X the Unknown*) films by becoming a grand adventure, highlighted by moments of sadistic pleasure: the mad, lecherous German character, infected by Caltiki, the scantily clad heroines, constantly in danger of losing their costumes, Caltiki graphically searing the flesh of victims. *L'Orribile Segreto del Dr. Hichcock*, one of Freda's better early efforts, is a delirious tale of a turn-of-the-century physician's failing attempts to control his own unbridled urges for necrophilia. The follow-up, *Lo Spettro*, another equally entertaining early effort, is a tale of jealousy and revenge that reaches to and from beyond the grave.

In 1969 Freda dabbled in the *giallo* genre with *A Doppia Faccia*, a supposed Edgar Wallace adaptation that featured Klaus Kinski in one of his more likable roles, involved in murderous intrigue, bisexuality and a plot device that involves a McGuffin of many types.

In this German-Italian co-production, Kinski falls in love with a woman (the sole heir to a fortune) and then they are married. However, he discovers that his new love is a lesbian who refuses to sleep with him. He is grief-stricken when she is killed in a car accident that seems suspicious. Kinski then makes the rounds idly sleepwalking through the places that he and his late lover once visited. He meets an alluring woman who, it turns out, has recently made love (on film) to a woman who not only looks exactly like his departed love, but could actually be her. In a film filled with surprises and twists, Kinski then embarks on a crusade to find out the true identity of the woman who he thinks is his wife.

Of course, Freda often blows the credibility of the film's noirish atmosphere and an above-average performance from the usually stoic lead actor suffers by surrounding Kinski with an uneven cast and silly dialogue. For example, one alluring female reveals to Kinski during his search: "I wanted to see you, but then I fell asleep like mischievous children do."

Freda returned to the horror cinema with *L'Iguana dalla Lingua di Fuoco* (1971), a nasty and vicious entry in the *giallo* thriller genre, complete with the hindrance of an unlikable cast of villains and suspects. *Follia Omicida* (1980) is Freda's best film, although it doesn't make much sense. It's the kind of horror movie that loves to play with the limitations of the genre and seeks to exceed the demands of its audience at the same time. A motion picture crew making a vicious splatter film about a maniacal killer of women break for the weekend to spend time at the isolated mansion of one crew members. Gratuitous nudity abounds as everyone pairs off into couples before becoming slice-and-dice victims of a real-life murderer. Freda constantly confounds the viewer with hallucinations, red herrings galore and a decidedly downbeat ending.

Riccardo Freda died on December 20, 1999, in Rome, Italy.

Riccardo Freda Filmography (selected films)

A Doppia Faccia

A.k.a. *Double Face* (English translation and title); a.k.a. *Das Gesicht im Dunkeln* (German title); a.k.a. *The Puzzle of Horror* (English title) (1969) (It., Fr., W.G.); D: Riccardo Freda; Prod. Co.: Colt Produzioni Cinematografiche/s.r.l.Rome, Mege Film/s.p.a. Rome (Italy)/Rialto Film Preben Philipsne GMBH and Co. KG Berlin (West Germany); P: Oreste Coltellacci, Horst Wendlandt; SC: Riccardo Freda, Lucio Fulci, Paul Hengge, Romano Migliorini, Gianbattista Mussetto, based on a story by Edgar Wallace; C: Gabor Pogany; M: Nora Orlandi a.k.a. Joan Christian; S: Klaus Kinski a.k.a. Klaus Gunther Nakszynksi, Margaret Lee, Annabella Incontrera, Christiane Kruger, Gunther Stoll, Sydney Chaplin, Barbara Nelli, Alice Arno.

Agi Murad, il Diavolo Bianco

A.k.a. *The White Warrior* (English title) (1959) (It., Yugo); D: Riccardo Freda; Prod. Co.: Majestic Films International/Loccen Film; SC: Luigi De Santis, Akos Tolnay; C: Mario Bava, Frano Vodopivec; M: Roberto Nicolosi, Pier Unvini; S: Steve Reeves, Georgia Moll, Scilla Gabel, Renato Baldini, Gerard Herter, Nikola Popovic, Mavid Popovic.

Caltiki, il Mostro Immortale

A.k.a. *Caltiki, the Immortal Monster* (English translation and title); a.k.a. *Caltiki*; a.k.a. *The Immortal Monster* (English title) (1959) (It., U.S.); D: Riccardo Freda, Mario Bava (uncredited); P: Samuel Schneider; Prod. Co.: Galatea Film (Milan)/Climax Pictures (Los Angeles)/Allied Artists (U.S.); SC: Filippo Sanjust; C: Mario Bava; M: Roman Vlad, Roberto Nicolosi; SP E: Mario Bava; S: John Merivale, Gerard Herter, Didi Perego, Daniela Rocca, Gay Pearl, Daniele Vargas, Giacomo Rossi-Stuart, Arturo Dominici.

Coplan FX 18 Casse Tout

A.k.a. *Agente 077 Summergame*; a.k.a. *Agente 777 Missione Summergame* (alternate Italian titles); a.k.a. *The Exterminators*; a.k.a. *FX 18 Superspy* (English titles) (1965) (It., Fr.); D: Riccardo Freda; P: Jeanu Maumy; SC: Riccardo Freda, based on the novel *Stoppez Coplan* by Paul Kenny; C: Henri Persin; M: Michel Magne; S: Richard Wyler, Robert Manuel, Jany Clair, Maria-Rosa Rodriguez. Gil Delamare.

Follia Omicida

A.k.a. *Deliria* (alternate Italian title); a.k.a. *L'Ossessione Che Uccide* (alternate Italian title); a.k.a. *Unconscious* (French title); a.k.a. *Satan's Altar* (G.B.); a.k.a. *The Wailing* (alternate G.B. title); a.k.a. *Fear*; a.k.a. *Murder Obsession*; a.k.a. *Murderous Obsession*; a.k.a. *Murder Syndrome*; a.k.a. *Unconscious* (English titles) (1980) (It., Fr.); D: Riccardo Freda; P: Pino Collura, Enzo Boetani, Simon Mizrahi; Prod. Co.: Dionysio Cinematografica S.r.l. (Rome)/Société Nouvelle Cinevog (Paris); SC: Riccardo Freda, Antonio Cesare Corti, Fabio Piccioni, Simon Mizrahi; C: Cristiano Pogany; M: Franco Mannino, utilizing the music of Bach and Liszt; S: Stefano Patrizi, Anita Strindberg, Laura Gemser, John Richardson, Martine Brochard, Silvia Dionisio, Fabrizio Moroni.

L'Iguana dalla Lingua di Fuoco

A.k.a. *The Iguana with the Tongue of Fire* (English translation and title); a.k.a. *Gli Esorcisti* (Italian re-release title; translation: *The Exorcists*); a.k.a. *L'Iguana a la Langue de Feu* (French title) (1971) (It., Fr., W.G.); D: Riccardo Freda; Prod. Co.: Oceania Film (Rome)/Les Films Corona (Nanterre-France)/Terra Filmkunst (Munich); SC: Riccardo Freda, Alessandro Continenza, Gunther Ebert, based on the novel *A Room Without a Door* by Richard Mann; C: Silvano Ippoliti; M: Stelvio Cipriani; S: Valentina Cortese, Luigi Pistilli, Dagmar Lassander, Dominique Boschero, Anton Diffring, Werner Pochath, Renato Romano, Sergio Doria, Riccardo Freda.

Maciste all'Inferno

A.k.a. *Maciste in Hell* (English translation); a.k.a. *The Witch's Curse* (English title) (1961) (It.); D: Riccardo Freda; P: Luigi Carpentieri, Ermanno Donati; Prod. Co.: Panda Societá per L'Industria Cinematografica Italiana; SC: Oreste Biancoli, Piero Pierotti, Ennio De Concini, Ermanno Donati; C: Riccardo Pallottini; M: Carlo Franchi; SP E: Serge Urbisaglia; S: Kirk Morris a.k.a. Adriano Belli, Helene Chanel, Virna Silenti, Andrea Bosic, Angelo Zanolli, John Karlsen.

L'Orribile Segreto del Dr. Hichcock

A.k.a. *The Terror of Dr. Hichcock*; a.k.a. *The Terrible Secret of Dr. Hichcock*; a.k.a. *Raptus* (English title) (1961) (It.); D: Riccardo Freda; P: Luigi Carpentieri, Ermanno Donati; Prod. Co.: Panda Societá per L'Industria Cinematografica; SP: Ernesto Gastaldi, Riccardo Freda; C: Raffaele Masciocchi; M: Roman Vlad; S: Robert Flemyng, Barbara Steele, Teresa Fitzgerald a.k.a. Maria Teresa Vianello, Silvano Tranquili, Harriet Medin White.

Lo Spettro

A.k.a. *The Spectre* (English translation); a.k.a. *The Ghost* (English title) (1963) (It.); D: Riccardo Freda; P: Luigi Carpentieri, Ermanno Donati; Prod. Co.: Panda Societa per Industria Cinematografica; SC: Riccardo Freda, Robert Davidson (pseudonym for ?); C: Raffaele Masciocchi; M: Frank Wallace (?); S: Barbara Steele, Peter Baldwin, Elio Jotta, Harrite Medin White, Umberto Raho.

I Vampiri

A.k.a. *The Vampires* (English translation) and *I, Vampire* (mistaken English verison); a.k.a. *The Lust of the Vampire*; a.k.a. *The Devil's Commandment* (English titles) (1956) (It.); D: Riccardo Freda, Mario Bava (uncredited); P: Ermanno Donati, Luigi Carpentieri; Prod. Co.: Titanus/Athena Cinematografica; SC: Riccardo Freda, Piero Regnoli, Rik Sjostrom; C: Mario Bava; M: RomanVlad; S: Giannia Maria Canale, Antoine Balpetre, Paul Mueller, Carlo D'Angelo, Wandisa Guida, Dario Michaelis, Renato Tontini, Riccardo Freda.

Mario Gariazzo

The bulk of Mario Gariazzo's (1930–82) films are sexploitative offerings intended to capitalize on the male audience's demand for imaginative sex and violence. *Lasciapassare per il Morto* (1961), starring Alberto Lupo and Helene Chanel, is a violent mystery-drama that precedes the groundbreaking *giallo* of *La Ragazza Che Sapeva Troppo* by one year.

Gariazzo's horror film *L'Ossesa* (1974) is as delirious as they come. In it, a beautiful (and repressed) archaeologist-artist finds a statue of a crucified man, supposedly a figure of one of the thieves crucified along with Jesus Christ. The statue is of an uncommonly handsome man, and the woman spends many hours working on the restoration and preservation of it. In a hallucinatory scene (complete with thunder and lightning raging outside the confines of her small studio), the statue comes to life. Eventually we learn that this statue actually encases a demonic presence, the Devil himself, perhaps?

After a suitably sexploitative but promising beginning, Garriazo's film becomes reduced to highlighting various sexual encounters before moving into the realm of exorcism rituals that are a standard of the possession genre. Despite all, *L'Ossessa* is a naughty, indecent and blasphemous film that is worth a look. Likewise, *Incontro Molto ... Ravvicinatti del Quattro Tipo* (1979) is a delirious sexploitation version of the popular American film *Close Encounters of the Third Kind* (1977), but made for an audience chiefly interested in seeing shapely naked women. As a schoolteacher is embarrassed, humiliated and abused by her charges, all manners of sexual couplings take place. Being an Italian sexploitation film, the filmmakers take the subject matter lightly and treat everything as a comedic affair.

In *Occhi dalle Stelle* (1978), Gariazzo's science fiction thriller, a photographer and a model hear strange metallic sounds in the woods, followed by a big gusty wind. Then all is silent. When the photographer develops his film, he discovers strange images on the negatives. Seeking assistance from a journalist who may help him prove the existence of extraterrestrials, they are

Mario Gariazzo

met by scorn and then threats in the form of a super-secret branch of the secret service who, for some reason, are protecting the secret of the aliens' arrival. Gariazzo's film is low-budget and overlong but it also is a bit intriguing and almost becomes a thriller at times. Popular '60s cinematic spy and espionage hero Giorgio Ardisson stars as a sinister man in black who leads the brutal agents to exterminate all those who posses information about the alien visitors.

Gariazzo's later cinematic exercise in the thriller genre *Play Motel* (1979) is an awful thriller that tells of a roadside motel where various couples go to achieve their sexual fantasies, only to be blackmailed by a mysterious killer. After several murders, a seemingly disinterested police inspector (Antonio De Teffe) stumbles across the killer. After a brief and disastrous theatrical run, Gariazzo took the film and re-cut it into an even more exploitable offering. With the addition of hardcore pornographic inserts (featuring members of the original cast, including porno actresses Marina Frajese, Anna-Maria Rizzoli and Patrizia Webley), it was re-released under the same title!

In *La Schiave Blanca* (1984), which Gariazzo co-directed with Franco Prosperi, the waning Italian mondo and cannibal film genres that were popular in the '70s and '80s are turned into a *giallo* thriller. After cannibals attack her family, and a young woman's parents are murdered and eaten before her eyes, the cannibals make the young girl their goddess. When she grows to adulthood (played by Elvire Audray), the woman returns to civilization and murders people she blames for the deaths of her parents. The film is told as a flashback as she awaits conviction on the charge of murder!

Mario Gariazzo Filmography (selected films)

Incontro Molto ... Ravvicinati del Quattro Tipo

A.k.a. *Very Close Encounters of the Fourth Kind* (English translation and title); a.k.a. *A Coming of Aliens* (G.B.) (English title) (1979) (It.); D: Mario Gariazzo; Prod. Co.: Midia Cinematografica; SC: Mario Gariazzo, August Finocchi; C: Aldo Greci; M: Alessandro Alessadroni; S: Maria Baxa, Monica Zanchi, Mario Maranzana, Marina D'Aunia, Alessio Pigna, Orazio Donati, Calogero Butta.

Lasciapassare per il Morto

A.k.a. *Passport for a Corpse* (English title) (1961) (It.); D: Mario Gariazzo; Prod. Co.: Produzione Aldo Calossa per Antonelliana Cineproduzione; SC: Mario Gariazzo, Gennaro Arendo, Carlo Ferrero; C: Jean Josipovici; M: Claudio Racca; S: Alberto Lupo, Helene Chanel, Linda Christian, Erno Crisa.

L'Ossessa

A.k.a. *The Sexorcist* (English translation and title); a.k.a. *Sexorcist Devil* (U.S. re-release with pornographic inserts); a.k.a. *Statue of the Antichrist*; a.k.a. *Devil Obsession*; a.k.a. *Enter the Devil*; a.k.a. *The Eerie Midnight Horror Show*; a.k.a. *The Tormented* (English titles1) (1974) (It.); D: Mario Gariazzo; P: Riccardo Romano, Paulo Azzoni; Prod. Co.: Tiberia Film International; SC: Mario Gariazzo, Amroglio Molteni, Mario Gariazzo, Ted Rusoff (additional dialogue added to English version); C: Carlo Carlini; M: Marcello Giombini; SP E: Paolo Ricci; S: Lucrezia Love, Stella Carnacina, Chris Avram a.k.a. Christea Avram, Luigi Pistilli, Ivan Rassimov, Gabriele Tinti, Umberto Raho, Giuseppe Addobbati, Piero Gerlini, Elisa Mantellini.

Play Motel

(1979) (It.); D/SC: Mario Gariazzo; P: Armando Novello, Renato Fe; Prod. Co.: Midia Cinematografica; C: Aldo Greci, Alfredo Senzacqua, Fabrizio Vicari; M: Ubaldo Continello; S: Raymond Lovelock, Anna Maria Rizzoli, Anthony Steffan a.ka. Antonio De Teffe, Mario Cutini, Antonella Antinori, Patricia Behn, Enzo Fisichella, Marina Frajese a.k.a. Marina Hedman a.k.a. Marina Lotar, Antonio Sabato, Marina Masé, Patrizia Di Rossi a.k.a. Patrizia Webley.

La Schiave Blanca

A.k.a. *The White Slave* (English translation and title); a.k.a. *Schiave Blanca: Violenza in Amazzonia*; a.k.a. *Violenza in Amazzonia*; a.k.a. *Violenza un Amazzonia*; a.k.a. *Amazzonia* (alternate Italian titles); a.k.a. *Amazonia — The Catherine Mills Story*; a.k.a. *The Catherine Miles Story*; a.k.a. *Forest Slave*; a.k.a. *Captive Women VII: White Slave*; a.k.a. *White Slave* (English titles) (1984) (It.); D: Mario Gariazzo, Franco Prosperi; SC: Mario Gariazzo, Franco Prosperi; C: Silvano Ippoliti; M: Franco Campanino; S: Elvire Audray, Neal Berger, James Boyle, Jessica Bridges, Alvaro Gonzales.

Gianfranco Giagni

Giagni's *Il Nido del Ragno* (1990) is one of the most obscure and atmospheric modern Italian horror films. In Budapest, a secret organization representing the Catholic Church is attempting to discover the identity of a strange cult. A scientist (who is also a religious scholar) is chosen to follow-up the investigations of his predecessor who was assigned to the same case, but has mysteriously stopped contacting the Vatican. The new investigator (Roland Wybenga) searches down a path of political corruption filled with strange malevolent people as he discovers that the man who came before him had discovered a deadly secret with apocalyptic overtones.

Mysterious, alluring women, strange, twisting alleyways and corridors and an overall sense of dread are featured in this film, along with a truly shocking climax. Giagni filmed *Il Nido del Ragno* in a style that is both contemporary (a lot of quick cutting to emphasize the influence of the music video age) and classic (much of the film is photographed with an emphasis on fantastic colors). It echoes Dario Argento's own work as a director in the sense of communicating dread and changes in mood and atmosphere through the use of photography, music and the placement of the camera. In Argento's world, life is but a surreal landscape, one separate from reality. In *Il Nido del Ragno* Giagni communicates to the audience a similar presence.

Before directing this film, Giagni was also a co-director on the Italian television miniseries *Valentina* (1988) starring Demetra Hampton and based on the '60s *fumetti* by Guido Crepax.

Gianfranco Giagni Filmography

Il Nido del Ragno

A.k.a. *In the Grip of the Spider* (English translation); a.ka. *The Spider's Labyrinth* (English title) (1990) (It.); D: Gianfranco Giagni; P: Tonino Cervi; Prod. Co.: Retitalia/Splendida; SC: Tonino Cervi, Riccardo Arragno, Cesare Frugoni, Gianfranco Manfredini; C: Nini Celeste; M: Franco Piersanti; S: Roland Wybenga, Paola Rinaldi, Marghareta Von Krauss, Claudia Muzli, William Berger, Stephane Audran, Valeriano Santinelli, Massimiliano Pavine, Arnaldo Dell'Aqua.

Valentina

(1988) (It.); D: Gianfranco Giagni, Giandomenico Curi; SC: Gianfranco Manfredi; C: Roberto Forges Davanzati; M: Eio Zanetti; S: Demetra Hampton, Russel Case, Assumpta Serna, Kim Rossi-Stuart, Andrea Liberovici.

Enzo Girolami

Born in Rome, Italy, on July 29, 1938, Enzo Girolami spent much of his cinematic career using the pseudonym of Enzo G. Castellari. Many of the male members of the Girolami household also became involved in the Italian cinema: Romolo and Marino Girolami (Enzo's father) were directors and Ennio (Enzo's brother) an actor.

Enzo became a proficient action film director, working in the Western genre (his *Keoma* [1976] is considered a classic) and the police action films that became popular in the latter '70s, before directing a number of early–'80s science fiction films in the popular post-nuclear apocalypse genre. A seldom-acknowledged master of the moving camera, Girolami made action films that often displayed a hyperkinetic style.

In Girolami's *Il Cacciatore di Squalli* (1979), Franco Nero (with blonde hair) stars as a former member of the Italian mob who spends his time hunting for treasure and sharks beneath the sea. Nero hatches a plan to recover millions of dollars in mob money that has been submerged in the waters off a nearby island. Along the way, Nero must battle many sharks and the local crime lords. It was little more than a manqué of *Jaws* (1975) and *The Deep* (1977. Girolami improved upon this film with his next movie.

Enzo Girolami, a.k.a. Enzo G. Castellari

Of all the *Jaws* rip-offs, *L'Ultimo Squalo* (1981) is the most obvious: When a group of oceanic wind surfers are attacked by a vicious shark, James Franciscus (in a mix of the Roy Scheider and Richard Dreyfuss characters from *Jaws*), a local writer takes his small boat out to search for survivors. Vic Morrow (in "the Robert Shaw part"), the crusty old hunter of the great whites, has been hired by the local politicians and the tourism board to kill the beast before a planned celebration and a boating regatta is scheduled to begin.

Despite brazenly copying the Steven Spielberg film, Girolami's movie does contain many exciting sequences, and Franciscus and Morrow (with a ridiculous Scottish accent) as the heroes strike their chivalrous poses and attempt to save the town. MCA/Universal, the producers and distributors of *Jaws*, slapped an injunction on Film Ventures, the U.S. distributor of *L'Ultimo Squalo*, claiming it bore too close a resemblance to the *Jaws* series. The film was pulled from theaters days before exhibition was scheduled to begin. The same thing happened in England when legal action prevented a similar planned release. Nowadays, the film is relatively hard to locate, but it did receive a video release (uncut and in English) in Venezuela.

Aside from the controversial *Jaws* clone *L'Ultimo Squalo*, Girolami's major contribution to the genre came with *Sensitività* (1979), a languid and surreal tale of sexual power, witchcraft and corruption and one of his best films. Lillian, a young woman (Leonora Fani), returns to her hometown where, years before, her mother had been murdered. She then inhabits the ancestral castle and deals with a witch named Kyra, nicknamed the Lady of the Lake, who has put a curse upon her. After years directing films in the numerous subgenres of the Italian horror film, Girolami finally achieves a poetic grandeur with this sensual, erotic horror tale.

In *I Nuovi Barbari* (1982), an excessively violent *Mad Max* clone set in a post-apocalyptic time, a fierce band of vicious thugs go on a spree of death and destruction, raping all in their path, men and women. Fred Williamson (starring as Nadir) and Timothy Brent (as Skorpion) team up to battle George Eastman a.k.a. Luigi Montefiori and his band of warriors and their decapitation vehicle (a four-wheeled roadster) that does pretty much that — easily chops off the heads of anyone in its path.

The follow-up science fiction film *1990 I Guerrieri del Bronx* (1982) was influenced by *The Road Warrior* (a.k.a. *Mad Max 2* [1982]), *The Warriors* (1979) and *John Carpenter's Escape from New York* (1981). It is a tale ripe for any late night television watching when you want something violent and nonsensical. In the then-future year of 1990, Manhattan has become a war-torn island of violence. Barbaric roaming gangs cause death and destruction. Only when

Enzo Girolami's *Jaws* imitation *La Ultimo Squalo*, in a Swedish poster (1981, Produzioni/ Horizon Produzioni [Rome]).

the police seal off Manhattan and create an enclosed structure do the warring gangs have no one to battle but each other. A young heiress escapes into the war zone and a heroic loner named Trash (Mark Gregory) must protect her against the assassin squad of police led by Vic Morrow's character (named Hammer). The film also stars Christopher Connelly, Fred Williamson and George Eastman. A sequel, *Fuga dal Bronx*, appeared the next year; Mark Gregory returned as Trash, the hero of an oppressed society battling a governmental extermination squad led by Henry Silva.

In *Sinbad* (1986), Lou Ferrigno, who previously played the role of Hercules in two films for director Luigi Cozzi, played the title role. He is joined by another body builder, Teagan, and perennial Italian villain John Steiner portrays the villain. Director Girolami made this adventure film on location in the Middle East, but even the producers deemed the end result terrible. The film was shelved as unreleasable, then re-worked and re-edited with new footage directed by Luigi Cozzi in 1989. In the new Cozzi footage, Daria Nicolodi is featured in a wraparound narrative device as a woman who reads the story of Sinbad to her young child and helps to explain the rambling plot to the audience. This version of the film was not released until the mid–1990s.

In recent years, Girolami has directed the television miniseries *Il Ritorno di Sandokan* (1996) and *Deserto di Fuoco* (1997).

Enzo Girolami Filmography (selected films)

Il Cacciatore di Squalli

A.k.a. *Guardians of the Deep*; a.k.a. *The Guardians of the Deep*; a.k.a. *The Shark Hunter* (English titles); a.k.a. *El Cazador de Tiburones* (Spanish title) (1979) (It., Mexico, Sp.); D: Enzo Girolami a.k.a. Enzo G. Castellari; P: Fabrizio De Angelis, Enzo Doria, Jaime Comas Gil, Francisco Flores; SC: Tito Carpi, Jaime Comas Gil, Jesus R. Folgar, Alfredo Giannetti, Gisella Longo; C: Raul Perez Cubero; M: Guido De Angelis, Maurizio De Angelis; S: Franco Nero, Werner Pochath, Jorge Luke, Michael Forest, Patricia Rivera, Mirta Miller, Eduardo Fajardo.

Deserto di Fuoco

A.k.a. *Desert of Fire* (English translation and title); a.k.a. *Prinzessin Amina* (German title) (1997) (It., Fr., G.F.R.); D: Enzo Girolami a.k.a. Enzo G. Castellari; P: Guido Lombardo); SC: Faliero Rosati, George Eastman a.k.a. Luigi Montefiori, Patrizia Pistagnesi; C: Giancarlo Ferranco; M: Stefano Mainetti; S: Anthony Delon, Franco Nero, Mandala Tayde, Stephane Freiss, Matthieu Carriere, Marie Laforet, Virna Lisi, Jean Sorel, Claudia Cardinale, Vittorio Gassman, Fabio Testi, Giulianno Gemma.

1990 I Guerrieri del Bronx

A.k.a. *1990 The Bronx Warriors* (English translation and title); a.k.a. *The Bronx Warriors* (English title) (1982) (It.); D: Enzo Girolami a.k.a. Enzo G. Castellari; P: Fabrizio De Angelis; SC: Enzo Girolami a.k.a. Enzo G. Castellari, Elisa Briganti, Dardano Sacchetti; C: Sergio Salvati; M: Walter Rizzati; S: Mark Gregory, Stefania Girolami, Fred Williamson, Vic Morrow, Joshua Sinclair, Christopher Connelly, George Eastman a.k.a. Luigi Montefiori, Ennio Girolami.

Fuga dal Bronx

A.k.a. *Escape from the Bronx* (English translation and title); a.k.a. *Escape 2000*; a.k.a. *Bronx Warriors 2* (English titles) (1984) (It.); D: Enzo Girolami a.k.a. Enzo G. Castellari; P: Fabrizio De Angelis; SC: Enzo Girolami a.k.a. Enzo G. Castellari, Tito Carpi, Dardano Sacchetti; C: Blasco Giurato; M: Francesco De Masi; S: Mark Gregory, Henry Silva, Valeria D'Obici, Timothy Brent a.k.a. Giancarlo Prete, Ennio Girolami, Moana Pozzi.

Keoma

A.k.a. *Keoma, il Vendicatore* (alternate Italian title); a.k.a. *Django Rides Again*; a.k.a. *Django's Great Return*; a.k.a. *The Violent One* (English titles) (It., Sp.) 1975); D: Enzo G. Castellari a.k.a. Enzo Girolami; P: Uranus Cine/Ponchielli; SC: Enzo G. Castellari a.k.a. Enzo Girolami, George Eastman a.k.a. Luigi Montefiori; C: Aiace Parolini; M: Guido and Maurizio De Angelis; S: Franco Nero, Woody Strode, William Beger, Olga Karlatos.

I Nuovi Barbari

A.k.a. *The New Barbarians* (English translation and title); a.k.a. *2019 I Nuovi Barbari* (alternate Italian title); a.k.a. *Metropolis 2000*; a.k.a. *Warriors of the Wasteland* (English titles) (1982) (It.); D: Enzo Girolami a.k.a. Enzo G. Castellari; P: Fabrizio De Angelis; SC: Enzo Girolami a.k.a. Enzo G. Castellari, Tito Carpi, Antonio Visone; C: Fausto Zuccoli; M: Claudio Simonetti; S: Timothy Brent a.k.a. Giancarlo Prete, Fred Williamson, Venantino Venantini, Massimo Vanni, Giovanni Frezza, Iris Peynoda, Andrea Girolami, Ennio Girolami, Mark Gregory, Zora Kerova.

Il Ritorno di Sandokan

A.k.a. *The Return of Sandokan* (English translation and title) (1996) (It.); D: Enzo Girolami a.k.a. Enzo G. Castellari; P: Guido Lombardo, Anselmo Parrinello; SC: Adriano Bolzoni, George Eastman a.k.a. Luigi Montefiori; C: Giancarlo Ferrando; M: Guido De Angelis, Maurizio De Angelis; S: Kabir Bedi, Matthieu Carriere, Romina Power, Mandala Tayde, Fabio Testi, Franco Nero.

Sensitività

A.k.a. *Kyra: La Signora del Lago* (alternate Italian title); a.k.a. *Kyra: The Lady of the Lake* (English translation); a.k.a. *L'Ultima Casa Vicino al Lago* (alternate Italian title); a.k.a. *Sensitiva* (alternate Italian title); a.k.a. *Last House Near the Lake* (English title) (1979) (It., Sp.); D: Enzo G. Castellari a.k.a. Enzo Girolami; P: Diego Alchimede; SC: Lella Buongiorno, Jose Maria Nunes; C: Alessandro Ulloa; M: Guido and Maruruzio De Angelis; S: Leonora Fani, Caterina Boratto, Wolfgang Soldati, Vincent Gardenia, Antonio Mayans, Patricia Adriani.

Sinbad

A.k.a. *Sinbad of the Seven Seas* (alternate English and export title) (1986) (It., U.S.); D: Enzo Girolami a.k.a. Enzo G. Castellari, Luigi Cozzi (uncredited), Tim Kincaid (uncredited); P: Enzo Girolami a.k.a. Enzo G. Castellari, Menahem Globus, Yoram Globus, Tim Kincaid; SC: Tito Carpi, Enzo Girolami a.k.a. Enzo G. Castellari, Luigi Cozzi (uncredited), Tim Kincaid (uncredited); C: Blasco Giurato; M: Dov Seltzer; S: Lou Ferrigno, John Steiner, Roland Wybenga, Yehuda Efroni, Alessandra Martines, Teagan Clive, Stefania Girolami, Daria Nicolodi, Giada Cozzi.

La Ultimo Squalo

A.k.a. *The Last Shark* (English translation); a.k.a. *The Last Jaws*; a.k.a. *Great White*; a.k.a. *The Great White Shark* (English titles) (1981) (It.); D: Enzo G. Castellari a.k.a. Enzo Girolami; P: Maurizio Amati, Ugo Tucci, Edmondo Amati; Prod. Co.: Produzioni/Horizon Produzioni (Rome); SC: Vincenzo Mannino; C: Alberto Spagnoli, Giovanni Bergamini; M: Guido and Fabrizio De Angelis; SP E: Antonio Corridori; S: James Franciscus, Vic Morrow, Joshua Sinclair, Micky Pignatelli, Timothy Brent a.k.a. Giancarlo Prete, Stefania Girolami, Marko Lari.

Marino Girolami

Marino Girolami was born on February 1, 1914. He started work as a scriptwriter in 1943 and moved on to assistant directorial work later that same year. By 1953 he began a long career as a director and made his first genre film in 1960, *Il Mio Amico Jekyll*, a tale about Prof. Fabius (Raimondo Vianello), who invents a machine which changes him into a handsome schoolteacher played by Italian matinee idol Ugo Tognazzi.

Girolami spent much of his career making dramas and comedies, and even contributed to the waning mondo film cycle (popular in Italy in the 1960s) with *Nude-Odeon* (1978), a movie about scandalous public and private sex acts. His lone horror film, *Zombi Holocaust* (1979) is something else entirely, a rampaging trip through a gory atmosphere of dread and dismemberment that attempts (unsuccessfully) to combine the popular cannibal and zombie film genre of the time. *Zombi Holocaust*'s story is an odd one for a film attempting to bridge both genres: After body parts vanish from a New York hospital, one of the orderlies, an Indian, is later found bloodily munching on a fresh human heart. The police investigate and an anthropologist becomes involved. On an expedition to the South East Asian island from which they believe the orderly came, the team (featuring Ian McCullough, Alexandra Della Colli and Sherry Buchanan) meets a group of ruthless cannibals and a mysterious doctor (Donald O'Brien) who experiments on both the dead and the living, seeking to extend the lifespan of humans by making them zombies! Yes, zombies! Which is how this film got its title, in the confrontation between cannibals and zombies. The American film distributor, Aquarius Releasing, took footage from an uncompleted film (*Tales to Rip Your Heart Out*) by American director Roy Frumkes (*Street Trash*) and incorporated it into the film, providing the bulk of the footage that appears at the beginning.

Marino Girolami died on February 20, 1994. His son Enzo Girolami a.k.a. Enzo G. Castellari is also a prominent director in Italy.

Marino Girolami Filmography (selected films)

Il Mio Amico Jekyll

(1960) (It.); D/P: Marino Girolami; Prod. Co.: M.G. Cineproduzioni; SC: Marino Girolami, Giulio Scarnicci, Renzo Tarabusi, Carlo Veo; C: Luciano Trasatti; M: Alessandro Derewitsky; S: Ugo Tognazzi, Raimondo Vianello, Abbe Lane, Helene Chanel.

Nude-Odeon

A.k.a. *Nudeodeon* (1978) (It.); D: Marino Girolami; S: Dorothy Flower, Mary Govert, Margareth Harrison, Kerina Mulligan.

Zombi Holocaust

A.k.a. *Zombie Holocaust* (English translation and title); a.k.a. *La Regina dei Cannibali* (alternate Italian title); a.k.a. *The Queen of the Cannibals* (English translation and title); a.k.a. *Zombie 3*; a.k.a. *Island of the Last Zombies*; a.k.a. *Dr. Butcher M.D.*; a.k.a. *Dr. Butcher — Medical Deviate* (English titles) (1979) (It.); D: Marino Girolami; P: Fabrizio De Angelis, Gianfranco Couyoumdjian; SC: Fabrizio De Angelis, Walter Patriarca, Romano Scandariato; C: Fausto Zuccoli; M: Nico Fidenco; S: Ian McCullough, Alexandra Della Colli, Sherry Buchanan a.ka. Cheryl Lee Buchanan, Peter O'Neal, Donald O'Brien.

Features additional footage from the uncompleted film *Tales to Rip Your Heart Out*, directed by Roy Frumkes, produced by Ron Harvey, music by Walter F. Sear. Terry Levene produced the *Dr. Butcher M.D.* composite print.

Aldo Lado

Aldo Lado is a director of uneven films. His *La Corta Notte delle Bambole di Vetro* (1972) is an effective thriller that will remain in your thoughts days after viewing it. The movie is a successful mix of all kinds of cinematic and literary influences, from the Cold War espionage thriller to the conspiracy film to outright horror. Jean Sorel portrays a reporter assigned to Budapest to discover the whereabouts of a scientist who developed new forms of brainwashing techniques to counter the missions of foreign secret service agents. His search leads him through mysterious alleys and passages, meets all manners of strange people and briefly befriends and romances a young woman (Barbara Bach)—only to one day awaken and find her missing. Sorel's search leads him to a sect of black magic worshippers who exchange their aging bodies with the youthful ones of kidnapped men and women. His initial assignment is forgotten as he finds himself in deadly peril and, finally, put into a cataleptic trance by his enemies. The film ends with Sorel, his icy cold body laid out on an operating table, assumed dead, about to be dissected while he struggles to break free of the strange bonds that hold him in this state. He attempts to force his body to move, his mouth to scream, but he cannot.

Lado's thriller *Chi l'Ha Vista Morire?* (1972) is another involving puzzler. A sadistic murderer of young children kills the small daughter of a couple (George Lazenby and Anita Strindberg) and what follows is the story of the father's agonizing search for the murderer amidst a landscape filled with sexual deviates and cynicism. *Chi l'Ha Vista Morire?* contains one of Lazenby's best performances (he is saddled with a voice not his own in English-dubbed prints). The film's coda even extends to distrust for authority figures as the police inspector takes credit for solving the crimes, when it was the detective work done by the father that was responsible for revealing the identity of the killer.

Unfortunately, Lado's other '70s horror shocker, *L'Ultimo Treno della Notte* (1975), is a wretched, violent exploitation film about a group of crazed overage youths who threaten the passengers of a train with violence, rape

Aldo Lado

and murder. The film is little more than a remake of *Last House on the Left* on the rails. In 1979, Lado co-directed (with Antonio Margheriti and others, all uncredited) the lavishly budgeted science fiction fantasy *La Umanoide*. As entertaining a film as it was, it was written off by even the most undemanding of Italian critics as little more than a cheap *Star Wars* clone. This obscure space opera stars Corinne Clery as the daughter of a brilliant scientist who teams up with heroic space cowboy Leonard Mann to battle an evil intergalactic masked villain (Ivan Rassimov), his equally sinister temptress queen (Barbara Bach) and the evil ruler of the galaxy (Arthur Kennedy). Former James Bond villain Richard Kiel co-stars as a kindly space jock affected by a strange device that turns him into an unstoppable killing machine. Containing Saturday morning children's show thrills and a load of violence, this film never received a wide export release to other countries.

Rito d'Amore (1989) appears to be a return to Lado's exploitative period when he was churning out offensive garbage like *L'Ultimo Treno della Notte*. *Rito D'Amore* is about a buxom Italian woman who meets a handsome Eurasian man who professes his love for her in such an all-consuming manner that he tells her of his fantasy to actually eat her flesh, then does it! Allegedly based on true events, the film features Valeria Bosch and Beatrice Ring. Among Lado's last films of note is the 1992 production *Alibi Perfetto*. This film is a return of sorts to the *giallo* thriller. In this age of sexual permissiveness and awareness, *Alibi Perfetto* rivals the most lurid and sensationalist Italian thrillers of the '60s and seems more concerned with exhibiting the nude flesh of its actresses (Kay Sandvik, Carla Cassola and Gianna Paola Scaffidi) and any sadistic moments of torture that they might endure on the way to the film's climax.

Aldo Lado Filmography (selected films)

Alibi Perfetto

A.k.a. *Perfect Alibi* (English translation); a.k.a. *Circle of Fear* (English title) (1992) (It.); D: Aldo Lado; Prod. Co.: P.A.C. Produzioni Atlas Consorziate; SC: Aldo Lado, Dardano Sacchetti, Robert Brodie Booth; C: Luigi Kuveiller; M: Romando Mussolini, Francesco Santucci; S: Michael Woods, Kay Sandvik, Annie Girardot, Carla Cassola, Gianna Paola Scaffidi, Burt Young, Philippe Leroy.

Chi l'Ha Vista Morire?

A.k.a. *Who Saw Her Die?* (English translation and title) (1972) (It., W.G., Yugo.); D: Aldo Lado; P: Enzo Passadore a.k.a. Enzo Doria, Dieter Geissler; Prod. Co.: Doria G. Film/Roas Produzioni (Rome)/Dieter Geissler Filmproduktion (Munich)/Jadran Film (Zagreb); SC: Aldo Lado, Massimo D'Avak, Francesco Barilli; C: Franco Di Giacomo; M: Ennio Morricone, Bruno Samale; S: George Lazenby, Anita Strindberg, Peter Chattel, Adolfo Celli, Dominique Boschero, Rosemarie Lindt, Nicoletta Elmi.

La Corta Notte delle Bambole di Vetro

A.k.a. *The Short Night of the Glass Dolls* (English translation and title); a.k.a. *La Corta Notte delle Farfalle* (alternate Italian title; translation: *The Short Night of the Butterfly*); a.k.a. *Malastrana* (German title); a.k.a. *Unter dem Skapel des Teufels* (alternate German title; translation: *Under the Scalpel of Devils*); a.k.a. *Die Kurze Nacht der Schmetterlinge* (alternate German title); a.k.a. *Das Todes Syndrom* (German TV title; translation: *The Death Syndrome*); a.k.a. *Paralyzed*; a.k.a. *Butterfly by Night* (English titles) (1972) (It., W.G., Yug.); D: Aldo Lado; P: Dieter Geissler, Enzo Passadore a.k.a. Enzo Doria; Prod. Co.: Jadran Film (Zagreb)/Dieter Geissler Filmproduktion (Munich)/Doria G. Film (Rome) in association with Dunhill Cinematografica (Rome); SC: Aldo Lado, Ruediger Von Spiehs; C: Giuseppe Ruzzolini; M: Ennio Morricone, Bruno Nicolai; S: Jean Sorel, Barbara Bach, Ingrid Thulin, Mario Adorf, Jurgen Drews, Fabian Sovagovic, Jose Quaglia.

Rito d'Amore

A.k.a. *Love Ritual* (English title) (1989) (It.); D: Aldo Lado; Prod. Co.: Futura Film/Chance Film; SC: Aldo Lado, C. Spagnol; C: Gabor Pagony; M: Pino Donaggio; S: Beatrice Ring, Valeria Bosch, Larry Huckmann, Natalia Bizzi.

La Ultimo Treno della Notte

A.k.a. *Violenza sull Ultimo della Notte* (alternate Italian title); a.k.a. *Senza Bisogno Indagine* (Italian pre-production title); a.k.a. *Late Night Trains*; a.k.a. *(Don't Ride On) Late Night Trains*; a.k.a. *Night Train Murders*; a.k.a. *The Night Train Murders*; a.k.a. *The Second Last House on the Left*; a.k.a. *The Last House on the Left Part Two*; a.k.a. *The New House on the Left* (English titles) (1975) (It.); D: Aldo Lado; P: Paolo Infascelli, Pino Buricchi; Prod. Co.: European Inc. Produzione; SC: Aldo Lado; C: Gabor Pogany; M: Ennio Morricone, the song "A Flower Is All You Need" performed by Dennis Roussos; S: Flavio Bucci, Gianfranco De Grossi, Macha Meril, Franco Fabrizi, Laura Angelo, Dalila Di Lazzaro, Enrico Maria Salerno, Marina Berti, Irene Miracle.

La Umanoide

A.k.a. *The Humanoid* (English translation and title) (1979) (It.); D: Aldo Lado, Antonio Margheriti (uncredited), Enzo Girolami a.k.a. Enzo G. Castellari (uncredited); Prod. Co.: Merope Film; SC: Aldo Lado, Adriano Bolzoni; C: Silvano Ippoliti; M: Ennio Morricone; SP E: Antonio Margheriti; S: Corinne Clery, Leonard Mann, Barbara Bach, Ivan Rassimov, Arthur Kennedy, Richard Kiel, Massimo Serato, Attilio Duse, Vito Fornari.

Mario Landi

Two of the films of Mario Landi (1920–92), *Giallo a Venezia* (1979) and *Patrick Viva Ancora* (1980), are perfect examples of how a filmmaker can go too far in his quest to achieve the perfect synthesis of horror and repulsion. Landi's films are the true successor to the Grand Guignol theater of the turn of the century. These are repulsive, misogynist and miserable productions that seek to entertain and, finally, make you wonder just what kind of person Mario Landi really was.

Giallo a Venezia is an exercise in the sexual corruption of a couple. The man and wife enjoy performing sexual games involving complete strangers, even to the point of danger. The man watches from a hidden spot when his lover is brutally assaulted and raped by a gang of roughs. As their sick sex games come closer to dancing with death, in a nearby part of town a maniacal killer is kidnapping women for his own abnormal, sexual pleasure. This sadistic killer cuts off portions of his victim's anatomy so that they won't attempt to escape. Eventually, these two plots converge into one. Apparently, this was a very popular film upon its initial release in Italy, but Italian film censors quickly ordered cuts. It was briefly withdrawn (after its initial theatrical release), then re-released minus offending footage (courtesy the Italian film censor board). The footage in question has been restored to some (but not all) Italian videocassette prints.

Patrick Viva Ancora is a little tamer, but not much. Based on the 1978 Australian film *Patrick* by Richard Franklin, this is an unauthorized remake of that film. In this version, a young man is hit in the head by a bottle which was carelessly thrown from a speeding vehicle. As he lies in a comatose state, his psychokinetic powers grow stronger by the day. His array of doctors, nurses and relatives, however, are less concerned with his well-being than they are in sharing each other's bed. The extrasensory powers of Patrick soon come to the fore as he causes the death and destruction of all those around him and compels a young, shapely nurse to strip for him. It's hard to see what else director Landi could have been hoping for other than a film that was ripe for the sexploitation market. Some severely disturbing, graphic murders were censored even in the original Italian theatrical prints, including Mariangela Giordano's gruesome demise via a long metal pipe. For true aficionados of Italian sleaze, this film could be a worthy addition to your collection for the female catfight between busty starlets Carmen Russo and Mariangela Giordano alone.

Mario Landi Filmography (selected films)

Giallo a Venezia

A.k.a. *Death in Venice* (English translation and title); a.k.a. *Thrilling in Venice* (pre-sales export title); a.k.a. *Executioner of Venice*; a.ka. *Gore in Venice* (English titles) (1979) (It.); D: Mario Landi; P: Gabriele Crisani; Prod. Co.: Elea Cinematografica; SC: Aldo Serio; C: Franco Villa; M: Berto Pisano; S: Leonora Fani, Gianni Dei, Jeff Blynn, Mariangela Giordano, Vassili Karras a.k.a.Vassili Karamesinis, Michele Renzullo, Eolo Capritti, Maria Mancini.

Patrick Viva Ancora

A.k.a. *Patrick Still Lives*; a.k.a. *Patrick Lives Again*; a.k.a. *Patrick Is Still Alive* (English translations and titles); a.k.a. *Il Ritorno di Patrick* (Italian pre-production title; translation: *The Return of Patrick*); a.k.a. *Patrick 2* (1980) (It.); D: Mario Landi; P: Gabriele Crisani; Prod. Co.: Stefano Film; SC: Piero Regnoli, Gabriele Crisanti; C: Franco Villa; M: Berto Pisano; S: Sascha Pitoeff, Gianni Dei, Carmen Russo, Paola Giusti, Mariangela Giordano, Franco Silva, Anna Veneziano.

Sergio Martino

Born in 1938, Sergio Martino is a filmmaker with many credits. His gritty crime film *Milano Trema: La Polizia Vuole Giustizia* (1973) is an outstanding and extremely violent contribution to the Italian genre of "maniac killers vs. the police" films. Martino's *La Montagna del Dio Cannibale* (1978) is one of those cannibal adventure yarns usually made by directors the likes of Ruggero Deodato and Umberto Lenzi. Martino's film tells of a sexy adventuress (Ursula Andress) who seeks her missing husband in the darkest jungles of South America. This film's much-discussed highlight comes at the climax, when Andress is captured by a cannibal tribe and her nude body is covered with slime, a ritual to make her a goddess.

Italian poster art for Sergio Martino's wild thriller *Tutti i Colori del Buio* (1972, Lea Film/National Cinematografica [Rome]/Compagnia Astro [Madrid]).

Martino's other genre films of note are *La Coda dello Scorpione* (1971), *Lo Strano Vizio della Signora Wardh* (1970), *Tutti i Colori del Buio* (1972), *Il Tuo Vizio È una Stanza Chiusa e Solo Io Ne Ho la Chiave* (1972) and *I Corpi Presantano Tracce di Violenza Carnale* (1973).

La Coda dello Scorpione begins with a couple lying in bed. Then a woman (Anita Strindberg) receives news that her husband has perished in a plane crash, resulting in her being awarded $1,000,000 in life insurance money. This is only the first in a series of puzzling events as Strindberg travels to Greece to collect her money and meets with a variety of ruthless people who want the money for themselves. The twisty thriller really takes a turn at the climax as she prepares to meet her lover in Japan and then ... a razor-wielding killer murders her — but who could this latest fiend be?

Lo Strano Vizio della Signora Wardh stars Edwige Fenech as the victim in a plot to drive her insane. Perennial *giallo* thriller presence George Hilton appears as a red herring in order to confuse the audience as to the identity of the hero and the killer.

In *Tutti i Colori del Buio*, a sick woman (Fenech again) is chosen by a sect of black magic worshippers as the target of their aggression. She succumbs to the forces of darkness when all those from whom she seeks salvation are revealed to

Italian poster art for Sergio Martino's *Lo Strano Vizio della Signora Wardh* (1970, Devon Film [Rome]/Copercines [Madrid]).

be members of the cult. George Hilton appears in the cast as a possible savior. *Il Tuo Vizio È una Stanza Chiusa e Solo Io Ne Ho la Chiave* also features Fenech but this time the actress who usually plays heroines in thrillers is a bisexual danger from hell, as she beds nearly the entire cast before their sudden demise. Who is committing the murders? Is it likely suspect Fenech, or the virginal and prim Anita Strindberg, who is terrorized by nearly everyone and everything in this film?

I Corpi Presantano Tracce di Violenza Carnale is a notorious slasher film. Suzy Kendall portrays a woman who by the end of the film will have barely survived a seemingly hopeless situation when a powerful, nearly unstoppable maniac killer wielding sharp and deadly instruments of murder invades the mansion where she and her fellow female friends are staying. Sex and violence at its most extreme.

Martino's stock in trade as a successful director of violent, erotically charged thrillers seemed to be in danger when he abandoned the *giallo* format for the film *L'Isola degli Uomini Pesci* (1979). This film is a delirious, campy re-working of ideas procured from the writings of H.G. Wells and Robert Louis Stevenson that tells of escaped convicts who end up on an island where a mad scientist is experimenting with genetic mutations. *Assassino al Cimitero Etrusco* (1982) is a boring mix of the Italian crime film, a possession movie and a *giallo* thriller. Based on a seven-part Italian television miniseries, the edited feature version is incomprehensible. American actor Van Johnson co-stars as an archaeologist who uncovers an ancient Etruscan tomb that releases a demon — or is there really an unseen killer? The edited feature version of the miniseries also asks many other questions such as: Is there really a supernatural killer on the loose or are the murders the result of a drug deal gone sour? Could the murderer who reduces the number of supporting players be someone out for revenge using a hoary scapegoat like superstition as a cover? Is the daughter of the archaeologist possessed by an ancient Etruscan goddess? By the film's climax, you'll be asking yourself: Who knows? And by the time most audiences manage to figure out what was happening, the film will have long since ended.

In 1983, Martino made the violent science fiction film *2019 Dopo la Caduta di New York*, which successfully paved the way for another, inferior dabble in that genre *Vendetta dal Futoro* (1986).

Martino's ***Tutti i Colori del Buio*** (1972, Lea Film/National Cinematografica [Rome]/Compagnia Astro [Madrid]) was re-titled *They're Coming to Get You!* in the U.S.

Martino returned to the thriller format for the miniseries *Delitti Privati* (1992). It features a virtual who's who of popular Italian thriller personalities (Edwige Fenech, Ray Lovelock and Alida Valli, among others). *Spiando Marina* (1992), an unsuccessful attempt to revive the thriller format of the '70s for the more liberally sex conscious '90s, came next. Besides the appearance of Debora Caprioglio as the shapely femme fatale, the film is little more than a series of softcore sex episodes, enlivened by weak moments of violence and drama.

Of late, Martino has attempted to regain past glories by returning to the thriller format with the erotic thriller *Graffiante Desiderio* (1993) and the comedy-thriller miniseries *L'Inspettore Giusti* (1999) for Italian television. Although his most recent film has been *L'Ultimo Sogno* (2000), his science fiction thriller *La Regina degli Uomini Pesce*, a post-apocalyptic adventure film, made in 1995, only recently turned up on Italian television screens.

Sergio Martino Filmography (selected films)

Assassino al Cimitero Etrusco

A.k.a. Murders in the Etruscan Cemetery (English translation); a.k.a. *Lo Scorpione a Due Code* (alternate Italian title; translation: *The Scorpion with Two Tails*); a.k.a. *Crimes au Cimetière Etrusque* (French title; translation: *Crimes in the Etruscan Cemetery*); a.k.a. *The Scorpion with Two Tails* (English title) (1982) (It., Fr.); D: Sergio Martino; P: Luciano Martino; Prod. Co.: Dania Film S.r.l./Medusa Distribuzione S.r.l./Imp.Ex Ci. S.A. (Nice)/Les Films Jacques Leitienne (Paris); SC: Ernesto Gastaldi, Dardano Sacchetti, Maria Chianetta, Jacques Leitienne; C: Giancarlo Ferrando; M: Fabio Frizzi; SP E: Paolo Ricci; S: Elvire Audray, Paolo Malco, Claudio Cassinelli, Marilu Tolo, Luigi Rosso, Van Johnson, Sonia Viviani, John Saxon a.k.a. Carmine Orrico, Wandisa Guida, Gianfranco Barra, Mario Cecchi. Originally a seven-part Italian TV series titled *Il Misterio degli Etrusci*.

La Coda dello Scorpione

A.k.a. *The Tail of the Scorpion*; a.k.a. *The Scorpion's Tail* (English translations and titles); a.k.a. *La Cola del Escorpion* (Spanish title); a.k.a. *Sting in the Tail* (English title) (1971) (It., Sp.); D: Sergio Martinto; P: Luciano Martino; Prod. Co.: Devon Film (Rome)/Copercines (Madrid); SC: Eduardo Maria Brochero, Ernesto Gastaldi, Suaro Scavolini, Lewis Ciannelli; C: Emilio Foriscot, Giancarlo Ferrando; M: Bruno Nicolai; S: Anita Strindberg, Evelyn Stewart a.k.a. Ida Galli, George Hilton, Luigi Pistilli, Janine Reynaud, Alberto De Mendoza, Luis Barboo, Annalisa Nardi.

I Corpi Presentano Tracce di Violenza Carnale

A.k.a. *The Corpses Show Evidence of Rape*; a.k.a. *The Bodies Bear Traces of Carnal Violence* (English translations and titles); a.k.a. *Torso* (English title) (1973) (It.); D: Sergio Martino; P: Carlo Ponti Cinematografica, Antonio Cervi; Prod. Co.: Compagnia Cinematografica Champion; SC: Sergio Martino, Ernesto Gastaldi; C: Giancarlo Ferrando; M: Guido amd Maurizio De Angelis; S: Suzy Kendall, Tina Aumont a.k.a. Marie Christine Salomons, Luc Merenda, John Richardson, Angelo Covello, Carla Brait, Cristiana Conchita Airoldi, Patrizia Adiutori, Roberto Bisacco.

Delitti Privati

(1992) (It.); D: Sergio Martino; SC: Franco Marotta; C: Giancarlo Ferrando; S: Edwige Fenech, Ray Lovelock, Alida Valli, Annie Girardot, Vittoria Belvedere, Manuel Bandera, Gudrun Landgrebe.

2019 Dopo la Caduta di New York

A.k.a. *2019: After the Fall of New York* (English translation); a.k.a. *2019 Après la Chute de New York* (French title); a.k.a. *After the Fall of New York* (English title) (1983) (It., Fr.); D: Sergio Martino; Prod. Co.: Nuova Dania Cinematografica/Medusa/Imp. Ex. (Nice)/Films Jacques Leitienne (Paris)/Films du Griffon; SC: Sergio Martino, Ernesto Gastaldi; C: Giancarlo Ferrando; M: Guido and Maurizio De Angelis; S: Michael Sopkiw, Valentine Monnier, George Eastman a.k.a. Luigi Montefiori, Anna Kanakis, Romano Puppo, Edmund Purdom, Ken Wood a.k.a. Giovanni Cianfriglia.

Graffiante Desiderio

A.k.a. *Craving Desire* (English translation and title) (1993) (It.); D: Sergio Martino; Prod. Co.: Dania Film/Devon CInematografica; SC: Sergio Martino, Maurizio Rasio; C: Giancarlo Ferrando, Eugenio Alabassio; M: Natale Massara; S: Vittoria Bellevedere, Serena Grandi, Simona Borioni, Alessia Franchini.

L'Inspettore Giusti

A.k.a. *Inspector Justice* (English translation and title) (1994/99) (It.); D: Sergio Martino; P: Adriano Arie, Guglielmo Arie; SC: Sergio Donati, George Eastman a.k.a. Luigi Montefiori, Marcotullio Barboni; C: Emilio Loffredo; M: Carmelo La Bionda, Michelangelo La Bionda; S: Enrico Montesano, Mietta, Paola Saluzzi, Nicola Arigliano, Francesco Casale, Luigi Montini.

L'Isola degli Uomini Pesci

A.k.a. *Island of the Fishmen* (English translation); a.k.a. *Island of Mutations*; a.k.a. *Something Waits in the Dark*; a.k.a. *The Fishmen*; a.k.a. *Screamers* (English title) (1979) (It.); D: Sergio Martino; P: Luciano Martino, Gianni Sarago; Prod. Co.: Dania Film/Medusa Distribuzione; SC: Sergio Martino, Cesare Frugoni, Sergio Donati; C: Giancarlo Ferrando, Ulli Knudsen, Gianlorenzo Battaglia, Daniele Nannuzi; M: Luciano Michelini; SP E: Paolo Ricci, Cataldo Galiano; S: Barbara Bach, Claudio Cassinelli, Richard Johnson, Beryl Cunningham, Franco Javone, Roberto Posse.

Additional footage for Screamers (U.S. version): D: Chris Walas, Gary Graver, ?; C: Gary Graver; SP E: Chris Walas; S: Mel Ferrer, Cameron Mitchell.

Martino dabbles into the cannibal genre with *La Montagna del Dio Cannibale* (1978, Dania Film).

Milano Trema: La Polizia Vuole Giustizia

A.k.a. *The Violent Professionals* (English title) (1973) (It.); D: Sergio Martino; P: Carlo Ponti; Prod. Co.: Dania Film/Compagnia Cinematografica Champion; SC: Ernesto Gastaldi; C: Giancarlo Ferrando; M: Guido and Maurizio De Angelis; S: Luc Meranda, Silvano Tranquilli, Richard Conte, Martine Brochard, Carlo Alghiero, Chris Avram a.k.a. Christea Avram, Luciano Bartoli.

La Montagna del Dio Cannibale

A.k.a. *The Mountain of the Cannibal God* (English translation); a.k.a. *The Prisoner of the Cannibal God*; a.k.a. *The Slave of the Cannibal God*; a.k.a. *The Mountain in the Jungle*; a.k.a. *Primitive Desires* (English titles) (1978) (It.); D: Sergio Martino; P: Luciano Martino, Gianni

Sarago; Prod. Co.: Dania Film; SC: Sergio Martino, Cesare Frugoni; C: Giancarlo Ferrando; M: Guido and Maurizio De Angelis; S: Ursula Andress, Stacy Keach, Claudio Cassinelli, Antonio Marsina, Franco Fantasia, Lanfranco Spinola, Carlo Longhi.

La Regina degli Uomini Pesce

A.k.a. *The Queen of the Fish Men*; a.k.a. *The Queen of the FishMen*; a.k.a. *The Fishmen and Their Queen* (English translations and titles) (1995) (It.); D: Sergio Martino; P: Marco Grillo Spina; SC: Sergio Martino, Sauro Scavolini; C: Roberto Girometti; M: Luigi Ceccarelli; S: Giuliano Gensini, Michael Velez, Natascia Castrignano, Donald Hodson, Antonella Troise, Al Yamanouchi a.k.a. Haruiko Yamanouchi.

Spiando Marina

A.k.a. *Spying on Marina* (English translation and title); a.k.a. *Foxy Lady* (English title) (1992) (It.); D: Sergio Martino; Prod. Co.: Dania Film/National Cinematografica; SC: Sergio Martino, Piero Regnoli; C: Giancarlo Ferrando; M: Luigi Ceccarelli; S: Debora Caprioglio a.k.a. Debora Kinski, Steve Bond, Sharon Twomey, Leonardo Treviglio, Raffaella Offidani.

Lo Strano Vizio della Signora Wardh

A.k.a. *The Strange Vices of Signora Wardh* (English translation); a.k.a. *La Perversa Senora Wardh* (Spanish title; translation: *The Perverse Signora Wardh*); a.k.a. *Next!*; a.k.a. *The Next Victim*; a.k.a. *Blade of the Ripper* (English titles) (1970) (It., Sp.); D: Sergio Martino; P: Luciano Martino, Antonio Crescenzi; Prod. Co.: Devon Film (Rome)/Copercines (Madrid); SC: Eduardo Maria Brochero, Ernesto Gastaldi, Vittorio Caronia; C: Emilio Foriscat; M: Nora Orlandi, Paolo Ormi; S: Edwige Fenech, George Hilton, Cristina Conchita Airoldi, Manuel Gli, Alberto De Mendoza, Ivan Rassimov, Carlo Alighiero, Bruno Corazzari, Marella Corbi, Miguel Del Castilo.

Tutti i Colori del Buio

A.k.a. *All the Colors of the Darkness*; a.k.a. *All the Colors of Darkness*; a.k.a. *All the Colors of the Dark* (English translations and titles); a.k.a. *Una Stranha Orichidea con Cinque di Sangue* (alternate Italian title); a.k.a. *Todos los Colores de la Oscuridad* (Spanish title; translation: *All the Colors of Darkness*); a.k.a. *They're Coming to Get You!*; a.k.a. *Day of the Maniac*; a.k.a. *Demons of the Dead* (English titles) (1972) (It., Sp.); D: Sergio Martino; P: Mino Loy, Luciano Martino, Fabio Diotallevi; Prod. Co.: Lea Film/National Cinematografica (Rome)/Compagnia Astro (Madrid); SC: Ernesto Gastaldi, Sauro Scavolini, Santiago Moncada; C: Giancarlo Ferrando, Miguel F. Mila; M: Bruno Nicolai; S: Edwige Fenech, George Hilton, Ivan Rassimov, Susan Scott a.k.a. Nieves Navarro, Julian Ugarte, Georges Rigaud, Marina Malfatti, Luciano Pigozzi.

Il Tuo Vizio È una Stanza Chiusa e Solo Io Ne Ho la Chiave

A.k.a. *Your Vice Is a Locked Room and Only I Have the Key*; a.k.a. *Your Vice Is a Closed Room and Only I Have the Key* (English translations and titles); a.k.a. *Excite Me* (G.B.); a.k.a. *Gently, Before She Dies*; a.k.a. *Eye of the Black Cat* (English titles) (1972) (It.); D: Sergio Martino; P: Luciano Martino; Prod. Co.: Lea Film (Rome); SC: Ernesto Gastaldi, Luciano Martino, Adrian Bolzoni, Sauro Scavolini, based on "The Black Cat" by Edgar Allan Poe; C: Giancarlo Ferrando; M: Bruno Nicolai; S: Edwige Fenech, Anita Strindberg, Luigi Pistilli, Ivan Rassimov, Franco Nebbia, Riccardo Salvino, Daniela Giordano, Ermelinda De Felice, Luciano Pigozzi.

L'Ultimo Sogno

A.k.a. *One Last Dream* (English title) (2000) (It.); D: Sergio Martino; C: Roberto Girometti; S: Giampiero Bianchi, Johannes Brandrip, Antonella Fattori, Gino Lavagetto, Leslie Malton, Marina Viro.

Vendetta dal Futoro

A.k.a. *Vengeance of the Future* (English translation); a.k.a. *Atomic Cyborg*; a.k.a. *Hands of Steel* (English titles) (1986) (It.); D: Sergio Martino; Prod. Co.: National Cinematografica Dania Film/Medusa Distribuzione; SC: Sergio Martino, Elisa Livia Briganti, Sauro Scavolini; C: Giancarlo Ferrando; S: Daniel Greene, Janet Agren, John Saxon a.k.a. Carmine Orrico, George Eastman a.k.a. Luigi Montefiori, Amy Werb, Claudio Cassinelli, Anna Galiena.

Stelvio Massi

Born in 1929, Stelvio Massi is primarily a director of violent crime films. His two horror movies, *Cinque Donne per l'Assassino* (1974) and *Arabella, l'Angelo Nero* (1989), are somewhat interesting thrillers with an emphasis on sexploitative couplings; the latter is by far the better of the two.

In *Cinque Donne per l'Assassino*, a physician (veteran British character actor Francis Matthews) arrives home to find out that his wife and child have been murdered. As the body count begins to grow, all suspicions point to the doctor as the killer. When the physician is told that he is in fact sterile and would have been unable to conceive his own child, he investigates on his own. But who is the killer and what is his motive?

For *Arabella, l'Angelo Nero*, director Massi gives his acting discovery Tini Cansino (the niece of Rita Hayworth) full rein and the woman is a monster! The shapely actress wallows in her key role as a wife to a paralyzed man (she bit off an important part of his anatomy during sex play while driving) and, since the husband is unable to satisfy her demands, she seeks the sexual company of anyone she meets. The film starts with Cansino frequenting a sex club for perverts and nymphos. When two people are found knifed to death (one of them a police inspector who was interested in Cansino), a tough lesbian detective is called into the case to try to prevent more murders and to keep Cansino from sexually exhausting the rest of the cast with her fiery passion!

Other questionably entertaining productions from Massi include *Mondo Cane 3* (1986), its follow-up *Mondo Cane Oggi* (1986) and *Mondo Cane 2000 l'Incredibile* (1988). Directing under his Max Steel pseudonym, Massi has also churned out a number of passably entertaining action thrillers like the Fred Williamson vehicle *Il Cobra Nero* (1987) and *Taxi Killer* (1988). Still making movies in the '90s, *La Pista Bulgara* (1994) is among his more recent films.

Stelvio Massi Filmography (selected films)

Arabella, l'Angelo Nero

A.k.a. *Arabella, the Black Angel* (English translation and title); a.ka. *Arabella*; a.k.a. *The Black Angel* (English titles) (1989) (It.); D: Stelvio Massi, Arduino Sacco (uncredited); P: Francesco Vitulano; Prod. Co.: La Arpa International S.R.L.; SC: R. Filipucci, Vittorio Ferrero; C: Stefano Catalano; M: Serfran; S: Tini Cansino, Valentina Visconti, Francesco Casale, Carlo Mucari, Renato D'Amore, Evelyn Stewart a.k.a. Ida Galli.

Cinque Donne per l'Assassino

A.k.a. *Five Women for the Killer* (English translation) (1974) (It., Fr.); D: Stelvio Massi; Prod. Co.: Thousand Cinematografica (Rome)/Les Films La Boetie (Paris); SC: Roberto Gianviti, Gianfranco Clerici, Vincenzo Mannino; C: Sergio Rubini; M: Giorgio Gaslini; S: Francis Matthews, Pascale Rivault, Giorgio Albertazzi, Howard Ross a.k.a. Renato Rossini, Katia Christine, Catherine Diamant, Cicciolina a.k.a. Ilona Staller.

Il Cobra Nero

A.k.a. *Black Cobra* (English translation and title) (1987) (It.); D/C: Stelvio Massi; P: Luciano Appignani; SC: Danilo Massi; M: Stelvio Cipriani; S: Fred Williamson, Eva Grimaldi, Karl Landgren, Maurice Poli, Vassili Karras a.k.a. Vassili Karamesinis, Sabrina Siani, Jack Palance a.k.a. Vladimir Dalamik.

Mondo Cane Oggi

A.k.a. *Mondo Cane Oggi — L'Orrore Continue* (alternate Italian title) (1986) (It.); D: Stelvio Massi; P: Gabriele Crisanti for General Cine International Film, Film 2; SC: Stelvio Massi, Piero Regnoli; M: Walter Martino.

Mondo Cane 2000 l'Incredibile

(1988) (It.); D: Gabriele Crisanti, Stelvio Massi; P: Gabriele Crisanti for General Cine International Film, Film 2; SC: Luigi Mangini; C: Roberto Cimpanelli; M: Claudio Cimpanelli.

Mondo Cane 3

(1986) (It.); D: Stelvio Massi.

La Pista Bulgara

A.k.a. *Balkan Runner* (English title) (1994) (It.); D/C: Stelvio Massi; SC: Danilo Massi, Salvatore Paretti; M: Antonello Libonati; S: Stephane Ferrara, Isabel Russinova, Daisy White, Giovanni Oliveri.

Taxi Killer

(1988) (It.); D/C: Stelvio Massi; P: Fred Williamson; SC: Mario Gariazzo, Paola Pascolini; M: Stelvio Cipriani; S: Chuck Connors, Walter D'Amore, Catherine Hickland, Van Johnson.

Camillo Mastrocinque

Camillo Mastrocinque (1901–69) directed his first feature film, *Regina della Scala*, in 1937. He helped to give birth to the Italian horror film with his fantastic comedy feature *Toto all'Inferno* (1954). He waited another 14 years before venturing into the genre again, with more serious fare.

La Cripta e l'Incubo (1964), an atmospheric entry in the Gothic horror genre, tells of a count (Christopher Lee) who seeks to prevent the possible possession of his daughter by a centuries-dead ancestor who was a practitioner of witchcraft. *Un Angelo per Satana* (1966) is another film that deals with possession and black magic. Barbara Steele gives an intense performance as a prim and proper woman possessed by a statue of a long-deceased woman said to have certain powers. Long on talk and meaningful stares and atmospherics, this film is one of the last of the black-and-white Italian gothic horror films.

Camillo Mastrocinque Filmography (selected films)

Un Angelo per Satana

A.k.a. *An Angel for Satan* (English translation and title) (1966) (It.); D: Camillo Mastrocinque; P: Lilliana Biancini, Giuliano Simonetti; Prod. Co.: Discobolo Cinematografica; SC: Camillo Mastrocinque, Giuseppe Mangione; C: Giuseppe Acquari; M: Francesco De Masi; SP E: Antonio Ricci; S: Barbara Steele, Anthony Steffan a.k.a. Antonio De Teffe, Claudio Gora, Ursula Davis a.k.a. Pier Ana Quaglia, Aldo Berti, Marina Berti, Vassili Karras a.k.a. Vassili Karamesinis.

La Cripta e l'Incubo

A.k.a. *The Crypt of Horror* (English translation and title); a.k.a. *La Maldición de los Karnstein* (Spanish title); a.k.a. *Terror in the Crypt*; a.k.a. *The Karnstein Curse*; a.k.a. *The Crypt of the Vampire*; a.k.a. *The Vampire's Crypt*; a.k.a. *Karnstein*; a.k.a. *The Crypt and the Nightmare*; a.k.a. *The Curse of the Karnsteins*; a.k.a. *Carmilla* (English titles) (1964) (It., Sp.); D: Camillo Mastrocinque; P: William Mulligan a.k.a. Mario Mariani; Prod. Co.: MEC Cinematografica (Rome)/Hispamer Film (Madrid); SC: Ernesto Gastaldi, Bruno Valeri, Maria Del Carmen, Martinez Ramon, Jose L. Monter; C: Giuseppe Acquari, Julio Ortas; M: Carlo Savina; S: Christopher Lee, Adriana Ambessi, Ursula Davis a.k.a. Pier Ana Quaglia, Jose Campos, Nela Conjiu, Vera Valmont, Jose Villasante, Angela Minervini.

Regina della Scala

(1937) (It.); D: Camillo Mastrocinque, Guido Salvini; P: G.V. Sampiere for l'Aprilia Film; SC: Guido Salvini, Camillo Mastrocinque, Raffaele Calzini; C: Vaclav Vich; M: Antonio Veretti et al.; S: Marghertita Carosio, Giovanni Cimara, Mario Ferrari, Nieves Poli.

Toto all'Inferno

A.k.a. *Toto in Hell* (English translation and title) (1954) (It.); D: Camillo Mastrocinque; P: Carlo Ponti Cinematografica; Prod. Co.: Excelsa/Carlo Ponti Cinematografica; SC: Antonio Vincenzo Stefano Clemente a.k.a. Antonio De Curtis a.k.a. Toto, Alessandro Continenza, Vittorio Metz, Italo Di Tuddo, Lucio Fulci, Gino Mangini; C: Aldo Tonti; M: Pippo Barzizza; S: Toto a.k.a. Antonio De Curtis a.k.a. Antonio Vincenzo Stefano Clemente, Maria Frau, Tino Buazzalli, Ubaldo Lay, Fulvia Franco, Dante Maggio.

Emilio Miraglia

Emilio Miraglia's *La Notte Che Evelyn Uscì dalla Tomba* (1971) is a wonderfully sleazy and often incoherent tale of a wealthy man (Antonio De Teffe) who has spent the better half of his adult life in a sanitarium due to mental illness. De Teffe picks up women and then, in a drug-induced hallucinatory stupor, attacks them. Is the man truly a killer? Why is the director trying so hard to gain sympathy from the audience for this killer? Is it possible that what we have been shown are *not* the actual events taking place? Is this all some kind of labyrinthine plot device to get at a possible inheritance? You bet it is!

La Dama Rossa Uccide Sette Volte (1972) is a richly photographed thriller that begins with the psychopathic corruption of a young child's mind. In the coming years of adulthood, this young woman will become a killer. The film is a decent thriller but little more.

Emilio Miraglia Filmography

La Dama Rossa Uccide Sette Volte

A.k.a. *The Red Queen Kills Seven Times*; a.k.a. *The Lady in Red Kills Seven Times* (English translation and titles); a.k.a. *Horror House* (German title); a.k.a. *The Corpse Which Didn't Want to Die*; a.k.a. *Blood Feast*; a.k.a. *Feast of Flesh* (English titles) (1972) (It., W.G.); D: Emilio P. Miraglia; P: Fabio Pittorru; Prod. Co.: Phoenix Cinematografica (Rome)/Romano Film G.M.B.H. (Munich)/Traian Boeru (Munich); SC: Emilio P. Miraglia, Fabio Pittorru; C: Alberto Spagnoli; M: Bruno Nicolai; S: Barbara Bouchet a.k.a. Barbel Goutscher a.k.a. Barbel Gutchen, Marina Malfatti, Ugo Pagliai, Maria Pia Giancaro, Marino Mase, Fabrizio Moresco, Sybil Danning a.k.a. Sybille Johanna Danninger.

La Notte Che Evelyn Uscì dalla Tomba

A.k.a. *The Night Evelyn Came Out of the Tomb*; a.k.a. *The Night Evelyn Came Out of the Grave*; a.k.a. *The Night That Evelyn Came Out of the Grave* (English translations and titles); a.k.a. *The Night She Rose from the Tomb* (G.B.); a.k.a. *Sweet to Be Kissed, Hard to Die* (English titles) (1971) (It.); D: Emilio P. Miraglia; P: Antonio Sarno; Prod. Co.: Phoenix Cinematografica; SC: Emilio P. Miraglia, Fabio Pittorru, Massimo Felisatti; C: Gastone Di Giovanni; M: Bruno Nicolai; S: Anthony Steffan a.k.a. Antonio De Teffe, Marina Malfatti, Giacomo Rossi-Stuart, Umberto Raho, Erica Blanc a.k.a. Erica Bianchi Colombatto, Rod Murdock.

Sergio Pastore

The prolific Sergio Pastore (1932–87) directed *Sette Scialli di Setta Gialli* (1972), one of the very best of the *giallo* thrillers. Of course, Pastore steals from the best when he cribs some basic plot devices and the character of his main protagonist (played by Antonio De Teffe) from Dario Argento's *Il Gatto a Nove Code*. De Teffe is a blind composer and amateur detective who, with the aid of his trusty servant (Umberto Raho), gets around quite well. When a maniacal killer murders De Teffe's lover, he is thrust into a murderous plot. Models at a fashion institute are being brutally murdered (shades of Mario Bava's *Sei Donne per l'Assassino*). As the body count rises, everyone becomes a suspect including De Teffe. The murders are committed in a unique fashion, by an ordinary house cat whose claws are dipped in poison.

After spending much of the '80s making vapid thrillers and television dramas, Pastore returned to the *giallo* format when he co-directed (with his wife Giovanna Lenzi) the thriller *Delitti* (1986). This is an awful film. Pastore and Lenzi attempted to make another thriller in the old-fashioned *giallo* mold of the early '70s, but an amateurish cast, very low budget and ridiculous, incoherent plot leaves the audience clamoring to claim back their 90 minutes of life.

Sergio Pastore Filmography (selected films)

Delitti

A.k.a. *Crimes* (English translation) (1986) (It.); D: Giovanna Lenzi, Sergio Pastore (uncredited); Prod. Co.: Il Mezzagiorno Nuovo d'Italia; SC: Giovanna Lenzi, based on the play *La Parisienne* by Henri Becque; C: Domenico Paolerico; M: Guido and Maurizio De Angelis; S: Saverio Vallone, Michela Miti, Tony Valente, Michel Clifford, Debora Ergas, Giorgio Ardisson, Jeanette Len a.k.a. Giovanna Lenzi.

Sette Scialli di Setta Gialla

A.k.a. *Seven Shawls of Yellow Silk* (English translation); a.k.a. *Seven Crimes of the Black Cat*; a.k.a. *The Crimes of the Black Cat* (English titles) (1972) (It.); D: Sergio Pastore; P: Edmondo Amati; Prod. Co.: Capitolina Produzione Cinematografica; SC: Sergio Pastore, Alessandro Continenza, Giovanni Simonelli; C: Guglielmo Mancori; M: Manuel De Sica; SP E: Eugenio Ascani, Renato Marinelli; S: Anthony Steffan a.ka. Antonio De Teffe, Sylva Koscina, Giacomo Rossi-Stuart, Jeanette Len, Renato De Carmine, Umberto Raho, Annabella Incontrera, Shirley Corrigan, Romano Malaspina.

Renato Polselli

Renato Polselli has always been a bit of a mystery among Italian filmmakers. He rarely gives interviews about his work. Little is written about him and yet his horror movies are some of the most original, hallucinatory and sleazy, low-budget productions in the genre, some with reputations approaching the mythical. *L'Amante del Vampiro* (1960) and *Il Mostro dell'Opera* (1964) are two of Polselli's earliest films. They combine vampire themes that occurred so often in early Italian horror features with overtly sexual themes and, in some instances, brief nudity. Polselli seemed to have been deeply affected by the British Hammer vampire movies, for his two early productions are steeped in nice-looking atmospheric sets and cast with busty, bodice-ripping actresses.

Polselli's *Riti, Magie Nere e Segrete Orge del Trecento* (1973), considered a lost film for decades, suddenly appeared in 1998 on Italian video in a heavily butchered version. Cut to 56 minutes, Polselli's film is virtually incoherent, seeming like little more than a random assembly of sequences from some bizarre erotic tableau, featuring shapely vampire maidens baring fangs, women being whipped, cast members glaring at the screen in wide-eyed stares, etc.

However, in 1999, the American DVD company Image released an uncut *Riti, Magie Nere e Segrete Orge del Trecento*. The film barely makes much more sense than the previously released, truncated Italian video version. In the contemporary Italy of the '70s, Mickey Hargitay portrays a modern-day Count Dracula who plans on marrying off his young daughter to a dull village nobleman. However, Dracula is plagued by the loss of his beloved Isabel, who centuries before was burned at the stake for being a vampire and a witch. The castle that hosts the reception and wedding party for the count's daughter just also happens to be the headquarters for a satanic sect attempting to resurrect the naked and bloody corpse of Isabel by performing a series of bloody rituals upon a handful of nubile victims during the cycle of the full moon. With actors staring off into the camera, sometimes about to break out in laughter, and with a succession of near-pornographic sexual encounters taking place every ten minutes or so, the film seems amateurish and unwatchable.

Delirio Caldo, also known as *Delirium* (1972), is a Polselli film that seems to have been entirely forgotten. His savage film will most likely leave some viewers wondering whether it would have been best to leave it that way. During a hallucinatory prologue that recalls *Apocalypse Now* (but on a budget that would barely buy one's lunch), we see a man tormented by the horrors of the Vietnam War. Years later, this man (Mickey Hargitay) becomes a well-respected police surgeon who occasionally snaps out of reality, returns (via flashbacks) to the horrors of war and goes on a killing spree. Hargitay kidnaps women, assaults them sexually and then brutally mutilates their bodies. When his understanding wife develops suspicions, he confesses all, then their tender lovemaking session turns sour when he violates her with strange objects. When the ridiculously slow (and stupid) police finally kill him, the viewer will sigh in relief. Of note is that the original Italian version of the film differs greatly; there are no Vietnam War traumas (as there are in the export English versions) to explain Hargitay's murder spree.

Another film to look out for is *Mania* (1973), a seldom-seen thriller about a scientist (Brad Euston) obsessively working on a project involving death who lives in a castle peopled by relatives and hangers-on, all with another strange obsession ... sex. Polselli finally released the film to Italian theaters in 1976, but it quickly disappeared into oblivion. There are rumors that a video (with hardcore inserts) appeared via a small Italian label.

Casa dell'Amore ... La Polizia Interviene (1976) is Polselli's offensive film about a group of hedonistic archeologists (two women and a man) searching for something in a forest. They come across members of a black magic sect burying the body of a woman sealed in plastic. Instead of immediately reporting this to the authorities, the group follows the killers to a mansion where they discover a plot to kidnap women for live sacrifices. The foolish trio audiotapes the proceedings (in between random bouts of euphoria-fueled sexual gymnastics) and the whole movie becomes totally confusing and incoherent before it appears to randomly end.

Polselli's output since this film has been sporadic, aside from some other horror films that appear to be unfinished and have yet to see the light of day. He filmed a hysterically ridiculous film about the horrific confessions of a sex therapist titled *Rivelazioni di uno Psichiatra sul Mondo Perverso* (1973) and reportedly also worked on a few porno features (with his frequent collaborator Bruno Vanni) during the '80s. There does not seem to be any new horror films coming any time soon from this director. Maybe this is a blessing.

Renato Polselli Filmography (selected films)

L'Amante del Vampiro

A.k.a. *The Loves of the Vampire* (English translation); a.k.a. *The Vampire's Lover*; a.k.a. *The Vampire and the Ballerina* (U.S. title); a.k.a. *The Dancer and the Vampire* (English titles) (1960) (It.); D: Renato Polselli; P: Bruno Bolognesi; Prod. Co.: Consorzio Italiano Films; SC: Renato Polselli, Giuseppe Pellegrini, Ernesto Gastaldi; C: Angelo Balstrocchi; M: Aldo Pigga; SP E: Leopoldo Rosi, Raffaele Del Monte; S: Helene Remy, Walter Brandi, Tina Gloriana, Maria Luisa Rolando, Isarco Ravaioli.

Casa dell'Amore ... La Polizia Interviene

A.k.a. *The House of Love ... The Police Intervene* (English translation); a.k.a. *La Casa dell'Amore* (Italian pre-production title; translation: *The House of Love*); (1976) (It.); D: Renato Polselli, Bruno Vanni* (uncredited); P: Sergio Baldacchino, Giovanni Luchetti; Prod. Co.: Simma Cinematografica; SC: Bruno Vanni; C: Saverio Diamanti, Fernando Campiotti; M: Giorgio Farina; S: Mirella Rossi, Iolanda Mascitti, Tony Matera, Katia Cardinali, Matilde Antonelli, Gianni Pesola, Nicola Morelli, Cesare Nizzica, Elsio Mancuso, Zaira Zoccheddu, Salvatore Carrara.

The film includes footage from *La Verità Seconda Satana* (credited to Bruno Vanni and Renato Polselli).

Delirio Caldo

A.k.a. *Hot Delirium* (English translation); a.k.a. *Delirium* (English title)(1972) (It.); D: Renato Polselli; P: Mario Maestelli; Prod. Co.: G.R.P. Cinematografica/Cinamerica International Film; SC: Renato Polselli; C: Ugo Brunelli; M: Gianfranco Reverberi; S: Mickey Hargitay, Rita Calderoni, Carmen Young, Gaetano Cimarosa, Krysta Barrymore, William Darnio, Katia Kardinali, Stefano Oppedisano.

Mania

(1973) (It.); D/P/Renato Polselli; Prod. Co.: G.R.P. Cinematografica; SC: Renato Polselli, Bruno Vani; C: Ugo Brunelli; M: Umberto Cannone; S: Ivana Giordano, Brad Euston, Isarco Ravaioli, Mirella Rossi, Eva Spadaro.

Il Mostro dell'Opera

A.k.a. *The Monster of the Opera* (English translation and title); a.k.a. *Il Vampiro dell'Opera* (alternate Italian title; translation and title: *The Vampire of the Opera*) (1964) (It.); D: Renato Polselli; Prod. Co.: N.I.F. (Nord Industrial Film); SC: Renato Polselli, Ernesto Gastaldi; C: Ugo Brunelli; M: Aldo Piga; S: Giuseppe Addobbati, Vittoria Prada, Marco Mariani, Carla Cavelli.

Riti, Magie Nere e Segrete Orge del Trecento

A.k.a. *Black Magic Rites ... Reincarnations*; a.k.a. *Secrets, Black Magic Rites and Reincarnation* (English translations and titles); a.k.a. *The Reincarnation of Isabel*; a.k.a. *The Horrible Orgies of Count Dracula*; a.k.a. *The Ghastly Orgies of Count Dracula* (English titles) (1973) (It.); D: Renato Polselli; Prod. Co.: GRP; SC: Renato Polselli, Bruno Vanni; C: Ugo Brunelli; M: Romolo Forlai, Gianfranco Reverberi; S: Mickey Hargitay, Rita Calderoni, Max Dorian, Consolata Moschera, Marcello Bonini.

Rivelazioni di uno Psichiatra sul Mondo Perverso

A.k.a. *Revelations of a Psychiatrist in a World Full of Perversion* (English translation and title) (1973) (It.); D: Renato Polselli; Prod. Co.: G.R.P. Cinematografica; SC: Renato Polselli, Bruno Vanni; C: Ugo Brunelli; M: Umberto Cannone; S: Isarco Ravaioli, Franca Gonella, Marisa Salli.

La Verità Seconda Satana

(1974) (It.); D: Renato Polselli, Bruno Vanni (co-director); Prod.Co.: G.R.P.; SC: Renato Polselli; C: Ugo Brunelli; M: Gianfranco Di Stefano; S: Rita Calderoni, Isarco Ravaioli, Marie-Paul Bastine, Sergio Ammirata, Gino Donato, Antonio Zambito.

Massimo Pupillo

Massimo Pupillo started his film career as an assistant to the French director Marcel Pagnol on *La Femme du Boulanger* (1938). Continuing to work with Pagnol in the capacity of an assistant director, Pupillo returned to Italy and became noted as a director of short films and documentaries.

Pupillo's first genre film *Il Boia Scarlatto* (1965) is an exercise in homophobia and the debasement of women masked as entertainment. Mickey Hargitay (former real-life muscleman, peplum actor and, once, the husband of Jayne Mansfield) stars as a narcissistic former actor who relishes his "perfect body" in such a manner that he has little time for anything other than to terrorize and torture the female

A possible victim in Massimo Pupillo's *Il Boia Scarlatto* (1965, M.B.S. Cinematografica/International Entertainment/Ralph Zucker [Massimo Pupillo]).

members of the cast who have been stranded (along with a few males) near the grounds of his isolated castle.

Hargitay's performance is so hysterically overwrought that the film comes off more as a trashy Grade Z movie. This author suggests that the film can be best appreciated if watched under the influence of artificial stimulants to more properly accept the film for the wondrous garbage that it is.

Pupillo's feature *Cinque Tombe per un Medium* (1966) is an improvement. The film stars female horror icon Barbara Steele as a widow whose late husband was an alchemist who dabbled in the black arts. It seems that the late occultist has found a way to summon the dead to avenge his murder. This is a handsomely photographed black-and-white feature containing atmospheric scenes of the dead being recalled to life.

La Vendetta di Lady Morgan (1966) is Pupillo's attempt to merge much more of an erotic tone into the gothic horror genre. The ghost of a dead woman seeks vengeance upon the descendants of those who contributed to her demise, but falls in love with one of them. *La Vendetta di Lady Morgan* is fairly dull, full of static, labored shots of the Italian countryside and little of the horrific chills one associates with these kind of films, which leaves little question as to why it was released only in Italy.

For decades, Pupillo had been confused with the real-life film producer Ralph Zucker, but they were two separate people, for Ralph Zucker died in 1982. In a 1996 interview with journalist Lucas Balbo for the book *Shock*, Pupillo stated, "Because I didn't care about the film *Cinque Tombe per Medium*, I let the producer Ralph Zucker take the credit. Also we made a deal for two films and he didn't want the same name on both films. So to please him, I let him sign [his name to] *Cinque Tombe per Medium* and I put my name on *Il Boia Scarlatto*…"

La Vendetta di Lady Morgan also seems to be Pupillo's last genre feature film. "I wasn't interested in making any more horror films and I turned down a lot of propositions (because I was making these kinds of movies)." Pupillo claimed to have contributed (uncredited) to the screenplay for Luigi Scatttini's *Svezia, Inferno e Paradiso* (1967), but there is little information available to substantiate this claim.

Pupillo's last film, *Sa Jana*, a documentary about Sardinian fishermen (a remake of his own 1961 documentary short subject *Gli Amici dell'Isola*), remains unreleased.

Other noteworthy genre contributions by Massimo Pupillo: As writer, or contributing writer, Pupillo worked on *Il Plenilunio delle Vergini* (1973), but had nothing to do with *Eva, la Venere Selvaggia* (1968), a film which Ralph Zucker produced.

Massimo Pupillo Filmography

Il Boia Scarlatto

A.k.a. *The Crimson Executioner*; a.k.a. *The Scarlet Hangman*; a.k.a. *The Red Hangman* (English translations and titles); a.k.a. *Bloody Pit of Horror* (English title) (1965) (It., U.S.); D: Massimo Pupillo; P: Francesco Merli, Massimo Pupillo; Prod. Co.: M.B.S. Cinematografica/International Entertainment/Ralph Zucker; SC: Roberto Natale, Romano Migliorini; C: Luciano Trasatti; M: Gino Peguri; S: Mickey Hargitay, Walter Brandi, Luisa Baratto, Massimo Pupillo, Alfredo Rizzo, Femi Benussi a.k.a. Eufemia Benussi, Barbara Nelli, Moha Thai, Nando Angelini.

Cinque Tombe per un Medium

A.k.a. *Five Graves for a Medium* (English translation); a.k.a. *The Tombs of Horror*; a.k.a. *Coffin of Terror*; a.k.a. *Terror Creatures from the Grave* (English titles) (1966) (It., U.S.); D: Massimo Pupillo; P: Massimo Pupillo, Ralph Zucker, Frank Merle; Prod. Co.: M.B.S. Cinematografica/GIA Cinematografica/International Entertainment Corporation; SC: Roberto Natale, Romano Migliorine; C: Carlo Di Palma; M: Aldo Pigga; S: Barbara Steele, Walter Brandi, Mirella Maravidi, Alfredo Rizzo, Riccardo Garrone, Luciano Pigozzi, Tilde Till, Ennio Balbo.

La Femme du Boulanger

A.k.a. *The Baker's Wife* (English title) (1938) (Fr., It., Sp.); D: Marcel Pagnol, Massimo Pupillo (uncredited); P: Leon Bourrely, Charles Pons; SC: Marcel Pagnol, Jean Giono; C: Georges Benoit; M: Vincent Scotto; S: Raimu, Ginette Leclerc, Robert Vattier, Robert Bassac, Fernand Charpin.

Some sources claim this was Massimo Pupillo's first directorial assignment. Previously, he had been an assistant director to Pagnol.

La Vendetta di Lady Morgan

A.k.a. *The Vengeance of Lady Morgan* (English translation) (1966) (It.); D: Massimo Pupillo; P: Franco Belotti; Prod. Co.: Morgan Film; SC: Gianni Grimaldi; C: Oberdan Trojani; M: Piero Umiliani; S: Gordon Mitchell a.k.a. Charles Pendleton, Erica Blanc a.k.a. Erica Bianchi Colombatto, Barbara Nelli, Paul Muller a.k.a. Paul Mueller.

Giulio Questi

Giulio Questi's career is a mystery in itself. After Questi came from nowhere as a technical assistant on Italian films in the early '60s, he made his first great picture, *Se Sei Vivo Spara* (1967), one of the most violent and gritty of the Spaghetti Westerns of that decade, elevating the saga of man seeking vengeance into a nasty, nihilistic, blood-soaked oater.

La Morte Ha Fatto l'Uovo (1968) is Questi's surreal "what the hell is it all about?" film. Starring Ewa Aulin, Gina Lollobrigida and Jean-Louis Trintignant, the movie is a seriously sick flick about the sexual corruption that invades, then influences, the breeding farm for a new kind of genetic food supply. With a plot that is nearly indescribable, *La Morte Ha Fatto l'Uovo* has garnered a cult following over the years. There are murders, genetically mutated giant chickens and the visual delights of both Aulin and Lollobrigida in various states of undress. *Arcana* (1972) is a pretentious drama masking as a surreal art film. The (implied) incestuous relationship between a medium and her son reaches apocalyptic proportions when the son's own experiments with the supernatural reach into other dimensions. He influences others to commit sexual acts with him, causes death and decay and, by the film's end, when he tires of all the chicanery, he re-imagines everything back to normal ... almost.

Questi seemed to disappear from filmmaking for several years and then, in 1991, he returned to directing with *Non Aprire l'Uomo Nero* and *Il Segno del Com-*

mander, two weak, dull thrillers. Recent productions for Italian television are the '90s thrillers *Vampirismus* and *L'Uomo della Sabbia*.

Some film reference sources erroneously list Giulio Questi as a pseudonym for the prolific Italian film producer Italo Zingarelli, but there is little factual information to substantiate this claim and it seems unlikely.

Giulio Questi Filmography (selected films)

Arcana

(1971) (It.); D: Giulio Questi; P: Gaspare Palumbo; SC: Giulio Questi, Franco Arcalli; C: Dario Di Palma; M: Romolo Grano, Berto Pisano; S: Lucia Bose, Maurizio Degli Espositi, Tina Aumont a.k.a. Marie Christine Salomons, Dario Vigano, Gianfranco Pozzi.

La Morta Ha Fatto l'Uovo

A.k.a. *Death Laid an Egg* (English translation and title); a.k.a. *La Mort a Pondu un Oeuf* (French title); a.k.a. *Le Sadique de la Chambre 24* (alternate French title); a.k.a. *A Curious Way to Love* (G.B.); a.k.a. *Plucked*; a.k.a. *Death Trap* (English titles) (1968) (It., Fr.); D: Giulio Questi; Prod. Co.: Summa Cinematografica/Cine Azimut (Rome)/Les Films Corona (Paris); SC: Giulio Questi, Franco Arcalli; C: Dario Di Palma; M: Bruno Maderna; S: Gina Lollobrigida, Jean-Louis Trintignant, Ewa Aulin, Jean Sobiesky, Renato Romano, Giulio Donnini.

Non Aprire all'Uomo Nero

A.k.a. *Don't Open the Door for the Man in Black* (English translation and title) (1991) (It.); D: Giulo Questi; P: Lina Bernardi, Mario Cotone; SC: Giulio Questi, David Grieco; M: Pino Donaggio, A. Goodwin, C. Josephs; C: Franco Fraticelli; S: John Phillip Law, Aurore Clement, Giuliano Gemma, Stefania Orsolo Garello, Renato Cecchatto, Yves Collignon.

Se Sei Vivo Spara

A.k.a. *If You Live, Shoot* (English translation); a.k.a. *Gringo Uccide* (alternate Italian title); a.k.a. *Oro Maldito* (Spanish title); a.k.a. *Django Kill* (English title) (1967) (It., Sp.); D: Giulio Questi; Prod. Co.: G.I.A. Cinematografica/Hispamer Film (Madrid); SC: Giulio Questi, Franco Arcalli; C: Franco Della Colli; M: Ivan Vandor; S: Tomas Milian a.k.a. Tomas Rodriguez, Piero Lulli, Milo Quesada, Paco Sanz, Roberto Camardie, Marilu Tolo, Raymond Lovelock.

Il Segno del Commander

A.k.a. *The Sign of the Commander* (English translation) (1992) (It.); D: Giulio Questi; P: Arturo Le Pegna, Olvia Le Pegna; S: Robert Powell, Elena Sofia Ricci, Michel Bouquet, Jonathan Cecil, Fanny Bastien.

L'Uomo della Sabbia

(1992) (It.); D: Giulio Questi.

Vampirismus

(1992) (It.); D/SC: Giulio Questi; C: Angelo Sciarra; M: Renzo Rizzone; S: Antonio Salines, Mariagrazia Marescalchi, Francesca Archibugi, Gerardo Panipucci.

Piero Regnoli

Besides contributing to numerous Italian horror films as a writer for over two decades (including *I Vampiri, Malabimba, Patrick Viva Ancora, Le Notti del Terrore, Incubo sulla Contaminata* and *La Bimba di Satana*), Piero Regnoli is also notable for directing the colorful sword-and-sandal peplum adventure *Maciste nelle Miniere di Re Salomone* (1964), *L'Ultima Preda del Vampiro* (1960), an entertaining, completely exploitative sexy vampire film, and *Ti Aspetterò all'Inferno* (1960), one of the first of the early *giallo* thrillers.

L'Ultima Preda del Vampiro is the tale of a group of show business types who become stranded at the castle of a count (Walter Brandi); it gave '60s grindhouse audiences many titillating glimpses of bare flesh. It alternates between romantic interludes (featuring the count and one of the female entertainers), sexy horror (the count has a twin, also played by Brandi) and a monstrous vampire who attacks the cast members.

His last production as a director is *Cerentola e la Principessa sul Pisello* (1974).

Piero Regnoli Filmography (selected films)

Cerentola e la Principessa sul Pisello

(1974) (It.); D: Piero Regnoli.

Maciste nelle Miniere di Re Salomone

A.k.a. *Maciste in King Solomon's Mines* (English translation and title); a.k.a. *Samson in King Solomon's Mines* (English title) (1964) (It.); D/SC: Piero Regnoli; P: Luigi Carpentieri, Ermanno Donati; C: Mario Capriotti, Luciano Trasatti; M: Francesco De Masi; S: Reg Park, Wandisa Guida, Dan Harrison, Giuseppe Addobbati.

The times were certainly changing for horror films with the introduction of blatant eroticism in Piero Regnoli's *L'Ultima Preda del Vampiro* (1960, Nord Film Italiana).

Ti Aspetterò all'Inferno

A.k.a. *I'll See You in Hell* (English translation and title) (1960) (It.); D: Piero Regnolli; Prod. Co.: Verdestella Film; C: Luciano Trasatti; M: Giuseppe Piccillo; S: Eva Bartok, John Drew Barrymore, Massimo Serrato, Moira Orfei, Tonino Pierfederici.

La Ultima Preda del Vampiro

A.k.a. *The Last Prey of the Vampire*; a.k.a. *The Last Victim of the Vampire*; a.k.a. *The Vampire's Last Victim*; a.k.a. *Desires of the Vampire*; a.k.a. *Daughters of the Vampire*; a.k.a. *Curse of the Vampires*; a.k.a. *The Vampires and the Playgirl*; a.k.a. *The Playgirls and the Vampire* (English titles) (1960) (It.); D: Piero Regnoli; P: Tiziano Longo; Prod. Co.: Nord Film Italiana; C: Ugo Brunelli; M: Aldo Piga; S: Walter Brandi, Lyla Rocco, Maria Giovannini, Tilde Damiani, Corinne Fontaine, Erika Di Centa, Marisa Quattrini, Alfredo Rizzo.

Mario Siciliano

Born in 1925, Mario Siciliano is known as a maker of exploitation movies. His directing career made a downturn into pure sexploitation when, before his death in 1987, the last of his films were revealed to be pornographic movies that he directed using a variety of pseudonyms. Among his better later productions as a director were *La Zia Svedese* (1980) featuring Marina Frajese and *Erotic Family* (1980) with Karen Well, Raquel Evans and Giorgio Ardisson. This last film is sometimes also credited to Sergio Bergonzelli, but it could have been a co-directing stint.

Siciliano also directed the odd and bizarre pornographic horror film *Orgasmo Esotico* (1982), about a night spent in a villa where an undead sorceress seduces the cast (including Marina Frajese). Equally strange is *Orgasmo Non-Stop* (1982), featuring mainstream Italian actress Paola Senatore's porno film debut.

Siciliano's best film in the horror genre is undoubtedly *Malocchio* (1975), an obscure picture about the occult. Made as an Italian co-production with Mexico, it's an inventive film about a mysterious man (Jorge Rivero) who seeks the assistance of his friend (Antonio De Teffe) when he is plagued by nightmarish visions of a sect of naked people who beckon him. Eventually Rivero is surrounded by corpses, and suspected of murder. When an investigator (Richard Conte) accepts the innocence of Rivero and attempts to solve the bizarre reasons for the killings, he too is murdered, as is the majority of the cast by the film's climax.

Siciliano seems more interested in the undraped bodies of his female cast members than the plot. Still, *Malocchio* remains a strange film that deserves more recognition for being ... different.

Mario Siciliano Filmography

Erotic Family

A.k.a. *Las Veredes Vacaciones de una Familia Bien* (Spanish title) (1980) (It., Sp.); D: Mario Siciliano, Sergio Bergonzelli; Prod. Co.: Metheus Film (Rome)/Llorca Films (Madrid)/. Films Dara (Barcelona) C: Juan Gelpi; M: Nico Fidenco; S: Karin Well, Raquel Evans, Giorgio Ardisson, Alfonso De Real, Berta Cabre.

Sergio Bergonzelli is credited as the sole director on the Italian video release, which also features pornographic footage, possibly directed by Siciliano (the film appears on his credits on numerous occasions) and added to the film after the initial Italian theatrical release.

Malocchio

A.k.a. *Evil Eye* (English translation and title); a.k.a. *The Evil Eye*; a.k.a. *Eroticfollia* (alternate Italian title); a.k.a. *Los Espectros* (Spanish title); a.k.a. *Mal de Ojo* (alternate Spanish title) (1975) (It., Sp., Mex.); D: Mario Siciliano; Prod. Co.: Metheus Cinematografica (Rome)/Emaus Film (Madrid) Producciones Gonzalo Elvira (Mexico); SC: Mario Siciliano, Federico De Urrutia, Julio Buchs; C: Otello Colangeli; M: Stelvio Cipriani; SP E: Paolo Ricci; S: Anthony Steffan a.k.a. Antonio De Teffe, Richard Conte, Pilar Velasquez, Jorge Rivero, Eduardo Fajardo, Daniela Giordano, Pia Giancarlo, Luis La Torre, Eva Vanicek, Luciano Pigozzi.

Orgasmo Esotico

A.k.a. *Exotic Orgasm*; a.k.a. *Orgasmo Erotico* (English titles) (1982) (It.); D: Mario Siciliano; P: Carlo Leone; Prod. Co. Metheus Film; C: Luigi Ciccarese; M: Carlo Maria Cordio/C.A.M. Music; S: Marina Frajese a.k.a. Marina Hedman a.k.a. Marina Lotar, Sonia Bennett, Michel Curie, Peter Brown, Eugenio Gramignano, Mimo Losy.

Orgasmo Non-Stop

A.k.a. *Non-Stop Orgasm* (English translation); a.k.a. *Paola Senatore — Non Stop* (English title) (1982) (It.); D/SC: Mario Siciliano; P: Carlo Leone; Prod. Co. Metheus Film; C: Luigi Ciccarese; S: Paola Senatore, Marina Frajese a.k.a. Marina Hedman a.k.a. Marina Lotar, Sonia Bennett, Maria Ramunno. Eugenio Gramignano, Daniela Samueli.

La Zia Svedese

A.k.a. *My Swedish Aunt* (English translation and title); a.k.a. *Hot Nights* (German title?) (1980) (It.); D: Mario Siciliano; P: Robert Ruschioni; Prod. Co.: Metheus Film; SC: Mario Siciliano; C: Luigi Ciccarese; M: Carlo Maria Cordio; S: Marina Frajese a.k.a. Marina Hedman a.k.a. Marina Lotar, Peter Thompson, Laura Levi a.k.a. Gabriella Tricca, Giuseppe Curia, Ermino Bianchi.

Paolo Solvay

Paolo Solvay is probably better known as Luigi Batzella, one of his many pseudonyms (the others being Ivan Katansky, Paul Hamus and Gigi Batzella). Solvay is generally not considered a very good filmmaker. The majority of his films are undemanding exploitation pictures with which one merely passes the time, while others are horrid exercises in dementia — part of the savage and, thankfully, short-lived cycle of Nazi women's prison torture films. *Kaput Lager: Gli Ultimi Giorni delle SS* (1976) and *La Bestia in Calore* (1977) are two examples of his contributions to this genre.

Il Plenilunio delle Vergini (1973) is a delirious sexploitation-vampire film. Featuring Rosalba Neri (billed here as Sara Bay), the film also stars Mark Damon (in dual roles) as an archaeologist and his twin brother. In Transylvania, one brother finds the long-lost ring of the Niebelungen, but this item is really the property of the vampire Countess de Vries (Neri). After turning one brother into a manic vampire with her body and fangs, she goes after the other. Of course, in between bouts of heterosexual couplings, Neri does find time to scour the countryside for full-bodied, nubile maidens to suck their blood.

In 1974, Solvay directed the obscure erotic possession film *Nuda per Satana*, a demented exercise into semi-pornographic skin flick horror (most of the female cast members are repeatedly, and often, nude) and very low-budget Italian gothic shenanigans. In this crazy quilt tale, a man (James Harris), who may or may not have been in an automobile accident, becomes infatuated with a voluptuous woman (Rita Calderoni) whom he drags from a crashed vehicle ... or does he? Filled with wacky flashbacks and psychedelic editing, the film continually shows various viewpoints of the same situation, each one different. There's a sinister castle, a foreboding count (who may be the Devil) and lots of naked flesh; after several viewings, the whole thing still makes no sense. It is possibly Solvay at his most gratuitous and bizarre.

Other noteworthy genre contributions by Paolo Solvay: He directed the thriller *Blackmail* (1968) with Brigitte Skay; appeared as an actor in the film *La Strage dei Vampiri* (1962); and directed his last feature film *La Guerre du Pétrole* (*Black Gold*) in 1978.

Paolo Solvay Filmography (selected films)

La Bestia in Calore

A.k.a. *The Beast in Heat* (English translation and title); a.k.a. *SS Hell Camp*; a.k.a. *SS Experiment Part 2*; a.k.a. *Horrifying Experiments of SS Last Days* (English titles) (1977) (It.); D/SC: Paolo Solvay; P: Ciro Papa, Natalino Gullo; Prod. Co.: Eterna Film; C: Ugo Brunelli; M: Giuliano Sorgini; S: Macha Magall, Brad Harris, Kim Gatti, Salvatore Borghese, Xiro Papas, Alfredo Rizzo, Brigitte Skay.

Kaput Lager: Gli Ultimi Giorni delle SS

A.k.a. *Kaput Camp: The Last Days of the SS* (English translation); a.k.a. *Achtung! The Desert Tigers*; a.k.a. *The Desert Tigers* (English titles) (1976) (It.); D/SC: Paolo Solvay; P: Ciro Papa, Enrico Bomba; Prod. Co.: International Cine Holiday; C: Ugo Brunelli; M: Marcello Giombini; S: Richard Harrison, Isarco Ravaioli, Lea Kruger a.k.a. Lea Leander, Agnese Kalpagos, Gordon Mitchell a.k.a. Charles Pendleton, Brad Harris, Zaira Zoccheddu.

Nuda per Satana

A.k.a. *Nude for Satan* (English translation and title) (1974) (It.); D/SC: Paolo Solvay; P: Remo Angioli; C: Antonio Maccoppi; M: Alberto Baldan Bembo; S: James Harris a.k.a. Giuseppe "Pino" Mattei, Stelio Candelli, Rita Calderoni, Barbara Lay.

Il Plenilunio delle Vergini

A.k.a. *Full Moon Full of Virgins* (English translation); a.k.a. *Pleine Lune* (alternate Italian title); a.k.a. *The Season of the Virgin*; a.k.a. *Countess Dracula*; a.k.a. *The Devil's Wedding Night* (English titles) (1973) (It.); D: Paolo Solvay; P: Massimo Pupillo, Walter Bigari; Prod. Co.: Virginia CInematografica; SC: Paolo Solvay, Massimo Pupillo, Walter Bigari; C: Aristide Massaccesi; M. Vasil Kojucharov; S: Rosalba Neri a.k.a. Sara Bay, Mark Damon, Francesca Romana Davila, Esmerelda Barros, Xiro Papas, Sergio Pislar, Stefano Oppedisano.

EPILOGUE

The Future of Italian Horror Films

The future of Italian horror films appeared quite bleak until 2001. In fact, the whole Italian film industry was in a shambles. Beginning in the early '80s, signs of the downward turn became evident when the Italian box office was down to less than half of its mid–'70s audience strength and lessening each year. This trend was tied to the generally weak economic structure of the country and rising inflation. Within a short time, admission ticket prices rose dramatically. Despite this, several Italian film companies persevered and continued to make films that were drawing fewer audiences than ever in their homeland, but fared better as export releases or on the home video market. In the early '80s, there had been approximately 3,500 theaters; by 1992 that number had fallen to 1,200. It has been claimed that outmoded sound systems and a general lack of quality homegrown product all contributed to the decline in cinema audiences.

By the early '90s, Italian cinemas were experiencing their worse performance since the days of World War II and there was no end in sight. Since a lot of Italian films are subsidized by government money, which was in short supply, television corporations that sensed the seriousness of the situation stepped in as the problem began to affect, and eventually put out of business, smaller producers and distributors. By the early '90s, a many productions were financed by RAI, Radio Televisione Italiana (the state-owned television system), Fininvest and Penta Film, a company owned by Mario and Cecchi Gori. It is estimated that together these major television corporations provided up to 90 percent of the financing for all Italian movies in 1991. Many of the deals that involved television financing for feature films demanded that some of these productions be shown at some point before any theatrical release would take place.

Unfortunately, the rising cost of theatrical distribution (and the abysmal performance of many so-called prestige productions) would mean that many of these features never even made it to a theater and some of them have yet to appear on video in Italy. Consequently, the investors' interest in making horror films was minimal and a potential boon to any producers seeking tax write-offs from the government.

Many of the horror features that Lucio Fulci, Ruggero Deodato and Lamberto Bava worked on during this period were relegated to late-night television airings (and even then, for some, shown at obscure times of the night).

The Italian cinema output had dwindled to about 100 productions a year. The public displayed apathy towards movies that did not pique their current interest. Many filmmakers, and horror filmmakers for certain, found it increasingly difficult to get any sort of a theatrical release in a market already overly crowded with foreign films, many of them American hits.

These are some of the many reasons that some Italian horror films were sent directly to video, where they performed better in terms of sales. Or they were exported to other countries, where their box office success enabled the filmmaker would deliver more productions to television or design them for overseas audiences and tastes. At the beginning of each and every year since 1992, Italian film publicists proclaimed in the press that the next year would be better — which it was not.

In 1996, the worst was yet to come. Only 75 films were produced for that year, 60 of which were financed by television corporations with the remaining 15 productions paid for by foreign investors or by the few remaining, struggling independents. Things got even worse as government assistance for films drew back and provided less than one percent for all of the arts — not just film, but funding for all of the arts in total.

The time of the classic Italian horror films had long since passed. The days of the classic Gothics, *gialli* and the popular exploitation cycles, influenced by popular foreign films, are long since gone although there always remains the possibility of a renewed interest from filmmakers and audiences alike. Of the directors highlighted within this book, quite a few have contributed much in terms of providing groundbreaking entries in the genre of horror. Some that have survived the recent tough economic years continue to be involved in the filmmaking process and have moved on to specializing in other forms of cinematic entertainment. For example, the ever-prolific Aristide Massaccesi spent the last decade (until his untimely death) turning out an endless stream of pornographic films.

The few recent works of horror from Italian filmmakers worth mentioning have already been discussed at length elsewhere in this volume. They include Dario Argento's *Nonhosonno*, Michele Soavi's *Dellamorte, Dellamore*, Ruggero Deodato's *Vortice Mortale*, Mario Baino's *Dark Waters* and Sergio Stivaletti's *M.D.C.— La Maschera di Wax*.

There are now renewed hopes that the future of Italian horror films lay in the hands of one of its largest proponents, Dario Argento. Argento has been independently producing his own films for years. One of the reasons that it takes so long for a new Argento production to appear is that he finances his films partly with his own production company's money and partly from foreign investors.

It would be a great sign for the continuance of the Italian horror film if Argento's newest production, *Il Cartaio (The Card Player)*, a planned return to the classic *giallo* format, would be the film to spur more filmmakers to great heights. Since *Nonhosonno* had become a great success both critically and financially in Italy and has gained interest in other countries. Could this next film be the one to influence other Italian directors to once again take chances on a film genre that has been obviously lacking in powerful, quality product for the last few years?

Mario Bava's classic film *Diabolik* (1968, Dino De Laurentiis Cinematografica [Rome]/Marianne Productions [Pairs]) was a hybrid of many film genres. Possibly, something like it in the future will pave the way for a whole new generation of Italian genre filmmakers.

I met with Aristide Massaccesi in the fall of 1999 and spoke with him about his plans for the future. After becoming financially secure due to a string of profitable pornographic films, the director was planning on a comeback with a new horror production based on Michele Soavi's *Deliria*.

Essentially, Massaccesi said that the new project would be the same film, only different. Wonderful words of wisdom from a man who copied others. However, Massaccesi succumbed to a heart attack and died on January 23, 1999. His plans for a new horror film were never realized. Maybe some new director will come forth and provide a work of startling innovation. Maybe some veteran of the heyday of Italian horror will once again find the right elements and make another grand film that in its wake will spawn more of its kind. This is becoming more and more unlikely as the years pass and the filmmakers age. Many of the masters of the golden years of Italian horror that are still alive are in their seventies and eighties; some have retired; and those who still work in the business have contributed less and less to the genre which gave them their reputations.

For now, the legacy of the finest years of Italian horror will keep us entertained and cowering in fear, the reflections in black that they are.

APPENDIX

Important Horror (and Other Genre) Films by Other Directors

Abbreviations and Explanation of Terms

A.k.a.	Also known as	***Countries***	
		Fr.	France
Credits		G.	Germany (before 1939)
D:	Director	G.B.	Great Britain
P:	Producer	G.F.R.	German Federal Republic
S:	Starring	It.	Italy
SC:	Screenplay	Mex.	Mexico
C:	Cinematographer	Sp.	Spain
Prod. Co.:	Production Company	U.S.	United States
SP E:	Special Effects	W.G.	West Germany
Co.:	In Collaboration With	Ven.	Venezuela
		Yug.	Yugoslavia

Ad Ogni Costo

A.k.a. *Diamantes A Go-Go* (Spanish title); a.k.a. *Grand Slam*; a.k.a. *Top Job* (English titles) (1967) (It., Sp., W.G.); D: Giuliano Montaldo; P: Arrigo Colombo, Giorgio Papi, Franco Serino; Prod. Co.: Jolly Film (Rome)/Coral Producciones Cinematograficas/Constantin Film; SC: Augusto Caminito, Marcello Fondato, Jose Antonio De La Loma, Mino Roli; C: Antonio Macasoli; M: Ennio Morricone, Bruno Nicolai; S: Edward G. Robinson, Janet Leigh, Robert Hoffman a.k.a. Max Lindt a.k.a. Hans Schmidt, Klaus Kinski a.k.a. Klaus Gunther Nakszynksi, Jorge Rigaud, Riccardo Cucciolla, Adolfo Celli.

Agente 3S3: Massacro al Sole

A.k.a. *Agent 3S3 Massacre in the Sun* (English translation); a.k.a. *Agente 3S3 Massacre au Soleil* (French title; translation: *Agent 3S3 Massacre in the Sun*); a.k.a. *Agente 3S3 Enviado Especial* (Spanish title); a.k.a. *Hunter of the Unknown* (English titles) (1966) (It., Sp., Fr.); D: Sergio Sollima; Prod: Cineproduzione Associate (Rome)/Cesareo Gonzalez Producciones (Spain)/Films Copernic (France); SC: Alfonso Balcazar; C: Carlo Carlini; M: Piero Umiliani; S: Giorgio Ardisson, Frank Wolff, Fernando Sancho, Barbara Simons, Seyna Seyn, Evi Marandi, Michel Lemoine, Salvatore Borgese.

Agente 3S3: Passaporto per l'Inferno

A.k.a. *Agent 3S3 Passport to Hell*; a.k.a. *Agent 3S3 Passport for Hell* (English translations); a.k.a. *Agente 3S3: Operazione Inferno* (alternate Italian title); a.k.a. *Agente 3S3: Pasaporte para el Inferno* (Spanish title); a.k.a. *Passport to Hell* (English titles) (1965) (It., Fr., Sp.); D: Sergio Sollima; Prod Co.: Cineproduzioni Associate/Films Copernic/Producciones Cinematograficas Blacazar; SP: Sergio Sollima; C: Carlo Carlini; M: Piero Umiliani (Italian version only); S: Giorgio Ardisson, Barbara Simons, Jose Marco, Georges Riviere, Salvatore Borgese, Seyna Seyn.

Alien 2 sulla Terra

A.k.a. *Alien 2 on Earth* (English translation); a.k.a. *Alien Terror* (G.B.); a.k.a. *Alien 2* (English titles) (1980) (It.); D/SC: Ciro Ippolito; P: Ciro Ippolito, Angelo Stella; C: Silvio Fraschetti, Ordone Bernadini, Federico Del Zoppo; M: The Olivier Onions (Guido and Maurizio De Angelis); S: Belinda Mayne, Michele Soavi.

Amanti d'Oltretomba

A.k.a. *Lovers Beyond the Tomb* (English translation); a.k.a. *Night of the Doomed* (G.B.); a.k.a. *Nightmare Castle*; a.k.a. *The Faceless Monster*; a.k.a. *Orgasmo* (English titles) (1965) (It.); D: Mario Caiano; P: Mario Caiano; Prod. Co.: Produzioni Cinematografica Emmeci; SC: Mario Caiano, Fabio De Agostini; C: Enzo Barboni; M: Ennio Morricone; S: Barbara Steele, Paul Muller a.k.a. Paul Mueller, Helga Line a.k.a. Helga Lina Stern, Giuseppe Addobbati, Rik Battaglia.

Amico, Stammi Lontano Almeno un Palmo

A.k.a. *The Ballad of Ben and Charlie*; a.k.a. *Ben and Charlie*; a.k.a. *Amigo, Stay Away*; a.k.a. *Humpty Dumpty Gang* (English titles) (1972) (It.); D: Michele Lupo; Prod. Co.: Jupiter Generale Cinematografica; SC: Sergio Donati, George Eastman a.k.a. Luigi Montefiori; C: Aristide Massaccesi; M: Gianni Ferrio; S: Giuliano Gemma, George Eastman a.k.a. Luigi Montefiori, Vittorio Congia, Giacomo Rossi-Stuart, Marisa Mell a.k.a. Marlies Moitzi.

Arrivano Django e Sartana ... È la Fine

A.k.a. *Django and Sartana Are Coming ... It's the End* (English translation); a.k.a. *Django and Sartana ... Showdown in the West*; a.k.a. *Django Against Sartana*; a.k.a. *Sartana, If Your Left Arm Offends, Cut It Off* (English titles) (1970) (It.); D: Demofilo Fidani; Prod. Co.: Tarquinia Film; SC: Demofilo Fidani, Valenza; C: Aristide Massaccesi; M: Lallo Coriolani Gori; S: Hunt Powers, Chet Davis, Simone Blondell, Krista Nell.

L'Atleta Fantasma

(1919) (It.); D: Raimondo Scotti; P: A. De Giglio; Prod. Co: A. De Giglio; SC: Renee De Liot; S: Elsa Zara, Mario Guaita-Ausonia, Gaetano Rossi, Dino Bonaiuti.

Autostop Rosso Sangue

A.k.a. *Hitch-Hike Red Blood* (English translation); a.k.a. *Hitch-Hike*; a.k.a. *Hitch Hike*; a.k.a. *Death Drive*; a.k.a. *Never Give a Lift to a Stranger* (English titles) (1977) (It.); D: Pasquale Festa Campanile; P: Bruno Turchetto, Mario Montanari, Diego Alchimede; Prod. Co.: Explorer Film International S.r.l./Medusa Distribuzione S.r.l. SC: Aldo Crudo, based on Peter Kane's novel *The Violence and the Fury*; C: Franco Di Giacomo, Giuseppe Ruzzolini; M: Ennio Morricone; S: Franco Nero, Corinne Clery, David A. Hess, Gianni Loffredo, Carlo Puri, Pedro Sanchez, Monica Zanchi.

La Avventura di Annabella

(1937) (It.); D: Leo Menardi; Prod. Co.: A.C.I. (Alleanza Cinematografica Italiana); SC: Leo Menardi, Luigi Giacosi, Vittorio Metz, and Steno a.k.a. Stefano Vanzina.; C: Mario Bava; M: Gino Filippini; S: Fioretta Dolfi, Paola Borboni, Maurizio D'Ancora, Anna Magnani, Giuditta Rissone.; Production on this film is rumored to have begun in 1937 and finished in 1943.

Baba Yaga

A.k.a. *Black Magic*; a.k.a. *The Devil Witch*; a.k.a. *Kiss Me, Kill Me* (English titles) (1973) (It.); D: Corrado Farrina; P: Simone Allouche; SC: Corrado Farrina, Guido Crepax, based on *fumetti* created by Crepax; C: Aiace Parolin; M: Piero Umiliani; S: Carroll Baker, George Eastman, Isabelle De Funès, Daniela Balzaretti.

Il Baccio

A.k.a. *The Kiss* (English translation and title) (1974) (It.); D: Mario Lanfranchi; SC: Mario Lanfranchi, Pupi Avati; C: Claudio Collepiccolo; M: Piero Piccioni; S: Maurizio Bonuglia, Eleonora Giorgi, Martine Beswick, Vladek Sheybal.

La Bambola

A.k.a. *The Puppet*; a.k.a. *The Doll* (English translations) (1972) (It.); D: Mario Foglietti; P: Dario Argento; Prod. Co.: RAI Radiotelevisione Italiana presents a SEDA Spettacoli S.p.A. (Rome) Production; SC: Mario Foglietti, Marcella Elsberger; C: Elio Polacchi; M: Giorgio Gaslini; S: Mara Venier, Robert Hoffman a.k.a. Hans Schmidt a.k.a. Max Lindt, Erika Blanc a.k.a. Erika Bianchi Colombatto, Gianfranco D'Angelo; Episode of the Italian television program *La Porta sul Buio* (a.k.a. *The Door to Darkness*).

La Bambola di Satana

A.k.a. *Satan's Baby Doll* (English translation); a.k.a. *Satan's Doll* (English title) (1969) (It.); D: Ferruccio Casapinta; Prod. Co.: Cinediorama; SC: Ferruccio Casapinta, Carlo Lori, Giorgio Cristallini; C: Francesco Attenni; M: Franco Potenza; S: Erna Schurer a.k.a. Erna Scheurer, Roland Carey, Aurora Battista, Ettore Ribotta, Lucia Bornez, Manlio Salvatori, Franco Daddi.

Il Bambule

(1979) (It.); D/P/SC: Marco Modugno; C: Michele Penelope, Michele Soavi; M: Marco Modugno, Marcello Modugno; S: Marco Modugno, Dario Silvagni, Cico Diaz, Fulvia Midulla, Michele Soavi.

La Battaglia di Maratona

A.k.a. *The Battle of Marathon* (English translation); a.k.a.*The Giant of Marathon* (English title) (1959) (It., Fr.); D: Jacques Tourneur, Bruno Vailati, Mario Bava (uncredited); P: Bruno Vailati; Prod. Co.: Titanus/Galatea Film (Milan)/Lux Film (Rome)/Société Cinématographique Lyre (Paris); SC: Bruno Vailati, Ennio De Concini, Augusto Frassinetti, Raffaello Pacini, Alberto Barsanti; C: Mario Bava; M: Roberto Nicolosi; S: Steve Reeves, Mylene Demongeot, Danielle Rocca, Sergio Fantoni, Ivo Garrani, Alberto Lupo, Philippe Hersent, Daniele Varga, Miranda Campa.

Caligola

A.k.a. *Caligula* (English translation and title) (1979) (U.S./It.); D: Tinto Brass, Bob Guccione, Giancarlo Lui (additional material); P: Bob Guccione, Franco Rossellini, Jack H. Silverman; Prod. Co.: Penthouse Films (New York)/Felix Cinematografica (Rome); SC: Gore Vidal, Masolino D'Amico; C: Tinto Brass, Silvano Ippolito; M: Paul Clemente, featuring music by Khatchaturian, Prokofiev; S: Malcolm McDowell, Teresa Ann Savoy, Helen Mirren, Peter O'Toole, John Gielgud, Adriana Asti, Guido Mannari, Giancarlo Badessi, Mirella D'Angelo, Gerardo Amato, Leopoldo Trieste, Lori Wagner.

La Carrozza d'Oro

A.k.a. *The Golden Coach* (English translation and title); a.k.a. *La Carrosse d'Or* (French title?) (1952) (It., Fr.); D: Jean Renoir; P: Francesco Alliata; Prod. Co.: Panaria Film/Hoche Productions; SC: Jean Renoir, Jack Kirkland, Renzo Avanzo, Giulio Macchi, based on the play by Prospero Merimee; C: Claude Renoir; M: Antonio Vivaldi; S: Anna Magnani, Duncan Lamont, Paul Campbell, Riccardo Rioli, Edoardo Spadaro.

Il Castello dei Morti Vivi

A.k.a. *The Castle of the Living Dead* (English translation and title); a.k.a. *Le Chateau des Morts Vivants* (French title); a.k.a. *Crypt of Horror* (English title) (1964) (It., Fr.); D: Luciano Ricci, Warren Keifer (uncredited), Michael Reeves (uncredited); P: Paul Maslansky; Prod. Co.: Serena Film (Rome)/Francinor (Paris); SC: Warren Keifer, Michael Reeves (uncredited); C: Aldo Tonti; M: Angelo Francesco Lavagnino; S: Christopher Lee, Gaia Germani, Philippe Leroy, Mirko Valentin, Antonio De Martino, Donald Sutherland, Jacques Stanislawski, Luciano Pigozzi.

Il Castello della Paura

A.k.a. *The Castle of Fear* (English translation); a.k.a. *Il Castello dell'Orrore* (alternate Italian title); a.k.a. *Il Castello delle Donne Maldette* (alternate Italian title); a.k.a. *Terror Castle*; a.k.a. *Terror*; a.k.a. *The House of Freaks*; a.k.a. *The Monsters of Frankenstein*; a.k.a. *Frankenstein's Castle of Freaks* (English titles) (1973) (It.); D: Robert H. Oliver a.k.a. Ramiro Oliveros; P: Dick Randall, Robert Straub; Prod. Co.: Classic Films International (Rome);

C: Mario Mancini; M: Marcello Ciccarella; S: Rossano Brazzi, Michael Dunn, Edmund Purdom, Christiane Rucker, Salvatore Borgese, Gordon Mitchell a.k.a. Charles Pendleton, Luciano Pigozzi, Xiro Papas, Simone Blondel, Eric Mann.

C'era una Volta il West

A.k.a. *Once Upon a Time in the West* (English translation and title); (1968) (It., U.S.); D: Sergio Leone; P: Sergio Leone, Fulvio Moresella; Prod. Co.: Rafran Cinematografica/San Marco Cinematografica/Euro; International Films/Paramount Pictures Corporation; SC: Sergio Leone, Sergio Donati, Dario Argento, Bernardo Bertolucci; C: Tonino Delli Colli; M: Ennio Morricone; S: Henry Fonda, Charles Bronson, Jason Robards, Claudia Cardinale, Gabriele Ferzetti, Keenan Wynn, Paola Stoppa, Lionel Stander, Jack Elam, Woody Strode, Enzio Santianello.

Chi Sei?

A.k.a. *Who?* (English translation); a.k.a. *The Devil Within Her*; a.k.a. *Beyond the Door* (English titles) (1974) (It.); D: Oliver Hellman a.k.a. Ovidio Assonitis, Sonia Assonitis (uncredited), Roberto D'Ettore Piazzoli (uncredited); P: Enzo Doria, Oliver Hellman a.k.a. Ovidio Assonitis, Giorgio C. Rossi; Prod. Co.: A. Erre Cinematografica; SC: Oliver Hellman a.k.a. Ovidio Assonitis, Sonia Assonitis, Roberto D'Ettorre Piazzoli, Antonio Gentilomo, Marini Aldo Crudo; C: Roberto D'Ettoree Piazzoli; M: Franco Micalizzi; SP E: SPEAC, supervised by Donn Davison (?), Wally Gentilomo; S: Juliet Mills, Richard Johnson, Gabriele Lavi, Nino Segurini, Elisabeth Turner, Carla Mancini, Barbara Fiorini, David Collin Jr., Vittorio Fanfoni.

Chicken Park

(1994) (It.); D: Jerry Cala; SC: Gino Capone, Galliano Juno; M: Giovanni Nuti, Umberto Smaila; C: Blasco Giurato; SP E: Antonio Margheriti; S: Jerry Cala, Demetra Hampton, Paolo Paolini, Simone Canosa, Rossy De Palma.

Cimitero Senza Croci

A.k.a. *Cemetery Without Crosses* (English translation and G.B. title); a.k.a. *Une Corde, un Colt* (French title) (1968) (Fr., It.); D: Robert Hossein; P: Jean-Charles Raffini, Jean-Pierre Labatut; Prod. Co.: Loisirs Du Monde S.A. (Paris)/Films Copernic (Paris)/Fono Roma (Rome); SC: Robert Hossein, Claude Desailly, Dario Argento; C: Henri Persin; M: Andre Jean Mandaroux; S: Robert Hossein, Michele Mercier, Lee Burton a.k.a. Guido Lollobrigida, Beatrice Altariba.

Commandamenti per un Gangster

A.k.a. *Commandments for a Gangster* (English translation) (1968) (It., Yugo.); D: Alfio Caltabiano; P: Salvatore Argento; Prod. Co.: Triumph Film 67/Prodi Cinematografica/Avala Film, Belgrade; SC: Alfio Caltabiano, Dario Argento; C: Milorad Markovic; M: Ennio Morricone; S: Ljuba Tadic, Al Northon, Syr John, Dante Maggio, Giancarlo Marrad, Dusan Janicijevic.

Dawn of the Mummy

(1981) (It., U.S., Egypt); D/P: Frank Agrama a.k.a. Farouk Agrama; Prod. Co.: Harmony Gold; SC: Frank Agrama a.k.a. Farouk Agrama, Daria Price, Ronald Dobrin; C: Sergio

Rubini; M: Shuki Y. Levy, Steve Rucker; SP E: Marizio Trani; S: Brenda King, Barry Sattels, George Peck, John Salvo, Joan Levy, Diane Beatty, Ibrahim Khan, Ali Gohar, Ahmed Ratib, Baher Saied, Ali Azab.

Il Decameron

(1970) (It.); D: Pier Paolo Pasolini; P: Alberto Grimaldi, Franco Rossellini; SC: Pier Paolo Pasolini, based on Giovanni Boccaccio's *Decameron*; C: Tonino Delli Colli; M: Pier Paolo Pasolini, Ennio Morricone; S: Franco Citti, Jovan Jovanovic, Vincenzo Amato, Giuseppe Zigaina, Gabriella Frankel, Silvana Mangana.

Delitto allo Specchio

A.k.a. *Crime in the Mirror* (English translation); a.k.a. *Delitto allo Specchio — Sexy Party* (alternate Italian title; translation: *Crime in the Mirror — Sexy Party*); a.k.a. *Les Possédées du Demon* (French title); a.k.a. *Sex Party* (English title) (1963) (It., Sp., Fr.); D: Jean Josipovici, Ambroglio Molteni; P: Jean Josipovici, Pasquale Tagliaferri; Prod. Co.: P.T. Cinematografica (Rome)/Jean Josipovici (Paris); SC: Jean Josipovici, Giorgio Stegani; C: Raffaele Masciocchi; M: Marcello De Martino; S: John Drew Barrymore, Antonella Lualdi, Gloria Milland, Michel Lemoine, Mario Valdemarin, Luisa Rivelli, Jose Greci, Maria Pia Conti.

Il Delitto del Diavolo

A.k.a. *The Crimes of the Devil* (English translation); a.k.a. *Les Sorcières* (French title); a.k.a. *Les Sorcières du Bord du Lac* (alternate French title); a.k.a. *Le Regine* (alternate French title); a.k.a. *Queens of Evil*; a.k.a. *Witches of the Lake* (English titles) (1971) (It., Fr.); D: Tonino Cervi; P: Raoul Katz, Alessandro Troisio; Prod. Co.: Flavia Cinematografica/Carlton Film Export/Labrador Film; SC: Tonino Cervi, Antonio Benedetti, Antonio Troisio; C: Sergio D'Offizi; M: Angelo Francesco Lavagnino; S: Raymond Lovelock, Haydee Politoff, Evelyn Stewart a.k.a. Ida Galli, Silvia Monti, Gianni Santuccio, Guido Alberti.

Django

(1967) (It., Sp.); D: Sergio Corbucci; P: Sergio Corbucci, Manolo Bolognini; Prod. Co.: B.R.C. Produzione/TECISA; SC: Bruno Corbucci, Sergio Corbucci; C: Enzo Barboni; M: Luis Enriquez Bacalov; S: Franco Nero, Loredana Nusciak, Jose Bodalo, Angel Alvarrez, Eduardo Fajardo.

Un Dollaro a Testa

A.k.a. *A Dollar a Head* (English translation and title); a.k.a. *Navajo Joe* (English title) (1966) (It., Sp.); D: Sergio Corbucci; P: Ermanno Donati, Luigi Carpentieri; Prod. Co.: Dino Di Laurentiis Cinematografica/C.B. Films; SC: Fernando Di Leo, Mario Pierotti; C: Silvano Ippoliti; M: Ennio Morricone; S: Burt Reynolds, Aldo Sanbrell a.k.a. Aldo Sambrell a.k.a. Alfredo Sanchez Brell, Nicoletta Machiavelli, Fernando Rey, Tanya Lopert, Franca Polesello.

Due Mafiosi Contra Goldginger

A.k.a. *Two Mafia Guys Vs. Goldginger* (English translation and title); a.k.a. *Operación Relampago* (Spanish title); a.k.a. *The Amazing Dr. G* (English title) (1965) (It., Sp.); D: Giorgio Simonelli; Prod. Co.: Fida Cinematografica/Epoca Films; SC: Marcello Ciorciolini, Sandro

Continenza, Bautista Lacasa Nebot, Amedeo Sollazo, Dino Verde; C: Isidoro Goldberger, Juan Ruiz Romero; M: Piero Umiliani, Angelo Francesco Lavagnino; S: Franco Franchi, Ciccio Ingrassia, Gloria Paul, Fernando Rey, George Hilton, Lino Banfi.

Emanuelle Nera N.2

A.k.a. *Black Emanuelle No. 2* (English translation); a.k.a. *Black Emanuelle 2*; a.k.a. *The New Black Emanuelle* (G.B.) (English titles) (1976) (It.); D: Adalberto Bitto Albertini; P: Mario Mariani, Agostino Pane; Prod. Co.: San Nicola Produzione Cinematografiche; SC: Adalberto Bitto Albertini, Palmabrogio Molteni, Mario Mariani; C: Guglielmo Mancori; M: Don Powell, Alfonso Zenga, songs "Love Rock" and "Going to Hawaii" performed by Don Powell and The Peppers; S: Emanuelle Neri a.k.a. Shulasmith Lasri, Angelo Infanti, Sharon Leslie, Don Powell, Percy Hogan, Dagmar Lassander, Peter McCoy a.k.a. Pietro Torrisi, Franco Daddi, Attilio Dottesio, Danielle Ellison, Franco Cremoni.

Ercole e la Regina di Lidia

A.k.a. *Hercules and the Queen of Lydia* (English translation); a.k.a. *Hercules Unchained* (English title) (1959) (It., Fr.); D: Pietro Francisci; P: Bruno Vailati; Prod. Co.: Lux Film (Rome)/Galatea Film (Milan); SC: Pietro Francisci, Ennio De Concini; C: Mario Bava; M: Enzo Masetti; S: Steve Reeves, Sylva Koscina, Sylvia Lopez, Patrizia Della Rovere, Primo Canera, Carlo D'Angelo, Sergio Fantoni, Andrea Fantasia, Gianni Loti.

Un Esercito di Cinque Uomini

A.k.a. *The Five Man Army* (English title) (1969) (It., Sp.); D: Don Taylor, Italo Zingarelli (Italian version credit only); P: Italo Zingarelli; Prod. Co.: Tiger Film; SC: Dario Argento, Marc Richards; C: Enzo Barboni; M: Ennio Morricone; S: Peter Graves, James Daly, Bud Spencer a.k.a. Carlo Pedersoli, Tetsuro Tamba, Nino Castelnuovo, Daniela Giordano, Claudio Gora, Annabella Andreoli, Giacomo Rossi-Stuart, Marc Lawrence.

L'Esorciccio

(1975) (It.); D: Ciccio Ingrassia; P: Rosario Cali; C: Guglielmo Mancori; M: Franco Godi; S: Ciccio Ingrassia, Ubalda Lay, Lino Banfi, Didi Perego, Barbara Nascimbene.

Eva, la Venere Selvaggia

A.k.a. *Eve, the Wild Woman*; a.k.a. *Eve, the Savage Venus* (English translations and titles) (1968) (It.); D: Roberto Mauri; P: Ralph Zucker, Walter Brandi, Dick Randall; SC: Ralph Zucker; C: Mario Mancini; M: Roberto Pregadio; S: Esmeralda Barros, Brad Harris, Marc Lawrence, Ursula Davis, Adriana Alben.

Le Fatiche di Ercole

A.k.a. *The Labors of Hercules* (English translation); a.k.a. *Hercules* (English title) (1957) (It.); D: Pietro Francisci; P: Ferruccio De Martino, Joseph E. Levine (U.S. version credit only); Prod. Co.: O.S.C.A.R. Film/Galatea Film (Milan); SC: Pietro Francisci, Ennio De Concini, based on *Argonautica* by Apollonius of Rhodes; C: Mario Bava; M: Enzo Masetti, Carlo Savina; SP E: Mario Bava; S: Steve Reeves, Sylva Koscina, Gianna Maria Canale, Fabrizio Mioni, Ivo Garrani, Arturo Dominici, Mimmo Palmara, Lidia Alfonsi, Luciana Paluzzi.

La Figlia di Frankenstein

A.k.a. *The Daughter of Frankenstein* (English translation); a.k.a. *Frankenstein's Daughter*; a.k.a. *Madame Frankenstein*; a.k.a. *Lady Frankenstein* (English titles) (1971) (It.); D/P: Mel Welles; Prod. Co.: Condor International; SC: Eduardo Di Lorenzo; C: Riccardo Pallottini; M: Alessandro Alessesandroni; SP E: C.I.P.A., Carlo Rambaldi; S: Sara Bay a.k.a. Rosalba Neri, Joseph Cotten, Mickey Hargitay, Paul Mueller, Herbert Fuchs, Renata Kashe, Ada Pometti, Lorenzo Terzon, Giovanni Lofredo, Romano Puppo.

4...3...2...1...Morte!

A.k.a. *Quattro ... Tre ... Due ... Uno ... Morte*; a.k.a. *Four ... Three ... Two ... One ... Death* (English translation); a.k.a. *Orbita Mortal*; a.k.a. *Operazione Stardust* (alternate Italian titles); a.k.a. *Perry Rhodan — SOS Aus Dem Weltall* (German title); a.k.a. *Alarm im Weltall* (alternate German title); a.k.a. *4-3-2-1–Muerto* (Spanish title); a.k.a. *Mission Stardust* (English title) (1967) (It., Sp., W.G.); D: Primo Zeglio; Prod. Co.: P.E.A.-Produzioni Europee Associate (Naples)/Aitor Films/Tritone Filmindustria Roma/Theumer Film (Munich); SC: Primo Zeglio, K.H. Vogelmann, Sergio Donati; C: Riccardo Pallottini; M: Marcello Giombini; S: Essy Persson, Lang Jeffries, Luis Davila, Daniele Martin, Gianni Rizzo.

Frankenstein '80

A.k.a. *Frankenstein Mosaico* (alternate Italian title); a.k.a. *Mosaico* (alternate Italian title); a.k.a. *The Orgies of Frankenstein*; a.k.a. *Midnight Horror*; a.k.a. *Frankenstein 2000* (English titles) (1973) (It.); D: Mario Mancini; P: Benedetto Graziani; Prod. Co.: M.G.D. Film; SC: Mario Mancini, Ferdinando Di Leo; C: Emilio Varriano; M: Daniele Patucchi; SP E: Carlo Rambaldi; S: John Richardson, Renato Romano, Xiro Papas, Gordon Mitchell a.k.a. Charles Pendleton, Dalia Di Lazzaro.

I Fratti Rossi

A.k.a. *The Red Monks* (English translation and title) (1988) (It.); D: Gianni Martucci; P: Pino Buricchi; Production Supervisor: Lucio Fulci; Prod. Co.: Natmas Productions; SC: Gianni Martucci, Pino Buricchi; C: Sergio Rubini; S: Gerardo Amato, Lara Wendel, Malisa Longo, Claudio Pacifico, Mary Maxwell, Ronald Russo.

Fuga dalla Morte

A.k.a. *Escape from the Dead*; a.k.a. *Bloody Moon* (English titles) (1989) (It.); D: Enzo Milioni; SC: Enzo Milioni, Giovanni Simonelli; M: Paolo Gatti, Alfonso Zenga; S: Zora Kerova a.k.a. Zora Ulla Keslerova Tschechin, Jacques Semas, Barbara Blasco, Alex Berger.

Furia in Marrakech

A.k.a. *Fury in Marakesh* (English translation and title); a.k.a. *Death Pays in Dollars* (English title) (1965) (It., Fr.); D: J. Lee Donan A.k.a. Mino Loy, Luciano Martino; P: Mino Loy and Luciano Martino; Prod. Co.: Zenith Cinematografica (Italy)/Radius Productions (France); SP: Ernesto Gastaldi, Luciano Martino; C: Floriano Trenker; M: Carlo Savina; S: Stephen Forsythe, Dominique Boschero, Jacques Ary, Cristina Gajoni, Mitsouko.

Genghis Khan

(1993) (It., Poland, Hungary); D: Ken Annakin; P: Enzo Rispoli; SC: Andrzej Krakowski; SP E: Antonio Margheriti; Begun production in 1991, and reportedly finished in 1993 for Italian television as a co-production.

I Giorni della Violenza

A.k.a. *Days of Violence* (English translation and title) (1967) (It.); D: Alfonso Brescia; P: Bruno Turchetto; SC: Antonio Boccaci, Mario Amendola, Gian Luigi Buzzi, Paolo Lombardo; C: Fausto Rossi; M: Bruno Nicolai; S: Peter Lee Lawrence, Rosalba Neri, Beba Loncar, Andrea Bosic.

Giovanni dalle Bande Nere

(1952) (It.); D: Sergio Grieco; P: Ottavio Poggi; Prod. Co.: P.O. Film; SC: Alessandro Cotinenza, Italo De Tuddo, Ottavio Poggi, Carlo Veo, based on a novel by Luigi Capranica; C: Alvaro Mancori; M: Roberto Nicolosi; S: Vittorio Gassman, Anna Maria Ferrero, Gerard Landry, Constance Smith, Phillipe Hersent.

Giù la Testa

A.k.a. *Duck! You Sucker!* (English translation and title); a.k.a. *A Fistful of Dynamite* (English title) (1971) (It.); D: Sergio Leone; P: Fulvio Morsella, Claudio Mancini, Ugo Tucci; Prod. Co.: Rafran Cinematografica/San Marco Cinematografica/Miura; SC: Sergio Leone, Sergio Donati; C: Giuseppe Ruzzolini, Franco Delli Colli; M: Ennio Morricone; S: Rod Steiger, James Coburn, Romolo Valli, Maria Monti, Rik Battaglia, Antoine Saint Jean, Franco Graziosi.

Goldface, il Fantastico Superman

A.k.a. *Goldface, the Fantastic Superman* (English translation and title) (1967) (It., Sp.); D: Adalberto Abelterini; Prod. Co.: Cineproduzioni Associate (Rome)/Producciones Cinematograficas Balcazar (Barcelona); SC: Alberto Albertini, Ambroglio Molteni, Italo Fasan; C: Carlo Fiore; M: Franco Pisano; S: Robert Anthony a.k.a. Espartaco Santoni, Evi Marandi, Manuel Monroy, Ugo Pimentel, Big Matthews, Micaela Pignatelli.

Hansel e Gretel

A.k.a. *Hansel and Gretel* (English translation and title) (1989) (It.); D/SC: Giovanni Simonelli; P: Luigi Nannerini, Antonio Lucidi; Prod. Co.: Cold Duck; C: Silvano Tessicini; M: Lanfranco Perini; S: Elisabete Pimenta Boaretto, Vincenzo Lotti, Lucia Prato, Ronald Russo, Giorgio Cerioni, Maurice Poli.

L'Interno di un Convento

A.k.a. *The Interior of a Convent* (English translation); a.k.a. *Behind Convent Walls*; a.k.a. *Behind the Convent Walls* (English titles) (1977) (It.); D/SC: Walerian Borowczyk, based on the novel *Promenade dans Rome* by Stendahl; P: Giuseppe Vezzani, Carmelo Bianco; Prod. Co.: Trust International Films; C: Luciano Tovoli; M: Sergio Montori, song "La Rosa È il Più Bel Fiore" performed by Ligia Branice; S: Ligia Branice, Marina Pierro, Gabriella Giaccobe, Loredana Martinez, Mario Maranzana, Rodolfo Dal Prà, Renato Rossini, Olivia Pascal.

Interzone

(1986) (It.); D: Deran Sarafian; P: Aristide Massaccesi; Prod. Co.: Filmirage/Transworld Entertainment (?); C: Lorenzo Battaglia; SC: Claudio Fragrasso, Deran Sarafian, Carol Marini, Rossella Drudi (Fragrasso's wife) [uncredited]; S: Bruce Abbott, Beatrice Ring, Teagan Clive, John Armstead, Kiro Wehara, Alain Smith, Franco Giogene, Laura Gemser.

Isabel, Duchessa del Diavoli

A.k.a. *Isabel, Duchess of the Devils* (English translation and title) (1969) (It., Monaco); D: Bruno Corbucci; P: Prod. Co.: Cinescolo/INDIEF/Hape Film; SC: Giorgio Cavedon, Mario Amendola, Elisabeth Forster; C: Fausto Zuccoli; S: Brigitte Skay, Tino Scotti, Mimmo Palmara, Fred Williams a.k.a. Frederick Williams, Emina De Witt, Salvatore Borgese, Renato Baldini, Enzo Andronico.

L'Isola del Tesoro

A.k.a. *Treasure Island* (English translation and title) (1972) (It., G.B., Fr., Sp., W.G.); D: Andrea Bianchi, John Hough; P: Harry Alan Towers, George Davis; Prod. Co.: Massfilms/Productions F.D.L./C.C.C. Filmkunst/Eguiluz Films (Madrid); SC: Orson Welles, Wolf Mankowitz, based on the novel *Treasure Island* by Robert Louis Stevenson; C: Cecilio Paniagua, Ginger Gemmell; M: Natale Massara; S: Orson Welles, Kim Burfield, Lionel Stander, Walter Slezak, Angel Del Pozo, Rik Battaglia, Maria Rohm, Paul Mueller, Jean Lefevbre, Aldo Sanbrell a.k.a. Aldo Sambrell a.k.a. Alfredo Sanchez Brell, Victor Israel.

L'Isola della Svedesi

A.k.a. *The Island of the Swedes* (English translation); a.k.a. *Twisted Girls* (English title) (1969) (It.); D: Silvio Amadio; P: Gino Mordini; Prod. Co.: Claudia Cinematografica; SC: Silvio Amadio, Roberto Natale, Gino Mordini; C: Aristide Massaccesi; M: Roberto Pregado; S: Ewa Green, Catherine Daimant, Nino Segurini, Wolfgang Hillinger.

Johnny Oro

(1966) (It.); D: Sergio Corbucci; P: Joseph Fryd; Prod. Co.: Sanson Film; SC: Amelia Zurlini, Adriano Bolzoni, Franco Rossetti; C: Riccardo Pallottini; M: Carlo Savina; S: Mark Damon, Valeria Fabrizi, Franco De Rosa, Giulia Rubini, Andrea Aureli, Ettore Manni, Ken Wood a.k.a. Giovanni Cianfriglia.

Libido

(1966) (It.); D/P: Ernesto Gastaldi; Prod. Co.: Nucleo Film; SC: Ernesto Gastaldi, Vittorio Salerno, Mara Maryl a.k.a. Maria Chianetta; C: Romolo Garroni; S: Giancarlo Giannini, Dominique Boschero, Mara Maryl a.k.a. Maria Chianetta, Luciano Pigozzi.

La Llama nel Corpo

A.k.a. *A Blade in the Body*; a.k.a.*The Knife in the Body*; a.k.a. *The Blade in the Body* (English translations and titles); a.k.a. *Les Nuits de l'Épouvante* (French title; translation: *The Nights of Terror*); a.k.a.*The Murder Clinic*; a.k.a.*The Murder Society*; a.k.a. *The Revenge of the Living Dead* (English titles) (1966) (It., Fr.); D: Elio Scardamaglia, Domenici De Felice (uncredited); P: Elio Scardamaglia, Francesco Scardamaglia; Prod. Co.: Leone Film (Rome)/Orphee Productions (Paris)/Société Française de Cinématographique (Paris); SC: Ernesto Gastaldi, Luciano Martino, based on the novel *A Knife in the Body* by Robert Williams; C: Marcello Masciocchi; M: Francesco De Masi; S: William Berger, Francoise Prevost, Mary Young a.k.a. Anna Maria Polani, Barbara Wilson, Delphine Maurin, Massimo Righi, Harriet Medin White, Phillipe Hersent.

La Lunga Notte di Veronique

A.k.a. *The Long Night of Veronique*; a.k.a. *Veronique's Long Night* (English translations and titles); a.k.a. *But You Were Dead?* (English title) (1966) (It.); D: Gianni Vernuccio; P: Oscar Righini; Prod. Co. Mercurfilm Italiana; SC: Gianni Vernuccio, Enzo Ferraris.; M: Giorgio Gaslani; S: Alex Morrison a.k.a. Sandro Luporini, Alba Rigazzi, Walter Poggi, Cristina Gajoni, Tony Bellani, Gianni Ruben, Marco Righini.

M.D.C.—La Maschera di Wax

A.k.a. *Wax Mask*; a.k.a. *Gaston Leroux's House of Wax* (English titles) (1997) (It., Fr.); D: Sergio Stivaletti; P: Dario Argento, Giuseppe Colombo; Prod. Co.: Cine 2000/Mediaset/France Film International; SC: Lucio Fulci, Daniele Stroppa, based on the original story by Gaston Leroux; C: Sergio Salvatti; M: Maurizio Abeni; S: Robert Hossein, Romina Mondello, Riccardo Serventi Longhi, Gabriella Giorgelli, Valery Valmond, Aldo Massasso.

Maciste Contro il Vampiro

A.k.a. *Maciste Against the Vampires* (English translation); a.k.a. *Goliath Vs. the Vampires*; a.k.a. *Goliath and the Vampires*; a.k.a. *The Vampires* (English titles) (1961) (It.); D: Sergio Corbucci, Giacomo Gentilomo; P: Paola Moffa, Dino De Laurentiis; Prod. Co.: Societa' Ambrosiana Cinematografica; SC: Sergio Corbucci, Duccio Tessari; C: Alvaro Mancori; M: Angelo Francesco Lavagnino; S: Gordon Scott, Gianna Maria Canale, Leonora Ruffo, Annabella Incontrera, Guido Celano, Jacques Sernas, Rocco Vitolazzi, Mario Feliciani.

Malenka—La Nipote del Vampiro

A.k.a. *Malenka, the Niece of the Vampire* (English translation and title); a.k.a. *Malenka—La Subrina del Vampiro*; a.k.a. *La Nipote del Vampiro* (Spanish titles); a.k.a. *Malenka*; a.k.a. *Fangs of the Living Dead* (English titles) (1968) (Sp., It.); D/SC: Amando De Ossorio; Prod. Co.: Cobra Films Productions, Victory Film (Rome)/Triton Films (Madrid); C: Fulvio Testi; M: Carlo Savina; S: Anita Ekberg, Julian Ugarte, Gianni Medici, Diana Lorys, Adriana Ambesi, Rosanna Yanni, Paul Mueller.

Il Medium

A.k.a. *The Medium* (English title) (1951) (It., U.S.); D: Gian-Carlo Menotti, Alexander Hackenschmied; P: Walter Lowendahl; Prod. Co.: Walter Lowendahl Productions/Transfilm Productions; SC: Gian-Carlo Menotti, based on his original opera "The Medium"; C: Enzo Serafin; Musical Conductor: Thomas Schippers; S: Marie Powers, Anna Maria Alberghetti, Leo Coleman, Belva Kibler, Donald Morgan, Beverly Dame.

Metamorphosis

A.k.a. *Regenerator* (G.B.) (English title) (1989) (It.); D/SC: George Eastman a.k.a. Luigi Montefiori; P: Aristide Massaccesi; Prod. Co.: Filmirage; C: Lorenzo Battaglia; M:

Pahamian; S: Gene Le Brock, Catherine Carson, David Wicker, Stephen Brown, Jason Arnold, Anna Colona, Laura Gemser, Allison Stokes.

Metti, Una Sera a Cena

A.k.a. *One Night at Dinner* (English translation and title); a.k.a. *The Love Circle* (G.B.) (English title) (1968) (It.); D: Giuseppe Patroni Griffi; P: Marina Cicogna, Giovanni Bertolucci; Prod. Co.: Red Film/Finanziaria San Marco; SC: Giuseppe Patron Griffi, Dario Argento, Carlo Patroni Griffi, based on the play by Griffi; C: Tonino Della Colli; M: Ennio Morricone, Bruno Nicolai; S: Tony Musante, Jean-Louis Trintignant, Florinda Bolkan a.k.a. Florinda Bulcao, Lino Capolicchio.

La Monaca Musulmana

A.k.a. *The Muslim Nun* (English translation); a.k.a. *Flavia, la Monaca Musulmana* (alternate Italian title); a.k.a. *Flavia, the Muslim Nun* (English translation); a.k.a. *Flavia, Priestess of Violence*; a.k.a. *Flavia, the Heretic* (English titles) (1974) (It., Fr.); D: Gianfranco Mingozzi; Prod. Co.: P.A.C./ROC; SC: Gianfranco Mingozzi, Raniero Di Giombattista, Sergio Tai, Francesco Vieltri, Fabrizio Onofri, Bruno Di Geronimo; C: Alfio Contin; M: Nicola Piovani; S: Florinda Bolkan a.k.a. Florinda Bulcao, Maria Casares, Claudio Cassinelli, Spiros Focas.

Moses, the Lawgiver

A.k.a. *Moses*; a.k.a. *Moses in Egypt* (alternate English titles) (1973/75) (It., G.B.); D: Gianfranco De Bosin; P: Vincenzo Labella; Prod. Co.: Radiotelevisione Italiana/ITC; SC: Gianfranco De Bosin, Anthony Burgess, Vittorio Bonicelli; C: Marcello Gatti; M: Ennio Morricone, Dov Seltzer; SP E: Mario Bava; S: Burt Lancaster, Anthony Quayle, Ingrid Thulin, Irene Papas, Aharon Ipale, Yousef Shiloah, Marina Berti, Mariangela Melato, Umberto Raho, Paul Mueller, narration by Richard Johnson (in English version only).

Il Mostro di Frankenstein

A.k.a.*The Monster of Frankenstein* (English translation); a.ka. *Frankenstein's Monster* (English title?) (1920) (It.); D: Eugenio Testa; P: Luciano Albertini; Prod. Co.: Albertini Film; SC: Giovanni Drivetti; C: Alvaro De Simone; S: Luciano Albertini, Umberto Guarracino.

Il Mostro di Venezia

A.k.a. *The Monster of Venice* (English translation); a.k.a. *The Embalmer* (English title) (1965) (It.); D: Dino Tavella; P: Antonio Walter a.k.a. Christian Marvel; Prod. Co.: Gondola Film; SC: Dino Tavella, Antonio Walter; C: Mario Parapetti; M: Marcello Gigante; S: Maureen Lidgard Brown, Gino Marturano, Luciano Gasper, Anita Todesco, Alcide Gazzotto, Alba Brotto, Elmo Caruso, Viki Del Castillo.

Nel Nido del Serpente

A.k.a. *The Snake House*; a.k.a. *Bloody Psycho* (English titles) (1989) (It.); D: Leandro Lucchetti; Prod. Co.: Cold Duck; SC: Leandro Lucchetti, Giovanni Simonelli; C: Silvano Tessicini; M: Lanfranco Perini; S: Peter Hinz, Louise Kamsteeg, Nubia Martini, Brigitte Chri.

No Grazie, il Caffè Mi Rende Nervoso

A.k.a. *No Thanks, the Coffee Makes Me Nervous*; a.k.a. *No Thanks, the Caffeine Makes Me Nervous* (English translations and titles) (1982) (It.); D: Ludovico Gaspari; Prod. Co.: Titanus-Yarno; P: Mauro Berardi; SC: Lello Arena, Michael Pergolani, Massimo Troisi; C: Pasquale Rachini; M: James Senese; S: Lello Arena, Magdalena Crippa, Massimo Troisi, James Senese, Anna Camperi.

Nosferatu a Venezia

A.k.a. *Nosferatu in Venice* (English translation and title) (1988) (It.); D/P/SC: Augusto Caminito; P: Augusto Caminito; Prod. Co.: Scena Film/Reteitalia; C: Tonino Nardi; SP E: Franco Corridoni, Sergio Angeloni, Luigi Rocchetti; S: Klaus Kinski a.k.a. Klaus Gunther Nakszynksi, Barbara De Rossi, Yorgo Voyagis, Donald Pleasence, Christopher Plummer, Anne Knecht.

La Notte dei Dannati

A.k.a. *Night of the Damned* (English translation and title) (1971) (It.); D: Filippi Walter Maria Ratti; P: Nicola Addario, Lucio Carnemolla; Prod. Co.: Primax; SC: Aldo Marcovecchio; C: Girolama La Rosa; S: Pierre Brice, Patrizia Viotti, Angelo De Leo, Mario Carra, Antonio Pavan, Daniele D'Agostini, Irio Fantini, Carla Mancini.

L'Occhio nel Labirinto

A.k.a. *Eye in the Labyrinth* (English translation and title); a.k.a. *Blood* (English title) (1971) (It., W.G.); D: Mario Caiano; P: Nello Santi, Hans Pfluger; Prod. Co.: Transeuro Film/TV 13; SC: Giovanni Ciarlo; SP E: Giannetto De Rossi; S: Rosemary Dexter, Adolfo Celli, Horst Frank, Alida Valli, Franco Ressel, Benjamin Lev, Sybil Danning a.k.a. Sybille Johanna Danninger, Gigi Rizzi.

Oggi a Me ... Domani a Te

A.k.a. *Today It's Me ... Tomorrow You*; a.k.a. *Today It's Me ... Tomorrow It's You!* (English translations and titles) (1968) (It.); D: Tonino Cervi; Prod. Co.: P.A.C.—Produzioni Atlas Consorziate/Splendid Film; SC: Tonino Cervi, Dario Argento; C: Sergio D'Offizi; M: Angelo Francesco Lavagnino; S: Brett Halsey, Bud Spencer a.k.a. Carlo Pedersoli, Wayde Preston, Jeff Cameron, William Berger, Tatsuya Nakadai.

Ossessione

A.k.a. *Obsession* (English translation and title); a.k.a. *The Postman Always Rings Twice* (English title) (1942) (It.); D: Luchino Visconti; Prod. Co.: Industrie Cinematografiche Italiane; SC: Luchino Visconti, Mario Alicata, Giuseppe De Santis, Gianni Puccini, based on the novel, *The Postman Always Rings Twice* by James M. Cain; C: Aldo Tonti, Domenico Scala; M: Giuseppe Rosati; S: Massimo Girotti, Clara Calamai, Juan Da Landa, Dhia Cristiani, Rlio Marcuzzo, Michele Riccardini, Vittorio Duse.

Per un Pugno di Dollari

A.k.a. *A Fistful of Dollars* (English translation and title) (1964) (It., W.G., Sp.); D: Sergio Leone; P: Arrigo Colombo, Giorgio Papi; Prod. Co.: Jolly Film (Rome)/Constantine Film

(Munich)/Ocean Films (Madrid); SC: Sergio Leone, Duccio Tessari; C: Massimo Dallamano; M: Ennio Morricone; S: Clint Eastwood, Gian Maria Volonte, Marianne Koch, Pepe Calvo, Wolfgang Lukschy, Sieghardt Rupp, Antonio Prieto, Margarita Lozano.

Piccole Labbra

A.k.a. *Little Lips* (English translation) (1978) (It.); D: Mimmo Cattarinichi; C: Sandro Mancori; M: Stelvio Cipriani; S: Katya Berger, Ugo Bologna, Pierre Clementi, Michele Soavi.

Piranha Paura

A.k.a. *Piranha Fear* (English translation); a.k.a. *Piranha II: Flying Killers*; a.k.a. *Piranha II — The Spawning*; a.k.a. *The Spawning* (English titles) (1981) (It., Netherlands?); D: James Cameron, Ovidio Gabriele Assonitis (uncredited); P: Chako Van Leuwen, Jeff Schechtman; Prod. Co.: Brouwersgracht Investments/Chako Film Company; SC: H.A. Milton (?); C: Roberto D'Ettore Piazzoli; M: Steve Powder (?); SP E: Giannetto De Rossi, Gino De Rosi, Antonio Corridori, Gilberto Carbonaro; S: Lance Henriksen, Tricia O'Neil, Steve Marachuk, Ricky Paul, Ted Richert, Leslie Graves.

Probabilità Zero

A.k.a. *Probability Zero* (English translation and title) (1968) (It.); D: Maurizio Lucidi; P: Dario Argento, Salvatore Argento; Prod. Co.: Auriga Film '68; SC: Dario Argento, Maurizio Lucidi, Giuseppe Mangione, Vittorio Vighi; S: Henry Silva, Luigi Castellato, Ezio Sancrotti, Franco Giornelli, Marco Guglielmi, Katia Kristine.

Qualcono Ha Tradito

A.k.a. *Every Man Is My Enemy*; a.k.a. *Everyman Is My Enemy* (English titles) (1967) (It., Fr.); D: Franco Prosperi; Prod. Co.: Tiki Film/Greenwhich Film Productions; S: Robert Webber, Elsa Martinelli, Jean Servais, William Bosh, Emil Messina, Marina Berti.

La Rivoluzione Sessuale

A.k.a. *The Sexual Revolution* (English translation and title) (1968) (It., Sp.); D: Riccardo Ghione; P: Italo Zingarelli, Roberto Palaggi; Prod. Co.: West Film; SC: Riccardo Ghione, Dario Argento, based on the novel by Wilhelm Reich; C: Alessandro D'Eva; M: Teo Usuelli; S: Christian Aleghy, Laura Antonelli, Maria Luisa Bavastro, Andres Jose Cruz, Riccardo Cucciolla.

Santa Sangre

(1989) (It.); D: Alejandro Jodorowsky; P: Claudio Argento; Prod. Co.: Intersound; SC: Alejandro Jodorowsky, Claudio Argento, Roberto Leoni; C: Daniele Nannuzzi; SP E: Marcelino Pacheco; S: Axel Jodorowsky, Blanca Guerra, Guy Stockwell, Thelma Tixou, Sabrina Dennison.

Sartana

A.k.a. *Se Incontri Sartana Prega per la Tua Morte* (alternate Italian title; translation: *If You Meet Sartana, Pray for Your Death*); a.k.a. *Gunfighters Die Harder* (English title) (1968) (It., W.G.); D: Gianfranco Parolini; Prod. Co.: Etoile Film/Parnass Film; SC: Gianfranco Parolini,

Renato Izzo; C: Sandro Mancori; M: Piero Piccioni; S: Gianni Garko, Klaus Kinski a.k.a. Klaus Gunther Nakszynksi, Fernando Sancho, William Berger, Sydney Chaplin, Gianni Rizzo.

Satanik

(1968) (It., Sp.); D: Piero Vivarelli; P: Romano Mussolini; Prod. Co.: Rodiacines/Copercines (Spain); SC: Eduardo M. Broschero; C: Silvano Ippoliti; S: Magda Konopka, Julio Pena, Armando Calvo, Umberto Raho, Luigi Montini, Mimma Ippoliti, Antonio Pica, Isarco Ravaioli.

Scusi, Lei È Favorevole o Contrario?

A.k.a. *Excuse Me, Are You for Or Against?* (English translation) (1966) (It., W.G.); D: Alberto Sordi; Prod. Co.: Fono Roma/C.C.C. Filmkunst; SC: Alberto Sordi, Sergio Amidei; C: Benito Frattari; M: Piero Piccioni; S: Alberto Sordi, Anita Ekberg, Bibi Andersson, Tina Marquand, Paola Pitagora, Silvana Mangano, Giulietta Masina, Dario Argento.

Seddok

A.k.a. *Seddok, la Erede Satana* (alternate Italian title); a.k.a. *Atom Age Vampire*; a.k.a. *Blood Fiend* (English titles) (1960) (It.); D: Anton Giulio Majano; P: Mario Fava; Prod. Co.: Lion Film; SC: Anton Giulio Majano, Pierre Monviso, Gino De Santis, Alberto Bevilacqua C: Aldo Giordani; M: Armando Trovaioli; SP E: Ugo Amadoro, Euclide Santoli; S: Alberto Lupo, Susanne Loret, Sergio Fantoni, Franca Parisi.

Sigpress Contro Scotland Yard

A.k.a. *Sigpress Vs. Scotland Yard* (English translation); a.k.a. *Mr. Zehn Prozent Miezen* (German title); a.k.a. *Psychopath* (English title) (1967) (It., W.G.); D: Guido Zurli; Prod. Co.: Cinescolo (Rome); S: George Martin, Paolo Carlini, Klaus Kinski a.k.a. Klaus Gunther Nakszynksi, Ingrid Schoeller, Andrea Aureli.

La Sorella di Satana

A.k.a. *Il Lago di Satana* (alternate Italian title); a.k.a. *The Curse of Satan*; a.k.a. *Satan's Sister*; a.k.a. *The Revenge of the Blood Beast*; a.k.a. *The She Beast* (English titles) (1965) (It.); D: Michael Reeves; P: Paul Maslansky; Prod. Co.: Leith Productions; SC: Michael Reeves; C: Amerigo Gengarelli; S: Barbara Steele, Ian Ogilvy, Mel Welles, John Karlsen, Jay Riley, Richard Watson.

La Sorella di Ursula

A.k.a. *Ursula's Sister* (English translation) a.k.a. *The Curse of Ursula* (English title) (1978) (It.); D/SC: Enzo Milioni; P: Armando Bertuccioli; Prod. Co.: Supercine; C: Vittorio Bernini; M: Mimmi Uva, Franco Bernardi; S: Barbara Magnolfi, Stefania Amario, Vann Materassi, Marc Porel, Anna Zinneman.

La Stagione di Sensei

A.k.a. *The Season of Senses* (English translation and title?) (1970) (It.,W.G.); D: Massimo Francoisa; P: Italo Zingarelli; Prod Co.: West Film (Rome)/Rapid Film (Munich); SC: Dario

Argento, Barbara Alberti, Franco Ferrari, Peter Kintzel.; C: Alessandro D'Eva; M: Ennio Morricone; S: Eva Thulin, Laura Belli, Edda Di Benedetto, Udo Kier, Suzanne Von Sass.

La Strage dei Vampiri

(1962) (It.); D/SC: Roberto Mauri; Prod. Co.: Mercur; C: Ugo Brunelli; M: Aldo Piga; S: Walter Brandi, Dieter Eppler, Graziela Granata, Paolo Solvay.

La Streghe

A.k.a. *The Witch* (English translation); a.k.a. *Witch Story* (English title) (1989) (It.); D: Alessandro Capone; P: Mauro Morigi, Giuseppe Pedersoli; Prod. Co.: Claudio Bonivento/United Entertainment Corporation; SC: Alessandro Capone, Rosario Galli, Jeff Moldovan; C: Roberto Girometti; SP E: Rick Gonzales; S: Ian Bannen, Christopher Peacock, Michelle Vannucchi, Deanna Lund, Gary Kerr, Amy Adams, Jeff Bankert, Charon Butler, Todd Conatser, Nancie Sanderson, Suzanne Law.

Un Sussurro nel Buio

A.k.a. *A Whisper in the Dark*; a.k.a. *Whispers in the Dark* (English translations and titles) (It.) (1976); D: Marcello Aliprandi; P: Enzo Gallo; SC: Maria Teresa Rienzi, Nicolo Rienzi; C: Claudio Cirillo; M: Pino Donaggio; S: John Phillip Law, Nathalie Delon, Olga Bisera, Joseph Cotten, Lucrezia Love.

Tempi Duri per Vampiri

A.k.a. *Hard Times for Vampires* (English translation); a.k.a. *Hard Times for Dracula*; a.k.a. *Uncle Was a Vampire*; a.k.a. *My Uncle the Vampire* (English titles) (1959) (It.); D: Steno a.k.a. Stefano Vanzina; P: Mario Cecci Gori; Prod. Co.: Maxima Film/CEI Incom Montflour Film; SC: Edoardo Anton, Dino Verde, Alessandro Continenza, Lucio Fulci (uncredited); C: Marco Scarpelli; S: Christopher Lee, Sylva Kocina, Renato Rascel, Lia Zoppelli, Kai Fischer, Franco Scandurra.

La Terrificante Notte del Demonio

A.k.a. *The Long Night of the Devil* (English translation); a.k.a. *La Notte Più Lunga del Diavolo* (alternate Italian title); a.k.a. *La Plus Longue Nuit du Diable* (French title); a.k.a. *Au Service du Diable* (alternate French title); a.k.a. *Les Nuit des Petrifiées* (alternate French title); a.k.a. *The Devil's Nightmare*; a.k.a. *The Devil Walks at Midnight*; a.k.a. *Succubus*; a.k.a. *Vampire Playgirls*; a.k.a. *Satan's Playthings*; a.k.a. *Castle of Death* (English titles) (1971) (Fr., It., Belgium); D: Jean Brismee, Andre Hunnebelle; P: Charles Lecocq; Prod. Co.: Compagnie Europenne (Brussels)/Delfino Cinematografica (Rome); SC: Charles Lecocq, Patrice Rhomm; M: Alessandro Alessandroni; S: Erica Blanc a.k.a. Enrica Bianchi Colombatto, Jean Servais, Daniel Emilfork, Jacques Monseau, Ivana Novak, Shirley Corrigan, Colette Emmanuelle, Lorenzo Terzon, Lucien Raimbourg.

Toto a Colori

(1952) (It.); D: Steno a.k.a. Stefano Vanzina; P: Dino De Laurentiis, Carlo Ponti; SC: Steno a.k.a. Stefano Vanzina, Agenore Incrocci, Mario Monicelli, Furio Scarpelli, Toto a.k.a. Antonio De Curtis a.k.a. Antonio Vincenzo Stefano Clemente; C: Tonino Delli Colli; M:

Felice Montagnini; S: Toto a.k.a. Antonio De Curtis a.k.a. Antonio Vincenzo Stefano Clemente, Mario Castellani, Isa Barzizza, Virgilio Riento.

Tutti Defunti Tranne i Morti

(1977) (It.); D: Pupi Avati; SC: Pupi Avati, Antonio Avati, Gianni Cavina, Maurizio Costanzo; C: Pasquale Rachini; M: Amedeo Tommasi; S: Gianna Cavina, Francesca Marciano, Carlo Delle Piane, Greta Vajan, Michele Mirabella, Flavia Giorgi, Andrea Matteuzzi.

Un Urlo dalla Tenebrae

A.k.a. *A Cry in the Darkness* (English translation); a.k.a. *Un Urlo nelle Tenebre* (alternate Italian title); a.k.a. *L'Esorcista N.2* (alternate Italian title); a.k.a. *Naked Exorcism* (G.B.); a.k.a. *Exorcist III — Cries and Shadows* (G.B. video title); a.k.a. *The Possessor* (English titles) (1976) (It.); D: Elo Pannaccio; P: Luigi Fedeli, Otello Cocchi; Prod. Co.: Manila Cinematogrfica; SC: Elo Pannaccio, Aldo Crudo, Franco Brocani; C: Franco Villa, Maurizio Centini, Gaetano Valle; M: Giuliano Sorgini; S: Richard Conte, Francoise Prevost, Elena Svevo, Patrizia Gori, Jean-Claude Verne, Sonia Viviani, Mimma Monticelli, Franco Garofalo.

La Villa delle Anime Maldette

A.k.a. *The House of the Damned* (English translation); a.k.a. *La Villa delle Anime Dannate* (alternate Italian title); a.k.a. *Don't Look in the Attic* (English title) (1982) (It.); D/S/C: Carlo Ausino; P: Michele Peyretti, Carlo Ausino; Prod. Co.: Antonelliana Cinematografica for Cinevinci; M: Stelvio Cipriani; S: Beba Loncar, Jean-Pierre Aumont, Annamaria Grapputo, Giorgio Ardisson, Paul Teicheid, Fausto Lombardi.

Zombi: Dawn of the Dead

A.k.a. *Zombi* (alternate Italian title); a.k.a. *Dawn of the Dead* (English title) (1979) (U.S., It.); D: George A. Romero; P: Dario Argento, Richard P. Rubinstein; Prod. Co.: Laurel Group Productions/Dawn Associates; SC: George A. Romero; C: Michael P. Gornick; SP E: Tom Savini; S: Ken Foree, David Emge, Scott H. Reininger, Gaylen Ross, David Crawford, David Early.

BIBLIOGRAPHY

Andriano, Joseph. *Immortal Monster: The Mythological Evolution of the Fantastic Beast in Modern Fiction and Film.* Westport, CT: Greenwood Press, 1999.
Annuario del Cinema Italiano. Rome, Italy: Centro Studi di Cultura, Promozione e Diffusioni del Cinema. Annual 1953-54 and 1971-72.
Baumann, Hans D. *Horror: Die Lust am Grauen.* Weinheim, Germany: Beltz, 1989.
Black, Andy. *Necronomicon: The Journal of Horror and Erotic Cinema.* England: Creation Books International, 1992–1995, annual.
Brown, Paul J., and Nigel Burrell. *Uncut: Worldwide Cinema Weirdness.* Huntingdon, England: Midnight Media and FAB Press, 1996–2003.
Bruschini, Antonio, and Antonio Tentori. *Nudi e Crudeli: I Mondo Movies Italiani.* Bologna, Italy: PuntoZero, 2000.
Bryce, Alan. *Video Nasties: From Absurd to Zombie Flesh-Eaters; A Collector's Guide to the Most Horrifying Films Ever Banned.* Cornwall, England: Stray Cat, 1998.
Butler, Ivan. *The Horror Film.* London, Zwemmer; New York: A.S. Barnes, 1967.
Caunce, Ian. *Absurd: The World of Exploitation on Film and Video: The Films of Jess Franco.* Rochdale, Lancs., England: Ian Caunce, 1988.
Cholewa, Michael, and Kartsen Thurau. *Der Terror Furht Regie: Italienische Gangster und Polizeifilme 1968–1982.* Germany: Terrorverlag, 1999.
Clarke, Frederick S. *Cinefantastique.* Elmwood Park, IL: Frederick S. Clarke, 1970–1994.
Constantini, Daniele, and Francesco Dal Bosco. *Nuovo Cinema Inferno: L'Opera di Dario Argento.* Milan, Italy: Pratiche Editrice, 1997.
Cozzi, Luigi. *Il Cinema dei Mostri: Da Godzilla a Dario Argento.* Rome, Italy: Fanucci, 1987.
Creed, Barbara. *The Monstrous Feminine: Film, Feminism, Psychoanalysis.* London and New York: Routledge, 1993.
Curci, Loris. *Shock Masters of the Cinema.* Key West, FL: Fantasma Books, 1996.
De Quincey, Thomas. *Confessions of an Opium-Eater.* Otley, England, and Washington, DC: Woodstock Books, 2002.
_____. *Selected Writings of Thomas DeQuincey.* Selected and edited with an introduction by Philip Van Doren Stern. New York: Random House, 1937.
Fenton, Harvey. *Flesh and Blood.* Guildford, England: FAB Press, 1996–2003.
_____, and David Flint. *Ten Years of Terror: British Horror Fims of the 1970s.* Guildford, England: FAB Press, 2001.
Fentone, Steve. *AntiCristo: The Bible of Nasty Nun Sinema and Culture.* Guildford, England: FAB Press, 2000.

Flynn, John L. *Cinematic Vampires: The Living Dead on Film and Television, from* The Devil's Castle (1896) *to* Bram Stoker's Dracula (1992). Jefferson, NC: McFarland & Co., 1992.

Gallant, Chris, et al. *Art of Darkness: The Cinema of Dario Argento*. Guildford, England: FAB Press, 2000.

George, Bill. *Eroticism in the Fantasy Cinema*. Pittsburgh, PA: Imagine Press, Inc., 1984.

Giovanni, Fabio. *Dario Argento: Il Brivido, il Sangue, il Thrilling*. Bari, Italy: Dedalo, 1986.

Grossini, Giancarlo. *Dizionario del Cinema Giallo: Tutto il Delitto dalla A alla Z*. Bari, Italy: Dedalo, 1985.

Hahn, Ronald M., and Rolf Giesen. *Das Neue Lexicon des Horror Films: Alles über die Dunkle Seite des Kinos: Mehr Als 1800 Horrorfilme mit Inhaltsangaben, Filmografien und Kritiken*. Berlin, Germany: Schwarzkopf & Schwarzkopf, 2003.

Hardy, Phil, ed. *Horror*. London, England: Aurum Press, 1993; New York: Overlook Press, 1997.

Helt, Marie and Richard. *West German Cinema Since 1945: A Handbook*. Lanham, MD: Scarecrow Press, 1987.

Howarth, Troy. *The Haunted World of Mario Bava*. Guildford, England: FAB Press, 2002.

Jaworzyn, Stefan. *Shock: The Essential Guide to Exploitation Cinema*. London: Titan, 1996.

Jones, Alan, and Paul J. Brown. *Mondo Argento*. Upton, Cambs, England: Media Publishing, 1996.

Jung, Fernand. *Der Horror Film: Regisseure, Stars, Autoren, Spezialisten, Themen und Filme von A–Z*. Munich, Germany: Roloff und Seesslen, 1977.

Kerekes, David, and David Slater. *Killing for Culture: An Illustrated History of Death Film from* Mondo *to* Snuff. London and San Francisco: Creation Books, 1995, 1998.

_____, and _____. *See No Evil: Banned Films and Video Controversy*. Manchester, England: Critical Visions, Headpress, 2000.

Kramp, Joachim. *Hallo! Hier Spricht Edgar Wallace: Die Geschichte der Deutschen Kriminalfilmserie von 1950–1972*. Berlin, Germany: Schwarzkopf & Schwarzkopf, 1998.

Lane, Margaret. *Edgar Wallace: The Biography of a Phenomenon*. New York: Doubelday, Doran, 1939.

Ledbetter, Craig. *European Trash Cinema (ETC)*. Kingwood, TX: Craig Ledbetter, 1987–98.

Lentz, Harris M. *Science Fiction, Horror and Fantasy Film and Television Credits: Over 10,000 Actors, Actresses, Directors, Producers, Screenwriters, Cinematographers, Art Directors, and Make-Up, Special Effects, Costume, and Other People; Plus Cross References from All Films and TV Shows*. Jefferson, NC: McFarland & Co., 1983.

Lindop, Grevel. *The Opium-Eater: A Life of Thomas De Quincey*. London: Dent, 1981.

Lucantonio, Gabrielle. *Il Cinema Horror in Italia: Dario Argento, Luigi Cozzi, Antonio Margheriti, Michele Soavi e Altri*. Roma, Italy: D. Audino, 2001.

_____. *Dario Argento, Autore-Cahiers*. L'Aquila: Textus, 1999.

Lucas, Tim and Donna. *Video Watchdog*. Cincinatti: Tim and Donna Lucas, 1990–2003.

Martin, John. *Giallo Pages: Exploitation all'Italiana*. Mansfield, Notts, England: On-Line Publishing, 1992–1994.

_____. *Giallo Pages: The Journal of Exploitation all'Italiana*, Vol. 1. Nottingham, England: Procrustes; Yellow Press, 1999.

_____. *Deep Red Diva: Daria Nicoldi*. Nottingham: Yellow Press, 1997.

Martinet, Pascal. *Mario Bava*. Paris: Edilig, 1984.

McDonagh, Maitland. *Broken Mirrors/Broken Minds: The Dark Dreams of Dario Argento*. London, England: Sun Tavern Fields, 1991.

Moore, Darrell, W. *The Best, Worst, and Most Unusual Horror Films*. New York: Beekman House, 1983. Distributed by Crown Publishers.

Murphy, Michael J. *The Celluloid Vampires: A History and Filmography, 1897–1979*. Ann Arbor, MI: Pierian Press, 1979.

Newman, Kim, ed. *The BFI Companion to Horror*. London: Cassell, 1996.

Palmerini, Luca M., and Gaetano Mistretta. *Spaghetti Nightmares: Il Cinema Italiano della Paura e del Fantastico Visto Attraverso gli Occhi dei Suoi Protagonisti*. Rome: M&P, 1998.

_____. *Spaghetti Nightmares: Italian Fantasy-Horrors As Seen Through the Eyes of Their Protoganists*. Translated by Gilliam M.A. Kirkpatrick. Key West, FL: Fantasma Books, 1996.

Paul, Louis. *Blood Times*. Brooklyn, NY: Louis Paul. 1983–1994.

_____. *Inferno Italia: Der Italienische Horrorfilm*. Munich: Bertler & Lieber, 1998.

_____. "Operatic Gore: Dario Argento and Suspiria," published in *It's Only a Movie*. Vol. 1, No. 1. Chicago, IL: Michael Flores, 1990.

_____, and Tom Lisanti. *Film Fatales: Women in Espionage Films and Television, 1962–1973*. Jefferson, NC: McFarland & Co. 2002.

Paxton, Timothy, and David Todarello, et al. *Naked! Screaming! Terror!* Oberlin, OH: Kronos Publications, 198?.

Pezzotta, Alberto. *Mario Bava*. Rome: Il Castoro, 1995 Photon. Brooklyn: Mark Frank, 1963–1977.

Piselli, Stefano, Roberto Guidotti, and Riccardo Morrocchi. *Cinefiles: Sadici and Sadiani: Sadistic and Sadean Movies*. Italy: Glittering Images, 199?.

Poppi, Roberto, Pecorari, Marco, and Lancia, E. Dizionario. *Del Cinema Italiano I Film 1910–2000*. Rome: Gremese, 1991–2000.

Pulchalski, Steven. *Slimetime*. Stockport, England: Headpress, 1996.

Rea, Luca. *I Colori Del Buio: Il Cinema Thrilling Italiano Dal 1930 al 1979*. Firenze, Italy: I. Molino, 1999.

Reich, Jacqueline, and Piero Garofalo. *Re-Viewing Fascism: Italian Cinema, 1922–1943*. Bloomington, IN: Indiana University Press, 2002.

Reteuna, Dario. *Cinema Di Carta: Storia Fotografica Del Cinema Italiano*. Alessandria: Falsopiano, 2000.

Rondolini, Gianni. *Catalago Bolaffi del Cinema Italiano, 1966–1975: Tutti I Film Italiani Degli Ultimi Dieci Anni*. Turin, Italy: G. Bolaffi, 1975.

_____, and Ornella Levi. *Catalago Bolaffi del Cinema Italiano: Tutti I Film Italiani del Dopoguerra*. Turin, Italy: G. Bolaffi, 1967.

Sargent, Robert. *Videooze: Your Guide to Obscure Horror and Exploitation on Videotape*. Alexandria, VA: Robert Sargent, 1990–1993.

Senn, Bryan, and John Johnson. *Fantastic Cinema Subject Guide: A Topical Index to 2500 Horror, Science Fiction, and Fantasy Films*. Jefferson, NC: McFarland & Co., 1992.

Skal, David J. *V is for Vampire: An A to Z Guide to Everything Undead*. New York: Plume, 1996.

Slater, Jason J., and Harvey Fenton, et al. *Diabolic: Il Cinema Fantastico Italiano: 1–2*. Guildford, England: FAB Press, 1997.

Smith, Adrian-Luther. *Delirium: A Guide to Italian Exploitation Cinema: 1975–1979*. London: Media Publications, 1997.

_____. *Delirium: Italian Exploitation Cinema: 1970–1974*. London: Media Publications (date unknown).

_____, and Trevor Barley. *Delirium: The Essential Reference Guide to Trash Cinema: Italian Exploitation Cinema Part Two: 1975–1979*. Old Marston, Oxford: Media Publications, 1992.

_____, and _____, et al. *Delirium: The Essential Reference Guide to Delirious Cinema: Part 3: Italian Cinema, 1980*. London: Media Publications (date unknown).

_____, and _____, et al. *Delirium: The Essential Reference Guide to Delirious Cinema: Part 4: Italian Cinema, 1981*. London: FAB Press (date unknown).

_____, _____, and Harvey Fenton, et al. *Delirium: The Essential Guide to Bizarre Italian Cinema 1982*. London: FAB Press (date unknown).

Stover, George M., Jr. *Black Oracle*. Baltimore, MD: George M. Stover, Jr., 1969–1977.

_____. *Cinemacabre*. Baltimore, MD: George M. Stover, Jr., 1978–1988.

Svehla, Gary J. *Midnight Marquee*. Baltimore, MD: Gary J. Svehla, 1977–1998.
Tentori, Antonio. *Dario Argento: Sensualità dell'Omicidio*. Alessandria: Edizioni Falsopiano, 1997.
_____. *Joe D'Amato: L'Immagine del Piacere*. Rome: Castelvecchi, 1999.
Thrower, Stephen. *Beyond Terror: The Films of Lucio Fulci*. Guildford, England: FAB Press, 1999.
_____. *Eyeball: Sex & Horror in World Cinema*. Guildford, England: FAB Press, 1994–2002.
Tombs, Pete. *Mondo Macabre: Weird & Wonderful Cinema Around the World*. New York: St. Martin's Griffin, 1998.
_____, and Cathal Tohill. *Immoral Tales: European Sex and Horror Movies, 1956–1984*. New York: St. Martin's Griffin, 1995.
Toufic, Jalal. *Vampires: An Uneasy Essay on the Undead in Film*. Sausalito, CA: Station Hill Press, 1993; The Post-Apollo Press, 2000.
Tses, Christos. *Der Hexer, der Zinker, und Andere Mordere: Hinter den Kulissen der Edgar Wallace-Filme*. Essen, Germany: Klartext, 2002.
Unitalia Film. *Unitalia Film: Italian Film Production, 1950-51–1973*. Rome: Unitalia Film, 1950-51–1973.
Ursini, James, and Alain Silver. *The Vampire Film*. South Brunswick, NJ: A.S. Barnes, 1975.
Variety film reviews 1907–1980. 16 volumes. New York: Garland Publishing, 1983.
Variety Portable Movie Guide. New York: Berkeley Boulevard Books, 1999.
Weldon, Michael. *The Psychotronic Video Guide*. London: Titan Books, 1996.
_____, Charles Beesley, Bob Martin, and Akria Fitton. *The Psychotronic Encyclopedia of Film*. New York: Ballantine Books, 1983.
Willis, Donald C. *Horror and Science Fiction Films I, II, III*. Metuchen, NJ: Scarecrow Press, 1980–1984.
_____. *Horror and Science Fiction Films IV*. Lanham, MD: Scarecrow Press, 1997.
Willis, John. *Screen World*. New York: Crown, annual.
Wolf, Leonard. *Horror: A Connoisseur's Guide to Literature and Film*. New York: Facts on File, 1989.

INDEX

A Doppia Faccia 276, 277
A 077 Challenge to the Killers see *A 077 Sfida ai Killers*
A 077 Sfida ai Killers 163, 171
A 008 Operation Exterminate see *A 008 Operazione Stermino*
A 008 Operazione Stermino 143–144, 151
Aames, Willie 117
Abbott, Bruce 332
Abraham, F. Murray 232
Absurd see *Anthropophagus II*
Achtung! The Desert Tigers see *Kaput Lager: Gli Ultimi Giorni delle SS*
Ad Ogni Costo 122, 323
Addobbati, Giuseppe 307, 312
Addormentarsi 55
Adorf, Mario 65, 77–78, 80, 115, 117, 261, 290
The Adventures of Baron Munchausen 222
The Adventures of Hercules (1984) see *Le Avventura di Ulisse*
The Adventures of Hercules see *Le Avventure dell'Incredibile Ercole*
The Adventures of Mary Read see *Le Avventura di Mary Read*
The Adventures of Stella Starr see *Scontri Stellari Oltre la 3a Dimensione*
The Adventures of Ulysses see *Le Avventura di Ulisse*
Aenigma 131, 135
Africa Sexy 210, 245
After the Fall of New York see *2019 Dopo la Caduta di New York*
Afternoon see *Pomeriggio Caldo*
Agente Segretissimi see *002 Agente Segretissimi*
Agente 3S3: Massacro al Sole 210, 324
Agente 3S3: Passaporto per l'Inferno 20, 324
L'Agguato sul Fondo 166, 171–172
Agi Murad, il Diavolo Bianco 85, 274, 277
Agrama, Farouk 327–328
Agrama, Frank *see* Agrama, Farouk
Agren, Janet 117, 139, 148, 155, 248–249, 299
Ahrens, Christopher 218, 246
Al Capone 198
Aladdin X see *Aladino X*
Aladino X 196
Albert, Edward 173
Albertini, Adalberto "Bitto" 184, 237, 329, 331
Albertini, Luciano 11
L'Alcova 194
L'Alcova dei Perversi Piaceri 196, 199
The Alcove see *L'Alcova*
The Alcove of Perverse Desires see *L'Alcova dei Perversi Piaceri*
The Alcove of Perverse Pleasures see *L'Alcova dei Perversi Piaceri*
Alda, Robert 100, 104, 173
Alda, Rutanya 262
L'Aldila 127, 130, 135, 191, 263
Alex l'Ariete 261
Alfonsi, Lydia 91, 108, 329
Alibi Perfetto 289–290
Alien 214
Alien Contamination see *Contaminazione*
Alien degli Abissi 169–170, 172
Alien from the Abyss see *Alien degli Abissi*
Alien 2 see *Alien 2 sulla Terra*
Alien 2 on Earth see *Alien 2 sulla Terra*
Alien 2 sulla Terra 220, 324
Aliens from the Abyss see *Alien degli Abissi*
Aliens from the Deep see *Alien degli Abissi*
Aliprandi, Marcello 29, 338
All the Colors of the Dark see *Tutti Colori nel Buio*
All the Colors of the Darkness see *Tutti Colori nel Buio*
All'Onorevole Piacciono le Donne...Nonostante le Apparenze e Purchè la Nazione Non le Sappia... 124, 135
All'Ultimo Minuto 110
Alt, Carol 115, 118
Alta Tensione 75, 80–83
L'Altro Inferno 211, 215
Amadio, Silvio 181, 332
L'Amante del Vampiro 14–15, 19, 304, 306
Amanti d'Oltretomba 19, 324
Amare e Morire 55
The Amazing Dr. G see *Le Spie Vengono dal Semifreddo*
Amazonia see *La Schiave Blanca*

Amazonia: The Catherine Mills Story see *La Schiave Blanca*
Ambessi, Adriana 302, 333
Gli Amici dell'Isola 309
Amico, Stammi Lontano Almeno un Palmo 181, 324
Amigo, Stay Away see *Amico, Stammi Lontano Almeno un Palmo*
The Amityville Horror 261
Amityville II: The Possession 261–262
Amleto 198
And God Said to Cain see *E Dio Disse a Caino*
Andersen, Susy 108, 171
Anderson, Susan see Andersen, Susy
Andre, Carole 81, 177
Andress, Ursula 77, 80, 292, 298
Andrews, Dana 166, 178
Andy Warhol's Dracula see *Dracula Cerca Sangue di Vergine...È Morì di Sete!*
Andy Warhol's Frankenstein see *Il Mostro È in Tavola...Barone Frankenstein*
Andy Warhol's Young Dracula see *Dracula Cerca Sangue di Vergine...È Morì di Sete!*
An Angel for Satan see *Un Angelo per Satana*
Angeli, Pier see Pierangeli, Anna Maria
Un Angelo per Satana 20, 301
Anger in His Eyes see *Con la Rabbia agli Occhi*
Angiolini, Alessandro 24
Annakin, Ken 331
Anno 2020: I Gladiatori del Futuro 194, 199, 220
Antefatto see *Ecologia del Delitto*
Anthar l'Invincibile 161, 172
Anthony, Robert see Santoni, Espartaco
Anthropophagus 190–192, 199
Anthropophagus — The Beast see *Anthropophagus*
Anthropophagus II 193, 199, 220
L'Anticristo 184, 264, 266
Antonelli, Laura 107, 135, 336
Antonioni, Michelangelo 120
Any Time, Any Place see *Ogni, Volta, un Gioco*
L'Apache Bianco 212, 215
Apocalisse Domani 166–167, 172
Apocalisse sul Fiume Giallo 143, 151–152
Apocalypse Now 112, 167, 305
Apocalypse on the Yellow River see *Apocalisse sul Fiume Giallo*
Appuntamento a Trieste 213, 215
Aquarius see *Deliria*
Arabella, l'Angelo Nero 299–300
Arabella, the Black Angel see *Arabella, l'Angelo Nero*
Arana, Tomas 76, 79, 81, 225–226
Aranda, Angel 107
Arcana 311
The Arcane Enchanter see *L'Arcano Incantatore*
L'Arcano Incantatore 230–232
L'Arciere delle Mille e Una Notte 160
Arcobaleno Selvaggio 167, 169, 172
Arden, Mary 106, 155
Ardisson, George see Ardisson, Giorgio
Ardisson, Giorgio 103–104, 161, 176, 236–237, 280, 304, 314–315, 324, 339
Argento, Asia 37, 57–58, 60–61, 63–65, 79, 225
Argento, Claudio 63–64, 336
Argento, Dario 1–3, 6, 22, 25, 32–33, 37–65, 67–68, 71–72, 74–75, 77–79, 89, 92, 98, 113, 131, 134, 144, 155, 220–222, 224–226, 233, 246, 251–257, 282, 303, 320–321, 325, 327, 329, 333–339
Argento, Fiore 37, 64, 79
Argento, Salvatore 37, 43, 55, 62–65, 336
Arizona Bill see *La Strada per Fort Alamo*
The Ark of the Sun God see *Sopravvissuti della Città Morta*
Arkin, Adam 117
Arkoff, Samuel Z. 107
Armida, il Dramma di Una Sposa 210, 215
Arno, Alice 204, 277
Arrivano Django e Sartana...È la Fine 183, 324
Arriverderci Amore, Ciao 224
Arsan, Emmanuelle 184
Ashton, Julie 203
Assassino al Cimitero Etrusco 294–296
Assassino dei Giorni di Festa 261–262
L'Assassino...È al Telefono (1973) 181, 264, 266
L'Assassino...È al Telefono (1994) 214, 215
L'Assassino È Costretto ad Uccidere Ancora 42, 251–253

Assignment Outer Space see *Spazzio Uomini*
Assonitis, Ovidio 101, 117, 327, 336
Atlantis Interceptors see *Predatori di Atlantide*
L'Atleta Fantasma 10, 325
Atom Age Vampire see *Seddok*
Atomic Cyborg see *Vendetta dal Futuro*
Ator l'Invincibile 194, 200, 220
Ator, the Fighting Eagle see *Ator l'Invincibile*
Ator the Invincible see *Ator l'Invincibile*; *Ator 2 l'Invincible Orion*
Ator II see *Ator 2 l'Invincible Orion*
Ator 2 l'Invincible Orion 194, 199
Attempt on the Three Great Powers see *Attentato ai Tre Grandi*
Attentato ai Tre Grandi 144, 152
Attrazione Pericolosa 214, 215
Aubriot, Didier 201
Audran, Stephane 282
Audray, Elvire 280–281, 296
Auger, Claudine 103
Aulin, Ewa 183–184, 204, 310–311
Aumont, Jean-Pierre 339
Aumont, Tina 296, 311
Aunt Martha Does Dreadful Things see *Non Avere Paura della Zia Marta*
Ausino, Carlo 31, 339
Autopsy see *Macchie Solari*
Autostop Rosso Sangue 325
Avallone, Marcello 229–230
Avalon, Frankie 94
Avati, Antonio 67, 81, 232, 339
Avati, Pupi 6, 67, 81, 124, 136, 230–232, 339
Avram, Chris see Avram, Christea
Avram, Christea 103, 202, 281, 297
L'Avventura di Annabella 84, 325
Le Avventura di Mary Read 143, 152
Le Avventura di Ullise 66, 97, 105
Le Avventure dell'Incredibile Ercole 251–253

Baal, Karin 258–260
Baba Yaga 27–28, 325
Babbao Natale 55, 74, 77, 252
Babenco, Hector 115

Index

Baccaro, Salavatore 28
Il Baccio 67, 325
Bach, Barbara 288–291, 297
Back from Hell see *Per Sempre*
Baino, Mariano 233–234, 320
Baker, Carroll 28, 122, 144–146, 153, 155–156, 272–273, 325
Baker, Stanley 122, 124, 138
Baldi, Ferdinando 39
Baldwin, Peter 18, 278
Balkan Runner see *La Pista Bulgara*
The Ballad of Ben and Charlie see *Amico, Stammi Lontano Almeno un Palmo*
Balpetre, Antoine 108
Balsam, Martin 63, 115, 173, 262
Il Bambino Rapito 55, 74, 78, 252
La Bambola 44, 325
La Bambola di Satana 24–25, 325
Il Bambule 220, 325
Bannen, Ian 338
Baratto, Luisa 309
I Barbari e Co. 113, 115–116
The Barbarians see *I Barbari e Co.*
The Barbarians and Company see *I Barbari e Co.*
Barbeau, Adrienne 56, 63
Barberini, Urbano 55, 63, 79, 82, 254
Barilli, Francisco 7, 131, 156, 234–235
Baron Blood see *Gli Orrori del Castello di Norimberga*
Baron Vampire see *Gli Orrori del Castello di Norimberga*
Barros, Esmeralda 175, 317, 329
Barrymore, John Drew 18, 313, 328
Bartok, Eva 106, 313
Battaglia, Rik 19, 142, 157, 242, 320, 331–332
La Battaglia di Maratona 85–86, 102, 326
The Battle of Marathon see *La Battaglia di Maratona*
Battle of the Commandos see *La Legione dei Dannati*
The Battle of the Worlds see *Pianeta degli Uomini Spenti*
Batzella, Luigi see Solvay, Paolo
Bauchau, Patrick 64
Bava, Eugenio 181
Bava, Lamberto 6, 52, 66–83, 102, 107–108, 110, 118, 150–151, 220–222, 252, 320
Bava, Mario 1, 6, 13–14, 16–20,
22–23, 29, 33, 39–40, 49–50, 63, 66–67, 70, 74–75, 83–108, 113, 181, 272, 275–278, 303, 321, 325–326, 329, 334
Baxa, Maria 280
Baxter, Les 91, 104–108
The Beast see *Cruel Jaws*
The Beast in Heat see *La Bestia in Calore*
Beatrice Cenci 122, 135
Bed of a Thousand Pleasures see *Finalmente…Le Mille e Una Notte*
Bedi, Kabir 286
Behind Convent Walls see *L'Interno di un Convento*
Behind the Convent Walls see *L'Interno di un Convento*
Beir, Fred 237
Bella, Anjelica 208
Belle, Annie 116, 175, 198
Bellevedere, Vittoria 297
Belli, Agostina 266–267, 272
Ben and Charlie see *Amico, Stammi Lontano Almeno un Palmo*
Benedict, Dirk 246
Bengel, Norma 107
Bennett, Joan 64
Bennett, Sonia 204, 315
Benussi, Eufemia see Benussi, Femi
Benussi, Femi 106, 166, 174–175, 240–243, 253, 309
Berenson, Marisa 117, 172
Berger, Helmut 258, 260
Berger, Katya 336
Berger, Senta 115, 117
Berger, William 21, 69, 82, 98, 103, 117, 213, 215, 229–230, 252, 254, 282, 285, 333, 335, 337
Bergerac, Jacques 267
Bergonzelli, Sergio 189, 235–237, 314–315
Berruti, Giulio 7, 238–239
Berryman, Michael 117
Bertolucci, Bernardo 38–39, 327
La Bestia in Calore 315–316
Beswicke, Martine 257, 262, 325
Betti, Laura 106
Beware, the Blob see *Son of Blob*
The Beyond see *L'Aldila*
Beyond the Darkness see *Buio Omega*
Beyond the Door see *Chi Sei?*
Beyond the Door II see *Shock*
Bianchi, Andrea 132, 137, 171, 239–243, 332
Bianchi, Daniela 267
Bianchi (Montero), Mario 132, 137, 243–246
Uno Bianco 224, 225
Bido, Antonio 7, 246–247
La Bimba di Satana 243–246, 312
The Bird with the Crystal Plumage see *L'Uccello dalle Piume di Cristallo*
Birkin, Jane 165
Bisset, Josie 156
Bite Me, Count see *Il Cavaliere Costante Nicosia Demoniaco, ovvero: Dracula in Brianza*
Bixby, Jerome 94
Black, Karen 117, 166, 171, 173
The Black Angel see *Arabella, l'Angelo Nero*
The Black Cat see *Il Gatto Nero* (1981); *Il Gatto Nero* (1991)
Black Cobra see *Il Cobra Nero; Eva Nera*
Black Demoni see *Demoni Neri*
Black Emanuelle see *Emanuelle Nera*
Black Emanuelle Goes East see *Emanuelle Nera — Orient Reportage*
Black Emanuelle N. 2 see *Emanuelle Nera N. 2*
Black Magic see *Baba Yaga*
Black Sabbath see *I Tre Volti della Paura*
Black Sunday see *La Maschera del Demonio* (1960)
A Black Veil for Lisa see *La Morte Non Ha Sesso*
Blackmail (1968) 316
Blackmail see *Il Ricatto*
A Blade in the Dark see *La Casa con la Scala nel Buio*
The Blade Master see *Ator 2 l'Invincible Orion*
Blade of the Ripper see *Lo Strano Vizio della Signora Wardh*
Blade Violent see *Violenza in un Carcere Femminile*
Blain, Gerard 237
Blanc, Erica (also Blanc, Erika; Blank, Erika) 11, 27, 44, 79, 96, 105, 153, 166, 174, 303, 310, 325, 338
The Blancheville Monster see *Horror*
Blasetti, Alessandro 1
Blastfighter 69, 78, 220
The Blob 13, 86, 275
Blondell, Simone 204, 324, 327
Blood see *L'Occhio nel Labirinto*

Blood and Black Lace see *Sei Donne per l'Assassino*
Blood Delirium see *Delirio di Sangue*
Blood Fiend see *Seddok*
Blood for Dracula see *Dracula Cerca Sangue di Vergine...È Morì di Sete!*
Blood Link see *Extrasensorial*
Blood Money see *La Dove Non Batte il Sole*
Blood Vengeance see *Emanuelle e Françoise: Le Sorelline*
The Bloodstained Shadow see *Solamente Nero*
The Bloody Pit of Horror see *Il Boia Scarlatto*
Bloody Psycho see *Nel Nido del Serpente*
Blount, Lisa 117
Blue Erotic Climax 189–190, 200
Blue Holocaust see *Buio Omega*
Blue Tornado 246
Bluebeard 131
Blynn, Jeff 292
Boccaci, Antonio 247–248, 331
The Bodies Bear Traces of Carnal Violence see *I Corpi Presantano Tracce di Violenza Carnale*
Body Count see *Camping del Terrore*
Body Puzzle see *Corpo Perplessità*
Il Boia Scarlatto 19–21, 307–309
Bolkan, Florinda 28, 37, 42, 122, 124, 138, 139, 334
Bolla, Robert see Kerman, Richard
Bolognini, Mario 1
Bond, Steve 298
Bono, Sonny 195
Boratto, Caterina 29, 286
Borel, Annik 268–269
Borelli, Illaria 115, 119
Borghese, Salvatore 136, 157, 173, 316, 324, 327, 332
Borgnine, Ernest 115, 117, 169, 172, 176
Borowczyk, Walerian 190, 331
Borromeo, Christian see Borromeo, Cristiano
Borromeo, Cristiano 64, 116, 152, 200, 269
Bosch, Valeria 289–290
Boschero, Dominique 172–173, 278, 290, 330, 332
Bose, Lucia 311
Bosic, Andrea 156–157, 267, 278, 331
Boswell, Simon 64, 78–83, 225

Bouchet, Barbara (Barbel Goutscher; also Gutschen) 139, 165, 173, 175, 264, 267, 303
Un Bounty Killer a Trinità 183, 200
A Bounty Hunter in Trinity see *Un Bounty Killer a Trinità*
A Bounty Killer in Trinity see *Un Bounty Killer a Trinità*
Bova, Raoul 226, 232
Brach, Gerard 60, 63
Bragaglia, Carlo Ludovico 109
Brandi, Walter 15–16, 20, 305, 309, 312–313, 329, 338
Brando, Marlon 112
Brandon, David 74, 79–82, 154, 200, 225
Brandon, Michael 42–43, 64
Brass, Tinto 2, 194, 326
Brazzi, Rossano 28, 136, 267, 273–274, 327
Brell, Alfredo Sanchez see Sanbrell, Aldo
Brent, Timothy 179, 284–286
Brescia, Alfonso 331
Briand, Annie see Belle, Annie
Brice, Pierre 27, 154, 158, 272, 335
Brismee, Jean 27, 338
Brivido Giallo 74, 78–79, 82
Brochard, Martine 83, 154, 277
Bronson, Charles (also Buchinski; Buchinsky) 327
The Bronx Warriors see *1990 I Guerrieri del Bronx*
Bronx Warriors 2 285
Brown, Frederic 39, 65
Brown, Jim 166, 178
Brown, Reb 177, 212, 218
Browne, Roger 144, 155, 157–158, 202
Browning, Tod 1
Brutal Nights see *Emanuelle in America*
The Brute and the Beast see *Colt Canatarono la Mort È Fu...Tempo di Massacro*
Bryant, Virginia 75, 78–79, 81, 116
Brynner, Yul 166, 173
Buchanan, Cheryl Lee 261, 287–288
Buchanan, Sherry see Buchanan, Cheryl Lee
Bucholz, Horst 77, 80
Buckman, Tara 207
Buio Omega 189, 197, 200
A Bullet for the General see *Quien Sabe?*
Buona Fine È Migliore Principio 55, 74, 78, 252

Buono, Victor 264, 267
El Buque Maldito 3 see *The Cursed Ship*
Burgess, Anthony 334
Burial Ground see *Le Notti del Terrore*
Buried Alive see *Buio Omega*
Burnett, Don 158
Burton, Lee see Lollobrigida, Guido
Buzzanca, Lando 121–122, 124, 135–136, 139

I Cacciatori del Cobra d'Oro 167, 173
Il Cacciatore di Squalli 283, 285
Caged Women see *Emanuelle — Violenza in un Carcere Femminile*
Cahn, Edward L. 94
Caiano, Mario 19, 27, 237, 324, 335
Cala, Jerry 171, 327
Calderoni, Rita 306–307, 316
Caligola 194, 326
Caligola e Messalina 212, 215
Caligola — La Storia della Raccontata 194, 200, 220
Caligula and Messalina see *Caligola e Messalina*
Caligula Reincarnated as Nero see *Nerone e Poppea*
Caligula — The Untold Story see *Caligola — La Storia della Raccontata*
Caligula 2: The Forbidden Story see *Caligola — La Storia della Raccontata*
Call to You God...and Die see *Joko, Invoca Dio...e Muori*
Caltiki see *Caltiki, il Mostro Immortale*
Caltiki, the Immortal Monster see *Caltiki, il Mostro Immortale*
Caltiki, il Mostro Immortale 13, 23, 85–86, 102, 275, 277
Calvo, Armando 121, 155, 337
Camerini, Mario 1
Cameron, James 336
Cameron, Jeff 183, 200, 335
Caminito, Augusto 31, 138, 335
Camping del Terrore 113, 116
Canale, Gianna Maria 17, 85, 108, 278, 329, 333
Canara, Gabriele 216
Candy 183
Cani Arrabbiati 66, 101–102
Cannibal Apocalypse see *Apocalisse Domani*
Cannibal Ferox 149, 152

Cannibal Holocaust 67, 111–112, 116
Cannibal Massacre see *Cannibal Holocaust*
Cansino, Tini 299–300
Can't Shake the Beat see *Prison Dancer*
Cantafora, Antonio 105, 175, 178, 200
Canter, Kieran 189, 200
Capolicchio, Lino 231–232, 247, 334
Capone, Alessandro 33, 338
Caprioglio, Debora see Kinski, Debora
Captain Yankee see *La Leggenda del Rubino Malese*
Captive Women VII: White Slave see *La Schiave Blanca*
Capucine 74, 80
Car Crash see *Carrera Salvaje*
Caracciolo, Rosa 208
Caraibi 77–78
Carati, Lilli 198, 204
Caravati, Lileana see Carati, Lilli
Cardinale, Claudia 42, 285, 327
Carey, Roland 325
Carlini, Carlo 165, 257, 281
Carnacina, Stella 281
Carnage see *Ecologia del Delitto*
Carne per Frankenstein see *Il Mostro È in Tavola...Barone Frankenstein*
Carnimeo, Giuliano 248–249
Carnival of Souls 133
Caroit, Phillipe 115, 119
Carol Will Die at Midnight see *Morirai a Mezzanotte*
Carpenter, John 56, 193, 284
Carrera Salvaje 167, 173
Carrie 131
La Carroza d'Oro 181, 326
Carsten, Peter 173–174–175, 177
Il Cartaio 62, 321
Caruncula 233–234
La Casa con la Scala nel Buio 68–69, 71–72, 78, 220
La Casa dalle Finestre Che Ridono 230–232
La Casa del Sortilegio 133, 149
La Casa del Tempo 132–133, 136, 149
La Casa del Terrore 132–133, 136–137, 141, 149, 152
Casa dell'Amore...la Polizia Interviene 305–306
La Casa dell'Esorcismo see *Lisa e il Diavolo*
La Casa dell'Orco 72, 75, 78

La Casa delle Anime Erranti 133, 149, 152
La Casa dello Stradivari 55, 252, 253
La Casa No. 3 149, 153, 194
La Casa Privata per le SS 210, 216
La Casa Sperduta nel Parco 112, 114, 116
Casapinta, Ferruccio 24–25, 325
The Case of the Bloody Iris see *Perchè Quelle Strane Gocce di Sangue sul Corpo di Jennifer?*
Cash, Tabitha 205
Casini, Stefania 64, 174, 247
Cassidy, Joanna 260
Cassola, Carla 289–290
Castel, Lou 115, 117, 145, 155, 238, 262
Castellani, Renato 1
Castellari, Enzo G. see Girolami, Enzo
Il Castello dei Morti Vivi 18, 326
Il Castello della Paura 28, 326–327
Castelnuovo, Nino 329
Castle, William 12
Castle of Blood see *La Danza Macabre*
Castle of Death see *La Terrificante Notte del Demonio*
Castle of Terror see *La Danza Macabre*
The Castle of the Living Dead see *Il Castello dei Morti Vivi*
A Cat in the Brain see *Un Gatto nel Cervello*
The Cat O'Nine Tails see *Il Gatto a Nove Code*
The Cathedral see *La Chiesa*
The Cat's Victims see *Il Gatto dagli Occhi di Giada*
Cattarinichi, Mimmo 336
Il Cavaliere Costante Nicosia Demoniaco, ovvero: Dracula in Brianza 3, 124, 136
I Cavalieri Che Fecero l'Impesa 231–232
The Cave of the Golden Goose see *Fantaghiro*
Cecchi, Carlo 231–232
Celentano, Adriana 62, 121
Celli, Adolfo 27, 96, 103, 119, 267, 290, 323, 335
Cemerys, Eva see Czemerys, Eva
Cemetery Man see *Dellamorte, Dellamore*

Cemetery Without Crosses see *Cimitero Senza Croci*
Cena con il Vampiro 75, 78
Centro Sperimentale di Cinematografica 11
Cerentola e la Principessa sul Pisello 312
Certosino, Manlio see Shannon, Mark
Cerusico, Enzo 62, 65
Cervi, Gino 1
Cervi, Tonino 25, 282, 328, 335
Challenge to the Killers see *A 077 Sfida ai Killers*
Challenge to White Fang see *Il Ritorno di Zanna Bianca*
Chandler, Raymond 39
Chanel, Giulia 197–199, 205
Chanel, Helene 154, 278–280, 287
Changeling 2 see *Per Sempre*
Changeling 2: The Return see *Per Sempre*
Changeling 2: The Revenge see *Per Sempre*
Chaplin, Charles 12
Chariots of Fire 55
Charleson, Ian 55, 63
Checchi, Andrea 86, 104, 262
Chi l'Ha Vista Morire? 288–289, 290
Chi Sei? 101, 327
Chianetta, Maria see Maryl, Mara
Chiani, Caterina see Damon, Marzia
Chicken Park 171, 327
La Chiesa 52, 56, 222, 225, 255
Chimenti, Melissa 187, 189, 205
China and Sex 196, 200–201
Chinese Kama Sutra 196, 201
The Chosen see *Holocaust 2000*
Christie, Agatha 18, 51, 90, 98, 133
The Church see *La Chiesa*
Ciak Si Muore 55, 252, 253
Cianfriglia, Giovanni see Wood, Ken
Ciani, Sergio see Steel, Alan
Cicciabomba 149, 153
Cicciolina 211, 216, 300
Cicciolina, Amore Mio 211, 216, 300
Cimitero Senza Croci 38, 327
Le Cinque Bambola per la Luna d'Agosto 98–99, 103
Cinque Donne per l'Assassino 299–300
Le Cinque Giornate 44, 62
Cinque Tombe per un Medium 20, 308–309

Cipriani, Stelvio 102–103, 105, 141, 205, 246–247, 257, 260, 266, 269, 278, 300–301, 315, 336
Circle of Fear see *Alibi Perfetto*
City of the Dead 17
City of the Living Dead see *Paura nella Città dei Morti Viventi*
City of the Walking Dead see *Incubo sulla Città Contaminata*
Clair, Jany 107, 277
Claire 201
Clark, Christopher 197–199, 205
Clark, Ken 94, 105, 107, 144, 152, 267
Clemente, Vincenzo Stefano see De Curtis, Antonio (Toto)
Clery, Corinne 138, 177, 253, 261, 289, 291, 325
Clive, Teagan 284, 286, 332
Cliver, Al 110, 118, 135–140, 142, 198–199, 202, 204
Close Encounters of the Third Kind 279
Coatti, Eva (also Roberto Coati) see Robbins, Eva
Il Cobra Nero 300
Coburn, James 331
La Coda dello Scorpione 293, 296
Codename: Wildgeese see *Arcobaleno Selvaggio*
The Co-Ed Murders see *La Polizia Chiede Aiuto*
Cohen, Larry 264
Colli, Alexandra Della 141
Colli, Ombretta 177
Collin, David, Jr. 107, 327
Collins, Gary 172
Collins, Lewis 169, 172–173, 179
Collins, Ruth 205, 209
Colombatto, Enrica Bianchi see Blanc, Erica
Un Colpo de Pistola 1
Le Colt Canatarono la Mort È Fu…Tempo di Massacro 121, 136
Il Coltello del Vendicatore 94, 103
Coltello di Ghiaccio 144–145, 153
Colucci, Mario 249–251
Combat Shock 233
Come Rubammo la Bomba Atomica 121, 136
A Coming of Aliens see *Incontro Molto…Ravvicinatti del Quatro Tipo*

Commandamenti per un Gangster 37, 327
Commando Leopard 169, 173
Commandos 37, 256–257
Con la Rabbia agli Occhi 166, 173
Conan the Barbarian 193
The Concorde Affair 1979 see *Concorde Affaire 79*
Concorde Affaire 79 111, 116
El Conde Dracula 210
Confessione di un Commissario di Polizia al Procuratore della Repubblica 261–262
Confessions of a Police Captain see *Confessione di un Commissario di Polizia al Procuratore della Repubblica*
Connelly, Christopher 112, 118, 138, 169, 176, 212, 218, 284–285
Connelly, Jennifer 51–52, 64
Connery, Neil 267
Connors, Chuck 241–243, 301
Conquest 129, 136
Contamination see *Contaminazione*
Contaminazione 252–253
Conte, Richard 297, 314–315, 339
Conti, Pier Luigi see Cliver, Al
Contraband see *Luca il Contrabbandiere*
Il Contronatura 24, 42, 163–164, 173
Controrapina 166, 173
Cooper, Stan see Rossi, Stelvio
Cop Target 151, 153
Coplan FX 18 Casse Tout 274, 277
Copper Face see *Tutto per Tutto*
Coppola, Francis Ford 112
Corbucci, Bruno 136, 177, 180
Corbucci, Sergio 1, 17, 24, 106, 109, 174, 328, 332–333
Cord, Alex 257
Cormack of the Mounties see *Giubbe Rosse*
Corman, Roger 56
La Corona di Ferro 1
I Corpi Presantano Tracce di Violenza Carnale 293–294, 296
Corpo Perplessità 76–77, 79
Corpse Which Didn't Want to Die see *La Dama Rossa Uccide Sette Volte*
La Corta Notte delle Bambole di Vetro 32, 288, 290
Cortese, Valentina 106, 136, 278
Cosa Avete Fatto a Solange? 181, 258–260

Così Dolci…Così Perversa 144–145, 153
Così Fan Tutti 196
Cotten, Joseph 25, 99, 105, 111, 116, 154, 330, 338
Cottofavi, Vittorio 1
Cozzi, Luigi 41–43, 56, 63–65, 222, 251–256, 284, 286
Craven, Wes 56, 112
Craving Desire see *Graffiante Desiderio*
Crawlers see *Troll 3*
Creepers see *Troll 3*
Crenna, Anthony 263
Crepax, Guido 27–28
Cries and Shadows see *Un Urlo dalla Tenebrae*
Crimes see *Delitti*
The Crimes of the Black Cat see *Sette Scialli di Setta gialli*
I Criminali della Galassia 109, 162–163, 174
The Crimson Executioner see *Il Boia Scarlatto*
La Cripta e l'Incubo 18, 301–302
Crispino, Armando 7, 37, 256–257
La Cristina Monaca Indemoniata 236–237
Cristofani, Eleanora see Fani, Leonora
Cronenberg, David 72
Cruel Jaws 214, 216
The Crypt of Horror see *Il Castello dei Morti Vivi*; *La Cripta e l'Incubo*
Cucciolla, Riccardo 102, 141, 323
Cuginetta Amore Mio 210, 216
Cunningham, Beryl 297
Cunningham, Liam 62
Cunningham, Sean S. 193
Il Cuore Altrove 231–232
Cupisti, Barbara 82, 141, 156, 220, 225
Curci, Loris 132
The Curse 131
Curse of the Blood Ghouls see *La Strage dei Vampiri*
Curse of the Ghouls see *La Strage dei Vampiri*
Curse of the Living Dead see *Operazione Paura*
The Curse of Ursula see *La Sorella di Ursula*
The Cursed Ship 3 see *El Buque Maldito*
Curtis, Kelly 222, 224, 226
Cut and Run see *Inferno in Diretta*

Cyberflic see *Virtual Assassin*
Czemerys, Eva 236, 269

Da Corleone a Brooklyn 148, 153
D'Abbraccio, Milly 245
Dalbes, Alberto 156
Dallamano, Massimo 7, 29, 181, 258–261, 336
Dallesandro, Joe 165–166, 174, 177, 238
Dalli, Fabienne 105
Dalton, Timothy 43
Daly, James 38, 329
The Dam on the Yellow River see *Apocalisse sul Fiume Giallo*
La Dama Rossa Uccide Sette Volte 302–303
D'Amato, Joe see Massaccesi, Aristide
Damiani, Damiano 261–262
Damiano, Luca 196, 199, 205
Damon, Mark 23, 108, 144, 163, 178, 315–317, 332
Damon, Marzia 207
The Dancer and the Vampire see *L'Amante del Vampiro*
D'Angelo, Mirella 254, 326
Danger: Diabolik see *Diabolik*
Dangerous Attraction see *Attrazione Pericolosa*
Dangerous Obsession see *Il Miele del Diavolo*
Danieli, Emma 157
Danning, Sybil 218, 254, 303, 335
Danninger, Sybille Johnana see Danning, Sybil
La Danza Macabre 19, 160–162, 164, 174
Dario Argento: Master of Horror 254–255
Dario Argento's Museum of Horror see *Il Mondo di Dario Argento 3: Il Museo degli Orrori di Dario Argento*
Dario Argento's World of Horror see *Il Mondo di Dario Argento*
Dark Eyes of the Zombies see *Raptors*
The Dark Is Death's Friend see *L'Assassino È Costretto ad Uccidere Ancora*
Dark Waters 233–234, 320
Davila, Luis 156, 330
Davis, Chet 204, 324
Davis, Ursula 301–302, 329
Dawn of the Dead 48, 125, 191, 217, 339
Dawn of the Mummy 327–328

Dawson, Anthony 267
Day of the Maniac see *Tutti Colori nel Buio*
Days of Violence see *I Giorni della Violenza*
The Dead Are Alive see *L'Etrusco Uccide Ancora*
De Angelis, Fabrizio 135, 141, 142, 201–202, 209, 255, 263, 285–286, 288
Death at Midnight see *Morire a Mezzanotte*
Death in Venice see *Giallo a Venezia*
Death Laid an Egg see *La Morte Ha Fatto l'Uovo*
Death on the Edge of a Razor Blade see *Sul Filo del Rasio*
Death Rage see *Con la Rabbia agli Occhi*
Death Smiles on a Murderer see *Morta Ha Sorriso all'Assassino*
Death Smiles on Murder see *Morta Ha Sorriso all'Assassino*
De Bosin, Gianfranco 101, 334
Il Decameron 183, 328
De Concini, Ennio 86, 140
De Curtis, Antonio (also Clemente, Vincenzo Stefano; Toto) 12, 120–121, 138, 140, 302, 338–339
Deep Blue Sea 69
Deep Red see *Profondo Rosso*
Deep River Savages see *Il Paese del Sesso Selvaggio*
Deep Star Six 171
The Deerhunter 167, 195
De Funes, Isabelle 27–28, 325
Degradation of Emanuelle see *Emanuelle: Perchè Violenza alle Donne*
Dei, Gianni 292
De La Rosa, Nelson 248–249
De Laurentiis, Dino 96, 103, 105, 262, 328, 333
Deliria 194, 220–23, 225, 321
Delirio Caldo 305
Delirio di Sangue 236–237
Delirium (1972) see *Delirio Caldo*
Delirium (1987) see *Le Foto di Gioia*
Delitti 303–304
Delitti Privati 295, 296
Delitto allo Specchio 18, 328
Il Delitto del Diavolo 25, 328
Delitto in Rock 55, 252, 254
Un Delitto Poco Comune 113, 116

Della Colli, Alexandra 287–288
Dellamorte, Dellamore 224, 225, 320
Della Robbia, Luciana see Tamburi, Jenny
Delon, Alain 97
Delon, Anthony 285
Delon, Nathalie 338
Del Pozo, Angel 332
Del Prete, Dulio 141
De Martino, Alberto 181, 184, 264–268
De Masi, Francisco 141, 267, 285, 301, 333
De Mejo, Carlo 138–140, 215, 253, 257
De Mendoza, Alberto 138, 296, 298
Demongeot, Mylene 102, 326
Demoni 52–53, 69, 71, 79, 150–151, 220–222
Demoni Neri 151, 153–154
Demoni 2: L'Incubo Ritorna 53, 71–72, 79
Demonia 132, 136
Demons: The Ogre see *La Casa dell'Orco*
The Demon's Mask (1960) see *La Maschera del Demonio* (1960)
The Demon's Mask (1989) see *La Maschera del Demonio* (1989)
Demons of the Dead see *Tutti i Colori del Buio*
Demons 3 see *Demoni Neri*
Demons 3: The Ogre see *La Casa dell'Orco*
Demy, Valentine 206, 237
De Nava, Giovanni 128, 135, 140
Dennehy, Brian 175
Dentro al Cimitero 74, 75, 79
Deodato, Ruggero 6, 67–68, 109–119, 162, 179, 220, 292, 320
De Ossorio, Amando 3, 23, 149–150, 333
De Ponti, Cinzia 139, 141, 177, 215
Le Deporate della Sezione Speciale SS 268–269
Deported Woman of the SS Special Section see *Le Deporate della Sezione Speciale SS*
De Quincey, Thomas 47–48
De Rossi, Barbara 31, 335
De Rossi, Giannetto 125, 127, 135, 139–140, 142, 166, 172, 243, 263, 335–336
De Rossi, Patrizia see Webley, Patrizia

De Sade's Juliette 204
De Salle, Lorraine 116, 152, 217, 219
Desert Commandos see *Attentato ai Tre Grandi*
Desert of Fire see *Deserto di Fuoco*
The Desert Tigers see *Kaput Lager: Gli Ultimi Giorni delle SS*
Deserto di Fuoco 285
De Sica, Vittorio 105, 165–166, 174
Desideria 77, 79
De Simone, Anna Maria see De Simone, Ria
De Simone, Ria 137, 140, 210, 216–217
De Teffe, Antonio 26, 121, 172, 280–281, 301–304, 314–315
De Toth, Andre 58
The Devil in Miss Jones 190
Devil Walks at Midnight see *La Terrificante Notte del Demonio*
The Devil Witch see *Baba Yaga*
The Devil Within Her (1975) see *Chi Sei?*
The Devil Within Her (1976) 190
The Devil's 190
The Devil's Commandment see *I Vampiri*
The Devil's Honey see *Il Miele del Diavolo*
The Devil's Nightmare see *La Terrificante Notte del Demonio*
The Devil's Veil see *La Maschera del Demonio* (1989)
The Devil's Wedding Night see *Il Plenilunio delle Vergini*
Devouring Waves see *Rosso nell'Oceano*
Dexter, Rosemary 27, 335
Diabolik 66, 96–97, 103, 321
I Diafanoidi Vengono da Marte 109, 162, 174
Dial Help see *Ragno Gelido*
Diario Segreto da un Carcere Femminile 268–269
Diary of a Roman Virgin see *Novelle Licenziose di Vergine Vogliose*
Il Diavolo e i Morti see *Lise e il Diavolo*
1900 I Guerrieri del Bronx 284, 285
Diffring, Anton 278
Di Giandomenico, Stefania see Stella, Stefania
Di Lazzaro, Dalila 64, 177, 290, 330

Di Leo, Fernando 1, 119, 328
Dinner with the Vampire see *Cena con il Vampiro*
Il Dio Chiamato Dorian 258, 260
Dionisio, Silvia see Dionisio, Sylvia
Dionisio, Stefano 63, 231–232
Dionisio, Sylvia 110, 118–119, 174, 277
Di Paolo, Dante 106
Di Paolo, Marcello 111
Di Pietro, Carmen 242
The Dirty Dozen 144
Dirty Pictures see *Un Posto Ideale per Uccidere*
Di Silvestro, Rino 7, 217, 268–270
Di Silvestro, Salvatore see Di Silvestro, Rino
Di Stefano, Andrea 61, 63
Django 109, 328
Django Against Sartana see *Arrivano Django e Sartana...È la Fine*
Django and Sartana Are Coming...It's the End see *Arrivano Django e Sartana...È la Fine*
Django Kill see *Se Sei Vivo Spara*
Django Rides Again see *Keoma*
Django's Great Return see *Keoma*
D'Obici, Valeria 71, 82, 285
Dr. Butcher M.D. see *Zombi Holocaust*
Dr. Butcher — Medical Deviate see *Zombi Holocaust*
Dr. Goldfoot and the Bikini Machine 94
Dr. Goldfoot and the Girl-Bombs see *Le Spie Vengono dal Semifreddo*
La Dolce Casa degli Orrori 132–133, 137, 149
Il Dolce Corpo di Deborah 122
Un Dollaro a Testa 109, 328
Domergue, Faith 141, 264, 267
Dominici, Arturo 104, 329
Donaggio, Pino 65, 116–117, 137, 175–176, 226, 232, 253–254, 290, 311, 338
Donan, J. Lee 330
Donati, Sergio 201, 266, 297, 324, 327, 331
Donne...Botte e Bersaglieri 109, 117
Donne di Piacere 196
Don't Look in the Attic see *La Villa delle Anime Maldette*
Don't Look Now 29

Don't Open the Door for the Man in Black see *Non Aprire l'Uomo Nero*
Don't Torture the Duckling see *Non Si Sevizia un Paperino*
Don't Torture the Ugly Duckling see *Non Si Sevizia un Paperino*
The Door to Darkness see *Il Porta sul Buio*
The Doors to Silence see *Le Porte del Silenzio*
Doppio Bersaglio 212, 216
Dor, Karin 268
Double Face see *A Doppia Faccia*
Double Target see *Doppio Bersaglio*
Douglas, Kirk 89, 264, 266
Dourif, Brad 57, 65
La Dove Non Batte il Sole 166, 174
Dracula 14–15, 86
Dracula Cerca Sangue di Vergine...È Morì di Sete! 165–166, 174
Dracula in the Provinces see *Il Cavaliere Costante Nicosia Demoniaco, ovvero: Dracula in Brianza*
Dreyfuss, Richard 283
Duck! You Sucker! see *Giù la Testa*
Due Mafiosi Contra Goldginger 94, 328–329
Due Mafiosi dell F.B.I. see *Le Spie Vengono dal Semifreddo*
2019 Dopo la Caduta di New York 295, 296
Due Occhi Diabolici 56, 62, 255
Dunn, Michael 28, 327
Duri a Morire 189, 201
Dynamite Joe see *Joe l'Implacabile*

E...di Moda la Morte 55, 74, 79, 252
E Dio Disse a Caino 164, 174
Eastman, George 31, 74, 78, 80, 102, 184–185, 190–191, 193, 195, 199, 201–203, 205–206, 221–222, 225, 284–286, 296–297, 299, 324–325, 333–334
Eastwood, Clint 336
Eaten Alive see *Mangiati Vivi*
Ecologia del Delitto 66, 98–99, 103
The Eerie Midnight Horror Show see *L'Ossessa*
Eggar, Samantha 257
Eisley, Anthony 178

Ekberg, Anita 23, 39, 152–153, 238–239, 333, 337
El Topo 32
Elam, Jack 327
Eleven Days, Eleven Nights see Undici Giorni, Undici Notti
Eleven Days, Eleven Nights: The Final Chapter see Pomeriggio Caldo
Eleven Days, Eleven Nights, Part II see Top Model
11 Days, 11 Nights Part 3 see Pomeriggio Caldo
Eleven Days, Eleven Nights, the Sequel see Undici Giorni, Undici Notti 2
Eleven Days, Eleven Nights 2 see Undici Giorni, Undici Notti 2
Elles Font Tout 189, 201
Elmi, Nicoletta 29, 64, 79, 105, 177, 260, 290
Emanuelle and Françoise see Emanuelle e Françoise: Le Sorelline
Emanuelle and the Last Cannibals see Emanuelle e gli Ultimi Cannibali
Emanuelle and the Porno Nights of the World see Emanuelle e le Porno Notti
Emanuelle and the Porno Nights of the World N. 2 see Emanuelle e le Porno Notti del Mondo N. 2
Emanuelle and the White Slave Trade see La Via della Prostituzione
Emanuelle and the White Slave Trade Today see La Via della Prostituzione
Emanuelle Around the World see Emanuelle: Perchè Violenza alle Donne?
Emanuelle e Francoise see Emanuelle e Françoise: Le Sorelline
Emanuelle e Françoise: Le Sorelline 184–185, 201
Emanuelle e gli Ultimi Cannibali 186–188, 201
Emanuelle e le Porno Notti 189, 201
Emanuelle e le Porno Notti del Mondo N. 2 210, 216
Emanuelle in Africa see Emanuelle Nera — Orient Reportage
Emanuelle in America 185, 187, 201–202
Emanuelle in Bangkok see Emanuelle Nera — Orient Reportage
Emanuelle in Tahiti 185, 203
Emanuelle Nera N. 2 329
Emanuelle Nera — Orient Reportage 185, 202
Emanuelle on Taboo Island 185, 203
Emanuelle on the Island of the Zombies see Le Notti Erotiche dei Morti Viventi
Emanuelle: Perchè Violenza alle Donne? 187, 202
Emanuelle — Reportage de un Carcere Femminile 216
Emanuelle Reports from a Women's Prison see Emanuelle — Violenza in un Carcere Femminile
Emanuelle — Violenza in un Carcere Femminile 212, 216
Emanuelle's Amazon Adventure see Emanuelle e gli Ultimi Cannibali
Emanuelle's Escape from Hell see Violenza in un Carcere Femminile
Emanuelle's Revenge see Emanuelle e Françoise: Le Sorelline
The Embalmer see Il Mostro di Venezia
The Emerald Forest see Mangiati Vivi
Emerson, Keith 63, 131, 138, 225
Emge, David 339
Emilfork, Daniel 338
Emmanuelle: The Joys of a Woman 184
Emmanuelle Nera 184
Endgame see Endgame — Bronx Lotto Finale
Endgame — Bronx Lotto Finale 194, 202, 220
Eno, Brian 63
Eno, Roger 63
Enter the Devil see L'Ossessa
C'era una Volta il West 38, 327
Eraserhead 233
Ercole 254
Ercole al Centro della Terra 16–17, 88–89, 103, 181
Ercole alla Conquista di Atlantide 89
Ercole e la Regina di Lidia 85, 329
Erik, the Conqueror see Gli Invasori
Eroi all'Inferno 183, 203
The Erotic Adventures of Aladdin X see Aladino X
The Erotic Dreams of Aladdin X see Aladino X

The Erotic Dreams of Cleopatra see Sogno Erotici di Cleopatra
Erotic Family 236–237, 314–315
The Erotic Nights of the Living Dead see Le Notti Erotiche dei Morti Viventi
The Eroticist see All'Onorevole Piacciono le Donne...Nonostante le Apparenze e Purchè la Nazione non lo Sappia...
Escape from New York 284
Escape from the Bronx 285
Escape from the Dead see Fuga dalla Morte
Un Esercito di Cinque Uomini 38, 329
L'Esorciccio 29, 329
L'Etrusco Uccide Ancora 256–257
Euston, Brad 305
Eva, la Venere Selvaggia 309, 329
Eva Nera 185, 203
Evans, Raquel 237, 314–315
L'Evasa 55, 252, 254
Eve, the Savage Venus see Eva, la Venere Selvaggia
Eve, the Wild Woman see Eva, la Venere Selvaggia
Everett, Rupert 224–225
Every Man Is My Enemy see Qualcono Ha Tradito
The Evil Dead 33
The Evil Eye see Malocchio; La Ragazza Che Sapeva Troppo
Evils of Dorian Gray see Il Dio Chiamato Dorian
Excite Me see Il Tuo Vizio È una Stanza Chiusa e Solo Io Ne Ho la Chiave
The Executioner of Venice see Giallo a Venezia
The Exorcist 29, 101, 184
The Exterminators see Coplan FX 18 Casse Tout
Extrasensorial 264, 266
Eye in the Labyrinth see L'Occhio nel Labirinto
The Eye of the Evil Dead see L'Occhio del Mal
Eyeball see Gatti Rossi in un Labirinto di Ventro
Eyes Without a Face see Gli Occhi Dentro
Eyewitness see Il Testimone Oculare (1973)
Eyewitness see Il Testimone Oculare (1990)

Fabian (also Fabian Forte) 94, 107

Fajardo, Eduardo 104, 153, 158, 253, 285, 314–315, 328
Falchi, Anna 77–79, 82, 224–225
Falk, Rossella 62–63, 157, 266
The Fall and Rise of the Roman Empire see *Caligola e Messalina*
Fangs of the Living Dead see *Malenka — La Nipote del Vampiro*
Fani, Leonora 29, 234–235, 283, 286, 292
Fantaghiro 77
Fantaghiro II 80
Fantaghiro III 80
Fantaghiro IV 80
Fantaghiro V 80
Il Fantasma dell'Opera 3, 60–61, 63
I Fantasmi di Sodoma 131–132, 137
Farmer, Mimsy 42–43, 64, 111, 113, 116, 127, 137, 169, 172, 234–235, 255–256–257
Farrina, Corrado 27–28, 325
Farrow, Tisa 125, 142, 179, 191, 199
Fatal Frames see *Fotogrammi Mortali*
Father Hope 115
La Fatiche di Ercole 85, 329
Fear see *Follia Omicida*
Fehmiu, Bekim 105
Fellini, Federico 1, 96
La Femme du Boulanger 307, 310
Fenech, Edwige 98, 103, 113, 116, 124, 139, 165, 240–243, 249, 293–296, 298
Fenomenal e il Tesoro di Tutankhamen 109, 117
Ferida, Luisa 1
Ferrara, Abel 2
Ferrari, Sofia 203, 207
Ferrer, Mel 148, 154–155, 266, 297
Ferrigno, Carla 253
Ferrigno, Lou 218, 253–254, 284, 286
Ferrini, Franco 62–65, 69, 72, 79, 225
Ferroni, Giorgio 16, 92, 270–272
Ferzetti, Gabriele 141, 327
Festa, Al 4, 272–274
Fidani, Demofilo 181, 183, 204, 324
Fidenco, Nico 139, 201–203, 206, 209, 237, 257, 288, 314
La Figlia di Frankenstein 25–26, 330

Il Figlio delle Stelle 220
Figura, Kasha 115, 119
The Final Curtain see *L'Assassino...È al Telefono* (1973)
Finalmente...Le Mille e Una Notte 165, 175
La Finestra sul Cortile 55
A Fistful of Dollars see *Per un Pugno di Dollari*
A Fistful of Dynamite see *Giù la Testa*
Fitzgerald, Teresa 278
The Five Days (also *The Five Days in Milan*) see *Le Cinque Giornate*
Five Dolls for an August Moon see *Le Cinque Bambola per la Luna d'Agosto*
The Five Man Army see *Un Esercito di Cinque Uomini*
Five Women for the Killer see *Cinque Donne per l'Assassino*
Flashdance 131, 194
Flavia, la Monaca Musulmana see *La Monaca Musulmana*
Flavia, the Heretic see *La Monaca Musulmana*
Fleming, Ian 38
Flemyng, Robert 17–18, 278
Flesh for Frankenstein see *Il Mostro È in Tavola...Barone Frankenstein*
The Flower of Desire see *China and Sex*
Flynn, Sean 143, 157
Foglietti, Mario 44
Follia Omicida 276–277
Follie di una Notte 189, 203
Fonda, Henry 327
Foree, Ken 339
Formula for a Murder see *7, Hyden Park — la Casa Maledetta*
Formula 3 — I Ragazzi dell'Autodrommo 242
Forrest, Andy J. 149
Forrest, Frederic 57, 65
Forsythe, Stephen 97, 106, 330
Foschi, Massimo 119
Foster, Lisa 200
Le Foto di Gioia 72–74, 76, 80
Fotogrammi Mortali 4, 273–274
Four Flies on Gray Velvet see *Quattro Mosche di Velluto Grigio*
The Four Gunmen of the Apocalypse see *Quattro dell'Apocalisse*
The Four of the Apocalypse see *Quattro dell'Apocalisse*
4...3...2...1...Morte! 171, 330

Four Times That Night see *Quattro Volte...Quella Notte*
Foxy Lady see *Spiando Marina*
Fragrasso, Claudio 142, 195, 206, 208, 215, 217–219, 332
Frajese, Marina 189–190, 202–203, 205, 216, 217, 243, 245, 280–281, 314–315
Franchi, Franco 29, 94, 107, 121, 135–136, 141, 329
Franciosa, Anthony 50, 64, 164, 177
Francisci, Pietro 16, 85, 329
Franciscus, James 41, 63, 111, 116, 166, 172, 283, 286
Franco, Jess see Manera, Jesus Franco
Francoisa, Massimo 337
Franju, Georges 16
Frank, Horst 27, 63, 144, 152–153. 257, 335
Frankenstein all'Italiana 256–257
Frankenstein '80 28, 330
Frankenstein Italian Style see *Frankenstein all'Italiana*
Frankenstein 2000 see *Ritorno dalla Morte*
Frankenstein's Castle of Freaks see *Il Castello della Paura*
Franklin, Richard 291
I Fratti Rossi 132, 330
Freda, Riccardo 1, 7, 12–15, 17–18, 20, 75, 84–86, 102, 108, 274–278
Fredrick, Lynne 139, 203
Free Hand for a Tough Cop see *Il Trucido e lo Sbirro*
Frezza, Giovanni 139, 286
Friday the 13th 53, 113, 193
Frumkes, Roy 287–288
La Frusta e il Corpo 19, 90, 101, 104
Fuchs, Herbert 330
Fuchsberger, Joachim 173, 257–260
Fuga dal Bronx 285
Fuga dalla Morte 132, 137, 330
Fuga dall'Arcipelago Maledetto 167, 175
Fulci, Antonella 3–4, 6
Fulci, Lucio 1, 3, 6, 29, 33, 58, 69, 120–142, 150, 166–167, 184, 191, 193, 195, 213–214, 219–220, 241–243, 245, 252, 263, 266, 277, 302, 320, 330, 333, 338
Funari, Dirce 189–191, 199, 201, 203, 205–206
Funari, Patrize see Funari, Dirce

Funari, Patrizia *see* Funari, Dirce
Furia in Marrakech 330
Furlong, Edward 232
Furstenberg, Ira 103
Fury in Marrakesh see *Furia in Marrakech*
FX 18 Superspy see *Coplan FX 18 Casse Tout*

La Gabbia 131
Gainsbourg, Serge 165
Galbo, Cristina 253, 259–260
Galleana, Elyde *see* Galleani, Ely
Galleani, Ely 105, 141, 202–203, 209
Galli, Ida *see* Stewart, Evelyn
Gallone, Carmine 1
Gang War in Milan see *Milano Rovente*
Gangland Bangers 203
Gardenia, Vincent
Gariazzo, Mario 279–281, 301
Garko, Gianni 69, 76, 79, 82, 141, 249, 254, 270–272, 337
Garrani, Ivo 104, 326, 329
Gaspari, Ludovico 335
Gassman, Vittorio 285, 331
Gastaldi, Ernesto 22, 104, 116, 171, 175–176, 179, 249, 278, 296, 298, 302, 306–307, 330, 332–333
Gastaldi, Romano 183
Gaston Leroux's House of Wax see *M.D.C.— La Maschera di Wax*
Gaston Leroux's Wax Mask see *M.D.C.— La Maschera di Wax*
Gastoni, Lisa 42, 143, 152, 163, 174
The Gates of Hell see *Paura nella Città dei Morti Viventi*
The Gates of Hell (1989) see *Le Porte dell'Inferno*
Gatti Rossi in un Labirinto di Vetro 147–148, 154
Il Gatto a Nove Code 41–42, 63, 303
Il Gatto dagli Occhi di Giada 246
Un Gatto nel Cervello 133, 137
Il Gatto Nero (1981) 127, 137
Il Gatto Nero (1991) 56, 222, 252, 254
Gemma, Giuliano 64, 140, 285, 311, 324
Gemser, Laura 184–189, 191, 198, 200–203, 205–212, 216–219, 263, 277, 332, 334
Genghis Khan (1993) 171, 331

Gentilomo, Giacomo 333
Gentleman Costant Nicosia Is a Demon, or: Dracula in Brianza see *Il Cavaliere Costante Nicosia Demoniaco, ovvero: Dracula in Brianza*
Gently, Before She Dies see *Il Tuo Vizio È una Stanza Chiusa e Solo Io Ne Ho la Chiave*
George, Christopher 125, 127, 139
Germani, Gaia 326
Ghastly Orgies of Count Dracula see *Riti, Magie Nere e Segrete Orge nel Trecento*
Ghione, Riccardo 37, 336
The Ghost see *Lo Spettro*
The Ghost Galleon see *El Buque Maldito*
Ghost House see *La Casa No. 3*
Ghost House 2 see *La Casa dell'Orco*
The Ghost of Sodom see *I Fantasmi di Sodoma*
Ghosthouse see *La Casa No. 3*
The Ghosts of Sodom see *I Fantasmi di Sodoma*
Giagni, Gianfranco 7, 281–282
Giallo a Venezia 291–292
Giallo — La Tua Impronta del Venerdì 55
Giallo Natale 55, 252, 254
Gianasi, Rick 273–274
Giannini, Giancarlo 22, 232, 332
The Giant of Marathon see *La Battaglia di Maratona*
The Giants of Rome see *I Giganti di Roma*
Gibson, Michelle 206
Gielgud, John 326
I Giganti di Roma 162, 175
Gilliam, Terry 222
Gimpera, Teresa 272
Ginty, Robert 151, 153, 241–243
Il Gioko 75, 80
Giordano, Daniela 98, 105, 207, 255, 299, 314–315, 329
Giordano, Ivana 306
Giordano, Mariangela 176, 226, 240–244, 292
Giorni da Leone 234–235
I Giorni della Violenza 247, 331
Il Giorno dei Diavolo 67, 83, 101–102, 108
Giovanni dalle Bande Nere 210, 331
Gipsy Angel 273, 274
Girardot, Annie 37, 296
The Girl from Vondel Park see *Hanna D.*

The Girl Who Knew Too Much see *La Ragazza Che Sapeva Troppo*
Girolami, Andrea 286
Girolami, Ennio 263, 282, 285–286
Girolami, Enzo 29, 31, 125, 214, 263, 282–287, 291
Girolami, Marino 14, 282, 287–288
Girolami, Romolo 282
Girolami, Stefania 285–286
Girotti, Mario *see* Hill, Terence
Girotti, Massimo 1, 105, 335
Giù la Testa 171, 331
Giubbe Rosse 181, 184, 203
Giubetto Rosso 55, 74, 81
Giustiziere Sfida la Città 148, 154
Glass, Philip 224–225
Glass, Uschi 145–146, 157
Go Away! Trinity Has Arrived in Eldorado see *Scansati... Trinità Arriva Eldorado*
Go for Broke see *Tutto per Tutto*
Go Go World see *Il Pelo nel Mondo*
Goblin (musical group) 45–48, 52, 61, 64, 74, 200, 215, 217, 225, 246, 255
The Golden Arrow see *L'Arciere delle Mille e Una Notte*
The Golden Coach see *La Carroza d'Oro*
Goldface, the Fantastic Superman see *Goldface, il Fantastico Superman*
Goldface, il Fantastico Superman 210, 331
Goldfinger 94
Goldsmith, Jerry 178
Goliath and the Vampires see *Maciste Contro il Vampiro*
Goliath Vs. the Vampires see *Maciste Contro il Vampiro*
The Goodnight Girl see *Cicciolina, Amore Mio*
Gora, Claudio 257, 262, 301, 329
Gore in Venice see *Giallo a Venezia*
Goren, Annj 189–190, 201, 203, 205–206
Gori, Gabriele 214, 218
Gori, Lallo Coriolano 107, 135–136, 204, 269, 324
Gori, Patrizia 184–185, 201, 339
Gortner, Marjoe 255
Graffiante Desiderio 295, 297

Grand Slam see *Ad Ogni Costo*
Grandi, Serena 74, 76, 80, 191, 199, 253, 297
Granger, Farley 249–251, 261
Graver, Gary 297
Graves, Peter 38, 329
Gravina, Carla 264, 266
Graziani, Sergio 62
Great White see *L'Ultimo Squalo*
Greci, Jose 155
Greene, Daniel 299
Gregory, Mark 284–286
Gremlins 195
Grieco, Sergio 331
The Grim Reaper see *Anthropophagus*
The Grim Reaper II see *Anthropophagus II*
Grimaldi, Eva 76, 81, 249, 300
Guaita-Ausonia, Mario 10–11
Guardian from Hell see *L'Altro Inferno*
Guardian of the Deep see *Il Cacciatore di Squalli*
Guardians of the Deep see *Il Cacciatore di Squalli*
Guarracino, Umberto 11, 334
Guccione, Bob 326
Guerin, Florence 215, 254
Guerra, Blanca 32, 336
La Guerre du Pétrole 316
Guerrieri, Romolo 122
I Guerrieri dell'Anno 2072 131, 137
Guida, Wandisa 108, 163, 171, 175, 178, 278, 296, 312
Gunfighters Die Harder see *Sartana*
Gungala, the Nude Panther see *Gungala, la Pantera Nuda*
Gungala, la Pantera Nuda 110, 117
Gypsy Angel see *Gipsy Angel*

Una Hacha para la Luna de Miel see *Il Rosso Segno della Follia*
Hackenschmied, Alexander 333
Hagler, Marvin 169, 171, 175–176, 180
Hagman, Larry 86
Halloween 193
Halsey, Brett 97–98, 105–106, 131, 136–140, 141, 169, 179, 254, 335
Hammett, Dashiell 39
Hampton, Demetra 282, 327
Hands of Steel see *Vendetta dal Futoro*
Hanna D 212, 217, 268–269
Hansel e Gretel 132, 331

Hard Sensation see *Hard Sensations*
Hard Sensations 189, 203
Hard Times for Dracula see *Tempi Duri per i Vampiri*
Hargitay, Mickey 20–21, 304–309
Harlin, Renny 69
Harmon, Robert 151
Harmstorf, Raimund 140, 142
Harper, Jessica 47–49, 64
Harris, Brad 165, 176, 212, 218, 254, 316, 329
Harris, James 316
Harrison, Dan 312
Harrison, Richard 162, 171, 175–176, 191, 193, 205, 218, 237, 316
Hasselhoff, David 255
A Hatchet for the Honeymoon see *Il Rosso Segno della Follia*
Hauer, Rutger 151
Haughton, David Caine see Brandon, David
A Heart Elsewhere see *Il Cuore Altrove*
The Heart Is Everywhere see *Il Cuore Altrove*
Heavy Metal 55, 74, 81, 252
Hedley, Jack 141
Hedman, Marina see Frajese, Marina
Hell Below Deck see *Le Avventura di Mary Read*
Hell of the Living Dead see *Inferno dei Morti-Viventi*
Hell Penitentiary see *Emanuelle — Violenza in un Carcere Femminile*
Hellman, Oliver see Assonitis, Ovidio
Hell's Gate see *Le Porte dell'Inferno*
Hemingway, Susan 201
Hemmings, David 45, 64
Hemmingway, Margaux 166, 171–172
Henricksen, Lance 336
Hercules see *Ercole*
Hercules at the Center of the Earth see *Ercole al Centro della Terra*
Hercules in the Center of the Earth see *Ercole al Centro della Terra*
Hercules in the Haunted World see *Ercole al Centro della Terra*
Hercules, Prisoner of Evil see *Ursus il Terrore dei Kirghisi*
Hercules II see *The Adventures of Hercules; Le Avventure dell'Incredibile Ercole*

Hercules Unchained see *Ercole e la Regina di Lidia*
Hercules Vs. Karate see *Ming, Ragazzi!*
Heroes in Hell see *Eroi all'Inferno*
Hersent, Philippe 175, 267, 326, 331, 333
Herter, Gerard 102, 277
Herzog, Werner 31
Hess, David 112–114, 116–117, 325
Heyward, Louis M. 107
Heywood, Anne 264, 266
Hickland, Catherine 218, 301
High Finance Woman see *La Signora di Wall Street*
Hill, Craig 207, 246–247
Hill, Terence 171, 180
Hilton, George 75, 78, 112, 118, 136, 249, 253, 293–294, 296, 298, 328
Histoires Extraordinaires see *Tre Passi nel Delirio*
Hitch Hike see *Autostop Rosso Sangue*
Hitch-Hike see *Autostop Rosso Sangue*
Hitchcock, Alfred 12, 17–18, 89, 122
The Hitcher 151
Hitcher II 156; see also *Paura nel Buio*
Hoffman, Robert 147, 157, 258, 260, 323, 325
Holocaust 2000 264, 266
The Holy Mountain 32
Holzer, Hans 262
Hornsby e Rodriguez 151, 154
The Horribile Dr. Hichcock see *L'Orribile Segreto del Dr. Hichcock*
The Horrible Orgies of Count Dracula see *Riti, Magie Nere e Segrete Orge nel Trecento*
Horrifying Experiments of the SS Last Days see *La Bestia in Calore*
Horror 264, 267
Horror Castle see *La Vergine di Norimberga*
Horror Hotel see *City of the Dead*
Horror of Dracula see *Dracula*
Horror of the Zombies see *El Buque Maldito*
Hossein, Robert 10, 58, 327, 333
Hot Laps see *Formula 3 — I Ragazzi dell'Autodrommo*
Hot Love Life of Al Capone see *Al Capone*

Hough, John 171, 239, 242, 332
The House by the Cemetery see Quella Villa Accanto al Cimitero
The House of Clocks see La Casa del Tempo
The House of Exorcism see Lise e il Diavolo
The House of Horrors see La Casa del Terrore
House of Wax 58, 134
The House Outside the Cemetery see Quella Villa Accanto al Cimitero
House 3 see La Casa No. 3
House with the Dark Staircase see La Casa con la Scala nel Buio
House with the Dark Stairway see La Casa con la Scala nel Buio
House with the Windows That Laugh see La Casa dalle Finestre Che Ridono
House with the Windows That Laughed see La Casa dalle Finestre Che Ridono
The Houses of Doom see La Casa del Terrore
How to Steal an Atomic Bomb see Come Rubammo la Bomba Atomica
How We Stole the Atomic Bomb see Come Rubammo la Bomba Atomica
Hubschmid, Paul 268
Huff, Brent 213, 218
Huff, Karina 136, 141, 254
The Humanoid see La Umanoide
Hundar, Robert 155, 158
Hunnebelle, Andre 27, 338
Hunter, Kim 63
Hunter, Tab 160, 172
Hunter, Thomas 144, 155
Hunter of the Unknown see Agente 3S3: Massacro al Sole
Hunters of the Golden Cobra see I Cacciatori del Cobra d'Oro

I Am Sartana, Your Angel of Death see Sono Sartana, il Vostro Becchino
I, Vampire [sic] see I Vampiri
An Ideal Place to Kill see Un Posto Ideale per Uccidere
An Ideal Place to Murder see Un Posto Ideale per Uccidere
If You Meet Sartana, Pray for Your Death see Sartana
L'Iguana dalla Lingua di Fuoco 276, 278
The Iguana with the Tongue of Fire see L'Iguana dalla Lingua di Fuoco
I'll See You in Hell see Ti Aspetterò all'Inferno
Images in the Convent see Immagini di un Convento
Immagini di un Convento 190, 203
L'Impero 77, 81
L'Impronta dell'Assassino 56, 252, 254
In the Folds of the Flesh see Nelle Pieghe della Carne
In the Name of the Father see I Quattro del Pater Noster
In the Web of the Spider see Nella Stretta Morsa del Ragno
L'Inafferabile, Invincibile Mr. Invisible 164, 175
Incontrera, Annabella 249, 277, 304, 333
Incontro Molto...Ravvicinatti del Quattro Tipo 279-280
Gli Incubi di Dario Argento 53
Incubo sulla Città Contaminata 148-149, 154, 167, 312
Indio 169, 175
Indio II: The Revolt 169, 175
Indio III 169, 175-176
Inferno 49-50, 63, 67, 131, 233, 252
Inferno dei Morti-Viventi 211, 213, 217
Inferno in Diretta 112, 117
Inginocchiati Straniero...i Cadaveri Non Fanno Ombra! 181, 183, 204
Ingrassia, Ciccio 29, 94, 107, 121, 135-136, 273-274, 329
Innocent Blood 57
Innocents from Hell see L'Altro Inferno
Inspector Justice see L'Inspettore Giusti
L'Inspettore Giusti 295, 297
Interlenghi, Antonella see Keller, Almanta
Interlenghi, Antonellina see Keller, Almanta
L'Interno di un Convento 331
L'Interpretare l'Incubo Dario Argento 55
Interzone 194, 332
The Invaders see Gli Invasori
Invasion of the Flesh Hunters see Apocalisse Domani
Gli Invasori 89, 104
Il Invincibile Cavaliere Mascherato 143, 154
Ippolito, Ciro 220, 324

Ireland, John 119, 141, 144, 158, 265, 267
The Iron Crown see La Corona di Ferro
Isabel, Duchess of the Devils see Isabel, Duchessa del Diavoli
Isabel, Duchessa del Diavoli 24, 332
Isabell, a Dream 251
Island of Mutations see L'Isola degli Uomini Pesci
Island of the Living Dead see Zombi 2
Island of the Zombies see Le Notti Erotiche dei Morti Viventi
L'Isola degli Uomini Pesci 294, 297
L'Isola del Tesoro (1972) 171, 239, 332
L'Isola del Tesoro (1986) 169, 176
L'Isola della Svedesi 181, 332
It! The Terror from Beyond Space 94

Jaeckin, Just 184
Jailbird Rock see Prison Dancer
Je Brûle de Partout 189
Jeffries, Lang 330
Jodorowsky, Alexandro 31-32, 336
Jodorowsky, Axel 336
Joe l'Implacabile 163, 176
John il Bastardo 256-257
John the Bastard see John il Bastardo
Johnny Oro 109, 332
Johnson, Richard 29, 125, 142, 260-262, 327, 334
Johnson, Van 111, 116, 153, 263, 294-296, 301
Joko, Invoca Dio...e Muori 163, 176
Jones, Dean 164, 175
Josipovici, Jean 18, 328
Juering, Arno 174, 177
The Juke Box Girls see I Ragazzi del Juke Box
Jungle Heat see Tarzan X
Jungle Holocaust see Ultimo Mondo Cannibale
Jungle Raiders see La Leggenda del Rubino Malese
Jurgens, Curd 155
Jurgens, Curt see Jurgens, Curd
Justine 204
Justine and Juliette 189

Kaput Lager: Gli Ultimi Giorni delle SS 315-316
Karlatos, Olga 138, 285

Karamesinis, Vassili *see* Karras, Vassili
Karloff, Boris (also William Henry Pratt) 91–92, 100, 108
Karras, Vassili 216, 218, 236, 292, 300–301
Keach, Stacy 298
Keaton, Camille 259–260
Kedrova, Lila 260
Keifer, Warren 18, 326
Keitel, Harvey 56, 63
Keith, David 131
Keller, Almanta 141
Keller, Sarah 135
Kelly, Jack 257
Kelly, Jim 166, 178
Kendall, Suzy 40, 44, 65, 147, 157, 294
Kendall, Tony 90, 104, 261
Kennedy, Arthur 289, 291
Kensit, Patsy 246
Kenton, Erle C. 1
Keoma 31, 282, 285
Kerman, Richard *see* Kerman, Robert
Kerman, Robert 116, 148, 152, 155
Kerova, Zora 140, 141, 152, 219, 286, 330
Kiel, Richard 289, 291
Kier, Udo 64, 165–166, 174, 177, 338
Kill, Baby, Kill see Operazione Paura
The Killer (1989) 164
Killer Crocodile 263
Killer Crocodile II 263
Killer Fish see L'Agguato sul Fondo
The Killer Is on the Phone see L'Assassino...È al Telefono (1973 and 1994 versions)
The Killer Is on the Telephone see L'Assassino...È al Telefono (1973 and 1994 versions)
The Killer Must Strike Again see L'Assassino È Costretto ad Uccidere Ancora
The Killer Strikes Again see L'Assassino È Costretto ad Uccidere Ancora
The Killers Are Challenged see A 077 Sfida ai Killers
Killing Birds see Raptors
Kincaid, Tim 286
King, Stephen 51
King, Tony 118, 167, 172, 175, 179
Kinski, Debora 76, 81, 295, 298
Kinski, Klaus (also Klaus Gunther Nakszynski) 31, 164,
169, 172–175, 177, 183–184, 203–204, 249, 262, 276–277, 323, 335, 337
Kirkland, Sally 63
The Kiss see Il Baccio
Kiss Me, Kill Me 325
Klein, T.E.D. 57, 65
The Knife of Ice see Il Coltello di Ghiaccio
The Knights of the Quest see I Cavalieri Che Fecero l'Impesa
The Knives of Ice see Il Coltello di Ghiaccio
Knives of the Avenger see Il Coltello del Vendicatore
Koch, Marianne 173, 336
Koll, Claudia 77, 81
Konopka, Magda 24, 236, 269, 337
Koscina, Sylva 100, 121, 136, 304, 329, 338
Kretschmann, Thomas 64, 82, 232
Kriminal 144, 155
Kristel, Sylvia 184
Kruger, Christiane 277
Kruger, Lea *see* Leander, Lea
Krystye, Anthony *see* Boccaci, Antonio
Kubrick, Stanley 171
Kyra: Lady of the Lake see Sensitivita
Kyra: La Signora del Lago see Sensitivita
KZ9 Lager di Stermino 210, 218

Labbra Bagnate 190, 204
Lacy, Ronald 117
Ladies of the Night see Follie di una Notte
Lado, Aldo 7, 288–291
I Ladri 121, 137–138
Lady Frankenstein see La Figlia di Frankenstein
Ladyhawke 77
Laennac, Katell 240–243
Laforet, Marie 285
Lai, Me Me 111, 119, 147–148, 155–156
Lancaster, Burt 101, 334
Landi, Mario 291–292
Landis, John 57
Lane, Sirpa 187, 189, 205
Lanfranchi, Mario 67, 325
La Russo, Adrienne 135
Lasciapassare per il Morto 279–280
Lasri, Shulasmith (also Emanuelle Neri) 329
Lassander, Dagmar 106, 137, 140, 269, 278, 329

The Last Cannibal World see Ultimo Mondo Cannibale
The Last House Near the Lake see Sensitivita
The Last House on the Left 112, 289
Last House on the Left: Part 2 see Ecologia del Delitto
The Last Hunter see L'Ultimo Cacciatore
The Last Jaws see L'Ultimo Squalo
The Last Man to Kill see Un Milione di Dollari per Sette Assassini
The Last Survivor see Ultimo Mondo Cannibale
Lattanzi, Claudio 194, 206
Laurenti, Fabrizio 195
Laurie, Piper 57, 65
Lavi, Daliah 90, 104
Lavi, Gabriele 62–64, 230, 232, 327
Law, John Philip 96, 103, 236–237, 311, 338
Lawrence, Marc 329
Lawrence, Peter Lee 144, 158, 331
Lazar, Veronica 135
Lazaro, Francoise Hadji 224–225
Lazenby, George 288–290
Leander, Lea 102, 106, 316
Lear, Amanda 189, 203
Le Brock, Gene 31, 334
Lee, Bernard 267
Lee, Christopher 14, 17–19, 82, 88–90, 103–104, 120–121, 161, 179, 301–302, 326, 338
Lee, Margaret 260, 277
LeFanu, Sheridan 18
Legend 77
The Legend of the Maltese Ruby see La Leggenda del Rubino Malese
Legend of the She-Wolf see La Lupe Mannera
The Legend of the Wolf Woman see La Lupe Mannera
Legend of the WolfWoman see La Lupe Mannera
La Leggenda del Rubino Malese 169, 176
La Legione dei Dannati 38, 144, 155
Leigh, Janet 323
Lemoine, Michel 107, 174, 328
Len, Jeanette *see* Lenzi, Giovanna
Lennon, John 42
Lenzi, Giovanna 303–304

Index

Lenzi, Umberto 1, 6, 37–38, 72, 110, 133, 143–158, 167, 181, 194–195, 253, 292
Leonardi, Marco 232
Leone, Alfredo 100, 104–105
Leone, Sergio 1, 38, 171, 327, 331, 335–336
Lerici, Barbara 61
Leroux, Gaston 60, 63, 134
Leroy, Philippe 155, 169, 175–176, 290, 326
Levi, Laura 139, 189–190, 200, 315
Leviathan 171
Levin, Henry 88, 104–105
Lewis, Charlotte 113, 115, 118
Lewis, Geoffrey 140
Lewis, Jerry 121
Libido 22, 26, 332
Lieh, Lo 166, 174
Lightning Bolt see *Operazione Goldman*
Liljedahl, Marie 260
Linder, Christa 136
Lindt, Max see Hoffman, Robert
Lindt, Rosemarie 184–185, 201, 203, 290
Line, Helga 153, 155, 264, 267, 320
Lisa and the Devil see *Lise e il Diavolo*
Lise e il Diavolo 66, 99–101, 104
Lisi, Virna 140, 142, 285
Little Lips see *Piccole Labbra*
Live Like a Cop, Die Like a Man see *Uomini Si Nasce, Poliziotti Si Muore*
A Lizard in a Woman's Skin see *Una Lucertola con la Pelle di Donna*
La Llama nel Corpo 21, 332
LoCascio, Franco see Damiano, Luca
Lollobrigida, Gina 310–311
Lollobrigida, Guido 267–268, 327
Lom, Herbert 222–223, 226, 260
Lombardo, Godfrey 39
Loncar, Beba 331, 339
Lone Runner 113, 117
The Long Hair of Death see *I Lunghi Capelli della Morte*
The Long Night of Veronique see *La Lunga Notte di Veronique*
Longo, Malissa 137, 178, 237, 330
Lorys, Diana 163, 178, 333
Lotar, Marina see Frajase, Marina

Love and Death in a Women's Prison see *Diario Segreto da un Carcere Femminile*
Love Angels see *Prostituzione*
The Love Circle see *Metti, una Sera a Cena*
Love, Lucretia 110, 117, 119, 269, 281, 338
Love, Lucrezia see *Love, Lucretia*
Love Ritual see *Rito d'Amore*
Love Sacrifice see *Cuginetta Amore Mio*
Lovelock, Raymond 25, 110, 119, 131, 138, 145, 156, 257, 281, 295–296, 311, 328
Loy, Mino 330
Luca il Contrabbandiere 138
Luca, the Smuggler see *Luca il Contrabbandiere*
Lucchetti, Leandro 131, 137, 334
Una Lucertola con la Pelle di Donna 122, 124, 141
Lucidi, Antonini 242–243, 245, 331
Lui, Giancarlo 326
Luke, Jorge 285
Lund, Deanna 33, 338
La Lunga Notte di Veronique 21–22, 333
I Lunghi Capelli della Morte 19, 161, 168, 176
La Lupe Mannera 268–269
Lupo, Alberto 143, 151, 279–280, 326
Lupo, Michele 181, 324, 337
Lussuria 204
Lust see *L'Alcova*
Lustig, William 46
Lynch, David 233
Lynch, Richard 112, 116–118

Macabre see *Macabro*
Macabro 67, 81
Macchie Solari 255–257
MacColl, Catherine see MacColl, Catriona
MacColl, Catriona 125, 127–128, 135, 139–140
Machiavelli, Nicoletta 158, 328
Maciste all'Inferno 17, 89, 274, 278
Maciste Contro il Vampiro 17, 333
Maciste in Hell see *Maciste all'Inferno*
Maciste in King Solomon's Mines see *Maciste nelle Miniere di Re Salomone*
Maciste nelle Miniere di Re Salomone 312
Macumba Sexual 193

Mad Max 131, 167, 193–194, 211, 284
Madness in the Night see *Follie di una Notte*
Il Maestro del Terrore 75, 81
Magall, Macha 316
Magee, Patrick 127, 137
The Magnificent Seven 218
Magnolfi, Barbara 337
Magnoni, Agostina Maria see Belli, Agostina
Majano, Anton Giulio 16, 88, 337
Majors, Lee 166, 171
Make Them Die Slowly see *Cannibal Ferox*
Malabimba 239–243
Malco, Paolo 140–141, 246, 296
Malden, Karl 41, 63
Malenka — The Niece of the Vampire see *Malenka — La Nipote del Vampiro*
Malenka — La Nipote del Vampiro 23, 333
Malfatti, Marina 26, 303
Malizia Oggi 236–237
Malle, Louis 96
Malocchio 314–315
Mamma, Ci Penso Lo 115, 117
Mamma, I Can Do It Alone see *Mamma, Ci Penso Lo*
A Man Called Horse 147
The Man from Deep River see *Il Paese del Sesso Selvaggio*
A Man to Laugh see *Un Uomo da Ridere*
The Man Who Could Cheat Death 113
The Man Who Knew Too Much 89
The Man Who Would Not Die see *L'Uomo Che Non Volere*
The Man Who Wouldn't Die see *L'Uomo Che Non Volere*
Man with the Icy Eyes see *L'Uomo dagli Occhi di Ghiaccio*
Mancini, Mario 28, 330
Manera, Jesus Franco 1–2, 6, 189, 193, 201, 204, 210, 235, 241
Mangiati Vivi 148, 155
Manhattan Baby see *L'Occhio del Mal*
Mania 239–243, 305
Mann, Leonard 289, 291
Manni, Ettore 18, 140, 175, 179, 203, 249, 332
Mansfield, Jayne 307
Marandi, Evi 107, 324, 331
La Marca del Hombre Lobo 23

Margheriti, Antonio 1, 6, 18–19, 22–24, 42, 75, 109, 159–180, 212, 266–267, 289, 291, 327, 331
Marley, John 257
Marshall, E.G. 56, 63
Marsillach, Blanca 131, 138
Marsillach, Cristina 55, 63, 131
Martell, Peter (also Martellanz, Pietro) 177
Martin, Dean 121
Martin, George 337
Martin, Jared 135, 137
Martinelli, Elsa 141
Martines, Alessandra 80
Martino, Luciano 22, 175, 171, 249, 297–299, 330
Martino, Sergio 292–299
Martucci, Gianni Antonio 132, 330
Martucci, Joe *see* Martucci, Gianni Antonio
Maryl, Mara 22, 332
La Maschera del Demonio (1960) 14, 19, 66–67, 86–90, 104–105
La Maschera del Demonio (1989) 72, 75–76, 81, 222
The Mask of Satan see La Maschera del Demonio (1989)
The Mask of the Demon see La Maschera del Demonio (1989)
Maslansky, Paul 337
Massaccesi, Aristide 6, 31, 74, 133, 142, 151, 153, 181–209, 211, 220–222, 225, 260, 263, 266, 317, 320–321, 324, 332–334
Massacre 132, 137, 239–243
Massacre Time see Colt Canatarono la Mort È Fu...Tempo di Massacro
Massi, Stelvio 249, 300–301
Mastrocinque, Camillo 18, 20, 301–302
Mattei, Bruno 6, 131, 142, 201, 210, 217, 218, 269, 272
Mattei, Giuseppe "Pino" *see* Harris, James
Matthews, Francis 299–300
Mauri, Glauco 64
Mauri, Roberto 329, 338
Maxwell, Lois 267
Maya 229–230
Mayne, Belinda 324
McCloskey, Leigh 49, 63
McCullough, Ian 125, 142, 252–253, 287–288
McDowall, Malcolm 326
McKenna, Virgina 266–267
M.D.C.— La Maschera di Wax 58–59, 134, 320, 333

Il Mediaglione Insanguinato 29, 258, 260
Il Medium 12, 333
The Medium see Il Medium
Melato, Mariangela 334
Melchoir, Ib 107
Mell, Marisa (also Marlies Moitzi) 96, 103, 141, 145–146, 157, 324
Menotti, Giancarlo 12, 333
Meranda, Luc 201, 235, 296, 297
La Meraviglie di Aladino 88, 104–105
Mercier, Michelle 91, 105, 108, 164–165, 177, 327
Meril, Macha 64, 290
Merivale, John 102, 277
Merli, Maurizio 153
Messalina — Orgasmo Imperiale 194, 204
Metamorphosis 31, 195, 333
Metempsycho 247–248
Metti, Una Sera a Cena 37, 334
Miami Golem 264, 267
Miami Horror see Miami Golem
Midnight Killer see Morirai a Mezzanotte
Midnight Party 189, 204
Il Miele del Diavolo 131, 138
Milano Rovente 147, 155
Milano Trema: La Polizia Vuole Giustizia 292, 297
Milian, Tomas 135, 139, 140, 154, 158, 311
Un Milione di Dollari per Sette Assassini 144, 155
Milioni, Enzo 132, 137, 330, 337
The Mill of the Stone Women see Il Mulino delle Donne di Petra
A Million Dollars for Seven Assassins see Un Milione di Dollari per Sette Assassini
Mills, John 258, 260, 327
Milly: Photo Live 245
Ming, Ragazzi! 165, 176
Mingozzi, Gianfranco 28, 334
Il Mio Amico Jekyll 14, 287
Mio Dio Come Sono Caduta in Basso? 196
Miracle, Irene 49, 63, 290
Miraglia, Emilio 7, 26, 302–303
Mirren, Helen 326
Mission Stardust see 4...3...2...1...Morte!
Missione Mortale Molo 83 235
Missione Pianeta Errante 162–163, 177
Missione Speciale Lady Chaplin 264, 267

Mr. Hercules Vs. Karate see Ming, Ragazzi!
Mr. Superinvisible see L'Inafferabile, Invincibile Mr. Invisible
Mitchell, Cameron 69, 89, 92, 94, 103–104, 106, 257, 266, 297
Mitchell, Gordon (also Charles Pendleton) 28, 117, 202, 204, 207, 236–237, 249, 310, 316, 327, 330
Mitsouko 163, 171, 330
M.M.M. 83 see Missione Mortale Molo 83
Molnar, Stanko 67, 81
La Monaca Musulmana 28, 334
La Mondana Nuda 236–237
Mondo Cane l'Incredibile 300–301
Mondo Cane Oggi 300
Mondo Cane 3 300
Il Mondo di Dario Argento 52, 221, 225
Il Mondo di Dario Argento 2 56, 252, 254–255
Il Mondo di Dario Argento 3: Il Museo degli Orrori di Dario Argento 252, 255
Il Mondo di Yor 167, 177
Mondo Erotico see Le Notti Porno nel Mondo
Monreale, Cinzia 137, 140, 189, 200, 206
The Monster Hunter see Anthropophagus II
The Monster of the Opera see Il Mostro dell'Opera
The Monster of Venice see Il Mostro di Venezia
Monster Shark see Rosso nell'Oceano
La Montagna del Dio Cannibale 292, 297–298
Montaldo, Giuliano 122
Montefiori, Luigi *see* Eastman, George
Montero, Mario Bianchi *see* Bianchi (Montero), Mario
Montero, Roberto (Bianchi) 243
Monty Python and the Holy Grail 212
Moorcock, Michael 163
Moore, Jessica 137, 208, 246
More Filthy Canterbury Tales see Sollazzevoli Storie Moglie Gaudenti e Martiti Peniteni
More Sexy Canterbury Tales see Sollazzevoli Storie di Mogli Gaudenti e Martiti Peniteni
Morghen, John 79, 116, 139, 152, 172, 225

Moriarty, Michael 264, 266
Morirai a Mezzanotte 71–72, 82
Morricone, Ennio 40, 43, 57, 61, 63–64, 103, 119, 138, 157, 173, 255, 260, 266–267, 290, 323–325, 327–329, 331, 335, 338
Morris, Kirk (also Adriano Belli) 17, 89, 172, 274, 278
Morrissey, Paul 165–166, 174, 177
Morrison, Alex (also Sandro Luporini) 333
Morrow, Vic 283–286
Morta Ha Sorriso all'Assassino 183–184, 204
La Morte Ha Fatto l'Uovo 310–311
La Morte negli Occhi del Gatto 165
La Morte Non Ha Sesso 258, 260
La Morte Viene dal Pianeta Aytin 162–163, 177
Moschin, Gastone 175
Moses: The Lawgiver
Moses in Egypt see Moses: The Lawgiver
Moses: The Lawgiver 101, 334
Il Mostro dell'Opera 19, 304, 307
Il Mostro di Frankenstein 10, 334
Il Mostro di Venezia 20, 334
Il Mostro È in Tavola…Barone Frankenstein 165–166, 177
Moxey, John (Llewellyn) 17
Mueller, Paul see Muller, Paul
Il Mulino delle Donne di Petra 16, 270–272
Mulot, Claude see Pierson, Claude
Muller, Paul 19, 85, 108, 179, 242, 278, 310, 324, 330, 332–334
Munro, Caroline 252, 255
Murder Clinic see *La Llama nel Corpo*
Murder Obssession see *Follia Omicida*
Murder Rock see *Murderock— Uccide a Passo di Danza*
The Murder Secret see *Non Avere Paura della Zia Marta*
Murder to the Tune of Seven Black Notes see *Sette Notte in Nero*
Murderock— The Dance of Death see *Murderock— Uccide a Passo di Danza*
Murderock— Uccide a Passo di Danza 131, 138

Musante, Tony 37, 39–41, 65, 131, 213, 215, 334
Muti, Ornella 145, 156
My Uncle, the Vampire see *Tempi Duri per i Vampiri*
The Mysterious Encounter see *L'Arcano Incantatore*

Nagy, Christina 267
Nakadai, Tetsuo 335
Naked Exorcism see *Un Urlo dalla Tenebrae*
Nannerini, Luigi 242–243, 245, 331
Napier, Charles 113, 116, 151, 153–154, 172, 175
Naploetano, Annamaria see Goren, Annj
Naschy, Paul (Jacinto Molina) 23
Navajo Joe see *Un Dollaro a Testa*
Navarro, Nieves see Scott, Susan
Nebraska il Pistolero 105
Nel Nido del Serpente 132, 137, 334
Nella Stretta Morsa del Ragno 164–165, 177
Nelle Pieghe della Carne 235–237
Neri, Rosalba 25, 158, 247, 268, 315–317, 330–331
Nero, Franco 77, 79, 121, 124, 136, 140, 142, 174, 177, 184, 262, 283, 285–286, 325, 328
Nero and Poppea: An Orgy of Power see *Nerone e Poppea*
Nerone e Poppea 212, 214
Next! see *Lo Strano Vizio della Signora Wardh*
The Next Victim see *Lo Strano Vizio della Signora Wardh*
The New Barbarians see *I Guerrieri dell'Anno 2072; I Nuovo Barbari*
The New Black Emanuelle see *Emanuelle Nera N. 2*
New House on the Left see *L'Ultimo Treno della Notte*
The New York Ripper see *Lo Squartatore di New York*
Newton, Margit Evelyn 217
Nicholson, James H. 107
Nicolai, Bruno 63, 103, 117, 119, 138, 154, 178, 249, 266–267, 290, 296, 298–299, 303, 323, 331
Nicolodi, Daria 37, 45–46, 52, 55, 63–64, 74, 80, 83, 102, 107–108, 255, 284, 286
Nicolosi, Roberto 91, 104, 106, 108, 277, 331

Il Nido del Ragno 281
Nielsen, Brigitte 80
The Night Child see *Il Mediaglione Insanguinato*
The Night Evelyn Came Out of the Grave see *La Notte Che Evelyn Uscì dalla Tomba*
The Night Is the Phantom see *La Frusta e il Corpo*
Night of the Damned see *La Notte dei Dannati*
Night of the Devils see *Le Notte del Diavoli*
Night of the Doomed see *Amanti d'Oltretomba*
Night of the Living Dead 48
Night of the Zombies see *Inferno dei Morti-Viventi*
The Night That Evelyn Came Out of the Grave see *La Notte Che Evelyn Uscì dalla Tomba*
The Night Train Murders see *L'Ultimo Treno della Notte*
Nightmare Castle see *Amanti d'Oltretomba*
Nightmare City see *Incubo sulla Città Contaminata*
Nightmare Concert see *Un Gatto nel Cervello*
Nightmare of the Contaminated City see *Incubo sulla Città Contaminata*
1990: The Bronx Warriors see *1990 I Guerrieri del Bronx*
1990 I Guerrieri del Bronx 284, 285
99 Mujeres 210
No Grazie, il Caffè Mi Rende Nervoso 335
No Thanks, the Coffee Makes Me Nervous see *No Grazie, il Caffè Mi Rende Nervoso*
Non Aprire l'Uomo Nero 310–311
Non Avere Paura della Zia Marta 132, 137, 243, 245–246
Non Si Sevizia un Paperino 124, 139
Nonhosonno 3, 33, 46, 61–63, 320–321
North by Northwest 12
Nosferatu a Venezia 31, 335
Nosferatu in Venice see *Nosferatu a Venezia*
Nosferatu, Phantom der Nacht 31
Nostalgia Punk 55
La Notte Che Evelyn Uscì dalla Tomba 26, 302, 303
La Notte dei Dannati 26–27, 335

La Notte dei Diavoli 92, 270–272
Una Notte nel Cimitero see *Dentro al Cimitero*
Le Notti del Terrore 239, 240–241, 243, 312
Le Notti Erotiche dei Morti Viventi 191, 205
Le Notti Porno nel Mondo 210, 217
Le Notti Porno nel Mondo N. 2 189, 204–205
Nottorno con Grida 22
99 Mujeres 210
Novelle Galeotte d'Amore 165, 178
Novelle Licenziose di Vergine Vogliose 183, 205
Nucci, Laura 238, 247
Nuda per Satana 316
Nude for an Assassin see *Nude per l'Assassino*
Nude for Satan see *Nuda per Satana*
Nude-Odeon 287, 288
Nude per l'Assassino 239–240, 241, 243
Nude...Si Muore 22–23, 163, 178
I Nuovo Barbari 283–284, 286

O'Brien, Donald 139–140, 190, 195–196, 199, 201, 203, 206, 287–288
Obsession see *Ossessione*
Occhi dalle Stelle 279
Gli Occhi Dentro 214, 218
L'Occhio del Mal 129, 138
L'Occhio nel Labirinto 27, 335
Occhipinti, Andrea 68, 78, 129, 136, 141
Oceano 115, 117
O'Connor, Donald 105
Odata di Piacere 67
L'Odissea 66, 97, 105; see also *Le Avventura di Ullise*
The Odyssey see *L'Odissea*
Oggi a Me...Domani a Te 38, 335
Oglivy, Ian 337
Ogni Volta, un Gioco 194–195, 205
The Ogre see *La Casa dell'Orco*
Oh! Those Most Secret Agents see *002 Agente Segretissimi*
O.K. Connery 264, 267
O'Keefe, Miles 113, 117, 193, 200, 211–212, 216
Oliver, Robert H. see Oliveros, Ramino
Oliveros, Ramino 28, 326–327

Olson, James 262
The Omen 101
On Your Knees Stranger... Corpses Cast No Shadows! see *Inginocchiati Straniero...I Cadaveri Non Fanno Ombra!*
Once Upon a Time in the West see *C'era una Volta il West*
Ondata di Piacere 110, 118
One for All see *Tutto per Tutto*
One Just Man see *Giustiziere Sfida la Città*
One Last Dream see *L'Ultimo Sogno*
One on Top of the Other see *Una sull'Altra*
One Thousand and One Nights see *Finalmente...Le Mille e Una Notte*
1001 Oriental Nights 196, 205
O'Neil, Tricia 336
O'Neill, Jennifer 124–125, 141
Only Blackness see *Solamente Nero*
Onorato, Glauco 257
Opera 37, 53–54, 56, 61, 63, 220, 252, 255
Operation: Goldman see *Operazione Goldman*
Operation Kid Brother see *O.K. Connery*
Operation Lady Chaplin see *Missione Speciale Lady Chaplin*
Operation St. Peter see *Operazione San Pietro*
Operazione Goldman 163, 178
Operazione Luna see *002 Operazione Luna*
Operazione Paura 66, 75, 96–97, 105
Operazione San Pietro 121–122, 139
Orano, Alessio 82, 100, 104, 253
Orfei, Moira 136, 158, 313
Orgasmo 144–145, 155
Orgasmo Erotico see *Orgasmo Esotico*
Orgasmo Esotico 314, 315
Orgasmo Nero 191–193, 205
Orgasmo Non-Stop 314–315
L'Orribile Segreto del Dr. Hichcock 17–18, 275–276, 278
Gli Orrori del Castello di Norimberga 66, 99, 105
Ortolani, Riz 116, 118, 137, 139, 141, 157, 174, 177–179, 232, 257, 262–263
L'Ossessa 279–281
Ossessione 120, 335
Oswald, Gerd 39

The Other Hell see *L'Altro Inferno*
O'Toole, Peter 326
Ottaviani, Luciana see Moore, Jessica

Pacula, Joanna 76, 79
Il Paese del Sesso Selvaggio 147–148, 155
Paganini Horror 252, 255
Pagano, Bartolomeo 10–11
Pagni, Eros 64
Pagnol, Marcel 307, 310
Pakel, Vural 237
Palance, Jack (also Vladimir Dalamik) 38, 144, 156, 185, 203, 300
Pallottini, Riccardo 117, 119, 136, 156, 160, 171, 173, 174–175, 176, 177, 178, 179, 253, 278, 330, 332
Paluzzi, Luciana 258, 260, 329
Pani, Corrado 246
Pannaccio, Elo 29, 339
Paola Senatore—Non Stop see *Orgasmo Non-Stop*
Papas, Irene 105, 117, 139, 145, 156, 334
Papas, Xiro 28, 316–317, 327, 330
Papaya dei Caraibi 187, 189, 205
Papaya, Love Goddess of the Cannibals see *Papaya dei Caraibi*
Papaya of the Caribbean see *Papaya dei Caraibi*
Paralyzed see *La Corta Notte delle Bambole di Vetro*
Paranoia 144–146, 156, 181
Parenti, Mario Nicola 109, 117, 119
Park, Reg 88–89, 103, 162, 179, 312
Parks, Michael 149, 157
La Parola di un Fuorilegge...È Legge! 166, 178
Parolini, Gianfranco 336–337
Parra, Marissa see Demy, Valentine
Pasoloni, Piero Paolo 183, 328
Passalia, Antonio 215, 217
Passport for a Corpse see *Lasciapassare per il Morto*
Passport to Hell see *Agente 3S3: Passaporto per l'Inferno*
Pastore, Sergio 303–304
Patrick 131, 291
Patrick Still Lives see *Patrick Viva Ancora*
Patrick 2 see *Patrick Viva Ancora*

Patrick Viva Ancora 291–292, 312
Patrizi, Stefano 277
Patroni, Giuseppe 334
Paul, David 116
Paul, Gloria 329
Paul, Peter 116
Paura nel Buio 151, 156, 195
Paura nella Città dei Morti Viventi 123, 125, 127–128, 134, 139, 150, 220
Pedersoli, Carlo *see* Spencer, Bud
Il Pelo nel Mondo 161, 178
Pensione Paura 234–235
Per Sempre 74–75, 81
Per un Pugno di Dollari 38, 335–336
Perchè Quelle Strane Gocce di Sangue sul Corpo di Jennifer? 248–249
The Perfume of the Lady in Black see *Il Profumo della Signora in Nero*
The Perfume of the Woman in Black see *Il Profumo della Signora in Nero*
Perrot, Françoise 189, 204, 219
Persson, Essy 330
Perversion Story see *Una sull'Altra*
Pestriniero, Renato 94, 107
Peters, Werner 65
The Phantom Assassin see *Qualcosa Striscia nel Buio*
The Phantom of Death see *Un Delitto Poco Comune*
The Phantom of the Opera 60
The Phantom of the Opera see *Il Fantasma dell'Opera*
Phenomena 51–52, 63, 220, 225
Phenomenal and the Treasure of Tutankhamen see *Fenomenal e il Tesoro di Tutankhamen*
The Photos of Joy see *Le Foto di Gioia*
Pianeta degli Uomini Spenti 159, 178
Piccole Labbra 220, 336
Piccoli, Michel 96, 103
Pierangeli, Anna Maria 235–237
Pierreux, Jacqueline 91, 108
Pierson, Claude 119
Pignatelli, Fabio 64, 225
Pigozzi, Luciano 22–23, 104–105, 106, 154, 165, 172–179, 216, 218–219, 249, 298–299, 309, 326–327, 332
Piranha Paura 336
Piranha II see *Piranha Paura*
Piranha II: The Spawning see *Piranha Paura*

The Pirates of Malaysia see *I Pirati della Malesia*
I Pirati della Malesia 143, 156
La Pista Bulgara 300–301
Pistilli, Luigi 103, 278, 281, 296, 298
A Pistol for One Hundred Coffins see *Una Pistola per Cento Bare*
Una Pistola per Cento Bare 144, 158
Pitoeff, Sascha 292
Pixote 115
Planet of the Vampires see *Terrore nello Spazio*
Planet on the Prowl see *Missione Pianeta Errante*
Platoon 167
Play Motel 279–281
The Playgirls and the Vampire see *L'Ultima Preda del Vampiro*
Pleasence, Donald 31, 52, 64, 113, 116, 169, 179, 216, 222, 224, 230, 255, 273–274, 335
Il Plenilunio delle Vergini 184, 309, 315–317
Plucked see *La Morte Ha Fatto l'Uovo*
Plummer, Christopher 31, 255, 335
Pochath, Werner 140, 176, 278, 285
Podesta, Rossana 161, 172, 179
Polanski, Roman 60, 165–166, 174
Poli, Maurice 102–103, 137, 142, 157, 187, 189, 205, 207, 242, 246, 300, 331
Politoff, Haydee 328
La Polizia Chiede Aiuto 258, 261
Pollard, Michael J. 140
Polselli, Renato 3, 14–15, 19, 304–307
Pomeriggio Caldo 194, 206
Porel, Marc 83, 108, 119, 139, 141
Porno Erotic Love see *Porno Esotic Love*
Porno Esotic Love 185, 206
Porno Holocaust 190, 206
La Porta sul Buio 44, 75, 251, 256, 325
Le Porte del Silenzio 133, 139, 195
Le Porte dell'Inferno 137, 149–150, 156
The Possessor see *Un Urlo dalla Tenebrae*
The Postman Always Rings Twice 120

Un Posto Ideale per Uccidere 145, 156
Potter, Madeline 63
Powell, Don 202, 329
Powell, Robert 311
Powers, Hunt (also Jack Betts) 204, 324
Pozzi, Moana 285
Prati, Pamela 253
Predatori di Atlantide 112, 118, 220
The Predators of Atlantis see *Predatori di Atlantide*
Preiss, Wolfgang 16, 155, 272
Preston, Wayde (also William Erskine Strange) 335
Prete, Giancarlo *see* Brent, Timothy
La Pretora 124, 139
Prevost, Francoise 333, 339
Price, Vincent 58, 94, 107, 134
Primal Instinct 198, 206
Primus, Barry 257
The Prince of Terror see *Il Maestro del Terrore*
The Princess and the Pauper see *La Principessa e il Povero*
La Principessa e il Povero 77, 82
Prine, Andrew 262
Prinzessin Alisea see *Sorelina e il Principe del Sogno*
Prison Dancer 194, 206
The Prisoner of the Cannibal God see *La Montagna del Dio Cannibale*
Probabilità Zero 38, 336
Probability Zero see *Probabilità Zero*
Prochnow, Jurgen 82
Profondo Rosso 37, 40, 44–46, 69
Il Profumo della Signora in Nero 234–235
Prosperi, Franco 37, 88, 103, 106, 215, 280–281, 336
Prostituzione 268–269
The Psychic see *Sette Notte in Nero*
Psycho 12, 89
Psychopath see *Sigpress Vs. Scotland Yard*
Pupillo, Massimo 19–22, 207, 269, 307–310, 317
Purdom, Edmund 111, 116, 200, 213, 215, 232, 260, 296, 327
Pussycat 197–199, 205

Quaglia, Pier Ana *see* Davis, Ursula
Qualcono Ha Tradito 37, 336
Qualcosa Striscia nel Buio 249–251

Quando Alice Ruppe lo Specchio 131, 137, 139
Quarshie, Hugh 225
Quatermass II 275
The Quatermass Xperiment 86
I Quattro del Pater Noster 110, 118
Quattro dell'Apocalisse 124, 140
Quattro Mosche di Velluto Grigio 42–43, 57, 72
4...3...2...1...Morte! 171, 330
Quattro Volte...Quella Notte 66, 98, 105–106
Quayle, Anthony 267, 334
The Queen of the Cannibals see *Zombi Holocaust*
Queen of the Fish Men see *La Regina degli Uomini Pesce*
Queens of Evil see *Il Delitto del Diavolo*
Quella Villa Accanto al Cimitero 126, 128–129, 140, 263
Quella Villa in Fondo al Parco 248–249
Questi, Giulio 7, 310–312
Quien Sabe? 261, 262
A Quiet Place to Kill see *Paranoia*
Quigley, Linnea 273–274
Quinn, Anthony 176
Quinn, Francesco 175

Radice, Giovanni Lombardo see Morghen, John
La Ragazza Che Sapeva Troppo 17, 19, 39–40, 89–90, 92, 105, 113
Ragazza del Vondel Park see *Hanna D*
I Ragazzi del Juke Box 121, 140
Ragno Gelido 113, 115, 118
Raho, Umberto 65, 105, 156, 174, 269, 272, 278, 281, 303–304, 334, 337
Raiders of Atlantis see *Predatori di Atlantide*
Raiders of the Golden Cobra see *I Cacciatori del Cobra d'Oro*
Raiders of the Lost Ark 169
Raimi, Sam 33
Rains, Claude 159, 178
Ralli, Giovanni 261
Rambaldi, Carlo 122, 138, 174, 177, 272, 330
Rambo's Revenge see *Giustiziere Sfida la Città*
Ramirez, Lucia 191, 193, 203, 205
Randall, Dick 326–327
Randall, Monica 135
Ransenthaler, Peter see Carsten, Peter

Raptors 194, 206
Raptors — Dark Nights of the Scarecrow see *Raptors*
Raptus see *L'Orribile Segreto del Dr. Hichcock*
Rascel, Renato 14, 121, 338
Rassimov, Ivan 107, 111, 113, 116, 119, 147–148, 155–157, 202, 253, 281, 298–299
Rassimov, Rada 63, 105
Rathbone, Basil 56
Ratman see *Quella Villa in Fondo al Parco*
Rats — The Nights of Terror see *Rats — Notte di Terrore*
Rats — Notte di Terrore 212, 218
Ratti, Filippo Maria Walter 26–27, 335
Ravaioli, Isarco 305–307, 316, 337
Rear Window 12
Reazione a Catena see *Ecologia del Delitto*
Red Coat see *Giubbe Rosse*
The Red Light Girls see *Prostituzione*
The Red Monks see *I Fratti Rossi*
Red Ocean see *Rosso nell'Oceano*
The Red Queen Kills Seven Times see *La Dama Rossa Uccide Sette Volte*
Reeves, Michael 18, 20, 326, 337
Reeves, Steve 102, 143, 156–157, 274, 277, 326, 329
Regenerator see *Metamorphosis*
La Regina degli Uomini Pesce 295, 298
Regina della Scala 301–302
Register, Meg 136
Regnoli, Piero 15–16, 108, 136, 141, 154, 243, 178, 292, 312–313
Reign of Fire see *Holocaust 2000*
The Reincarnation of Isabel see *Riti, Magie Nere e Segrete Orge nel Trecento*
Reiner, Thomas 106
Reininger, Scott H. 339
Remy, Helene 305
Rennie, Michael 23, 163, 178
Renoir, Jean 120, 326
Renzi, Eva 65
Return from Death see *Ritorno dalla Morte*
The Return of Sandokan see *Il Ritorno di Sandokan*
The Return of the Hitcher see *Paura nel Buio*

The Return of White Fang see *Il Ritorno di Zanna Bianca*
Revenge of the Dead see *Zeder*
The Revenge of the Vampire see *La Maschera del Demonio* (1960)
Rey, Fernando 328–329
Reynaud, Janine 163, 171, 296
Reynolds, Burt 328
Il Ricatto 115, 118
Ricci, Barbara 115, 118
Ricci, Luciano 18, 326
Rice-Davies, Mandy 218
Richardson, John 86, 104, 154, 225, 257, 277, 296, 330
Rickman, Alan 60
Rigazzi, Alba 22
Rinaldi, Nadia 61, 63
Ring, Beatrice 79, 142, 219, 289–290, 332
The Rip-Off see *Controrapina*
Ripley, Isabelle 206
The Ripper see *Lo Squartatore di New York*
Riti, Magie Nere e Segrete Orge nel Trecento 3, 304–305, 307
Riti Notturni 55
Rito d'Amore 289–290
Ritorno dalla Morte 193, 195–196, 198, 206–207
Il Ritorno di Sandokan 285–286
Il Ritorno di Zanna Bianca 124, 140
Rivelazioni di uno Psichiatra sul Mondo Perverso 306–307
Rivero, Jorge 129, 136, 314–315
Riviere, Georges 160–162, 164, 174, 179, 324
La Rivoluzione Sessuale 37, 336
Rizzoli, Anna-Maria 280–281
The Road to Fort Alamo see *La Strada per Fort Alamo*
The Road Warrior 211, 284
Robards, Jason 327
Robbins, Eva (also Eva Robins, Eva Coatti, Roberto Coatti) 51, 64, 253, 254
Robins, Eva see Robbins, Eva
Robinson, Edward G. 121–122, 139, 323
Robowar 214, 218
Rocca, Danielle 102, 326
Rocca, Stefania 62
Rodriguez, Tomas see Milian, Tomas
Roeg, Nicolas 29
Rohm, Maria 242, 260, 332
Roma Contra Roma 18
Roman, Leticia 89–90, 106
Romando, Renato 330
Romay, Lina 201, 204, 2

Rome, Sydne 253
Rome 2072: The New Gladiators see *I Guerrieri dell'Anno 2072*
Romero, George A. 48, 56, 62, 125, 147, 157, 191, 339
Rose, Kristine 209
Ross, Gaylen 339
Ross, Howard 103, 105, 141, 300, 331
Rossellini, Roberto 6, 12, 84, 109
Rossi, Franco 105
Rossi, Mirella 305–306
Rossi, Stelvio 207
Rossi-Drago, Eleanora 235–237
Rossi-Stuart, Giacomo 96, 102–103, 105, 156–157, 177, 202, 204, 277, 303–304, 324, 329
Rossi-Stuart, Kim 80, 225, 282
Rossini, Renato see Ross, Howard
Rosso nell'Oceano 69, 82
Rosso Sangue see *Anthropophagus II*
Il Rosso Segno della Follia 66, 97, 106
Roussos, Tiffany 204
Roy Colt e Winchester Jack 66, 97, 106
Rubinstein, Richard P. 339
Ruffo, Leonora 103, 333
Russell, Ken 190
Russell, Tony 163, 174
Russo, Adriana 246
Russo, Carmen 292
Russo, James 57, 65
Rustichelli, Carlo 104–106, 142, 175–176, 200, 203, 268
Rydell, Christopher 65

Sa Jana 309
Sabato, Antonio 145–146, 155, 157, 264, 267, 281
Sacchetti, Dardano 63, 68–69, 71–72, 78–82, 103, 107, 116–118, 125, 135, 137–141, 142, 158, 179, 230, 261–263, 285, 290, 296
Sacrifice! see *Il Paese del Sesso Selvaggio*
Salerno, Enrico Maria 65, 290
Salerno, Vittorio 22, 332
Salier, Mary 137
Salomons, Marie Christine see Aumont, Tina
Salter, Louise 233–234
Salvino, Riccardo 65
Sambrell, Aldo see Sanbrell, Aldo

Sammy 55
Samson and the Slave Queen see *Zorro Contro Maciste*
Samson in King Solomon's Mines see *Maciste nelle Miniere di Re Salomone*
Samuels, Sandy (also Clare Colosimo) 200
San Francesco 224
Sanbrell, Aldo 105, 140, 242, 245, 328, 332
Sancho, Fernando 237, 324, 337
Sandokan see *Sandokan, La Tigre di Mompracem*
Sandokan il Maciste della Giungla 143, 157
Sandokan la Tigre di Mompracem 143, 157
Sandokan, the Great see *Sandokan la Tigre di Mompracem*
Sands, Julian 60–61, 63
Sandvik, Kay 289–290
Sangue per Dracula see *Dracula Cerca Sangue di Vergine…È Morì di Sete!*
Santa Sangre 32, 336
Santoni, Espartaco 104, 331
Sarayevo Inferno di Fuoco 151
Sartana 336–337
Sartana, the Gravedigger see *Sono Sartana, il Vostro Becchino*
Satanik 24, 337
Satan's Altar see *Follia Omicida*
Satan's Baby Doll see *La Bimba di Satana*
Satan's Doll see *La Bambola di Satana*
Satan's Playthings see *La Terrificante Notte del Demonio*
Satan's Sister see *La Sorella di Satana*
Savage, John 133, 139. 195
Savage Gringo see *Nebraska il Pistolero*
The Savage Island see *Anthropophagus*
Savalas, Telly (also Aristotle Savalas) 100, 104, 264, 266
Savina, Carlo 104, 171, 173–176, 178, 330
Savini, Tom 56, 63, 339
Savoy, Teresa Ann 326
Saxon, Glen (also Roel Bos) 155
Saxon, John (also Carmine Orrico) 50, 64, 90, 106, 149, 157, 166–167, 172, 296, 299
Scaffidi, Gianna 289–290

Scala, Gia 158
Scalps 212, 218
Scandinavian Erotica see *Le Notte Porno nel Mondo No. 2*
Scansati…Trinità Arriva Eldorado 183, 207
Scarciofolo, Geofreddo see Cameron, Jeff
Scardamaglia, Elio 21, 332–333
Scattini, Luigi 309
Scenes from a Murder see *L'Assassino…È al Telefono* (1973)
Scheider, Roy 282
Scheure, Erma see Scheurer, Erna
Scheurer, Erna 24–25, 269, 325
Schiaffino, Rosanna 261–262
La Schiave Blanca 280, 281
Schivazappa, Piero 105
Schizoid see *Una Lucertola con la Pelle di Donna*
Schmidt, Hans see Hoffman, Robert
Schoeller, Ingrid 135, 144, 151, 337
School of Fear see *Il Gioko*
The School That Couldn't Scream see *Cosa Avete Fatto a Solange?*
Schoolgirl Killer see *Nude…Si Muore*
Schubert, Karin 202, 217, 269
Schurer, Erna see Scheurer, Erna
Sclavi, Tiziano 224–225
Scola, Ettore 1
Scola, Gioia Maria 74, 81–82, 118, 136
Scontri Stellari Oltre la 3a Dimensione 251–252, 254–255
The Scorpion with Two Tails see *Assassino al Cimitero Etrusco*
Scorsese, Martin 2
Scott, Gordon 17, 333
Scott, Susan (also Nieves Navarro) 191, 193, 201, 205, 298
Scotti, Raimondo 325
Screamers see *L'Isola degli Uomini Pesci*
Screaming Mimi 39, 65
Scusi, Lei È Favorevole o Contrario? 37, 337
Se Sei Vivo Spara 310–311
Secret Agent 00 see *O.K. Connery*
The Secret Killer see *Gatti Rossi in un Labirinto di Ventro*
The Secret of Dorian Gray see *Il Dio Chiamato Dorian*
The Sect see *La Setta*

Seddok 16, 88, 337
Seggiani, Sabrina *see* Siani, Sabrina
Il Segno del Commander 310–311
Il Segreto di Cristina 110
Sei Donne per l'Assassino 19, 40, 89, 92, 94–95, 97, 106, 303
Sella d'Argento 125, 140
Semaforo Rosso see *Cani Arrabbiati*
Senator Likes Women...Despite Appearances and Provided the Nation Doesn't Know see *All'Onorevole Piacciono le Donne...Nonostante le Apparenze e Purchè la Nazione Non le Sappia...*
Senatore, Paola 148, 155, 190, 202–203, 269, 314–315
Sensitività 29, 31, 283, 286
The Sentinel 128
Serafian, Deran 142, 194, 219, 332
Sernas, Jacques 83, 213, 215, 330, 333
Servais, Jean 27, 336, 338
La Setta 52, 56, 222–224, 226, 255
7, Hyden Park — la Casa Maledetta 264, 266–267
I Sette Magnifici Gladiatori 212, 218
Sette Notte in Nero 124–125, 140–141
Sette Orchidee Macchiate di Rosso 145–146, 150, 157
Sette Scialli di Setta gialli 303–304
Seven Crimes of the Black Cat see *Sette Scialli di Setta gialli*
Seven Doors to Death see *L'Aldila*
7, Hyden Park — la Casa Maledetta 264, 266–267
The Seven Magnificent Gladiators see *I Sette Magnifici Gladiatori*
Seven Notes in Black see *Sette Notte in Nero*
Seven Orchids for the Murderer see *Sette Orchidee Macchiate di Rosso*
Seven Orchids Stained in Red see *Sette Orchidee Macchiate di Rosso*
Sex and Chinese Food 196, 207
Sex and Zen 196
Sex Party see *Delitto allo Specchio*
Sex Slayer see *Prostituzione*
The Sexorcist see *L'Ossessa*
Sexorcist Devil see *L'Ossessa*

The Sexual Revolution see *La Rivoluzione Sessuale*
Sexy Night Report see *Le Notti Porno nel Mondo*
Sexy Night Report N. 2 see *Le Notte Porno nel Mondo No. 2*
Sexy Nights of the Dead see *Le Notti Erotiche dei Morti Viventi*
Sexy Party see *Delitto allo Specchio*
Seyn, Seyna 157, 176, 324
Shalima 197
Shannon, Mark 189–191, 199–200, 203–206
The Shark Hunter see *Il Cacciatore di Squalli*
Sharks: Deep Blood 195, 207
The She Beast see *La Sorella di Satana*
Shepard, Patty 166, 174
She's Seventeen and Anxious see *Emanuelle: Perchè'Violenza alle Donne?*
Sheybal, Vladek 325
Shining Sex — La Fille aux Brillant 189, 204
Shock 66, 70, 74–75, 101–102, 106–107
Shocking Dark see *Spectres à Venise*
Shocking Dark Terminator 2 Alien 3 see *Spectres à Venise*
The Short Night of the Glass Dolls see *La Corta Notte delle Bambole di Vetro*
Siani, Sabrina 136, 199–200, 300
Siciliano, Mario 236–237, 314–315
Siffredi, Rocco 197, 208
La Signora di Wall Street 195, 207
Sigpress Vs. Scotland Yard 181, 337
Silva, Henry 38, 158, 284–285, 336
Silver Saddle see *Sella d'Argento*
Simonelli, Giorgio 94, 165, 248, 328
Simonelli, Giovanni 132, 137, 173, 176, 178–179, 267, 304, 330–331, 334
Simonetti, Claudio 52, 59, 63–64, 74, 79, 82, 117, 119, 136, 157, 225, 255, 286
Simons, Barbara 324
Sinbad 284, 286
Sinbad of the Seven Seas see *Sinbad*

La Sindrome di Stendahl 57
Six Women for the Killer see *Sei Donne per l'Assassino*
Six Women for the Murderer see *Sei Donne per l'Assassino*
Skay, Brigitte 24, 103, 105, 316, 332
Slaughter of the Vampires see *La Strage dei Vampiri*
The Slave Merchants see *Anthar l'Invincibile*
The Slave of the Cannibal God see *La Montagna del Dio Cannibale*
Sleepless see *Nonhosonno*
Slezak, Walter 242, 332
The Smugglers see *Luca il Contrabbandiere*
The Snake House see *Nel Nido del Serpente*
Snow Devils see *La Morte Viene dal Pianeta Aytin*
Snyder, William 216
So Sweet, So Perverse see *Così Dolci...Così Perversa*
Soavi, Michele 6, 52, 56, 64, 68, 76, 78–79, 81, 118, 194, 199, 200, 202, 220–226, 253–254, 320–321, 324, 326, 336
Sodoma's Ghosts see *I Fantasmi di Sodoma*
Sogno Erotici di Cleopatra 268, 270
Solamente Nero 246–247
Solar, Sylvia 154, 237
Soldati, Mario 1
Solima, Sergio 1, 324
Sollazzevoli Storie di Mogli Gaudenti e Martiti Penitenti 183, 207
Solvay, Paolo 315–317, 338
Some Like It Hard 207
Something Creeping in the Dark see *Qualcosa Striscia nel Buio*
Something Is Creeping in the Dark see *Qualcosa Striscia nel Buio*
Something Strikes in the Dark see *Qualcosa Striscia nel Buio*
Something Waits in the Dark see *L'Isola degli Uomini Pesci*
Sommer, Elke 99–100, 104, 105, 121, 140
Son of Blob 86
Sono Sartana, il Vostro Becchino 248–249
Sopkiw, Michael 69, 78, 82, 296
Sopravvissuti della Città Morta 169, 170, 178–179

Index

Sordi, Alberto 37, 337
Sorel, Jean 32, 122, 138, 156, 285, 288–290
Sorellina e il Principe del Sogno 77, 82
La Sorella di Satana 20, 337
La Sorella di Ursula 337
Sotto il Cielo dell'Africa 115, 118
Southwood, Charles 97, 106
Spaak, Catherine 63, 178
Spasmo 147, 157
Spataro, Diego 183, 205, 207
Spazzio Uomini 159, 179
Special Mission Lady Chaplin see *Missione Speciale Lady Chaplin*
Spectres see *Spettri*
Spectres à Venise 214, 218
Spencer, Bud 38, 42–43, 64, 329, 335
Spettri 229–230
Lo Spettro 18, 275–276, 278
La Spiaggia del Terrore 149, 157
Spiando Marina 295, 298
The Spider's Labyrinth see *Il Nido del Ragno*
Le Spie Amano i Fiori 144, 157
Le Spie Vengono dal Semifreddo 66, 94, 107, 328
Spies Love Flowers see *Le Spie Amano i Fiori*
Spinell, Joe 255
Spirits of the Dead see *Tre Passi nel Delirio*
Sposarsi È un Po Morire 56, 252, 255
The Spy Who Loved Flowers see *Le Spie Amano i Fiori*
Spying on Marina see *Spiando Marina*
Lo Squartatore di New York 129, 141
The Squeeze see *Controrapina*
SS Experiment Part 2 see *La Bestia in Calore*
SS Extermination Camp see *KZ9 Lager di Stermino*
SS Girls see *La Casa Privata per le SS*
SS Girls Camp see *La Casa Privata per le SS*
SS Hell Camp see *La Bestia in Calore*
Staccioli, Ivano 217
Stafford, Frederick (also Frederick Strobel Von Stein) 269
La Stagione di Sensei 37, 337–338
Staller, Ilona see Cicciolina
Stallone, Sylvester 263
Stamp, Terence 42, 96

Stander, Lionel 119, 135, 203, 242, 327, 332
Star Crash see *Scontri Stellari Oltre la 3a Dimensione*
Star Wars 167
Starr, Ringo (also Richard Starkey) 42
Steel, Alan 153, 158
Steele, Barbara 14, 17–21, 86–87, 104, 160–161, 164–165, 174, 176, 278, 301, 308–309, 320, 337
Steffan, Anthony see De Teffe, Antonio
Stegers, Bernice 67, 81
Steiger, Rod 331
Steiner, John 50, 64, 107, 110, 116–118, 124, 136, 140, 167, 169, 173, 177, 179, 269, 284, 286
Stella, Luciano see Kendall, Tony
Stella, Stefania 273–274
The Stendahl Syndrome see *La Sindrome di Stendahl*
Steno see Vanzina, Stefano
Stern, Helga Lina see Line, Helga
Stewart, Evelyn 103, 141, 153, 260, 296, 300, 328
Stiglitz, Hugo 154
The Sting in the Tail see *La Coda dello Scorpione*
Stivaletti, Sergio 58–59, 63, 71, 76, 79–81, 134, 230, 320, 333
Stockwell, Guy 32, 336
Stone, Oliver 167
Stoppa, Franca 200, 215, 219
Storraro, Vittorio 40
La Strada per Fort Alamo 66, 94, 107
La Strage dei Vampiri 316, 338
The Stranger and the Gunfighter see *La Dove Non Batte il Sole*
Stranger That Kneels Beside the Shadow of the Cross see *Inginocchiati Straniero…i Cadaveri Non Fanno Ombra!*
Lo Strano Vizio della Signora Wardh 293–294, 298
Street Trash 287
La Strega 55
La Strega in Amore 261–262
Le Streghe 33, 338
Strike Commando 212, 218
Strike Commando 2 213, 218
Strindberg, Anita 135, 141, 266, 269, 277, 288–289, 293–294, 296, 298
Strip Nude for the Killer see *Nude per l'Assassino*

Strip Nude for Your Killer see *Nude per l'Assassino*
Strode, Woody 285, 327
Succubus see *La Terrificante Notte del Demonio*
Sul Filo del Rasio 198, 207
Sullivan, Barry 107, 166, 178
Sullivan's Marauders see *Commandos*
Suor Omicidi 238–239
Superseven Calling Cairo see *Superseven Chiama Cairo*
Superseven Chiama Cairo 144, 158
Suska, Almanta see Keller, Almanta
Suspicion 89
Suspiria 37, 46–49, 51, 64, 68, 131, 233
Un Sussurro nel Buio 29, 338
Sutherland, Donald 326
Svenson, Bo 216, 241
Svezia, Inferno e Paradiso 309
Swan, Kitty 117
The Sweet House of Horrors see *La Dolce Casa degli Orrori*
Swinn, Monica 204
Syndicate Sadists see *Giustiziere Sfida la Città*

The Tail of the Scorpion see *La Coda dello Scorpione*
Take a Hard Ride see *Parola di un Fuorilegge…È Legge!*
Tales of Terror 56
Tales to Rip Your Heart Out 287–288
Tamba, Tetsuro 329
Tamburi, Jenny 141, 257, 269
Tani, Yoko 157
Tarantino, Quentin 2
Tarzan X 198, 208
Tarzan X: The Shame of Jane see *Tarzan X*
Tati, Jacques 12
Taurog, Norman 94
Tavella, Dino 20, 334
Il Taxi Fantasma 56, 252, 255
Taxi Killer 300–301
Taylor, Don 38, 329
Taylor, James 42
Taylor, Ronnie 55, 61–63
Tedesco, Paola 65, 246
Tempi Duri per i Vampiri 13, 120, 338
The Temple of the White Elephants see *Sandokan il Maciste della Giungla*
The Tempter see *L'Anticristo*
Tenebrae 50–51, 54, 68–69, 255
Tenebre see *Tenebrae*

The Terminator 214
Terminator 2 Alien 3! see *Spectres à Venise*
La Terrificante Notte del Demonio 27, 338
Terror Castle see *La Vergine di Norimberga*
Terror Creatures from the Grave see *Cinque Tombe per un Medium*
Terror in the Crypt see *La Cripta e l'Incubo*
Terror in the Opera see *Opera*
The Terror of Dr. Hichcock see *L'Orribile Segreto del Dr. Hichcock*
Terrore nello Spazio 20, 66, 94, 96, 107
Terry-Thomas 103
Terzano, Ubaldo 88, 104, 106, 108
Tessari, Duccio 88, 103–104, 333, 335
Tessier, Robert 255
Testa, Eugenio 11, 334
Testi, Fabio 138–140, 184, 203, 258–260, 285–286
Il Testimone 224, 226
Il Testimone Oculare (1973) 44, 65
Il Testimone Oculare (1989) 75, 82
Teutscher, Pauline 204
Tharus, Figlio di Attila 210
The Thief see *I Ladri*
The Thieves see *I Ladri*
Thinking About Africa see *Sotto il Cielo dell'Africa*
1001 Oriental Nights 196, 205
The Three Faces of Fear see *I Tre Volti della Paura*
The Three Faces of Terror see *I Tre Volti della Paura*
Thrilling in Venice see *Giallo a Venezia*
Thulin, Ingrid 290, 334, 338
Ti Aspetterò all'Inferno 15, 312–313
Tiger Joe see *Fuga dall'Arcipelago Maledetto*
Tinti, Gabriele 104, 117, 201–203, 206, 209, 212, 217, 219, 246, 281
To Die at Midnight see *Morirai a Mezzanotte*
Today It's Me...Tomorrow It's You see *Oggi a Me...Domani a Te*
Today It's Me...Tomorrow You see *Oggi a Me...Domani a Te*
Todd, Richard 260
Tognazzi, Ugo 14, 287
Tolo, Marilu 44, 62, 65, 106, 257, 262, 296, 311
Tomb of Torture see *Metempsycho*
Top Job see *Ad Ogni Costo*
Top Model 194, 208
El Topo 32
The Tormented see *L'Ossessa*
Tornado 167, 179
Tornado Strike Force see *Tornado*
Torso see *I Corpi Presantano Tracce di Violenza Carnale*
Torture Chamber of Baron Blood see *Gli Orrori del Castello di Norimberga*
Toto see De Curtis, Antonio
Toto a Colori 120, 338
Toto all'Inferno 12, 301–302
Touch of Death see *Quando Alice Ruppe lo Specchio*
Tough to Kill see *Duri a Morire*
Tourneur, Jacques 85, 102, 326
Towers, Harry Alan 141, 242, 332
Il Tram 44, 65
Tranquilli, Silvano 297
Trap Them and Kill Them see *Emanuelle e gli Ultimi Cannibali*
Trauma 57–58, 65
Travolta, Joey 167, 173
Tre Passi nel Delirio 96
I Tre Volti della Paura 18, 85, 90–93, 100, 107–108, 113, 272
Treasure Island see *L'Isola del Tesoro* (1972); *L'Isola del Tesoro* (1986)
Treasure Island in Outer Space see *L'Isola del Tesoro* (1986)
Treasure Island in Space see *L'Isola del Tesoro* (1986)
Treviglio, Leonardo 71, 82, 298
Triangle of Fear see *Il Triangolo della Paura*
Il Triangolo della Paura 169, 179
Triangolo Rosso 110
Tricca, Gabriella or Gabrielle see Levi, Laura
Trintignant, Jean-Louis 42, 145, 153, 310–311, 334
Il Trionfo di Robin Hood 143, 158
The Triumph of Robin Hood see *Il Trionfo di Robin Hood*
Les Trois Visages de la Peur see *I Tre Volti della Paura*
Troll 2 195, 208
Troll 3 195, 208

Tromba, Alberto 261
Trotter, Laura 154, 215, 265, 267
Il Trucido e lo Sbirro 148, 158
True Story of the Nuns of Monza see *La Vera Storia della Monaca di Monza*
Trussardi Action 52
Tschechin, Zora Ulla Keslerova see Kerova, Zora
Il Tunnel Sotto il Mondo 251
Il Tuo Vizio È una Stanza Chiusa e Solo Io Ne Ho la Chiave 293–294, 298–299
Turner, Elisabeth 172, 327
Turner, John (also Valimir Brajovic) 217
Turno di Notte 55, 77–79, 81, 252–254
Tutti Defunti Tranne Io Morti 339
Tutti i Colori del Buio 293–294, 295, 298
Tutto per Tutto 144, 158
2019 Dopo la Caduta di New York 295, 296
2020 Texas Gladiators see *Anno 2020: I Gladiatori del Futoro*
Twisted Girls see *L'Isola della Svedesi*
Twisted Nerve 41
Twitch of the Dead Nerve see *Ecologia del Delitto*
Twitch of the Death Nerve see *Ecologia del Delitto*
Two Evil Eyes see *Due Occhi Diabolici*
Two Mafia Guys Vs. the F.B.I. see *Le Spie Vengono dal Semifreddo*
2001: A Space Odyssey 171

L'Uccello dalle Piume di Cristallo 25, 30–31, 37–39, 44, 72
Ugarte, Julian 23, 174, 298, 333
Ulisse 198, 208
L'Ultima Pallottola 224, 226
L'Ultima Preda del Vampiro 15–16, 312–313
L'Ultimo Cacciatore 167, 179
Ultimo Mondo Cannibale 67, 110–111, 113, 118–119
L'Ultimo Sogno 299
L'Ultimo Squalo 214, 283, 286
L'Ultimo Treno della Notte 289–290
Ultimo 2 — La Sfida 224, 226
Ulysses see *Ulisse*
La Umanoide 289, 291
Umiliani, Piero 107, 135, 203

Una sull'Altra 122, 124, 131, 141
Uncle Was a Vampire see *Tempi Duri per i Vampiri*
Unconscious see *Follia Omicida*
Undari, Claudio see Hundar, Robert
Undici Giorni, Undici Notti 195, 208
Undici Giorni, Undici Notti 2 195, 208
The Unnaturals see *Il Contronatura*
Uno Bianco 224, 225
Unsane see *Tenebrae*
Until Death see *Per Sempre*
Uomini Si Nasce, Poliziotti Si Muore 110, 119
L'Uomo Che Non Volare 75, 83
Un Uomo da Ridere 121, 141
L'Uomo dagli Occhi di Ghiaccio 264, 267
L'Uomo della Sabbia 311–312
Upperseven: The Man to Kill see *Upperseven l'Uomo da Uccidere*
Upperseven l'Uomo da Uccidere 264, 268
Un Urlo dalla Tenebrae 29, 339
Ursus il Terrore dei Kirghisi 109, 162, 179

Vacanze sulla Costa Smeralsa 109, 119
Vacation on the Emerlad Isle see *Vacanze sulla Costa Smeralsa*
Vadis, Dan 212, 218
Vailati, Bruno 102, 172, 326
Valentina 282
Valeri, Tonino 115, 118
Valli, Alida 64, 100, 104, 238–239, 266, 273–274, 295–296, 335
Valli, Simona 197–199, 205
Vallone, Saverio 303
The Vampire and the Ballerina see *L'Amante del Vampiro*
The Vampire and the Playgirls see *L'Ultima Preda del Vampiro*
The Vampire of the Opera see *Il Mostro dell'Opera*
Vampire Playgirls see *La Terrificante Notte del Demonio*
The Vampires see *Maciste Contro il Vampiro*
I Vampiri 12–15, 20, 84–85, 108, 275, 278, 312
Vampirismus 311–312
Van Cleef, Lee 37, 166, 169, 173–174, 176, 178–179, 257

Van Hooven, Keith 83, 136, 154
Vanni, Bruno (also Bruno Vani) 305–307
Van Nutter, Rik 176, 179
Vanzina, Stefano 13, 120, 325, 338–339
Vari, Giuseppe 18
Vaughn, Robert 206
Velasquez, Pilar 315
Vendetta dal Futoro 295, 299
La Vendetta di Lady Morgan 21–22, 308, 310
La Venere dell'Ille 66–67, 83, 102, 108
Vengeance see *Joko, Invoca Dio...e Muori*
2019 Dopo la Caduta di New York 295, 296
The Venus d'Ille see *La Venere dell'Ille*
Venus im Pelz 210
La Vera Storia della Monaca di Monza 211, 218
La Vergine di Norimberga 18, 161–162, 179
La Verità Seconda Satana 3, 307
Il Verme 55
Vernuccio, Gianni 22, 333
Veronique's Long Night see *La Lunga Notte di Veronique*
Very Close Encounters of the Fourth Kind see *Incontro Molto...Ravvicinatti del Quattro Tipo*
La Via della Prostituzione 187, 209
Via delle Streghe 56, 252, 255
Vianello, Maria Teresa see Fitzgerald, Teresa
Vianello, Raimondo 14, 287
Il Vicino di Casa 44, 151, 256
The Victim see *Macchie Solari*
Videodrome 72
The Vikings 89
La Villa delle Anime Maldette 31, 339
Villagio, Paolo 110, 118
Violence in a Women's Prison see *Violenza in un Carcere Femminile*
The Violent Professionals see *Milano Trema: La Polizia Vuole Giustizia*
Violenza in un Carcere Femminile 212, 219
The Virgin of Nuremberg see *La Vergine di Norimberga*
Virtual Assassin 171, 180
Virtual Weapon see *Virtual Assassin*

Virus see *Inferno dei Morti-Viventi*
Visconti, Luchino 1, 120, 335
Vivarelli, Piero 24, 121, 140, 202, 337
Il Vizio Infinito 196
Voci del Profondo 133, 141
Voglia di Rock 222
Voices from Beyond see *Voci del Profondo*
Voices from the Beyond see *Zeder*
Volonte, Gian Maria 261–262, 336
Von Sydow, Max 62–63
Voodoo Baby see *Orgasmo Nero*
Vooren, Monique Van 177
Vortice Mortale 115, 119, 320
Voyagis, Yorgo 119, 335

The Wailing see *Follia Omicida*
Walas, Chris 297
Walken, Christopher 50
Wall Street Woman see *La Signora di Wall Street*
Wallace, Bryan Edgar 38, 65
Wallace, Edgar 6, 38, 92, 146, 276–277
Wallace, Tommy Lee 262
Walsh, Raoul 84
War Between the Planets see *Missione Pianeta Errante*
War of the Planets see *I Diafanoidi Vengono da Marte*
Warbeck, David 127–128, 135, 137, 151, 154, 167–169, 173, 175–176, 179, 212, 214–215, 248–249, 265–267, 273–274
Ward, Simon 264, 266
Warhol, Andy 165–166, 177
Warner, David 246
The Warriors 284
Warriors of the Wasteland see *I Nuovo Barbari*
Warriors of the Year 3000 see *I Guerrieri dell'Anno 2072*
The Washing Machine see *Vortice Mortale*
Watch Me When I Kill see *Il Gatto dagli Occhi di Giada*
Waves of Lust see *Ondata di Piacere*
Web of the Spider see *Nella Stretta Morsa del Ragno*
Webber, Robert 336
Webley, Patrizia 242, 280–281
Weird Wicked World see *Il Pelo nel Mondo*
Welcome to Spring Break see *La Spiaggia del Terrore*
Well, Karin 237, 243, 314–315
Welles, Mel 25–26, 329, 337

Welles, Orson 242, 332
Wendel, Lara 64, 82, 153, 206, 330
Werewolf Woman see *La Lupe Mannera*
Wet Lips see *Labbra Bagnate*
Whale, James 1
What! see *La Frusta e il Corpo*
What Are Those Strange Drops of Blood Doing on the Body of Jennifer? see *Perchè Quelle Strane Gocce di Sangue sul Corpo di Jennifer?*
What Have They Done to Our Daughters? see *La Polizia Chiede Aiuto*
What Have They Done to Solange? see *Cosa Avete Fatto a Solange?*
What Have You Done to Solange? see *Cosa Avete Fatto a Solange?*
When Alice Broke the Mirror see *Quando Alice Ruppe lo Specchio*
The Whip and the Body see *La Frusta e il Corpo*
A Whisper in the Dark see *Un Sussurro nel Buio*
Whispers in the Dark see *Un Sussurro nel Buio*
White, Harriet Medin 104, 106, 108, 278, 333
White Apache see *L'Apache Bianco*
White Fang see *Zanna Bianca*
White Slave see *La Schiave Blanca*
The White Warrior see *Agi Murad, il Diavolo Bianco*
Who Saw Her Die? see *Chi l'Ha Vista Morire?*
Why Those Strange Drops of Blood on the Body of Jennifer? see *Perchè Quelle Strane Gocce di Sangue sul Corpo di Jennifer?*
Wide-Eyed in the Dark see *Gatti Rossi in un Labirinto di Ventro*
Wild Dogs see *Cani Arrabbiati*
The Wild Geese 169
Wild Wild Planet see *I Criminalli della Galassia*
Williams, Fred (also Frederick Williams) 332

Williamson, Fred 137, 166, 178, 284–286, 300–301
Willow 77
Wilson, Ajita 189, 193, 205, 235
The Witch see *La Strega in Amore; Le Streghe*
The Witch in Love see *La Strega in Amore*
Witch Story see *Le Streghe*
The Witches of the Lake see *Il Delitto del Diavolo*
The Witch's Curse see *Maciste all'Inferno*
Witney, William 1
Wolff, Frank 249, 324
Women in Cell Block 7 see *Diario Segreto da un Carcere Femminile*
Women's Camp 119 see *KZ9 Lager di Stermino*
Women's Penitentiary see *Emanuelle—Violenza in un Carcere Femminile*
Women's Prison see *Emanuelle—Violenza in un Carcere Femminile*
Women's Prison Massacre see *Emanuelle—Violenza in un Carcere Femminile*
Wonders of Aladdin see *La Meraviglie di Aladino*
Woo, John 164
Wood, Ken 296, 332
Woolrich, Cornell 6, 39, 146
The World of Dario Argento see *Il Mondo di Dario Argento*
Wybenga, Roland 281, 286
Wyler, Richard 277
Wynn, Keenan 267, 327

X Hamlet (Hamlet, Hamlet II) see *Amleto*
X the Unknown 86, 275

Yamanouchi, Al 117, 152, 199, 202, 298
Yamanouchi, Haruiko see Yamanouchi, Al
Yanni, Rosanna 333
Yeh, Karen 174
Les Yeux Sans Visage 16
Yor, Hunter from the Future see *Il Mondo di Yor*
York, Michael 42, 113, 116, *You Will Die at Midnight* see *Morirai a Mezzanotte*

Young, Burt 262, 290
Young, Mary (also Anna Maria Polani) 333
Young, Sarah 199
Young Dracula see *Il Cavaliere Costante Nicosia Demoniaco, ovvero: Dracula in Brianza*
The Young, the Evil, and the Savage see *Nude...Si Muore*
Your Vice Is a Locked Room and Only I Have the Key see *Il Tuo Vizio È una Stanza Chiusa e Solo Io Ne Ho la Chiave*

Zada, Ramy 56, 63
Zalewska, Halina 161, 176–177
Zanchi, Monica 280, 325
Zanger, Ziggy (also Zizi Zanger) 216
Zanna Bianca 124, 141–142, 184
Zeder 230–232
Zeglio, Primo 171, 330
Zenabel 110, 119
002 Agente Segretissimi 121, 135
002 Most Secret Agents see *002 Agente Segretissimi*
002 Operazione Luna 121, 135
002 Operation Moon see *002 Operazione Luna*
La Zia Svedese 314–315
Zingarelli, Italo 311, 329, 336
Zombi 48
Zombi: Dawn of the Dead 48, 125, 339; see also *Dawn of the Dead*
Zombi 2 125, 142, 166, 191, 252, 263
Zombi 3 131, 142, 213–214, 219
Zombi Holocaust 287–288
Zombie Creeping Flesh see *Inferno dei Morti-Viventi*
Zombie Flesh Eaters see *Zombi*
Zombie Holocaust see *Zombi Holocaust*
Zombie 6: Monster Hunter see *Anthropophagus II*
Zombie 3 see *Zombi 3*
Zombie 3: The Nights of Terror see *Le Notti del Terrore*
Zombies see *Zombi 2*
Zorro Contro Maciste 143, 158
Zucker, Ralph 309–310, 329
Zurli, Guido 181, 337

www.ingramcontent.com/pod-product-compliance
Lightning Source LLC
Chambersburg PA
CBHW081535300426
44116CB00015B/2638